MILTON IN CONTEXT

Few early modern poets engaged more fully with their historical circumstances than John Milton. A pamphleteer, government employee, and writer of occasional verse, Milton did not retreat from public life even after his political hopes were dashed by the Restoration. This volume investigates the various ways in which Milton's works and experiences emerged from the culture and events of his time. In a series of concise, engaging essays, an international group of scholars examines both the social conditions of Milton's life and the broader intellectual currents that shaped his writings and reputation. A uniquely wide range of topics is covered: from biography to translations, from astronomy to philosophy, and from the English Church to the civil wars. *Milton in Context* is an accessible reference work that both students and scholars will turn to again and again to enrich their understanding of Milton's writings and his world.

STEPHEN B. DOBRANSKI is Professor of English at Georgia State University. He is the author of *Milton, Authorship, and the Book Trade* (Cambridge, 1999); *Readers and Authorship in Early Modern England* (Cambridge, 2005); and *A Variorum Commentary on the Poems of John Milton: "Samson Agonistes"* (2009). He is also co-editor, with John Rumrich, of *Milton and Heresy* (Cambridge, 1998).

MILTON IN CONTEXT

STEPHEN B. DOBRANSKI

CAMBRIDGE
UNIVERSITY PRESS

CAMBRIDGE UNIVERSITY PRESS
Cambridge, New York, Melbourne, Madrid, Cape Town, Singapore,
São Paulo, Delhi, Dubai, Tokyo

Cambridge University Press
The Edinburgh Building, Cambridge CB2 8RU, UK

Published in the United States of America by Cambridge University Press, New York

www.cambridge.org
Information on this title: www.cambridge.org/9780521518987

First published 2010

Printed in the United Kingdom at the University Press, Cambridge

A catalogue record for this publication is available from the British Library

Library of Congress Cataloguing in Publication data
Milton in context / edited by Stephen B. Dobranski.
p.   cm.
Includes index.
ISBN 978-0-521-51898-7 (hardback)
1. Milton, John, 1608–1674 – Criticism and interpretation.   2. Milton, John, 1608–1674 –
Knowledge – England.   3. Milton, John, 1608–1674 – Knowledge – History.   4. Milton, John,
1608–1674 – Political and social views.   5. Milton, John, 1608–1674 – Contemporaries.
6. England – Intellectual life – 17th century.   I. Dobranski, Stephen B.   II. Title.
PR3583.M57   2009
821′.4 – dc22   2009030742

ISBN 978-0-521-51898-7 Hardback

for Audrey Irene

Contents

List of illustrations   *page* xi
Illustration acknowledgments   xiii
Notes on contributors   xiv
Preface   xxi
Abbreviations   xxv

PART I: LIFE AND WORKS

1   Biography   3
    Annabel Patterson

2   Composition process   15
    Juliet Lucy

3   Early lives   26
    Edward Jones

4   Letters, verse letters, and gift-texts   35
    Cedric C. Brown

5   Milton on himself   46
    Stephen M. Fallon

6   Poetic tradition, dramatic   58
    Ann Baynes Coiro

7   Poetic tradition, epic   68
    Anthony Welch

8   Poetic tradition, pastoral   78
    Barbara K. Lewalski

9   Prose style   94
    Walter S. H. Lim

10 Verse and rhyme   105
    John Creaser

PART II: CRITICAL LEGACY

11 Critical responses, early   119
    John Rumrich

12 Critical responses, 1825–1970   130
    P. J. Klemp

13 Critical responses, recent   143
    J. Martin Evans

14 Later publishing history   155
    John T. Shawcross

15 Translations   169
    Christophe Tournu

16 Visual arts   180
    Wendy Furman-Adams

PART III: HISTORICAL AND CULTURAL CONTEXTS

17 Astronomy   213
    Dennis Danielson

18 The book trade   226
    Stephen B. Dobranski

19 The Caroline court   237
    Nicholas McDowell

20 Catholicism   248
    Joan S. Bennett

21 The civil wars   258
    James Loxley

22 Classical literature and learning   270
    Stella P. Revard

23 Education   281
    Gregory Chaplin

24 The English Church   292
    Neil Forsyth

25 The Interregnum   305
    David Loewenstein

26 Italy   318
    Catherine Gimelli Martin

27 Law   328
    Lynne Greenberg

28 Literary contemporaries   338
    Albert C. Labriola

29 Logic   349
    Phillip J. Donnelly

30 London   361
    Ian W. Archer

31 Manuscript transmission   372
    Randall Ingram

32 Marriage and divorce   382
    Shigeo Suzuki

33 Music   394
    Diane McColley

34 The natural world   406
    Karen L. Edwards

35 The New World   418
    Amy Boesky

36 Pamphlet wars   429
    N. H. Keeble

37 Philosophy   439
    Pitt Harding

38 Reading practices   449
    Elizabeth Sauer

39 The Restoration   460
    Joad Raymond

40 Theology   475
    William Poole

Appendix: chronology of Milton's major works   487
Juliet Lucy

Further reading   498
Index   509

Illustrations

Fig. 1   Drafts of three sections of *Lycidas* in the Trinity College
          Manuscript. Cambridge University.   *page* 19

Fig. 2   Jan Bruegel the Elder (1568–1625), *Paradise*.
          Gemaldegalerie, Staatliche Museen zu Berlin.   181

Fig. 3   Frontispiece to the Geneva Bible (1610). Henry
          Huntington Library, San Marino, California.   183

Fig. 4   Bernard Lens, illustration to book IV of *Paradise Lost*
          (1688). William Andrews Clark Library, University of
          California, Los Angeles.   184

Fig. 5   Louis Chéron, headpiece to book IV of *Paradise Lost*
          (1720). Huntington Library.   186

Fig. 6   Francis Hayman, *Adam and Eve in Paradise*, illustration to
          book V (1749). Clark Library.   187

Fig. 7   Richard Westall, *Adam with Sleeping Eve*, illustration to
          book V (1794). Huntington Library.   188

Fig. 8   Richard Westall, *Eve Among Her Flowers*, illustration to
          book VIII (1794). Huntington Library.   190

Fig. 9   Edward Burney, *Adam Wooing Eve*, illustration to book
          VIII (1799). Huntington Library.   191

Fig. 10   Edward Burney, *Eve's Temptation*, illustration to book IX
          (1799). Huntington Library.   192

Fig. 11   William Blake, *Raphael's Visit with Adam and Eve*,
          illustration to book V (1808). Museum of Fine Arts,
          Boston.   193

Fig. 12   William Blake, *Raphael's Visit with Adam and Eve*,
          illustration to book V (1807). Huntington Art Collections,
          San Marino, California.   194

Fig. 13   John Martin, *Eve and Her Reflection in the Liquid Plain*,
          illustration to book IV; plate 9 in a series of twenty-four

made for Septimus Prowett (1825–27). Special Collections, University of Southern California Library, Los Angeles. 196

Fig. 14 John Martin, *Raphael Instructing Adam and Eve*, illustration to books v–viii; plate 15 (1825–28). University of Southern California. 197

Fig. 15 Jane Giraud, title page to *Paradise Lost. The Flowers of Milton* (1846). Collection of Virginia Tufte. 198

Fig. 16 Jane Giraud, "Awake / My fairest . . ." *The Flowers of Milton* (1846). Collection of Virginia Tufte. 199

Fig. 17 Carlotta Petrina, *Adam and Eve in Paradise*, illustration to book iv (1936). Clark Library. 201

Fig. 18 Carlotta Petrina, *Eve Grieving*, illustration to book ix (1936). Clark Library. 202

Fig. 19 Mary Elizabeth Groom, decorative headpiece to book iv (1937). Clark Library. 203

Fig. 20 Mary Elizabeth Groom, *Adam and Eve in Paradise*, illustration to book iv (1937). Clark Library. 204

Fig. 21 Alexis Smith, *Snake Path* (1992). Stuart Collection. University of California, San Diego. Photography by Philipp Scholz Rittermann. 205

Fig. 22 Alexis Smith, granite volume of *Paradise Lost* (detail). 206

Fig. 23 Alexis Smith, garden and bench (detail). 207

Fig. 24 Thomas Digges' diagram of the extended Copernican cosmos. Private copy. 214

Fig. 25 John Milton Senior's "Thou God of Might" from William Leighton's *The Teares or Lamentacions of a Sorrowfull Soule* (1614). The Folger Shakespeare Library. 396

Figs. 26–27 Opening from George Sykes' *The Life and Death of Sir Henry Vane* (1662), showing Milton's sonnet to Vane, with annotations by a near-contemporary reader. Private copy. 463–64

Illustration acknowledgments

The photograph of Bruegel's *Paradise* (fig. 2) is reproduced by permission of Bildarchiv PreuBischer Kulturbesitz/Art Resource, New York. The frontispiece to the Geneva Bible, 1610 (fig. 3) and images by Louis Chéron, Richard Westall, and Edward Burney (figs. 5 and 7–10) were reproduced by permission of the Huntington Library, San Marino, California, whose staff produced the digital images. Special thanks are due to Aaron Greenlee of the Rare Books Department. Images by Bernard Lens and Francis Hayman (figs. 4 and 6) come from photographs provided by the William Andrews Clark Library, University of California, Los Angeles. William Blake's 1808 illustration to *Paradise Lost*, book v (fig. 11) is reproduced by permission of the Boston Museum of Fine Art, whose staff produced the original photograph. Blake's 1807 illustration of the same scene (fig. 12) is reproduced by permission of the Huntington Art Collections, San Marino, California, whose staff produced the digital image. The photographs of John Martin's mezzotints (figs. 13–14) were made by the Special Collections staff at the University of Southern California Library, Los Angeles. The two images from Jane Giraud's *Flowers of Milton* (figs. 15–16) were taken by Dawn Finley from a copy of the work owned by Virginia James Tufte. Images by Carlotta Petrina (figs. 17–18) come courtesy of the Limited Editions Club and the Clark Library; those by Mary Elizabeth Groom (figs. 19–20) by courtesy of the Golden Cockerel Press and the Clark Library. Images of Alexis Smith's *Snake Path*, 1992 (figs. 21–23) are used by permission of the Stuart Collection, University of California, San Diego, photography by Philipp Scholz Rittermann. The image of William Leighton's *The Teares or Lamentacions of a Sorrowfull Soule* is by permission of the Folger Shakespeare Library.

Notes on contributors

IAN W. ARCHER is Fellow, Tutor, and University Lecturer in History at Keble College, Oxford. He is the author of *The Pursuit of Stability: Social Relations in Elizabethan London* (Cambridge, 1991) and various articles on the social and political history of early modern London. He is Literary Director of the Royal Historical Society and General Editor of its online Bibliography of British History. With Paulina Kewes and Felicity Heal he co-directs the Oxford Holinshed Project.

JOAN S. BENNETT is Professor of English at the University of Delaware. She is the author of *Reviving Liberty: Radical Christian Humanism in Milton's Great Poems* (Cambridge, MA, 1989). Her articles on Milton have appeared in journals such as *PMLA* and *Milton Studies* as well as in collections such as *Milton and Heresy* (Cambridge, 1998), *The Cambridge Companion to Milton* (Cambridge, 1999), and *Milton in the Age of Fish* (Pittsburgh, PA, 2006).

AMY BOESKY is Associate Professor of English at Boston College, Massachusetts. She is the author of *Founding Fictions: Utopias in Early Modern England* (Athens, GA, 1996) and co-editor, with Mary Crane, of *Form and Reform in Renaissance England: Essays in Honor of Barbara Kiefer Lewalski* (Newark, 2000).

CEDRIC C. BROWN is Professor of English and former Dean of Arts and Humanities at the University of Reading. In Milton studies he is the author of *John Milton's Aristocratic Entertainments* (Cambridge, 1985); *John Milton: A Literary Life* (Basingstoke, 1995); and numerous essays. He is general editor of the series *Early Modern Literature in History* (forty volumes to date), and his present interests concern the discourses of friendship exchange.

GREGORY CHAPLIN is Assistant Professor of British Literature at Bridgewater State College in Massachusetts. He is co-editor, with John

Rumrich, of *Seventeenth-Century British Poetry, 1603–1660* (New York, 2005). He has published articles on Ben Jonson and Milton in *ELH*, *Modern Philology*, and *PMLA*, and he is currently working on a study of Milton and Renaissance friendship.

ANN BAYNES COIRO is Associate Professor of English at Rutgers, The State University of New Jersey. She is the author of several essays on Milton as well as *Robert Herrick's "Hesperides" and the Epigram Book Tradition* (Baltimore, 1988). She is co-editor, with Thomas Fulton, of the forthcoming collection, *Rethinking Historicism: Essays in Early Modern Literature and Culture*, and she is presently completing a book on Milton and drama.

JOHN CREASER is Emeritus Professor of Royal Holloway, University of London, and Emeritus Fellow of Mansfield College, Oxford, and until recently had for many years been Executive Secretary of the Malone Society. He has edited plays by Middleton and Jonson (including *Bartholomew Fair* for the forthcoming *Cambridge Works of Ben Jonson*), and written extensively on Milton, Jonson, and other seventeenth-century poets.

DENNIS DANIELSON is Professor of English at the University of British Columbia, Vancouver. He is the author of *Milton's Good God: A Study in Literary Theodicy* (Cambridge, 1982) and *The First Copernican: Georg Joachim Rheticus and the Rise of the Copernican Revolution* (New York, 2006); and editor of *The Cambridge Companion to Milton* (Cambridge, 1989, 1999) and *Paradise Lost, Parallel Prose Edition* (Vancouver, 2008).

STEPHEN B. DOBRANSKI is Professor of English at Georgia State University. He is the author of *Milton, Authorship, and the Book Trade* (Cambridge, 1999); *Readers and Authorship in Early Modern England* (Cambridge, 2005); and *A Variorum Commentary on the Poems of John Milton: "Samson Agonistes"* (Pittsburgh, PA, 2009). He is also co-editor, with John Rumrich, of *Milton and Heresy* (Cambridge, 1998; rpt. 2008).

PHILLIP J. DONNELLY is Associate Professor of Literature in the Honors College at Baylor University, Texas, where he teaches in the Great Texts Program and the English Department. He is the author of *Milton's Scriptural Reasoning: Narrative and Protestant Toleration* (Cambridge, 2009).

KAREN L. EDWARDS is Senior Lecturer in the English Department at the University of Exeter. She is the author of *Milton and the Natural World:*

Science and Poetry in "Paradise Lost" (Cambridge, 1999) and of *Milton's Reformed Animals: An Early Modern Bestiary* (currently being published in twice-yearly issues of *Milton Quarterly*).

J. MARTIN EVANS is William R. Kenan Professor in the English Department, Stanford University. He is the author of *"Paradise Lost" and the Genesis Tradition* (Oxford, 1968); *The Road from Horton* (Victoria, 1983); *Milton's Imperial Epic* (Ithaca, NY, 1996); and *The Miltonic Moment* (Lexington, KY, 1998). He is also editor of *John Milton: Twentieth Century Perspectives* (New York, 2003)

STEPHEN M. FALLON is John J. Cavanaugh Professor in the Humanities at the University of Notre Dame, Indiana. He is the author of *Milton Among the Philosophers: Poetry and Materialism in Seventeenth-Century England* (Ithaca, NY, 1991) and *Milton's Peculiar Grace: Self-Representation and Authority* (Ithaca, NY, 2007). He is also co-editor, with William Kerrigan and John Rumrich, of *The Complete Poetry and Essential Prose of John Milton* (New York, 2007).

NEIL FORSYTH is Professor of English at the University of Lausanne in Switzerland. He also teaches in Geneva. He co-edited *Milton, Rights and Liberties* (Bern, 2006) and is the author of *The Old Enemy: Satan and the Combat Myth* (Princeton, 1989) and *The Satanic Epic* (Princeton, 2003), as well as the recent *John Milton: A Biography* (Oxford, 2008).

WENDY FURMAN-ADAMS is Professor of English at Whittier College, California. She is co-editor of *Renaissance Rereadings: Intertext and Context* (Urbana, IL, 1988) and a special edition of *Milton Studies*, volume 28, *Riven Unities: Authority and Experience, Self and Other in Milton's Poetry* (1993). Her articles on Milton – many written in collaboration with Virginia Tufte – have appeared in *Philological Quarterly, Huntington Library Quarterly, Milton Quarterly,* and *Milton Studies*, as well as in various multi-author collections.

LYNNE GREENBERG is Associate Professor of English at Hunter College, New York. She has published several articles on Milton and is the author of *The Body Broken* (New York, 2009) and editor of *Legal Treatises* in *The Early Modern Englishwoman: A Facsimile Library of Essential Works* (Aldershot, UK, 2005).

PITT HARDING is Associate Professor at Jacksonville State University, Alabama. He is the author of " 'Strange point and new!': Satan's Challenge to Nascent Christianity," in *Uncircumscribed Mind: Reading Milton*

Deeply, ed. Charles W. Durham and Kristin A. Pruitt (Selinsgrove, PA, 2008), and "Milton's Serpent and the Birth of Pagan Error," *Studies in English Literature* 47 (2007).

RANDALL INGRAM is Professor of English and Director of the Humanities Program at Davidson College, North Carolina. He is the author of essays on early modern media and poetry, including "The Writing Poet" on Milton's 1645 *Poems* in *Milton Studies* (1997).

EDWARD JONES is Associate Professor of English at Oklahoma State University and the editor of *Milton Quarterly*. In addition to authoring several articles on Milton, he is preparing a new edition of Milton's state papers for the *Oxford Complete Works of John Milton* and serving as the commentary editor for books VII and VIII of *Paradise Lost* for *A Variorum Commentary on the Poems of John Milton*.

N. H. KEEBLE is Senior Deputy Principal and Professor of English Studies at the University of Stirling, Scotland. His publications include *Richard Baxter: Puritan Man of Letters* (Oxford, 1982); *The Literary Culture of Nonconformity in Later Seventeenth-Century England* (Leicester, 1987); *The Restoration: England in the 1660s* (Oxford, 2002); a two-volume *Calendar of the Correspondence of Richard Baxter* (Oxford, 1991, with Geoffrey F. Nuttall); and editions of texts by Baxter, Bunyan, Defoe, Hutchinson, and Marvell.

P. J. KLEMP is Professor of English at the University of Wisconsin, Oshkosh. The Senior Editor of *Milton Quarterly* and Associate General Editor of *A Variorum Commentary on the Poems of John Milton*, he is the author of bibliographies of Milton and essays on Andrewes, Laud, Spenser, Dante, and Petrarch.

ALBERT C. LABRIOLA passed away while this book was in production. He was Acting Dean of the McAnulty College and Graduate School of Liberal Arts at Duquesne University, Pennsylvania, and General Editor of *A Variorum Commentary on the Poems of John Milton*. He was also editor of *Milton Studies*, and Secretary (1974–2009) of The Milton Society of America.

BARBARA K. LEWALSKI is William R. Kenan Professor of History and Literature and of English at Harvard University. Her books include *The Life of John Milton: A Critical Biography* (Oxford, 2000; rpt. 2003); *"Paradise Lost" and the Rhetoric of Literary Forms* (Princeton, 1985); and *Milton's Brief Epic: The Genre, Meaning, and Art of "Paradise Regained"*

(London, 1966). She is also editor of *Paradise Lost*, an original language edition (Oxford, 2007) and is editing volume III (*The Shorter Poems*) for the new *Oxford Complete Works of John Milton*.

WALTER S. H. LIM is Associate Professor of English Literature at the National University of Singapore. He is the author of *The Arts of Empire: The Poetics of Colonialism from Ralegh to Milton* (Newark, NJ, 1998) and *John Milton, Radical Politics, and Biblical Republicanism* (Newark, NJ, 2006). He is co-editor, with Debra Johanyak, of *The English Renaissance, Orientalism, and the Idea of Asia* (forthcoming).

DAVID LOEWENSTEIN is Marjorie and Lorin Tiefenthaler Professor of English at the University of Wisconsin-Madison. His publications include *Milton and the Drama of History: Historical Vision, Iconoclasm, and the Literary Imagination* (Cambridge, 1990); *Milton: "Paradise Lost,"* in the Cambridge Landmarks of World Literature series (Cambridge, 1993; rpt. 2004); and *Representing Revolution in Milton and His Contemporaries: Religion, Politics, and Polemics in Radical Puritanism* (Cambridge, 2001). He is also co-editor, with Janel Mueller, of *The Cambridge History of Early Modern English Literature* (Cambridge, 2002).

JAMES LOXLEY is Senior Lecturer in English Literature at the University of Edinburgh. He is the author of *Royalism and Poetry in the English Civil Wars* (Basingstoke, 1997), *Ben Jonson* (London, 2002), and *Performativity* (London, 2007).

JULIET LUCY, formerly Juliet Cummins, is an honorary research adviser in English at the University of Queensland, Australia, and a practicing lawyer. She is co-editor, with David Burchell, of *Science, Literature and Rhetoric in Early Modern England* (Aldershot, UK, 2007); editor of *Milton and the Ends of Time* (Cambridge, 2003); and author of *Water Regulation: The Laws of Australia* (Pyrmont, NSW, 2008).

DIANE McCOLLEY is Professor II Emeritus of Rutgers, The State University of New Jersey, Camden. Her books are *Milton's Eve* (Urbana, IL, 1983); *A Gust for Paradise: Milton's Eden and the Visual Arts* (Urbana, IL, 1993); *Poetry and Music in Seventeenth-Century England* (Cambridge, 1997; rpt. 2007); and *Poetry and Ecology in the Age of Milton and Marvell* (Aldershot, UK, 2007).

NICHOLAS McDOWELL is Associate Professor in the Department of English at the University of Exeter. He is the author of *The English Radical Imagination: Culture, Religion, and Revolution, 1630–1660* (Oxford, 2003) and *Poetry and Allegiance in the English Civil Wars: Marvell and the Cause of Wit* (Oxford, 2008). He also is co-editor, with Nigel Smith, of *The Oxford Handbook of Milton* (Oxford, 2009), and is editing Milton's regicide tracts for volume VI of the *Oxford Complete Works of John Milton*.

CATHERINE GIMELLI MARTIN is Professor of English at the University of Memphis, Tennessee. Her publications include *The Ruins of Allegory: "Paradise Lost" and the Metamorphosis of Epic Convention* (Durham, NC, 1998), and two edited collections, *Milton and Gender* (Cambridge, 2004) and, with Julie R. Solomon, *Francis Bacon and the Refiguring of Early Modern Thought* (Aldershot, UK, 2005).

ANNABEL PATTERSON is Sterling Professor of English, Emeritus, at Yale University. Her publications include several essays on Milton as well as *Early Modern Liberalism* (Cambridge, 1997; rpt. 2006); *The Long Parliament of Charles II* (New Haven, 2008); and *Milton's Words* (Oxford, forthcoming 2009). She also edited the Longman Critical Reader on Milton (London, 1992).

WILLIAM POOLE is Galsworthy Fellow and Tutor in English at New College, Oxford. He is the author of *Milton and the Idea of the Fall* (Cambridge, 2005) and co-directed the project "Language-planning and free-thinking in late seventeenth-century England," funded by the Arts and Humanities Research Council.

JOAD RAYMOND is Professor of English Literature at the University of East Anglia. He is the author of *Pamphlets and Pamphleteering in Early Modern Britain* (Cambridge, 2003); *The Invention of the Newspaper: English Newsbooks, 1641–1649* (Oxford, 1996); and of articles on early modern literature, politics, print culture, and news, as well as editor of several collections. He is presently completing a book on angels and editing *The Oxford History of Popular Print Culture*, vol. I.

STELLA P. REVARD is Professor Emerita of Southern Illinois University at Edwardsville. She is the author of *The War in Heaven* (Ithaca, NY, 1980); *Milton and the Tangles of Neaera's Hair* (Columbia, MO, 1997); *Pindar and the Renaissance Hymn-Ode: 1450–1700* (Tempe, AZ, 2001); and *Politics, Poetics, and the Pindaric Ode: 1450–1700* (Tempe, AZ, 2008). She is also editor of *Milton's Complete Shorter Poems* (Oxford, 2009).

JOHN RUMRICH is Thaman Professor of English at the University of Texas at Austin. He is the author of *Matter of Glory: A New Preface to "Paradise Lost"* (Pittsburgh, PA, 1987) and *Milton Unbound: Controversy and Reinterpretation* (Cambridge, 1996). He has also co-edited

Milton and Heresy (Cambridge, 1998); the *Norton Critical Edition of Seventeenth-Century British Poetry, 1603–1660* (New York, 2005); and *The Complete Poetry and Essential Prose of John Milton* (New York, 2007).

ELIZABETH SAUER is Professor of English at Brock University, Canada. She has authored two books, including *"Paper-Contestations" and Textual Communities in England* (Toronto, 2005), and eleven editions/co-editions, including *Milton and Toleration*, with Sharon Achinstein (Oxford, 2007); *Milton and the Climates of Reading: Essays by Balachandra Rajan* (Toronto, 2006); *Reading Early Modern Women*, with Helen Ostovich (New York, 2004); and *Reading the Nation in English Literature*, with Julia Wright (New York, 2009). A book on Milton, toleration, and nationhood is in progress.

JOHN T. SHAWCROSS is Professor of English, Emeritus, at the University of Kentucky. Recent publications include *The Development of Milton's Thought: Law, Government, and Religion* (Pittsburgh, PA, 2008) and companion volumes edited with Michael Lieb, *"Paradise Lost": A Poem Written in Ten Books: An Authoritative Text of the 1667 First Edition* and *Essays on the 1667 First Edition* (Pittsburgh, PA, 2007).

SHIGEO SUZUKI is Professor of English at the Graduate School of Languages and Cultures at Nagoya University, Japan. In addition to publishing in English on Milton, he is the author of two books in Japanese, one on Michel Foucault (Hiroshima, 2005) and the other on multicultural studies (Tokyo, 2007). He is also co-author of *Polyvalenz und Multifunktionalitat der Emblematik* (Frankfurt, 2002) and co-translator of *Sprechen Sie Lateinisch?* (Tokyo, 1993).

CHRISTOPHE TOURNU is Professor of English at the University of Strasbourg. He is the author of *Théologie et politique dans l'œuvre en prose de John Milton* (Villeneuve-d'Ascq, 2000) and *Milton et Mirabeau, rencontre révolutionnaire* (Paris, 2002). He made the first translation into French of *The Doctrine and Discipline of Divorce* (Paris, 2005) and is co-editor, with Olivier Abel, of *Milton et le droit au divorce* (Geneva, 2005) and, with Neil Forsyth, of *Milton, Rights and Liberties* (Bern, 2007).

ANTHONY WELCH is Assistant Professor of English at the University of Tennessee, Knoxville. His essays on Milton, Davenant, and Dryden have appeared in *ELR, Modern Philology, Milton Studies*, and in *Uncircumscribed Mind: Reading Milton Deeply*, ed. Charles W. Durham and Kristin A. Pruitt (Selinsgrove, PA, 2008).

Preface

In the middle of *Paradise Lost*, John Milton offers what has proven to be an enduring image of his poetic creation. The epic speaker pauses in his invocation of the muse to lament that he has "fall'n on evil days" and now composes his poem "In darkness . . . / And solitude," surrounded by the "barbarous dissonance / Of Bacchus and his revellers" (VII.25, 27–28, 32–33). Certainly this portrait of the author seems plausible: in 1661, the blind poet could have sat alone in his house in Jewin Street and fearlessly composed his heroic poem, undaunted by the distant noise of royalist celebrations. But Milton's Orphic self-conception in this and similar passages has also contributed to an implausible mythos of an ever-isolated genius. Again and again in his works, Milton emphasizes his achievements by casting himself as a solitary figure. Even in treatises commissioned by the Commonwealth government, he often frames his work rhetorically as an act of individual heroism, describing how he defeated the French intellectual Salmasius "in single combat" (*CPW* IV:556), for example, and interrupting his *Pro Populo Anglicano Defensio Secunda* to defend his own life and writings.

The eight biographies of Milton written within sixty years of his death reflect and have contributed to this perception of Milton's autonomy. Often published with editions of his works, these early lives echo Milton's strong authorial voice in encouraging readers to approach his writings in terms of his individual identity. Collectively, the biographies depict Milton as a poet, like Shakespeare, "not of an age but for all time" – or, as one early biographer less eloquently puts it, "the best of Writers our Nation hath in any Age brought forth" (*EL* 50). Still today, the traditional divisions of British literary history continue to separate Milton from his contemporaries. Born at the end of the English Renaissance but publishing his greatest poetic works after the Restoration, Milton defies easy categorization and is most often studied in a single-author course, best suited to reading all twelve books of *Paradise Lost*.

The problem with this perspective is that it obscures the rich historical and cultural conditions that helped to shape Milton's life and writings. Few early modern poets engaged more fully or more directly with their historical circumstances. A pamphleteer, government employee, and writer of occasional verse, Milton did not retreat from public life even after his political hopes were dashed by the Restoration. That during his trip to Italy in 1638 Milton began to sign his name "John Milton, Englishman" – and cut short his continental journey as the threat of war loomed at home – suggests that he conceived his identity as a citizen of England and was deeply invested in the period's political and religious conflicts. Even the autobiographical digressions in some of Milton's works, while implying his individual achievements, reveal upon closer scrutiny his engagement with contemporary events. If we return to the above passage from *Paradise Lost*, Milton underscores the isolation he feels because of his blindness, but with expressions such as "evil days" and "dangers" he also seems to allude to the recent restoration of monarchy.

This volume pursues such contextual details in order to remedy the myth of authorial autonomy that Milton himself sometimes encouraged. The essays in the collection investigate the author's life and works within his changing cultural and historical circumstances. Building on the efforts of recent scholars who have successfully uncovered relevant, local contexts for reading Milton's poetry and prose, all of these essays contain original arguments and analyses. The contributors re-assess the milieu of Milton's writings and reveal various ways that Milton's works and experiences emerged, directly and indirectly, from his culture.

The volume comprises three parts, with the essays in each section arranged alphabetically for ready reference. The book's first section, "Life and works," contains ten chapters. It begins with a brief biography and a discussion of Milton's process of composition. A separate chapter on Milton's correspondence focuses on humanist conventions of letter-writing and the insight that Milton's epistles provide into his career, character, and habits. Two additional essays address, respectively, the author's acute self-concern and the versions of Milton's life constructed by early biographers. The final five essays in this section pertain to the literary contexts of Milton's works: a chapter on Milton's prose style compares his early and late polemical method, and four chapters on his poetry offer fresh examinations of his verse and rhyme as well as the dramatic, epic, and pastoral traditions in which he composed his major poetic works.

The book's second section, "Critical legacy," turns to the reception of Milton's works in six chapters that trace the interpretive threads that have interested scholars over the past three and a half centuries. Rather than attempting to provide a comprehensive overview of changing critical trends, each essay actively intervenes in the issues and interests of its respective historical period. The goal of the first three essays is to improve our understanding of how various readers – and various schools of thought – have read Milton and how his literary reputation has accordingly evolved. The other three essays in this section also address the way that Milton has been reconfigured posthumously – in later editions, through translations, and in paintings and illustrations inspired by his works. The authors of these three essays explore how subsequent generations of readers have paid homage to Milton's poetry and prose while re-interpreting his works in new forms.

The book's third and longest section, "Historical and cultural contexts," offers a series of original arguments and engagements with existing and emergent contexts in Milton studies. The writers of these twenty-four essays discuss the ways in which an understanding of seventeenth-century issues and institutions sheds new light on Milton's works and helps today's readers re-assess traditional interpretations. Not only do the book's contributors examine Milton's personal experience within these contexts – as in, for example, the chapters on education and the Interregnum – but the contributors also analyze the broader social conditions and intellectual currents that subtly affected Milton's writings – as in the chapters on Catholicism and the New World.

The overarching goal of this book is not to argue for a single version of Milton but to piece together various glimpses of his life and works from multiple critical perspectives and within a selection of interrelated contexts. Like Milton, the collection's contributors are necessarily influenced and limited by their own historical situations. So as to capture most effectively the range and depth of Milton's changing circumstances, I have assembled a diverse group of contributors. The writers of these essays consist of both seasoned scholars and up-and-coming, younger critics. Geographically, the contributors represent Australia, Canada, England, France, Japan, Scotland, Singapore, Switzerland, and the United States; methodologically, they represent bibliographers, eco-critics, feminists, formalists, historians, materialists, Marxists, and psychoanalytic critics. I am grateful to all the contributors for their cooperation and goodwill throughout the editing process.

When Milton in one of his early prose works asserted that "he who would . . . write well hereafter in laudable things, ought him selfe to bee a true Poem" (*CPW* 1:890), he was suggesting the intimate relationship between a writer's life and works. The essays in this collection begin with that premise. My hope is that *Milton in Context* will enrich readers' understanding of Milton and his writings by demonstrating how his historical moment and personal experiences helped to shape some of the greatest works in English literary history.

Abbreviations

CPEP	*The Complete Poetry and Essential Prose of John Milton*, ed. William Kerrigan, John Rumrich, and Stephen M. Fallon (New York, 2007).
CPW	*The Complete Prose Works of John Milton*, gen. ed. Don M. Wolfe, 8 vols. (New Haven, 1953–82).
EL	Helen Darbishire, ed., *The Early Lives of Milton* (London, 1932).
LR	J. Milton French, ed., *The Life Records of John Milton*, 5 vols. (New Brunswick, NJ, 1949–58).
WJM	Frank Allen Patterson, ed., *The Works of John Milton*, 18 vols. (New York, 1931–38).

Citations and line numbers for Milton's poetry, unless otherwise noted, are taken from *CPEP*, which uses modernized spellings. Milton's prose works are quoted in their original spelling and punctuation, except for those tracts that are translated from the Latin. Citations to classical works are to the Loeb editions published by Harvard University Press. All translations from Greek or Latin, unless otherwise indicated, are taken from the editions cited.

PART I

Life and works

CHAPTER I

Biography

Annabel Patterson

John Milton lived a long and tumultuous life. He was born in 1608, just a few years after the death of Queen Elizabeth, and died about halfway through the reign of Charles II, in 1674. He was intended to be either a clergyman or some form of independent scholar/author – his father and he may have disagreed on the value of the latter, but the clerical option was soon dropped. Instead, his life was irrevocably shaped by what happened in the middle of the seventeenth century – the first English revolution against Charles I, father of Charles II, which produced first a civil war, then a republic, then a dictatorship under Oliver Cromwell, and finally came full circle with the recall of Charles II to the English throne. Milton was drawn deep into this conflict as it continued through the middle twenty years of the century. He became first what we today would call a public intellectual, second an apologist for the revolutionary government that had just executed their king, and eventually a figure in the international press of Europe, to which he contributed in Latin, earning himself both admirers and vociferous enemies.

In 1660, when Charles II returned to England, Milton was obviously in some danger for his attacks on the king's father. He was also completely blind, a condition that developed during, and was exacerbated by, his work for the revolutionary government. He survived the Restoration, after a brief spell in prison, by returning to a very restricted version of private life, writing poetry almost exclusively, and depending heavily on readers and secretaries, including his daughters. We are the beneficiaries of this downward turn in his fortunes, for what emerged in 1667 was *Paradise Lost*, and in 1673, the year before his death, *Paradise Regained* and *Samson Agonistes*. These late poems made him a famous canonical author and justify his secure place in the international pantheon. But one cannot understand the man nor his great poems without also knowing his political views and arguments, as worked out in the heat of controversy, between 1640 and 1660.

There are at least two commonsense questions to consider before writing a life of John Milton: the first, obviously, what readers today want or need to know about the facts of Milton's life; the second, what would Milton himself have wished them to know. For one of the many things that made Milton remarkable was his determination to interpret his life along the evaluative lines he preferred, for his readers at the time, retrospective piece by piece. Without actually sitting down to write his life, Milton managed to insert large chunks of autobiography into other projects, to such a degree that John Diekhoff was able to publish these "digressions" under the title of *Milton on Himself* (New York, 1939). Their testimony needs to be taken with a pinch of salt. Most autobiographers shape their stories to make themselves seem more (or sometimes less) admirable than they really were. But Milton's desire to control the record is *itself* one of the more interesting biographical facts about him.[1]

At Cambridge, where his well-off scrivener father sent him to get a gentleman's education, Milton's sense of himself as designed for a great literary future was expressed in an important personal notebook, the "Trinity Manuscript," named after the college library that preserves it, as distinct from Milton's own college, which was Christ's. In this manuscript he recorded his early poems in the order in which they were composed, sometimes noting the dates of composition or the age at which he wrote them. But in his later autobiographical digressions Milton did not specify dates. This means that biographers and critics have for years struggled to create, or to agree on, an exact chronology of his life and works. Also, Milton's admirers tend to have a theory about his life, to which the undisputed facts are not so much bent as lent. Some of these theories are political, as in John Toland's late seventeenth-century Whig *Life*, or Barbara Lewalski's modern insistence that Milton was a coherent liberal thinker from beginning to end.[2] Some are sexual, as in William Kerrigan's Freudian account of Milton's relations with his parents, or Anna Beer's view that all three of Milton's marriages were inhibited by an early passionate commitment to a fellow undergraduate, Charles Diotati.[3] More recently, Blair Worden has argued for a long-standing collaboration between Milton and the Commonwealth journalist Marchamont Nedham, a side of Milton's career less high above the fray than he liked to suggest.[4] Some biographers believe that Milton was "unchanged," to use his own term from *Paradise Lost*, from college to the grave. Others see a story of drift, changes of intention, opportunism, and even an implicit retraction, in his great poems, of his most important contributions to English political life.

This, however, is a more or less uninterpreted summary of what we know, situating the man not only in a chronology but in relation to his works, his historical circumstances, his friends, his employers, his family – in last place because Milton almost never discussed his family members in his own writing. The most important exceptions are the early but undatable letter to his father (*Ad Patrem*) pleading, in Latin, to be allowed to pursue a literary vocation, and the late sonnet about the death of his wife – but which of his three wives he mourned, he left unclear!

It used to be the fashion for biographers to dwell on Milton's earliest years, his excellent schooling, his time at Cambridge, his period of private study at his father's estate at Horton, and his extended tour of Italy, the social and conventional culmination of his education. This was the period of "intellectual development," as Harris Fletcher called it, thought to explain the poet he became.[5] What Milton himself felt, however, was that he suffered from writer's block. In 1632 he complained: "my late spring no bud or blossom shew'th. / . . . And inward ripeness doth much less appear, / That some more timely-happy spirit endu'th" (Sonnet 7). In bulk, at least half of his output was in Latin, and the so-called "prolusions" were required university essays. The form of block that he suffered was, perhaps, unrealistic ambition. In 1628, at the age of nineteen, performing a public exercise on the topic of Aristotelian logic, he outlined the grand metaphysical or heroic subjects he hoped in future to address. But by 1642 he had still not decided what kind of great poem to write, as he admits in a long autobiographical aside in *The Reason of Church-Government,* one of the earliest of the pamphlets by which his original goal had been derailed.

Nevertheless, Milton did write some successful poems before his continental tour. In the first of these, dated 1629, he established a claim to become a major new religious poet. This was "On the Morning of Christ's Nativity," which goes far beyond the stable in Bethlehem, however beautifully rendered, to consider the eventual redemption of the world by Christ, all folded into a brilliant prolepsis that is withdrawn as soon as it is offered: "But wisest Fate says no, / This must not yet be so" (lines 149–50). The next religious poem he tried, "The Passion," collapsed after eight stanzas. It would take thirty-five years to prove his claim good.

At Cambridge Milton had also started to write sonnets, in Italian and English, a genre to which he would remain committed for the next twenty years. In 1630 he wrote, or at least dated, a sonnet-like poem in praise of Shakespeare, which had the honor of being included in the second folio of Shakespeare's plays when it appeared in 1632. Possibly as a result, in 1634 he received a rather important dramatic and social commission – to write a

masque for the installation of John, Earl of Bridgewater, as Lord President
of Wales. The intermediary was Milton's friend Henry Lawes, a musician
with court connections. Generically, the *Mask* sits uncertainly between the
court masques of the day and something more intellectually and morally
demanding. It was published by Henry Lawes, but still anonymously,
in late 1637 or early 1638, and its anonymity led, ironically, to its being
appropriated to the canon of his greatest college rival, Thomas Randolph.[6]
Finally, in 1638, not long before he left for Italy, one of his most ambitious
poems was published with his name attached: *Lycidas*, an elegy for a young
man he had known at Cambridge and who had drowned in a shipwreck in
the Irish Channel, was included with other elegies in a university memorial
volume.[7] Thus by the time he left on his own sea-voyage Milton had, in
real terms as adjudged by publication, accomplished very little, not nearly
as much as other aspiring young writers such as Randolph or Abraham
Cowley, two of the "more timely happy spirits" to whom he had compared
himself in Sonnet 7.[8]

Most of what we know about Milton's continental tour is thanks to a
very retrospective account he himself provided in 1654, in the Latin tract,
Pro Populo Anglicano Defensio Secundo, written to explain and defend the
English revolution and regicide, and his own role therein. It is devoid of
dates but packed with assertions of Milton's respectability and acceptability
to European literati, including Giovanni Battista Manso, the famous patron
of Torquato Tasso. Milton had gone with a letter of introduction, he
tells us proudly, from Sir Henry Wotton, "who had long served King
James' ambassador to the Venetians," and in Paris Lord Scudamore, the
present ambassador to France, had introduced him to Hugo Grotius "then
ambassador from the Queen of Sweden to the King of France" (*CPW*
IV:614–15). Impeccable credentials; but whether he really gained from this
trip *at the time* "a great boost of self-confidence in the rightness of his chosen
vocation as poet"[9] is an inference from an autobiographical passage in
The Reason of Church-Government, written three years later. Then Milton,
asserting his qualifications as an author, described having recited some of
his poems to the Italian academicians, their praise reinforcing an "inward
prompting . . . that by labour and intent study (which I take to be my
portion in this life)" he might indeed become a great poet (*CPW* I:810).
He did write a Latin letter of compliment and gratitude to Manso, and a
pastoral elegy in Latin for Charles Diodati, who had died in August 1638.
The second was certainly written after Milton's return to London, and the
first very probably so. Both, in a sense, were required. Both poems, to the
delight of Milton scholars, contain statements of a great literary ambition,

to write a British epic based on Arthurian materials. The statements are all we have. After that there were no signs of poetic activity for several years.

In the *Defensio Secunda* Milton tells us that his plans to visit Sicily and Greece were interrupted by the "sad tidings of civil war from England" (*CPW* IV:619). This could only have been have been the First Bishops' War against the Scots, declared late in January 1639. Seeing himself in the light of 1654, Milton wrote, "I thought it base that I should travel abroad at my ease for the cultivation of my mind, while my fellow-citizens at home were fighting for liberty" (*CPW* IV:619). This was an odd description of the war to put down the Scottish rebellion over the imposition of the English prayer-book, and in fact Milton did not immediately return home, but spent several more months in Florence, and visited Venice, where he spent a month sightseeing and buying books. He returned home in late July or early August 1639, by which time the war was in abeyance; but the Scots had, significantly, changed the structure of their church government, replacing the hierarchical and ritual structure of episcopacy (bishops at the top) with the somewhat more egalitarian organization of presbytery. Would this model spread to England?

Milton's behavior on his return was consistent with the program of "labour and intent study" he saw as his future, and had nothing to do with "the fight for liberty" he later claimed brought him home. Significantly, he left his family home at Horton for the more professional venue of London, and in the autumn of 1639 or early in 1640 rented lodgings near Fleet Street. He had agreed with Thomas Agar, the second husband of his sister Anne, to take on the education of his two young nephews, John and Edward Phillips, and both the little boys and their uncle began a rigorous program of study. Milton re-opened a notebook he had used at Horton as a record of his reading, and now rapidly filled it with references to, and citations from, new research. This "Commonplace Book" was already divided into four sections: ethical, economic, political, and a theological one which has not survived. Although Elizabeth Sauer has a detailed account of the Commonplace Book in chapter 38 of this volume, it is worth stating here that the new entries show a new interest in British history or political thought, especially Holinshed's *Chronicles* (the most frequently quoted work). By 1644 Milton had turned to European history, such as Paolo Sarpi's *Historia del Concilio Tridentino*, to which he makes thirteen references. Milton's Political Index, much the longest index in his Commonplace Book, has an overflowing section under the heading "King" and another under "Tyrant." While this might be a broad program of humanist reading, such as Sauer and others posit, it will turn out to have political applications. It was not a seedbed for poetry.

For it must have become increasingly difficult to ignore what was happening outside the walls of the study and private schoolroom. In 1640 Bishop Joseph Hall responded to the threat of spreading Presbyterianism by publishing *Episcopacie by Divine Right*, a provocative title if ever there were one. In March 1641 five Presbyterian ministers, one of whom, Thomas Young, had been Milton's private tutor, wrote jointly *An Answer* to a second pamphlet by Hall. The *Answer* was followed by an anonymous "Postscript" attacking episcopacy on historical grounds, with references to the English historical sources, Holinshed, Speed, and Stow, that Milton had just been reading – including several of the same page references! Don Wolfe therefore infers that the anonymous author was John Milton (*CPW* 1:79–80), and the inference is supported by the appearance, in May 1641, of another anonymous tract in the conflict about the bishops: *Of Reformation Touching Church-Discipline in England*, which was largely an expansion, with some splendid metaphors, of the "Postscript". This was Milton's entrée into the world of political polemic – for political it was, despite the focus on church affairs. By the early spring of 1642 Milton had written four more tracts against the bishops, to the third of which, *The Reason of Church-Government Urg'd against Prelaty,* he put his name. And into it he inserted the first of his famous autobiographical passages, telling his audience not only about his education and Italian trip but about his literary ambitions, and how painful he found it to put them aside "to imbark in a troubl'd sea of noises and hoars disputes" (*CPW* 1:821).

But embarked he was, and getting better at polemic by the moment. On February 7, 1642, the House of Lords assented to the bill excluding all the bishops from their House, and Milton might reasonably have returned to his "calme and pleasing solitarynes" (*CPW* 1:821) in the belief that he had marginally contributed to this reform. But what happened next surprised everybody, including, perhaps, Milton himself. In the summer of 1642, just after his fifth antiprelatical tract appeared, Milton suddenly decided to get married. His choice was at first sight unfortunate (though perhaps it was love at first sight that was to blame). At thirty-three, after a very short courtship, he married Mary Powell, the seventeen-year-old daughter of Richard Powell, a royalist gentleman in Oxfordshire, who owed Milton a substantial sum of money. For this episode, we have the colorful testimony of Edward Phillips, his nephew and pupil, himself twelve at the time.[10] The young bride, brought back to London, soon became miserable in this rigorously scholarly household, and asked permission to go back to Oxfordshire until the end of September. Meanwhile, the looming civil war between king and parliament had actually broken out. Oxford became a royalist stronghold (with Milton's brother Christopher among the king's supporters). Mary did not return at the appointed time, and her family refused communications with the deserted husband. By January 1643 the House of Commons forbade traffic with Oxford. By August 1, Milton had written the first of four pamphlets advocating a change in England's divorce laws, which were still regulated by canon law. Though he never mentions Mary Milton, we can easily read between the lines of the first divorce pamphlet, *The Doctrine and Discipline of Divorce,* to recover his massive disappointment in his young wife and his consequent insistence that canon law, by allowing divorce only on the grounds of adultery or non-consummation, was entirely missing the point. Marriage was always, since Genesis, Milton now argued, intended to be less for sex or procreation than for emotional solace or intellectual support, a meeting of minds.

Between May 1641 and August 1644 Milton had published five pamphlets on church reform, four on reform of the divorce laws; and some of these tracts were long. Suddenly he had become a published author of some standing. That intensive study was still going on was advertised, if not proven, by his publication also of *Of Education* in June 1644, a fearsome account of the pedagogical regime that Milton was presumably attempting on behalf of his nephews. But meanwhile his divorce pamphlets were causing a scandal. The Presbyterians, whose cause Milton thought he had assisted in the church reform pamphlets, were now insisting on the need to control radical or "wicked" ideas in the marketplace of print. The House of Commons charged a committee to seek out and prosecute the authors, printers, and publishers of "the Pamphlet against the Immortality of the Soul, and concerning Divorce" (*CPW* II:142). Everybody knew that the latter referred to Milton, who had signed the preface to the second expanded edition of the *Doctrine.* William Prynne, whose own cruel treatment by Charles I for writing against the court had made him a revolutionary hero and martyr, now recommended that the Grand Council should suppress "Atheistical opinions, as of the soules mortality, divorce at pleasure, &c." (*CPW* II:142). And a very long, though anonymous, pamphlet "answering" the *Doctrine* appeared in November. Any thought that Milton might have had of retiring to "the quiet and still air of delightfull studies" (*CPW* I:821–22) was put aside by these challenges. The result was, in the eyes of literary scholars, Milton's most brilliant piece of prose, *Areopagitica,* a defense of the freedom of the press. Self-defense put Milton in a flame which generated forward-looking principles he might not have previously thought through. Despite the occasional cavil (from those who object to Milton's exempting Catholic publications from such freedom), it still stands as one of the founding texts of early modern and modern liberalism. But in late November 1644, it utterly failed to achieve its specific goal of persuading the Long Parliament to repeal its new licensing act, which largely reinstated the censorship legislation and mechanisms of Charles I.

Milton now leased a larger house in Cripplegate, apparently with the intention of expanding his school and possibly of marrying again. He was having trouble with his eyesight, and needed domestic help. But in the summer of 1645, a reconciliation between Milton and his estranged wife was effected by friends. Mary returned to her husband's house, to help him run what was now a much larger establishment. At this point Milton collected and published almost all his early poems, both in English and Latin (although his publisher, Humphrey Moseley, stated that it was he who sought out the author on the basis of his reputation) and worked on several scholarly projects, including a history of Russia (Moscovia), a history of early Britain, and textbooks on grammar and logic. Was this a deliberate withdrawal from the political arena, or lack of other opportunities? In 1654 he complained that his polemical skills had received no recognition or reward, whereas "other men secured offices at no cost to themselves." "As for me, no man has ever seen me seeking office . . . clinging with suppliant expression to the doors of Parliament . . . I kept myself at home for the most part" (*CPW* iv:627). He wrote some politically inflected sonnets, including two that mocked the negative reception of his divorce pamphlets. Meanwhile, it had become clear that Charles I was losing the civil war, and that the new government would consist of some blend of the Long Parliament with the army leaders, of whom Oliver Cromwell was preeminent. On December 6, 1648 Colonel Pride and his forces arrested or excluded two-thirds of the Presbyterian MPs who had been negotiating with the king. Milton now knew that those in charge were the eighty-odd remaining parliamentarians, who became known as the Rump Parliament. On January 4, 1649, the Rump formally declared the kingdom a republic, and the army leaders determined to try Charles I on a charge of high treason against his subjects. The trial began on January 20, and on January 30 the king was executed.

These events brought to a close Milton's second retreat into pure scholarship. After nearly four years of silence in the public sphere, he suddenly reappeared as the author of a revolutionary pamphlet justifying the king's trial, its title, *The Tenure of Kings and Magistrates*, marking a foray into hardcore political theory. Once again, he managed to obscure the motives and the process of this volte-face, by claiming, in 1654, that he wrote as a private citizen, that he had only been drawn to defend the regicide after Charles had already been condemned to death, and that he had had no intention of influencing the trial. The *Tenure* was indeed published after the king's death, on or about February 13, 1649. But it is highly likely that Milton was asked to write something theoretical justifying the trial, perhaps by John Bradshaw, the presiding judge, whose connections with both Milton and Nedham have been documented by Blair Worden.[11] Milton had to work fast, a talent he had already displayed in his previous bursts of polemic. One reason he was able to do so now was that he could turn back to his Commonplace Book, where ready to hand was his Political Index, with its entries on "The State," "Laws," "King," "Subject," "The Tyrant," "Liberty," and "Various Forms of Government," a virtual textbook of political theory, though as yet undigested. Having been handed a new occasion for the use of his talents (and his notes), Milton rose to it with an energy and eloquence that can still seem shocking, given the nature of the argument.

On March 13 or 14, 1649, in obvious exchange for services rendered, Milton was offered one of those "offices" he later claimed most scrupulously not to have sought: he was made Latin Secretary to the revolutionary Council of State, to write foreign correspondence and the occasional "official" response to a crisis, such as the royalist threat in Ireland. More important, he was instructed to counter the impact of the newly published *Eikon Basilike*, the royalist representation of the king's execution as a martyrdom. So enormously popular was the "king's book" that in its first year it sold thirty-five editions in London and twenty-five more in Ireland and Europe. In October or November 1649, Milton was ready with his riposte, *Eikonoklastes* (literally, "the image-breaker"), a title which attempted to undo the emotional affect of the famous frontispiece to the *Eikon*, picturing the king on his knees, discarding his earthly crown for a heavenly one. Alas for Milton's reputation, there were only two editions of *Eikonoklastes*, an alarming sign of where popular sentiment still lay. But almost immediately he was given a new commission, to reply to the *Defensio Regio pro Carolo I* by the French scholar Claude de Saumaise (known to Milton as Salmasius), who took it upon himself to speak for Europe on the unlawfulness of England's proceedings. Had Salmasius been successful in arousing European intervention, Charles II might have been returned to the throne by force in 1650, instead of having to wait another decade.

In all, Milton wrote three Latin defenses, the first of the English Commonwealth (*Pro Populo Anglicano Defensio*, 1651), the second of what had become Cromwell's Protectorate (*Pro Populo Anglicano Defensio Secunda*, 1654) and the third (*Pro Se Defensio*, 1655) of himself and his polemical conduct, which today seems far from unblameworthy. The first cost him the loss of his remaining good eye. Milton saw this as a heroic sacrifice in defense of principles. The *Defences* established him as the primary spokesman for the English experiment in government, and foreigners visited him as a great man. But meanwhile Mary Milton died giving birth to a daughter, shortly followed by the death of their baby son John. A second marriage, to Katherine Woodcock in 1656, was followed two years later by her death. On the domestic front everything was misery. On the political, there are hints that Milton was disillusioned by the regime he had praised so effusively in the *Second Defence*, and he never attached himself in personal loyalty to Cromwell, the route taken by his friend Andrew Marvell. As the Presbyterians had turned out to be as bad as the bishops they displaced, so Cromwell, by assuming supreme power in the state, was hardly to be distinguished from the monarch he had executed.

On September 3, 1658, Oliver Cromwell died. From Milton's perspective, for his son Richard to succeed him as Protector was almost as bad as hereditary monarchy. But actual hereditary monarchy was the chief threat. Amid the chaos of political deal-making and breaking, the return of the Rump Parliament, and the appearance of another military leader, General George Monck, Milton braced his "left hand" once more and wrote two versions of a pamphlet whose very title ironized the situation: *The Readie & Easie Way to establish a Free Commonwealth; and the Excellence therof Compar'd with the inconveniencies and dangers of readmitting Kingship in this Nation* (1660). No longer under the protection of the Council of State, Milton had to return to the status of independent public intellectual, and face the risks. No printer could be found for the second edition willing to sign his name to it. It appeared just a few days before Charles II himself returned to England.

1660, therefore, was another turning point for Milton, marking his enforced and perhaps truly desired final retreat from controversy. Despite a period of actual danger, when he could have been executed along with other leading regicides, a brief imprisonment which may have been an administrative error, and an escape from both the plague and the Great Fire of 1666, he settled in to what his early biographers describe as an orderly compositional routine. In 1663 he had solved some of his personal difficulties by a third marriage, to Elizabeth Minshull, a much younger woman who contracted to cook and keep a comfortable house for him. And whether or not he had begun *Paradise Lost* in 1658, by 1665 he had an extensive draft of the poem, and by the end of April 1667, a publisher, Samuel Simmons, whose father Matthew had published the *Tenure* and *Eikonoklastes*. When *Paradise Lost* appeared it was immediately recognized as a highly original masterpiece.

But, as usual with Milton, one thing led to another in the same genre. Piqued by a comment by his young Quaker friend and clerical assistant, Thomas Ellwood, that he had mastered the loss of Paradise but omitted to describe its restoration, Milton produced to order *Paradise Regained*, which may have originally been written as a play and expanded with epic trappings. Perhaps as an afterthought, the publisher, the redoubtable Whig John Starkey, supplemented this still rather short poem in 1671 with something that was undoubtedly written as a play, though "never intended" for the stage, *Samson Agonistes* (*CPEP* 708). And then, as if to summarize his career as disengaged *littérateur*, Milton arranged to have his early poems republished in 1673, adding to them the sonnets he had written since 1645 – all but four. Three of these had been written to revolutionary heroes: Sir Thomas Fairfax, Oliver Cromwell, and Sir Henry Vane; the fourth had been addressed to his personal friend Cyriack Skinner, on the subject of Milton's blindness. Milton wrote in 1655 that he lost his eyes "[i]n liberty's defense, my noble task, / Of which all Europe talks from side to side" (Sonnet 22). It would take Milton's nephew Edward Phillips, in his 1694 edition of his uncle's state letters, to resurrect these poems as a group. This extraordinary fact of book history, often unmentioned by modern scholars, suggests that the long internal debate between the public figure, who loved the limelight and feared nobody, and the private author/scholar, who felt safer in the ivory tower, had still not been resolved.

NOTES

1 Milton's self-representation is discussed in Stephen Fallon's chapter in this volume.
2 John Toland, "The Life of John Milton," in *A Complete Collection of the Historical, Political and Miscellaneous Works of John Milton* ("Amsterdam" [London], 1698); and Barbara K. Lewalski, *The Life of John Milton* (Oxford, 2000).
3 William Kerrigan, *The Sacred Complex: On the Psychogenesis of "Paradise Lost"* (Cambridge, MA, 1974); and Anna Beer, *Milton: Poet, Pamphleteer and Patriot* (London, 2008).
4 Blair Worden, *Literature and Politics in Cromwellian England* (Oxford, 2007).

5 Harris F. Fletcher, *The Intellectual Development of John Milton*, 2 vols. (Urbana, IL, 1956–61).

6 See Ann Baynes Coiro, "Anonymous Milton, or, *A Maske* Masked," *ELH* 71 (2004): 609–29.

7 In *Obsequies to the memorie of Mr. Edward King*, Part 2 of *Justa Eduardo King Naufrago* (Cambridge, 1938).

8 Cowley actually published a volume entitled *Poetical Blossoms* in 1633; and by 1631 Randolph had written and/or published several verse plays, including the pastoral drama *Amyntas*, acted before the king and queen in 1631. In 1632 *The Jealous Lovers* was also performed before the king, and published by the university press. Only three years older than Milton, Randolph must have made Milton feel small with such a prodigious and elegant output.

9 Lewalski, *Life*, 87.

10 Available in *EL* 49–82. See also Edwards Jones' discussion of Phillips' biography in chapter 3 of this volume.

11 Worden, *Literature and Politics*, 45–47.

CHAPTER 2

Composition process

Juliet Lucy

John Milton helped to forge a new kind of authorship in an age in which the modern author was beginning to emerge. This has contributed to the significant amount of surviving evidence we have about how and when Milton wrote his poetry and prose. Shakespeare, born forty-four years earlier than Milton, left notoriously little information about his character or his views, or how he wrote. Milton, on the other hand, was acutely conscious of the significance of his own authorial identity and wrote about himself and his role as a writer to an unprecedented degree. Milton fully participated in the pamphlet wars brought about by the advent of print, and often used his prose works and even his poetry to project a carefully crafted authorial persona. Over the course of the seventeenth century, people became increasingly interested in the personality of authors and their life histories. The flourishing of the genre of short biography, or "lives," means that we have several early accounts of Milton's life, which inform us about Milton's patterns of writing and dictating and about when he wrote some of his major works. Added to this we have manuscripts, such as the Trinity Manuscript, which show Milton planning and revising his writing, and we have printed works which Milton has altered in different editions, helping us to understand his methods of composition and revision. There are still large gaps in our knowledge about exactly when Milton wrote many of his works, but there is enough information to be fairly certain about some dates of composition, and to make educated guesses about others.[1]

Understanding when and on which occasions Milton composed his works suggests that his compositions were predominantly social or interactive acts. Milton's image of himself composing "In darkness . . . / And solitude" in *Paradise Lost* (VII.27–28) is misleading if it is taken to represent him as *generally* isolated from society and conversation, rather than as a likely reference to his situation immediately after the Restoration. Milton's prose works often reply to the works of other authors and participate in or generate current debates (such as with the divorce tracts). As Secretary for Foreign Tongues, Milton wrote at the behest of the government, also reacting to political imperatives and the works of other authors such as Salmasius. Sometimes Milton's poems respond to particular events, including the death of a relative, friend, or acquaintance, or a political incident such as the Gunpowder Plot. The date of a particular work can be a significant aspect of its meaning, as it changes how we situate the work in a biographical or political context. This is particularly the case with Sonnet 23, "Methought I saw my late espousèd saint," where scholars have argued for different dates of composition on the basis of their views as to whether Milton's first or second wife is the subject of the poem. Sometimes the relationship between Milton's works and contemporary history is less apparent, but nevertheless remains significant. Works such as *Paradise Lost, Paradise Regain'd, Samson Agonistes*, and *The History of Britain* express a different kind of creative impulse from the more occasional pieces, and are the products of a longer process of composition and development, but they too allude to contemporary events and concerns.

The timing of Milton's compositions was a subject which concerned Milton himself, in that he appears to have been confident of his ability to produce a great work of poetry fairly early in his career, but also anxious about his belatedness in doing so.[2] In his early thirties, in *The Reason of Church-Government* (1641), Milton recalls that while in Italy he came to the view "that by labour and intent study" and with his own ability he might "leave something so written to aftertimes, as [others] should not willingly let it die" (*CPW* 1:810). Although history has proved Milton right, it was not until he was nearly sixty that the great epic for which he is best known was first published. This evolved over a long period of time – more than thirty years if we include the revisions Milton made in preparation for the second edition of the poem. Milton wrote lists of characters for a drama on the subject of "Paradise Lost" in the Trinity Manuscript probably in the latter half of 1640, and Milton's nephew Edward Phillips told John Aubrey that he read what is now book IV, lines 32–41 around 1642.[3] The revisions of the surviving manuscript of book I of *Paradise Lost* are in many hands, suggesting that many different friends, acquaintances, or amanuenses assisted in amending the poem before it was first published in 1667.[4] The process of writing this poem, then, was collaborative and prolonged. This can be contrasted with other occasions on which Milton seems to have composed works very quickly and independently; the *Tenure of Kings and Magistrates*, for example, may have been largely written within two weeks,[5] the Nativity Ode purports, at least, to have been written by Milton on Christmas Day, 1629, and Milton remarks in a letter to his friend Alexander Gil Jr. that he translated an ode, probably Psalm 114, "before daybreak a week ago – almost in bed."[6]

Resolving questions about how and when a particular work was composed depends upon forming a view of what composition entails, which itself involves value judgments about the significance of different aspects of the creative process. Milton conceived the process of composition to include the preliminary stages of reading, researching, and consulting, as well as the later stages of revising a draft after it had been produced. In *Areopagitica* (1644), Milton defends writers' right to control their works in the context of an argument against licensing. He describes his understanding of the writing process as follows: "When a man writes to the world, he summons up all his reason and deliberation to assist him; he searches, meditats, is industrious, and likely consults and conferrs with his judicious friends; after all which done he takes himself to be inform'd in what he writes, as well as any that writ before him" (*CPW* II:532). Milton's own practices affirm this description, particularly in his "industrious" preparation for writing. His own "ceaselesse round of study and reading" (*CPW* I:891) was an essential part of his practice of composition, and his works generally reflect his extensive knowledge of classical and contemporary texts. As a young child, Milton "studied very hard and sate-up very late," thereby producing "many Copies of verses," and even in Milton's later years, after he became blind, he had a man read to him several times daily, which helped stimulate his poetry.[7] Milton's early biographers report that his evenings were "spent in reading some choice Poets . . . to store his Fancy against Morning" and that Milton "had a man read to him" at four in the morning, then again at seven, "and then read to him and wrote till dinner: the writing was as much as the reading."[8] The image Milton evokes in *Areopagitica* of an author consulting with friends before beginning to write is also very likely taken from his own experience.[9] As Stephen Dobranski has shown, Milton's writing involved much more social interaction and input from others than has generally been recognized.[10]

The hypothetical author Milton pictures in *Areopagitica* continues to think about the work after it appears to be finished, and Milton remarks that it may happen "to the best and diligentest writers" that "many things well worth the adding" occur to mind "after licensing, while the book is yet under the Presse" (*CPW* II:532). Milton's own tendency to revise his works was even greater than that of his imagined counterpart; he often continued to revise *after* a book had been published.[11] John Shawcross describes

Milton's attitude to revisions as "the fastidiousness of getting things just right" and sees it as a symptom of Milton's "anality."[12] There certainly is something of the perfectionist, sometimes bordering upon the obsessive, in Milton's apparent dissatisfaction with his finished works, and his inability or unwillingness to stop changing them. As Shawcross points out, Milton totally rewrote *The Doctrine and Discipline of Divorce* (1st edn., 1642), doubling its original length, and revised *The Tenure of Kings and Magistrates* (1649) and *Eikonoklastes* (1649) within a year of first publication. He also made changes to much of his poetry in manuscript form and after initial publication. For example, "At a Solemn Music" was revised drastically, so that only six lines of the first draft survived in the final version. He revised the 1667 edition of *Paradise Lost* in 1673 or 1674, including by changing the format from ten books to twelve, adding five lines to the new book xii, and adding a captivating image of the angels "quaff[ing] immortality and joy" in book v (line 638).

Evidence of Milton crafting and substantially revising his poetry, both in manuscript and print, disturbs the Romantic myth of the inspired genius which Milton himself helped to promote. The early nineteenth-century poet and writer Charles Lamb recoiled in mock horror at discovering the manuscript version of Milton's *Lycidas*:

I had thought of the "Lycidas" as of a full-grown beauty – as springing up with all its parts absolute – till, in an evil hour, I was shown the original written copy of it . . . How it staggered me to see the fine things in their ore! interlined, corrected! as if their words were mortal, alterable, displaceable at pleasure! as if they might have been otherwise, and just as good! as if inspirations were made up of parts, and those fluctuating, successive indifferent![13]

The passage alternates between irony and a real sense of shock to find the apparently integrated, seamless whole, the aesthetic object, de-constructed or, perhaps more aptly, pre-constructed. The Trinity Manuscript which gave rise to Lamb's comments contains drafts of *Lycidas*, written in November 1637 (according to Milton's dating), when Milton was nearly thirty. It is likely that Milton wrote earlier drafts of the poem which have not survived, before copying the poem into the Trinity Manuscript, since the verse appears quite well developed in this draft.

The Trinity Manuscript version of the poem allows us to imagine Milton's thought processes as he crosses out words and makes corrections, and looking at the manuscript is almost like seeing Milton composing the poem (figure 1). The draft of the opening lines reads:

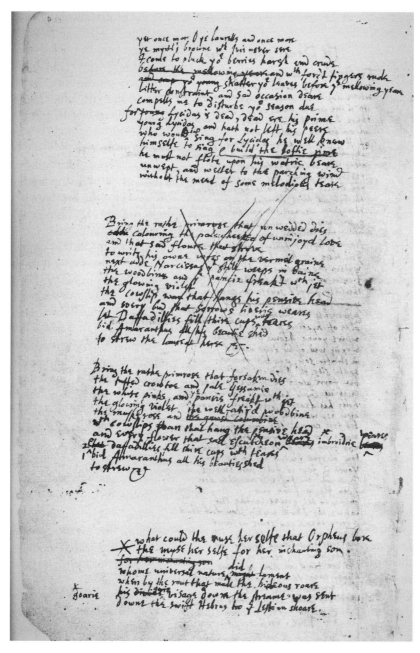

Fig. 1 Drafts of three sections of *Lycidas* in the Trinity College Manuscript

yet once more O ye laurels and once more
ye myrtl's browne wth Ivie never sere
I come to pluck yor berries harsh and crude
~~before the mellowing yeare~~ and wth forc't fingers rude
~~and crop yor young~~ shatter yor leaves before ye mellowing yeare[14]

Examining the emendations allows us to speculate as to why Milton chose the words he did. The substitution of "shatter" for "crop" adds force to the fifth line, and the transfer of the phrase "before the mellowing yeare" from line 4 to the end of line 5 allows Milton to sustain the imagery of premature, violent plucking of life with harsh-sounding words ("forc't fingers rude," "shatter") before a shift to a more peaceful image of natural ripening or aging with the soft-sounding "mellowing yeare." The next verse in the manuscript, beginning "Bring the rathe primrose," is crossed through with a large "X" and substantially changed in another draft of the same verse, written underneath. In the published version of the poem, this verse has been moved to line 142, with further changes made to the wording. Even a brief examination of the Trinity Manuscript points to an ongoing process of composing, revising, and re-ordering, a process of critical self-evaluation.

This process continued, in a more restrained form, after publication. *Lycidas* was first published in 1638 under the initials "JM" in a collection of poems in tribute to Edward King – *Justa Edouardo King*. Milton published it again under his name in 1645 in his *Poems*, with "several unnerving differences."[15] The changes included identifying the "faithless shepherds" of the poem as the "corrupted clergy" in the headnote, in a safer political climate to do so. Not only does this show Milton re-evaluating his compositions; it also demonstrates a different attitude to a "work" as not necessarily inviolable and fixed, but as a more fluctuating text or evolving process; as in manuscript culture, subject to change. Further, it demonstrates Milton's understanding that the meaning of the work is not merely a product of authorial intention, but is tied to the social and political context in which it is received.

Milton's progressive composition and revision of the earlier *A Mask Presented at Ludlow Castle* (1634) also challenges the Romantic image of the authoritative, canonical poet, composing in solitude, with complete responsibility for an original, inspired artifact. Firstly, *A Mask* is a piece of theatre, written for performance. Secondly, Milton wrote *A Mask* in circumstances where he was not clearly or solely in control of the work.[16] It was commissioned by the Egerton family, and the musician Henry Lawes, who wrote the music, oversaw the staging, made revisions to the manuscript, and probably obtained Milton the commission.[17] The printed edition in 1637 is dedicated by Lawes to Lord Brackley, who played the Elder Brother, and presented as "a legitimate off-spring" of the anonymous "Author" although "not openly acknowledg'd" by him.[18] Thirdly, as Randall Ingram discusses in chapter 31 of this book, *A Mask* takes various forms: two surviving and different manuscript versions, in the Bridgewater and Trinity Manuscripts; the performance in 1634; publication by Lawes in 1637; publication in Milton's *Poems* of 1645, and republication in the *Poems* of 1673, in which version references to the Egerton family and commendatory letters from Lawes and Sir Henry Wotton are removed.[19] The removal of these letters, and the presentation of the work as part of the collected poems of John Milton, known by the 1670s as a great epic poet, frames the masque as a work of independent authorship in the later edition of the *Poems*.[20] *A Mask* is therefore not a single text, but several texts, their meanings affected by the circumstances of their performance or publication. The entertainment makes the journey from an aristocratic performance embedded in a culture of patronage to becoming part of Milton's assertion of autonomous poetic authorship in a print culture.

The evidence of Milton making extensive revisions to his works, including manuscripts which show Milton in the process of creating his poems, provides us with a sense of the industry and diligence with which he composed his poetry and prose. These revisions also indicate his continuing engagement with his writing, and his tendency to keep evaluating it. And yet when Milton describes the way in which he writes he emphasizes the experience of being inspired, and the need for "devout prayer to that eternall Spirit who can enrich with all utterance and knowledge." Milton presents "studious ways" and "industrious and select reading" as necessary, but insufficient in themselves, the accomplishment of "wise and artfull" writing lying "in a power above mans to promise" (*CPW* 1:819–21).

It is important not to discount what was for Milton the most significant factor in his ability to compose great poetry. *Paradise Lost* opens with an invocation to the "heav'nly Muse" and a prayer to the "Spirit" who "brood[ed] on the vast abyss" at Creation (1.6, 17, 21). Throughout Milton's poetry and prose there are references to the need for divine inspiration to create well, and to the importance of the poet's role as prophet. Biographical accounts are also indicative of the inspired nature of Milton's compositions. Milton generally wrote in the mornings, the verse having come to him during the night. Milton's nephew, John Phillips, recalled that, upon waking early, Milton "had commonly a good Stock of Verses ready against his Amanuensis came; which if it happend to bee later than ordinary, hee would complain, Saying *hee wanted to bee milkd.*"[21]

According to John's older brother, Edward, such inspiration only came to Milton during the colder part of the year. Milton's "Vein never happily flow'd, but from the *Autumnal Equinoctial* to the *Vernal*" and if he attempted to compose poetry during summer "though he courted his fancy never so much" the results were "never to his satisfaction."[22]

Milton's sense of being divinely inspired is connected with his understanding of and feeling for his poetry as sound. While the nature of this connection is not straightforward, it is an aspect of the phonocentric tradition according to which speech is associated with the logos and presence, while writing is associated with death and absence.[23] In *Paradise Lost*, for example, Milton calls on Urania, the heavenly muse, who "Visit'st [his] slumbers nightly" to "govern" his "song" (VII.29, 30). Inspiration is connected with singing, breathing (literally "inspiring") and with the voice. While industry is for Milton a necessary part of the preparation for composing good poetry, so too is prayer and an openness to divine aid which allows the verse to come to the poet through non-rational processes, "unpremeditated" (*Paradise Lost* IX.24).

Milton appears to have heard his poetry, as a composer might hear music, before dictating it or writing it down. As Leah S. Marcus observes, the "process of composition, as Milton appears to have imagined it, did not move from the creative faculties straight to the hand, as it would for most of us, but...from mind to voice to utterance."[24] As is illustrated by the appeals for inspiration in *Paradise Lost*, Milton often describes his compositions as vocal acts, either as song or speech.[25] His father was an amateur musician and composer who taught Milton music as a child and, according to his contemporaries, Milton "had an excellent ear" and a "delicate tuneable Voice."[26] In his later years, when "Blindness and Age confin'd him" Milton "play'd much upon an Organ he kept in the House" and also played the bass-viol.[27] As Diane McColley demonstrates in chapter 33 of this book, the musical nature of Milton's imagination enriched and stimulated his poetic compositions. This is evident in the sound and rhythm of Milton's great poetry, in Milton's use of blank verse to create "true musical delight" through "apt numbers, fit quantity of syllables, and the sense variously drawn out from one verse into another" (*Paradise Lost*, "The Verse," (*CPEP* 291).

Milton's early biographers report that Milton mentally composed one or several verse paragraphs of his poetry at a time and then dictated or wrote these lines all at once. Jonathan Richardson claimed that he had been told that Milton "would Dictate many, perhaps 40 Lines as it were in a Breath, and then reduce them to half the Number."[28] Richardson also reported that Milton asked visitors "to Write a Quantity of Verses he had ready in his Mind, or what should then occur."[29] Edward Phillips reported that he "had the perusal" of *Paradise Lost* "from the very beginning," and that it was transcribed "in a Parcel of Ten, Twenty, or Thirty Verses at a Time."[30] These accounts indicate Milton's ability to hold the verses in his mind as sound and suggest the inspired nature of his compositions, while also acknowledging Milton's impulses toward revisions and correction.

The importance of orality to Milton's processes of composition is evident from his use of scribes even before his eyesight became weak.[31] Milton was blind in one eye by 1649, and he became fully blind in 1652. In 1654, he wrote to Leonard Philaras that he had first noticed his sight weakening ten years previously which, if accurate, would mean in 1644.[32] Yet he relied on others to transcribe poems and prose for him before this time, suggesting his participation in an oral culture in which reading scripture and poetry aloud, and dictating at school and elsewhere, were common practices. The sonnet "Captain or colonel, or knight in arms" (1642), in the Trinity Manuscript, is written by a scribe, and John Shawcross notes that scribal emendations occur in the Trinity Manuscript of *A Maske*, "which were probably made when the text for the first edition (1637–38) was prepared."[33] Edward Phillips reports that, when he was Milton's student, he had the task of "writing from his own dictation, some part, from time to time, of a Tractate which he thought fit to collect from the ablest of Divines" – presumably *De Doctrina Christiana*.[34] This was probably around 1645 or 1646.[35] We know that John Phillips served as scribe for Milton while living with him up until 1652, since certain of Milton's sonnets and letters are in his hand.[36] This early use of scribes, and Milton's ability to hold large passages of verse in his mind, may have been of assistance when Milton's blindness required him to rely on "the help of Amanuenses" to prosecute "the former design of his calmer studies."[37]

The Romantic image of Milton as a solitary and inspired genius is clearly inadequate to capture the full complexity of Milton's processes of composition. It is probably true that Milton did sometimes write his poetry alone, in the early morning, inspired by his heavenly muse or at least with a sense of being divinely inspired. But even in this writing process he was influenced by friends, and by his readings of other authors, and his writing was always informed by his social and reading experiences. The image of Milton as a solitary composer can only be sustained by ignoring the input and influence of others: printers, students, amanuenses, friends, even the intriguing presence of "ye mayde" who sat up late into the night with the young Milton as he read and wrote, according to his brother Christopher.[38] The works of

"John Milton, Author" embody Milton's practices of composition, which depend upon reading and contemplation as well as an active engagement with contemporary society, politics, and intellectual culture.

NOTES

1 My Chronology of Milton's major works in this volume's appendix sets out dates of composition on which scholars generally agree, and also identifies some of the dates which are contested.

2 See Stephen M. Fallon, *Milton's Peculiar Grace: Self-Representation and Authority* (Ithaca, NY, and London, 2007).

3 John T. Shawcross, *With Mortal Voice: The Creation of "Paradise Lost"* (Lexington, KY, 1982), 173.

4 Stephen B. Dobranski, *Milton, Authorship, and the Book Trade* (Cambridge, 1999), 34.

5 Gordon Campbell, *A Milton Chronology* (London, 1997), 97.

6 Letter 6 to Alexander Gil, December 4, 1634, *CPW* 1:321.

7 John Aubrey, "Minutes of the Life of Mr John Milton," in *EL* 10.

8 *EL* 33 and 6.

9 Fallon, *Milton's Peculiar Grace*, 139.

10 Dobranski, *Milton, Authorship, and the Book Trade*.

11 Amongst those to note Milton's habit of "revising" his works "sometimes substantially, even after they appeared in print" is Dobranski, *Milton, Authorship, and the Book Trade*, 7.

12 John T. Shawcross, *John Milton: The Self and the World* (Lexington, KY, 1993), 187–88.

13 Quoted in Leah S. Marcus, *Unediting the Renaissance: Shakespeare, Marlowe, Milton* (London, 1996), 177.

14 See *Poems, Reproduced in Facsimile from the Manuscript in Trinity College, Cambridge* (Menston, UK, 1970).

15 Marcus, *Unediting the Renaissance*, 178.

16 On Milton's lack of control over the production and composition, see William B. Hunter, Jr., *Milton's "Comus": A Family Piece* (Troy, NY, 1983), 4–5.

17 Ann Baynes Coiro, "Anonymous Milton, or, *A Maske* Masked," *ELH* 71 (2004): 609–29 (p. 609).

18 See *ibid.*, 611.

19 On the republication of *A Mask* in the 1673 *Poems*, see Barbara K. Lewalski, *The Life of John Milton* (Oxford, 2000; rev. edn. 2003), 504–05; and Stella P. Revard, *Milton and the Tangles of Neaera's Hair: The Making of the 1645 "Poems"* (Columbia, MO, 1997), 156, 206.

20 See Coiro, "Anonymous Milton," 613, 624–25.

21 *EL* 33.

22 *Ibid.*, 73.

23 See Jacques Derrida, *Of Grammatology*, trans. Gayatri Chakravorty Spivak (Baltimore, 1974), 13–16.

24 Marcus, *Unediting the Renaissance*, 210.
25 *Ibid.*, 210–11.
26 *EL* xv, 6.
27 The words are those of Milton's early biographer, John Toland: see *ibid.*, 194.
28 *Ibid.*, 291.
29 *Ibid.*, 209.
30 *Ibid.*, 73.
31 John T. Shawcross, "Amanuenses," in *A Milton Encyclopedia*, ed. William B. Hunter, Jr., 8 vols. (Lewisburg, PA, 1978), 1:41–43; and James Holly Hanford, "The Chronology of Milton's Private Studies," *PMLA* 36 (1921): 251–314.
32 See William Riley Parker, *Milton: A Biography*, 2nd edn., ed. Gordon Campbell, 2 vols. (Oxford, 1968), 88, 286, 894 n.
33 Hanford, "Chronology," 254; and Shawcross, "Amanuenses," 41.
34 *EL* 61.
35 Parker, *Milton: A Biography*, 293.
36 Shawcross, "Amanuenses," 41.
37 *EL* 28.
38 *Ibid.*, 10.

CHAPTER 3

Early lives

Edward Jones

Toward the end of his recent discussion of Milton's earliest biographers, Thomas Corns asks: "What value do the early lives really have for a modern biographer of Milton?"[1] His immediate answer, that "they contain some information not available elsewhere in the life records," while accurate, need not be construed as absolute.[2] Value resides as well in their methodology (how the early lives disclose information) and in their potential to assist future research (leads furnished through information disclosed). In other words, it is not only because of what they say but also how they say it that the seventeenth-century narratives by John Aubrey, Cyriack Skinner, Edward Phillips, and Anthony à Wood remain the foundation for the more than 100 biographies of John Milton that have followed them.

As Helen Darbishire has noted in her important edition of the first six attempts at a life of Milton, "the first four biographers stand together and form the first authority" and have "left a record . . . which has not been . . . superseded."[3] Authority has been readily accorded the accounts of Phillips and Skinner because of their personal acquaintance with Milton as his students, assistants, and, in the former case, his nephew. While not among Milton's close associates, Aubrey and Wood were his contemporaries, and the former, in particular, has been trusted because his *Minutes of the Life of Mr John Milton* makes clear that he interviewed his subject's widow, brother, and nephew. As Darbishire rightly observes, "[t]he relation of the four is intricate . . . and the[ir] tangled tale must be carefully unwound" (*EL* viii). In providing a sampling from these texts and attempting to unravel what they tell and do not tell us, this chapter will pay particular attention to how undocumented statements have enabled later commentators to add to our knowledge of Milton's life and in so doing have underscored the significance of the earliest attempts to tell his story.

While concurring with Darbishire's general sentiment that the four narratives pose a complex problem because of the way Wood uses the

26

materials of Aubrey and Skinner and because Phillips writes his uncle's life story independently from the others, this chapter departs from Darbishire's findings in two ways. First, it agrees with Peter Beal that her case for John Phillips as the author of the anonymous life found among Wood's papers falters in the face of the evidence of two autograph letters by Cyriack Skinner housed in the City of Hull archives. When these two letters are compared to Sonnets 21 and 22 in the Trinity Manuscript and MS Wood D.4, as Beal reports, "the handwriting here is in every respect so distinctive – even down to the peculiar style of deletion employed – as to leave no doubt whatsoever . . . that Cyriack Skinner was also responsible for page 49 in the Trinity Manuscript and for the 'Life' of Milton in Bodleian, MS Wood A [*sic* D].4, ff. 140–4."[4] Second, this chapter views the undocumented nature of the first four Milton biographies as distinct. It is John Toland, Milton's fifth biographer, who begins the practice in 1698 of citing sources that all subsequent biographers follow. What Toland offers, however, is far less than the full disclosure later scholars provide:

The amplest part of my Materials I had from his own Books, where, constrain'd by the Diffamations of his Enemys, he often gives an account of himself. I learnt som Particulars from a Person that had bin once his Amanuensis, which were confirm'd to me by his Daughter now dwelling in *London*, and by a Letter written to one at my desire from his last Wife, who is still alive. I perus'd the Papers of one of his Nephews, learnt what I could in Discourse with the other; and lastly consulted such of his acquaintance, as after the best inquiry, I was able to discover. (84–85)

Overt gestures of indebtedness like these are hard to find in Wood, Phillips, and Skinner, although a kinship exists with Aubrey's minutes in which comments appear after the names of those he interviewed. While it has long been known that Aubrey sent Wood his minutes, and that approximately half of Wood's account is taken word for word from Skinner's manuscript, Wood gives no hint that he is using the findings of others, even if that material is what we would call today hearsay evidence – personal recollections from friends and acquaintances. It may be, as Corns argues, that "[t]he discourse of criticism was still too underdeveloped" and "primary archival research, as it is now understood, was at best difficult and at worst impossible."[5]

Nevertheless, the lack of acknowledgment has not really hampered research. Readers of these accounts repeatedly encounter statements pointing them in profitable directions. When Edward Phillips, for example, declares that the ten-line soliloquy of Satan addressing the sun in *Paradise*

Lost was originally designed to begin a tragedy (72–73), he alerts later commentators to the importance of the "Outlines on Tragedy" found among his uncle's papers in the Trinity Manuscript. When Cyriack Skinner states that Milton had "sav'd two thousand pounds, which being lodg'd in the Excise, and that Bank failing upon the Restoration, hee utterly lost" (32), he provides enough information for Gordon Campbell to discover that Milton had in fact transferred an excise bond to Skinner on May 5, 1660.[6] Similarly, the closest indication that Aubrey may have met Milton is couched in a carefully distanced way ("He was scarce so tall as I am" [3]). At the heart of the biographical enterprise in the four early accounts are details that cannot be proved ("when he was very young he studied very hard and sate-up very late, comonly till 12 or one aclock at night" [10]) combined with others which appear settled but are not ("About *Whitsuntide* it was, or a little after, that he took a Journey into the Country; no body about him certainly knowing the Reason, or that it was any more than a Journey of Recreation: after a Month's stay, home he returns a Married-Man, that went out a Batchelor" [63]). Such passages convey the subtle complexities of the entwined tale that Darbishire believes must be carefully unwound. Filled with unsubstantiated claims, the early lives challenge their readers either to accept on faith what Milton's contemporaries have said or to verify what they say by finding evidence that is not based upon personal experience or hearsay (the option that has become the standard for later research). By recognizing the implications of this method of presentation, scholars can use the narratives of the early lives as springboards to learn more about Milton's life, though new discoveries will still prove hard to come by. Another look at the two examples just cited, one regarding Milton's study habits and the other his first marriage, provides a sense of the factors in play as well as the obstacles to overcome.

Biographies of Milton, whether of the expansive, annotated kind (Masson, Parker, and Lewalski)[7] or of a more reader-friendly nature (Brown, Wilson, and Flannagan),[8] have devoted significant time to verifying, expanding, correcting, or rejecting the assertions made by the early biographers – thus accepting on faith only those statements that do not lend themselves to corroboration other than personal testimony. If we take the often-cited comments of Christopher Milton regarding his brother's study habits, we face a typical challenge: a "fact" such as this one is hard to corroborate; thus most scholars have simply accepted and repeated it as if it were true, knowing that it could or could not be so. In such an instance, the recollection appears so in keeping with a particular profile of Milton that one suspects that many allow it as fact with little hesitation because in this instance, if there is no harm, there is no foul. If the bulk of Milton's career indicates his scholarly predilections, why begrudge him such tendencies as a youth? In the second instance, the circumstances leading to Milton's first marriage, there is a greater need for certainty and scholars have proceeded with much more caution. Edward Phillips admits not only to his own but to the ignorance of others regarding the circumstances leading up to Milton's first marriage ("no body about him certainly knowing the Reason" [63]). Have later commentators been able to improve upon his account?

Lacking a definitive answer from Milton's nephew, scholars have gone in search of one using the clues he has provided. In this case, they have discovered what the young Phillips may not have known at the time or possibly even later – that his uncle had financial dealings with Richard Powell prior to his alliance with Powell's daughter. On June 11, 1627, Milton's father loaned Richard Powell £300 at 8 percent interest, with biannual payments of £12 to be paid to his son; Powell honored the contract for a good part of two decades before defaulting in 1644.[9] Such knowledge provides a plausible correction of Phillips' "he took a Journey into the Country; no body about him certainly knowing the Reason, or that it was any more than a Journey of Recreation" (63). Milton's nephew, a boy of twelve at the time, apparently did not know that his grandfather and other uncle were living in Reading in 1642, although he certainly did know years later when he wrote his uncle's life ("His Father, who till the taking of *Reading* by the Earl of *Essex* his Forces, had lived with his other Son at his House there" [63]). Why Phillips did not consider that his uncle John most probably combined a visit with his grandfather and other uncle en route to his later destination outside Oxford is one of the many imponderables scattered throughout the early lives, accounts, as Corns accurately notes, that are "concerned with a small number of topics while silent on issues of massive significance."[10] In any event, once in Forest Hill Milton became acquainted with Mary Powell (whether for the first time or not has not been determined) and from there any number of possibilities leading to the marriage could have ensued. Unfortunately, the additional information concerning the financial dealings with Richard Powell and the Milton family residence at Reading has not significantly cleared away the ambiguity that informs Phillips' narrative: no record of the marriage, no discovery of a marriage settlement similar to one we know was prepared for the marriage of Milton's sister Anne to Edward Phillips in the 1620s (which Milton and his mother signed),[11] and not even a marriage allegation has been discovered in the Oxford parish records, the church courts, or other diocesan records. Thus with no information of this kind, Phillips' unsubstantiated assertion that no one knew why Milton traveled to Oxfordshire still holds – neither disproved nor contradicted in a significant way. A tangled tale has indeed appeared and continues to resist efforts to untie it.

Fortunately, Phillips' account of the peculiar alliance with the Powell family (which none of the early biographers appears to understand fully), the almost immediate falling out between bride and groom, and especially the reconciliation between Milton and Mary Powell, brought about by interested parties from both families, ends profitably, with details capable of shedding considerable light:

he was surprised to see one whom he thought to have never seen more, making Submission and begging Pardon on her Knees before him; he might probably at first make some shew of aversion and rejection; but partly his own generous nature, more inclinable to Reconciliation than to perseverance in Anger and Revenge; and partly the strong intercession of Friends on both sides, soon brought him to an Act of Oblivion, and a firm League of Peace for the future; and it was at length concluded, That she should remain at a Friends house, till such time as he was settled in his New house at *Barbican*, and all things for her reception in order; the place agreed on for her present abode, was the Widow *Webber's* house in *St. Clement's* Church-yard, whose Second Daughter had been Married to the other Brother many years before. (66–67)

While attention has been duly paid to Mary's "making Submission and begging Pardon on her Knees before him" and to Phillips' debatable characterization of his uncle's "generous nature, more inclinable to Reconciliation than to perseverance in Anger and Revenge," it is his closing comments ("the place agreed on for her present abode, was the Widow *Webber's* house in *St. Clement's* Church-yard, whose Second Daughter had been Married to the other Brother many years before") that have fostered biographical discovery four centuries later.

Naming a house, a location, a person, and a relative in a matter-of-fact fashion, Edward Phillips opens a door to information capable of providing a much fuller understanding of a significant event in Milton's life: his reconciliation with Mary Powell will lead to a family of four children born over the next seven years. Through Phillips' slightly opened door walk David Masson, J. Milton French, and William Riley Parker, whose combined efforts determine by 1968 that the Widow Webber was Isabel Webber, the wife of a tailor John Webber. The Webbers resided in the parish of St. Clement Danes in Westminster, had several children, and one of their daughters, Thomasine, married Christopher Milton prior to

1645.[12] Phillips' details turn out to be precise (as to the married status of Mrs. Webber), misleading (Christopher married the Widow's third daughter), and incomplete (Isabel Webber held leases on more than one house in St. Clement's Churchyard).[13] As do many of the best passages in the early lives of Milton, a circumstantial narrative leaves it up to later biographers to fill in gaps and determine essential matters of identification, location, and dates. Once answered by the likes of Masson, Parker, and French, such matters have been deemed settled, rarely if ever questioned, and even less frequently reexamined. And yet in the process of verifying Phillips' details, I recently discovered over fifty documents in the City of Westminster Archives Centre regarding the Webber family that alter and enhance Phillips' one-sentence report.

It turns out that by traversing the circuitous path created by the narratives of the early biographers one can discover how details in need of verification can become gateways to new biographical information. In this present case, the large number of documents ranging over matters typically the province of the parish chest – baptism, marriage, and burial registers, rate books for the maintenance of the poor and parish roadways, and churchwarden accounts – establishes a record of stability for a segment of the extended Milton family for approximately four decades (1609–52).[14] For the first time, scholars have a vantage point from which to gauge the changing fortunes of Christopher Milton's family during the civil war period and their impact upon his brother's life. Does Milton's acquaintance with Westminster parish life through the christenings and burials of his nephews and nieces during the 1640s figure into his decision to move his own family into the same area in the early 1650s? With his extended family residing nearby, can a fuller knowledge of their activities help account for one of his most ambiguous periods – the months involving the deaths of his first wife, his son, and the onset of blindness? Did the Widow Webber, for instance, furnish some of the same services she provided for Christopher Milton, the care of children during a difficult time? The discovery of these documents certainly increases the opportunities to provide more definitive answers to such questions. For example, it is now possible because of the extant parish rate books, to establish that by April 1644, the Widow Webber relocated within the parish of St. Clement Danes, an event we would be unable to determine by any other means. In both the poor rate and survey accounts for 1644, she is listed as residing in the Clement Inn area of the parish, specifically on Clement Lane, a location to which she can be linked as a resident from 1640. In 1645, however, the word "gone" appears next to her name for that residence, and her name and assessment rate reappear in the Middlerow Forestreet area of the parish, a row of dwellings facing the Strand just off St. Clement's Churchyard. By the time of Milton's reconciliation with Mary Powell, Edward Phillips has informed us properly, guided us to her new location, and we have the evidence to verify his accuracy.

An additional instance of information reported more than three centuries ago leading to greater understanding concerns Milton's move to Petty France in December 1651. Three of the four early biographers note the residency ("Hee had too at the first return of the Court in good manners left his house in Petty France, which had a door into the Park" [Skinner 32]); ("[H]e was more admired abroad, and By Foreigners, than at home; and was much visited by them when he liv'd in *Petty France*" [Wood 48]); but it is Phillips who once again gives the fullest account:

From this Apartment, whether he thought it not healthy, or otherwise convenient for his use, or whatever else was the reason, he soon after took a pretty Garden-house in *Petty-France* in *Westminster*, next door to the Lord *Scudamore's* and opening into St. *James's* Park; here he remain'd no less than Eight years, namely from the year 1652, till within a few weeks of King *Charles* the 2d's Restoration. (71)

This passage has been largely accepted as the basis for approximating the length of Milton's Petty France residency from 1652 to April 1660. The survival of a letter dated December 31, 1651 from Milton to Hermann Mylius, a diplomat from the small German principality of Oldenburg, corrects Phillips' date from 1652 to late 1651 with notable specificity: "Before I respond . . . to your letter to me dated December 17 . . . I should explain . . . [a] sudden moving to another house, which it so happened I began on that day when your letter was brought to me."[15] Similar to the situation regarding the Webber family in St. Clement Danes, newly discovered parish chest records from St. Margaret's, Westminster, have emerged during my verification of Phillips' account and Leo Miller's later research. They attest to the accuracy of Milton's and his nephew's statements. Poor relief returns found in the parish overseer account books for 1652 list Milton as a parishioner by March 25, the date of the first of the quarter days (June 24, September 29, and December 25, being the others) when collections for the year took place.[16] These accounts, apparently not consulted by Parker or French, chronicle Milton's time in the parish through 1659 (damaged during World War II, the records for 1660 have not survived, but the 1659 ledger confirms Milton's payments and therefore presence through Easter 1660, a date in April remarkably close to Phillips' estimation). Moreover, the organization of the records – listing parishioners house by house – verifies Phillips' claim that his uncle lived next door to Scudamore. The two names appear one after the other for eight years in the part of the parish designated as Petty France North.

Housed as well in the City of Westminster Archives Centre is a volume entitled "An Assessment Upon the Parissh [*sic*] of Margaret's Westminster for three months to the 25th of March 1652 toward four payments of goods for the maintenance of the Armies of England, Ireland, and Scotland raised by the authoritie of Parliament for the defense of this Commonwealth."[17] It is the first of nine extant rate books that record quarterly or half-year payments Milton made in support of the parliamentary army over a period of four years. This particular rate book, covering as it does the period from December 25, 1651 through March 24, 1651/52, lends further credence to Milton's explanation to Mylius that he had changed residencies on December 17, 1651. If Milton has his date correct, the parish took notice of its new member immediately and within eight days had him on its tax rolls. He is assessed on Christmas Day 1651 for 5 shillings for rents and 1 shilling, 6 pence for his estates. The ambiguity that marks events which take place in the Milton household during the next six months – details concerning the deaths and burial places of Mary Powell and Milton's son remain unknown – clearly did not extend to this aspect of the Petty France residency. Army assessment rate books for all of 1652 and 1653, and part of 1654 survive, and Milton appears in all of them. Thus, from Christmas Day 1651 through March 25, 1655, Milton made twelve payments in support of the parliamentary army; extant records of nine of these payments allow us, as with the poor relief returns, to determine his whereabouts every three months. This set of records transforms Phillips' approximations about the beginning and ending of Milton's Petty France residency into evidence-based facts. While it has taken more than three centuries to find that evidence, speculation can now give way to it for an important nine-year period of Milton's life.

The availability of the poor relief and army assessment returns for St. Margaret's provides scholars with two independent sources of evidence that can verify Milton's whereabouts for an extended period of time (two years for certain, four years if one believes army payments continued through all of 1655). It remains a rare luxury even in the study of one of England's most documented figures of the seventeenth century. But the greater lesson – that the seeds for such discovery reside in the four early lives – is one that must be embraced if a replete, documented life of Milton is to continue to emerge.

NOTES

1 Thomas N. Corns, "The Early Lives of Milton," in *Writing Lives: Biography and Textuality, Identity and Representation in Early Modern England*, ed. Kevin Sharpe and Steven N. Zwicker (Oxford, 2008), 87.

2 *Ibid.*

3 *EL* vii–viii. Subsequent page references to the early lives by Aubrey, Phillips, Skinner, Wood, and Toland discussed in this chapter are taken from this edition and appear parenthetically in the text. References in the chapter to Christopher Milton's observations are taken from Aubrey's account.

4 Peter Beal, *Index of English Literary Manuscripts, Volume II 1625–1700, Part 2 Lee-Wycherley* (London, 1993), 86. A full account of this matter will appear in my forthcoming essay, "Why the Anonymous Biography is no Longer Anonymous."

5 Corns, "The Early Lives," 88.

6 Gordon Campbell, *A Milton Chronology* (London and New York, 1997), 190.

7 David Masson, *The Life of John Milton*, 7 vols. (London, 1859–94); William Riley Parker, *Milton: A Biography*, 2nd edn., ed. Gordon Campbell (Oxford, 1996); and Barbara K. Lewalski, *The Life of John Milton* (Oxford, 2000).

8 Cedric C. Brown, *John Milton: A Literary Life* (London, 1995); A. N. Wilson, *The Life of John Milton* (Oxford, 1983); Roy C. Flannagan, *John Milton: A Short Introduction* (Oxford, 2002).

9 *LR* I:135–40; Campbell, *A Milton Chronology*, 32, 74–75.

10 Corns, "The Early Lives," 78.

11 *LR* I:67–74.

12 *LR* II:118–19; Masson, *Life*, III:435–42; and Parker, *Milton*, 297–99; 900, 925–28.

13 City of Westminster Archives Centre, St. Clement Danes, Parish registers (unpublished), vol. I (1558–1638/39) and vol. II (1639–53); and National Archives, PROB 11/67 Audley (will of John Webber).

14 City of Westminster Archives Centre, St Clement Danes, B2 (Surveyor Accounts 1609–38), B3 (Surveyor Accounts, 1638–58), B22 (Overseer and Churchwarden Receipts, 1609–26), B23 (Overseer and Churchwarden Receipts, 1627–53), B10 (Churchwarden Accounts, 1609–32), B11 (Churchwarden Accounts, 1633–53).

15 Leo Miller, *John Milton & the Oldenburg Safeguard* (New York, 1985), 124.

16 City of Westminster Archives Centre, St. Margaret's, E 166–173 (Overseer Accounts, 1652–60).

17 City of Westminster Archives Centre, St. Margaret's, E 1595–1603 (Army and Navy Assessments, 1651–54).

CHAPTER 4

Letters, verse letters, and gift-texts

Cedric C. Brown

Milton was not a frequent and instinctive social letter writer such as Virginia Woolf might have picked up in *The Common Reader*, but a deliberate composer of letters of mainly scholarly bent, frequently in Latin. Writing to his friend Henry Oldenburg in December 1659, he confesses a characteristic slowness: "*ipsa fortasse ad scribendum pigritia*" ("perhaps that sluggishness in writing").[1] The modest selection of familiar letters published in 1674 at the end of his life contains thirty-one texts and represents the humanist tradition of display for posterity, mainly featuring exchanges with learned men.[2] Yet some of these letters are interestingly composed, and we also need to take into account Milton's epistolary communications in other forms. Not surprisingly, for a dedicated poet, there are letters in verse, English and Latin, some wonderfully judged for their readers and occasions. Key to this chapter's methodology is recognition of the general practices of humanist exchange and "gift theory," and of the social practices of letter writing.[3] In this exchange culture, letters, verse letters, gift-poems, and gifts and loans of books were often associated. Some remarkable gift-poems are discussed in this chapter, and with Milton, in fact, most of the best documents of friendship come in verse form. Milton wrote a total of fourteen verse letters and gift-poems, a number that is still, however, small compared with those of a compulsive communicator in these forms such as John Donne.[4] The many other letters in Latin in which Milton had a hand as translator/drafter, when he was Secretary for Foreign Languages to the Council of State between 1649 and 1652, represent a body of work existing in many variants. These were originally intended to accompany the familiar letters in a twin volume in 1674, and need a different frame of reference from that in this chapter, which is concerned with communications of friendship and personal textual exchange.[5]

A crafted body of work in modest numbers is, then, what we are looking at, but there must have been other texts that have not survived. This we can deduce from the records of Milton's exchanges with Hermann Mylius, the envoy from the little German principality of Oldenburg.[6] Mylius had been sent to London to negotiate a treaty and communicated with Milton as an employee of the Council of State and as a fellow man of letters, in this case state business and scholarly acquaintance running together. The Oldenburg Staatsarchiv preserves seven letters from Milton, but only one appears in the 1674 volume, as Letter 11 of December 1651, a substantial composition also showing Milton in a positive light as active negotiator. Such selectivity must have been exercised with his other correspondence.[7] Did Milton keep a letter-book of fair copies of letters sent, which might have been selective, from which further selections were then made for the 1674 publication, with the help of his amanuenses during the years of blindness? His production is select in composition and presentation to the public, and his target audience can be fiercely select, too.

If we begin with the *Familiar Letters*, the range of associations and activities they deal with might be reviewed by grouping the parties addressed.[8] That four of the recipients are humanist diplomats neatly underlines the notice taken during the 1650s of Milton's republican and polemical writings by politically engaged continental scholars. Along with Hermann Mylius, there was Liewe van Aitzema, the envoy from the Hanse towns in 1652, who wrote in early 1655 about getting Milton's divorce tracts translated in the Netherlands, and to whom Milton's reply of February is preserved in the 1674 volume. Then there was the effusive Greek-born but Italian-educated envoy of Palma, Leonard Philaras, an admirer of Milton's writings, to whom Milton addresses two friendly letters acknowledging gifts and kindnesses. In Letter 12, of June 1652, thanking Philaras for a portrait, eulogy, and gracious letter, he praises the envoy as the true successor of free Greek learning, presumably in the same generous spirit as Philaras had shown. In Letter 15, of September 1654, Milton thanks him for a visit and solicitude about his blindness. Finally in this group there is Henry Oldenburg, at first the agent of Bremen on a mission to the Council of State, but from 1654 pursuing a scientific retirement in England. He stayed for a while in Oxford and tutored the son of Milton's friend Lady Ranelagh, Richard Jones, whom Milton seems also to have taught, then traveled with Jones in Europe before settling back in England and becoming in due course Secretary of the Royal Society. Milton sent Oldenburg copies of the *Defensio Secunda* to distribute. There are four letters to Oldenburg in the volume (four short ones also to young Jones), more than to any other correspondent, and I shall return to this series because of its frank manner. The humanist-diplomat group was a good one to publish in 1674: the correspondents showed European recognition of Milton's writings, and in each case there was exchange of textual gifts or the provision of services in connection with Milton's writings.

Not all scholarly correspondents were of course also diplomats. The arrangement of *Familiar Letters* is chronological, charting the development of Milton's education and reputation as a scholar-writer on a European scale, so the first seven letters, to Charles Diodati, Alexander Gil Jr., and Thomas Young, form a tribute to the men who most encouraged the first stages of that development. Of these three formative influences, Young was a zealous Scots Presbyterian pastor whom the family engaged as an early tutor, and to one of Milton's letters to him I shall briefly return. Young was also the recipient of one of Milton's verse letters in elegiacs (Elegy 4). Gil, some ten years older than Milton, was the son of the high master at Milton's school, St. Paul's, and also taught there. He was a considerable neo-Latin poet, and one of Milton's three published letters to him, Letter 5 of 1634, nine years after leaving St. Paul's, includes as gift-text a Greek rendition of Psalm 114. Milton was publicizing a connection with this scholar respected in the field of ancient languages. Diodati, a fellow schoolboy at St. Paul's and probably the most intimate friend of the whole of Milton's life, was the recipient not only of Familiar Letters 6 and 7, but also two verse letters in elegiacs (Elegies 1 and 6), probably all the Italian sonnets, and, in death, a wonderful *epitaphium*. I shall also come back to this series of letters to Diodati, which shows the two friends' mutual psychological support and their free-spirited mastery of languages. It involved Greek (from Diodati), Latin (the staple), Italian (the Diodati ancestral tongue), and English. Against the usual diplomatic tradition of replying in whatever language the incoming text had been written, these friends played freely with language variety.

Language is also one of the keys to the next group of letters, which celebrates Milton's tour to Italy in 1638–39, a crucial experience for him in his desire to escape insularity.[9] There are many courtesies exchanged in textual form in this group. Letter 8, to Benedetto Buonmattei, a Florentine academy member, shows Milton's engagement with issues of good language. The next letter, to Lucas Holste, the Vatican librarian, records Holste's generosity in Rome, in the library and with introductions to learned men. In Letter 10, written years later in 1647 and a revealing text to which I shall return, Milton confesses to Carlo Dati, the popular Florentine academy member, all his fond and grateful memories of literary exchange in Florence, which he cannot match in England. There are also verse messages to Giovanni Salzilli, a Roman poet, and Giovanni Battista Manso, the celebrated humanist scholar-patron in Naples, to both of which I will also return. *Epitaphium Damonis* (1640?), his memorial poem for Diodati, who had died whilst Milton was abroad, is partly aimed at his Italian friends. They, like Diodati, had served as genial humanist companions, with whom Milton could share an appreciation of good writing as well as his literary plans. There are later letters to European scholars printed in 1674; to Ezekiel Spanheim in 1655, a Genevan theologian and scholar who supported Milton against Salmasius; to Emeric Bigot in 1657, of Rouen, a book collector; and to Jean de Labadie in 1659, a reforming French divine whom Milton never met but wrote to with advice partly on behalf of the French church in London. These men acknowledge and admire Milton, but with none of these does one get the sense of engagement that appears in some of the earlier letters. It also has to be said of the familiar letters, verse letters, and gifts in verse, that the exchanges fall away after the Restoration, when Milton as supporter of regicide was for a while in danger or ostracized. The lack of such exchanges after 1660 might be thought of as corroborating the isolation he so vividly mythologized in *Paradise Lost* (VII.24–39).

There is another group of characteristically shorter letters represented in *Familiar Letters*, and they are to former pupils or young scholars. In these Milton plays the authoritative role of educator-advisor, fitting well with his humanist self-presentation. Richard Jones has already been mentioned in connection with Oldenburg, but there is also Richard Heath, whom Milton calls *alumnus* (foster-son or pupil), though marking his Latin as less than perfect; Henry de Brass, who consulted Milton on Latin historians; and a young German admirer and republican, Peter Heimbach. Although it is not clear whether Milton developed a relaxed and equal friendship with these correspondents, some of the other letters preserved in the 1674 volume suggest that Milton did form lasting friendships in part through his letter-writing. I shall look at the case of Charles Diodati in the 1620s and 1630s across verse and prose; Henry Oldenburg in the 1650s; and, though in a single text, Carlo Dati in 1647.

The Milton–Oldenburg correspondence is the most substantial of Milton's mature years. Four letters from Milton are preserved in *Familiar Letters* (14, 19, 24 and 29), and we have copies of five from Oldenburg, and a knowledge of the content of two others.[10] The period is from 1654, after the two men had met and discussed the regicide controversies, until the eve of the Restoration in 1659, when Milton firmly rejects the insensitive suggestion that he should write a history of the revolution. Of the two, Oldenburg, a compulsive communicator and networker, is the outgoing initiator, but much can be learned from this exchange, partly because both parties prefer unflattering, unaffected discourse, and frank reactions.

It was important that Oldenburg continued to show interest in Milton's books, and Milton sent him copies when Oldenburg was abroad. Socially, too, it probably helped that they had mutual interests in the education of young Jones, that they shared a group of friends (Lady Ranelagh, Jones, and Oldenburg), and that Oldenburg and Jones visited often enough to know Milton's scholar-helpers such as Cyriack Skinner. Oldenburg and Milton may also have shared a good number of religious views. For all that, considerable differences in temperament are also evident. Letter 14 (1654) rejects Oldenburg's advice that Milton should not spend all his time on continued regicide controversies, for he was in fact obsessed with his opponents, Salmasius and Alexander More. Letter 18 (1656) is dismissive of the intellectual environment in Oxford and skeptical about ideas of a new non-Mosaic chronology. Letter 24 is testy about Oldenburg's diplomatic decision not to distribute *Pro Se Defensio* in Saumur in 1657 except on demand. The older Milton could be hard to handle, in fact, having fierce opinions, which he did not hide from his more irenic friend. But that ability to speak frankly also indicates the two men's confidence in their relationship: "*mequis in tuis numera*" ("reckon me amongst your friends"), Milton signs off in Letter 14.

If frankness is a mark of friendship in the Oldenburg exchanges, then ironic playfulness is the characteristic of Milton's exchanges with Charles Diodati. It is an important feature, showing a comfortable familiarity with and a trust in the reactions of his friend. The Milton–Diodati exchanges range across forms and languages. Two early short letters from Diodati are in Greek, and they depend on well-established roles or habits in friendship: Diodati plays the convivial companion; he casts Milton as melancholic solitary scholar; both letters tease him away from excessive bookwork. Milton's earliest texts to Diodati, Elegies 1 and 6, adopt jocular ironies in response, the first presenting so many reversals on the pattern of Ovid's rustication from Rome to Tomis as to tease readers as to which town, London or Cambridge, is the place of rustication. In a context like this, "active" readership means following the ironic game.[11] The second poem limits Diodati's discourse of conviviality by figuring the opposite extreme, Pythagorean abstinence, despite the Christmas season. There are also two prose letters from Milton to Diodati, Letters 6 and 7, both much later, from late 1637. The first seeks to re-establish contact (Diodati had for years been based around Chester) and shows disappointment at his friend's failure to make contact during London visits. Letter 7, written after Diodati's prompt reply, is extraordinary. It expatiates on true friendship in a way that scholars have compared with the famous case of Montaigne and de la Boétie. Its playful beginning, reacting to Diodati's repeated enquiries after Milton's health, leads to a reaffirmation of friendship – "*veterem meam . . . Benevolentiam*" ("my old goodwill") – and then to a rapt Platonizing celebration of Diodati as one of beautiful mind, whom he, as a seeker of the idea of the beautiful, cannot but love always. This outpouring, unique among Milton's letters but also illustrative of the affective design of familiar letters in humanist circles, also helps to explain the charged language of the memorial poem, *Epitaphium Damonis*.[12]

Given Milton's substantial correspondence with both Diodati and Oldenburg, it might be invidious to put too much stress on a single text, that of Letter 10 to Carlo Dati in Florence in 1647. But this letter also reveals strong feelings and likewise depends on memories of personal contact. Milton never forgot the generous exchanges about language and literature that he encountered in the Italian academies, but he seems to have felt inhibited in keeping up contacts because he was uncertain about differences in religion – he had been unapologetic about his Protestantism while abroad. To his relief, he now discovers from Dati's recent letter that the Florentine had sent three previous letters that had been lost, showing that friendship was equal and mutual in both parties. That discovery unleashes an extraordinary account of Milton's current intellectual loneliness, rather like the outpourings to Diodati: here in London he is "*in perpetua fere solitudine*" ("in almost perpetual solitude"), not in numbers, because the house is crowded with his wife's family, but in any kind of intellectual compatibility. His true friends are in distant places, or, like Diodati, dead. He is currently reading with pleasure Dati's funeral oration for Louis XIII, and he will soon send a copy of his collection of Latin poems to his Florentine friends, whom he greets anew. We have Dati's reply, in Italian (a deliberate compliment to Milton's multilingualism), requesting him to join other notable scholars in composing a funerary eulogy for Francesco Rovai, and adding a free-running discussion of the use of *rapidus* and *rabidus* in various classical poems.[13] Quite like old times. It is fascinating, though, to see how often Milton waited on approaches from others: he seldom initiated exchanges himself.

If we now turn to the fourteen verse letters and gift-poems, each with its own occasion, we might note as a common feature amongst them a versatility in technique: humanist practice in textual exchange allowed for different approaches to different readers in different situations. As with the letters, and even with Milton's didactic habits, there is inventiveness and care in finding the "right" idea. This flexibility of invention can be seen in the simple example of Sonnet 10 (1642?), for Lady Margaret Ley, a little gift that praises her by way of the cherished memory of her distinguished father, the Earl of Marlborough, a former Lord Chief Justice, Lord High Treasurer, and President of the Council. That may have pleased her. Or we could take Sonnet 14 (1646), presumably to Milton's friend George Thomason, the bookseller and collector, on the death of his wife Catherine, written in a completely different register. The definition of a virtuous woman is stereotyped, but the drafts in the Trinity College Manuscript show how carefully the gift-poem was prepared to comfort his friend, pious clichés being replaced by a stronger emphasis on the personification of Faith and Love.[14] Or, with more exuberant invention, there is *Ad Salzillum*, written in Rome in 1638 or 1639 in the unusual metre of scazons.[15] Milton and Salzilli had previously shared their verses with each other at an Italian academy, and Salzilli had written an encomiastic epigram on the English visitor's multilingual skills (reproduced in the 1645 poems), but as well as acknowledging these courtesies Milton responded to the occasion of Salzilli being ill. His clever idea was to send him, as it were in sympathy, "limping" verses.

There are cases in this group of poems in which the fit to the addressee has not been sufficiently emphasized by literary critics, for example in Elegy 4, to Thomas Young in 1627, when Milton was nineteen. His boyhood tutor was now pastor to the English merchants in Hamburg. Milton's affectionate and respectful poem to him, long delayed so the more elaborately wrought, and remembering the earlier gift of a Hebrew bible, is a display piece in vocabulary and range of allusion, as might please its reader, and also shows appropriate meta-epistolary effects – the letter itself becomes the messenger. But the picture of Young as good shepherd, exiled by a heartless England to fields dangerously close to religious wars, often taken simply as evidence of Milton's own zealous interventionalism at this time, might also be seen as using a language suitable for this Puritan reader.

The most substantial and well-calculated Latin examples are, however, *Ad Patrem* (1631–32), *Mansus* (1638–39), and *Ad Joannem Rousium* (1647). All show intricacies of textual and gift exchange, and all contribute considerably to the range of subjects in the 1645 collection. Milton's poem to his father is a gift of thanks, showing honor and duty to the provider of his ample education. Milton rehearses the acquisition of five languages, giving him access to wide learning. But *Ad Patrem* is also a negotiation: written in defense of the pursuit of poetry, when other professions might have been pressed on him, it beguilingly presents poetry, in poetry, as the sister art to his father's precious avocation of music. The elegant Latin also renders thanks in appropriate kind. Equally well conceived, and also spoken as by

a poet-son, was Milton's poem of tribute and thanks in Italy to the elderly
Giovanni Battista Manso, Marquis of Villa and founder of an academy.
Manso had treated Milton generously in Naples, despite Milton's frankness about his Protestantism. *Mansus* responds to the marquis' generosity
in furnishing introductions and probably to the gift of two of his books,
but also specifically to the commendatory distich reproduced in the 1645
poems. Manso's reputation as a patron of the arts is richly exploited and the
approach carefully judged: Manso had been patron to the famous Tasso,
who had repaid him with the dedication of a treatise on friendship, then
subsequently he befriended and served as patron to the epic poet Giambattista Marino. In writing his gift-poem to the scholar-patron Milton reveals
his ambitions for English poetry and also enrols himself in the company
of Tasso and Marino, whom Manso had generously supported. The mischievous last line, showing that even a Protestant poet might be received
on Olympus, can only really be understood as a witty response-in-kind to
Manso's pointed lines adapting the remark attributed to Gregory the Great
about pagan English boys: "*Ut mens, forma, décor, facies, mos, si pietas sic /
Non Anglus, verum hercle Angelus ipse fores*" ("If your religion were equal to
your mind, figure, grace, face and manners, by Hercules, you would be an
angel, not an Englishman").[16]
     Completely different, a virtuoso display designed for one of the univer-
sities though for a select person, is the ode *Ad Joannem Rousium*, addressed
to the librarian of the Bodleian Library. This free ode, with three strophes,
three antistrophes, and a concluding epode, must be read in humanist
terms. Rouse was independent-minded, putting the free collection of learning ahead of political correctness, even collecting Milton's radical tracts.
"*Aeternorum operum custos fidelis*" ("faithful guardian of eternal works")
Milton calls him (line 54). Milton had earlier sent Rouse a copy of his 1645
Poems, but it had gone astray in the wartime chaos. The ode accompanies
a second copy of the volume (still in the Bodleian Library with this introductory poem) and uses more meta-epistolary effects: the text of the poem
addresses the 1645 collection, and the book embodies the poet.[17] The loss
of the first copy allows Milton to express to Rouse the tensions between
civilizing poetry and the barbarity of civil war, their generous exchange
reinforcing the point.[18] *Ad Rousium* is also fiercely exclusive in its challenging form and its guarded distance from "*lingua procax vulgi*" ("the unruly
tongue of the mob") (line 79).
     As I have said, some of Milton's best texts to friends come as gifts in
verse. I want to end with three English sonnets to younger men who gave
him companionship and practical support with reading and writing in the

1650s. Two sonnets survive to Cyriack Skinner. "Cyriack, this three years' day" (1655) enlists him as "friend" (line 10) and answers the question that seems to have been put to him: "What supports me [in blindness]?" (line 9). The answer is heroic: Milton is comforted to have ruined his sight by over-employing it in "my noble task, / Of which all Europe talks" (lines 11–12), his revolutionary writings. An intimate confession, the poem was not included in the second, enlarged edition of Milton's occasional poems in 1673, presumably because of its intransigent republicanism, but it was printed in 1694 with the *Letters of State*, as contributing to the myth of his heroic service to the republic. More social, but not without a political edge, is Sonnet 21, in which the opening recalls Skinner's maternal grandfather, Sir Edward Coke, a champion of the law against the abuses of church and state. Written as to a student, it celebrates the benefits of time off from hard study, and of a moderate mirth. In combination, these two poems suggest a developed friendship, and the repeated gifts of verse indicate thankfulness and a measure of Skinner's companionship with the blind master beyond the familiar discourse of any of the letters to former pupils. But the most stylishly accomplished gift-in-thanks to a younger scholar comes in the urbane Sonnet 20, to Edward Lawrence. This beautifully crafted elite gift-text to a cultivated young friend is written in light-hearted, ironic Horatian mode.[19] A political orientation is, however, again in view: the first line, "Lawrence of virtuous father virtuous son," refers to his father, Henry, another scholar-writer, who had been a member of the republican Council of State and its chairman from early 1654. The mode is interesting: the poem is partly in the invitation to supper tradition, though redefined towards moderate conviviality, leading to the appreciation of delicate arts:

> What neat repast shall feast us, light and choice,
>   Of Attic taste, with wine, whence we may rise
>   To hear the lute well touched, or artful voice
> Warble immortal notes and Tuscan air?
>
> (lines 9–12)

This celebration of civilized companionship is however generalized, not specific to one invitation. Written in thanks and appreciation, the poem asks "Where shall we sometimes meet...?" (line 3) during the winter months, and thus celebrates the pleasures of a continuing relationship. Such a poem defines the urbane companionship that Milton configures as desirable in letters, verse letters and gift-texts, and in its exquisite exclusivity also helps to explain the loneliness, intellectual and aesthetic, that he sometimes lamented. Epistolary texts often sought to maintain relation-ships, or compensated for absences.

NOTES

1 *CPW* VII:515 (translated); *WJM* XII:108–11 (Latin and English). Brief Latin translations are my own.

2 The foundational study of this humanist tradition, demonstrating "manipu-lations of writing and printing," is Lisa Jardine, *Erasmus, Man of Letters: the Construction of Charisma in Print* (Princeton, 1993). An exception to the Latin in Milton's case is the so-called "Letter to a Friend" (early 1633?) in two anx-ious drafts in the Trinity College Manuscript. This letter, enclosing a copy of Sonnet 7, addressed a senior advisor who had been pressing him to enter the ministry rather than study longer.

3 On gift theory, see more generally Natalie Zemon Davies, *The Gift in Sixteenth-Century France* (Oxford, 2000), a book making many references to English culture. On letter-writing there are two recent bibliographies by James Daybell: "Recent Studies in Seventeenth-Century Letters," *ELR* 36 (2006): 135–70, and "Recent Studies in Sixteenth-Century Letters," *ELR* 35 (2005): 331–62.

4 The fourteen are: Elegies 1, 4 and 6; Sonnets 4, 9, 10, 14, 20, 21, "Cyriack, this three years' day"; *Ad Patrem, Ad Salzillum, Mansus,* and *Ad Rousium.* Categorizations are contestable and texts were used for more than one purpose.

5 The bookseller Brabazon Aylmer had intended a collection of Milton's state letters for the Commonwealth government for the second part of *Epistolarum Familiarum Liber Unus* (1674). Permission not being granted, the volume was bulked out with academic exercises (Prolusions). The state letters appeared in various editions from 1676.

6 The range of texts is in *CPW* IV:828–50 (translated), *WJM* XII:337–79 (Latin and English), augmented by Leo Miller's documentary and analytical study, *John Milton and the Oldenburg Safeguard* (New York, 1985).

7 On selectiveness, if we take the sense of *Epistolarum Familiarum Liber Unus* literally, further *familiar* letter texts would be implied.

8 A translated title is used throughout and the original numbering, not the re-numbering in *CPW*. The Latin text is in *WJM* XII:1–115.

9 On Milton's Italian connections, see chapter 26 in this volume.

10 Information on this exchange can be found in *CPW* IV:865–67 and VII:489–516.

11 For a recent overview of "active" reading encouraged in the early modern period, see Stephen B. Dobranski, *Readers and Authorship in Early Modern England* (Cambridge, 2005), 21–62. A groundbreaking essay is that of Lisa Jardine and Anthony Grafton, "'Studied for Action': How Gabriel Harvey Read his Livy," *Past and Present* 129 (1990): 30–78.

12 On the affective design of humanist familiar letters, see the exploratory essay of Lisa Jardine, "Reading and the Technology of Textual Affect: Erasmus's Familiar Letters and Shakespeare's *King Lear*," in *The Practice and Representa-tion of Reading in England*, ed. James Raven, Helen Small, and Naomi Taylor

(Cambridge, 1996), 77–101; also in her *Reading Shakespeare Historically* (London, 1996), 78–97.

13 Originals of Milton's letter and Dati's reply are in the New York Public Library. This letter, which had been taken to Italy by a bookseller friend, is only one of two holographs surviving, the other being *Ad Rousium* in the Bodleian Library (below, note 17).

14 *Poems, Reproduced in Facsimile from the Manuscript in Trinity College, Cambridge* (Menston, UK, 1970), 41–42. There are three drafts, two autograph, one by an amanuensis. The manuscript shows alterations for publication, including the deletion of the title ("On ye religious memorie of Mrs Catharine Thomason / my christian friend deceas'd 16 Decem 1646") and substitution of [Sonnet] number 14.

15 Scazons are iambics disrupted by a spondee or trochee in the final foot, though in Milton's free version there is variation also in the penultimate foot. On Milton, Salzilli and the *Fantastici* in Rome, see James A. Freeman, "Milton's Roman Connection: Giovanni Salzilli," in *Urbane Milton: The Latin Poetry*, ed. James A. Freeman and Anthony Low, special issue of *Milton Studies* 19 (1984): 87–104. On responses to gifts of praise, see also Estelle Haan, "'Written Encomiums': Milton's Latin Poetry in its Italian Context," in *Milton in Italy: Contexts, Images, Contradictions*, ed. Mario A. di Cesare (Binghamton, NY, 1991), 521–48.

16 The fullest account of the response to Manso is Antony Low, "*Mansus*: in Its Context," in Freeman and Low, *Urbane Milton*, 105–26. My comments push the response further.

17 The presentation text, apparently holograph, is now shelved at MS. Lat. Misc. d. 77. It was formerly pasted into the presentation copy of the book (8°M.168.Art).

18 The fullest account of *Ad Rousium* in context is Stella P. Revard, ch. 8, "*Ad Joannem Rousium*: Milton's Farewell to his Book," in *Milton and the Tangles in Neaera's Hair: the Making of the 1645 "Poems"* (Columbia, MO, 1997), 237–66.

19 Some of the habitual Horatian configurations of this desire for shared reading and companionship are briefly explored in my "Horatian Signatures: Milton and Civilised Community," in di Cesare, *Milton in Italy*, 329–44.

CHAPTER 5

Milton on himself

Stephen M. Fallon

If Shakespeare is our great anonymous poet, invisible even in works that bear his name, Milton is his great mirror opposite, unavoidably present even in his unsigned works. The autobiographically promiscuous Milton, to borrow Hamlet's simile, unpacks his heart like a whore. He never misses, and sometimes he invents, occasions to write about himself. Readers have found Milton not only in the voice of the prose works and the speakers and narrators of the poetry but also in his characters, for example in Abdiel, Samson, and even Satan. Today's readers are liable to value Shakespeare's reticence, the epitome of Keatsian "negative capability," along with the variety to which it gives rise, over Milton's single-minded, demanding earnestness. Samuel Taylor Coleridge, however, gives us a way to think about the value of the peculiarly Miltonic perspective:

There is a subjectivity of the poet, as of Milton, who is himself before himself in everything he writes; and there is a subjectivity of the *persona*, or dramatic character, as in all Shakespeare's great creations... [I]t is a sense of [his] intense egotism that gives me the greatest pleasure in reading Milton's works. The egotism of such a man is a revelation of spirit.[1]

Himself before himself. Coleridge's reflexive construction voices the involutions of writing about the self. Milton is before himself in the sense that he is to himself an object of contemplation. In the temporal sense he is the precursor; the story of John Milton precedes and occupies the center of his diverse works. In the absence of a poet who is "him selfe ... a true Poem," as he phrases it in *An Apology against a Pamphlet* (1642), there can be no great poem, so Milton set about the task of composing himself over the course of his career, in prose and poetry (*CPW* 1:890). Reading Milton on himself raises questions about the complicated relation between a constructed image and the self discovered or concealed behind it.

The relation between constructed image and living author is radically complicated in Milton's case by the fact that he tells an impossible story

46

about himself. While sharing the Christian beliefs, particularly emphasized in his time, in the depravity of the fallen human race and the need
for divine grace to precede and make possible any good action, Milton in
the explicitly autobiographical digressions in his prose writes about himself
as if he is without blame. In doing so, he rejects the story of sin, conviction, repentance, and regeneration rehearsed in countless contemporary
autobiographies. While the genre was particularly popular among Calvinist
Puritans, writers from across the theological spectrum published their lives.
Their autobiographies and autobiographical digressions followed a script,
derived from the examples of Paul's letters and Augustine's *Confessions*: a
trajectory from youthful sinfulness, through conviction of sin, reception
of the Word, regeneration of the spirit, and sanctification, with each step
attended by enabling grace. Milton did more than reject this obligatory
story, he makes impossible claims for his imperviousness to sin. The same
set of beliefs that made admission of sin part of the ethical proof for Milton's
contemporaries, for a conviction of sin is a necessary prelude to godliness,
destabilizes the story of sinlessness that he chooses to tell. To follow the
career of Milton's autobiographical writing is to follow the seismic effects
of the collision between the story that Milton's beliefs dictated and the
story that Milton nonetheless chooses to tell about himself.

Because Milton writes about himself so often and under so many guises,
I will focus on salient instances of three modes of writing about the self.
For Milton's explicit autobiographical digressions in his prose, a category
that includes familiar and revealing sections of *The Reason of Church-
Government* (1642) and *Pro Populo Anglicano Defensio Secunda* (1654), I
will examine the remarkable digression in *An Apology against a Pamphlet*.
For Milton's practice of veiling representations of himself (from himself
as well as from his readers), I will look to *The Doctrine and Discipline of
Divorce* (1643; 2nd edn. 1644). And for Milton's deployment of his poems'
speakers and narrators as self-revelation, I will look at the invocations of
Paradise Lost.

The autobiographical sections of the *Apology* are the most intimate
that Milton wrote. Answering an attack on his *Animadversions* (1641) that
portrayed him as unlearned, delinquent, profligate, unaccomplished, and
licentious, and promising his readers "the discovery of my inmost thoughts"
(*CPW* 1:889), Milton describes his daily routines, his literary education and
aspirations, the high regard of his university teachers, his present ideals of
chastity and honor, and his future aims. He reacts to the "conceit that all
who are not Prelaticall, are grosse-headed, thick witted, illiterat, shallow."
"Can nothing then," an exasperated Milton asks, "but Episcopacy teach

men to speak good English, to pick & order a set of words judiciously?" (*CPW* 1:873). Milton turns the implication around, arguing that eloquence is the exclusive possession of the virtuous, as opposed to the grasping bishops: Milton constructs his own image to demonstrate that he is both good and learned, suggesting, as he had in *The Reason of Church-Government*, that goodness and learning, as manifest in eloquence, are inseparable: "how he should be truly eloquent who is not withall a good man, I see not" (*CPW* 1:874).

The pose of seamless continuity between the moral writer and his writing is complicated by Milton's recounting of his internal monologues. The literary may emerge from and reveal the man, but the literary goes all the way down. The self is, ineluctably, constructed. The Confuter, who does not know Milton, must "fetch his character from some scattered passages in his own writings."[2] Milton replies that the resulting hostile portrait derives not from his own words but "from some penurious Book of Characters" (*CPW* 1:883).[3] Despite their opposition, they agree that the Confuter has gathered the character from a text, not from an observed life. And while Milton will counterpose his life to the Confuter's textual fantasy, he writes as if the "self" is itself a textual production: "I conceav'd my selfe to be now not as mine own person, but as a member incorporate into that truth whereof I was perswaded" (*CPW* 1:871). "Conceives" looks in two directions; Milton understands himself and creates himself. The self is inseparable not only from the truth, but from the texts that proclaim the truth.

In *Areopagitica*, Milton would suggest that books are living things; here in *An Apology*, he suggests that men can be books: "I was confirm'd in this opinion, that he who would not be frustrate of his hope to write well hereafter in laudable things, *ought him selfe to bee a true Poem*, that is, *a composition*, and patterne of the best and honourablest things" (*CPW* 1:890; my emphasis). Skeptical that autobiographical portraits give us access to unmediated selves, we remind ourselves that they are artifacts. Milton, once again, was there ahead of us. The self, even before making its mediated way into writing, is already textual; Milton sees himself as composing himself even before taking up his pen.

Reading the best authors has inspired Milton to emulate the poetry and the virtues celebrated (*CPW* 1:889–90); given his identification of poet and poem they amount to the same thing. He singles out Dante and Petrarch, "the two famous renowners of *Beatrice* and *Laura*," for their sublimity and purity (*CPW* 1:890). Milton's aspiration to be a great poet and true poem depends upon sexual purity. The purity of virgin lady, chaste reader, and honorable author animate one another. Even granting the pressure of the rhetorical situation and the requirements of the ethical proof, Milton's claims to purity are hyperbolic. They are, moreover, in tension with the doctrine of inherited sinfulness. Despite his claim to have conducted an "unfained and diligent inquiry of mine owne conscience at home" (*CPW* 1:869), his examination of conscience unearths no sins. Milton articulates his ethic of chastity and literary excellence in secular terms. Christianity enters as an afterthought. Although stipulating that he mentions training in Christian precepts last "as perfection is last" (*CPW* 1:892), he implies that literary training and natural disposition are sufficient for chastity: "though Christianity had bin but slightly taught me, yet a certain reserv'dnesse of naturall disposition, and morall discipline learnt out of the noblest Philosophy was anough to keep me in disdain of farre less incontinences then this of the Burdello" (*CPW* 1:892). If there is no true learning without goodness, it seems as if learning, with the possible addition of a promising disposition, can make grace unnecessary.

Milton's description of himself implies an exemption from the universal condition of fallenness. While he cannot have intended to make a claim that violates his understanding of the fall, he omits the gestures of conviction that were second nature to his contemporaries. The result is an instability at the heart of Milton's representation of himself. Images and ideas do not lie still; under the pressure of untenable claims they oscillate and reverse themselves. This is the case in the charged discussion of stained garments:

With me it fares now, as with him whose outward garment hath bin injur'd and ill bedighted; for having no other shift,[4] what helpe but to turn the inside outwards, especially if the lining be of the same, or, as it is sometimes, much better. So if my name and outward demeanour be not evident anough to defend me, I must make tryall, if the discovery of my inmost thoughts can. (*CPW* 1:888–89)

Milton's meaning is clear. If his public image has been muddied, he will reveal what lies within. Turning what was inside to the outside, he will reveal the unspotted lining of the soiled garment. But the play of inside and outside in the image is unstable. The lining, even if normally turned in, is part of a covering. In being turned out, it is now just what the outside of the garment had been, a public face that covers the speaker even as it purports to discover him. Once reversed, the garment more aptly resembles that state of affairs that a garment metaphor might be expected to signify: a spotted inside covered and disguised by "finer" appearance.

In writing the text, Milton has conceived and given birth to himself. The *Apology* argues for the continuity between a virtuous interior, a name, and a reliable self-representation. But this continuity is unsettled by a discontinuity between an unmediated self and a constructed self, between the man and his textual self-representation. It is unsettled, in addition, by the hyperbolic and, given his stated understanding of the fall, untenable claims for virtue in his self-representation. The pressures generated by this impossible story will erupt in the divorce tracts.

In *The Doctrine and Discipline of Divorce*, Milton refrains from recounting his own life. His avoidance of autobiography in this work and in *Areopagitica* (1644) may have something to do with his ambivalence about having a personal stake in an argument. He assures readers in *Areopagitica* that his opposition to the licensing law "is not... the disburdening of a particular fancie, but the common grievance of all" who study and write for the public good (*CPW* II:539). In the *Doctrine and Discipline*, on the other hand, he laments "how cold, how dull, and faree from all fellow feeling we are, without the spurre of self-concernment" (*CPW* II:226). Taking the place of professedly autobiographical digressions in these works are micro-narratives in the third persons of men who look very much like Milton. In the *Doctrine and Discipline* these proxy autobiographies wrestle with what was excluded in the antiprelatical tracts: the possibility of sin and alienation.

Milton has two problems in the divorce tracts. His own marriage in ruins (he and Mary Powell would later reconcile), he finds himself needing a divorce, a remedy apparently forbidden by Christ. The remedy, moreover, is adapted to human weakness after the fall, a weakness Milton does not acknowledge in himself elsewhere. The strained, counterintuitive argument – Christ permits divorce, his apparent prohibition only a trap for the Pharisees – coupled with Milton's painful situation, work against his familiar self-construction as heroically virtuous.

The result is the splintering of Milton's self-representation. On the one hand, Milton casts himself as a benefactor of humankind, possessed of prophetic insight into Christ's intentions. On the other hand, he displaces identifiably autobiographical detail onto a hypothetical third person. Veering between antithetical extremes, he will claim heroic stature, grounded in virtue, even as he contemplates obscurely and behind veils the possibility of guilt and mortal error. We recognize Milton's life experiences in the third-person description of those "soberest and best govern'd men" who, because they "have spent their youth chastly" and "are lest practiz'd in these affairs," are liable to innocent error in choice of a marriage partner (*CPW* II:249). When this happens, the natural burning for companionship is frustrated, giving rise to an innocent hate, "not that Hate that sins" (*CPW*

II:253). The paradox suggests that the blamelessness of Milton's veiled self-representation is sustained tenuously at best. Moments later this other self teeters at the edge of a chasm:

> though he be almost the strongest Christian, he will be ready to *dispair* in vertue, and mutin against divine providence: and this doubtles is the reason of those lapses and that melancholy despair which we see in many wedded persons, *though they understand it not . . .* and is of extreme danger; therefore when human frailty surcharg'd, is at such a losse, charity ought to venture much, and use bold physick, lest an over-tost faith endanger to shipwrack. (*CPW* II:254; my emphasis)

The struggle for equilibrium marking the tract is played out here in small compass. I am the strongest Christian, Milton seems to say, and I am ready to divorce virtuously, or to "dis-pair in vertue"; though the strongest Christian, owing to an intolerable law I am in danger of despair, loss of faith, and mutiny against God.

The distance between Milton's acknowledged and unacknowledged self-representations is betrayed in a passage recalling the *Apology*'s declarations of heroic virtue:

> hee who shall indeavour the amendment of any old neglected grievance in Church or State, or in the daily course of life, if he be gifted with abilities of mind that may raise him to so high an undertaking, I grant he hath already much whereof not to repent him; yet let me arreed him, not to be the foreman of any mis-judged opinion, unless his resolutions be firmly seated in a square and constant mind, not conscious to it self of any deserved blame. (*CPW* II:224)

Milton again distances himself from any blame and derives his authority from his purity. Examinations of conscience yield assurance rather than conviction. But of how many actions can it be said, as Milton said of the natural hatred of ill-yoked spouses, that it "hath not the least grain of a sin in it" (*CPW* II:253)? Substantial psychological and theological pressures attend a claim of freedom from "any deserved blame."

These pressures inevitably betray themselves. The reformer of divorce laws such as Milton will share the fate of the "foreman of any mis-judged opinion." While Milton clearly means that one's opinion may be misjudged as false, the syntax allows a reading of the "foreman's" misjudgment. What if the tract's rereading of Christ's apparent proscription of divorce in Matthew 19 and its opposition to overwhelming opinion results from improper judgment? What if the same faulty judgment fails to recognize "deserved blame"? When Milton offers one of his typical, knotted negatives, "he hath already much whereof not to repent him," the cumbersome construction evokes what Milton means to exorcize, the taint of guilt.[5]

Milton argues in the *Doctrine and Discipline* from above and from below. Milton speaks as if alongside God and above human frailty, as if untouched by human misery, and as if free from sin. At the same time, Milton speaks from below, out of painful, fallen experience. He demonstrates that divine law concerning marriage and divorce is properly adapted to fallen weakness. If it were not so adapted, a person of good will saddled with the blameless hatred that is not sin would be led to despair, the sin against the Holy Spirit: "the whole worship of a Christian mans life should languish and fade away beneath the waight of an immeasurable grief and discouragement" until he (as opposed to she) is driven "through murmuring and despair to thoughts of Atheism" (*CPW* II:259–60). Even if a bad marriage does not damn him, it can kill him: "they ofttimes resent one anothers mistake so deeply, that long it is not ere grief end one of them" (*CPW* II:273). The third-person portrait that culminates in this language of despair is at the outset indistinguishable from Milton himself; it contributes to a self-construction more disguised but no less authentic than the familiar heroic one.

The implicit admission of imperfection, even morally blameless imperfection, runs counter to Milton's former practice and deep inclination. He argues that blameless thralldom in an unfit marriage can lead to neglect of duty toward God, "if there be not a miracle of vertue on either side" (*CPW* II:260). But Milton has consistently represented himself as miraculously virtuous, as uniquely worthy of blessing. In a particularly revealing moment, Milton argues that divorce is necessary for the man (such as himself) who finds himself in an unhappy marriage, "unless he be a thing heroically vertuous, and that are not the common lump of men for whom chiefly Laws ought to be made, though not to their sins, yet to their unsinning weaknesses" (*CPW* II:253–54). Within ten lines of implicitly associating himself with the "common lump of men," Milton externalizes and neutralizes this admission by describing the wife as "an image of earth and fleam [i.e., phlegm]" (*CPW* II:254). Now he associates the *woman* with natural and blameless weakness. By the time he comes to write *Tetrachordon*, which repeats the argument for mutual incompatibility, Milton increasingly traces unfit marriages to the woman's moral failure. In both works, his self-representations as imperfect are unstable, in part because Milton cannot for long think of himself as common and in part because he has difficulty keeping culpable and non-culpable imperfection separate.

Thus Milton's implicit acknowledgment of imperfection triggers a volatile, double reaction. Unable or unwilling to maintain the distinction of culpable and blameless weakness upon which his own argument depends, Milton contemplates despair and alienation, a typical Puritan experience most familiar to us perhaps in Bunyan. And immediately, in a counterreaction, Milton reasserts his freedom from imperfection, and thus implicitly and inconsistently dissociates himself from the fall.

From the time of the divorce tracts, Milton's writing about himself is marked by a tension between explicit assertions of virtue and prophetic power on the one hand and implicit and veiled contemplation of error and alienation on the other. Increasingly, self-praise alternates with anxious, veiled contemplation of sin. This dialectic informs *Paradise Lost*, notably in the echoes of Milton's self-representations in Abdiel and Satan. It is particularly salient in the words of the narrator. While we are used to being cautioned to think of narrators as characters rather than as unmediated voices of authors, I believe the caution unnecessary in Milton's case. If Milton's narrator is constructed, he is so in the sense that any self-description is a construction. Thomas Newton, a sharp-eyed early editor, had no doubt that Milton's narrator speaks as and for Milton:

These prologues, or prefaces, of Milton to some of his books, speaking of his own person, lamenting his blindness, and preferring his subject to those of Homer and Virgil and the greatest poets before him, are condemned by some criticks: and it must be allowed that we find no such digression in the *Iliad* or *Æneid*; it is a liberty that can be taken only by such a genius as Milton, and I question whether it would have succeeded in any hands but his ... He gratifies the curiosity he has raised in me about his person.[6]

Newton's comment will seem naïve to those who insist that literary texts' authors not be confused with their narrators and speakers. But Milton has told us that the true poet must be a "composition, and patterne of the best and honourablest things." He must compose himself, and he does so in all his works. An insistence on a categorical difference between the speaker of a prose work and the narrator in the epic succumbs to the illusion that in prose works authors can directly transcribe some extra- or pre-literary self. In both prose and poetry, to write about oneself is to create a character; in the case of *Paradise Lost*, Milton's narrator repeatedly echoes the self-constructions of Milton's prose. In the epic, as in the prose, Milton describes his motivations, his aims, his lived experience (most notably, his isolation at the Restoration in VII.25–28), and his signature anxieties (as in his identification with Orpheus in VII.32–39).

Where earlier epics begin with a human hero (Homer with Achilles and Odysseus, Virgil with Aeneas, Abraham Cowley's Christian epic *Davideis* with David), Milton's epic begins by highlighting the temporal gap between "man's first disobedience" and the arrival of "one greater man" (I.1,4). In the invocation's emphasis on his heroic ascent (his "advent'rous song" will take "no middle flight" [1.13,14]), Milton offers himself in place of those heroes. His flight leads him to a confident assertion of his prophetic status; at a time when raising the question of divine justice was viewed as presumptuous, Milton will "assert eternal providence / And justify the ways of God to men" (1.25–26). The recollection of Satanic pride immediately following the invocation raises a specter that will trouble Milton as the epic proceeds: what if my pretensions to prophecy mask damnable presumption?

This nascent anxiety colors the invocation in book III. Invoking the "holy light" of God, Milton asks, "May I express thee unblamed?" (III.3), in effect questioning whether he has accurately expressed the relation between physical light and an eternal God. But there is a residue of meaning, allowed by syntactic ambiguity: will my writing about God betray pride and presumption? An anguished lament for physical blindness ("but thou / Revisit'st not these eyes" [III.22–23]) is succeeded by gratitude for the compensating gift of prophetic vision, which is itself replaced by another anguished lament ("But cloud instead, and ever-during dark / Surrounds me" [III.45–46]) and then renewed gratitude. The repetition of the dialectic unsettles the apparently conclusive consolation, suggesting the possibility of fresh despair over blindness.

The dialectic between confident self-praise and anxious self-doubt is most apparent in the third invocation, in book VII. About to turn from heaven to earth, Milton addresses Urania:

> Up led by thee
> Into the Heav'n of Heav'ns I have presumed,
> An earthly guest, and drawn empyreal air,
> Thy temp'ring; with like safety guided down
> Return me to my native element:
> Lest from this flying steed unreined, (as once
> Bellerophon, though from a lower clime)
> Dismounted, on th'Aleian field I fall
> Erroneous there to wander and forlorn.
>
> (VII.12–20)

The general sense is clear: writing of heaven, Milton has courted presumption. Bellerophon turns out to be a particularly apt figure not only because he, like Milton, spent his final years blind, but also because competing versions of his myth anticipate the tensions in Milton's competing self-constructions.[7] Homer's Bellerophon is chaste and heroic; he rejects Queen Anteia's lascivious advances and performs a series of superhuman feats (*Iliad* 6.155–210). At the end of his life, however, he is left wandering the Aleian plain, grieving for a son and daughter killed by gods. Plutarch (*Concerning the Virtues of Women*, 9) and Horace (*Odes* III.7) echo Homer on Bellerophon's chastity and heroism. In Pindar's Seventh Isthmian Ode, however, Bellerophon is a figure of foolish presumption, who falls to his death from Pegasus.

Milton thus inherited the Bellerophon myth in significantly different versions. The variations resonate in the brief allusion in the invocation to book VII. The allusion re-enacts in brief compass longstanding patterns of self-representation, with an uncomplicated and naïve confidence in divine election to prophetic status, an election validated in large part by chastity, on the one hand, and, on the other, the entertainment of doubts and misgivings potentially damaging to that claim.

Milton begins book VII by placing himself in the position of Bellerophon just before his fall: "above th'Olympian Hill I soar, / Above the flight of Pegasean wing" (VII.3–4). Without the protection of muse Urania (VII.2), Milton has less between him and the earth than did the presumptuous Bellerophon. The equipoise of confidence and anxiety is captured in a paradoxical claim: "Into the Heav'n of Heav'ns I have *presum'd*, / An earthly *guest*" (VII.13–14). Milton, a guest who has presumed, has crashed a party to which he has been invited. If he is still one of the "selected heralds" of God, he is safe (*CPW* I:802); otherwise he is in grave danger.

With the Bellerophon allusion Milton attempts to inoculate himself from the threatened danger. Bellerophon represents both the danger of presumptuous flight and the wisdom and chastity that will protect Milton from that danger. Protected by the true muse and his own virtue, Milton can exchange the fate of the foolish Bellerophon for that of the wise and virtuous one: "Standing on earth, not rapt above the pole, / More safe I sing" (VII.23–24). The relief is short-lived. Precisely at this point, as Milton has erected a pale around himself as a protection from danger, danger floods back into the poem. His voice is

> unchanged,
> To hoarse or mute, though fall'n on evil days,
> On evil days though fall'n, and evil tongues;
> In darkness, and with dangers compassed round,
> And solitude.
>
> (VII.24–28)

Milton here reflects bitterly on his desperate situation after the Restoration. The depth of anxiety is difficult to overstate, given that Milton's self-description echoes language with which he had had Sin describe

herself earlier. Sin sits by the Hell-gates "in perpetual agony and pain, /
With terrors and with clamors compassed round" (II.861–62). In the small
step from "With terrors and with clamors compassed round" to the metri-
cally identical "In darkness, and with dangers compassed round," Milton
uncovers to us and to himself what he wishes to remain covered.

The mirroring of lines is only the most salient instance of the presence
in book VII's invocation of language associated with Satan and the fallen
angels. Milton's fear that he will fall to earth, "Erroneous there to wander
and forlorn" (VII.20) echoes one of Satan's first questions, "Seest thou yon
dreary plain, forlorn and wild?" (I.180). The exploring devils of book II
are similarly described as "roving on / In confused march forlorn" (II.614–
15). The narrator's echoing of Satan's and Sin's words undercuts Milton's
exorcism of the danger of presumption.

Anxiety and a hint of transgression return at the end of the invocation,
in the familiar allusion to Orpheus:

> But drive far off the barbarous dissonance
> Of Bacchus and his revellers, the race
> Of that wild rout that tore the Thracian bard
> In Rhodope, where woods and rocks had ears
> To rapture, till the savage clamour drowned
> Both harp and voice; nor could the Muse defend
> Her Son. So fail not thou, who thee implores:
> For thou art Heav'nly, she an empty dream.
>
> (VII.32–39)

As with the Bellerophon allusion, Milton attempts here to secure himself
from the fate of a figure that resembles him. And again there are significantly
different versions of the myth. Some credited Orpheus with chastity for
spurning the Bacchantes. Ovid, on the other hand, implies that Orpheus
angered the Bacchantes by his practice and advocacy of sodomy.[8] Some
viewed Orpheus' spurning of the women as a refusal to honor the god
Dionysius. The allusion points to chastity and license, to piety and to
impiousness. Milton is either secure or headed for the same fate as Orpheus.
The recoil or return from Bellerophon to Orpheus, like the recoil and
return from blindness to blindness in book III, can point as easily toward
an unceasing oscillation between despair and confidence as it can to the
final laying to rest of doubt. If a second reassurance is needed, why not a
third, fourth, fifth, and so on indefinitely?

In the invocations Milton introduces himself and attempts to establish
his authority as a prophetic poet, but what might be called the authorized
presentation of the author is accompanied and unsettled by intimations of

alienation and error. In exploring the possibility of error, Milton, however unintentionally, is writing about himself. In the invocations one can see the lineaments of two conflicting self-constructions that have been unfolding together since the divorce tracts. These self-constructions will inform *Paradise Regained* and *Samson Agonistes* as well, with the Son of God modeled uncannily on Milton's self-representation as virtuous and Samson reflecting both Milton's heroic self-construction and his more obscure contemplation of fallibility.[9]

NOTES

1 From *Specimens of the Table Talk of the Late Samuel Taylor Coleridge*, ed. Henry Nelson Coleridge, 2 vols. (London, 1835), 1:129–30 and II:240–41 (May 12, 1830 and August 18, 1833).

2 *A Modest Confutation*, "To the Reader," A3r. Reprinted in William Riley Parker, *Milton's Contemporary Reputation* (1940; New York, 1971), 121.

3 Traceable to Theophrastus (fourth century BCE), the "Character" was a familiar seventeenth-century genre,

4 A "shift" is both a strategy or expedient and an undergarment. Milton will appear, figuratively, naked before us.

5 Arthur Barker argued that in his unhappy marital experience Milton "had proof of his own infirmity and imperfection" and that by the time he wrote the divorce tracts Milton had been forced to recognize his own humanity" (*Milton and the Puritan Dilemma, 1641–1660* [Toronto, 1942], 115, 116).

6 Newton, as cited in *Poetical Works of John Milton*, ed. Henry J. Todd, 5th edn., 6 vols. (London, 1826), III:135.

7 For Bellerophon's incarnations in poetry and mythograhy, see Marianne Shapiro's "Perseus and Bellerophon in *Orlando Furioso*," *Modern Philology* 81 (1983): 109–30.

8 *Metamorphoses* 10.78–85, 11.6–7; I owe this observation to John Rumrich.

9 The arguments in this chapter are treated more fully in my *Milton's Peculiar Grace: Self-Representation and Authority* (Ithaca, NY, 2007).

CHAPTER 6

Poetic tradition, dramatic

Ann Baynes Coiro

Milton's dramatic influences range across Western literature, from Greek tragedy to Restoration drama. The extent of his debt to Greek tragedy is unique in the early modern period, and he draws as well on a rich tradition of humanist drama, an international vehicle for education and for political commentary. Although Milton grew increasingly uneasy about spectacle and actorly role-playing, the vibrant, generically disparate drama of sixteenth- and seventeenth-century England supplied him with characters, plot constructions, metric innovation – and a high native bar. The major works that frame his career – 1634's *A Mask Presented at Ludlow Castle* (aka *Comus*) and 1671's *Samson Agonistes* – demonstrate Milton's shifting influences and attitudes but also testify to the abiding importance of drama for his poetry.

The closing of the theaters in 1642 divides Milton's career as a Caroline poet with a strong interest in contemporary theater, particularly masques, from his later years as an epic poet. Yet in trying to gauge Milton's dramatic contexts, it is important to avoid grand cultural narratives about the Renaissance and the Restoration. His career is a complex bridge between Shakespeare and Dryden, masque and opera, university culture and popular print culture, and theater and drama. If Milton had died young like his classmate Edward King, we would know him today as a gifted writer with a bent toward dramatic forms. "On Shakespeare," part of the front matter of the second folio of Shakespeare's plays (1632), was Milton's first published poem in English. It is a powerful act of both praise and oedipal resistance.[1] The "great heir of Fame" (line 5) has built his kingdom "in our wonder and astonishment" (line 7), in "our fancy" (line 13). His "easy numbers flow" (line 10). But in the process Shakespeare has killed our fancy, made us his sepulcher. The poem is Milton's opening gambit in a career that will repeatedly find inspiration in Shakespeare as well as creative energy in denying him.

Herbert Berry's discovery that Milton's father was one of the trustees who managed Burbage's share in Blackfriars for his widow and children is evidence that Milton and his family were, like many Puritans, comfortable with the professional stage.[2] As a boy at St. Paul's he would have acted in plays as part of his humanist training. When Milton was a student at Cambridge in the 1620s and early 1630s, theater was an important but, given the increasing influence of strict Puritanism there, a controversial part of university culture. Yet during his college years Milton was far from a stereotypically antitheatrical Puritan. In his first Elegy, addressed to Charles Diodati probably in 1626 near the beginning of his Cambridge years, Milton tells his friend that while at home in London and tired of studying, "*Excipit hinc fessum sinuosi pompa theatri*" ("When I am tired the spectacle of the curved theater attracts me," line 27). Some critics have argued that the plays Milton goes on to describe are Greek tragedies and Roman comedies, not plays he would have seen on the London stage. Since English drama borrows liberally from classical conventions, however, arguments that isolate Milton from London theater in his youth probably have more to do with a preconceived scholarly narrative than with the kind of rich theatrical experience Milton almost certainly had.

The paired speakers of *L'Allegro* and *Il Penseroso*, poems Milton wrote around the time he wrote "On Shakespeare," refer, respectively, to theater and to drama, neatly demonstrating what was to prove a complicated polarity for Milton. The companion poems have often been seen as a sequence and the serious studiousness of *Il Penseroso* understood as autobiographical. But if the exaggerated persons of the companion poems are Milton, they are each Milton playing parts. As lyric versions of the seventeenth-century character genre, Allegro and Penseroso display a relationship with theater and drama that is consonant with each speaker's personality. The apparently joyful man, for example, is driven by a fear of loneliness. Yet, although he restlessly seeks company, he is always a spectator, never part of the groups he moves among. For him the city is a place of busy refuge once darkness falls, and:

> Then to the well-trod stage anon,
> If Jonson's learned sock be on,
> Or sweetest Shakespeare, Fancy's child,
> Warble his native wood-notes wild.
> (lines 131–34)

The reclusive pensive man, Allegro's matched opposite, reads plays rather than attending the theater. At night in his study he asks

> Sometime let gorgeous Tragedy
> In sceptered pall come sweeping by,
> Presenting Thebes, or Pelops' line,
> Or the tale of Troy divine.
>
> (lines 97–100)

The learned Penseroso prefers Greek tragedy, which in his typically florid manner he describes as "gorgeous" and "divine." Like the lark and the nightingale or Euphrosyne and Melancholy, theater and drama weigh in the balance of these paired poems.

And indeed, while Milton held dramatic literature in high esteem, he also had a pronounced theatrical inclination. As a Cambridge undergraduate he wrote and played a starring role in a punning philosophical entertainment for his classmates at the end of the 1628 school year.[3] "Salting," an intermittent Cambridge tradition, was an end-of-term show featuring beer, undergraduate cleverness, gross jokes, and intellectual showing-off. Milton did not publish his college theatrical until the end of his life and then only in pieces in separate volumes ("At a Vacation Exercise" in the *Poems* of 1673 and Prolusion 6 in 1674's *Epistolae Familiares* and *Prolusiones*), but his early performance as "Ens," or Absolute Being, is his first public performance of himself as England's great poet. When Ens/Milton speaks in Latin he is mildly embarrassed about playing a "fool" but also endearingly grateful that the peers he thought disliked him for his intellectual rigor wanted him to entertain them. He obliges with a scatological roasting based on the predicaments of Aristotle. When Ens/Milton turns to English, however, he openly confesses his ambition. In front of Milton's peers, his character tells his native English language that he "had rather, if I were to choose, / Thy service in some graver subject use" (lines 29–30). In order to announce himself as a serious poet Milton plays a role in a performance of his own devising.

After leaving Cambridge to study at home, Milton wrote two commissioned pieces for performance, *Arcades* and *A Mask Presented at Ludlow Castle*. *Arcades*, the script Milton provided for the Egerton family to honor their matriarch, Alice, Dowager Countess of Derby, combines music and dance with charming lyrics. Although Milton called it an "entertainment," *Arcades* certainly shares some of the techniques and sensibility of early modern masques, which wove elaborate compliments around slight narratives, often borrowed loosely from classical mythology. Yet, while masques are usually associated with the court, *Arcades* focuses on a family and was performed at the Dowager Countess' country estate. And although its action gravitates toward the honoree's "shining throne" (line 15), *Arcades* is more interested in the dramatic possibilities of music than in the specta-cle normally associated with the masque form. The Genius of the Wood, who plays the role of master of ceremonies, is able to hear "the celestial sirens' harmony" (line 63) in the night, and he confesses an impossi-ble longing, often expressed in Milton's works, to achieve "the heavenly tune, which none can hear / Of human mold with gross unpurgèd ear" (lines 72–73).

Music is an increasingly significant component of dramatic practice throughout the seventeenth century. In 1634, soon after the pastoral lyricism of *Arcades*, Milton collaborated with Henry Lawes, famous court composer and singer, on a full-scale masque for the Egerton family. Milton wrote the role of the Attendant Spirit for the man he fondly called "Harry" ("To Mr. H. Lawes," line 1), and Lawes wrote the music for the masque, acted as the music tutor for the Egerton children who played the Lady and the Elder and Younger Brothers, and served as the on-site director at Ludlow. Like *Arcades*, *A Mask Presented at Ludlow Castle* builds upon the Caroline masque, but here Milton fully realizes the dramatic potential of the form by opening it to recent masque innovations and by folding in his interest in Shakespeare's comedies and romances. It is conventional to refer to this work by the name of its seductive antagonist, Comus. But it is surely important that Milton titled the piece *A Mask*, strongly signaling that he is deliberately working in this modern genre.

Since the masque is generally associated with the court, Milton's serious interest in the form is initially surprising. But important aspects of the masque genre are compatible with Milton's poetic ambitions.[4] Although they were designed to be extravagant compliments for the monarchs and aristocrats who sponsored them, masques presented moral principles and sought to instruct the country's elite. In *The Reason of Church-Government*, written eight years after *A Mask* and only months before the closing of the theaters, Milton encouraged the Commonwealth's magistrates to "manag[e] . . . our publick sports, and festival pastimes," procuring "wise and artfull recitations sweetned with eloquent and gracefull inticements to the love and practice of justice, temperance and fortitude, instructing and bettering the Nation" (*CPW* 1:819). The state-sponsored entertainments he proposes can be understood as more popular versions of the nation-building and moral uplift that were at the heart of the court masque's lavish spectacle.

Milton did not restrict himself, however, to straightforward moral instruction in his masque.[5] In contrast to court masques, Milton's ver-sion not only has a complex plot and character development, but its conclusion is fraught with ambiguity. Many critics have been disturbed by the conclusion of Shakespeare's *Measure for Measure* where the Duke steps out of his surveillance role and claims a newly silent Isabella as his wife. The Lady's position at the end of *A Mask* is similarly disturbing – her father has watched her heroic chastity throughout the body of the masque, but in the end she is silent, delivered to his court ready for marriage. Milton finds other important sources of imaginative complexity in early modern theater. The Attendant Spirit echoes *The Tempest*'s Ariel, and Comus' bestial crew enacts a dark version of Bottom's temporary fate in *A Midsummer Night's Dream*. Comus himself is an early version of brilliantly seductive Satan, but he is also a dramatic development of Ben Jonson's crucial masque innovation, the comic or threatening antimasque, in which disruptive, carnivalesque forces such as witches, Welshmen, or drunks began the performance and were then counteracted and defeated by the opposing forces of order and morality. Milton transformed the antimasque into a dramatic through-line, producing a work much closer to a fully developed play. Indeed, we might call Milton's version a "problem masque." Jonson deployed a charming, drunken stumblebum version of Comus as the leader of a troupe of dancing bottles and kegs in *Pleasure Reconciled to Virtue* (1618), for example, an opponent both amusing and easy to overcome. Milton's Comus, in contrast, has a razor-sharp intellect, a sinister goal, and he is wholly integrated into the plot of *A Mask*, escaping in the end to cast a shadow of danger over the work's final triumphant celebration.

The range of contemporary masques and plays from which Milton directly borrowed turns on its head any separatist notion of Milton as above his own culture. Milton used John Fletcher's *Faithful Shepherdess*, a pastoral play first performed in 1608–09 but revived by Henrietta Maria at court in 1633, as a significant source. He borrowed lines from his Cambridge classmate, the scholar and playwright Thomas Randolph, and he is directly in dialogue with the masques presented at court in the early 1630s. Henry Lawes, Milton's collaborator, was involved in virtually every masque performed at court from 1629 on. Two court masques of particular significance for Milton's 1634 work are Aurelian Townshend's *Tempe Restored*, performed in 1632, and Thomas Carew's *Coelum Brittanicum*, performed just months before Milton's masque was presented at Ludlow Castle (the Egerton children participated in both these masques). The cult of heroic chastity fostered by the masques of Charles I and Henrietta Maria's court appealed to Milton's idealism, and he used his commission to produce the most sensuously beautiful example of the form.

Milton did not die young, and theatrical performance is not the first and perhaps almost the last thing we think of in connection with him now. Nevertheless, drama continued to be an important source for Milton. The years between the publication of *Lycidas* in 1638 and *Paradise Lost* in 1667 were momentous not only for Milton but for his country. In 1638 and 1639 Milton traveled in Italy, and he returned to a changed life in England, beginning almost twenty years of active engagement in polemical prose writing. Milton continued, however, to consider his literary career. In the autobiographical digression at the beginning of book two of *The Reason of Church-Government*, for example, Milton wonders whether "Dramatick constitutions, wherein *Sophocles* and *Euripides* raigne shall be found more doctrinal and exemplary to a Nation" than epic poetry (*CPW* 1:814–15). Such a play seems to be what Milton was imagining when, in his Commonplace Book under the heading "Public Shows," he rebuts as "absurd beyond measure" Lactantius' rejection of drama. For "what in all philosophy is more important or more sacred or more exalted than a tragedy rightly produced, what more useful for seeing at a single view the events and changes of human life?" (*CPW* 1:491).

The Reason of Church-Government was published in February 1642, but by September 1642 parliament had closed the theaters. Although this may have been meant as a temporary measure, the theaters remained closed until the Restoration. Once again, an automatic association of Milton with Puritan antitheatricality distorts our understanding of his interests. Starting soon after he returned from Italy in 1639, Milton worked on a number of ideas for plays in his workbook (now called the Trinity Manuscript), and he frequently returned to these plans, revising and expanding them. In the end, Milton did not write for the stage, but these notes make clear that he was thinking in the 1640s of writing plays for performance. Although the section of his notebook devoted to plays is often called Milton's plans for tragedies, Milton's ideas imply a range of genres from tragedies to pastoral comedies, from rhetorical contests to dark masques. He considered about sixty-four biblical possibilities, thirty-three British subjects and five ideas he lists under "Scotch stories or rather brittish of the north parts."[6] Milton generally tried to find ideas that would be workable within the constraints of the unities of time, place, and action, and he relied on messengers, choruses, and narrators to supply off-stage action. He was not squeamish about composing an old-fashioned finale piled with dead bodies, and his thoughts about British and Scottish plays appear to be indebted to English tragedies and history plays, particularly Marlowe's and Shakespeare's.

But the preponderance of his ideas, and those he develops most extensively, are drawn from the Bible. In it, as he points out in *The Reason of Church-Government*, there are important dramatic precedents: "Scripture also affords us," he muses, the model of "a divine pastoral Drama" from the Song of Songs or "the majestick image of a high and stately Tragedy" (*CPW* 1:815) that he finds in the Apocalypse of St. John. Milton could find models for biblical tragedy outside the Bible as well. He had a vigorous English precedent in the drama of John Bale (1495–1563), monk turned ardent Protestant reformer, who wrote what is regarded as the first English history play, *King Johan*, and jauntily colloquial biblical plays on such subjects as Christ's temptation in the wilderness and John the Baptist preaching. As a humanist and as a teacher, Milton would have been particularly interested in neo-Latin plays by leading Protestant intellectuals such as George Buchanan and Hugo Grotius, Milton's admired contemporary. Buchanan's tragedies, *Jephthes* and *Baptistes*, are part of the mid sixteenth-century wave of what are called Christian Terence plays: modeled on the structure of Terence's plays, based on biblical subjects, and usually driven by a Reformed agenda. Buchanan wrote his plays to be performed by his students (including Montaigne), but they were also widely published. Buchanan's *Baptistes* (London, 1577) was reprinted a remarkable number of times, in many countries and languages, often at moments of political turmoil. The English parliament, for example, ordered a translation of Buchanan's play in 1642 as *Tyranicall-Government Anatomized: A Discourse Concerning Evil-Councellors*. Hugo Grotius, whom Milton sought out in Paris in 1638 and who is virtually the only modern authority Milton cites in *Doctrine and Discipline of Divorce* (1643 and 1644), wrote three highly regarded plays, including *Adamus Exul* (1601), which has frequently been suggested as a model for *Paradise Lost*. When Milton was in Italy we know he saw an opera at the Barbarini court. He would almost certainly also have been present at oratorios, performances of sacred stories where singers sang individual parts. Especially because music was so important to Milton, these dramatic musical stories are intriguing influences. It is also possible that Giambattista Andreini's play *L'Adamo* (1613) suggested aspects of *Paradise Lost*.[7] And Joost van den Vondel's brilliant *Lucifer* (1654) in Dutch has been put forward as a Miltonic influence. Although the direct influence of any of these works is difficult to determine, we can certainly conclude that the interest across Europe in dramatic representations of biblical stories, particularly Satan and the fall, frames Milton's turn to this subject in *Paradise Lost*.

A drama of the fall attracts Milton's attention more than any other idea, and it grows and changes as he plays with possible characters and plot. There are four versions in the Trinity Manuscript (as well as a simple title, "Adam in Banishment," which may have been the idea for another play entirely). The first two are lists of characters, with Michael the narrator in the first and Moses in the second. A more detailed version, titled "Paradise Lost," is outlined in five acts, divided by choruses, and Moses is again the narrator. The final version is written out in narrative form and called "Adam Unparadiz'd." Gabriel is now the narrator, and he "causes to passe before [Adam's] eyes in shapes a mask of all the evils of this life & world."[8] These surviving notes inhabit a tantalizing middle space – hinting at past influences, sketching unrealized possibilities, and suggesting elusive connections with *Paradise Lost*. The one firm connection we have is Edward Phillips' testimony that the first lines of Satan's soliloquy to the sun in *Paradise Lost* (IV.32–41) were originally part of the opening scene of a tragedy.[9]

In *Eikonoklastes* (1649), published in the wake of the king's execution and full of disgust for those who fell under the theatrical spell of Charles, Milton mocks Charles for reading Shakespeare as he prepares for his death. Nevertheless, drama's presence is profound and pervasive in *Paradise Lost*.[10] First, the blank verse of *Paradise Lost* was associated in English almost exclusively with the stage. Milton cites Homer's Greek and Virgil's Latin as his precedent, but in his native language Milton says it is "our best English tragedies" that have "long since" understood the "ancient liberty" of blank verse and its ability to draw "the sense variously . . . from one verse into another" ("The Verse," *CPEP* 291). The plot, the characters, and the dialogues of *Paradise Lost* pull from a range of dramatic genres: tragedy in books IX and X, but also comedy for the scenes of Edenic marriage, masque for the construction of Pandemonium and for the education of Adam in book XI, and, in the end, the Christian tragicomedy of the fortunate fall. Satan resembles a Renaissance revenge tragedy antihero, and the choirs of angels perform the role of heavenly chorus. The nuanced roles of Satan, Eve and Adam, their tragic flaws, and the turning point when they act upon them and bring tragedy upon their heads are all portrayed in lively dialogue and in dramatic soliloquies.

But unease about theatricality also saturates Milton's great Restoration poems. *Paradise Regained*'s actorly Satan makes a mockery of the stage, a platform for which Milton says his enigmatic tragedy, *Samson Agonistes*, was "never . . . intended."[11] Instead, Milton carefully provides other contexts for his dramatic work in the brief essay that prefaces *Samson Agonistes*,

"Of the Sort of Dramatic Poem which is Called Tragedy." He defends tragedy as "the gravest, moralest, and most profitable of all other poems," but "as it was anciently composed." Aeschylus, Sophocles, and Euripides are "the three tragic poets unequalled yet by any, and the best rule to all who endeavor to write tragedy." Euripides particularly attracted Milton. (In 1634, while pursuing his private course of study at Hammersmith, Milton purchased a two-volume edition of Euripides, now in the Bodleian Library, which he worked through and annotated carefully at least twice.) Yet while *Samson Agonistes* is a careful imitation of a Greek tragedy, it is an imitation so authentically Miltonic that it is difficult to assert any particular Greek tragedy as his model.[12] In fact, rather than clarify, Milton's brief critical essay has occasioned almost as much disagreement as the work it prefaces. He begins, for example, with Aristotle's definition, in Greek, in Latin, and then in English: tragedy has the "power by raising pity and fear, or terror, to purge the mind of those and such-like passions, that is to temper and reduce them to just measure with a kind of delight, stirred up by reading and seeing those passions well imitated." Milton's choice of words and his homeopathic understanding of tragedy's effects open the possibility that his interpretation of Aristotle agrees with such Italian commentators as Minturno or Castelvetro and thus allows for a redemptive reading. But Irene Samuels' authoritative essay, "*Samson Agonistes* as Tragedy," demonstrates how irremediably tragic the poem remains if we accept Aristotle's *Poetics* directly as Milton's guide.[13]

What does seem certain, at least at first, is Milton's unrelenting rejection of the current stage. He must defend tragedy because of "the small esteem, or rather infamy, which . . . it undergoes at this day." Tragedy has been demeaned because "comic stuff" has been intermingled "with tragic sadness and gravity." "Trivial and vulgar persons" people the stage, which the "judicious" know is "absurd" but is done "corruptly to gratify the people." Yet here at the end of Milton's career, Shakespeare, "Dear son of memory," remains a brilliant presence ("On Shakespeare," 5). *Antony and Cleopatra*, with all of its "comic stuff" and vulgarity, is, for example, a constant and revealing intertext for Milton's dramatic poem. What Milton may be rejecting then is the bawdiness and bombast of Restoration drama. Yet even this is wonderfully uncertain – for Milton pleasantly agreed when Dryden asked him if he could adapt *Paradise Lost* into a rhymed opera, *The State of Innocence*. And Milton's works have been adapted for musical, dance, and theater performances in hundreds of ways since. Milton, whom we think we know personally, disappears, like Shakespeare, into the dramas he wrote.

NOTES

1 See John Guillory, *Poetic Authority: Spenser, Milton, and Literary History* (New York, 1983).

2 Herbert Berry, "The Miltons and the Blackfriars Playhouse," *Modern Philology* 89 (1992): 510–14; and Gordon Campbell, "Shakespeare and the Youth of Milton," *Milton Quarterly* 33 (1999): 95–105.

3 John K. Hale, "Milton Plays the Fool: The Christ's College Salting, 1628," *Classical and Modern Literature* 20 (2000): 51–70; and Ann Baynes Coiro, "Anonymous Milton, or, *A Maske* Masked," *ELH* 71 (2004): 609–29.

4 John G. Demaray, *Milton and the Masque Tradition: the Early Poems, "Arcades," and "Comus"* (Cambridge, MA, 1968).

5 Stephen Orgel, "The Case for Comus," *Representations* 81 (2003): 31–45.

6 *Poems, Reproduced in Facsimile from the Manuscript in Trinity College, Cambridge* (Menston, UK, 1970), 39.

7 John Arthos, *Milton and the Italian Cities* (London, 1968).

8 *Poems*, 38.

9 *EL* 13, 72–73.

10 See Paul Stevens, *Imagination and the Presence of Shakespeare in "Paradise Lost"* (Madison, WI, 1985); and Barbara K. Lewalski, *"Paradise Lost" and the Rhetoric of Literary Forms* (Princeton, 1985).

11 This and subsequent references to Milton's preface to *Samson Agonistes* are to *CPEP* 707–08.

12 William Riley Parker, *Milton's Debt to Greek Tragedy in "Samson Agonistes"* (Baltimore, MD, 1937).

13 Irene Samuels, *"Samson Agonistes* as Tragedy," in *Calm of Mind*, ed. Joseph A. Wittreich, Jr. (Cleveland, OH, 1971), 235–57.

CHAPTER 7

Poetic tradition, epic

Anthony Welch

Milton made it his life's work to compose a great epic that would rival Homer and Virgil. He was not alone. Many of Milton's contemporaries shared John Dryden's view of epic poetry as "the greatest Work which the Soul of Man is capable to perform."[1] Scores of poets nursed epic ambitions, and they flooded Renaissance Europe with heroic poems. Most promptly sank without a trace. Others were celebrated as deathless masterpieces, only to fall out of the canon within a generation or two. But while these poems have few modern champions, they remain valuable to us. Like rare fossils, they preserve the anatomy of a literary genre at a key moment in its long history of evolutionary adaptation. They also tell us a story about Milton. His epic masterpieces, *Paradise Lost* and *Paradise Regained*, grapple triumphantly with the Greco-Roman classics, yet they are in many ways poems of their time. They take part in a common cultural enterprise, a shared struggle to craft a modern heroic vision out of the materials of an ancient literary form.

What did Milton's epic tradition look like? At its core remained the bright, alien worlds of Homer's *Iliad* and *Odyssey*, and the Roman historical vision of Virgil's *Aeneid*. It became fashionable in Milton's time to compare the merits of Homer and Virgil; most critics favored Virgil. They complained that Homer's heroes were brutish, his gods ridiculous, and his style garrulous and undisciplined; he was "the greatest talker of all Antiquity," grumbled René Rapin.[2] Europe in any case knew Virgil more intimately than it knew Homer. While manuscripts of the Homeric epics, lost to the West in late antiquity, did not surface again until the fourteenth century, the *Aeneid* was read and admired throughout the Middle Ages. European Christendom tended to allegorize Virgil's hero, Aeneas, as an ideal everyman, and it found its own spiritual life reflected in his struggle to carry the burden of empire. The poem was already laden with centuries of moralizing commentary when the early humanists pushed it to the center of their educational curricula and consolidated Virgil's reputation as the most gifted of classical poets. When Petrarch, who had tried but failed to learn Greek, set about writing the first humanist epic of the Renaissance, he naturally took Virgil as his model.

Petrarch did not complete his neo-Latin *Africa*, an account of Scipio Africanus' triumph in the Second Punic War. Undeterred, other poets followed him in trying to claim Virgil's mantle. Surely, they felt, Christianity could produce a modern epic to rival the ancients in their own language and idiom. But it soon became clear that the future of the genre lay in vernacular culture. In the thirteenth century, French Carolingian war epics had fused with the love stories of Arthurian legend to form the wildly successful genre of chivalric romance. Widely circulated in manuscript and later in print, and orally performed by itinerant *cantastorie*, these soon found a home in the aristocratic courts of northern Italy. At the hands of the Ferrarese poets Boiardo and Ariosto, romance reshaped the humanist epic. Ariosto's brilliant *Orlando Furioso* (1516, 1532) cast a spell over readers as far away as England, where Spenser's *Faerie Queene* (1590, 1596) overlaid its magical quest romance with Protestant allegory. In Italy, however, reactions to Ariosto were mixed. Commentary on Aristotle's recently rediscovered *Poetics* began to coalesce into a formal system of "rules" for writing epic poetry. The rules – which, in effect, called for strictly imitating Virgil's *Aeneid* – soon hardened into dogma. The neo-Aristotelian critics were infuriated by Ariosto's multiplying plotlines, his magical machinery, his flaunting of classical epic norms. Many of those critics found a rallying point in Torquato Tasso's influential epic about the First Crusade, *Gerusalemme Liberata* (1581). Tasso did his best to absorb Ariostan romance into a poem of militant literary and religious orthodoxy. His crusaders' conquest of Jerusalem marks the triumph not just of Counter-Reformation Catholicism over pagan apostasy, but of Virgilian epic form over the structural and stylistic "error" of modern romance.

Tasso's poem cast a long shadow over European literary culture. Dozens of neoclassical epics took up stories of holy war. Their plots were generally the same: a military campaign bundling together political and religious imperatives in the person of an idealized hero fighting for a divine cause. A backdrop of Christian supernatural machinery rose up around the main plot action; God's angels ranged themselves under the banners of ever more perfect martial heroes while Satan oversaw the resistance of their hard-hearted pagan enemies. Such a model applied equally well to the primeval war in heaven (e.g., Erasmo di Valvasone, *Angeleida*, 1590), to epics of Old Testament warfare (e.g., Jacques de Coras, *Josué*, 1665), or to the campaigns of national warrior-saints (e.g., Jean Chapelain, *La Pucelle*,

1656). Yet even this popular format was only one of many. The late six-teenth and seventeenth centuries witnessed an explosion of epic writing: Ovidian epyllia, hexameral creation poems, versified chronicle histories, epics of colonial discovery and conquest, allegorical and philosophical epics, and a flurry of new translations of the classics, from Homer to Silius Italicus. English poets made efforts in many of these categories, and they produced at least one work of acknowledged greatness, Spenser's *Faerie Queene*.

Surrounded by all of this activity, why did Milton worry that he lived in "an age too late" for heroic poetry (*Paradise Lost*, IX.44)? Some of his contemporaries shared his concern. The royalist poet William Davenant voiced similar misgivings in his unfinished epic, *Gondibert* (1651):

> Dead to Heroick Song this Isle appears,
> The ancient Musick of Victorious Verse:
> They tast no more, than he his Dirges hears,
> Whose useless Mourners sing about his Herse.[3]

Both poets had some reason for pessimism. They were, first of all, writing in the wake of the English civil wars, which are often said to have left the epic genre weak and demoralized. One sign of malaise is the period's attraction to Lucan's anti-epic about the loss of political liberty, *De Bello Civili*, which became a literary model for royalist and republican authors alike. Abraham Cowley composed a fragmentary *Civil War* (*c.* 1643); Davenant's *Gondibert* features civil conflict in eighth-century Lombardy; *Paradise Lost* links its rebel-tyrant Satan with Lucan's Caesar.

But it is important to approach Milton's art, as he did, against a broad European backdrop, and the Renaissance epic's troubles stretched wider and deeper. The genre faced challenges on many fronts. The spread of gunpowder weapons had launched modern mass warfare and doomed the feudal knight-errantry of epic romance. Decades of European religious con-flict sapped readers' appetite for martial heroism. The early modern state's centralization of political and economic power weakened the aristocracy and shrank its patronage of would-be epic poets. Scientific rationalism ate into the genre's trade in supernatural marvels. Hard-line Aristotelian criticism, making its way from Italy to France and England, stifled for-mal innovation. An increasingly bourgeois reading public came to view the celebration of heroic violence, which had never fully reconciled itself to Christian ethics, as a distasteful anachronism. The bewildering formal variety of the seventeenth-century epic, then, bears witness above all to the genre's cultural insecurity, its struggle to adapt to an environment that had grown skeptical of heroic fictions.

Milton's own epic ambitions evolved slowly. In his teens he announced his hope to sing, like Homer's Demodocus, of "kings and queens and heroes old" ("At a Vacation Exercise," line 47). Milton's travels in Italy confirmed his early desire to "recall our native kings into song" (*Mansus*, line 80) and to write a great national epic rooted in Arthurian legend (*Epitaphium Damonis*, lines 162–71). He pored over the available models: his verse and prose allude to epics by Homer, Apollonius Rhodius, Virgil, Statius, Claudian, Pulci, Boiardo, Ariosto, Vida, Tasso, Camões, Du Bartas, Spenser, Marino, Giles and Phineas Fletcher, and more. He attentively studied epic theory from Aristotle to Tasso (he seems to have had little interest in French criticism). Because Milton left us no formal *ars poetica* like those of Tasso or Sidney, his views must be extrapolated from hints scattered throughout his writings, such as his choice to forgo Latin and write an epic in his native tongue – in *The Reason of Church-Government* he cites Ariosto's *Furioso* as a precedent (*CPW* I:811) – and his eventual rejection of rhyme. In the same prose tract, Milton's tantalizingly brief discussion of "that Epick form whereof the two poems of *Homer*, and those other two of *Virgil* and *Tasso* are a diffuse, and the book of *Job* a brief model" points to an expanding definition of religious epic (Job was widely thought to be written in "epic" hexameters), but Milton still proposes a "K[ing] or Knight before the conquest" as his probable hero (*CPW* I:813). In the years that followed, Milton's alienation from the Stuart monarchy, his growing doubts about the historical veracity of Arthurian legend, and his disappointment over England's failure to embrace his eschatological hopes led him to abandon epic nationhood as unworthy of his ambition. Milton's late poetry would rise above the polity and focus its heroic vision on "the individual soul as it stands before God."[4]

Paradise Lost does, however, show some affinities with the popular neo-classical epics of holy warfare. The poem takes up the full formal apparatus of the genre, its catalogues of troops, war councils, single combats, flytings, epic games, and so on, all answering to the devils' call for "eternal war" with God (I.121). Milton's Satan, like the neoclassical poets, frames his story as a cosmic theomachy, a divine contest of force between good and evil, and he often resembles their epics' stock pagan villains. Compare the Saracen king of Egypt in Pierre Le Moyne's *Saint Louis* (1653, 1658), leaguing with demonic forces to foil the invasion of Louis IX's Christian army:

> Si le Ciel ne m'y sert, l'Enfer m'y servira:
> Ce que le droit ne peut, le crime le pourra:
> Et le crime se change, & cesse d'estre crime,
> Quand la necessité l'a rendu legitime.[5]

[If Heaven will not serve me in this, Hell will serve me; what law cannot do, crime will achieve. For crime is altered, and ceases to be crime, when necessity has made it lawful.]

Here we can see the familiar outlines of Satan's impious ambition – "Better to reign in Hell, than serve in Heav'n" (1.263) – and his self-deceiving criminality – "with necessity, / The tyrant's plea, [he] excused his devilish deeds" (IV.393–94). Milton would have known that he was evoking epic commonplaces. Satan, a "great sultan" (1.348) linked with eastern decadence and tyranny, becomes an archetype for the interchangeable pagan despots who crowd the poems of Milton's contemporaries.

Since it is madness to fight against an omnipotent God, the neoclassical poets often portrayed their villains as demonically possessed. A favorite epic source was Virgil's account of the Fury Allecto filling Turnus with jealous rage against Aeneas (*Aeneid* 7.406–66). Thus, for example, Allecto inspires Tasso's Solimano to launch a night assault on the crusaders' camp (*Gerusalemme Liberata* 9.1–12); the allegorical figure of Envy rises from hell to inflame Saul's fury against David in Cowley's *Davideis* (1.227–310); and Milton's youthful brief epic on the Gunpowder Plot, *In Quintum Novembris*, opens with Satan visiting the sleeping pope to press him into action against the English:

> Dormis nate? Etiamne tuos sopor opprimit artus?
> Immemor O fidei, pecorumque oblite tuorum,
> Dum cathedram venerande tuam, diademaque triplex
> Ridet Hyperboreo gens barbara nata sub axe[.]
>
> (lines 92–95)

[Are you sleeping, son? Does sleep still oppress your limbs? O forgetful of your faith, and oblivious of your flock, while a barbarous nation born under the Hyperborean sky mocks your throne and triple diadem.]

The human actors in the neoclassical epic tend to be mere tools or proxies in the cosmic battle between God and Satan. Divine agents move them like chess pieces across the epic landscape, guiding their moral choices and orchestrating their campaigns. This kind of writing allows for absolute moral clarity. The hero embodies perfect piety; the villain seethes with blind rage. At the same time, by transferring agency from human to supernatural forces, the poet manages to avoid the problem of motive: to focus on the external *forms* of heroism – what the critics called the epic's "manners" – without inquiring too deeply into the characters' inner lives.

In this Manichaean literary universe, epic villains could hardly avoid caricature and ridicule. The narrator's mockery of Satan in *Paradise Lost*, given such emphasis by critics from C. S. Lewis to Stanley Fish, looks milder when compared to the derision heaped on Satan-figures in Tasso's *Liberata*, or Odorico Valmarana's *Daemonomachiae* (1623), or Phineas Fletcher's *Apollyonists* (1627): "O let him serve in hell, who scornes in heaven to raigne!"[6] Milton's satire is rarely so bluntly wielded. Always conscious of epic precedent, its forms can range from the angry polemicism of Lucan to the high comic burlesque of Tassoni or Scarron. Milton's late poems, taking shape in a great age of European mock epic, use their scorn not for crude scapegoating but for moral self-scrutiny. When *Paradise Lost* laments political discord – "men only disagree / Of creatures rational . . . / As if (which might induce us to accord) / Man had not hellish foes enow besides" (II.497–504) – it stakes out common ground with its royalist cousin, Samuel Butler's *Hudibras* (1663, 1678):

> Have we not enemies *plus satis*,
> That *Cane et angue pejus* hate us?
> And shall we turn our fangs and claws
> Upon our own selves, without cause?[7]

Both poems are indignant responses to civil war; both are troubled by a fractured human polity; and both systematically demolish the ideal of martial glory, which they recast as the pernicious legacy of an epic tradition held captive to its violent past. *Paradise Lost* pointedly sums up the classical epic in three words, "wrath," "rage," and "ire" (IX.14–18), and dismisses heroic warfare as the Satanic work of "Death's ministers, not men" (XI.676).

Moreover, Milton's Satan is a far more complex literary creation than the grimacing, fire-snorting devils of many earlier Christian epics. This is partly because *Paradise Lost* reaches far beyond its peers in the scope and nuance of its engagement with the epic past. No other long poem of this era is held together by such a thickly woven texture of allusion. Satan alone incorporates more than a dozen prior epic protagonists from Claudian's Pluto to Camões' Vasco da Gama. Furthermore, Milton's redeployment of the Allecto motif in *Paradise Lost* – "why sleep'st thou Eve?" (V.38) – shows that his mature epic vision has left its models behind in its probing analysis of individual psychology. While other poems' demonic visitations imply a lack of human agency, Eve's dream is precisely about the intricate workings of the human will, about the painful reality of moral choice.[8]

The poem's rich questioning of motive and volition exfoliates in the leisurely, pastoral space of Milton's Paradise, a traditional epic *locus amoenus*. Since Homer's *Odyssey*, these magical islands and pleasure gardens had dotted the epic landscape, zones of idyllic ease and rest. In epic romance, they took the form of a temptation: decadent, enervating, presided over by Circe-like seductresses, they offered weary warriors a refuge from epic history. "This is the Port of rest from troublous toyle," sing the mermaid-sirens to Spenser's Guyon as he nears the Bower of Bliss, "The worlds sweet In, from paine and wearisome turmoyle."[9] The hero's task in these regions is to imitate Aeneas' abandonment of Dido, to tear himself away from amorous repose and commit himself wholly to his martial epic purpose. Yet certain seventeenth-century epics refused to forsake their paradisal gardens. The most extreme case is Marino's *Adone* (1623) – one of the most famous poems of its day, praised in Milton's *Mansus* and heralded by the French critic Jean Chapelain as a pioneering "epic poem of peace"[10] – in which Adonis, a languid antihero, spends many thousands of verses shuttling between the gardens of Venus and Falsirena, two competing outposts of pastoral *otium*. Such garden enclaves usually symbolized sensual corruption, but they could also celebrate human artistry and imagination. Like the period's aristocratic prose romances, they mapped the inner contours of the self in a space of cultured leisure. Milton's *locus amoenus* similarly swells to dominate *Paradise Lost*. One of Milton's most daring innovations is to plant this enclave of domestic intimacy at the heart of his epic cosmos, a new kind of romance garden featuring companionate marriage, creative work, and dynamic growth. The task of Spenser's Guyon now passes to Satan, who despoils the golden world of Adam and Eve. Yet the love affair of "our first parents" (IV.6), profoundly remaking the customary epic motif of dynastic marriage, stands as the origin and ethical touchstone for human history.

Marino and Milton form part of a widespread counter-movement in the European baroque epic, an attraction to passive heroes, static or episodic plots, extensive description and dialogue, and a revisionist critique of the martial epic tradition. Saint-Amant called his 1653 *Moyse Sauvé* an "idyle heroïque"; its infant hero spends the poem afloat on the Nile in his basket of reeds, and the plot's most dramatic event is a thwarted attack by a crocodile. Vondel's *Joannes de Boetgezant* (1662) infuses its tale of John the Baptist's ministry with sensuous northern Catholic mysticism. Signs in Milton's early poetry, furthermore, point to his interest in epic-length scientific-philosophical creation poems on the model of Guillaume du Bartas' vast *Semaines* (1578, 1584), which spawned hundreds of editions and many imitations. The poem not only informs numerous local touches in *Paradise Lost* – such as its famous image of the Holy Spirit "brooding on the vast abyss" (1.21), a figure also imitated in Lucy Hutchinson's hexameral *Order and Disorder* (1679)[11] – but also its core ethical premise, that "to create / Is greater than created to destroy" (VII.606–07).

We might place Milton's *Paradise Regained* inside a smaller, overlapping circle of European epics that showcase key events in the life of Christ. The trend began in earnest with Marco Girolamo Vida's important *Christiad* (1535), admired in the young Milton's "The Passion." Among its many successors are Diego de Hojeda's *La Christiada* (1611), Nicolas Frénicle's *Jésus Crucifié* (1636), and Giles Fletcher's Spenserian allegory, *Christ's Victory and Triumph* (1610). Barbara Lewalski has widened this circle, moreover, to include a diverse group of "brief epics" on religious subjects, many of them taking a single biblical episode and adorning it with classical epic trappings: an invocation, councils in heaven and hell, extended similes and catalogues, flashbacks and prophecies, and a heroic central figure.[12] Milton may have found none of these poems wholly satisfactory; the only example of brief epic that he cites in *The Reason of Church-Government*, we recall, is the biblical book of Job (*CPW* I:813). In many respects, *Paradise Regained* remains *sui generis*. From beginning to end, despite its plain style and its cold attitude toward pagan literature, Milton's poem revisits and reframes the epic tradition. Its first lines echo the opening passage that typically appeared in Renaissance editions of Virgil's *Aeneid*. Milton gives us not one but two traditional demonic councils (here revealed in their true nature as purely ornamental excrescences, irrelevant to the poem's outcome). The poem teases us with military symbolism, but its heroic single combat between Jesus and Satan takes a wholly intellectual and spiritual form. And in making Satan carry Jesus to the pinnacle of the Temple "without wing / Of hippogrif" (IV.541–42), alluding to Ariosto's famous magical beast, Milton comments enigmatically on the period's endless theoretical debate over the role of the "Christian marvelous" in heroic poetry.

Indeed, Milton's epic theory in *Paradise Regained*, far from being tucked away in a learned preface, rests to a striking degree on the surface of the poem itself. Again and again, the period's critical arguments over the fate of Christian epic become grounds for debate between Milton's Jesus and Satan. The poem constantly makes an issue, for example, of its own lack of narrative action. The words "act," "action," and their variants appear eleven times in *Paradise Regained*: nine times in the mouth of Satan, once in reference to him. Satan presses Jesus to understand his world, and his mediatorial function, in terms of worldly narratives – the attainment of wealth, glory, empire – that are bound by false human measures of time and agency. In the process, of course, Satan is offering a series of templates for an epic plot. John Dryden similarly argued that heroic poems should relate "some great Action of War," a show of "Active Virtue," while Thomas Rymer insisted that "it is rather the *actions* than his sufferings that make an *Heroe*."[13] Milton's Jesus differs: "Who best / Can suffer, best can do; best reign, who first / Well hath obeyed; just trial ere I merit / My exaltation without change or end" (III.194–7). His passive indifference defeats the sequential, cause-and-effect logic of the Aristotelians, and confirms his faith in a providential design "without change or end" that transcends all teleological plots based on the illusion of human power.

It is fitting that Satan's beloved neoclassical epic was soon to collapse under the pressure of cultural change, while Milton's fascination with human interiority was to find an abiding home in the modern novel. Approaching *Paradise Lost* as a brilliant comic pastiche, T. J. B. Spencer claimed that "the death of epic was, in Milton's hands, a glorious and perfectly staged suicide."[14] Milton would likely have disagreed. He believed that he was transforming and redeeming an ancient genre, not immolating it. He seized on those elements of the epic tradition which still had a future, and he pried them free from the creaky external trappings which obsessed the neoclassicists. He was extraordinarily nimble in his handling of the troubled genre that was changing around him. Yet at the core of *Paradise Lost* and *Paradise Regained* rest the fundamental concerns that had always inspired epic literature: the meaning and cost of individual human effort, the relationship between humanity and the divine, the struggle to come to terms with mortality. Even more than Milton's technical mastery of his form, it is his determination to face these great questions that places his poetry in the front ranks of the European epic tradition.

NOTES

1 *The Works of John Dryden,* gen. ed. H. T. Swedenberg, Jr., 20 vols. (Berkeley, 1956–89), V:267.

2 René Rapin, *Observations on the Poems of Homer and Virgil,* trans. John Davies (London, 1672), 84.

3 *Sir William Davenant's "Gondibert,"* ed. David Gladish (Oxford, 1971), 253 (3.7.2).

4 C. M. Bowra, *From Virgil to Milton* (London, 1945), 195.

5 Pierre Le Moyne, *Oeuvres Poétiques du P. Le Moyne* (Paris, 1671), 57 (my translation).

6 Phineas Fletcher, *The Locusts, or Apollyonists*, 1.18.9, in *The Poetical Works of Giles and Phineas Fletcher*, ed. Frederick S. Boas, 2 vols. (Cambridge, 1908–09), 1:133.

7 Samuel Butler, *Hudibras*, ed. John Wilders (Oxford, 1967), 23 (1.1.741–4). On this and other parallels see Michael Wilding, *Dragons' Teeth: Literature in the English Revolution* (Oxford, 1987), 173–204.

8 An argument recently elaborated in Tobias Gregory, *From Many Gods to One: Divine Action in Renaissance Epic* (Chicago, 2006), 192–95.

9 Edmund Spenser, *The Faerie Queene*, ed. A. C. Hamilton (London, 1977), 286 (2.12.32.8–9).

10 Jean Chapelain, preface to *Adone* (1623), in *Opuscules Critiques*, ed. Alfred C. Hunter (Paris, 1936), 78.

11 Du Bartas, *La Semaine* (1578), 1.1.323–30; and Hutchinson, *Order and Disorder*, 1.297–304.

12 Barbara Kiefer Lewalski, *Milton's Brief Epic: The Genre, Meaning, and Art of "Paradise Regained"* (Providence, RI, 1966).

13 Dryden, *Works*, IV:16; and Thomas Rymer, Preface to Rapin's *Reflections on Aristotle's Treatise of Poesy* (1674), in *Critical Essays of the Seventeenth Century*, ed. J. E. Spingarn, 3 vols. (Oxford, 1957), II:171.

14 T. J. B. Spenser, *"Paradise Lost*: The Anti-Epic," in *Approaches to "Paradise Lost,"* ed. C. A. Patrides (London, 1968), 98.

CHAPTER 8

Poetic tradition, pastoral

Barbara K. Lewalski

In his uses of pastoral, Milton could draw upon a rich array of subjects, topics, and genres from a variety of sources. In the Renaissance, pastoral had become a mode, identified by subject matter, attitude, tonality, and topics, and it interpenetrated works or parts of works in several genres.[1] Its personages are herdsmen of various sorts – shepherds, goatherds, cowherds – and occasionally fishermen; their principal activities are love and song and the (undemanding) work of watching animals; and those activities take place in Sicily, Arcadia, or some other idyllic place. The highest value is *otium*, contentment, care-lessness[2] – in contrast to the sophistication of city dwellers and courtiers with their opposing value of *neg/otium*, busy-ness, involving ambition, war, civic and political action, glory (values associated with epic). Pastoral can accommodate unrequited love and death as part of the natural cycle: spring (youth), summer (maturity), autumn (age), winter (death). Typically, humankind is depicted in harmony with a nature that reflects and responds to human emotions and circumstances. Also, the community of herdsmen-singers and sometimes mythic figures hear and share in lovers' joys and laments and mourners' sorrow. In Renaissance literature, pastoral offered ways to explore the relation of humans and nature, art and nature, the poet and his world.

Pastoral or bucolic poetry was never the creation of rustics but rather of sophisticated court or city poets who imagine themselves and their fellow poets in the personae of poet-herdsmen engaged in dialogue (eclogues) and several kinds of song. The Greek poet Theocritus, the first pastoral poet, presented in ten of his *Idyls* the imagined lives and activities and poems of shepherds, goatherds, and other country-folk. His subjects include singing-contests and wagers, a day-long harvest festival (no. 7 "The Harvest-Home"), the joys and tribulations of love, and the death of Daphnis. Virgil's ten *Eclogues* continue but also extend the range of subjects, with Eclogue 1 beginning a long tradition of reading pastoral as political allegory.[3] Its dialogue contrasts the lamenting Meliboeus, whose lands have been confiscated and who is going into exile, with the peace and contentment of Tityrus, who praises Rome (Augustus) fulsomely for allowing him to remain in his delightful fields. Eclogue 4, more elevated in style than most others, celebrates (probably) the birth of the Roman consul Pollio's son, taking that birth to herald a new Golden Age; by Christian commentators it was often taken as an allegorical prophecy of the birth of Christ. Most Renaissance editions of the *Aeneid* include opening lines in which Virgil supposedly records his advance from pastoral to georgic to epic themes,[4] a career trajectory imitated by Spenser and Milton, who accepted the Renaissance commonplace that pastoral is the lowest of the genres and therefore the appropriate starting point for a young poet.

Renaissance pastoral also incorporated topics pertaining to the classical Golden Age and the biblical Eden. Ovid in *Metamorphoses,* book 1, described the Golden Age under Saturn as needing neither laws nor armies because men were just and content; spring was perpetual, producing warm breezes and blooming flowers; the earth yielded fruits and grain in abundance without tilling; and milk, nectar, and honey flowed freely. Subsequently, nature and human life declined through the silver, bronze, and finally the iron age. The topic of the *locus amoenus,* the pleasant place, incorporated features of the Golden Age into many descriptions of gardens and idyllic landscapes replete with the loveliness of spring: rolling hills, green grasses, grazing sheep, cool breezes, burgeoning flowers, birdsong, and murmuring streams.[5] The biblical Eden was often depicted as a counterpart to the Golden Age, where an eternal spring brought forth fruits, flowers, frolicking animals, and all the goods and glories of nature in abundance without labor or tools or fire, and where Adam and Eve led a peaceful, serene life untroubled by passion or sex – until the fall. The Golden Age associations led some critics, among them René Rapin, to designate pastoral as not the lowest but the noblest of the genres: "Pastoral is . . . a perfect image of the state of Innocence, of that golden Age, that blessed time, when Sincerity, Innocence, Peace, Ease, and Plenty inhabited the Plains . . . [As much as] the Golden Age is to be preferr'd before the Heroick, so much *Pastoral* must excell *Heroick* Poems."[6]

Virgil's *Georgics* praise the activities and responsibilities of farmers and beekeepers, a far more laborious life than that of herdsmen, although sometimes associated with pastoral in that both contrast the happy country life to that of city or court. That motif is also developed in several of Horace's *Odes* and *Epodes*, also voiced by city-dwellers.[7] Georgic was usually associated with the Silver Age under Jove, which brought in seasonal change, agriculture, and the use of domestic animals, but in one famous passage Virgil celebrates the georgic "happy husbandmen" as enjoying "the life golden Saturn lived on earth."[8] In that same passage Virgil links the work and joys of the philosopher of nature and the poet with those of the husbandman, but he treats the georgic labors of the mind and of the body as alternative life choices. Biblical parallels – Christ the good shepherd, the psalmist David as erstwhile shepherd, the apostles and their successors referred to as pastors of the Christian flock – associate the georgic ethos of duty and responsibility with pastoral, providing further grounds for couching moral and political critique and ecclesiastical satire in the pastoral mode.[9]

The major genres of ancient pastoral were eclogues – dialogues in which two or more herdsmen discuss love, festivals, myths, and their poet-companions – and pastoral songs of various kinds, usually set within such dialogues. Spenser's *Shepheardes Calendar* (1579) domesticated those genres in English poetry. His twelve eclogues treat a range of topics in deliberately archaic language and an amazing variety of verse forms; they also incorporate many kinds of pastoral song – lovers' laments, blazons, funeral elegy, poets' complaints – often within singing contests. Another influential collection of eclogues and songs is *England's Helicon* (1600). Separate pastoral lyrics set to music are everywhere – Marlowe's "Come live with me and be my Love," and Ralegh's witty answer, followed by Donne's imitation of Marlowe, "The Bait," in wryly comic, piscatory terms. There were also pastoral epithalamia, the most impressive and influential being Spenser's lofty "Epithalamion" (1595); the Cavalier poet Sir John Suckling produced a parody of the genre and that model featuring real rustics, "A Ballad upon a Wedding" (1646). Many pastoral funeral elegies poured forth for the untimely death of Sir Philip Sidney in 1586 and others for Prince Henry in 1612. There were pastoral eclogues such as Michael Drayton's *Idea: The Shepherds Garland* (1593), and pastoral hymns such as Crashaw's "A Hymne of the Nativity: Sung by the Shepherds" (1646). Pastoral dramas include John Fletcher's *The Faithful Shepherdess* (*c.* 1610) which is indebted to continental dramas by Guarini and Tasso. Also, pastoral scenes and characters – rustic, stereotypical, disguised – are central to Shakespeare's *As You Like It* (1599) and *The Winter's Tale* (1611). Several long narratives mix heroic and pastoral. Sir Philip Sidney's *Old Arcadia* takes place in a pastoral countryside whose native shepherds present all varieties of pastoral songs and eclogues, but its courtly visitors import comedic, satiric, and some heroic elements; his unfinished *New Arcadia* retains these elements but recasts the whole in more heroic terms.[10] Sidney's niece Lady Mary Wroth also mixed pastoral and heroic in her *Countess of Mountgomeries Urania* (1621). And Spenser included a pastoral book (book 6) in his romantic epic, *The Faerie Queene* (1590, 1596) as well as other passages that employ Golden Age and garden motifs.[11]

English Renaissance theorists emphasized the uses of pastoral for covert political allegory. In his *Arte of English Poesie,* George Puttenham allows that shepherds may well have been the first to form communities and engage in conversation and song, but he flatly denies the Italian critic Scaliger's claim that pastoral poetry was the earliest kind, with simple rustic characters, base matter, and low style.[12] Rather, Puttenham insists that classical poets devised their eclogues "to counterfait or represent the rusticall manner of loves and communication: but under the vaile of homely persons, and in rude speeches to insinuate and glaunce at greater matters, and such as perchance had not been safe to have been disclosed in any other sort."[13] He cites Virgil's Eclogue 1 as the prime example of such political allegory and Mantuan as illustrating the use of pastoral for moral teaching, "for the amendment of mans behavior."[14] Sir Philip Sidney also cites Virgil's Eclogue 1 as moral and political allegory, displaying in Meliboeus "the miserie of people, under hard Lords and ravening souldiers," and in Tityrus the blessedness the lowly may derive "from the goodnesse of them that sit highest"; he concludes that pastoral "Sometimes under the prettie tales of Woolves and sheepe, can enclude the whole considerations of wrong doing."[15] Such theory invites attention to the political and ecclesiastical satire in the May, July, and September eclogues of Spenser's *Shepheardes Calendar,* and to the moral and political import of Sidney's own *Arcadia.* Along with the idea of pastoral as oblique allegory came, often, an emphasis on the fragility of the pastoral life and world, on the ease with which it may be destroyed or at least revealed as partial and temporary. In the *Arcadia,* Sidney's King Basilius brings near-complete ruin to his family and realm when he retreats from his kingly duties to a pastoral retreat in fearful response to an oracle; in Spenser's *Faerie Queene* the peaceful pastoral community headed by Meliboeus is utterly destroyed by brigands; and in Shakespeare's *As You Like It* and *Winter's Tale* the characters who find refuge from dangers at court as well as love, pleasure, and sometimes education in pastoral places must at length return to their proper social roles.

When Milton took up his pastoral pen in the 1620s and 1630s, the vogue for pastoral lyrics, eclogues, funeral elegies, and dramas had largely passed. But the mode was taken over by the Stuart court in several masques by Ben

Jonson and Aurelian Townshend – *Pan's Anniversary* (1620), *Cloridia* (1631), and *Tempe Restored* (1632) – which associate the court with the ideality of Arcadia and Tempe, and the king with Pan. Also, Queen Henrietta Maria performed in a long pastoral romance by Walter Montagu, *The Shepherd's Paradise* (1633), and sponsored a revival of Fletcher's *Faithful Shepherdess* (1634).[16]

In his Nativity Ode, *L'Allegro, Lycidas, Arcades, A Mask,* and *Epitaphium Damonis* – and much later in *Paradise Lost* – Milton makes extensive and strikingly original use of pastoral, often emphasizing its fragility. His first great poem, "On the Morning of Christs Nativity," already displays qualities that remain constants in Milton's poetry: allusiveness, revision-ism, mixture of genres, stunning originality, cosmic scope, and prophetic voice. In the four-stanza proem the speaker locates himself among Beth-lehem's shepherds as a pastoral poet and proposes, in the chronology of the Nativity event, that his muse arrive with her "humble ode" (24) before the Magi come with their ostentatious gold, frankincense, and myrrh. Behind this identification is Virgil's Eclogue 4, but Milton's poem revises that celebration of an imminent restoration of the Golden Age with the birth of Pollio's son, to laud instead the true Messiah who alone can restore the Golden Age – though only at the Millennium. He also asso-ciates his poem with the angels' hymns at the Nativity, describing it as a "hymn, or solemn strain" (line 17) and himself as an inspired prophet-poet like Isaiah, whose lips were purified by an angel with a burning coal.[17] He thereby presents his poem as pastoral ode, literary hymn, and prophecy.

The "Hymn" proper has a grand theme: not simply the Nativity story but the uneasy encounter of the natural order with a supernatural event, revealing by stages the meaning of the Incarnation for humankind, nature, and the entire cosmos. This poem inaugurates a poetic technique charac-teristic of Milton, in which a particular event is made to encompass all time and space and history. It begins with the manger scene, then moves quickly to the cosmos as Nature, personified as the paramour of the Sun, attempts unsuccessfully to hide her "guilty front with innocent snow" (line 39) and the Sun itself fears that the natural order is about to be supplanted by the supernatural. Then the focus shifts back to a local, distinctly pastoral, scene – "The shepherds on the lawn, / Or ere the point of dawn, / Sat simply chatting in a rustic row" (lines 85–87) – unaware that the "mighty Pan" (Christ conflated with the shepherds' God) has come to live with them. Moving out again to the cosmos, the poet describes the angelic choirs hymning Christ's nativity, and his imagination is carried back to the Creation and forward to the Millennium when that music was before and will again be heard – leading him to expect that the Golden Age is imminent. Other stunning shifts of perspective move between the Nativity moment and all that must occur before the Golden Age can be restored, including the flight of all the pagan deities (idols old and new) from all their dark places throughout the earth. The final stanza returns to the Bethlehem scene and the "courtly stable" (line 243) – an oxymoron emblematic of the poem itself as a pastoral ode/hymn, a humble yet exalted celebration of the paradox of the Incarnation.[18]

The graceful, urbane companion poems, *L'Allegro* and *Il Penseroso*, written a few years later, explore the ideal pleasures appropriate to their respective lifestyles – "heart-easing Mirth" (line 13) and "divinest Melancholy" (line 12) – that a poet might choose, or might choose at different times, or in sequence. Milton took seriously the linkage they treat so delightfully between choice of lifestyle and kind of poetry.[19] The title personages of both poems are drawn with some playfulness, as ideal but exaggerated types, representing two kinds of art and life. Yet Milton seems to imply a progression. Both poems are modeled on the classical hymn celebrating an allegorical deity – for L'Allegro (the Happy Man) it is the Grace Euphrosyne (Mirth), and for Il Penseroso (the Thoughtful Man), it is the allegorized goddess, Melancholy.[20] Each poem incorporates a mix of generic elements gathered within a dominant mode: pastoral for *L'Allegro*, romance for *Il Penseroso*. The first five sections of the two poems are closely paralleled, save that those in *Il Penseroso* are a little longer and its eight-line coda has no parallel in *L'Allegro*. The final couplet of each poem echoes and answers the question posed in Marlowe's pastoral seduction poem, "Come live with me and be my love."

L'Allegro is a praise of youthful mirth, innocent joy, lighthearted pleasure, freedom from care – the values of pastoral, which are displayed in appropriate activities and in literary genres harmonious with pastoral: rural folk and fairy tales of Queen Mab and Goblin, love songs in the Lydian musical mode, and romantic comedies in which "sweetest Shakespeare, Fancy's child, / Warble[s] his native wood-notes wild" (lines 133–34). The speaker derives the Grace Euphrosyne from sources evocative of springtime: Zephyr, the West Wind; and Aurora, the Dawn. Her associates are Jests, Sports, and Laughter, and her special companion and defining quality is "The mountain nymph, sweet Liberty" (line 36). The sociable daytime activities of Mirth's devotee are presented in delightful pastoral scenes that mix classical shepherds and shepherdesses – Corydon, Thyrsis, Phyllis – with the sights and sounds and sunshine holidays of rural England. Then the speaker turns from pastoral to depict in briefer compass the nocturnal pleasures L'Allegro seeks in "Towered cities" (line 117): festivals, knightly jousts, court masques, and stage comedies.

In *Il Penseroso* the activities, pleasures, and values of a solitary scholar-errant are rendered chiefly in a medievalizing romance mode. The literary genres Il Penseroso enjoys are more exalted than those L'Allegro delights in: allegorical romances rather than folk tales, tragedy instead of comedy, Christian hymns as opposed to Lydian airs. Also, the eight-line coda of *Il Penseroso* disrupts the poems' parallelism by opening to the future. *L'Allegro* portrays the lifestyle of youth as a cyclic round, beginning with Mirth's man awakening from sleep and ending with the drowsing Orpheus. Melancholy's devotee begins with evening and ends with a waking ecstatic vision of heaven, an all-embracing knowledge of nature, and "something like prophetic strain" (line 174) – the creation of prophetic poetry. Some readers have seen surprising affinities with the Cavalier poets in L'Allegro's pastoralism and his attendance at masques and stage plays[21] but Milton here reclaims pastoral from debased courtly uses for innocent delight. Nevertheless, though not tainted, the life devoted to Mirth seems to be limited, and the pastoral ethos defining it fragile, giving way naturally as youth gives way to age.

Milton's *Arcades*, an entertainment for the Countess of Derby probably written and performed in 1632, proposes more directly to reclaim pastoral from the court. The entertainment was a genre usually employed to praise royalty or their surrogates when they visited a noble house and supposedly brought to it the benefits and virtues of the court. The label was also applied to the pastorals sponsored by Catholic Queen Henrietta Maria. In Milton's Reformed entertainment the visitors – the countess' grandchildren and others – come in pastoral guise from the "Arcadian" court to pay homage to the noble Protestant countess (an erstwhile patron of Spenser) as a far superior rural queen of a better Arcadia: "Such a rural queen / All Arcadia hath not seen" (lines 108–09). The work insists on the superiority of these festivities at Harefield to the queen's suspect pastorals. Genius, the gardener/guardian of Harefield who directs the performance, embodies the curative and harmony-producing powers of music and poetry, indicating that the virtues of Harefield are nurtured by good art as well as by the ruling lady. His last song calls on the visitors to leave off their Arcadian dances (several of the countess' grandchildren had recently danced in court masques) to serve this more excellent queen, associating the better aesthetics Milton is promoting with the virtues of a soundly Protestant aristocracy.

A Mask, commonly called *Comus*, first acted at Ludlow in 1634 to honor the Earl of Bridgewater as Lord Lieutenant of Wales and published in expanded form in 1637 and 1645, carries on this program. It is a Reformed masque in form, theme, and spirit, projecting Reformist religious and political values, in part through pastoral motifs.[22] The tempter, Comus, deceptively claims the world of pastoral by his shepherd's garb, but instead of leading the Lady lost in the dark wood to a "low / But loyal cottage" (lines 319–20) as he promises, he takes her to a decadent court. In masque terms an audience would expect the court scene to be the main masque after the antimasque of the dark wood, but instead it is another antimasque: the court is Comus' own residence. He embodies the refined, licentious, dissolute Cavalier lifestyle with his mesmerizing *carpe diem* seductions and "gay rhetoric" (line 790), his elaborate banquet, and his beast-headed entourage.[23] A masque audience would also expect the monarch or at least the earl to be the agents of rescue and cure. But the lady's rescue is accomplished by the Attendant Spirit in the guise of the shepherd Thyrsis, and by a female spirit, Sabrina, who, among other associations, is a personage in Spenser's poem and a singer herself. Then the supposed shepherd Thyrsis guides the Lady and her two brothers to their Father's castle, Ludlow, where their first sight is of shepherds performing rustic dances – features that recuperate pastoral from Comus' and the court's deformation of it. Formal masque songs and dances follow, imaging the pleasure, beauty, and art that accord with the life of virtue, best nurtured in the households of the country aristocracy.

Lycidas is the *chef-d'oeuvre* of Milton's early poetry and arguably the finest funeral elegy in the English language. A Cambridge volume of funeral elegies for Edward King, *Justa Edouardo King Naufrago,* in Latin and English, appeared in 1638 with *Lycidas* as its last and longest contribution and the only pastoral.[24] The Miltonic speaker is presented in pastoral terms as an "uncouth swain" (line 186) who must sing a funeral elegy before his poetic gifts are ripe, shattering with "forced fingers rude" (line 4) the unripe laurel and myrtle leaves, time-honored symbols of poetic accomplishment. The opening phrase, "Yet once more" (line 1), recalls the long series of pastoral funeral elegies by classical, neo-Latin, and vernacular Renaissance poets, and virtually every line echoes Theocritus, Virgil, Petrarch, Mantuan, Spenser, and many more.[25] Yet no previous, or I think subsequent, funeral poem has the scope, dimension, poignancy, and power of *Lycidas*; it is at once, paradoxically, the most derivative and most original of elegies.

Milton's poem calls upon the rich symbolic resonances pastoral had come to embody in the Renaissance, but Milton radically transforms pastoral funeral elegy. For one thing, the passionate emotion in this poem is not prompted by personal grief for Lycidas/King, who was not a close friend, but by Milton's perception of him as a kind of alter ego: three years younger, suddenly killed in a shipwreck, and like Milton just beginning a career as poet, scholar, and cleric. His death causes Milton to explore his own most profound anxieties about vocation, early death, belatedness and unfulfillment, the worth of a poetic vocation, and the worth of service to the church, since it seems to demonstrate the uselessness of exceptional talent, lofty ambition, and noble ideals, with human life and nature alike given over to meaningless chaos.

The most profound transformation is the way in which the poem evokes the pastoral ethos again and again, and then enacts its collapse, as its fundamental assumptions about the harmony of nature, humans, and art prove unable to deal with the wanton destruction of youth and beauty and talent. The dead poet and the living mourner are first presented in a poignantly nostalgic scene as youthful companion shepherds singing and tending sheep in a *locus amoenus* – an idealized Cambridge University characterized by pastoral *otium,* in which nature, humankind, and poetic ambition seem to be secure, unthreatened by the fact or even the thought of mortality. Lycidas' early death shatters this idyll, revealing in nature as in human life not the orderly seasonal processes that pastoral assumes, but rather indiscriminate devastation: the blighted rosebud, the taintworm destroying the weanling sheep, and frostbitten flowers in early spring. The Nymphs do not protect their Bards, who may be subject to the mindless violence symbolized in the myth of Orpheus, the archetypal poet whose song had power to charm the very sticks and stones, but who was torn limb from limb by the Maenads, embodying the dark forces of savagery whose noise can so easily overcome the fragile civilizing arts. If poetic talent, labor, and the noble desire for fame can be so early and so easily snuffed out, why not live a simple pastoral life of ease and pleasure: why not "sport with Amaryllis in the shade, / Or with the tangles of Neaera's hair?" instead of devoting laborious days to "the thankless muse?" (lines 66–69). The swain's bitter disillusion is rendered in graphic, appalling metaphors of the "blind Fury" and the "thin-spun life" (lines 75–76). Apollo's response, in a "higher mood" (line 87), promises enduring fame in heaven from the "perfect witnes of all-judging Jove" (line 82) – figuring God in the aspect of best critic.

This consolation, though partial, enables the swain to recall the oaten flute of pastoral and turn to another topic of pastoral elegy, questioning the nature deities and the classical gods as to why they did not prevent this death. But their denial of all responsibility places this death outside the order of nature and pastoral, as does Milton's assignment of blame to "that fatal and perfidious bark / Built in th'eclipse, and rigged with curses dark" (lines 100–01). The metaphor suggests sailing on the sea of life in the frail bark of the human body, cursed because of the fall to suffer mortality – the reason pastoral assumptions cannot adequately account for this or any death.

Then St. Peter, in his role as chief pastor of Christ's church, launches into a long and fiercely satirical denunciation of the Laudian church and clergy – much fiercer than other ecclesiastical satire in Renaissance pastoral. His scornful paradox, "Blind mouths," exposes the ignorance, ambition, and greediness of those bad shepherds who seek only to feed their bellies, leaving their hungry sheep unfed, "swoll'n with wind," and subject to the ravages of the Roman Catholic "grim wolf" raging freely in the Caroline court (lines 119–29).[26] By identifying Lycidas/King as one good pastor among so many wicked, Peter seems to underscore the random chaos of human life. But his invective promising imminent divine retribution supplies a kind of consolation – an apocalyptic prophecy that some formidable if ambiguous "two-handed engine" stands ready "at the door" (line 130) to smite the guilty and cleanse the church.[27]

Then the swain again recalls pastoral – the river Alpheus and the Sicilian muse were frightened away by Peter's jeremiad – and develops another common pastoral topic, a flower passage echoing numerous others but surpassed by none in its delicacy and loveliness. He imagines Lycidas' funeral bier heaped with the flowers into which classical figures were often transformed, providing immortaliy in nature and displaying nature's sympathy with humankind. But this pastoral consolation collapses with the swain's bitter recollection that it is based on "false surmise" (line 153): Lycidas' body is not here to receive nature's floral tribute but instead is weltering in the sea, subject to the horrors of the monstrous deep. From this nadir the movement to true consolation begins, catching up earlier intimations of resurrection in the stories of Orpheus, Hyacinth, Amaranthus, and St. Peter. At length the swain envisions a perfected pastoral scene in which Lycidas enjoys true *otium* beside heavenly streams, with both his vocational roles preserved: as poet he participates in the "unexpressive nuptial song" (line 176) of the Lamb, and as pastor he is now the "genius of the shore," guiding all who wander in the "perilous flood" of human life (lines 183–85) – perhaps by means of his exemplary story immortalized in Milton's poem. Pastoral dissolves again, but now into the higher mode of prophetic vision. Although painfully inadequate to the fallen human condition, pastoral has its true locus in heaven.

The new voice introduced in the eight-line coda – apparently a more mature poetic self who has been voicing the uncouth swain's monody – reports the swain's movement from despair to affirmation as, after his vision, he rededicates himself to the "Doric lay" of pastoral (line 189). However, by looking beyond the daily cycle of pastoral – forth at dawn, home at evening – the coda also suggests its limitations, promising new fields of endeavor, personal and literary: "Tomorrow to fresh woods, and pastures new" (line 193).

Three years later, Milton composed another pastoral elegy, *Epitaphium Damonis* (219 lines in dactyllic hexameter), for his dearest friend, Charles Diodati, who had died while Milton was abroad.[28] It is the most impressive of his many Latin poems, and it everywhere exhibits profound personal grief. In *Lycidas* the issue for the Miltonic speaker is why he should devote himself to poetry and God's service when the death of Lycidas seems to indicate that the world is chaotic and the poet's life meaningless. In *Epitaphium Damonis* his problem is how he can bear to go on with his life, his duty to God and country, and his poetic projects, given the terrible loneliness caused by the loss of his most intimate companion. Even more than *Lycidas* this poem reverberates with echoes from the entire pastoral tradition, most insistently Virgil's *Eclogues* and *Georgics*; and it also challenges pastoral norms, though in quite different ways.[29] There is no pathetic fallacy: the crops and the sheep do not suffer because of sorrow for Damon/Diodati but because Thyrsis/Milton neglects them. The shepherds and shepherdesses do not form a procession of mourners for Damon, but try vainly to console Thyrsis; nor do figures from the classical or Christian supernatural answer questions or offer consolation. Also, reversing Virgil's Eclogue 10 in which the poet bids farewell to pastoral by sending his young goats home fully fed, Thyrsis reiterates seventeen times in a repeated refrain his shocking refusal to fulfill his pastoral duties in the wake of Damon's loss: "Go home unfed, lambs; your master has no time for you now" (line 19). At length Thyrsis sketches out plans for a projected epic, an Arthuriad, but his new pipes have broken; however, at the last occurrence of the refrain (line 179) he dismisses his lambs in confidence of a new poetic direction. And in contrast to the pastoral imagery in the apotheosis and coda of *Lycidas*, *Epitaphium Damonis* concludes with an ecstatic vision of Damon/Diodati enjoying sanctified bacchic revelries and festal orgies at the celestial marriage feast (lines 214–19). This turn from pastoral is decisive: Milton wrote no more pastoral lyrics.

More than twenty years later, however, Milton incorporated into *Paradise Lost* (1667, 1674) a full spectrum of genres and modes, including pastoral, in keeping with a commonplace of Renaissance critical theory that viewed epic as a heterocosm or compendium of subjects, literary kinds, and styles.[30] He used those kinds in complex ways, to evoke and evaluate the values attaching to them – most radically in defining his epic against the traditional epic subject, wars and empire, and the traditional epic hero as the epitome of courage and battle prowess. His protagonists are a domestic pair, the scene of their action is a pastoral garden, and the primary challenge intended for them is, "under long obedience tried" (VII.159), to make themselves, their marital relationship, and their garden – the nucleus of the human world – ever more perfect.[31]

The pastoral mode figures in the portrayal of Heaven and Eden, in ways that undermine readers' stereotypes of those places as static and unchanging. To portray the wholeness of angelic life in Heaven Milton calls upon a mix of modes. The angels enjoy the *otium* of pastoral but without its limitation to rustic things: their *locus amoenus* mixes imagery of fruits, flowers, harvests, living streams, and the Tree of Life with the courtly magnificence of jewels, gold, and gleaming surfaces; and their activities involve singing hymns, dancing, feasting, and sex. They also undertake the responsibilities of georgic without the drudgery of laboring in farm or garden or beehive, as they care for God's garden in Eden and cultivate the minds of Adam and Eve. And they engage in martial pageantry and in battle, manifesting the valor, military prowess, and magnificence of the heroic without its usual emphasis on personal *aristeia* and glorification of war.[32]

In its essence Adam and Eve's life in Eden is defined by the qualities of Golden Age pastoral: freedom and leisure, the perfect harmony of humans and nature, an abundance of natural goods satisfying all human needs, a range of activities consisting primarily of love, song, and pleasant conversation – and *otium*, contentment. Yet from the outset Milton's Edenic pastoral contains georgic concerns, for the garden is far from static, and Adam and Eve themselves are intended to grow in perfection to something closer to angelic condition. Their husbandry, though unlaborious, is absolutely necessary to the maintenance of the garden lest it revert to wild, and their emotions, impulses, and potential mistakes also require appropriate and continual control.[33] Indeed, the challenge to them is properly to integrate into their pastoral life the georgic and even heroic challenges that arise from their work, their complex love relationship, their intellectual curiosity fed by the education that Raphael supplies, their individual moral responsibilities in a hierarchical universe, and their heroic duty to resist and conquer evil. Such integration is essential to provide ballast to the otherwise fragile pastoral state.

To portray Adam and Eve's Edenic life as an extended period of growth and change in innocence, Milton presents them first (in book IV) in a kind of pastoral idyll in which topics and genres pertaining to the pastoral mode are emphasized, and then shows them incorporating ever larger elements of georgic into their lives. In book IV the entire landscape is a *locus amoenus* – "A happy rural seat of various view" (line 247) – with groves of trees, lawns or level downs, flowery valleys lovelier than Proserpine's fields of Enna, thornless roses, umbrageous grots and caves, crystal rivers, ambrosial fruits, soft breezes. At evening, the most tranquil time of the pastoral day, Adam and Eve rest on a flowery bank to watch the playful antics of their herd (the animals of Eden), take their supper fruits, and engage in eclogic dialogue. That dialogue includes Eve's autobiographical narrative of a courtship happily concluded, and her exquisite pastoral love song to Adam. At their nuptial bower they offer a psalmic night prayer and the Bard celebrates their marital love and sexual union with a rapturous epithalamion.

With book V georgic is emphasized as Adam and Eve go forth to perform their necessary task of caring for their external world, pruning "where any row / Of fruit-trees over-woody reached too far / Their pampered boughs, and needed hands to check / Fruitless embraces" or leading "the vine / To wed her elm" (v.212–16).[34] But whereas Virgil presented the georgic labors of the mind and of the body as alternatives, in Eden they are necessary complements. Adam and Eve's gardening labors are analogous to the pruning and direction required to keep their own emotions and desires as well as their marital relationship in order. For this mental gardening the implement is dialogue – both among themselves as when they cope with Eve's Satan-inspired dream, and with the angel Raphael (books V–VIII) about philosophical, historical, theological and scientific matters. But in the marital dispute and the temptation scenes they fail to meet the dialogic challenges, and fall.

Because of the fall Adam and Eve are expelled from Eden into a nature not in harmony with human needs, marked by bitter weather, resistant soil, and predatory animals, a nature requiring their harsh and painful labor in the fields and in childbirth. The angel Michael, however, promises that they can gain through faith and love "A paradise within thee, happier far" (XII.587) – raising the question of whether this dictum discounts their happy pastoral-georgic life in Eden and promotes a retreat from the external world. But the examples in Michael's prophetic account of Enoch, Noah, Moses, and others suggest that, however temporary their victories, some of the just are called in every age to defy whatever Nimrods, and Pharaohs, and persecuting clerics, and tyrannous kings seek to enslave their people. Rather, Adam and Eve are to recognize, like the swain in *Lycidas*, that Golden Age pastoral-cum-georgic will never again be the mode for nature and human life in the fallen external world until the promised restoration of all things at the Millennium. But the *otium* of pastoral can be experienced within – in the mind and spirit.

In the thematic statement of *Paradise Regained* (1671), Jesus, by with-standing Satan's temptations to the whole panoply of vices and wrong values, as well as to false and faulty models of church and state, is said to have "Recovered Paradise to all mankind, / . . . And Eden raised in the waste wilderness" (1.3–7). At the end, the angelic hymn celebrating Jesus' victory over Satan makes clear that, while his followers await that ultimate millennial restoration of the earth as Eden, they can inhabit the "paradise within" that he has exemplified and so obtain its pastoral *otium* now:

> For though that seat of earthly bliss be failed,
> A fairer Paradise is founded now
> For Adam and his chosen sons, whom thou
> A savior art come down to reinstall.
> Where they shall dwell secure, when time shall be
> Of tempter and temptation without fear.
>
> (IV.612–17)

NOTES

1 See Alastair Fowler, *Kinds of Literature: An Introduction to the Theory of Genres and Modes* (Cambridge, MA, 1982); and Rosalie L. Colie, *Genre-Theory in the Renaissance* (Berkeley, 1973).

2 See Paul Alpers, *What is Pastoral?* (Chicago, 1996); and Renato Poggioli, *The Oaten Flute: Essays on Pastoral Poetry and the Pastoral Ideal* (Cambridge, MA, 1975).

3 See Annabel Patterson, *Pastoral and Ideology: Virgil to Valéry* (Berkeley, 1987).

4 The *Aeneid*'s opening lines read, "Ille ego, qui quondam gracili modulatus avena / carmen, et egressus silvis vicina coegi / ut quamus avido parerent arva colono, / gratum opus agricolis; at nunc horrentia Martis." ("I am he who once tuned my song on a slender reed, then, leaving the woodland, constrained the neighboring fields to serve the husbandmen, however grasping – a work welcome to farmers: but now of Mars' bristling.") Virgil may or may not be the author. The opening lines of Milton's *Paradise Regained* echo these lines, wittily implying that this poem about Christ's victory over Satan is more heroic and epic-like than *Paradise Lost,* his earlier (pastoral!) poem about a "happy garden" (*PR* I.1).

5 See Ernest Curtius, *European Literature and the Latin Middle Ages,* trans. Willard B. Trask (New York, 1953), 183–202.

6 René Rapin, "Dissertatio de Darmine Pastorali," Peface to *Eclogae Sacrae,* trans. Thomas Creech, *The Idylliums of Theocritus* (Oxford, 1684), 2–6.

7 See especially Epode 2, "Beatus ille." See Maren-Sofie Rostvig, *The Happy Man: Studies in the Metamorphoses of a Classical Ideal,* 2 vols., vol. 1, 1600–1700 (Trondheim, 1962).

8 Virgil, *Georgics,* 2.458–540.

9 For the uses of georgic especially in seventeenth-century England see Anthony Low, *The Georgic Revolution* (Princeton, 1985).

10 The *Old Arcadia,* probably written 1577–80, was unpublished in Sidney's lifetime but circulated in manuscript. The unfinished *New Arcadia* was published (with the last two books supplied from the *Old Arcadia*), in 1593.

11 Especially the Bower of Bliss (book 2, canto 12) and the Garden of Adonis (book 3, canto 6).

12 Julius-Caesar Scaliger, *Poetices libri septem* 1.3, 1.4 (Geneva, 1561), 6–10.

13 [George Puttenham], *The Arte of English Poesie* (London, 1589), 30–31.

14 *Ibid.,* 31.

15 Phillip Sidney, *The Defence of Poesie* (London, 1595), sig. E 3v.

16 Walter Montagu, *The Shepherd's Paradise. A Comedy* (London, 1650), written 1629, performed 1633; and John Fletcher, *The Faithful Shepherdess* (first performed *c.* 1610).

17 Isaiah 6:6–7; Nativity Ode, 27–28.

18 See Stella Revard, *Milton and the Tangles of Neaera's Hair: The Making of the 1645 "Poems"* (Columbia, MO, 1997), 64–90; and Rosemond Tuve, *Images and Themes in Five Poems by Milton* (Cambridge, MA, 1957), 37–72.

19 See Barbara K. Lewalski, *The Life of John Milton,* rev. edn. (Oxford, 2003), 46–52.

20 See Revard, *Neaera's Hair,* 91–127; Tuve, *Images and Themes,* 15–36.

21 Annabel Patterson, "'Forc'd fingers': Milton's Early Poems and Ideological Constraint," in *The Muses Common-Weale,* ed. Claude Summers and Ted-Larry Pebworth (Columbia, MO, 1997), 9–22.

22 See Barbara K. Lewalski, "Milton's *Comus* and the Politics of Masquing," in *The Politics of the Stuart Court Masque,* ed. David Bevington and Peter Holbrook (Cambridge, 1998), 296–320.

23 See Cedric C. Brown, *John Milton's Aristocratic Entertainments* (Cambridge, 1985), 12–56.

24 *Justa Edouardo King Naufrago* (Cambridge, 1638); the English section (Part 2) carries a separate title page, *Obsequies to the memorie of Mr. Edward King. Lycidas* appears on pages 20–25.

25 See *A Variorum Commentary on the Poems of John Milton,* vol. II.2, ed. A. S. P. Woodhouse and Douglas Bush (New York, 1972), 544–734; Revard, *Neaera's Hair,* 179–90; and Tuve, *Images and Themes,* 75–111.

26 Cedric C. Brown, "Milton and the Idolatrous Consort," *Criticism* 35 (1993): 429–30, notes that the wolf's predations point especially to a string of

notorious female converts in the circle of the Roman Catholic queen, Henrietta Maria.

27 See *Variorum* II.2: 686–704 for a survey of interpretations of this image, the poem's most-debated crux.

28 The title aligns the poem with the Greek *epitaphios*, a generic label that often designates laments expressing a strong sense of personal loss. See Gordon Campbell, "Imitation in *Epitaphium Damonis*," in *Urbane Milton: The Latin Poetry*, ed. James A. Freeman and Anthony Low, *Milton Studies* 19 (1984): 165–68.

29 The *Variorum* records some seventy citations of Virgil's *Eclogues* (especially nos. 5 and 10), thirty-five to the *Georgics*, and forty to the *Aeneid*.

30 Scaliger, *Poetices* I.3, III.25, pp. 5, 113.

31 See John R. Knott, *Milton's Pastoral Vision: An Approach to Paradise Lost* (Chicago, 1971).

32 See Lewalski, *"Paradise Lost" and the Rhetoric of Literary Forms* (Princeton, 1985), 140–72.

33 *Ibid.*, 198–219.

34 See Ken Hiltner, *Milton and Ecology* (Cambridge, 2003).

CHAPTER 9

Prose style

Walter S. H. Lim

Reading John Milton's prose works can often prove challenging owing to the need to grapple with certain stylistic features and characteristics – the densely involved syntactical structures; the heavy heaping of clause upon clause; the cumulative gathering of allusions to classical and scriptural authority for evidential support and argumentative substantiation. The primary working tools of the polemicist are rhetorical and emotive – the first to bring the auditor to a position through argument, the next to move the reader through a heightening of feelings. Both are at work in Milton's polemical production. Working with (fallen) language, Milton understood the Holy Spirit as capable of facilitating understanding in the minds of people, thus enabling them to arrive at correct decisions and undertake right action. Framing this understanding of God's working through language is, of course, Milton's conception of his prophetic identity: he is the conduit through which God communicates his vision of how the English Christian Commonwealth may best work.

In this chapter I set out to examine two prose works – *The Reason of Church-Government* (1642), published very early in Milton's pamphleteering career, and *The Tenure of Kings and Magistrates* (1649), written just prior to Charles I's execution and published almost immediately after. My aim is to analyze characteristic features of Milton's prose style and his polemical temper, and also to extrapolate from these features identifiable habits of thought. When we consider the diachronic development of Milton's pamphleteering career from *Reason* to *Tenure*, a development that is in many ways shaped by the pressures exerted by political and historical events, we find ourselves charting the pamphleteer's progress from registering a need to impress his abilities by promising great works in the future to his systematic and radical defense of tyrannicide. Both works yield certain common features: (1) Milton makes constant reference to various scriptural proof-texts to lend authority to the argument that is being forged; (2) he works to elicit an emotive response from his reader to a rhetorical exercise that often depends upon the affective dimensions of imagery and metaphor; (3) he appeals to a typological vision of history to frame and lend support to the polemical project.

The very title, *The Reason of Church-Government*, informs the reader that there is a God-given "reason" for endorsing a particular system of church-government and also that the tract aims to convince through "reason" and "reasonable" argument the logic of the pamphleteer's position on the subject. In an argument, nothing is more potent than making a direct appeal to God as the transcendent authority who has the final word on the subject. Milton does this by asserting "that Church governement is set downe in holy Scripture, and that to say otherwise is untrue" (*CPW* 1:756). Scripture, God's powerful Word itself, establishes that God is on the side of the Presbyterian system of church-government, a system with no place for the authority of the Anglican bishops. The effective reformation of the church, as we are told in Milton's first antiprelatical tract, *Of Reformation* (1641), will follow on the heels of the removal of prelates from their seat of power and authority.[1]

The citation of proof-texts from scripture for authoritative utterance is always indispensable for the pamphleteer wanting to generate the powerful impact of the Puritan sermon, a genre Milton had in mind when writing *Reason*. As Ralph A. Haug has noted, "characteristics of the Puritan sermon Milton's readers would recognize readily are the plain, sometimes homely style of speech, the imagery drawn from common life or the Bible, and the clear organization into divisions and subdivisions, headings and subheadings."[2] In addition to noticing characteristics of the Puritan sermon in *Reason*, Haug also notes that Milton strives to work with the pattern of the classical oration as defined by Cicero: "exordium, narratio, propositio, partitio, confirmatio, reprehensio, and peroratio, with an eighth, a digression, allowable before the peroration."[3] If adapting the structure of the classical oration is meant to augment the argument that Milton sets out to build from scripture, we may yet note its failure to accomplish quite this. The experience of reading *Reason* is not exactly an easy one; the invocation of scriptural proof-texts and the appeal to details do not carry the same impact as does the emotive force of image and metaphor belonging to the affective dimensions of the text. Commenting on the experience of reading *Reason*, Lana Cable notes that the abundance of details (such as those Milton mines from scripture) is, for example, by and large readily forgettable. By contrast, Milton's metaphors and images are highly vivid, the reason suggested being that they "develop from his assumptions of a higher reality, one that is eternal, suprarational, functionally (though not finally) dualistic, theocentric." In what Cable refers to as Milton's "metaphoric moral realm," meaning derives "not from rational and empirical interpretation, not from historical analysis, but from relationship to God."[4]

Image and metaphor are also at work in Milton's invocation of typology in *Reason*, this aimed at strengthening his argument against the supporters of prelacy and in particular those who had identified in the structures of the Aaronic priesthood a basic pattern for the prelatical system of church-government. In typology, the New Testament dispensation of grace has effectively relegated Old Testament modalities to obsolescence. This point is reinforced in Milton's emphasis on Timothy's "ordination by the hands of the Presbytery" (*CPW* 1:767), a New Testament focus grounded in the liberty enabled by grace. Milton's distinctive argument from typology is one that does not need to rely upon evidential authority built upon the amassing of textual details and proof-texts from scripture. Rather it depends upon the implied logic that any argument made by the supporters of prelacy on the basis of Old Testament paradigms cannot be sustained because these have been definitively superseded by Christ's superior spiritual dispensation of grace. In addition to bringing liberty, the Gospel, by its definition as a dispensation that brings a "religion [that is] pure, spirituall, simple, and lowly," also reveals what "the face of the ministery" must be (*CPW* 1:766). In the typological vision, what is material in the Old Testament gets translated into spiritual terms in the New Testament. In arguing that the Presbyterian system of church-government enjoys scriptural sanction, Milton makes the point that the temple of God must not be built since any physical construction of this temple must by definition entail an (illogical) reversion back to the old conditions of bondage and law. *Reason* instead sets out to locate the ideal vision of the architectural dimensions of God's church in the antitypical temple that is "that immortall stature of Christs body which is his Church, in all her glorious lineaments and proportions" (*CPW* 1:758).

In Milton's understanding, the authority for church discipline (understood in the Calvinistic sense as signifying both moral code and ideal of government) belongs to its ministers and deacons. For Milton the authority of the prelates cannot be borne out by scriptural evidence and *Reason* sets out to reinforce this point only to hammer away at the institution of prelacy through negative figurations and imagings. The prelates are false fathers who exercise an effeminizing influence, emasculating both state and church. Much like the womb of Sin in *Paradise Lost*, prelacy engenders monstrous forms that are self-consuming. In the institution of prelacy, which is created by custom, Milton identifies the distinctive presence of Roman Catholic structures. If he is allowed to carry on without opposition, the prelate will develop to a point where he will effectively function as an "Arch-primat, or Protestant Pope" (*CPW* 1:783). *Reason* also identifies the spiritual ancestor of the prelates in Lucifer, "the first prelat Angel" (*CPW* 1:762), who aspired above his order. In this antiprelatical tract, the pamphleteer had already arrived at a particular conception of the tyrant, which will later be given the following consolidated expression in *Paradise Lost*: "man over men / [God] made not lord; such title to himself / Reserving, human left from human free" (xii.69–71). If Presbyterianism is emblematized as a kind of Roman phalanx, formidable in its masculinist "truth and steadfastnesse," prelaty is figured as a pyramid (*CPW* 1:789). Standing for the extremely destructive schism generated between laity and priesthood, this image of the prelatical pyramid is positioned in stark contrast to the unifying horizontal structures of Presbyterianism and to Milton's distinctive vision of a Christianity that confers (classical) heroic status upon the community of the faithful.[5]

How the seventeenth-century reader read *Reason* has been a subject of much critical consideration, given the overall sense that this work does not appear to have been all that successful in deploying the structures of discursive reasoning (identified, for example, by Haug) to advance its controlling argument. In his reading of the text, Stanley Fish has located *Reason*'s most interesting feature in the difficulty with which the general reader is able to identify the informing structures of the text's formal reasoning, leading him to conclude that, if we must speak of reason(ing) in the text at all, then this must surely be a "self-validating reason" totally independent of any expectations for a systematic and logically unfolding argument tied to rational deliberation and progressive clarification.[6] Citing K. G. Hamilton's assessment that *Reason* is marked by a certain "ratiocinative emptiness," "lack of real intellectual content," and a discourse that jumps "up and down in one place," Fish arrives at the conclusion that Milton does not offer his reader any argumentative development because of the implied and explicit premise that obvious truth requires no proof: "Thus the reader who inclines to the party of the Prelates will be the reader who attends carefully to the order of the numbered chapters and to the unfolding argument they presumably carry, while to the eye of the Presbyterian (or illumined) reader, these divisions will be less pressuring than the truths that imply themselves at every point."[7] Anyone who has eyes to see will have them opened to the truth that God endorses the Presbyterian form of church-government. Fish's reader inhabits a Calvinistic and predestinarian universe because only to the regenerate will the Holy Spirit light the way to a discernment of truth while the unregenerate will not, or simply cannot, be so enlightened. In his reading Stanley Fish makes Milton out to be much more of a Presbyterian than is actually suggested by the text.

That Milton seems to have a hard time producing a controversialist pamphlet with a clearly defined argument that can be easily followed may have less to do with his discrediting of reason and its attendant machinery than with the challenges encountered when seeking out convincing evidence from scriptural proof-texts. It is clear from a reading of *Reason* that Milton tried his best to harness biblical passages to lend support to his argument without forgoing the appeal to figures and images. When rifling the text of Holy Writ does not successfully yield the needed materials for the convincing construction of an argument, Milton turns readily enough to the affective potential of resonance facilitated by image and metaphor. In fact the game is given away early on in *Reason* when Milton tells his reader: "And this seemes to be the cause why in those places of holy writ, wherein is treated of Church-government, the reasons thereof are not formally, and profestly set downe, because to him that heeds attentively the drift and scope of Christian profession, they easily imply themselves" (*CPW* 1:750). If the Presbyterian system of church-government is not formally and professedly set down in scripture, how then is the pamphleteer able to set up a convincing case in support of this system? The answer is in "the drift and scope of Christian profession" and in the "reasons" of Presbyterianism that "easily imply themselves." John F. Huntley tells us that "the drift and scope of Christian profession" refers to the intrinsic argumentative logic of the Bible's informing typological structure – the movement from the Old to the New Testament and "the motion from Genesis to Revelation" – which will impel the reader to respond to the message of scripture in the correct way without being necessarily reliant on specific citations.[8] "When Milton," Huntley elaborates, "urges that truly authoritative reasons for presbyterial government will 'easily imply themselves' . . . being sometimes 'for the plainnesse thereof a matter of eye sight, rather then of disquisition' . . . to one who attends Scripture, he suggests that the reader must also attend the interconnection of his arguments, the organizing principles of Scripture, and the rich texture of his prose."[9]

In Huntley's reading, Milton is not dealing with the problematics of scriptural interpretation or interruptions encountered in reading God's Word – the significant issue revolves around not losing sight of the whole by fixating on the parts or details of scriptural citations. When we look closely at Milton's line cited above, however, the pamphleteer appears in effect to be saying that the Bible is not always as clear as it might (ideally) be in effectively explaining the logic ("reasons") underwriting a particular system of church-government. This may be read as a concession to the experience that scripture may in fact be lacking in certain areas when called upon to communicate God's truth with clarity and precision, or rather, to lend substantive evidence to the oratory at hand. In those places where scripture is not forthcoming in terms of clarity, God's view of and position on things "easily imply themselves" – they are obvious to those who have eyes to see and ears to hear. In terms of literary discourse, the "connotative" can always be relied upon when the "denotative" proves inadequate. When Milton talks about "the drift and scope of Christian profession," he accepts a certain looseness ("drift") and vastness ("scope") in the hermeneutical reading and interpretation of scripture. If details from scriptural proof-texts are typically harnessed for the polemical purpose of building up a discursive structure to substantiate an argument, "drift and scope" make room for the functioning of the affective dimension that does not necessarily need to rely on formal rhetoric and textual evidence.

In *Reason*, the reader who attends to the "drift and scope" of scripture applies common sense instead of subscribing to the often overdetermined literalism of (revelatory) details. In Milton's understanding, such a reader works with the spirit of liberty that entered the world with the dispensation of grace. When Milton tells us in *Reason* that the message of scripture can be located in its general intention and import, we encounter a pamphleteer who deems it unnecessary to have to formulate an argument or arrive at understanding exclusively on the basis of divine fiat. The polemical and hermeneutical temper of *Reason* does not appear unduly influenced by the textualist and literalist imperative when it comes to the matter of scriptural interpretation. When scripture is not as plain or as perspicacious as it could have been, and where biblical interpretation unsettles because of inadequate clarification, tensions, or contradictions, Milton appeals to the spirit of Christian liberty that is greater than the narrow parameters associated with the literal letters of the text.

Definitions, it will be noticed, are important to Milton's polemical projects. Milton takes especial care to infuse particular words with positive or negative resonances and meanings. In *Reason*, for example, the reader becomes aware quickly enough that "prelate" is a supremely negative word, much more so than "bishop" or even "episcopacy." In this regard, Milton's use of the phrase "prelatical episcopacy" does not amount to a tautology, for "prelatical" functions as a negative adjective designed to qualify "episcopacy," a generally neutral word that simply refers to the overseeing of preaching and worship. Likewise *The Tenure of Kings and Magistrates* sets out to offer a definition of the tyrant, for it is only by properly delineating the political parameters of tyrannical authority that the English nation can be brought to recognize that the conditions of tyranny must be contested and challenged. Beginning with a critique of the Presbyterians who are now accused of siding with the royalist cause, Milton proceeds to define a tyrant as the ruler who first and foremost violates the social contract entered into between a people and the ruler to whose care the overall well-being of society is entrusted.

In *Tenure* Milton traces the origins of monarchy all the way back to the calamitous event of the theological fall. Because the fall gave rise to a violence that threatened to destroy everything, in particular the fabric of social and communal life, there was an urgent need to source out a mechanism whereby this innate propensity toward destruction could be hedged in and managed. Society therefore found it necessary to locate an ordering mechanism in the institution of monarchical rule, one whose primary purpose was to serve a practical function, that being to preserve "peace and common right" (*CPW* III:199). In Milton's theological framing of the emergence of political institutions, monarchy became a practical solution to the destructive problems of anarchy that entered the world through Adam and Eve's disobedience. Unlike Sir Robert Filmer's *Patriarcha* (1680), which traced the origin of monarchical authority all the way back to the overlordship of Adam himself, Milton argues that it is the people who make the laws and who are responsible for conferring authority on kings and magistrates. This delegation of authority upon trust serves a functional purpose tied to Natural Law. Its radical implication is that this authority can always be revoked without any reason being given. As Milton tells us in *Pro Populo Anglicano Defensio* (1651), the prerogative of revocation belongs to the "right of the people [that] is more ancient than that of kings" (*CPW* IV:405).

In *Tenure* allegiance is given to the monarch based on the contractual understanding that he will govern to protect the well-being of society. The operative word employed by Milton to designate the binding nature of the contract between the ruler and his subjects is "Cov'nant" (*CPW* III:199). First and foremost, a covenant is meant to be binding, its dislocation the occasion for retribution. Milton's emphasis on the idea of covenant in *Tenure* is fundamentally predicated upon the understanding that the ruler is under the Law of Nature and therefore accountable to the people should he choose to do wrong over right. In particular Milton makes appeal to this overarching moral system of the Natural Law because the entire framework of positive laws forged under the monarchical system is, by definition, compromised and unreliable. Natural Law refers to that higher law to which all men and women, including monarchs, are subject. Meant to protect the welfare of the people, this Law of Nature affirms the primacy of the people over the monarch. Any injury inflicted upon the people whose welfare the monarch is responsible for ensuring amounts to a violation of the fundamental trust granted him by society for its protection. Trangressing Natural Law thus entails a penalty because it infringes the grounding and foundational principles of transcendent justice itself. When Milton appeals to Natural Law to highlight its egregious violation by Charles I, he also appeals to the necessary exercise of reason to ensure that the demands of justice are met. Virtually synonymous with the idea of conscience in his political lexicon, reason, for Milton in *Tenure*, is then related to the fundamental ability to choose and judge between right and wrong.

In *Tenure* the word "reason" appears once again but this time to underscore the point that it is generally understood (as in the Natural Law) by cultures and civilizations that it is right for a people to rise up against a wicked ruler. In fact nothing short of "the Law of nature and right reason" (*CPW* III:197) informs the common man that any authority that makes it its practice to demolish the principle of equality which should rightly define and inform all human and social relationships, is a tyrant. Any rational and reasonable man will immediately see with the necessary clarity that all tyrants must be brought to account – this is a "universal" understanding shared by both non-Christian and Christian societies. If Milton invokes examples from events and characters from a variety of sources – ancient history, the Church Fathers, classical literature, and English history – to substantiate his radical argument that bringing a tyrant to trial finds incontrovertible basis in the authority of Natural and Divine Law, he also turns, significantly, to the Old Testament for analogies, lessons, and answers. This appeal to the invaluable lessons of God's dealings with his chosen people in the past that is Hebraic history entails more than simply a rhetorical invocation of the "transcendent" authority of Holy Writ that is, by definition, beyond critical interrogation. Attesting to Milton's typological view of history, it sets up revolutionary England and its anticipation of the decisive establishment of the English Commonwealth as none other than God's contemporary Israel itself. Within this typological framing – a framing we have already seen to be very much at work in the earlier *Reason of Church-Government* – Old Testament Israel functions as a mirror of history wherein lessons can be learned and disastrous errors not be made subject to repetition, and also where direct and important political lessons may be carefully identified and then emulated. Sometimes, however, a recalcitrant people may insist on turning their backs on the indispensable lessons of both history and scripture. Horrified recognition of this reality was what impelled Milton to produce *The Readie and Easie Way* (1660) in the twilight of the English republic. When appealing, in this pamphlet, to the English people not to forfeit the liberty for which they had fought so hard to secure, Milton pointed out that any embracing of political tyranny would be akin to a liberated Israel making the inexplicably perverse decision to return to the conditions of Egyptian bondage.

In the radical Reformation to which Milton found himself deeply indebted for his polemical and prophetic authority, the foundational Martin Luther loomed large as a controlling cultural figure moved by an extraordinary impulse to take on the world. However, unlike the reforming Luther who, appropriating St. Paul as a central model, presented himself as someone inelegant and plain-speaking, the pamphleteering Milton is unready to adopt the persona of the "fool." We see this clearly in his highly self-conscious syntactical constructions, his awareness of the iconoclastic potential of figures and imagery, and his desire to be given due recognition for his abilities. And where Luther had focused on ordinary reason as the great leviathan or beast because it operates on the basis of self-interest, the controversialist Milton found himself thinking of reason very much in relation to its close synonym – common sense.[10] The fit reader of Milton's pamphleteering prose is one who possesses the ability to respond to the issue or subject at hand with the benefit of common sense, a faculty that sometimes brings a distinctively large degree of flexibility (what Milton prefers to call "liberty") to the reception and interpretation of Holy Writ.

In Milton's prose works, common sense is brought to bear upon the deciphering of scriptural texts not only because Milton wishes to foreground the centrality of the rationalizing faculty but also because he owes a huge debt to a tradition of classical ethics that sometimes finds itself distinctively at odds with the emphasis of Christian ethics. One important feature of classical ethics Milton embraces and which he brings to bear upon expressions of his Puritan convictions is the "dignity" of the human subject generally set up in opposition to the Christian valorization of humility. As Richard Strier has noted, "In Milton's controversial prose, humility functions primarily as a negative term."[11] Milton's deep sense of his own dignity and abilities underwrites the various fashionings of his ethical authority, whether as a prophetic spokesman for God modeled on the likes of Moses, Jeremiah, and Isaiah, or as a Reformation saint like Luther who radically overturned the defining structures of the existing social and political status quo.[12] When reading such apparently differing texts as *Reason* and *Tenure*, we may extrapolate certain features of Milton's polemical temper and his relation to scriptural authority. As early as *Reason*, Milton had already given his reader major hints about his willingness to respond to Holy Writ with a fair degree of "liberty" (where it came to interpretation), and about his not being a strict textualist in the way that the Presbyterians generally were. That Milton did not find himself compelled to offer close and detailed ratiocinations as well as undertake necessarily detailed analyses of scripture in the rhetorical argument of *Reason* reveals a temper that opens him up to charges of heresy (his Arminianism and anti-Trinitarianism, for example) and also of loose engagements with conventional biblical interpretation (the argument for divorce, for instance). That he accords significance to common sense and rationalism also means that his argument from biblical proof-texts for the right to execute a tyrant (based upon the radical premise of an original social and governmental compact) is, importantly, framed and inflected by the developing culture of English political philosophy in the period. When we read Milton's prose works, we find ourselves involved not only in unpacking an individual pamphleteer's understanding of specific political and theological issues but also in appreciating the complex culture of royalist and republican debates central to the vibrant political culture of revolutionary England.

NOTES

1 For a fuller discussion of episcopacy and Milton's response to it, see Neil Forsyth's chapter in this volume.
2 Ralph A. Haug, Preface, *The Reason of Church-Government*, in *CPW* 1:741.
3 *Ibid.*, 1:740.
4 Lana Cable, *Carnal Rhetoric: Milton's Iconoclasm and the Poetics of Desire* (Durham, NC, and London, 1995), 54.
5 Richard Strier, "Milton Against Humility," in *Religion and Culture in Renaissance England*, ed. Claire McEachern and Debora Shuger (Cambridge, 1997), 258–86; see especially 265.
6 Stanley Fish, *Self-Consuming Artifacts: The Experience of Seventeenth-Century Literature* (Berkeley and Los Angeles, 1972), 265–302 (p. 274).
7 *Ibid.*, 277 and 297.
8 John F. Huntley, "The Images of Poet and Poetry in Milton's *The Reason of Church-Government*," in *Achievements of the Left Hand: Essays on the Prose of John Milton*, ed. Michael Lieb and John T. Shawcross (Amherst, MA, 1974), 83–120 (p. 90).
9 *Ibid.*

10 For an explanation of Luther's distrust of the faculty of reason as it operates in the realm of religion, see Richard Strier, *Love Known: Theology and Experience in George Herbert's Poetry* (Chicago, 1983), 29–31. Strier points out the importance of recognizing that Luther was not against reason when it functions as the capacity to understand concepts and make inferences or distinctions. Luther's distrust of reason is very much tied up with his theological understanding that fallen man is saved exclusively by grace through faith; reason becomes associated with the Beast when it insists that fallen man must be able to contribute something (merit) toward the attainment of his salvation.

11 Strier, "Milton Against Humility," 262.

12 For more on Milton's self-presentation, see Stephen Fallon's chapter in this volume.

CHAPTER 10

Verse and rhyme

John Creaser

Milton the poet is a radical conservative. He invariably writes in established genres, yet each poem is a critique of its genre and is innovative in poetic craft. For his first masterpiece, "On the Morning of Christ's Nativity," he created a complex stanza, blending the popular lyricism of the ballad with Spenserian elevation. For *Lycidas* – his transformation of that ancient genre, the pastoral elegy – the elaborate symmetries of the Italian *canzone* become a form exploratory as well as intricate. His sonnets turn English expectations inside out; they are unprecedented not only in their choice of the Italian form but also in the lordly freedom of handling of the form. *Samson Agonistes* has the first sustained passages in English of what can be called free verse. His supreme masterpiece, *Paradise Lost*, is as distinctive in craftsmanship as everything in its re-creation of the most celebrated of literary genres.

As the work of a heretic in religion, a revolutionary in politics, and a radical in literary values, *Paradise Lost* has always aroused resistance as well as admiration, in craft as well as content. Andrew Marvell, in his commendatory poem to the 1674 edition, seeks to defuse two objections, that it "ruin[s] . . . The sacred truths to fable and old song" and that it does not rhyme.[1] This second objection, to the form of the poem, was the first to show itself (apart from the political disquiet of the licenser Thomas Tomkins[2]). In the 1668 reissue of the first edition, the printer explains that he has procured the synopsis desired by many readers and also "that which stumbled many others, why the poem rhymes not." Milton's testy note on "The Verse" follows, dismissing rhyme as "the invention of a barbarous age . . . trivial and of no true musical delight." With precedent claimed in Homer and Virgil, the blank verse of the poem is declared the first example in English "of ancient liberty recovered to heroic poem from the troublesome and modern bondage of rhyming" (*CPEP* 291).

Yet for years to come what many readers found most "troublesome" was just this lack of rhyme. Eventually, Milton's example would establish blank verse as the inevitable metre for ambitious narrative and meditative poems such as James Thomson's *The Seasons* and William Wordsworth's *The Prelude*, as well as many shorter forms. But in Restoration England, blank verse was unknown outside drama, and even there was seriously challenged. While *Paradise Lost* was in press, John Dryden was running rings around his brother-in-law Sir Robert Howard, a friend of Milton's, in a debate over the merits of blank verse and rhyme in serious drama. In essence, Howard argued that rhyme was unnatural on the stage, especially when two speakers shared one rhyme, and Dryden responded that blank verse was equally unnatural and moreover made for verbosity, while the "quick and poignant brevity" of rhyme sharpened dialogue and concentrated expression.[3] Even Howard would have been uneasy with *Paradise Lost*, since he accepted that blank verse was "much too low" for verse on the page rather than the stage.[4]

The case for unrhymed verse originated in Italy with the *endecasillabi sciolti* (eleven-syllable lines freed from rhyme) of works such as Trissino's tragedy *Sofonisba* (1524) and epic *Italia liberata da' Goti* (*Italy Liberated from the Goths* [1547–48]). Such poems, and even Tasso's unrhymed *Le sette giornate del mondo creato* (*The Seven Days of the Creation of the World* [1607]), were, however, more important as experiments than achievements.[5]

The English approximation to the Italian hendecasyllables was unrhymed iambic pentameter – a norm of five beats per line, each rising from a lighter to a heavier stress – and this "blank verse," as it was soon known, was introduced as early as around 1540 by the Earl of Surrey in his translation of two books of *The Aeneid* (publ. 1554–57). But the influence of this, and of the original blank verse of George Gascoigne (*c.* 1534–77), and of Marlowe's translation of the first book of Lucan's *De Bello Civili* (*c.* 1590), was minimal. The occasional criticism of rhyme, such as Roger Ascham in *The Schoolmaster* (1570) on the need to avoid "our rude, beggarly rhyming" and Thomas Campion's *Observations in the Art of English Poesy* (1602) on "the childish titillation of riming," was expressed not in favor of blank verse but of the sterile attempts to cram English into the quantitative verse of the ancients.[6] Campion was firmly answered by Samuel Daniel in *A Defence of Rhyme* (1602), who argues that rhyme is natural in the strong stresses of English, whereas unrhymed verse is no more than "orderly prose," lacking "the pulse, life, and energie . . . which now we are sure where to have in our Rymes, whose knowne frame hath those due staies for the minde . . . though the varietie be infinite."[7]

Consequently, virtually no non-dramatic blank verse was written between Campion and *Paradise Lost*.[8] On the contrary, intrusively rhymed "heroic" forms, the pentameter couplet and quatrain, became predominant. Although Ben Jonson thought couplets "the bravest sort of verses,"[9] they are just one meter among many in the verse of his major contemporaries, and even Jonson's couplets are relatively open and free. But the heroic couplet, usually closed by a light stop after the first line and a heavier stop after the second, dominated English verse from around 1640 till the late eighteenth century. Among Milton's contemporaries, Abraham Cowley chose the heroic couplet for his pair of uncompleted epics, *The Civil War* (1643) and *Davideis* (1656), while the even stricter heroic quatrain – with a pause after the second line and a full stop after the fourth – was chosen by William Davenant for the epic *Gondibert* (1651) and by Dryden for his quasi-epic *Annus Mirabilis* (1667).

Milton's lack of rhyme was so incomprehensible to Dryden – as, even a century later, to Samuel Johnson – that, much as they admired his sublime powers, they assumed he was an incompetent rhymer. Though Dryden's admiration for Milton increased with time, as late as 1693, in "The Original and Progress of Satire," he asserts "whatever causes [Milton] alleges for the abolishing of rhyme . . . his own particular reason is plainly this, that rhyme was not his talent; he had neither the ease of doing it, nor the graces of it; which is manifest in his juvenilia."[10] But this is hardly borne out by Milton's rhyming. *Lycidas*, for example, weaves expressively in and out of intricate patterns, from the broken sonnet of the grief-stricken opening paragraph to the perfectly turned *ottava rima* (three alternating rhymes and a couplet) of the serene close. Much of the sustained power of Sonnet 18, "On the Late Massacre in Piedmont," comes from intensive rhyming on only two vowels, and those closely related – the octave rhymes on *–ones* and *–old* and the sestet on the bare vowels *–ay* and *–owe* – whereas the more typical Sonnet 19 on his blindness has five distinct rhyme sounds. Concentrated in the rhyme-words "groans" and "moans" in the octave and the echoing "way" and "woe" closing the sestet, the very monotony of the rhyming is a cry of lamentation throughout the poem.

But it may be that Dryden *needed* to misunderstand *Paradise Lost*, in revealing ways. Dryden the royalist came to his former colleague in Cromwell's service asking permission to revise the new work as an "opera" (then a rhyming play with dancing, scenic effects, and some music). According to John Aubrey, Milton "received him civilly" but was clearly skeptical: as another account of their meeting runs, "Well, Mr Dryden, says Milton, it seems you have a mind to Tagg my Points, and you have my Leave to Tagg 'em, but some of 'em are so Awkward and Old Fashion'd that I think you had as good leave 'em as you found 'em."[11] Milton's most acute early reader shared this skepticism, for Marvell's commendatory poem scorns Dryden the "town-Bayes" for threatening to tag the epic into "tinkling rhyme."

The re-working of *Paradise Lost* as *The State of Innocence* (1677) is as bizarre as any adaptation in the period. Dryden was out to control and tame what seemed to him its outrageousness, its challenge to the conservative principles he had espoused with the king's return. The emerging arbiter of literary values aimed to transform an unruly poem into an orderly script, tidying up the language and confining the characters and their thoughts within closed couplets. Hardly ever, for example, is a couplet shared between two speakers, apart from a few in hell in the opening scene and a few later where there is a speech but one line long. Dryden was to be the first to propose Satan as the hero of the poem, but Lucifer, the equivalent in the opera, has none of Satan's disquieting presence or tragic intensity.[12] Couplets give a sense of finality to his situation from his opening words:

> Is this the Seat our Conqueror has given?
> And this the Climate we must change for Heaven?
> These Regions and this Realm my Wars have got;
> This Mournful Empire is the Loser's Lot.
>
> (1.1.1–4)

Hence the movement of Dryden's verse is at odds with Miltonic freedom, and this reinforces something personal to Dryden in his taming of the epic. At this time he was still very responsive to the determinist thought of the philosopher Thomas Hobbes and skeptical of the existence of free will. In his preface to *The Rival Ladies* (1664), for example, he likens dramatic characters to living beings in the power of God: "They are moved . . . like the rational creatures of the Almighty Poet, who walk at liberty, in their own opinion, because their fetters are invisible . . . instead of an absolute power over their actions, they have only a wretched desire of doing that which they cannot choose but do."[13]

The most revealing of Dryden's innovations in *The State of Innocence* is the visit of archangels Raphael and Gabriel in 4.1 to warn Adam that the devil is nearby. Adam has been a defeatist since his creation, always feeling himself doomed by a harsh destiny (2.1.27), and also finding subjugation to Eve's beauty irresistible; even when he has seen her only in vision she is "My better half . . . To whom I yield my boasted Sovereignty" (2.3.5–6). In 4.1, the archangels are unable to persuade him that he is free to stand, and they become exasperated by the stubborn ingenuity of his determinist arguments. After they tell him to get on with it and leave, Adam is left in despair:

> Why am I trusted with my self at large,
> When [God]'s more able to sustain the charge?
> Since Angels fell, whose strength was more than mine,
> 'Twould show more grace my frailty to confine.
> Fore-knowing the success, to leave me free,
> Excuses him, and yet supports not me.
>
> (4.1.115–20)

This scene is the apotheosis of the heroic couplet. The characters are enclosed within their preconceptions, the angels smug in their piety, and Adam self-righteous in gloom. The characters' lack of what they feel as genuine choice is reinforced in the crisp repetitions of the verse. Heroic couplet and quatrain are the most intrusive of common forms, because rhyming and line-end pauses, reinforced by a caesura after the fourth, fifth, or sixth syllable, make for clearly structured antithesis and balance. Unless a poet undermines form by forcing syntax against the shape of the line – as Keats was to do in *Endymion* but no Restoration poet would have tolerated – the couplet imposes itself on syntax, utterance, and the perception of experience. Form proclaims order. Any rhymed verse brings a sense of destination to the line, and in tight couplets and quatrains that destination readily expresses a sense of finality, even destiny.

Milton's rejection of rhyme lies at the heart of his masterpiece. As an epic, *Paradise Lost* is defiantly unique and is, explicitly at the beginning of book IX, a reappraisal of its genre. Milton commandeers the venerated ancient epics for his "more heroic" Christian purposes (IX.14), and dismisses the "tedious havoc" of epic warfare, "hitherto the only argument / Heroic deemed" (IX.28–30), turning his back on the elaborate chivalry of Renaissance romantic epic and contravening the determined efforts of William Davenant and Thomas Hobbes to re-think the genre for modern times.[14] Crucial to the distinctiveness of *Paradise Lost* as an epic are the signs it bears of emerging from the experience of defeat. It was probably written primarily in 1658–63,[15] and serious work on it spread over Milton's growing disenchantment with Cromwell and increasing dismay at the confusion after his death, and then the disaster of the Restoration, which left him "fall'n on evil days, / . . . / In darkness, and with dangers compassed round" (VII.25–27).[16] Dryden goes so far as to say that Milton's "subject is not that of an heroic poem, properly so called. His design is the losing of our happiness; his event is not prosperous, like that of all other epic works."[17] Other epics enact a positive transformation of their people: with Hector dead, the Greeks are on the verge of victory over Troy; Odysseus eventually returns to cleanse his kingdom; Aeneas begins to establish a new Troy and the origins of Rome; Christian knights subdue the threat of paganism; Dryden contrives to transform mixed fortunes in war and a disastrous fire in London into a prophecy of regal and national triumph.

Against tradition, Milton's theme is one of loss; his poem ends outlining the disasters of human history. But paradoxically, defeat in Milton is the guarantee of human individuality and freedom. Epic had always been an authoritarian form. As Tasso wrote: "The most excellent poem belongs exclusively to the most excellent form of government. This is monarchy."[18] Moreover, earlier heroes, however great, are subordinated to the divine, for the benign transformation of their people. The gods are ubiquitous in Homer, and, despite their squabbling, the fall of Troy and purgation of Ithaca are divinely decreed; Aeneas is divinely compelled to subjugate his passion to his destiny; in *The Lusiads*, Vasco da Gama is merely an instrument of "the secret womb / Of pregnant FATE" (2.43).[19] The stated aim of *Paradise Lost*, in its turn, is "to assert eternal providence, / And justify the ways of God to men" (1.25–26), while Adam and Eve leave paradise with "providence their guide" (XII.647). Nevertheless, they, and the angels, and the Son himself live in freedom, a freedom both established and endorsed by their being always on trial. The newly created Adam has to keep on arguing his case for a human companion; Eve has to choose between the gentle image in the pool and the importunate male who is "[l]ess winning soft, less amiably mild" (IV.479); the Son makes a positive choice to die for man; Satan keeps on facing the promptings of conscience and remorse. All are constantly presented with real decisions and with alternatives about which to make rational choices. As God says, "reason also is choice" (III.108). The whole of *Paradise Lost* endorses what the younger Dryden could not persuade himself to accept, that divine supervision of life and absolute knowledge of the future in no way impinge on the freedom of individual will. The "[p]revenient grace" (XI.3) that descends on Adam and Eve enables but does not cause their loving reconciliation and growth into penitence in book X. As they are ushered from the Garden, one is less conscious of providence than that "the world was all before them" (XII.646): the fall enlarges into the new. As ever in Milton, a poem ends with a new trial and opportunity.

This epitomizes how for Milton life is a state of perpetual aspiration. For him (as I have written elsewhere) the possibilities of life are illimitable because truth, though it exists, can never be finally known by man. Consequently, man has a duty to search and develop. As *Areopagitica* puts it, in the great image of Isis and Osiris and the scattered fragments of truth: "We have not yet found them all, Lords and Commons, nor ever shall doe, till her Masters second comming … The light which we have gain'd, was giv'n us, not to be ever staring on, but by it to discover onward things more remote from our knowledge" (*CPW* II:549–50).[20] Moreover, politically *Paradise Lost* is republican rather than royalist in tendency, emphasizing Adam and Eve's individual authority[21] – hence Tomkins' reluctance to license the poem.

Paradise Lost is, then, the epic of free will and liberty of conscience, and Milton creates the profoundly apt medium for it. Whereas the shaping of rhyme reinforces a sense of destiny, Milton develops an unprecedented mode at once disciplined and unpredictably open-ended of what was, outside drama, a very rare prosody. Shakespeare, the supreme master of blank verse before Milton, created a medium appropriate for drama, free to the point of licentiousness. He mixes four- and six-beat lines among the five beats of the pentameter, and deviates freely from the already flexible prosodic norms developed intuitively by sixteenth-century poets. The best analytical account of these norms has been given recently by Derek Attridge, who starts from two fundamentals of spoken English: first, isochrony or the tendency to make stressed syllables fall, or be perceived as falling, at regular intervals of time; and second, the duple tendency toward an alternation of a stressed and a non-stressed syllable. In iambic verse, these combine to permit just three variations allowing endlessly varied rhythms: (1) *demotion*: in a sequence of three stressed syllables, the second is naturally given the time of a stress but rather less emphasis ("QUICK *BROWN* FOX"; "Say first, for HEAVEN *HIDES* NOTH-ing from thy view" (*Paradise Lost*, I.27); (2) *promotion*: in a sequence of three unstressed syllables, the second is, in careful speech and in verse, given the time and a little of the weight of a stressed syllable (as in "Tennis ON the lawn" rather than "tea on the lawn," or in the second "infinite" of IV.74: "IN-fin-ite WRATH and IN-fin-ITE de-SPAIR"); (3) *pairing*: with only two adjacent stresses, there is no demotion and the line becomes unbalanced; balance is restored by immediately preceding or following the two stresses with a pair of non-stresses. So pairings may be *stress-initial*, as in "For one re-STRAINT, LORDS of the world besides" (I.32), or *stress-final*, as in "Favoured of heaven so high-ly, to FALL OFF" (I.30).[22]

In addition, the pause of the line-turn is a real presence and may in specific circumstances act as a virtual syllable, stressed or unstressed, so that two rather than three syllables may permit promotion or demotion, and a single stress may permit pairing. In iambics, *promotion* occurs at the end of the line: "That to the height of this great ARG-u-MENT [#]" (I.24).

Conversely, *demotion* may occur at the start: "[#] *BROUGHT* DEATH into the world, and all our woe" (1.3). *Pairing* occurs as the familiar reversed stress beginning a line: "[#] ROSE out of chaos: or if Sion hill" (1.10).

Analysis of *Paradise Lost* on these lines reveals a paradoxical fusion of austerity and freedom. With very few exceptions, lines are strict decasyllables varying within the deviation rules, with the integrity of the individual line marked by a firm ending, usually a stressed monosyllable. Whereas the mature Shakespeare breaks the norms as often as one line in five, in *Paradise Lost* Milton writes such an aberrant line only once in 265. Not a single line-end is thrown away on a mere function word. Even feminine endings are rare, and every single paragraph ends at the end of a line. On the other hand, the verse is experienced as very free: some five lines in every six deviate in some non-aberrant way from a regular iambic tread, and the extensive freedoms within the deviation rules are fully exploited, not just for variety but for mimetic or emphatic ends. With this goes the rhythmic flexibility brought within the line by frequent elision, constant variation of the caesura – often away from the conventional syllables – and occasional but expressive use of feminine endings. Scanning a characteristic passage will show something of the rhythmic intensity achieved by Milton throughout. (Stressed syllables are in capitals, demoted syllables in italic caps, and promoted in small caps; the syllables of a pairing are linked by underlining and of elisions by italics; caesuras are marked by ||, and line-turn virtual syllables by #.)

> # *SAY* FIRST, || for HEAV'N *HIDES* NOTH-ing from THY VIEW
> # NOR the *DEEP* TRACT of HELL, || *SAY* FIRST what CAUSE
> # MOVED our *GRAND* PAR-ents || IN that HAP-py STATE,
> # FAV-oured of HEAV'N so HIGH-ly, || to FALL OFF
> From THEIR cre-A-tor, || AND trans-GRESS his WILL
> For ONE re-STRAINT, || LORDS of the WORLD be-SIDES?
> Who FIRST se-DUCED THEM to that FOUL re-VOLT?
> *The* in-FERN-al SER-pent; || HE it WAS, whose GUILE
> # STIRRED up with EN-vy AND re-VENGE, || de-CEIVED
> The MOTH-er OF man-KIND, || what TIME his PRIDE
> Had CAST him OUT from HEAV'N, || with ALL his HOST
> Of REB-el AN-gels, || by WHOSE AID || a-SPIR-ing
> To SET him-SELF in GLOR-*y* a-BOVE his PEERS,
> He TRUST-ed TO have E-qualled the MOST HIGH,
> If HE op-POSED; || and WITH am-BIT-*ious* AIM
> a-GAINST the THRONE and MON-arch-Y of GOD
> # *RAISED* IM-*pious* WAR in HEAV'N and BAT-tle PROUD
> With VAIN at-TEMPT.
>
> (1.27–44)[23]

None of these lines is aberrant (apart from the subordinate stresses on "deep" and "grand" in lines 28–29, which are not orthodox demotions but a mild license occasionally found on the third syllable after a reversed stress). Typically, almost every line marks the end with a firmly stressed syllable. Yet there is not a single completely regular pentameter here, even though a couple have only a single promotion, the quietest of deviations. Instead the lines are dense with the potent deviations of pairing and demotion; four successive lines begin with a variety of stressed syllable; overall, there are more spoken stresses than metrical beats, creating a weighty movement; with caesuras falling unpredictably, there is constant modulation of cadence. Within the prevailing sense of gravity, almost every line has some expressive nuance: the feminine ending on "aspiring" at 38 is a rarity, but so minute is Milton's concern for rhythmic nuance that these endings invariably express overreaching and opposition to God. Line 40, "He TRUST-ed TO have E-qualled the MOST HIGH," is subtle in the way that it goes to the limit of the acceptable, with only two full stresses in the first eight syllables. Like Satan himself, it is deviant yet kept within bounds.

Moreover, the passage is typical of what Milton presents in his note on the verse as essential to "true musical delight": having "the sense variously drawn out from one verse into another" (*Paradise Lost*, "The Verse," *CPEP* 291). Despite its packed emphasis, the verse of *Paradise Lost* is unprecedented in its fluid enjambment. Milton is rejecting not simply rhyme but the Restoration norm of closure. That norm was so unquestioned that the blank verse Dryden writes for one scene of *The State of Innocence* (2.2, Lucifer's meeting with Uriel) is almost entirely end-stopped. Even the first appreciative imitation of *Paradise Lost* – a cento of phrases abbreviating the war in Heaven in the Earl of Roscommon's "Essay on Translated Verse" (1685) – rarely runs on.[24] In the whole of *Paradise Lost*, however, as many as three lines in every five are enjambed. Sentences frequently end mid-line, and overall there are far more mid-line pauses than end-stops. With verse no longer moving line by line, syntax is released from metrical regularity; word order and syntactical form can be endlessly varied. Incessant changes of cadence and phrasing are felt all the more because the firm line-endings convey a clear underlying norm.

This pervasive enjambment has the major consequences of energy and unpredictability. Even though Milton makes pointed rhetorical use of short sentences – as in "Who first seduced them to that foul revolt?" – the subsequent sentence from "The infernal serpent..." of eighty-one words over ten lines is typical. Sentences like this, packed with meaning and unprecedented in length, create the most dynamic verse in English. Sustained and proliferating syntax drives on for line after line, creating mental energies in the reader, who must keep the whole complex in play. Moreover, Milton impels the verse along by placing most of his verbs, two-thirds of them in the passage cited, either side of the line-turn. In particular, kinetic verbs are placed there – "fall off," "stirred up," "had cast," "aspiring / To set," and "raised" – driving the verse over the turn or along the line.

The prolonged sentences also enhance the sense of unpredictability. Thomas Corns has shown how Milton's periods are distinctive in length and sustained vigor, through their growth into clause after clause and especially sub-clause after sub-clause.[25] Typically, the sentences are not "periodic" with one shaping rhythm, but "loose" in growth from member to member, as in the cited lines 34–44. This pervasive unpredictability of growth is sharpened by ironic or unexpected local turns, such as the bathos of "With vain attempt" after two grandiose lines unbroken by caesura.

In *Paradise Lost*, all is inevitable and nothing is predictable. The biblical matter is predetermined, but everything is explored afresh. Moreover, once undergone, the trial stretches on into the future. In Milton, the movement of verse is always an embodiment of meaning, never a neutral medium. Here, the local unpredictability of rhythm and syntax is essential to the epic of free will, and justifies "why the poem rhymes not." For Milton, man is absolutely dependent for salvation on Christ's sacrifice, and yet the world is all before us to explore, and life is an unending quest for the unknowable fullness of truth. The verse of *Paradise Lost*, with its continual variety of movement within the line and thrusting energies across many lines, demands unremitting discrimination and makes reading an act of perpetual discovery and revelation.

NOTES

1 Dryden's preface to *The State of Innocence* (1677) confirms that "our false Critiques [critics] have presum'd" to tax Milton "for his choice of a supernatural Argument" (*The Works of John Dryden*, 20 vols., gen. eds. Edward Niles Hooker, H. T. Swedenberg, Jr., and Vinton A. Dearing [Berkeley, 1956–2000], XII.97).

2 See Stephen Dobranski's chapter, "The book trade," in this volume.

3 George Watson, ed., *John Dryden: "Of Dramatic Poesy" and Other Critical Essays*, 2 vols. (London, 1962), 1:89.

4 D. D. Arundell, ed., *Dryden & Howard 1664–1668: The Text of "An Essay of Dramatick Poesy," "The Indian Emperor," and "The Duke of Lerma" with Other Controversial Matter* (Cambridge, 1929), 8.

5 See F. T. Prince, *The Italian Element in Milton's Verse* (Oxford, 1954).

6 Roger Ascham, *The Schoolmaster (1570)*, ed. Lawrence V. Ryan (Charlottesville, VA, 1967), 145; and Percival Vivian, ed., *Campion's Works* (Oxford, 1909), 37.

7 G. Gregory Smith, ed., *Elizabethan Critical Essays*, 2 vols. (1904), II:362.

8 See O. B. Hardison, Jr., "Blank Verse before Milton," *Studies in Philology* 81 (1984): 253–74; and John T. Shawcross, "Milton and Blank Verse Precedents," *ANQ: American Notes and Queries* 3 (1990): 160–63.

9 "Conversations with William Drummond," in *Ben Jonson: The Complete Poems*, ed. George Parfitt (Harmondsworth, 1975), 461.

10 Watson, *Dryden: Critical Essays*, II:84–5.

11 *EL* 7, 335.

12 Watson, *Dryden: Critical Essays*, II:233.

13 *Ibid.*, I:4.

14 See *Sir William Davenant's "Gondibert*," ed. David F. Gladish (Oxford, 1971), 3–55, for the author's preface addressed to Hobbes, and Hobbes' response, which *inter alia* reject poetic inspiration, archaic language, imitation of the ancients, and the inclusion of scenes set in heaven and hell, and favor writing that displays wit, the use of quatrains, and direct ethical and religious teaching through heroes who are models of virtue, acting in the world of courts and camps.

15 Nicholas von Maltzahn, "The First Reception of *Paradise Lost* (1667)," *The Review of English Studies* 47 (1996): 479–99 (p. 479).

16 David Armitage, Armand Himy, and Quentin Skinner, eds., *Milton and Republicanism* (Cambridge, 1995), esp. Martin Dzelzainis, "Milton and the Protectorate in 1658," 181–205, and David Armitage, "John Milton: Poet against Empire," 206–25.

17 Watson, *Dryden: Critical Essays*, II:84.

18 Torquato Tasso, *Discourses on the Heroic Poem*, trans. and ed. Mariella Cavalchini and Irene Samuel (Oxford, 1973), 37.

19 *Luís de Camões: The Lusiads*, trans. Richard Fanshawe, ed. Geoffrey Bullough (London, 1963), 96.

20 John Creaser, "'Fear of Change': Closed Minds and Open Forms in Milton," *Milton Quarterly* 42 (2008): 166.

21 See Armitage *et al.*, *Milton and Republicanism*; and David Norbrook, *Writing the English Republic: Poetry, Rhetoric and Politics 1627–1660* (Cambridge, 1999), 433–95.

22 See Derek Attridge, *The Rhythms of English Poetry* (Harlow, UK, 1982), and *Poetic Rhythm: An Introduction* (Cambridge, 1995). For a fuller exposition of Attridge and of my subsequent discussion of Milton's blank verse, see my "'Service is perfect freedom': Paradox and Prosodic Style in *Paradise Lost*," *The Review of English Studies*, new ser. 58 (2007): 268–315. The account of Shakespeare's verse is indebted to George T. Wright, *Shakespeare's Metrical Art* (Berkeley, CA, 1988).

23 Inevitably, a few alternative scansions are possible, e.g. promoting "from" rather than stressing "thy" in line 27.

24 Reprinted in John T. Shawcross, ed., *Milton: The Critical Heritage* (New York, 1970), 92–93. The only marked enjambment, "down they fell / By thousands," is lifted from 6.593–4.

25 Thomas N. Corns, *Milton's Language* (Oxford, 1990), 22–23.

PART II

Critical legacy

CHAPTER 11

Critical responses, early

John Rumrich

Postmodern reader-response theorists generally cite "interpretive communities" as the source of textual meaning and describe them as "completely independent from the author's original intentions."[1] When we set out to assess Milton's reception history, according to this view, we assess hermeneutic strategies deployed by a succession of such communities – *not* their responses to the writings of the seventeenth-century poet-polemicist with whom we, too, in our own historical circumstances, are concerned. Milton, on the contrary, or at least the interpretive strategies we label "Milton," insists on the real presence of the author in his works, though he acknowledges that readers are indispensable partners in an author's reception. In *The Reason of Church-Government*, for example, while presenting himself to his audience as an aspiring poet sidetracked by antiprelatical controversy, he claims that his youthful style exhibited "certain vital signes" (*CPW* 1:809). The notion of textually intrinsic authorial vitality is elaborated in *Areopagitica* when Milton insists that "Books are not absolutely dead things, but doe contain a potencie of life in them to be as active as that soule was whose progeny they are"; a "good Booke is the pretious life-blood of a master spirit, imbalm'd and treasur'd up on purpose to a life beyond life" (*CPW* 11:492–93).

These claims are made in figurative language that looks to us like insubstantial pageantry, but often in Milton's writings such figurative assertions are moored in a now unfamiliar system of human physiology. Instrumental spirits integrated in any individual person – the fingers tying "the subtle knot that makes us man," as John Donne puts it in "The Ecstasy" (line 64) – were generally considered sublimations of the blood that function at ascending levels of refinement: vital spirits sustaining life, animal spirits mediating sensation and response, and, uniquely in Milton's monist account of pneumatic biology, intellectual spirits constituting reason itself (see *Paradise Lost* v.482–90).[2] "Imbalm'd" in the inky cloak of print, "the pretious life-blood of a master spirit" awaits only a reader's extromitted "visual ray" to become active (*Paradise Lost* III.620), as in Richard Crashaw's "On Mr. G. Herbert's Book": "Divinest love lies in this book / Expecting fire from your eyes / To kindle this his sacrifice" (lines 2–4). Later in the seventeenth century Jonathan Swift satirizes this tendency to exalt the book's powers of spiritual mediation. In *Tale of a Tub* and *Battle of the Books*, he groups works of modern authorship under one type or another of what Robert Adams describes as "grotesque devices of elevation to facilitate the puffing of air into a multitude."[3] Swift's narrator analyzes these devices under three rubrics: the ladder, the pulpit, or the stage itinerant. Milton, writing before all Europe as the enthusiastic authorial defender of the English people, describes himself as elevated in just the oratorical posture later satirized by Swift: "I seem now . . . to be surveying from on high far-flung regions and territories across the sea, faces numberless and unknown, sentiments in complete agreement with mine" (*CPW* IV:554–55). What Milton writes of optimistically and Swift pessimistically depends on a shared idea about the printed vehicle of an author's spiritual potency. In a later pamphlet with the arch title *Milton Restor'd and Bentley Depos'd*, Swift thus characterizes Richard Bentley's edition of *Paradise Lost* as a homicidal assault on the author: "Milton alone has had the hard Fate of being murder'd by an Editor in sixty years space."[4]

A book may in Milton's view may hold "the purest efficacy and extraction of that living intellect that bred them," but that efficacy and extraction lie vulnerable to critics and theorists inclined to murder authors or, more commonly, to neglect them. Without fire from readers' eyes to cherish them, authors remain in suspended animation. Even the vital signs exhibited by Milton's youthful writings had first to be "found," detected "by them that had the overlooking" (*CPW* I:809). Milton's "labour" and "intent study" prepared him to write, and a "strong propensity of nature" undeniably invigorates his compositions, but for the preservation of what he has written, he looks to "aftertimes, as they should not willingly let it die" (*CPW* I:810). Milton persistently reaches out from his texts to propagate and influence successive generations of his reception.

The 1645 edition of his poems, for example, includes "an unparallel'd attestation of that renowned Provost of Eton, Sir Henry Wotton," in the words of publisher Humphrey Moseley (A3v). After reading *A Mask* and making Milton's acquaintance, Wotton in 1638 had written a generous letter saying that its lyrical part "ravish[ed him] with a certain Dorique delicacy . . . whereunto I must plainly confess to have seen yet nothing parallel in our Language" (E4r–v).[5] The public deployment of praise from a well-known and respected man might be discounted as a promotional tactic perpetrated by Moseley, but Milton himself must have supplied the letter (Wotton died in 1639). Similarly, the italicized revelations sprinkled in captions (seventeen of them) throughout the 1645 edition could not have originated with Moseley. In the first edition of his poems, obviously, and generally in books published from 1641 on, Milton attempts to frame the impression of him left on the printed page, and does so more insistently and obtrusively than any previous English author. John S. Diekhoff filled an entire volume (274 pages + appendices and index) with such passages.[6] In the 1645 *Poems*, beginning with a smug snippet engraved in Greek beneath William Marshall's uncomely frontispiece, Milton incrementally presents himself not only as an overpowering pleasure to read but also as an uncommonly erudite poet: urbane, sharp-witted, more precocious than he actually was, self-knowing, an exemplar of humanistic social and familial virtues, pious, and an inspired prophet.[7]

This readiness to insist on his vigorous talent, and to piggyback indicators of his character on works devoted to other concerns, is even more overt in the polemical prose. *The Reason of Church-Government* includes an account of his reception in "the privat Academies of *Italy*," where "trifles which I had in memory, compos'd at under twenty . . . met with acceptance above what was lookt for" and where other more serious efforts that he managed to "patch up . . . were receiv'd with written Encomiums, which the Italian is not forward to bestow on men of this side of the *Alps*" (*CPW* 1:809). Milton's full and frequent self-disclosures, defenses of himself, and reports of others' praise of him may be referred in part to his belief that an author's character is implicit in what he writes: "he who would not be frustrate of his hope to write well hereafter in laudable things, ought him selfe to bee a true Poem, that is, a composition, and patterne of the best and honourablest things" (*CPW* 1:890). The fierce ideological controversies in which Milton engaged, especially concerning the regicide, meant that the presumed correspondence of moral character and aesthetic value would in his case play out in a fractious reception history during his own lifetime and in subsequent generations. He anticipated as much. Milton's ode *Ad Joannem Rousium* appeals to John Rouse, the librarian of Oxford University, as a guardian of "the famous monuments of men" (line 51). The librarian will protect Milton's book from the "degenerate [*prava*] crowd of readers" and preserve his works for the sake of "a sane posterity" (lines 80, 86) – a group so often and so flatteringly invoked in late seventeenth-century print culture that Swift satirically dedicated *Tale of a Tub* to "His Royal Highness Prince Posterity."[8]

Milton's characterization of his contemporary detractors as depraved exemplifies a familiar, hermeneutic reflexivity: readers by their responses to the works of a good author render judgment on themselves. Hence the Son of God insists in *Paradise Regained* that some there are "Of whom to be dispraised were no small praise" (III.56). That Milton in 1645 was already enduring a storm of "no small praise" indicates how fierce the negative reaction to his divorce tracts had been. In 1644, a former ally in antiprelatical controversy, Herbert Palmer, cautioned parliament against toleration in a sermon that referred to Milton as the "impudent" author of "a wicked book... deserving to be burnt."[9] Stuart supporters later seized on Milton's advocacy of divorce as an early indicator of his bad character, which they deemed a prerequisite for employment by Cromwell's government. Richard Perrinchief in 1662 refers to Milton as a "base scribe," hired by Cromwell's minions after he "made himself notorious by some licentious and infamous Pamphlets, and so approved himself as fit for their service."[10] Francis Turner, later Bishop of Ely, in a sermon in 1681 commemorating Charles' death, identifies Milton similarly:

that same vile mercenary Satyrist that writ... in justification of this prodigious Murder... was the same Author... that writ also upon *Divorce*, to make Adultery as well as Murder lawful in themselves, as they were delightful to him. He, whom it pleas'd God to strike with blindness, as he struck those Sodomites that durst attempt to violate even Angelical Purity.[11]

The identification of Charles as angelical and Milton as a Sodomite comprehends both the sexual and political crimes for which royalist writers rebuked Milton.

Milton in *The Doctrine and Discipline of Divorce* preceded his detractors in recognizing the connection between his arguments for divorce and the right to change government: "He who marries, intends as little to conspire his own ruine, as he that swears Allegiance: and as a whole people is in proportion to an ill Government, so is one man to an ill mariage" (*CPW* II:229). In an apt and variously ironic coincidence, Palmer's early declaration that Milton's *Doctrine and Discipline* "deserv[ed] to be burnt" would in the 1650s be echoed and supplemented by John Egerton, who as a boy had played the chastity-championing Elder Brother in Milton's *Mask*. His copy of *Pro Populo Anglicano Defensio*, Milton's fullest justification of the trial and execution of Charles Stuart, bears this inscription: "*liber igni, Author furca, dignissimi*," which is to say, "the book richly deserves fire; the author the gallows."[12] Egerton's judgment was indeed carried out on Milton's *Defensio* in its first year of publication (1651), at least in France.

The author, however, escaped the gallows, narrowly it seems, and lived to guarantee his survival as a poet, too, by completing and publishing his verse masterpieces. *Paradise Lost* in particular became a synecdoche for the works of John Milton. If there is such a thing as a literary afterlife of the sort intimated by Milton, it has been largely mediated through his epic.

Even this survival was not uncomplicated. Through the generations, it has depended on protracted if largely implicit political negotiation, one still ongoing. As T. S. Eliot wrote in repenting his part in an early twentieth-century assault on Milton, "the Civil War of the seventeenth century, in which Milton is a symbolic figure, has never been concluded ... Of no other poet is it so difficult to consider the poetry simply as poetry, without our theological and political dispositions, conscious and unconscious, inherited or acquired, making an unlawful entry."[13] Eliot, who though born Protestant in St. Louis ultimately became an Anglo-Catholic subject of the British monarchy, is accurate and characteristically evocative in calling Milton a "symbolic figure" of the Civil War. The historical process of Milton's literary afterlife, with its symbolic freight, bears comparison to the process of dream-work articulated by Freud. In both processes latent content becomes manifest only after mechanisms of distortion have been applied – including displacement, condensation, and, *per* Eliot's suggestion, symbolization – which permit the individual dream or a cultural reception to ameliorate repression through indirect expression.[14]

Milton's development as a cultural symbol, however, has been an evolving social and political formation over centuries, not the outcome of an individual unconscious process. Milton himself initiated the history of his symbolization, moreover, especially within his writings as Latin Secretary. Under Cromwell's regime he participated in the effort to position "John Milton, Englishman" as the voice of the English people's aspiration to what he understood as political and religious liberty. The effort to efface that symbolic identification, the biographer David Masson long ago speculated, was also deliberate and initially pursued not by Milton's ideological enemies but by his friends.

In 1660, with the Restoration underway, these friends sought a way to preserve the defender of regicide from capital punishment. According to Masson, it was strategically conceded that Cromwell hired Milton's pen not to champion liberty but to attack Charles in *Eikonoklastes* and other works.[15] The deliberately reductive emphasis on harsh personal attacks led royalist critics to depict Milton as a wretched mercenary who slandered a dead king widely regarded as a martyred saint. As offensive as the strategic depiction of Milton might seem, it distracted attention from the radical political principles articulated in *The Tenure of Kings and Magis-trates* and other works. Inasmuch as Milton was not drawn and quartered, the selective distortion of his record worked to his immediate benefit. The widespread belief that Milton had libeled the dead king, however, inspired lasting, visceral indignation. Royalist literati generally agreed that Milton was a rhetorically gifted but vicious, unprincipled hireling, whose literary achievements had been rendered inconsequential by his villainy. Writing in 1687, William Winstanley epitomizes this line of attack:

> *John Milton* was one, whose natural parts might deservedly give him a place amongst the principal of our English poets, having written two Heroick poems and a Tragedy... But his Fame is gone out like a Candle in a Snuff, and his Memory will always stink, which might have ever lived in honorable Repute, had he not been a notorious Traytor, and most impiously and villanously bely'd that blessed Martyr King *Charles* the First.[16]

The royalists deplored Milton not as a republican who championed popular sovereignty but as a prostituted penman who published nasty lies about Charles in a sodomitical attempt to violate his "angelical purity." That Milton was far from mercenary in character and largely accurate in his attacks on Charles were at the time unspeakable propositions, which only gradually rose to cultural consciousness.

Similarly repressive pressures seem to have influenced Anthony Wood's 1691–92 account of Milton, *Fasti Oxonienses*, which drew on the detailed research of John Aubrey. Aubrey, himself a royalist, was a remarkably impartial collector of data and assumed a distinction between literary merit and political content that anticipates the eighteenth-century invocation of the sublime as an apolitical aesthetic category. He mentions, for example, "two admirable panegyrics" in praise of Cromwell and Fairfax (Sonnets 15 and 16). Having heard of their "sublimity of wit," Aubrey was eager to read these as yet unpublished poems despite their forbidden subjects: "were they made in commendation of the devil, 'twere all one to me: 'tis the *hoopsoos* [loftiness] that I look after" (*CPEP* xxix). But the facts Aubrey impartially recorded were at the disposal of Anthony Wood, to whom it was not "all one." Selecting from Aubrey's detailed research, he thus arranged a familiar judgment: Milton might have been remembered with honor "had he been but honestly principled."[17]

Royalist scorn of Milton in the late seventeenth century was genuine even if it was based in a distortion propagated to save the poet's life. George Lytellton in *Dialogues of the Dead* has Pope explain that "the Politics of Milton at that time brought his Poetry into disgrace."[18] The conventional wisdom of the first half of the eighteenth century was that until Joseph Addison (1672–1719) introduced the poet, Milton's artistic genius had simply gone unrecognized. Aaron Hill in 1731 attributed the delay to Britain's "stupid insensibility to such a prodigious Genius as Milton's, who had been thirty years dead before the force of his Poetry began to take Life among us."[19] Noting that thousands of copies of *Paradise Lost* were sold prior to 1688, however, Samuel Johnson posits a "subterraneous current" by which early appreciation of the epic stole its way "through fear and silence."[20]

We should not imagine that this subterraneous current sprang pure from Restoration dissenters predisposed to appreciate Milton, or to embrace his art for the same political reasons that the establishment disowned it. The evidence instead suggests that, as in the case of Eliot, the conflict aroused by Milton was as much internal as external. Consider the turmoil expressed by Thomas Yalden (1670–1736) in verses "On the Reprinting Milton's Prose Works with his Poems. Written in his *Paradise Lost*":

> We own the poet worthy to rehearse
> Heaven's lasting triumphs in immortal verse.
> But when thy impious, mercenary pen
> Insults the best of princes, best of men,
> Our admiration turns to just disdain,
> And we revoke the fond applause again.

The poem ends after identifying Milton with Satan and suggesting that the "apostate bard" has been condemned to hell.[21]

Similar testimony to the ambivalence of Englishmen reading *Paradise Lost* during its first 150 years occurs in Johnson's *Life of Milton* itself. The current of a strong political antipathy regularly breaks through his critical appreciation of Milton's art. Citing the narrator's lament in the invocation to book VII of *Paradise Lost* that he has "fall'n on evil days" and "evil tongues" (lines 25–26), Johnson thus expresses not sympathy but indignation. "He was fallen indeed on *evil days*; the time was come in which regicides could no longer boast their wickedness. But of *evil tongues* for Milton to complain required impudence at least equal to his other powers; Milton, whose warmest advocates must allow, that he never spared any asperity of reproach or brutality of insolence."[22] The internal dissonance that Milton, taken all in all, provoked in British subjects in the seventeenth and eighteenth centuries brought them to discriminate in sustaining his literary afterlife, to attend with much greater care to his poetry, especially as the definitive example of sublimity, and to avert their eyes insofar as possible from the impudent prose. The attention paid *Paradise Lost* in particular, especially as critics turned to identify its shortcomings, manifests the unspoken political opposition with which admiration of Milton had to negotiate. The two best examples of this critical-political phenomenon are the early and persistent response to his abandonment of rhyme and to the theological implications of the epic, especially the Arianism of the narrative and the vitalist monism of that narrative's setting.

A note from the printer introducing a defense of the verse was inserted in copies of the first edition in 1668, which demonstrates that the absence of end rhymes bothered Milton's Restoration audience from the very first (*CPEP* 291, n.1). The note on the verse appears to have been written by Milton inasmuch as it displays his characteristic "asperity of reproach," describing rhyme as "the invention of a barbarous age," "a thing of itself, to all judicious ears, trivial and of no true musical delight." The note further insists that the lack of rhyme is no "defect," regardless of what "vulgar readers" think, but "an example set, the first in English, of ancient liberty recovered to heroic poem from the troublesome and modern bondage of rhyming" (*CPEP* 291). Milton had previously claimed in his controversial prose to be recovering other ancient liberties, the right to divorce or change government, for example, and, following the pattern set in those controversies, here too he depicts his opposition as ill-informed and inclined to brutish servility.

Restoration critics did not value rhyme simply because they were stupid animals, however. For obvious circumstantial reasons, they were more likely to endorse the relatively uniform aesthetic principles of the absolutist French court than the brotherly dissimilitudes of the earlier Italian and Spanish neoclassical theorists embraced by Milton. The connection between rhyme and French absolutism was clear enough to be remarked on in the eighteenth century, as these lines by William Roberts (d. 1791), addressed to rhyme personified, demonstrate: "Go, mark the lettered sons of Gallia's clime / Where critic rules, custom's tyrant law, / Have fettered the free verse."[23] A century earlier, however, the aptly named Thomas Rymer, working from his narrow intellectual perch to snuff Milton's literary candle, sneered at *Paradise Lost* as a work "some are pleased to call a poem."[24] In 1694, he skips it altogether in an account of English heroic poetry that praises poems by royalists William Davenant (*Gondibert*) and Abraham Cowley (*Davideis*) as the prime examples.[25]

Although few writers over the next century endorsed Rymer's categorical exclusion of blank verse from poetry, rhyming verse, especially the heroic couplet, was considered more proper for serious subjects. The hammer and gavel of the closed heroic couplet was not for Milton the proper instrument of epic discourse, which in his view should be subject only to its own internally generated if divinely inspired rational discipline rather than to the externally imposed necessity of rhyme. Its beauty, Milton insists, is in the way it freely accommodates variety and unregularity. Earlier in the seventeenth century, Ben Jonson and his followers had not permitted the epigrammatic formal cast of the heroic couplet to prevent pursuit of a line of thought that overflowed the distich; in a community of reasonable men matters could not always be settled with an end-stopped rhyme. Similarly, Milton in his early adherence to the couplet form persistently resists "the bondage of rhyming" and early exhibits a tendency to draw out his sense freely "from one verse into another."[26] As late as his translation of Psalm 1 (1653), he shows himself able to follow the Jonsonian manner, but evidently when it came time to compose his epic, he had concluded that submission to the heroic couplet would be counterproductive.

Milton's note on the verse, challenging a poetic practice repeatedly championed by Dryden in the 1660s, made the political resonance of such an aesthetic choice palpable to Restoration and eighteenth-century poets. Dryden, despite his admiration for Milton's achievement in *Paradise Lost*, could not extend his theodicy to the verse, refusing to "justify Milton for his blank verse."[27] Critics such as Francis Atterbury, who could "wish the tyrant [rhyme] dethroned, and blank verse set up in its room" were few.[28] Johnson perhaps expressed the strategic consensus reached by most eighteenth-century writers when he maintained that while rhyme is the superior practice, he could not, in view of Milton's astonishing sublimity, wish Milton a rhymer: "he that thinks himself capable of astonishing may write blank verse; but those that hope only to please must condescend to rhyme."[29]

The other early response to Milton's epic that expresses obliquely the political consternation aroused by Milton and his part in the trauma of civil war is the early and persistent controversy over his theology, especially the Arianism and vitalist monism evident in the epic. John Rogers has argued at length that the "vitalist moment" of the mid-seventeenth century was a leveling metaphysical precursor to the political liberalism and popular sovereignty promulgated at the end of the century.[30] Similarly, Arianism was felt as a threat to monarchical government and, contrary to the repeated claims of twentieth-century Milton scholars, it was early on apparent to informed readers that the narrative of *Paradise Lost* takes Arian doctrine as a given. Indeed, it may have been difficult for early readers not to see it in the epic because they had been sensitized to such doctrinal deviations: "between

1687 and approximately 1700," as John Marshall has observed, "there was a major debate over the trinity in England which became known as the 'Unitarian Controversy.'"[31] Skepticism toward the ideological claims of supposedly sacred monarchs and a state church were defining traits of these heretics and, as I have argued elsewhere, their inclination to political and religious self-determination.[32] It is this set of attitudes to which readers like Defoe and Johnson were responding with their complaints over Milton's ontological demotion of the Son and "the confusion of spirit and matter."[33]

In each case examined here, Milton's early reception indeed reflects the strategies of "interpretive communities" and in each case strategies that grew up in a recently war-torn monarchy returned to peaceful times as a way of coping with the political enormity of a poet-regicide. What he wrote was real enough to scare as well as astonish them.

NOTES

1 The concept of "interpretive communities" was developed by Stanley Fish, *Is There A Text in This Class* (Cambridge, MA, 1980), 147–74. The quoted assertion of their complete independence appears in Cornelius Holtorf, *Monumental Past: The Life-histories of Megalithic Monuments in Mecklenburg-Vorpommern (Germany)*, electronic monograph (University of Toronto: Centre for Instructional Technology Development, 2000–2007), https://tspace.library.utoronto.ca/citd/holtorf/2.4.html.

2 Unless otherwise noted in what follows, quotations of seventeenth-century verse other than Milton's are cited by line number and follow John Rumrich and Gregory Chaplin, eds., *Seventeenth-Century British Poetry, 1603–1660* (New York, 2006). On early modern understanding of spiritual bodily processes, see, in the same volume, Lawrence Babb, "The Physiology and Psychology of the Renaissance," 749–63. On Milton's invention of intellectual spirits and its theological consequences, see Stephen M. Fallon, *Milton Among the Philosophers* (Ithaca, NY, 1991), 104–05.

3 Robert M. Adams, *Strains of Discord: Studies in Literary Openness* (Ithaca, NY, 1958), 156.

4 Jonathan Swift, *Milton Restor'd and Bentley Depos'd* (London, 1732), vii.

5 Wotton uses "delicacy" in an obsolete sense to mean a quality pleasurable to the palate (cf. *Paradise Lost* v.333).

6 John S. Diekhoff, *Milton on Himself* (New York, 1939).

7 For a thorough account of the 1645 edition, to which I am variously indebted in this paragraph, see Stephen B. Dobranski, *Milton, Authorship, and the Book Trade* (Cambridge, 1999), 82–103. Milton's self-representation is also discussed in Stephen Fallon's chapter in this volume.

8 "The Epistle Dedicatory," *Tale of a Tub*, in *Jonathan Swift: A Tale of a Tub and Other Works*, ed. Angus Ross and David Woolley (New York, 1986), 14.

9 Milton reacted defiantly, publishing a second edition of *The Doctrine and Discipline of Divorce* followed by another three pamphlets justifying divorce. The final one, *Colasterion* (Greek for "place of punishment"), calls an anonymous critic of his argument "this Pork," "this fleamy clodd of an *Antagonist*," and "a Boar" before wondering "what should a man say more to a snout in this pickle, What language can be low and degenerat enough?" (*CPW* II:737, 740, 747). A similarly vituperative spirit animates the two sonnets (11 and 12) responding to the scandal raised by his arguments: "a barbarous noise environs me / Of owls and cuckoos, asses, apes and dogs" (Sonnet 12, lines 3–4).

10 Richard Perrinchief and William Fulman, eds., BASILIKA: *The Workes of King Charles the Martyr* (London, 1662), 94.

11 Francis Turner, *A Sermon Preached before the King on the 30 of January 1681* (London, 1681), 17–18.

12 Henry John Todd, *Poetical Works of John Milton*, 4 vols. (London, 1842), 1:80.

13 T. S. Eliot, "Milton II," in *On Poetry and Poets* (London, 1957), 148.

14 Sigmund Freud, *The Interpretation of Dreams*, trans. Joyce Crick (Oxford, 1999). See especially chapter 6.

15 David Masson, *The Life of John Milton*, 7 vols. (London, 1859–94), VI:170–93.

16 William Winstanley, *Lives of the English Poets* (London, 1687), 195.

17 *EL* 39.

18 George Lytellton, *Dialogues of the Dead*, 2nd edn. (London, 1760), 123.

19 Quoted in John Walter Good, *Studies in the Milton Tradition* (Champaign-Urbana, IL, 1913).

20 Samuel Johnson, *Lives of the Most Eminent English Poets*, 3 vols. (London, 1896), 1:103.

21 *The Works of the English Poets, from Chaucer to Cowper*, ed. Alexander Chalmers and Samuel Johnson, 21 vols. (London, 1810), XI:74.

22 Johnson, *Lives*, 1:100.

23 William Roberts, "A Poetical Epistle to Christopher Anstey," *Critical Review* 35 (1773): 52.

24 Thomas Rymer, *The Tragedies of the Last Age* (London, 1678), 143.

25 Thomas Rymer, *Monsieur Rapin's Reflections on Aristotle's Treatise of Poetry* (London, 1694), B3r–v.

26 William Bowman Piper, *The Heroic Couplet* (Cleveland, OH, 1969), 273.

27 John Dryden, *Discourses on Satire and Epic Poetry* (Whitefish, MT, 2004), 12.

28 Francis Atterbury, "Preface," *The Second Part of Mr. Waller's Poems* (London, 1690).

29 Johnson, *Lives*, 1:134.

30 John Rogers, *Matter of Revolution* (Ithaca, NY, 1996).

31 John Marshall, *John Locke: Resistance, Religion, and Responsibility* (Cambridge, 1994), 389.

32 John Rumrich, "Milton Arianism: Why it Matters," in *Milton and Heresy*, ed. Stephen B. Dobranski and John P. Rumrich (Cambridge, 1998), 75–92; and *Milton Unbound* (Cambridge, 1996), 40–49.

33 Johnson, *Lives*, 1:129.

CHAPTER 12

Critical responses, 1825–1970

P. J. Klemp

More significant than the concerted efforts by twentieth-century scholars to effect Milton's "dislodgment" (F. R. Leavis), "dethronement" (Douglas Bush), and "discanonization and unconstellation" (Logan Pearsall Smith) from the literary firmament, a number of controversies dominated Milton criticism from 1825 to 1970.[1] Critics frequently staked out dichotomous positions when they addressed Satan's alleged hijacking of *Paradise Lost*, the identity of the epic's hero, and the value of the grand style. They also asked whether *Paradise Lost* was an intellectually vital poem, what Walter Raleigh called "a monument to dead ideas," or a vacuous work conveying no ideas.[2] These key issues received thorough discussions in a number of surveys of nineteenth- and twentieth-century Milton criticism.[3] Remarking on the direction criticism took in the mid twentieth century, Robert Martin Adams fretted that "a major overreading" of some of the shorter poems caused them to replace *Paradise Lost*, *Paradise Regained*, and *Samson Agonistes* as Milton's major works.[4] But this brief trend represented an aberration, for critics consistently focused on the epic from the period immediately following the Romantics' commentaries on Milton to the point when poststructuralist theories began to influence Anglo-American literary studies. Emphasizing *Paradise Lost*, I will provide an overview of the two interpretive approaches that dominated Milton studies during those years: author-centered and reader-oriented criticism.

In the practice of literary interpretation, context is everything. Our understanding of Milton's writing changes dramatically when we make the decision, consciously or otherwise, to see it through the lens of, say, contemporary political events, gender issues, or biography. Milton's reflections on his lived experience – including his relationships with family members, education, travel, and career as an author – invite readers to view his writings as autobiographical.[5] However, Bush, speaking for many twentieth-century readers, dismissed biographical analyses by noting that "it is axiomatic in modern criticism that our concern is with an author's works and not his personal character," and Balachandra Rajan rejected readings based on psycho-biography by claiming that "A poem cannot be defined genetically through its evolution in the mind of the poet."[6] Yet generations of readers have accepted Milton's tacit invitation and used his life and mind as the foundation on which to construct interpretations. Many critics sketched out or implied connections between the artist's life and literature – what Denis Saurat called "the harmony between Milton's ideas and Milton's character"[7] – but E. M. W. Tillyard in 1930 offered one of the most explicit formulations of the biographical approach as it applied to Milton's writing. Tillyard contended that a given text related actual experiences and was therefore "really about . . . the true state of Milton's mind when he wrote it"; that is, the poetry and prose provided insights into the author's daily life and inner world.[8] Some critics reversed this approach, bringing evidence from Milton's life to bear on his texts, though most, including Tillyard, fluttered back and forth between biography and writing. That the biographical approach was not universally accepted was made clear when Tillyard and C. S. Lewis attempted to debate it in 1939, calling their book *The Personal Heresy: A Controversy*. Milton's forceful personality ensured that one of the most significant interpretive issues from 1825 to 1970 dealt with whether "I like Milton as a person" (William Riley Parker) or "I cannot like him" (John Middleton Murry) and, often implicitly, with what place readings based on biography should occupy in Milton studies.[9]

Because of Milton's conspicuous literary persona and political allegiance during the English Revolution, few commentators felt indifferent toward or ambivalent about his personality and psychology. The result was a relentlessly dualistic critical landscape, one divided between those who have been termed Miltonists and anti-Miltonists. The heroic Milton, who, according to Thomas Babington Macaulay in 1825, struggled more than any other poet with "unfavourable circumstances," characterized much of the nineteenth-century response to the man and his writings.[10] Ralph Waldo Emerson, in addition to observing that Milton's "true greatness is a perfect humility," believed that "no man in these later ages, and few men ever, possessed so great a conception of the manly character."[11] The step from biography to literary analysis proved to be a short one, given Macaulay's belief that Milton's works were "coloured" by his "personal feelings" and Emerson's claim that throughout Milton's poetry, "one may see, under a thin veil, the opinions, the feelings, even the incidents of the poet's life, still reappearing . . . It was plainly needful that his poetry should be a version of his own life."[12] From this perspective, to borrow the Lady's assertion of a commonplace in *A Mask*, "none / But such as are good men can give good things" (lines 702–03). Therefore, despite some grumbling about Milton's political prose, a man portrayed for most of the nineteenth century as magnanimous, as Emerson claimed, and modest and in possession of "a high and flawless excellence," as Matthew Arnold described him, obviously could produce only works that displayed noble attributes.[13] In Thomas De Quincey's judgment, Milton wrote, not the literature of knowledge ("What do you learn from *Paradise Lost*? Nothing at all"), but instead the far superior literature of power, which moved readers and gave the "exercise and expansion to your own latent capacity of sympathy with the infinite."[14] Whether Milton wrote the literature of knowledge or of power, near the end of the nineteenth century Mark Pattison observed that *Paradise Lost* "has been more admired than read," in part because of Milton's "unsympathetic disposition." Since Pattison recognized no boundary between poem and personality, it is unclear whether his memorable remark that "An appreciation of Milton is the last reward of consummated scholarship" applied to the man, his epic, or both.[15] When Raleigh, writing in 1900, continued to connect biographical and literary matters by maintaining that "Milton's life and his art seem to cohere, and to express the pride and the power of his character," he also acknowledged some of this interpretive strategy's weakness: "But enough of this vein of criticism, which is justified only by the pleasure of detecting Milton too imperfectly concealed behind his handiwork."[16]

Enough of this kind of criticism was not enough, for, accompanying a steady stream of praise for Milton's character and writing, a vocal contingent of anti-Miltonists argued that none but such as are bad men can write bad poems. Opposing these critics, the Miltonists, following Macaulay's lead, described a heroic author whose epic appropriately distributed virtue and vice among its chief characters, particularly God and Satan, even if some commentators worried that Milton lavished excessive attention on the devil. Avoiding biographical interpretations, these so-called traditionalists saw Milton's God as a figure of "right reason" and eternal love (Bush) and his Satan as "malicious and idiotic" (Charles Williams), "'(in the long run) an ass'" (Lewis), and the "first liar" (Rajan), who displayed the "perverted quality of parody-heroism, of which the essential quality is destructiveness" (Northrop Frye).[17] However, the anti-Miltonists found much to condemn in Milton's God and much to praise in his Satan, basing their views on harsh judgments of the author's character and psychology. Murry, after pausing to express concern that he had "perhaps a childish criticism to make of Milton," charged that the author of *Paradise Lost* was "deficient in love."[18] Whether childish or just mean-spirited, this claim did affect the critical response to Milton's writing. Within ten years, hints of Murry's biographical speculation appeared in A. J. A. Waldock's assessment of Milton's epic characterization: although "it does not come very naturally to Milton to suggest a loving God," the portrait of evil was closer to hand because Milton was "able, in a marked degree, to conceive of Satan in terms of himself" and to make the devil an increasingly sympathetic character as his career progressed in *Paradise Lost*.[19] Raleigh, who was interested in Milton's proud and egotistic personality, described the struggle that occurred when the poet portrayed the rebel angel: with "chains of interest and sympathy stronger than he confessed or knew," Milton, "as if by some mediæval compact," discovered that "the relations are reversed, and the poet is in the service of the Devil."[20] The focus on Milton's pride and ego made it a straightforward matter to conclude that Satan prevailed over the poet and his poem. This victory, by reviving the Romantic reading that saw Satan as the epic's hero, defined the role of Milton's God as the "whimsical Tyrant" who opposed the heroic energy of both the poet and Satan, the character into whom "Milton pours out his own feelings" and in whom was "invested . . . all that Milton felt and valued most strongly."[21] Openly voicing Percy Bysshe Shelley's and especially William Blake's perspectives, Murry explained that, "in his magnificent picture of Satan, Milton is unconsciously uttering the rebellion of his own creative humanity against the false God whom his mind has enthroned."[22] The most forceful attack came from William Empson, whose study of *Milton's God* was not based on biographical claims. Yet generations of biographical analysis and the neo-Romantic view of Milton and his characters, both of which were amply documented in Empson's argument, provided the foundation for his description of Milton's God as "wicked" and "an infinite malignity," a character who rules through "trickery." Indeed, Empson announced that the contributions of God and Christianity made *Paradise Lost* "an impressive example of one of the more appalling things the human mind is liable to do."[23]

Milton's firm grasp of evil was complemented, from the anti-Miltonists' perspective, by the "deficiency of the human element in his imagination," as Pattison charged.[24] This deficiency soon developed into Raleigh's complaint that Milton "knew human nature only in the gross" and T. S. Eliot's that "he had little interest in, or understanding of, individual human beings."[25] This biographical insight about a lack of perceptiveness and empathy, which was consistent with the allegation that Milton was deficient in love, had profound interpretive consequences, for such an author's vision of the first couple in *Paradise Lost* must lack human interest.

Adam and Eve are, in Frye's witty phrase, "suburbanites in the nude," consumed by middle-class activities, or, in Tillyard's characterization of them, "Old Age Pensioners" in the "hopeless position of . . . enjoying perpetual youth."[26] While two early critics anticipated late twentieth-century feminist readings – Walter Savage Landor in 1846 found Milton's Eve a "more interesting" character than Adam, and Walter Bagehot in 1879 called her "one of the most wonderful efforts of the human imagination"[27] – these characters, unlike Milton's God and Satan, were not at the center of any ongoing critical controversy. It is noteworthy, however, that analyses that avoid biographical assumptions were more favorable to the first couple. Thus Frye sounded a unique note in Milton criticism when he praised Adam and Eve's "lively, even explosive personalities" and their "exuberance in the possession of language as a new and fresh form of intellectual energy."[28] But dramatically different results emerged when Raleigh seized on the biographical implications of Milton's portrayal of women: "To judge from some passages of his works, one half of the human race was to Milton an illusion to which the other half was subject."[29] An interpretation of Eve's fall as being caused by "mental triviality," as Tillyard explained it, was firmly rooted in patriarchal views based on assumptions about Milton's relationships with women and perceptions of gender.[30] The allegation that Milton was a misogynist was consistent with the claims that he had no understanding of human nature and was deficient in love.

When these accusations were compounded by the charge of a lack of charity, particularly in *The Doctrine and Discipline of Divorce* and *Samson Agonistes*, Murry was able to make a broad assault on Milton's final poetic vision. Unlike Shakespeare's *Tempest*, in which "there can be no doubt whatever of the spirit of charity," *Samson Agonistes* was "a monument of poetical desiccation" in which Milton's vision had "no charity at all."[31] We may never know whether Milton's tutor at Cambridge "whip't him," as John Aubrey reported, but the nineteenth- and twentieth-century anti-Miltonists certainly took their shots, mustering biographical details, assumptions, and inventions to try to repudiate him.[32] While there is much to recommend Bush's remark about the "plentiful evidence in Milton's writings and in the early biographies that he liked and was liked by a varied circle of friends," does an understanding of Milton's amiability help us better understand his poetry and prose? Bush stated that "one may doubt if Isaiah or Aeschylus or Dante was very likeable."[33] One may also doubt whether students of Virgil or Marvell or Ralph Ellison believe that an understanding of the author's personality will illuminate his texts, whether everything he wrote is in effect autobiographical. Or, to reinforce concerns that Bush raised, when Macbeth speaks, do we conclude that Shakespeare was filled with despair, cynicism, and demonic ambition?

Just as the personality behind the creation of Milton's texts received attention in critical discussions from 1825 to 1970, so a complementary discussion dealt with the recipient of those texts, Milton's reader. Without basing their critical responses on biographical matters, readers of *Paradise Lost* seemed compelled to acknowledge that they were participating in a relationship with the poem's main characters, themes, and style. Although readers always assume that texts have designs on them, Milton's conspicuous narrative voice and provocative characters ensure that the poem will act on us, pull us into a relationship. As Rajan observed, *Paradise Lost* "imposes its perspective on your feelings," an assessment of the epic as forceful, perhaps even bullying, that Waldock also advanced: "The poem thrusts on us a view, insists on an attitude."[34] Since passive reading is not a productive strategy when encountering such an aggressive epic, the active reader must discover when it is appropriate to respond with resistance, compliance, smugness, and guilt. In 1825, Macaulay described the relationship between Milton and his reader in thrilling terms – "He electrifies the mind through conductors" – and Lewis in 1942 used another metaphor to outline a similar relationship: "We are his organ: when he appears to be describing Paradise he is in fact drawing out the Paradisal Stop in us."[35] In 1967, Stanley Fish's *Surprised by Sin* presented a fully developed "programme of reader harassment," offering a reminder that the reader of the epic had a central role in the interpretive process.[36] Many studies included no examination of this reader's identity; instead, a given critic often plunged ahead with an analysis in which he was assumed to be the reader.[37] Yet some critics were more reflective. When Bagehot briefly raised this issue, he stumbled over the question of whether the reader and the critic and Bagehot were interchangeable terms: "The only way to criticise a work of the imagination, is to describe its effect upon the mind of the reader – at any rate, of the critic."[38] Critics rarely explored the reader's identity and how it affected interpretive strategies and conclusions in Milton's prose and shorter poems, but these were important issues in nineteenth- and twentieth-century studies of *Paradise Lost*.[39]

With the establishment of distinct reader-oriented theories in the 1960s and 1970s came the identification of a wide range of readers. The hermeneutic scene was suddenly populated by ideal readers, implied readers, narratees, guilty readers, informed readers, and their siblings. However, in Milton studies from 1825 to 1970, as in literary studies in general, the issue was usually handled in a less reflective manner. Tillyard, briefly moving beyond the autobiographical impulse that led the reader from evidence in the text to "some indication of the author's own experience," explained that the reader could find this experience by "record[ing] the dominant sensations a work of art arouses in him."[40] Tillyard ignored the second, reader-oriented part of this approach, but Waldock attended to it with a vengeance: "If we are ever to see the poem as it really is, our *impressions*, surely, are what we must first and last attend to . . . [T]hey constitute the facts of the poem." Waldock found that the reader of *Paradise Lost* witnessed "a fundamental clash" between the narrator's editorial remarks, which assert one thing (that the reader should despise Satan and condemn Adam's decision to fall, for example), and what the poem demonstrates in its narrative and "compels us to feel," such as sympathy for Satan and Adam.[41] Whether because Milton botched the job or was unaware of the difficulties posed by his biblical theme, the reader experienced the triumph of demonstration over assertion. Consequently, Waldock argued, the reader encountered a very different poem from the one Milton intended to write. In most studies of Milton's works, including Tillyard's and Waldock's, the reader's identity remained unclear. Was he an entity independent of the study's author and the individual he called "the critic" (who might or might not be identical)? Frequently, one suspects that the three terms were conflated, except when rhetorical necessity called for an ambiguous creature known as "the reader" to enter the analysis.

Instead of hiding behind a phantom reader, some critics looked for a nearly ideal reader, to whom they assigned a new identity in the interpretive process. These critics recognized that a reader's hermeneutics and the analysis he produced were largely based on part of his identity – but only part. Critics frequently focused on the ways in which the reader's identity was shaped by a time period, usually his own, and all of its cultural assumptions except those connected to gender, class, religious beliefs, and race. As a result, the reader was tacitly universalized as male, upper middle class, secular, and white. Illustrating this oversight, Lewis argued that the best reader expanded his historical perspective:

To enjoy our full humanity we ought, as far as is possible, to contain within us potentially at all times, and on occasion to actualize, all the modes of feeling and thinking through which man has passed. You must, so far as in you lies, become an Achaean chief while reading Homer, a medieval knight while reading Malory, and an eighteenth century Londoner while reading Johnson. Only thus will you be able to judge the work "in the same spirit that its author writ" and to avoid chimerical criticism.[42]

Just such a hypothetical individual informed Rajan's *"Paradise Lost" and the Seventeenth Century Reader.* As he attempted "to see *Paradise Lost* through the eyes of Milton's contemporaries" by "reconstruct[ing] the response of an alert and qualified reader of the epic," Rajan acknowledged a potential weakness in his analysis: "I hope I have prevented it from becoming wholly capricious by relating it persistently to the available facts." These facts, "the equipment which the typical reader" brought to *Paradise Lost,* included his "impossibly learned" nature, though Rajan noted that this reader might be unlearned yet willing to gain knowledge and read more; his knowledge of the Bible and reading of related texts; and his unquestioning belief in the truth of the scriptural argument on which Milton's epic was based. Encountering *Paradise Lost,* this reader "would have seen the epic in its proper proportions," recognized that the poem's outlines were "easily accessible," and found its subject straightforward and precisely the one the poet announces.[43] Notwithstanding Rajan's many perceptive observations about Milton's epic, the reader he constructed, like Lewis' idealized contemporary reader, disappeared (or was absorbed into Rajan the twentieth-century critic) for long stretches of his book and was based on no evidence about seventeenth-century literacy and reading practices, education, or heterodox interpretations of the Bible. The idea of assuming the identity of a seventeenth-century reader, complete with all of his equipment or cultural baggage, has a powerful appeal. Who would deny that we have much to learn from the assumptions that Milton's contemporary reader brings to the text? This reader is just close enough to our fantasies about Milton's ideal reader or intended audience that, in an instant, he can turn into the only valid portrait of Milton's reader.

Milton's contemporary reader, like the thoroughgoing nineteenth-century reader Landor posited when he claimed that *Paradise Lost* is "Founded on an event believed by nearly all nations, certainly by all who read the poem," was also monolithic and exclusively masculine.[44] All such constructions of Milton's reader have the same lure, peril, and reality as the "wand'ring fire" that "Misleads th' amazed night-wanderer from his way" (*Paradise Lost* IX.634, 640). A few critics admitted, not only that they were the readers in question, but that this role did not require them to shed their twentieth-century cultural assumptions and identities. If Arnold Stein issued a firm refusal to adopt one appealing role – "I have not tried to be a seventeenth-century reader of *Paradise Lost*" – Bush went further, dismissing even the possibility that "as a poem, it can now be read in the same spirit in which it was composed."[45] Taking on a seventeenth-century identity provided no certain resolution to interpretive questions; indeed, such a personality makeover might be, as Bush implied, humanly impossible. That it is hermeneutically unhelpful becomes apparent when the modern reader is confronted by Milton's apparently attractive Satan and despicable God. Frye did not allow that reader to seek refuge in what he termed "the Great Historical Bromide": "the assertion that such problems would not exist for the seventeenth-century reader, who could not possibly have felt such resentment against a character clearly labelled 'God,' and talking like a seventeenth-century clergyman."[46] Frye embraced the view that Stein and Bush had implied, that the most productive perspective a reader could hold was to be a more self-reflective version of himself.

Where Leavis proposed a different kind of reader, one victimized by the music of Milton's verse, which "lulls the mind out of its normal attentiveness," reader-oriented criticism required an active participant in the interpretive process.[47] Joseph Summers argued that in *Paradise Lost* Milton "did almost everything possible to keep the reader's every faculty alert," allowing him to pursue his goal of changing the reader, "in imagination at least." Explaining how this change occurred, Summers perceptively connected Milton's treatment of his reader in *Paradise Lost* with one of Henry James' narrative strategies. In some novels, Summers explained, James constructs a guilty reader who is involved in the story's moral action and seduced to identify initially with a perspective that seemed "at least human and sympathetic." As the plot develops, this perspective's limitations are revealed, teaching the guilty reader that "the original point of view was stupid, unimaginative, shabby, and evil."[48] The epic poet, like the novelist whose technique he anticipates, wants the reader to make judgments based on frequently faulty preconceptions, recognize his errors, and then feel diffident as he doubts those judgments. Acknowledging his debt to Summers' argument, Fish constructed a reader who experienced the moral pedagogy of *Paradise Lost* by being harassed, corrected, accused, manipulated, taunted, and rebuked. Fish operated from a more carefully articulated theoretical foundation, in which meaning was conceived as an event that occurred in the reader's mind and the poem's real subject was the reader himself, even if his reader, like Summers', was an ahistorical creature who did not reside in any specific era. Fish explored the poem's key pedagogical strategy, which is based on guiding the reader through a series of good temptations that lead him to fall repeatedly. Using the pattern of "mistake – correction – instruction," modeled in Adam and Eve's Edenic circumstances and Michael's teaching of Adam in book XI, *Paradise Lost* gives the reader the opportunity to undergo a "transformation or education": he gains the self-knowledge of how he came to be a fallen person, which brings him to humility; he learns a new way to read, based on a "distrust of our own abilities and perceptions"; and he is taught how to lead a postlapsarian existence as he prepares for the next life.[49] John Milton's life and inner world have been pushed off the epic's stage. *De te fabula narratur*: the story is about you, the reader.

The question of the place of biography in literary studies emerges when we ask whether it is more productive to analyze the relationship between Milton and his reader or between Milton's literary texts and their reader. Although Rajan believed that the style of *Paradise Lost* "involves no struggle, no movement toward conversion, no transfiguration through experience of the mind," most critics argued that Milton or his epic – or both – elicited powerful responses from the reader.[50] Macaulay explained that the reader would be moved to emulate "the Great Poet and Patriot" who created the epic, and Emerson said that Milton exerted an "influence purely spiritual" on the reader because he had "the power *to inspire*."[51] Equally stirring, the effects produced by the epic, according to De Quincey, moved the reader, leading him to take "a step upwards, a step ascending as upon a Jacob's ladder from earth to mysterious altitudes above the earth."[52] Anticipating Fish's view of the readers' presence in *Paradise Lost*, Lewis commented on our deep involvement in the poem, noting that "we also have our places in this plot, that we also, at any given moment, are moving either towards the Messianic or towards the Satanic position."[53] For three centuries, critics have disagreed about the identity of the hero of *Paradise Lost*. But the main candidates – Satan, God, the Son, Adam, or, in David Masson's judgment, "Humanity itself"[54] – are mere props compared to the two indispensable participants in the experience of the epic: Saurat proposed that "The hero of *Paradise Lost* is Milton himself," and Fish identified "still another hero to be noted in the universe of *Paradise Lost* – the reader."[55]

NOTES

1 F. R. Leavis, "Milton's Verse," *Scrutiny* 2 (1933): 123–36; rpt. in *Revaluation: Tradition and Development in English Poetry* (London, 1936), 42–67 (p. 42); Douglas Bush, *"Paradise Lost" in Our Time: Some Comments* (Ithaca, NY, 1945), 3; and Logan Pearsall Smith, *Milton and His Modern Critics* (London, 1940), 31.

2 Walter Raleigh, *Milton* (London and New York, 1900), 85. When *De Doctrina Christiana* was first published in 1825, critics had an opportunity to explore Milton's ideas, particularly his heterodox ones. But while his theological treatise received many reviews, it had little effect on commentary about his writings.

The most thorough study of the relationship between *De Doctrina Christiana* and *Paradise Lost* is Maurice Kelley's *This Great Argument: A Study of Milton's "De Doctrina Christiana" as a Gloss upon "Paradise Lost"* (Princeton, 1941), but Balachandra Rajan momentarily removed the epic from its historical context by pronouncing that "surely *Paradise Lost* should be sufficient unto itself" (*"Paradise Lost" and the Seventeenth Century Reader* [London and Toronto, 1947], 25). This view, with its hint of the New Criticism's assumptions, accords with much interpretive practice from 1825 to today.

3 Historical perspectives on the critical response to Milton's writings are provided by William Kolbrener, *Milton's Warring Angels: A Study of Critical Engagements* (Cambridge, 1997); Patrick Murray, *Milton: The Modern Phase. A Study of Twentieth-Century Criticism* (London and New York, 1967); W. W. Robson, "*Paradise Lost*: Changing Interpretations and Controversy," in *From Donne to Marvell*, ed. Boris Ford, rev. edn. (Harmondsworth, 1982), 239–59; and John P. Rumrich, *Milton Unbound: Controversy and Reinterpretation* (Cambridge, 1996). For discussions of Satan's role in *Paradise Lost*, see Amadeus P. Fiore, O.F.M., "Satan is a Problem: The Problem of Milton's 'Satanic Fallacy' in Contemporary Criticism," *Franciscan Studies* 17 (1957): 173–87; and John M. Steadman, "The Idea of Satan as the Hero of *Paradise Lost*," *Proceedings of the American Philosophical Society* 120 (1976): 253–94. Because these essays raised questions about the epic's hero, they are connected to three other important studies by Steadman, *Milton and the Paradoxes of Renaissance Heroism* (Baton Rouge, LA, and London, 1987), *Milton and the Renaissance Hero* (Oxford, 1967), and *Milton's Epic Characters: Image and Idol* (Chapel Hill, NC, 1968); two analyses of Christ in *Paradise Regained*, Merritt Y. Hughes, "The Christ of *Paradise Regained* and the Renaissance Heroic Tradition," *Studies in Philology* 35 (1938): 254–77, and Frank Kermode, "Milton's Hero," *The Review of English Studies* new ser. 4 (1953): 317–30; and John Mulryan's study of "The Heroic Tradition of Milton's *Samson Agonistes*," *Milton Studies* 18 (1983): 217–34. Many scholars have published discussions of the complementary issues of Milton's style and ideas. For representative studies of style, see Paul J. Alpers, "The Milton Controversy," in *Twentieth-Century Literature in Retrospect*, ed. Reuben A. Brower (Cambridge, MA, 1971), 269–98; Cleanth Brooks, "Milton and Critical Re-Estimates," *PMLA* 66 (1951): 1045–54; and Christopher Ricks, *Milton's Grand Style* (Oxford, 1963). For studies of Milton's ideas, see James Holly Hanford, "Milton and the Return to Humanism," *Studies in Philology* 16 (1919): 126–47; and M. K. Starkman, "The Militant Miltonist; or, The Retreat from Humanism," *ELH* 26 (1959): 209–28.

4 Robert Martin Adams, *Ikon: John Milton and the Modern Critics* (Ithaca, NY, 1955), 1.

5 Milton's self-representation is discussed in Stephen Fallon's chapter in this volume.

6 Bush, "*Paradise Lost*," 12; Rajan, "*Paradise Lost*," 17.

7 Denis Saurat, *Milton: Man and Thinker* (London and New York, 1925), 106.

8 E. M. W. Tillyard, *Milton*, rev. edn. (1930; London and New York, 1967), 201.

9 William Riley Parker, *Milton: A Biography*, 2 vols. (Oxford, 1968), v; and John Middleton Murry, *Heaven – and Earth* (London, 1938), 160. With the exception of Parker's *Milton*, none of the studies cited in this section is a biography.

10 Thomas Babington Macaulay, "Milton" (1825), in *The Critical Response to John Milton's "Paradise Lost,"* ed. Timothy C. Miller (Westport, CT, and London, 1997), 152. This volume is hereafter cited as *Critical Response*.

11 Ralph Waldo Emerson, "Milton" (1838), in *Milton Criticism: Selections from Four Centuries*, ed. James Thorpe (New York, 1950), 366, 365. This volume is hereafter cited as *Milton Criticism*.

12 Macaulay, "Milton," 156; Emerson, "Milton," 367.

13 Matthew Arnold, "Milton" (1889), in *Milton Criticism*, 374, 373.

14 Thomas De Quincey, "The Poetry of Pope" (1848), in *Critical Response*, 170.

15 Mark Pattison, "Milton" (1887), in *Critical Response*, 189.

16 Raleigh, *Milton*, 178, 153.

17 Bush, *"Paradise Lost,"* 46, 41; Charles Williams, ed., *The English Poems of John Milton* (London, 1940), xiii; C. S. Lewis, *A Preface to "Paradise Lost"* (London, 1942), 95; Rajan, *"Paradise Lost,"* 96; and Northrop Frye, *The Return of Eden: Five Essays on Milton's Epics* (Toronto and Buffalo, 1965), 23.

18 Murry, *Heaven*, 150.

19 A. J. A. Waldock, *"Paradise Lost" and Its Critics* (Cambridge, 1947), 103, 75.

20 Raleigh, *Milton*, 91–92.

21 *Ibid.*, 130; Saurat, *Milton*, 214; and Tillyard, *Milton*, 1.

22 Murry, *Heaven*, 152.

23 William Empson, *Milton's God*, rev. edn. (1961; London, 1965), 17, 46, 47, 12–13.

24 Pattison, "Milton," 189.

25 Raleigh, *Milton*, 23; and T. S. Eliot, *Milton* (Oxford, 1947), rpt. as "Milton II," in *On Poetry and Poets* (London, 1957), 155.

26 Frye, *Return of Eden*, 66; Tillyard, *Milton*, 239.

27 Walter Savage Landor, "Southey and Landor" (1846), in *Critical Response*, 164; and Walter Bagehot, "John Milton" (1879), in *Critical Response*, 180.

28 Frye, *Return of Eden*, 66, 68.

29 Raleigh, *Milton*, 150.

30 Tillyard, *Milton*, 221.

31 Murry, *Heaven*, 162, 165.

32 John Aubrey, *Minutes of the Life of Mr. John Milton*, in *EL* 10.

33 Bush, *"Paradise Lost,"* 11.

34 Rajan, *"Paradise Lost,"* 106; Waldock, *"Paradise Lost,"* 55.

35 Macaulay, "Milton," 152; Lewis, *Preface*, 49.

36 Stanley Eugene Fish, *Surprised by Sin: The Reader in "Paradise Lost"* (New York and London, 1967), 4.

37 Only later, and rarely, did critics posit female readers of Milton's writing. See, for example, Joseph Wittreich, *Feminist Milton* (Ithaca, NY, and London, 1987); and Sandra M. Gilbert, "Patriarchal Poetry and Women Readers: Reflections on Milton's Bogey," *PMLA* 93 (1978): 368–82.

38 Bagehot, "John Milton," 176.
39 After 1970, more critics gave their attention to the reader in other writings by Milton. *How Milton Works* (Cambridge, MA, 2001), a collection of Stanley Fish's studies, illustrates the relevance of reader-oriented criticism to Milton's poetry, prose, and drama from the 1970s on.
40 Tillyard, *Milton*, 203.
41 Waldock, *"Paradise Lost,"* 26, 145.
42 Lewis, *Preface*, 64.
43 Rajan, *"Paradise Lost,"* 7, 17, 18–19.
44 Landor, "Southey," 164.
45 Arnold Stein, *Answerable Style: Essays on "Paradise Lost"* (Minneapolis, 1953), viii; and Bush, *"Paradise Lost,"* 29.
46 Frye, *Return of Eden*, 101.
47 F. R. Leavis, "Mr. Eliot and Milton," *Sewanee Review* 57 (1949): 1–30, rpt. in *The Common Pursuit* (London, 1952), 9–32 (p. 18).
48 Joseph Summers, *The Muse's Method: An Introduction to "Paradise Lost"* (Cambridge, MA, 1962), 26–27, 30, 31.
49 Fish, *Surprised by Sin*, 104, 161, 22.
50 Rajan, *"Paradise Lost,"* 111.
51 Macaulay, "Milton," 156; Emerson, "Milton," 364.
52 De Quincey, "Poetry," 170.
53 Lewis, *Preface*, 132.
54 David Masson, *The Life of John Milton*, 7 vols. (1859–94; New York, 1946), VI: 554.
55 Saurat, *Milton*, 220; Fish, *Surprised by Sin*, 206.

CHAPTER 13

Critical responses, recent

J. Martin Evans

More than twenty-eight years ago Stanley Fish confidently predicted that "there would be no new directions in Milton studies."[1] In the Introduction to her recently published collection of Balachandra Rajan's essays, Elizabeth Sauer implies that Fish was right, chiding Milton scholars for their "methodological prudence" and citing Joseph A. Wittreich's melancholy observation that Milton criticism "risks coming to a standstill" thanks to "its resistance to theory."[2] It seems to me, on the contrary, that John Shawcross was closer to the truth when he remarked in 2005 that although "there has been a persistence of past interpretations and supposed 'facts'" in studies of John Milton, "at the same time recent concerns – political, social, cultural, gender, philosophical – have provided an entrée into Milton's work and life that has created revisions of those past readings and supposed 'facts' and provided significant additions."[3] After all, a body of criticism that includes Fish's reader-response analyses (1965–), Donald Bouchard's structural commentary (1974), Christopher Hill's Marxist approach (1977), Sandra Gilbert's feminist critique (1978), the Jungian analyses of Joan Webber (1979) and James P. Driscoll (1993), William Kerrigan's Freudian studies (1983), Herman Rapaport's poststructural readings (1983), Claude Summers' investigations of homoerotic themes in Milton (1997), Balachandra Rajan's postcolonial perspective (1999), Diane McColley's ecologically oriented interpretations (1994–), Blair Hoxby's application of free market economic ideas to Milton's works (2002), and Peter Herman's postmodernist treatment of them (2005) can hardly be characterized as unadventurous. Far from being methodologically prudent, Milton criticism since 1970 has experimented with virtually every theoretical tool available.[4] The problem of describing this wildly heterogeneous body of material, then, lies precisely in its hermeneutical diversity.

The problem is compounded by another prominent feature of recent Milton criticism, namely the form in which much of it has been published. For although the stream of books, articles, and monographs continues unabated, over the past thirty or forty years Milton scholarship has exhibited a growing tendency to organize itself in the form of collected essays by various hands. Until the mid 1960s, the only significant collection of Milton criticism was Frank Kermode's *The Living Milton* (1960). But beginning with the appearance of A. E. Barker's *Milton, Modern Essays in Criticism* in 1965, the last decades of the twentieth century and the first decade of the twenty-first have seen the publication of an extraordinary number of compendia on various aspects of Milton's life and writings. Since 1970 at least sixteen essay collections have appeared in print not to mention the two editions of Dennis Danielson's *Cambridge Companion to Milton* (1989, 1999), the two *Blackwell Companions to Milton* (2001, 2007) edited by Thomas Corns and Angelica Duran respectively, the more than eighty volumes issued by *Milton Studies* (1969–) and *Milton Quarterly* (1967–), and the numerous proceedings of the International Milton Symposium and the South Eastern Conference on John Milton. Far from stagnating, the "Milton industry," as Stanley Fish and John Carey have called it, seems to be forging ahead at full throttle.

In the face of this overwhelming body of scholarly and critical material it is tempting to categorize its contents by the specific works on which each individual item focuses. But while this organizational strategy might be appropriate in a bibliography, it would inevitably obscure the larger critical and theoretical currents flowing beneath the surface. In what follows, therefore, I shall attempt to describe some of the most powerful and influential movements in recent Milton criticism and to suggest some of the ways in which they differ from or are connected to the interpretive tradition which preceded them.

CONSPICUOUS ABSENCES

Before I do so, however, it is worth taking a moment to note that several of the major themes and issues which figured most prominently in that earlier tradition no longer seem to be of much concern to Miltonists. For instance, the lively controversy over Milton's poetic style, ignited by T. S. Eliot and F. R. Leavis back in the 1930s, has largely petered out thanks in part at least to Christopher Ricks' brilliant defense of it in *Milton's Grand Style in "Paradise Lost"* (1963) and Archie Burnett's penetrating discussion of Milton's style in the shorter poems, *Paradise Regained*, and *Samson Agonistes* (1981), while the rather less controversial issue of Milton's prose style has been definitively treated in Keith W. Stavely's *The Politics of Milton's Prose Style* (1975) and Thomas N. Corns' study *The Development of Milton's Prose Style* (1982).

No less striking has been the relative lack of interest that Milton critics have shown during the last few years in the longstanding argument about Milton's Satan, initiated by John Dryden's famous comment that *Paradise Lost* would have had a stronger claim to epic status if Milton had not made Satan rather than Adam its hero. Following C. S. Lewis' provocative attack on the so-called Satanist school from Blake and Shelley to E. M. W. Tillyard in *A Preface to "Paradise Lost"* (1942), a vigorous debate took place over the next two decades or so concerning Milton's portrayal of the Devil in his two epics. Was Satan a hero as E. D. Stoll (1944), A. J. A. Waldock, (1948), and others maintained, or was he a fool, as C. S. Lewis (1942) and Joseph H. Summers (1962) insisted? Entertaining though it may have been, that debate now seems to have run its course. Indeed, with the notable exception of Neil Forsyth's two magisterial historical studies of *Our Old Enemy: Satan and the Combat Myth* (1987) and *The Satanic Epic* (2003), which came as close to being the last word on the subject as one can imagine, it is hard to think of any fresh contribution to the question of Satan's heroism that has appeared in print since 1970.

Finally, the traditional view of Milton as a pillar of Christian ortho-doxy promulgated by critics such as C. S. Lewis (1942), Sister Miriam Joseph (1954), and William B. Hunter, C. A. Patrides, and Jack H. Adam-son, the authors of *Bright Essence: Studies in Milton's Theology* (1971), has gradually been displaced by a growing awareness of the poet's heterodoxies. Despite the efforts of apologists like Peter Fiore (1981) and Georgia Christo-pher (1982), most modern Miltonists such as William Kerrigan (1975), Gordon Campbell (1979), Balachandra Rajan (1980), Michael Bauman (1987), John Rumrich (1988), Stephen Dobranski (1998), and Neil Forsyth (2003) have emphasized Milton's Arianism, Arminianism, mortalism, anti-trinitarianism, monism, materialism and denial of creation *ex nihilo* rather than his debts to St. Augustine or John Calvin. Far from being a monument of Protestant dogma, *Paradise Lost* in particular is coming to be recognized as a poem "bristling with heresies" written by "a lifelong nonconformist."[5] As Neil Forsyth puts it in the opening sentence of his Introduction to *The Satanic Epic*, *Paradise Lost* "is not an orthodox poem and it needs to be rescued from its orthodox critics."[6]

MILTON'S LEFT HAND

As this last example already suggests, the disappearance of some of the themes and issues which had occupied so much critical attention before 1970 created an interpretive vacuum which was rapidly filled by a new set of interests and methods. In some cases, including the question of Milton's orthodoxy, the new interpretive paradigm that emerged in the 1970s and 1980s was the exact converse of its predecessor, but more often it called attention to an aspect of Milton's writings which had previously been ignored or neglected. Perhaps the most dramatic example of this process has been the remarkable upsurge of critical interest in the prose works. Up until the early 1940s, when Don M. Wolfe's *Milton in the Puritan Revolution* (1941) and Arthur Barker's *Milton and the Puritan Dilemma* (1942) were published, detailed studies of Milton's prose tracts were few and far between. The appearance of Wolfe's monumental edition of *The Complete Prose Works of John Milton* in the years following 1953, however, galvanized critics into paying far closer attention to what Milton himself had dismissively described as the products of his "left hand" (*CPW* 1:808). The result is clearly reflected not only in the extraordinary number of books and articles about Milton's prose works which have appeared in the past forty years, but also in such collections as Michael Lieb and John T. Shawcross' *Achievements of the Left Hand* (1978) and David Loewen-stein and James G. Turner's *Poetics and Hermeneutics in Milton's Prose* (1990).

Since 1991, however, some of the most significant and influential work in this area has revolved around one tract in particular, the *De Doctrina Christiana*. At the International Milton Symposium in Vancouver in that year William B. Hunter announced that there were good reasons for believing that Milton did not write the treatise, and that as a result all those critical works which assumed that he did should be re-thought. Not surprisingly, Hunter's declaration provoked a vigorous response from the community of Milton scholars, many of whom had a major stake in Milton's authorship of *De Doctrina*. Barbara Lewalski (1992) and John Shawcross (1992) both replied immediately, soon followed by Christopher Hill and Maurice Kelley (1994). Three years later a scholarly committee consisting of Gordon Campbell, Thomas Corns, John Hale, and Fiona Tweedie was convened to investigate the evidence for and against the traditional attribution. It concluded that the manuscript of *De Doctrina* "has two principal strata, an ur-text [by an unknown author or authors] and a transformation of that text effected by a process of revision...by Milton."[7] These were by no means the last words on the subject, however; Michael Lieb (2002), John Rumrich (2003), and John Shawcross (2005) subsequently re-examined the issue afresh, and in 2007 in what might well prove to be the definitive analysis of the issue, the authors of the above-quoted report published a monograph arguing that the treatise "rightfully belongs in the Milton canon."[8]

At stake in this controversy, as John Rumrich and others have pointed out, is not only the question of attribution, important though that is. Upon the outcome of the debate will depend the view that critics take of the crucial issue I mentioned earlier, namely, was Milton a proponent of traditional Christian orthodoxy or was he the spokesman for a form of Christian heterodoxy so radical that most of his contemporaries would have branded it as heretical? One thing at least is certain. In the future, critics who want to support their interpretations of Milton's poems with material drawn from *De Doctrina Christiana* will need to make their views on its authorship clear from the outset.

THE FEMINIST CRITIQUE

Unlike the expanding critical focus on Milton's prose works, the feminist critique of his writings had its origins in a social and political rather than a literary phenomenon, the so-called "second wave" of the women's movement which developed during the 1960s and 1970s. Among its first expressions in the context of Milton criticism were Marcia Landy's seminal articles "Kinship and the Role of Women in *Paradise Lost*" (1972) and "A Free and Open Encounter: Milton and the Modern Reader" (1976), both in *Milton Studies,* and Sandra H. Gilbert's essay "Patriarchal Poetry and Women Readers: Reflections on Milton's Bogey" published in *PMLA* in 1978, which led many commentators to see Milton's poetry in a completely new light. For until those articles appeared in print, the "reader" posited by almost all Milton critics was resolutely male; in 1965 for example, Stanley Fish published an essay in which he declared that Milton's aim in *Paradise Lost* was "to recreate in the mind of the reader . . . the drama of the Fall, to make *him* fall again exactly as Adam did" so that he would be educated "to an awareness of *his* position and responsibilities as a fallen *man* and to a sense of the distance which separates *him* from the innocence once *his.*"[9] By the simple device of looking at the poem through the eyes of a female reader rather than a male one, Landy and Gilbert disclosed a whole series of issues relating not only to Milton's attitude to marriage but also to his view of gender relations in general. According to both critics, Milton was, in Virginia Woolf's phrase, "the first of the masculinists," "an embodiment of the misogynistic essence of patriarchal poetry," who promulgated a male supremacist version of woman's creation celebrating "male hegemony and female subordination."[10] And these conclusions were echoed a few years later by Christine Froula (1983) in an essay which extended the poem's female readers to include Eve herself.

Inevitably, these analyses provoked a vigorous response – from female as well as male Miltonists. Just two years after Landy's first article, Barbara Lewalski (1974) published a point by point rebuttal of Landy's arguments, Philip J. Gallagher (1979) and Joan Webber (1980) responded to Gilbert, and Edward Pechter (1984) attempted to refute Froula in an essay which, notwithstanding its critical shortcomings, must surely be awarded the prize for the most amusing title: "When Pechter Reads Froula Pretending She's Eve Reading Milton." (Froula countered immediately with "Pechter's Spectre: Milton's Bogey Writ Small"). Two years later William Shullenberger (1986) provoked a brief series of exchanges with Deirdre McChrystal (1987) and Lawrence Hyman (1987) by offering yet another defense of Milton against feminist critics, but by this point the argument was beginning to lose steam thanks, I suspect, to Diane McColley's forceful effort to rehabilitate Milton's Eve (1983) and Joseph Wittreich's provocatively titled *Feminist Milton* (1987), in which he suggested that the feminist critique of Milton was a reaction not to the original poem but to subsequent patriarchal distortions of it. Indeed, during the past three or four years the pendulum has begun to swing in the opposite direction, as demonstrated by Catherine G. Martin's *Milton and Gender* (2004), which "reevaluates the charge that Milton was antifeminine, pointing out that he was not seen that way by contemporaries but espoused startlingly modern ideas of marriage and the relations between the sexes."[11] Just a year later Peter C. Herman was able to declare confidently that "*Paradise Lost* is possibly the most thorough critique of misogyny in the English language."[12]

At the heart of these disagreements lies a fundamental theoretical issue which Landy had originally identified in her very first article: should Milton's works be read in the context of the values and attitudes which prevailed in his own time, an approach exemplified by James Turner's informative study, *One Flesh: Paradisal Marriage and Sexual Relations in the Age of Milton* (1987), or should they be interpreted in the context of our current values and beliefs? Almost invariably Milton's defenders have tended to choose the former course, claiming either that his views were conditioned by seventeenth-century attitudes to women or that his treatment of gender issues was in fact far more progressive than that of his contemporaries. His detractors, on the other hand, usually prefer the latter strategy, insisting on the primacy of the modern reader's response to the text. As a result, the two sides' arguments and counter-arguments have not always fully engaged each other, and it is refreshing to encounter a book like Martin's which embraces both approaches and builds on the insights each can provide.

GREEN READINGS

A second striking example of the influence of modern social and political movements on critical attitudes to Milton's poetry may be found in the recent development of "green" readings of *A Mask* and *Paradise Lost* in particular. The 1970s saw a spate of books and articles building on the literary insights of Bartlett Giamatti's *The Earthly Paradise and the Renaissance Epic* (1966) and John Armstrong's *The Paradise Myth* (1969). Milton's account of the garden of Eden was seen in relationship to the conventions of English pastoral (John R. Knott, 1971), to seventeenth-century English horticultural practices (C. F. Otten, 1973; John D. Hunt, 1981), to the landscapes of Italy (Hannah D. Demaray, 1974), to the paintings of Poussin (M. B. Garber, 1975), and to contemporary descriptions of the New World (J. Martin Evans, 1996). More recently, however, modern concern with environmental change in general and global warming in particular has generated a series of essays by Joan S. Bennett (1987), Ellen Goodman (1992), Richard J. DuRocher (1994–96), Karen Edwards (1999, 2005), Diane McColley, (1994, 1999, 2001), Jeffrey Theis (1996), Ken Hiltner (2003), and Juliet L. Cummins (2007), in which Milton's portrayal of unfallen nature is analyzed in more strictly ecological terms. The impact of this new approach can be measured by the fact that the 2007 conference on John Milton in Murfreesboro, Tennessee, included sessions not only on "Milton and the Environment" but also on "Milton and Ecocriticism."

The emphasis in these later studies is not on Milton's debt to the fictional and literal gardens with which he may have been familiar but rather on his "presentation of nature as animate and intimately connected with human identity," a presentation which "implicitly critiques the objectification and exploitation of nature often connected with the new science."[13] "Reading Milton greenly," Diane McColley consequently suggests, not only illuminates his poetry but may also serve as "an antidote to the ecological devastation that is the slow version of the apocalyptic final conflagration."[14]

When they are historicized, as they often are, studies of this kind can illuminate not only Milton's revolutionary treatment of the natural world but also environmental conditions in seventeenth-century England and some of the earliest efforts to improve them. If, on the other hand, ecocritics are more concerned with enlisting Milton's poetry in the service of a campaign to reverse the effects of industrial pollution and global warming, they run the risk of reducing it to a mere proof-text for environmental reform. It is one thing to bring modern values to bear on Milton's works, as many feminist critics have done. It is quite another to read modern values *into* them.

Another significant development in Milton criticism which can be traced back to the 1970s is the theme of Milton's imperialism. In the wake of the bicentennial celebrations in 1976 a number of ground-breaking literary and historical studies appeared which focused on the discursive consequences of the discovery of America and its aftermath.[15] Although none of them was specifically concerned with the writings of John Milton, they made it possible to think about his attitude to English imperial conquest in ways that would have been impossible in earlier decades, and Miltonists were not slow to do so. David Armitage's article "John Milton: Poet Against Empire" was published in 1990 soon followed by David Quint's *Epic and Empire* in 1993, Robert T. Fallon's *Divided Empire: Milton's Political Imagery* in 1995, and my own investigation of *Milton's Imperial Epic* three years after that. Paul Stevens' essay on *"Paradise Lost* and the Colonial Imperative" also appeared in 1996, Balachandra Rajan and Elizabeth Sauer's *Milton and the Imperial Vision* came out in 1999, and Anne-Julia Zwierlein's masterful study of the epic's afterlife, *Majestick Milton: British Imperial Expansion and Transformations of "Paradise Lost" 1667–1837*, was published in 2001.

Milton's political ideology, of course, had been discussed and analyzed over and over again in previous decades, and it continued to be the subject of scholarly investigation well into the new millennium. But this emphasis on the imperial theme in his writings was new, and it naturally attracted the attention of critics belonging to two relatively new theoretical schools, new historicism and postcolonialism. For both of them, the crucial question that needed answering was: did Milton approve or disapprove of England's colonial ventures in the New World and elsewhere? Was *Paradise Lost* "an indictment of European expansion and colonialism" as David Quint proposed, or was it a ringing endorsement of enterprises such as Jamestown and Plymouth Plantation?[16]

My own opinion is that Milton's imperial vision was bifocal. Milton's views on the subject seem to me as deeply divided as those expressed in the colonial discourse of seventeenth-century England. As I put it in *Milton's Imperial Epic*, "Imperial expansion, the poem implies, is morally neutral. When it is practiced by the virtuous, it is entirely admirable. When it is practiced by the wicked, it is one of the greatest evils the human race can endure."[17]

POLITICALLY CORRECT MILTON

The efforts of critics such as Quint to cast Milton as an enlightened opponent of English imperialism have their counterpart in recent attempts to depict him as a humanitarian advocate of non-violence. According to Wittreich's study *Interpreting "Samson Agonistes"* (1986), for instance, those readers who assume that the hero of Milton's play was a noble exemplar of redemptive faith whose ultimate triumph over his persecutors is held up for our admiration are wrong. Vengeance rather than divine impulsion prompted Samson's destruction of Dagon's temple, and the resulting slaughter of the Philistines was a barbarous perversion of his divine mission which Milton could not possibly have wanted us to approve. In short, Samson was a negative model, not, as generations of critics had assumed, a positive one.

Sixteen years later, on the first anniversary of 9/11, John Carey reinforced this reading with an article in the *Times Literary Supplement* in which he compared Samson to the terrorists who demolished the World Trade Center. Milton, he declared, was "a subtle-minded poet, not a murderous bigot" and critics who interpret the play "as a work in praise of terrorism" are treating it as "a license for any fanatic to commit atrocity."[18] Carey's target here was Fish, who in 2001 had argued that Samson's destruction of the temple of Dagon was "praiseworthy because he intend[ed] it to be answerable to the divine will . . . whether it was or not does not matter."[19] Carey insisted, on the contrary, that Milton could not possibly have regarded the slaughter of the Philistines as the praiseworthy act of an Israeli patriot, and that it is inconceivable that he could have intended us to rejoice with Manoa and the Chorus over Samson's bloodthirsty vengeance on his nation's enemies.

Carey's essay provoked a flurry of letters to the editor in subsequent issues of *TLS*, pointing out, among other things, that Samson had been cruelly abused by his captors, that his people had endured years of subjugation under the rule of the Philistines, and that Milton was careful to emphasize that only "Lords, ladies, captains, councellors or priests" the "choice nobility and flower" (*Samson Agonistes*, lines 1653–54) of the Philistine nation perished in the catastrophe whereas the common people all escaped. Eventually, the argument culminated in the publication of Michael Lieb and Albert Labriola's collection of essays, *In the Age of Fish: Essays on Authorship, Text, and Terrorism* (2006), in which David Loewenstein and Lieb offered their more historically informed perspectives on the issue and, for the first time, Fish himself responded in detail to Carey's attack.

Restricting the term "terrorist" to those who, like Milton's Satan, "are devoted to destruction as an end in itself," he concluded that Samson is not a terrorist but an antinomian.[20]

While I find Fish's defense less than persuasive, I agree with him that the play presents Samson's actions as praiseworthy. Carey and Wittreich, it seems to me, have superimposed their own humanitarian ideology on *Samson Agonistes* and on its author. But as I remarked in *The Miltonic Moment*, "the truth is that Milton and his revolutionary contemporaries were rather less scrupulous about destroying their adversaries than a peaceable, humane, and tolerant academic living in the aftermath of Belsen and Hiroshima is likely to be." The man who defended the execution of Charles I and applauded Cromwell's massacres in Ireland was not likely to lose much sleep over Samson's vengeance on his country's oppressors.[21]

POSTMODERNIST MILTON

Underlying most of the disagreements and debates I have described is a fundamental disjunction between those critics who believe that all Milton's writings have been shaped by what Rajan calls "the unifying imperative" and those who recognize, as he does, that they are "deeply self-contesting."[22] For many years, the interpretive community of Milton critics has usually taken it for granted either that the poet's works are free of tension or contradiction or that any tensions and contradictions they contain are finally resolved. As Fish put it in *How Milton Works*, "conflict, ambivalence, and open-endedness . . . are not constitutive features of the poetry but products of a systematic misreading of it."[23] This assumption has now been forcefully challenged not only by established critics such as Wittreich and Rajan but still more significantly, perhaps, by a younger generation of scholars including Dobranski, Herman, Rumrich, and Sauer. Milton's works are now beginning to be seen as sites of contention and conflict rather than unified verbal and intellectual structures or syntheses of heterogeneous ideas and values. The following statement by two eminent Miltonists suggests what future critical studies may look like: "Milton is a poet of contraries, whose poems, admitting to more than one interpretation, present 'two ways of seeing on two sides of a crisis,' not choosing between propositions but, instead, 'celebrat[ing] the world that is brought into being between them, the push and the pull of contrary understandings in the systole and diastole of the imagination.'"[24]

NOTES

1 Stanley Fish, *There's No Such Thing as Free Speech* (Oxford, 1994), 257.

2 Elizabeth Sauer, ed., *Milton and the Climates of Reading* (Toronto, 2006), 3; and Joseph Wittreich, *Shifting Contexts: Reinterpreting "Samson Agonistes"* (Pittsburgh, 2002), xi.

3 John T. Shawcross, *Rethinking Milton Studies* (Newark, NJ, 2007), 9.

4 See Roy Flannagan in *A Concise Companion to Milton*, ed. Angelica Duran (Oxford, 2007), 55: "Milton scholars have explored in ever-expanding formats every critical area that represents the fads and fascinations of the last third of the twentieth century: colonialism, post colonialism, psychology, feminism, queer theory, structuralism, history of the book, computer-generated stylistics, ecological criticism, semiotics, multiculturalism, new historicism – you name it."

5 Balachandra Rajan, "Surprised by a Strange Language," in Sauer, *Milton and the Climates of Reading*, 48.

6 Neil Forsyth, *The Satanic Epic* (Princeton, 2003), 1.

7 Gordon Campbell, Thomas N. Corns, John K. Hale, and Fiona J. Tweedie, "The Provenance of *De Doctrina Christiana*," *Milton Quarterly* 31 (1997): 120.

8 Gordon Campbell, Thomas N. Corns, John K. Hale, and Fiona J. Tweedie, *Milton and the Manuscript of "De Doctrina Christiana"* (Oxford, 2007).

9 Stanley Fish, "The Harassed Reader in 'Paradise Lost,'" *Critical Quarterly* 7 (1965): 162. My italics. See also P. J. Klemp's discussion of Fish's reader-centered critical method in the preceding chapter.

10 Sandra M. Gilbert, "Patriarchal Poetry and the Woman Reader: Reflections on Milton's Bogey," *PMLA* 93 (1978): 368–69.

11 See John Halkett, *Milton and the Idea of Matrimony* (New Haven, 1970).

12 Peter C. Herman, *Destabilizing Milton: "Paradise Lost" and the Poetics of Incertitude* (New York, 2005), 154.

13 Juliet Lucy Cummins, "The Ecology of *Paradise Lost*," in Duran, *A Concise Companion to Milton*, 161.

14 Diane McColley, "Beneficent Hierarchies: Reading Milton Greenly," in *Spokesperson Milton*, ed. Charles W. Durham and Kristin P. McColgan (Selinsgrave, PA, 1994), 246.

15 See, for instance, Fredi Chiappelli, ed., *First Images of America: The Impact of the New World on the Old* (Berkeley, 1976); Peter Hulme, *Colonial Encounters* (London, 1986); Stephen Greenblatt, *Marvelous Possessions: The Wonder of the New World* (Chicago, 1991); and Anthony Pagden, *European Encounters with the New World* (New Haven, 1993).

16 David Quint, *Epic and Empire* (Princeton, 1993), 265.

17 J. Martin Evans, *Milton's Imperial Epic: "Paradise Lost" and the Discourse of Colonialism* (Cornell, 1996), 146–47.

18 John Carey, "A Work in Praise of Terrorism? September 11 and *Samson Agonistes*," *Times Literary Supplement* (September 6, 2002), 15–16.

19 Stanley Fish, *How Milton Works* (Cambridge, MA, 2001), 428.

20 Michael Lieb and Albert Labriola, eds. *Milton in the Age of Fish* (Pittsburgh, PA, 2006), 264.
21 J. Martin Evans, *The Miltonic Moment* (Lexington, KY, 1998), 128.
22 Rajan, "Surprised by a Strange Language: Defamiliarizing *Paradise Lost*," in Sauer, *Milton and the Climates of Reading*, 46–47.
23 Fish, *How Milton Works*, 14.
24 Joseph Wittreich quoting Balachandra Rajan, "'His More Attentive Mind,'" in Sauer, *Milton and the Climates of Reading*, 156.

CHAPTER 14

Later publishing history

John T. Shawcross

As with most authors, Milton's reputation and reading public depended often upon the availability of his works; contemporary issues such as political, social, and religious concerns; and changing responses to the nature and style of his writing. With his death in November 1674 came what has been seen as a void of readership for *Paradise Lost*, the second edition of which appeared in July of that year, until the publication of its fourth edition in 1688, after which his poetic reputation began to soar without cessation, despite some brief periods of decline.[1] This cannot be accurate, for in 1675 the poem was reissued, and in 1678 its fifth edition appeared; in 1677 (with further editions in 1677, 1678, and 1684) John Dryden's tagged version, *The State of Innocence, and Fall of Man*, was published; in 1682 the first European translation of the diffuse epic by Ernst Gottlieb von Berge, *Das Verlustigte Paradeis*, appeared; and in 1686 a Latin translation of book 1 by J. C. came out. Dryden's "opera" (for which no music exists) is the first of many staged and/or musical versions of one of Milton's poems.[2] Von Berge's translation is the first of many poems to be published in different languages, as Christophe Tournu discusses in chapter 15 of this volume. In both cases it is *Paradise Lost* that is most frequently so honored. Later publishing history establishes a continued availability and presence of Milton's poetry, especially the major poems and popular shorter ones, as well as much of the prose, particularly after the beginning of the nineteenth century.

The second, combined edition of *Paradise Regained* and *Samson Agonistes* in 1680 and the third edition in 1688 (plus reprintings of "Old Hobsons Epitaph" and "On Shakespeare" in *Witt's Recreations*, 1683, and three issues of the fourth Shakespeare folio, 1685), as well as printed references and poems by authors exhibiting influence during these years, attest to an awareness of the poet among, at least, a learned public. Notably the question of blank verse in *Paradise Lost* was raised in 1678 and continued unabated through the eighteenth century, with both antagonistic rejection and much flattering (though often incompetent) imitation in what were called "Miltonicks" (ten-syllable unrhymed lines).

Milton as "authority" in things biblical emerged in Matthew Poole's *Annotations upon the Holy Bible* (1683, though unacknowledged) and Henry Hare, Baron Coleraine's *Situation of Paradise Found Out* (1683).[3] In these same years, 1674–88, Milton's prose writings maintained a presence with the public, and various comments or discussions recalled earlier works: in 1676, the Cromwellian State Papers, *Literæ Senatûs Anglicani*, in two editions, one of which was a pirated printing in Brussels; in 1677 and 1678, two issues of a second edition of *The History of Britain*; in 1680, a retitled *Hirelings*, that is, *A Supplement to Dr. Du Moulin, Treating Of the likeliest Means to Remove Hirelings*; in 1681, *Character of the Long Parliament*; in 1682, *A Brief History of Moscovia*, as well as an English translation of the State Papers, *Miltons Republican-Letters*. Fairly numerous citations and brief quotations emerge in arguments for and against Milton's positions on Charles I and *Eikon Basilike*, the Salmasian controversy (particularly allusions to *Pro Populo Anglicano Defensio*), divorce, tithing, government and anti-monarchism, toleration and popery (including the fabrication of Milton as papist). These matters created both a positive and negative reputation, with Milton's being employed as "proof" of one's belief or as offering false opinion. The unsettled controversy over licensing and censorship brought forth telling employment and adaptations of *Areopagitica*: see Andrew Marvell's *An Account of the Growth of Popery, and Arbitrary Government in England,* 1677; Charles Blount's adaptation and discussion in *A Just Vindication of Learning,* 1679, and William Denton's in *Jus Caesaris et Ecclesiæ Vere Dictæ,* 1681, which also summarizes *Civil Power* and refers to *Tenure*; and Blount again in an adaptation in *Reasons Humbly Offered for the Liberty of Unlicens'd Printing* (1693, and assigned to J. M.). We should also note Thomas Hunt's adaptation of *Defensio prima* in the "Postscript" to *Mr. Hunt's Argument for the Bishops Right* (1682). Despite the Copyright Act of 1709 that grew out of the preceding debate, settlement was not firmly achieved for literary copyright until 1842. Piracies of Milton's poetry by Robert Walker in 1739 became part of the legal action taken under Lord Hardwicke; and Milton's arguments emerged significantly in Catharine Macaulay (Graham)'s *A Modest Plea for the Property of Copy Right* (1774). Such evidence of Milton's presence in literature and fields of learning continues through the century and well beyond.

The fourth edition of *Paradise Lost* in 1688 is a milestone not only for Milton's reputation but for publishing history in England. Planned in 1686, it is a large folio (as differentiated from its prior quarto and octavo forms), on large paper, in copies whose edges often were gilded, using 14-point type and wide margins, in three issues, with twelve illustrations (thus one of the earliest such productions for an English poem), published by subscription (the first undertaken by one of the publishers, the important and prolific Jacob Tonson), and the result of highly political efforts (centered at Christ Church College, Oxford) by such Whigs as Henry Aldrich and Francis Atterbury. The more than 500 subscribers, however, included a range of political, religious, and literary personages. The illustrations, one for each book of the poem, were by artists Sir John Baptist Medina, Henry Aldrich, and Bernard Lens, and engravers Michael Burghers (Burgesse) and Peter Paul Bouche. It has been demonstrated that the illustrations for books I and II depicting Satan are a satiric rebuke of James II, who had been attacked as king on various issues, including his Roman Catholicism, and who was forced to abdicate in the Glorious Revolution in December of that same year, 1688. Satan's garb is that of James in a well-known public statue. The frontispiece is an engraved portrait of Milton by Robert White, based on William Faithorne's in the 1670 edition of *The History of Britain*, with John Dryden's often reprinted epigram that asserted that Milton united, and thus surpassed, the loftiness of thought of Homer and the majesty of Virgil.[4]

The portrait and illustrations – frequently in poor and even ludicrous redrawings – are used over and over again in the ensuing years and following century.[5] The text is based on the 1678 third edition, and becomes the copy-text for the 1691/1692/1693 fifth edition (three issues, the third labeled "The Fourth Edition") and, with corrections from the 1674 second edition, is the source of the 1695 sixth edition printings. A folio (third) edition of *Paradise Regained* and *Samson Agonistes* also appeared in 1688 and again (corrected) in 1695 (the fourth edition, but not so designated). Copies exist of the 1695 *Paradise Lost* alone as well as copies with 1688 or 1695 *Paradise Regained/Samson Agonistes* attached. A folio *Poems Upon Several Occasions* appeared in 1695, the third edition, with the poems printed in a different arrangement from that in the 1673 version. Omitted, as in 1673, are the "political" Sonnets 15, 16, 17, 22, but also, apparently because they are in Greek, *Philosophus ad regem* and *In Effigiei Ejus Sculptorem* (which do appear in 1673).[6]

In the 1690s Latin translations of *Paradise Lost* also were produced. Thomas Power's verse renditions of book I complete (*Paradisi Amissi*, 1691) and sections from books III, IV, V (in separate issues of *The Gentleman's Journal*, 1694) were published. His basically complete version is found in manuscripts in the libraries of Trinity College (Cambridge) and the

University of Illinois. Eve's dream in book v by Charles Blake is included in his *Lusus Amatorius* (1694). The significant translation by William Hog was joined by *Paradise Regained* and *Samson Agonistes* in *Paraphrasis Poetica in Tria* (1690, reissued in 1699). In 1747–51, William Lauder (abetted by Samuel Johnson) employed the "sublime" Milton as scapegoat in an effort to advance the reputation of Scottish poets against Alexander Pope's dismissal of them. Lauder inserted Hog's translation of various passages and lines from *Paradise Lost* into the work of Jacopo Masenius and Hugo Grotius's *Adam Exsul* to charge Milton with plagiarism. In addition to other articles and books on the subject, a detailed refutation by John Douglas of Lauder's *An Essay on Milton's Use and Imitation of the Moderns, in His Paradise Lost* (1750, actually late 1749 but issued with a new preface shortly afterward) appeared as *Milton Vindicated from the Charge of Plagarism, Brought Against Him by Mr. Lauder, and Lauder Himself Convicted of Several Forgeries and Gross Impositions on the Public* (1751). Further volumes pertinent to the notorious affair appeared, one of which was an *Apology*, passed off as Lauder's but really the work of Johnson.

The *Poetical Works of Mr. John Milton* (1695) presents the 1695 *Paradise Lost*, to which are added the *Table*, the *Annotations on Milton's Paradise Lost*, a reissue of the 1688 or 1695 *Paradise Regained/Samson Agonistes*, and a reissue of the folio 1695 *Poems*. The foregoing editions of *Paradise Lost* were printed for Jacob Tonson; his "ownership" continues with the companion volumes *Paradise Lost*, "The Seventh Edition" (illustrations are from 1688 redrawn by Henry Eland and J. Gweere), and *Paradise Regain'd . . . To which is added Samson Agonistes. And Poems upon several Occasions . . . The Fourth Edition* in 1705 as well as the continued printings of both individual volumes thereafter. It will be noticed that the title page of the *Poetical Works* (really referring to *Paradise Regained* and *Samson Agonistes*) errs in calling this the "fourth" edition, and that the separate internal title page for *Poems* also errs in calling it "The Third edition"; it returns to the earlier arrangement. A *Table* and *Annotations*, aids for a general reading public, had been announced on the title page of the separate issues of *Paradise Lost*, but only the former was included. "A Table of the Most remarkable Parts of Milton's *Paradise Lost*, Under the Three Heads of Descriptions, Similes, and Speeches" is repeated in editions of the earlier eighteenth century, where it is usually called "The Index." "Annotations" is the extensive and learned work of P. H., identified as Patrick Hume, and appears as pp. 1–321 in a separate printing from that of the poem. As the separate title page records, "Texts of Sacred Writ are Quoted"; "Parallel Places and Imitations of the most Excellent Homer and Virgil, Cited and Compared"; "All the

Obscure Parts render'd in Phrases more Familiar"; as well as "The Old and Obsolete Words, with their Originals, Explain'd and made Easie to the English Reader." Scholars are still paying attention to Hume's annotations, some of which were employed in future editions and studies, for example, by Thomas Newton in his edition of 1749.

In other words, in the quarter of a century after Milton's death his poetic works were readily available in special and expensive editions as well as in handy, cheaper volumes for a wider popular audience. Individual poems were reprinted and translated, and demonstrate Milton's influence upon other authors. At the same time the epic was accorded full scholarly treatment, and the beginning of a still continuing tradition of illustration and of portraiture of the author arose. The 1688 elaborate edition helped to establish Milton as poet for a wider audience and elicited such praise as Addison's in "An Account of the Greatest English Poets."[7] However, Addison goes on to lament Milton's political positions in his prose (we have observed this bifurcation earlier), where *Eikonoklastes* and *Defensio prima* are particularly intended, works that had been confiscated and burned in France, and through decrees by Charles I at Oxford University. Sermons on the anniversaries of Charles I's execution likewise condemned these tracts. Despite this repeated criticism, individual prose texts and collected works were printed from 1689 onward, a result not only of censorship questions but of antagonists against Milton's anti-monarchic and governmental works.

Ascribed to James Tyrrell, *Pro Populo Adversus Tyrannos: or the Sovereign Right and Power of the People over Tyants, Clearly Stated, and plainly Proved* (1689), was actually a slightly altered printing of Milton's *Tenure*. We can conclude that it was well known because of references and many catalogues detailing ownership. "Sir Walter Ralegh's" *The Cabinet-Council*, which Milton had published in 1658, reappeared as *The Arts of Empire* (1692) and *The Secrets of Government* (1694); Milton's *The History of Britain* was re-published in 1695 in two issues; and *Sententiæ*, edited by Edmund Elys, from Milton's *Animadversions* and *Defensio secunda*, appeared in 1699. In addition, Milton's State Papers (in 1690), plus individual letters in volumes dealing with Cromwell and the Interregnum (from 1691 through the eighteenth century), were published in Gregorio Leti's *Vita di Oliviero Cromvele* (1692, with a number of new editions in various languages following into the next century; a different collection is found in Johann Christian Lünig's three-volume 1712 *Literae Procerum Europae*), in an English translation, *Letters of State* (1694), by Milton's nephew Edward Phillips, and in *Oliver Cromwell's Letters to Foreign Princes and States* (1700). As the title page of

Phillips' edition relates, the publication also includes "An Account of his Life," "several of his Poems," and "a Catalogue of his Works, never before Printed." The poems (in garbled texts) are Sonnets 15, 16, 17, 22, which were excised from the 1673 edition because of their political content; only number 17, to Henry Vane, had been previously published. All parts of this volume have had deep influence on publication and biographical/political knowledge and criticism of Milton.

Arguments over Milton's political position and the authorship of *Eikon Basilike* emerged with the publication of *Eikonoklastes* (1690, printed in London although the title page says Amsterdam in an attempt to get around censorship) and Joseph Washington's English translation of *Pro Populo Anglicano Defensio* (1695, two issues). The latter brought before the general public what the Latin had obscured for them, and made clear the impugning of Milton in such a tract as *An Essay upon the Original and Designe of Magistracie; or, A Modest Vindication of the Late Proceedings in England* (Edinburgh, 1689) and the positive use of Milton's argument against Salmasius made by P. Georgeson in *The Defence of the Parliament of England in the Case of James the II* (1692, in Latin and translated by S. Rand). Most copies of the new *Eikonoklastes* have a Preface discussing the controversy over *Eikon Basilike*; some have "An Advertisement" and the Earl of Anglesey's "Memorandum," which are specifically concerned with authorship. The "Memorandum" alleges the authorship of John Gauden, Charles I's chaplain; a letter from Gauden to Edward Hyde, Lord Clarendon, dated March 13, 1661/62, is printed in various later tracts arguing both for and against this attribution. There are allusions to the republication of Milton's work in manuscript letters in the Bodleian Library, from George Hickes to Arthur Charlett, dated September 6, 1690, and from John Willes to Charlett, dated September 9, 1690. In 1691 alone there are four volumes provoked by the *Eikonoklastes* printing that deal with the issue and with Milton's criticism of Charles for plagiarizing a prayer spoken by Pamela from Philip Sidney's *Arcadia*. Like these, most of the ensuing discussions champion Charles, but we should note the anonymous (often ascribed to John Toland), *A Defence of the Parliament of 1640. And the People of England, Against King Charles* (1698), in which Pamela's prayer is printed in parallel citations from Sidney and from *Eikon Basilike*, and Anglesey's "Memorandum" and Clarendon's letter and other documents are quoted in the review of the controversy over authorship. The authorship question and Milton's relationship to it continued through the eighteenth and early nineteenth centuries, some discredit being charged to Milton for his attack on Charles and the plagiary from Sidney.

There were two posthumous collections of Milton's prose works, the first in 1697, perhaps an attempt to divert attention from the expected publication of the second in 1698. The 1697 collection is a single large folio of most of the English prose with approximations of title pages on separate pages, and partial title pages above texts for the rest. The second edition of *Tenure* is given, but the first of both *Eikonoklastes* and *The Readie and Easie Way*. Omitted are *Of Education, Accedence Commenc't Grammar, The History of Britain, Declaration, The Character of the Long Parliament*, and *Brief History of Moscovia*. The volume seems, at best, to have been little used or even known. The well-known collection with a new and important life by John Toland in the first volume (thus inaccurately sometimes called "Toland's edition") is *A Complete Collection of the Historical, Political, and Miscellaneous Works of John Milton, Both English and Latin. With som Papers never before Publish'd. In Three Volumes, Containing, Besides the History of his Works, Several Extraordinary Characters of Men and Books, Sects, Parties, and Opinions*. Again, the place of publication was London although the title page says Amsterdam, published, it has been shown, by John Darby. The first volume, surely because of more extensive demand, was re-issued later in the same year, this time in and by "the Book-sellers of London and Westminster." The "Life" reflects much of Toland's interest in non-orthodoxy, particularly Socinianism (the "Sects, Parties, and Opinions") rather than Milton's. Volumes I and II print the English works. *The History of Britain*, in vol. I, is a version allegedly revised and augmented by Milton, and an Index for it follows. Volume II includes material after the text of *Eikonoklastes* about Pamela's prayer, Charles' duplicity, Charles II's proclamation for confiscation, the "Memorandum," and other items; it also contains Joseph Washington's translation of *Defensio prima* and Phillips' translation of *Literæ. Tenure* and *Eikonoklastes* are the first edition, and *Readie and Easie Way* the second. It omits *The Character of the Long Parliament*, but it includes the first printings of *Letter to a Friend* (1659) and *Present Means and Brief Delineation of a Free Commonwealth* (1660). Volume III presents the Latin works (with a Latin title page), and includes John Phillips' *Responsio* (1652). Thus, as the new century began, Milton's work, poetic and prose, was available and his reputation as poet soared, while his status as a political writer depended upon a critic's own position.

Succeeding centuries exhibit most of the concerns and the patterns of publication noted above. Individual poems and some prose were produced, especially (with earliest date, where applicable, since original publication), *True Religion* (1719), *Areopagitica* (1738, with a preface by James Thomson),

Of Education (1746, a slightly augmented edition), *The History of Britain*, *Eikonoklastes*, *Hirelings* (the first Milton work published in the colonies in 1770), State Papers, *Civil Power* (1790), and *Readie and Easie Way* (1791). (See the next paragraph for the wide availability of *Of Education* from 1713 onward.) Parts of many of these poems and tracts occur in various books from 1701 to the present. *Scriptum dom. Protectoris* (the 1655 Spanish manifesto from Cromwell) was published in a translation by Thomas Birch and attributed, in its Latin form, to Milton in 1738, as *A Manifesto of the Lord Protector of the Commonwealth of England, Scotland, Ireland, &c.* Its second edition immediately followed, the third in 1741, and a different version in the same year, *A true Copy of Oliver Cromwell's Manifesto Against Spain, Dated October 26, 1655.* Excerpts appeared in popular magazines in 1740. The original had great significance, for it came out in the midst of the much opposed war with Spain, launched over hegemony in the West Indies. The British fleet claimed victory, established Jamaica as a British center, and achieved what has been argued was the real reason for the war, establishment of Protestantism. In 1738–41 the impetus for republishing was the continued rivalry for domination of the sea, trade, and land ownership, and the *asiento* (slave trade) passed at the Treaty of Utrecht in 1713, and most specifically opposition to Robert Walpole and the Prime Minister's foreign policies. Reprinted again for the election of 1741, the *Manifesto* aided in forcing Walpole to resign in 1742.

Georg Friedrich Handel's musical settings of "L'Allegro ed Il Penseroso" (with libretti by Charles Jennens, who added a third section, "Il Moderato," not always included) and of "Samson: An Oratorio" (with a libretto by Newburgh Hamilton) were published with music but more often without it, from 1640 and 1642 onward. Editions of *Paradise Lost* are plentiful, and piracies (some in English but printed in France) abound. In 1713 the volume of "other" poems, a duodecimo (in contrast to the 1705 octavo companion book, but still published for Tonson), added *Of Education* (as in 1673), which became standard for many years. It brought this tract before a general public and enabled a number of discussions and new printings by others, with some apparent adaptation of ideas in educational practices in England and the colonies. Illustrations in the 1713 volume are by Michael vander Gucht and Nicholas Pigné, engraver, as well as a redrawn 1645 portrait by William Marshall as frontispiece. In 1719 a separate printing of Addison's *Spectator* Papers, which originally appeared in the periodical in 1712, was frequently added to a duodecimo *Paradise Lost*. (The preliminary papers were also included in printings of *Paradise Lost* as a "Critique"; at other times later editions presented the papers on the individual books of the epic as well. Some readers apparently used Addison's work as a crib sheet with the long and difficult text.) An elaborate edition of the *Poetical Works* in 1720, a large quarto in two volumes, known as Thomas Tickell's edition, has the "Critique" and new illustrations. It adds the verses from Milton's prose and the poem on Salmasius in Latin and English. The edition of 1725 (the source for many further printings) adds Elijah Fenton's brief "Life," which, being brief, is very frequently copied through the century and into the next. *Paradise Lost* and *Paradise Regained* were published together by George Grierson in Dublin in 1724, but the first totally separate publication of *Paradise Regained* is 1793 (two different editions) and of *Samson Agonistes*, 1796.

The first variorum edition of *Paradise Lost* by Thomas Newton in 1749 presents a frequently reprinted "Life"; the text is the basis for many future editions and the long biography reappears frequently. The notes are of major significance and derive from a number of critics or sources, but not always from published criticism. The notes are repeated in many further editions, actually even up to recent times. Addison's "Critique," "The Index," and a "Verbal Index" are included. The "Verbal Index" was by Alexander Cruden, in a separate printed edition in 1741; it was often repeated in editions after 1749. The large quarto was made available through subscribers and has new illustrations. The companion volume to the foregoing is Newton's variorum edition of *Paradise Regained, Samson Agonistes*, and *Poems* in 1752, without *Of Education* and with the attributed Latin poem "Ad Christinam" (by Fleetwood Shepherd). The illustrations in some copies are by Francis Hayman, engraved by Johann S. Müller (Miller), Charles Grignion, or Simon François Ravenet. The frontispiece is Vertue's fanciful picture of Milton at age forty-two with a moustache.

Two more notable editions of the poetical works should be remarked. The three-volume, large folio *Poetical Works*, published by John and Josiah Boydell and George Nicol (1794, 1795, and 1797), prints William Hayley's "Life" and numerous illustrations and portraits by various artists and engravers. Hayley's edition of William Cowper's examination of the poems and his translations (including Testimonies), in 1792–99, appeared in 1808, with "The Fragment of an Intended Commentary on Paradise Lost," covering books 1 through part of book III; notes are by Cowper, Hayley, and others.

Paradise Regained was accorded a most important separate variorum treatment by Charles Dunster in 1795. Notes from various critics are extensive, with corrections, supplementary notes, and summaries by Dunster. A foldout "Map of Places mentioned in the Paradise Regained, chiefly from

Orbis veteribus notus of M. D'Anville" and a dedicatory poem, dated September 20, 1799, also are included.

In addition to printings of individual prose works noted above, there were two major collected editions: Thomas Birch's two-volume large quarto *A Complete Collection of the Historical, Political, and Miscellaneous Works of John Milton: Correctly Printed from the Original Editions. With an Historical and Critical Account of the Life and Writings of the Author; Containing several Original Papers of His, Never before Published* (1738) and its revised edition in 1753. Birch's "Life" gives some shorter items or excerpts and transcriptions from the newly discovered Trinity Manuscript. Various critics are quoted at length (including Voltaire and Bernard Routh); part of Richard Dawes' Greek translation of part of *Paradise Lost* book 1; Alexander Pope's sonnet hoax "In a glass window at Chalfont," ascribed to Milton; and John Ward's letter on Milton's daughter Deborah. Two informational dissertations are appended: the controversy over *Eikon Basilike* and the commission given by Charles I to the Irish. In vol. II are *Scriptum dom Protectoris* and *The History of Britain,* called "History of England," which inserts the text of *Character of the Long Parliament.* The publication of 1653 by Richard Baron has a separate preface by the editor, the 1740 Spanish *Manifesto,* and a letter from Moses (called John) Wall to Milton in 1659, which in 1781 was separately published; it also appeared in books on Cromwell in the intervening years. The first edition of *Eikonoklastes* is used, except that in some copies that has been replaced with Baron's separate quarto edition of 1756 from the second edition, which includes Wall's letter with a note by Baron, dated June 20, 1756; a reprint is an octavo from 1770.

Two other matters of great importance are: Richard Bentley's "corrected" edition of *Paradise Lost* and the revised, musical adaptation of *A Mask* in 1738. In the years before 1732, Bentley made proposals to "correct" the text of the long epic but attempts to dissuade him in person and in print failed. Because Milton, blind, could not have written down his text or seen it through the press, Bentley argued, "The Faults therefore in Orthography, Distinction by Points, and Capital Letters, all of which swarm in the prior Editions, are here very carefully, and it's hop'd, judiciously corrected."[8] The notorious and conventionally misinterpretive result, Bentley's publication of *Paradise Lost* (1732), elicited both invective and caricature, but two corrections (the result of printer's foul case) have been generally accepted: "Soul," VII.451 (for "Fowle / Foul") and "swelling," VII.321 (for "smelling"). Two editions listing *Dr. Bentley's Emendations on the Twelve Books of Milton's Paradise Lost* made them available, as one of the title pages puts it, "For the Benefit of those who are possess'd of the former Editions." But Jonathan

Swift countered with *Milton Restor'd, and Bentley Depos'd* (1732), and provided discussion of the matter and *Paradise Lost* 1.1–32 in rhyme. Such periodicals as *The Gentleman's Magazine, The Grub-Street Journal,* and the *London Magazine* were filled with articles denouncing Bentley, and Zachary Pearce presented full, detailed refutations in *A Review of the Text of Milton's "Paradise Lost"* (1732, 1733). The reputation of *Paradise Lost* and Milton experienced some negativity (in religious matters) from the public but also strong positive readings and approval from broad audiences, as references in books and periodicals make clear. Bentley's efforts were generally dismissed.

In 1738 the first edition of *Comus, a Mask: (Now adapted to the Stage) As Alter'd from Milton's Mask* by John Dalton and with music by Thomas Arne was published, therewith altering the title of Milton's poem for posterity and misemphasizing its thesis. Printings (with and without the music) and performances were numerous throughout the century and occasional after 1800 to the present; songs (with and without music) were excerpted as Milton's although many of the texts were entirely Dalton's (though not realized by listeners or readers). George Colman revised the text to two acts in 1772, largely through excision and simplification; it also enjoyed many printings and performances. Additionally, new editions of Milton's masque occurred, including Henry John Todd's scholarly version in 1798. Todd reprinted Henry Lawes' and Henry Wotton's letters, discussed Ludlow Castle and the Egerton family, included remarks on Lawes and Thomas Warton's discussion of the origin of *A Mask*, and then gave original readings, notes, editions, and the Ashridge Manuscript (that is, the Bridgewater Manuscript). A new edition of the work in 1799 (apparently evoked in competition) reprints Todd's discussion of Ludlow Castle and some of his notes and Warton's "Origin of Comus," and adds "The General Opinions of Various Critics Concerning the Beauties and Faults of Comus," *L'Allegro, Il Penseroso*, and four illustrations. Not only had "A Mask" become well known and repeatedly printed in some version, but it enjoyed in its musical settings widespread performances throughout England, not only in London.

After 1800 through the present, publications of Milton's works remained frequent, some with illustrations, some with notes. Rather recently many editions from the past have been reprinted, often in facsimile, and some original printings have been available in facsimiles. Four further variora of the poetry came from Todd in 1801, 1809, 1826, and 1842; a continuation of the *Variorum Commentary* begun in 1970 is currently in progress. Some important editions of the poetry were produced by Thomas Keightley in 1859; R. C. Browne and Henry Bradley in 1894 (the English poems);

Harris Francis Fletcher, *Complete Poetical Works, Reproduced in Photographic Facsimile*, 4 vols., in 1943–48; Merritt Y. Hughes in 1957 (a popular modernized text with selected prose); and John Carey and Alastair Fowler in 1968. Separate editions of *Paradise Lost* (some with notes, many aimed at scholastic audiences, particularly within the last few years) are very numerous, as are other single or coupled poems. *The Sonnets* with introduction and notes by John S. Smart (1921), and a new edition by E. A. J. Honigman in 1966, and *The Latin Poems* in English prose translation by Walter MacKeller (1930) provide important information. The Trinity Manuscript became available in facsimile by William Aldis Wright in 1899, reproduced (as *The Cambridge Manuscript*) in 1933, and again by the Scolar Press, improved, in 1970. S. E. Sprott edited *John Milton: "A Maske," the Earlier Versions* in 1973. *The Manuscript of Paradise Lost. Book 1* (the only extant manuscript form) was made public in 1931 in an edition by Helen Darbishire; it also is found in Fletcher's vol. II, noted above.

The prose works with a new life, translations, and critical remarks were edited by Charles Symmons in seven volumes in 1806, and were followed by other editions by Robert Fletcher (1833), by R. W. Griswold (1845), by John Mitford, together with the poetry in eight volumes (1851); and in five volumes by J. A. St. John, [1848]–1881, now including *De Doctrina Christiana*. In 1824 Milton's *De Doctrina Christiana* was discovered in the Public Record Office, London, and published by Charles R. Sumner both in Latin and in an English translation in 1825. Sumner's translation was revised at the press by his proofreader, the classics scholar William Sidney Walker, who often fraudulently used lines from *Paradise Lost* where he thought them appropriate. This discovery and publication disturbed scholars and continues to do so. Its accounts of the Son of God and of the Holy Spirit argue a separation between God the Father and God the Son as well as a denial of orthodox Trinity. Its translated reading has brought a label of Arian upon such heterodoxy and has led to questioning of the authorship of the treatise. Another recovered manuscript, A Commonplace Book, appeared in 1876 in facsimile with an introduction by Alfred Horwood, who, in the same year, oversaw a revised edition by The Camden Society. As with the poetry, individual prose works (or some in small gatherings) were published or in excerpts, over the years from 1800 on. The still most important and only complete publication of *The Works* (thus also including the poetry in the first two volumes) was printed from 1931 through 1938, eighteen volumes in twenty-one, from Columbia University Press (the "Columbia Edition"). Included are all foreign language texts (with translations) and a volume of "Uncollected Works," vol. XVIII. Introductions are slight and notes are textual. Published from 1953 through 1982, eight volumes in ten of the *Complete Prose Works* published by Yale University Press (the "Yale Prose") provide texts in English only (thus new translations of original foreign language works), with extensive introductions and notes, and with original pagination indicated.

In all, the poetry and most of the prose have been readily available to the public continuously over the centuries, and the immediate future is already slated to provide continuingly useful and updated editions of all Milton's works.

NOTES

1 Two similar inaccurate misconceptions are that the poem was little read and appreciated until Joseph Addison's *Spectator* Papers appeared in 1712 and that other poems, particularly the shorter ones, were not known until Thomas Newton's edition of them in 1752. Such beliefs have been confuted both by the frequent publications of Milton's works and by attention to a fuller bibliography of imitations of, allusions to, quotations from, and critical discussions of Milton's oeuvre. See John T. Shawcross, *Milton: A Bibliography for the Years 1624–1700 (Revised) and for the Years 1701–1799*, 4 vols. (Tempe, AZ, forthcoming; online at www.IterGateway.org).

2 Others include *Paradise Regained, Samson Agonistes, A Mask* ("Comus"), *Arcades, Lycidas,* the Nativity Ode, "Song on May Morning," *L'Allegro, Il Penseroso,* "At a Solemn Music," "On Time," Sonnet 1, and Psalms 8, 82, 84, and 136.

3 Later, Milton's *The History of Britain* was given authoritative inclusion in *A Complete History of England,* ed. John Hughes (1719), and by such annotations as Richard Lewis' notes to his poem *Muscipula* (1728), 43–44.

4 It is based upon the Latin encomium, in *Poems,* 1645, by "Selvaggi," that is, David Codner.

5 Among other items, see Marcia R. Pointon, *Milton and English Art* (Toronto, 1970).

6 Hog also translated *Lycidas,* which is one of two poems in *Paraphrasis Latina. In Duo Poemata* (1694), with facing English and Latin texts, and *A Mask* in *Comoedia Joannis Miltoni, Viri clarissimi* (1698). Some of the Latin poems reappear in Dryden's collections, and John Hopkins' altered text *Milton's Paradise Lost. Imitated in Rhyme. In the Fourth, Sixth and Ninth Books* came out in 1699.

7 Printed in John Dryden's collection, *The Annual Miscellany; for the Year 1694. Being the Fourth Part of Miscellany Poems* (London, 1694), 321–23: "But *Milton* next, with high and haughty stalks, / Unfetter'd in majestick numbers walks; / . . . ev'ry verse, array'd in majesty, / Bold, and sublime, my whole attention draws, / And seems above the critick's nicer laws." Milton has become the "sublime" poet, the constantly repeated and customary description that Mary Wollstonecraft objected to as idolatry; see *Thoughts on the Education of Daughters* (London, 1787), 52–53. She is objecting to the emptiness of the term that critical

repetition had created. Addison's reference to the "nicer laws" counters criticism, for example, that negatively viewed Milton's variations on "standard" epic form and the argument over blank verse (the "Unfetter'd . . . majestic numbers"). In the same poem, Addison wrote about Milton's prose, "Oh had the Poet ne'er profan'd his pen, / To vernish o'er the guilt of faithless men; / His other works might have deserv'd applause!"

8 Richard Bentley, *Milton's Paradise Lost. A New Edition* (London, 1732), A1r.

CHAPTER 15

Translations

Christophe Tournu

Milton's works were being translated when he was still alive.[1] If his fame has been built on his grand epic, Milton's first translated work was a prose tract: William Dugard's *ΕΙΚΟΝΟΚΛΑΣΤΗΣ, ou Réponse au Livre intitulé ΈΙΚΩΝ ΒΑΣΙΛΙΚΗ': ou Le Pourtrait de sa Sacrée Majesté durant sa Solitude & ses Souffrances* (London, 1652), and the last-to-date translations are also prose and in Japanese, Jun Harada's *Areopagitica* and *The Readie and Easie Way to Establish a Free Commonwealth* (Tokyo, 2008).

Milton has been translated for two main reasons: first, because of the Westernization of the world, his great poems being recognized as masterpieces of world literature; secondly, because of the representation of Milton with intellectuals as the eponymic figure of freedom since the French Revolution. (A significant number of translations occurred at the end of the eighteenth century.) As people move toward defining their identity as a nation, they appropriate Milton to themselves so as to make him part of their own culture.

William Dugard, in a foreword to the reader, apologizes for the Anglicisms in his translation; he explains he has kept the elegance of the author's style and language so as "not to lose the gracefulness of the original." In so doing, he notes, the French might in some places be perverted.[2] No doubt the new English government was trying to reply to the French translation of *Eikon Basilike* published in Rouen in 1649. Dugard accordingly addresses his translation of Milton's tract to a large audience, including the common people, at the time of the Fronde. He invites his readers to have more care for the substance – "so great & notable a change" in England – rather than the accidents of the language.[3]

The very first translation of Milton's great poems was William Hog's Latin version (1690), making them available to the fast-diminishing international community of the learned, a very restricted audience.[4] Today Milton's works, mainly his poetry, have been made known to an international audience – still a cultural elite. According to John K. Hale, German was the first vernacular to be given a translation of *Paradise Lost*.[5] The prose version of J. H. Bodmer appeared in 1732, and Friedrich W. Zachariä offered a verse translation in dactylic hexameters in 1762. The most recent German translation of *Paradise Lost* is Hans Heinrich Meier's (1969, rpt. 2006). *Paradise Regained* and *Samson Agonistes* were translated only in the twentieth century, respectively by Otto Hauser (1914) and Hermann Ulrich (1958). *Areopagitica* was translated in the middle of the nineteenth century and in 1925. Of Dutch translations, three translations of *Paradise Lost* appeared in the eighteenth century: Jacob van Zanten's was the first (1728), in unrhymed pentameters. Then came Lambert van der Broek's (1730) in Alexandrine couplets, and a prose version by Jan H. Reisig appeared in 1791. There were three translators of *Paradise Lost* in the nineteenth century: Johannes Philippus van Goethem (1843–45), J. F. Schimsheimer (1856), and Jan Jacob Lodewijk ten Kate (1875). The latest Dutch translation of Milton in the last hundred years or so is Peter Verstegen's *Paradise Lost*, with illustrations by Gustave Doré (2003). Most interestingly, there were Dutch translations of Milton's prose in the seventeenth century: one, *Tractaet ofte discours vande echt-scheydinge* (1655), was a translation of the first edition of *The Doctrine and Discipline of Divorce*, the other, *Verdedigingh des gemeene volcks van Engelandt* (1651), was a translation of *Pro Populo Anglicano Defensio*. H. van Dijk translated *Paradise Regained* in metric verses in 1901. Amazingly, there is still no Dutch translation of *Samson Agonistes*, whereas *L'Allegro* and *Il Penseroso* were translated by Otto Heinrich von Gemmingen in 1781.

Moving up north, we encounter Danish translations of *Paradise Lost*, *Paradise Regained*, and *Samson Agonistes* in 1790–92; and the translator was Johan Heinrich Schønheyder (1744–1831).[6] Uffe Birkedal (1852–1931), a Unitarian priest in Copenhagen, also published a translation of *Paradise Lost* (*Det Tabte Paradis* [1905]), which was reissued in 2005 to mark the 100th anniversary of the original edition, and he translated *A Mask* in 1908. A senior member of the Icelandic community in Copenhagen, Reverend Þorgeir Guðmundsson (1794–1871) acted as publisher of some of the most important contributions to Icelandic cultural, spiritual, and political life, including Jón Þorláksson's translation of *Paradise Lost* (1828), a work which was to have a deep effect on the development and thought of Jónas Hallgrímsson (1807–45), a nationalistic poet – he invoked nationalism in the hearts of the Icelandic people in the hopes of inciting a popular resistance against Danish rule.

The first Swedish translation of *Paradise Lost* appeared in Stockholm in 1815. Widely admired, *Det förlorade paradiset* was written by Johan Gabriel Oxenstierna (1750–1818), an aristocrat known as the representative of the neoclassical, Gustavian nature-poetry school and one of the greatest poets in Sweden. Frans G. Bengtsson (1894–1954), an essayist, novelist, poet, and biographer, best known for his Viking saga novel *Röde Orm*, which he wrote during World War II, made a second Swedish translation of *Paradise Lost* in 1926. Uno Lindelöf (1868–1944), a professor extraordinary in English at the University of Helsinki, Finland, translated *Samson Agonistes* (*Simson*, 1918). The only Finnish translation I have been able to find is *Kadotettu paratiisi: runoelma* (1933), a translation of *Paradise Lost* reissued in 1952 and 2000. It was the work of Yrjö Jylhä (1903–56), a member of a literature group of young writers formed in the mid 1920s called *Tulenkantajat* ("Torchbearers"). Their slogan was "Open the windows to Europe!" and consequently they introduced Finns to free verse, exotic themes, and urban romanticism. The very first Norwegian translation of *Paradise Lost*, *Det tapte paradis*, appeared only in 1993, and *Det gjenvundne Paradis* (*Paradise Regained*) was published in 2005. They were the works of Arthur O. Sandved, a retired professor of English and linguist at the University of Oslo.

Milton also reached the Baltic States – Estonia, Latvia, and Lithuania. Timotheos Kuusik (1863–1940) published an Estonian translation of *Paradise Lost* and *Paradise Regained* at the end of the nineteenth century[7] (*Samson Agonistes* has not yet been translated), and Henno Rajandi (1928–98), another man of letters, recently translated *Areopagitica* (Tallinn, 1987). Ernests Dinsbergs (1816–1902), a Latvian writer of patriotic and love poetry, produced a translation of *Paradise Lost* in 1899.[8] Interestingly, there is a Lithuanian translation, not of Milton's grand epic, but of his short poems: *Lycidas, l'Allegro, il Pensieroso* (Wilnius, 1830) were translated by Benedykt Lenartowicza.

Milton is also much present in Central and Eastern Europe. In Poland, for instance, Jacek Idzi Przybylski (1756–1819), a Cracow intellectual and a professor at the Krakow Academy, translated epic poetry into Polish, including Milton's (*Paradise Lost*, 1791; *Paradise Regained*, 1792). Franciszek Salezy Dmochowski (1762–1818), a Polish Romantic novelist, poet, translator, publisher, critic, and satirist, translated *Paradise Lost* (1803), which was re-translated by Władysław Bartkiewicz in 1902. Maciej Słomczyński, an eminent scholar (he translated the complete works of William Shakespeare) and a popular crime writer, translated *Paradise Lost* (*Raj utracony*, 1986). Michał Sprusiński translated *Samson Agonistes* (*Samson walczacy*, 1971).

Josef Jungmann (1773–1847), a leading figure of the Czech National Revival, laid the foundations of a modern written Czech language with his reputedly brilliant translation of *Paradise Lost* (*Ztracený ráj*, Prague, 1811).

A second translation, by Josef Julius David (1871–1941), appeared in 1900, seven years before he completed a translation of *Paradise Regained* (*Ráj opět nabytý*, 1893). A Czech translation of Milton's *Samson Agonistes*, by the poet Jarmila Urbánková, appeared only in 1996, and Josef Milde translated the only Milton prose work available in Czech, *Areopagitica* (1946).

It was not until the end of the nineteenth century that Milton was translated into Hungarian. Gusztáv Jánosi, a major contributor to *Budapesti Szemle*, a literary and learned journal, published *Az elveszett paradicsom* (*Paradise Lost*, 1890). István Jánosy, author of the verse novel *Rákóczi ifjúsága* (1958) about the youth of a prominent hero of national history, made a second translation of *Paradise Lost* in 1969, and the poet György Jánosházy published a second translation of *Samson Agonistes*, *A küzdö Sámson tragédia*, in 1975.[9] The two works were bound together and reissued in 1987. Apart from *Paradise Lost* and *Samson Agonistes*, there are no other works by Milton in Hungarian.

Alexander Shurbanov published the only available Bulgarian translation of a work by Milton, with introduction and notes: *Paradise Lost* (Sofia, 1981) based on the fairly recent edition by Alastair Fowler (1968). Another Eastern European translation of Milton is *Paradisul pierdut*, rendered into Romanian first by an Orthodox priest, Archimandrite Paulin Lecca (1997), and more recently by Adina Claudia Begu (2003).

The translator, poet, journalist, and film critic Marjan Strojan recently brought out the first Slovenian translation of *Paradise Lost*.[10] Today Marjan Strojan is the vice-president of the Slovene Pen Centre, a literary gathering whose aim is to be the meeting point between the East and the West. Milton's epic is closely associated with the assertion of freedom against oppression: for example, in Serbia, Milovan Đilas (1911–95), a Yugoslavian Communist politician, theorist and, ultimately, a dissident, translated *Paradise Lost* into Serbo-Croatian while he was in jail (first published in New York in 1969, reissued in 1989). Darko Bolfan, a literary translator from Belgrade, and Dušan Kosanović, a journalist, published a translation of both *Paradise Lost* and *Paradise Regained*, in 1989.[11] In 1990, Darko Bolfan made the first Serbian translation of *Areopagitica*. Ivan Krizmanić (1766–1852) had published his Croatian translation of *Paradise Lost* in 1827 (*Raj zgubljen*, reissued 2005).

In Russia, interest in Milton started in the middle of the eighteenth century when Baron A. G. Stroganov made the first Russian translation of *Paradise Lost* (1745). It was unpublished and incomplete, and its author translated not from the original English, but from the French version of Dupré de Saint Maur (1729). John Shawcross numbers no fewer than fifteen Russian translations of *Paradise Lost* up to 1956 (three were based on the French) and six translations of *Paradise Regained*.[12] *Samson Agonistes* was apparently translated only once, in 1911. A sixteenth translation of *Paradise Lost* was published in 1976, and a compilation of the translations of Milton's great poems was released in 2007. The Russian literary critic and historian D. S. Mirsky (1890–1939) chose to repatriate himself to the Soviet Union in 1932 after a dozen years of exile in London. In 1934, he set to work on an edition of *Paradise Lost* but he was arrested in 1937 and died in the Gulag (1939): his edition was never published.

A keen Zionist, Joseph Massel, born in Russia, migrated to Manchester as a printer and published his own translation of *Samson Agonistes* into Hebrew (1890). Isaac Edward Salkinsohn (1820–83), a converted Jew born in Belarus, translated *Paradise Lost* as "Vaygaresh et ha-adam" ("And He drove the man out," a phrase from Genesis 3:24) while he was in London (1871).

Turning to South Europe, we can see again Milton's remarkable presence as a poet, not as a polemicist. "Very little has been published on Iberian connections with Milton," John Shawcross has noticed.[13] Aníbal Galindo, from Columbia, translated *Paradise Lost* as early as 1868, and he proffered Milton's poem as inspiration in the struggle of Latin-American nations to attain liberty. The first Portuguese translation of *Paradise Lost*, followed by *Paraiso restauro*, appeared in Lisbon in 1789. It was a work in prose by José Amaro da Silva, and included Joseph Addison's essay and notes by Louis Racine. There are two verse translations, one by Francisco Bento Maria Targini (1823), the other by António José de Lima Leitão (1840) with illustrations by Gustave Doré. Fernando da Costa Soares' is the latest (2002). Manuel Frias Martins released a bilingual edition of *L'Allegro* and *Il Penseroso* (1987). As for Spanish translations, they include the first unrhymed version by Gaspar Melchor de Jovellanos, which was published in 1796, and José Hermida y Escoiquiz's verse translation, which appeared in Bourges in 1812. There have been at least sixteen published complete editions of Milton's works in translation (twelve in the twentieth century), including the latest by Enrique López Castelló (bilingual edition, 2005) and Bel Atreides (2005). *Samson Agonistes* was not translated before 1949 (and 1977), while *A Mask* appeared in 1862; *Of Education* in 1916, 1925; and *Sonnets* in 1977. A Spanish version of *Areopagitica* appeared in 1999. Josep M. Boix I Selva's *Paradise Lost* (1950) and Esteve Pujals' *Paradise Regained* (1994) are Catalan versions.

There have been no fewer than eighteen Italian translators of *Paradise Lost*, from Paolo Rolli (1758) to the poet and critic Roberto Sanesi (1987).

Lazzaro Papi's is the most popular version, with illustrations by Gustave Doré (1811, over thirty editions until 1987). A poet, Gerolamo Silvio Martinengo, made the first translation of *Paradise Regained*, which remained unpublished until 1975. In 1911 there appeared a hendecasyllabic version, which is practically impossible to find, illegible and without a critical apparatus. Daniele Borgogni, University of Turin, has just released a bilingual edition, and he endeavoured to respect the prosody, the rhythm, the assonances, in short, Milton's idiosyncratic language, providing a large amount of notes. There are five Italian translations of *Samson Agonistes*. The earliest translation of *A Mask* dates back to 1812, and the poem can be found in another translation in a bilingual edition of Milton's minor poems (including *Ode alla Natività, Ad un concerto sacro,* and *Arcadi*) published by Carlo Izzo in 1958. *L'Allegro* was translated alone in the last quarter of the eighteenth century and bound with *Il Penseroso* only in 1946. *Lycidas* and *Sonnets* were published in 1930. Only two of Milton's prose works have been translated: his brilliant apology of the freedom of the press, *Areopagitica,* and his treatise on educational reform, *Of Education.*

In Greece, there is apparently a lack of interest in Milton's Christian epic as *Paradise Lost* was not fully translated until 1990. Only selections existed before (1887–88, 1896), whereas George Henry Glass translated *Samson Agonistes* into Greek as early as 1788. John Plumptre translated *Lycidas* in 1797, and *A Mask* and *Il Penseroso* were first translated in 1832 and 1878, respectively.

Located at the frontier between Europe and Asia, Turkey has also showed little interest in Milton: in 2006, Enver Günsel published the first translation of *Paradise Lost* into Turkish ("Kayıp Cennet: Adem İle Havva'nın Cennetten Kovuluş Öyküsü").

Turning to Asia, we encounter Japanese, Korean, and Chinese translations of Milton. For Japan, we should add the following editions to the list supplied in the *Milton Encyclopedia*:[14] Arai Akira translated *Paradise Lost* (1978), *Paradise Regained,* and *Samson Agonistes* (1982); *The Reason of Church-Government* (with Hiroshi Tanaka, 1986); *The Judgment of Martin Bucer* (with Ayako Matsunmai and Hiroshi Tanaka, 1992); *The Doctrine and Discipline of Divorce* (with Hiroko Sano and Hiroshi Tanaka, 1998); and the two *Defenses* (with Yuko Noro, 2003). Jun Harada has recently translated *Areopagitica* and *The Readie and Easie Way to Establish a Free Commonwealth* (Tokyo, 2008). The quartercentenary of Milton's death (1974) provided an opportunity for Japanese Miltonists – Akira Arai, Takero Oiji, and Hiroshi Tanaka – to organize the Milton Society of Japan and to translate all of Milton's prose works. The project is pending owing to the small market for such academic books.

The first complete Korean translation of a work by Milton, *Paradise Lost*, was published in 1963 by two scholars, Jung-sik Rhyu (along with *Paradise Regained*) and Chang-bae Lee (along with *Samson Agonistes*). There are four other editions of *Paradise Lost* (1973–85) and five plagiarized editions of the epic. The earlier translations may have been from Japanese: Korea was liberated from Japan after forty-five years of occupation at the end of World War II, and many scholars in the following two decades were bilingual. The prose has not been translated, except for *Areopagitica* (Sang-won Lim, 1998, and Sang-ik Park in the following year).

The first translator of Milton in China was an English Congregationalist missionary, Rev. Dr. Walter Henry Medhurst: he translated Milton's sonnet on his blindness (1854). The most recent Chinese translator of Milton (and one of the most accomplished) is Jin Fashen: he translated most of Milton's poems, including *Paradise Lost, Paradise Regained, Samson Agonistes*, and minor poems (2004). In the intervening 150 years notable translators include Fu Donghua (1930), Zhu Weiji (1934), Yin Baoshu (1958), and Zhu Weizhi (1998). That *Areopagitica* (1958), *Pro Populo Anglicano Defensio* (1958), *Pro Populo Anglicano Defensio Secunda* (1958), and *The Readie and Easie Way to Establish a Free Commonwealth* (1964) should have been translated into Chinese is especially remarkable.

Shaukat Wasti produced an Urdu rendition of *Paradise Lost* in Pakistan (Peshawar, 1979). In India the Christian poet and translator, Isa Charan Sada (1870–1957), translated the three great poems between 1914 and 1927. In Arabic, only the first two books of *Paradise Lost* have been translated, Muhammad Inani's "Al-Firdaws al-Mafqud" (Cairo, 1982). As Jeffrey Eiboden points out, Inani's work was "the first academic endeavour . . . to translate and explain Milton's epic to Arab readers." It is penetrated by Qur'ānic language and "the interpolation of the language of the Qur'an into the English epic ultimately functions to dissolve the substantial historical, cultural and religious distance between [the] two texts."[15] There is an exception, though: "God and his Son [11.678]" is translated as "God and the Messiah," for the divine Sonship of Christ is utterly rejected by Islam. Farideh Mahdavi-Damghani translated *Paradise Lost* into Farsi (Teheran, 2002). As she explains, she translates classical books out of an interest in "immaterial, theosophical and religious issues," and because, "if we don't know classical books, we will not have any suitable academic knowledge." There is also a nationalistic urge behind her undertaking: "We shouldn't be weaker than Asian countries such as Egypt, India, and South Korea, Japan or China in reading books."[16]

French translations of Milton's poetry are well known through Jean Gillet's thesis on *Paradise Lost* (1974), which also addresses Mirabeau's translation of two of Milton's prose works, *Areopagitica* and *Pro Populo Anglicano Defensio*. I was commissioned by the French government to translate *The Doctrine and Discipline of Divorce* after Professor Olivier Abel had spoken about divorce in Protestant ethics before the Senate on January 29, 1999. Olivier Lutaud gave us a canonical version of *Areopagitica* in 1956. Armand Himy is the author of the latest translation of *Paradise Lost* (2001). All in all, there have been fifteen complete translations of *Paradise Lost* into French: Nicolas-François Dupré de Saint-Maur (1730); Louis Racine (1755); Henri-Claude-Marie Le Roy (1775); Jean-Baptiste Mosneron de Launay (1786, 1804); Pierre-Joseph-François Luneau de Boisjermain (*Cours de langue anglaise*, 1798); Jacques Delille (in verse, 1805); Jacques-Barthélemy Salgues (1807); Deloynes d'Auteroche (*L'Esprit de Milton*, which, the author claimed in the subtitle, was "freed from the lengths and superfluities that spoil the harmony of the poem," 1808); Chateaubriand (1836); Jean-Baptiste-Antoine-Aimé Sanson de Pongerville (1838); Paul Guérin (1857); Jean de Dieu (*La Perte d'Eden*, 1864); André Tasset (1867); Pierre Messiaen (1951–55); and Armand Himy (2001). Milton scholars translated most of the rest of his poetry in the twentieth century: Emile Saillens (*Sonnets*, 1930, *Lycidas*, 1971); Jacques Blondel (*Paradise Regained* 1955, *A Mask* 1964); and Floris Delattre (*Samson Agonistes*, 1972). A PhD candidate, Laïla Ghermani, translated *Of True Religion* in a book devoted to toleration (2002) and Renée and André Guillaume, two retired university professors, have recently undertaken to translate Milton's English prose works.

The most famous of all French translators of Milton is Chateaubriand. Though he was also a historian and politician, Chateaubriand is remembered as a great literary figure and is said to have ushered in the Romantic movement in France. Chateaubriand describes *Le paradis perdu de Milton* as "the work of [his] whole life."[17] While he also presented the translation as a bread-earning activity, Chateaubriand's reasons for translating Milton were not merely practical, but were part of his own spiritual quest.[18]

Chateaubriand deserves attention because his translation purported to be "une révolution dans la manière de traduire" ("a revolution in translating"): instead of competing with and embellishing the original version, the translator claimed he had stuck to the English text: "It is a literal translation . . . which a child as well as a poet can follow with the text, line for line, word for word, like a dictionary open before his eyes."[19] That literalness manifests itself, firstly, in a respect for the material presentation of the text (his was a bilingual edition) and typography. Contrary to what his predecessors had done, Chateaubriand did not cut any part of the text which was not pleasing to the French taste; for example, he kept the anti-monarchist and anticlerical critiques, the verses deemed heretical (Milton's Arianism), prelapsarian sexuality, and the materiality of the angels. He also refused to clarify Milton's text and he consequently reproduced the defects of the original – at the expense of the correctness and elegance of the French. What was revolutionary was the radicalism of Chateaubriand's literal translation: he held Milton's text in so much devotion that he scrupulously respected the genre, meaning, syntax, lexical richness, and the tone of the text. Thus he rendered Milton's obscure words into French in his translation and respected Milton's sometimes ambiguous vision of the world.

Yet his so-called "literal translation" is not so literal: Chateaubriand used false calques, i.e., expressions whose awkwardness leads us to believe mistakenly that he borrows from an English phrase, to convey the illusion of literality. Another strategy is to do superficial violence to the target language so as to welcome the linguistic strictures of the source language, i.e., the vigor and brutality of the style of *Paradise Lost* in the use of ellipses and inversions, present participles, unsteady verbal constructions, and lexical irregularity. Chateaubriand's translation is literal but still artful.[20] All his albeit superficial changes are meant to render the intensity of Milton's idiomatic language: did not "the English Homer" violate the rules of his own tongue? "Il traite sa langue en tyran."[21]

Why did Milton matter for Chateaubriand? With a translation he claimed to be literal, Chateaubriand voluntarily humbled himself before Milton's epic, which he regarded as sacred, and through his arduous task of translation, he hoped to establish a personal and privileged relationship with God. Thus his translation of *Paradise Lost* was a spiritual quest, and his reading of Milton played an important role in his vision of Christianity, which he was to express in *Vie de Rancé*.

Why does Milton matter for his posterity? "A poet translated is, in a way, a poet saved," wrote the prefacer to Alexander Shubarnov's *Frost-Flowers*.[22] Milton the poet has been saved from oblivion through translations. In particular, as I have shown, the French Revolution played a key role in prompting other poetic translations of Milton in Europe and enhancing his reputation as a champion of freedom to the whole world. As scholars continue to translate Milton the polemicist and poet – and as new readers discover his works – Chateaubriand's pronouncement continues to prove true: "il est devenu un homme de notre temps" ("he has become a man of our own times").[23]

NOTES

1 I restrict the term "translation" to the most widely recognized definition of the word among the dozen definitions in the *Oxford English Dictionary*, namely, "the product of the action or process of turning from one language into another." Hence I will only consider the purposefully accurate interlingual renditions of Milton's writings. I will not discuss the translations *into* English. I would like to express my gratitude to Hiroko Sano (Aoyama Gakuin University, Tokyo), Oydin Uzakova (Oklahoma State University, Stillwater), Jeffrey Einboden (Northern Illinois University, Dekalb), Katsuhiro Engetsu (Doshiba University, Kyoto), Hao Tianhu (Peking University, Beijing), Georgi Vasilev (State University of Library Studies and Information Technologies, Sofia), and Sung-kyun Yim (Sookmyung Women's University, Seoul) for their valuable help.

2 The full passage reads: "*Le Lecteur est prié de remarquer... que le Traducteur a été obligé par plusieurs considération, mais principalement, à cause de l'élégance du stile & du language de l'Auteur & de ses conceptions, de s'attacher entièrement à ses paroles & expressions, autant que la langue Françoise l'a pû permettre, de peur de perdre la grace... [de] l'Original*" (A3r).

3 The original French reads: "*... qui ne sert pas peu à justifier les procédures d'un Etat, tel que celui d'Angleterre, en un si grand & si notable changement, les frases & les termes ne doivent pas ètre recherchez, à l'égal des choses, qu'ils signifient*" (A3v).

4 *Paraphrasis poetica in tria Johannis Miltoni... poemata, viz. Paradisum amissum, Paradisum recuperatum, et Samsonem Agonisten* (London, 1690).

5 John K. Hale, "The Significance of the Early Translations of *Paradise Lost*," in *Milton as Multilingual: Selected Essays by John K. Hale*, ed. Lisa Marr and Chris Ackerley (Dunedin, New Zealand, 2005), 157–80.

6 *Det tabte Paradiis* (Copenhagen, 1790); *Det gienvundne Paradiis* (Copenhagen, 1792); and *Samson hiin Kæmper* (Copenhagen, 1815).

7 *Kadunud ja jälleleitud Paradiis* (Tallinn, 1895).

8 *J. Miltona pazaudēta paradīze: epose divpadsmit dziedājumos* (Liepaja, 1899).

9 A first translation by Tihamér Dybas, *Sámson: dráma*, with illustrations by Gustave Doré, had appeared twenty years before, in 1955.

10 *Izgubljeni raj* (Ljubljana, 2003). Moreover, to reach a wide audience, he turned his version into a twenty-five-episode radio play and produced a stage adaptation.

11 *Izgubljeni raj: Dvanaest pevanja, Raj ponovo stečen: četiri pevanja* (Belgrade, 1989; new edn., 2002).

12 John T. Shawcross, "Translations, poetic," in *A Milton Encyclopedia*, ed. William B. Hunter, Jr., John T. Shawcross, and John M. Steadman, 9 vols. (Lewisburg, PA, 1978–83), VIII:78–86 (p. 84).

13 John T. Shawcross, "John Milton and His Spanish and Portuguese Presence," *Milton Quarterly* 32.2 (1998): 41–52 (p. 41).

14 See *A Milton Encyclopedia*, IX:18, VIII:78–86.

15 Eid Abdallah Dahiyat, *John Milton and the Arab-Islamic Culture* (Amman, 1987), 86, quoted in Jeffrey Einboden, "A Qur'ānic Milton: From Paradise to al-Firdaws," *Milton Quarterly* 43.3 (October 2009), forthcoming.

16 See Atiban.com http://en.atiban.com/article.aspx?id=30. "Atiban" (literally "guardian of the future") is the leading website for literary reporters and writers without borders from Iran, Tajikistan, and Afghanistan. It aims to expand Persian literature and language across the world.

17 Chateaubriand, *Le paradis perdu; Essai sur la literature anglaise,* vol. XI of *Oeuvres complètes de Chateaubriand* (Paris, 1861; Klaus reprint, Nendeln [Liechtenstein], 1975). Available online at the digital library of the Bibliothèque Nationale de France: http://gallica2.bnf.fr. *Le paradis perdu* (pp. 1–477) opens with *Remarques* (pp. 3–13) and is followed by the *Essai sur la littérature anglaise* (pp. 479–793), which includes *Avertissement* (pp. 481–85). This quotation is taken from *Avertissement*, 482.

18 *Essai sur la littérature anglaise*, 793.

19 *Remarques*, 12, 4.

20 "Traduire . . . c'est se battre avec des mots" ("To translate . . . is to fight with words") (*Avertissement*, 482).

21 *Ibid.*, 483. The French translates as, "He deals with his own language as a tyrant."

22 Vladimir Trendafilov, Preface, in Alexander Shubarnov, *Frost-Flowers* (Princeton, 2002), 13.

23 *Avertissement*, 485.

CHAPTER 16

Visual arts

Wendy Furman-Adams

Despite blindness from mid-life and his famous iconoclasm, John Milton is one of the most visual poets England has yet produced. As Roland M. Frye argued three decades ago, Milton responded more deeply to his own extensive, firsthand experience of the visual arts than we might expect, creating his own immense universe – infernal, heavenly, and terrestrial – in conversation with a vast repository of traditional visual images.[1] Conversely, perhaps *because* he wrote of things "invisible to mortal sight," Milton's works are among the world's most frequently illustrated. During three and a half centuries, more than 190 artists have created illustrations for over twenty of Milton's works; more than 150 have attempted to give visual form to *Paradise Lost*. Joseph Wittreich's pioneering essay in *A Milton Encyclopedia* remains indispensable for its chronological list of those artists, as well as for his suggestion that the history of Milton illustration is a history not just of decoration, but of interpretation, of "nonverbal criticism."[2] From the first illustrated edition of *Paradise Lost*, published in 1688, to Alexis Smith's *Snake Path*, installed in 1992, artists have illuminated not only Milton's texts, but their own historically grounded readings of those texts. Each has emphasized different aspects of Milton's vision – different works, different scenes, and different themes. Each, as a reviewer of illustrator Mary Groom put it, has seen the works with "other eyes."[3]

One way to consider the history of Milton illustration is to look at the scenes various artists have chosen to embody in visual terms. Some ages belong to the Son of God, others to Satan. But as Milton referred to "lantskip" more often than to any other genre[4] – and was no doubt touched by early modern images of Paradise – so virtually all artists have in turn focused on Milton's representation of Eden. They have interpreted it, moreover, in a dazzling variety of ways: as an idealized environment evoking both a lost paradise and the green breast of the New World; as a stage set for the drama of gender and sex; as an eternal embodiment of the unity between the human and the divine; as a pastoral or georgic

Fig. 2 Jan Bruegel the Elder (1568–1625), *Paradise*

site – existing either for human delight or for human growth and fulfillment; as the externalized sign of human love and relatedness itself; as the
womb of all life; and as the last temptation, that of ignorance and perpetual childhood. All these possibilities are to some extent present in Milton's
text, but each artist foregrounds different elements – helping us as readers
literally to see them. For, as Milton illustrator Carlotta Petrina once said,
"All art is of its own time."[5]

The word "landscape" itself, so much evident in books IV–VII of *Paradise
Lost*, first came into English as "a technical term to describe the well-known
products of Dutch art."[6] And among Dutch artists, none was more famous
for his scenes of Paradise than Jan Bruegel the Elder (1568–1625). In one
such image, simply called *Paradise* (figure 2), we can easily read Milton's
own "sylvan scene" (IV.140). Here, too, "All beasts of th' earth, since wild"
(IV.341) dwell in peace, along with pairs of gloriously plumed tropical birds.
The viewer of Bruegel's image lies in the foreground, eye to eye with a brace
of ducks splashing in a shallow stream – and is beckoned, like Adam, to
rise, to walk, to breathe, to contemplate, and to name.

If early modern painters gave literal descriptive form to the garden of
Genesis, biblical illustrators underscored its typological – moral, spiritual,
and ultimately anagogical – meanings. The frontispiece to the Geneva
Bible (figure 3), like Milton's first invocation, summarizes all of human
history with an image of Adam and Eve – standing on either side of "that
forbidden tree, whose mortal taste / Brought death into the world, and all
our woe" (1.2–3). Visible only by his mysterious name, entirely swathed in
cloud and light, God the Father hovers over the central tree, from which
our first parents are in the very act of picking fruit. They are surrounded
by a veritable ark full of animals, all in pairs, as well as by the four rivers
of Eden. Beams of light emanating from the Divine Name suggest that,
as in Milton's book III, God here bends "down his eye, / His own works
and their works at once to view" (58–59). And banners in our first parents'
left hands announce the moral and spiritual meaning of their fatal choice:
"Desire to knowe / Hath wrought our woe. / By tasting this / Th' exile
of blisse." But that, of course, is not the whole story. The curse written
on a banner around the serpent's body ("Duste for to eate / Must be my
meate") balances and gives rise to the promise held in our parents' *right*
hands: "By promis made / Restored we be / To pleasures of Eternitye"
(cf. Genesis 3:14–15; *Paradise Lost* X.177–86). From initial creation to the
moment when "time stand[s] fixed" in "new heav'ns, new earth, ages of
endless date / . . . To bring forth fruits, joy and eternal bliss" (*Paradise Lost*

Fig. 3 Frontispiece to the Geneva Bible (1610)

Fig. 4 Bernard Lens, illustration to book IV of *Paradise Lost* (1688)

XII.555, 549, 551) – all this is neatly embodied spatially by the Geneva Bible's engraver, as it will be embodied temporally in Milton's epic.

The earliest illustrated edition of Milton's poetry was a 1688 *Paradise Lost*, with twelve engravings following designs by Dr. Henry Aldrich, John Baptist Medina, and Bernard Lens.[7] These designs clearly privilege narrative over description, to produce a close literal reading of each episode of the poem. Like the arguments Milton added in 1668, they were designed not to give a sensuous or emotional experience of Paradise, but to help readers navigate Milton's narrative and to take its moral instruction to heart. To this end, the artists borrowed the medieval technique of synoptic narration, representing several scenes within one design. Lens' representation of book IV (figure 4) is typical of the four designs set in Eden, in that the natural environment is sharply curtailed in favor of storytelling.

The viewer is called upon to *read* the picture, beginning at the center-right. Here a tiny Adam and Eve disport with their animal companions, as Satan perches over their heads, an outsized cormorant on the Tree of Life (IV.196, 194). The viewer's eye follows them, forward and left, to their evening prayer; then to their bower in the right foreground, where Ithuriel and Zephon discover Satan "[s]quat like a toad, close at the ear of Eve" (IV.800). Larger figures narrate the divine level of the story, as a massive Uriel "glides" on a cloud-banked sunbeam just to the right of mid-center – announcing the fiend's invasion to Gabriel and his angelic guards, who are seated "[b]etwixt . . . rocky pillars," while their "[c]elestial armory" hangs at the ready behind them (IV.549, 53). Lens represents the book's final episode in a tiny vignette to Uriel's right: Satan "hem[med] . . . round" by angels – whose "ported spears" are indeed "thick as . . . a field / Of Ceres ripe for harvest" (IV.979–81) – as the Father's "celestial sign" hangs overhead (IV.1011).

If the 1688 Eden is "about" satanic transgression hemmed in by Providence, eighteenth-century Edens are primarily "about" Adam and Eve, as Paradise becomes the stage-set for their romance. The pair shed much of their moral and spiritual baggage to become a man and woman in love (and stalked not by supernatural evil, but by a jealous rival). Earlier in the century, these images lean toward the domestic, becoming more frankly erotic during what Marcia Pointon has called the "English Rococo."[8] In a 1720 headpiece illustration to book IV (figure 5), Louis Chéron represents our first parents in a charming moment of domestic affection, surrounded by animal companions including a pair of large, affectionate-looking dogs.[9] Eden is rendered in a few deft strokes – just enough to display a garden of the new, "natural" style, inspired to some extent by Milton's poem and promoted by landscape architects such as Lancelot ("Capability") Brown

Fig. 5 Louis Chéron, headpiece to book IV of *Paradise Lost* (1720)

(1715–83). But the center of the eighteenth-century Eden is always the lovers, more lushly portrayed as the century progresses.

In a 1749 edition's sole illustration to book V (figure 6), Francis Hayman represents the lovers in a far more romantic pose – one reminiscent of French rococo painters such as Watteau and Fragonard.[10] As in his illustration to book IV, which shows the entwined lovers spied upon by a jealous Satan, the lovers here enjoy "[t]he happier Eden" of erotic love, "[i]mparadised" in their conversation (IV.507, 506). No narrative moment in book V accounts for the scene, which seems to represent, rather, the essence of the lovers' life together in Eden. Surrounded by lush foliage, the pair takes up fully a third of the pictorial space, Adam's leg equal in length to the trunk of the tree behind his seated form. The natural world is background here: a stage set for the drama of love between man and woman. Eve's full frontal nudity invites Adam's adoring gaze (along, presumably, with that of the gentleman reader), her "loose tresses" falling across her decorously bent left arm. Hayman's rococo message is simple: *this* is paradise, to love and be loved.[11]

At the end of the century, however, Richard Westall (1794–95) and Edward Burney (1799) initiate a new kind of erotic Paradise – in which the rococo *fête gallant* is replaced by an emerging romanticism: an intensely gendered dialectic between the sublime (represented by Satan, Sin, and Death) and the beautiful (represented by Eve and by the Eden with which she is increasingly identified).[12] They follow Chéron and Hayman in

Fig. 6 Francis Hayman, *Adam and Eve in Paradise,* illustration to book v (1749)

representing the couple's relationship as the essence of Eden, but their Eden appears more fragile, more fraught with the melancholy of impending loss.

We first encounter Westall's Adam and Eve in his illustration to book v, as Adam hangs enamored over his still sleeping wife (figure 7). Although he is surrounded by a lush, Constable-like landscape, and sunlight falls directly

Fig. 7 Richard Westall, *Adam with Sleeping Eve*, illustration to book v (1794)

on the couple, darkness pervades the surrounding forest, and Adam's face registers not just adoration but concern: his "wonder . . . to find unwakened Eve / With tresses discomposed, and glowing cheek, / As though unquiet rest" (v.9–11). The frank erotic intersubjectivity registered by Hayman – each loving and each beloved – gives way to a less reciprocal kind of longing: a sense that for Adam Eve *is* Eden – he the subject of paradise, she the ever-elusive object. Thus the fall is never more proleptically present than in their tenderest scenes. This romantic Adam will not fall, as previous artists have suggested, out of disobedience to God, but rather out of love for Eve, a love for which the world might indeed be well lost. Westall is also virtually unique among illustrators in representing book VIII with what is – in Milton's text and in Medina's synoptic narrative – a background image: Eve among her flowers (figure 8). In so doing, he sketches in the other side of the distinctly gendered universe so many readers since have read in (and perhaps into) *Paradise Lost*. As clearly representing "the beautiful" as the flowers she tends, Westall's Eve is proleptically "separate"– subjected to *our* gaze as she soon will be to Satan's: "oft stooping to support / Each flow'r of tender stalk . . . mindless the while, / Herself, though fairest unsupported flow'r, / From her best prop so far, and storm so nigh" (IX.427–33).

Burney likewise represents book VIII with a paradisal vision of Eve as object (figure 9) – in this case of Adam's gaze as she first appears to him, yet seems to turn away, as one "[t]hat would be wooed, and not unsought be won" (VIII.503). Adam shades his eyes as if "weak / Against the charm of beauty's powerful glance" (VIII.532–33) – again suggesting uxoriousness, not loss of faith, as the deepest cause of his fall. Burney's Eve, in fact, is so much a part of the landscape that her body echoes the sinuous folds of the snake in her almost comically lush temptation scene (figure 10) – a sinuousness representing the very antithesis of the stern masculine sublime Adam fails to embody. The couple take on a somewhat georgic role in Burney's design for book v, as Eve prepares for the arrival of the fast-approaching angel. But on the whole, Burney's Eve takes on full humanity only after the fall. Beforehand, she indeed possesses, as Milton's Adam worries, "Too much of ornament, in outward show / Elaborate, of inward less exact" (VIII.538–39) – and lures him, as "the link of nature" (IX.914), to self-betrayal. The romantic Eve, always somewhat "separate," has replaced the rococo couple as the soul of Paradise. And because, for the romantic Adam, she is its soul, she, far more than Satan, becomes its inevitable destruction.

Eve also stands at the center of William Blake's Eden, particularly in his 1808 illustration of the Edenic dinner party with Raphael (figure 11),

Fig. 8 Richard Westall, *Eve Among Her Flowers*, illustration to book VIII (1794)

Fig. 9 Edward Burney, *Adam Wooing Eve*, illustration to book VIII (1799)

Fig. 10 Edward Burney, *Eve's Temptation*, illustration to book IX (1799)

Fig. 11 William Blake, *Raphael's Visit with Adam and Eve*, illustration to book v (1808)

although she sits beside Adam in Blake's 1807 version of the scene (figure 12). In either case, the fall, for Blake, is about far more than gender, as Paradise is about much more than landscape. For Blake, in fact, Paradise is not a "place" at all, but an eternal state of human existence – the state of connection to the "true Vine" which is eternally Christ. Scholars have differed about the exact moment represented in Blake's two images – which

Fig. 12 William Blake, *Raphael's Visit with Adam and Eve*, illustration to book v (1807)

in turn illustrate not just Milton's book v, but Raphael's entire visit and Adam and Eve's entire experience of Eden. Clearly the setting is Adam and Eve's bower, the paradise in the heart of Paradise, with garden furniture that grows up directly out of the earth – sprouting, in turn, into vines and lilies, to evoke both the Song of Songs and the redemption to come through the Seed of the second Eve.

In the earlier version, Adam and Eve both sit listening to the angel's discourse; in the later version, Eve "minister[s] naked" as he speaks (v.444). But Raphael's discourse and every element in the scene point in two contrasting directions: toward the ever-present temptation to fall and toward the ever-present offer of redemption. Blake's Edenic landscape, in other words, is neither descriptive nor narrative. Rather, it is a window into the divine reality that Raphael attempts to mediate through human speech. In both views, albeit at different distances from the bower, the most salient feature of the garden is the forbidden tree, awaiting Adam and Eve's transgression even as they experience a eucharistic foretaste of the Heavenly Banquet. The snake enwrapping that tree is both the satanic serpent and the saving Christ, lifted up upon a stick in the wilderness (Numbers 21:4–9; John 3:14–15). The gourd in Eve's left hand is both a symbol of pride and the attribute of pilgrims – a prefiguration of Christ's supper at Emmaus; the grapes in her right signify both connection to Christ and the blood he will shed to heal humankind's revolt and self-separation. Prevenient grace and moral responsibility grow up together in Blake's Paradise, as inextricable as Psyche's Miltonic seeds.

Blake's Eden is the farthest removed of all artists' versions from what we ordinarily describe as *nature*. Our first parents and their angel guest fill at least three-fifths of the frame. Moreover, the natural elements that surround Blake's majestic figures are arranged so as to remove all reference to literal space and time, and to locate the viewer in an eternal symbolic universe outside what were, for Blake, the illusory dimensions of this world.[13] But in the second decade of the nineteenth century, something new emerged in Milton illustration: a focus on Paradise as an actual *place*, standing in for the fragile, time-bound, endangered earth itself. As the industrial revolution scarred the landscape with smoky tunnels and sulfurous pits; as botany became a national passion; and as the word "ecology" was about to come into use, artists begin to "read Milton greenly."[14]

The first of these artists was John Martin, who made two sets of mezzotint engravings of the epic between 1824 and 1827. The second was Jane Giraud, whose virtually unknown and anonymously published *Flowers of Milton* appeared in 1846, making her Milton's first woman illustrator. Both artists foregrounded – as Milton's earlier visual interpreters had not – the landscape of Eden and the earth's vulnerability to human choices. Both advanced this ecological awareness by focusing on the poem's natural environment rather than on the figures previously at the center of the drama. They did so, however, in gender-specific ways – using sharply contrasting definitions of place to define Paradise and to suggest its fragility. John

Fig. 13 John Martin, *Eve and Her Reflection in the Liquid Plain*, illustration to book iv; plate 9 in a series of twenty-four made for Septimus Prowett (1825–27)

Martin's enormous mezzotints presented a vast and endlessly evocative prospect – one that for the first time placed human figures in truly proportionate scale to their surroundings, thus underscoring their dependence upon their environment. Jane Giraud's delicate watercolors *reduced* Milton's vast landscape to the eloquent synecdoche of a flower, while foregrounding, like Martin's designs, a green understanding of human "dominion" (Genesis 1:28).

We first encounter Martin's Paradise as Eve discovers her image in the "liquid plain" (iv.455; figure 13). A tiny figure in a massive landscape of dappled light and shade, Martin's Eve is neither narcissist nor incipient feminist, but a human being coming to astonished consciousness of her place within the natural world. This new sense of scale marks all the images in Martin's series. In contrast to all previous artists, Martin does not place humankind at the center of his representation of Paradise. Adam and Eve matter greatly as conscious, responsible beings, whose fall tragically wounds the earth – a wound, Martin suggests, reflected in the excesses of the industrial age. If the fall comes of placing oneself at the center, redemption for Martin is to see one's true position in a world far larger

Fig. 14 John Martin, *Raphael Instructing Adam and Eve*, illustration to books V–VIII; plate 15 (1825–28)

than oneself – one covering "distance inexpressible / By numbers that have name" (VIII.113–14). This seems, in fact, the burden of Raphael's discourse (figure 14): the true meaning of the word *dominion* – expressed not, as Satan will argue, in *domination* over one's fellow creatures, but rather in learning to make a home within the vast *domus*, or "house," of nature.[15]

Jane Giraud underscores this same ecological insight by focusing her entire reading of the epic on flowers (figure 15) – a story that may on the surface seem too small to be taken very seriously. But for Giraud it is finally nothing less than the story of our equally fragile earth, which is in turn our own story – as human beings who are rooted in nature and are dependent upon it, like every other "fair creature" (IV.468), for our flourishing and survival. Giraud begins her representation of Milton's narrative by devoting two plates, of a total of seven, to Milton's description of Adam and Eve's bower: a "place / Chos'n by the sov'reign planter, when he framed / All things to man's delightful use" (IV.690–92). And having established this natural *domus* within the larger home of Eden, she focuses on Adam and Eve's Edenic work: a blend of meaningful labor and joyous contemplation of the natural world. In her illustration

Fig. 15 Jane Giraud, title page to *Paradise Lost*. *The Flowers of Milton* (1846)

wake; the morning shines, and the fresh field
Calls us; we lose the prime, to mark how spring
Our tended plants, how blows the **Citron** grove,
What drops the **Myrrh**, and what the **Balmy Reed**,
How nature paints her colours, how the bee
Sits on the bloom, extracting liquid sweet.

J.E.G. del & lith.

Book 5th Line 20

Fig. 16 Jane Giraud, "Awake / My fairest . . ." *The Flowers of Milton* (1846)

of Adam's dawn song (figure 16), Giraud bypasses the romance of its first three lines (so crucial to eighteenth-century readers), and moves directly to Adam's second "Awake" (v. 20–25), in which he goes on to describe the wonders of nature, inviting their attention both as gardeners and as observers. But as in Martin's universe our first parents' scale suggests the independent importance and value of the natural world, here their absence underscores – perhaps yet more strongly – that same perspective: nature is about more than human beings; dominion is, at its root, an ethic of care.

Milton illustration in the twentieth century is best represented by three extraordinary women: Carlotta Petrina, Mary Elizabeth Groom, and Alexis Smith. Although they were not aware of each other's existence, the American Petrina and English Groom were near contemporaries, producing deluxe illustrated editions of *Paradise Lost* just one year apart, in 1936 and 1937.[16] Still working today, Alexis Smith is a leading conceptual artist, specializing in large-scale installations – including her remarkable *Snake Path*, installed on the San Diego campus of the University of California in 1992. Together they bring a variety of feminist readings to the poem – readings that range from the despairing to the wittily hopeful.

For Petrina, as for earlier Romantic illustrators, Milton's Paradise is about the relationship between Adam and Eve – and about the search for the self in relation to the Other. That is certainly the subject of Petrina's heartbreaking illustration to book IV (figure 17). In Milton's text, the lovers sit down by a "brimming stream" to enjoy "their supper fruits" (IV.336, 331). In Petrina's design, however, the stream has the still and reflective character of a "clear / Smooth lake" (IV.458–59). Eve, moreover, looks intently, almost beseechingly at Adam's face, as if seeking there a missing clue to her own existence. Yet Adam, disconcertingly, gazes not at Eve, but directly, almost anxiously, at the viewer, as if seeking a clue to his *own* identity – an identity available neither in God, whose image he supposedly bears, nor in his wife, who supposedly bears his. For Petrina it is in the eye of the beloved that one finds one's truest self; yet these lovers seem already to have lost their bearings, to have discovered an existential placelessness that has cast them already out of Paradise into their irreducible difference.[17]

Petrina's representation of book IX (figure 18) may be the single most tragic image in all Miltonic illustration. But for her even the loveliest paradisal scene includes a sense of loss and erasure. One has to wonder how long Eve can continue to solicit this inattentive Adam, before turning her face again to the abandoned lake, or perhaps to a talking serpent, for reassurance of her reality. To do so, surely, would require not satanic vanity, but only the human need for a human thou: "In solitude / What happiness, who can enjoy alone, / Or all enjoying, what contentment find?" (VIII.364–66). In any case, if Eve seems fragile here, in the weeping scene her body seems almost to melt, eroding into non-being with the flow of her tears. Petrina's Eve, indeed, is the image of existential emptiness – reduced

Fig. 17 Carlotta Petrina, *Adam and Eve in Paradise*, illustration to book IV (1936)

Fig. 18 Carlotta Petrina, *Eve Grieving*, illustration to book IX (1936)

Fig. 19 Mary Elizabeth Groom, decorative headpiece to book iv (1937)

to her particularly vulnerable, feminine, and utterly deferred desire for wholeness.

Mary Groom's twenty-nine wood engravings of Milton's epic convey an altogether different kind of feminism: on the one hand, a Jungian celebration of the feminine in nature, and, on the other, a clear assertion of the absolute equality of the sexes and of their mutual sufficiency to stand. Eden, for Groom, is among other things "the field of this World," in which "the knowledge of good is . . . involv'd and interwoven with the knowledge of evil" (*CPW* ii:514) – and in which ethical seed-sorting, before and after the fall, is the daily task of human beings. Groom represents Paradise as a womb-like space, even in the decorative headpieces repeated at the beginning of each book (figure 19). Here viewers are challenged, like Adam and Eve, to discern the presence of both lurking temptation and prevenient grace. At first glance the design appears to be merely a profusion of leaves, stems, flowers, and fruit. But almost hidden in the upper corners, involved in the natural environment, the faces of Adam and Eve gradually emerge. Eve gazes thoughtfully at an enormous apple swelling beneath her; the apple in turn is involved in what looks to be foliage, but is actually the tail of a serpent, whose fanged head is disguised as a pear. But for all his capacity to deceive and dismay, to insinuate himself into the lushness of a good and fertile creation, the serpent is balanced by the also nearly hidden figure at the top-center of the design, where a gentle-faced deity extends leaflike hands in a gesture of prevenient blessing.

Groom's ultimate expression of Paradise, however, lies in her representation of the lovers. Once she has established their equality and mutuality and the seriousness of their ethical task, it is Eve and Adam's erotic connection that most fully represents the nature of Eden. In her design for book iv (figure 20), Groom engraves a great deal of Paradise into a tiny

More grateful, to thir Supper Fruits they fell,
Nectarine Fruits which the compliant boughes
Yeilded them, side-long as they sat recline
On the soft downie Bank damaskt with flours:
The savourie pulp they chew, and in the rinde
Still as they thirsted scoop the brimming stream;
Nor gentle purpose, nor endearing smiles
Wanted, nor youthful dalliance as beseems
Fair couple, linkt in happie nuptial League,
Alone as they. About them frisking playd
All Beasts of th' Earth, since wilde, and of all chase
In Wood or Wilderness, Forrest or Den;
Sporting the Lion rampd, and in his paw

110

Fig. 20 Mary Elizabeth Groom, *Adam and Eve in Paradise*, illustration to book IV (1937)

Fig. 21 Alexis Smith, *Snake Path* (1992)

space, on a completely human scale. She represents the "fruitful Earth" of Raphael's lines (VIII.96, 97), to which the rest of the cosmos is "[o]fficious" (as Adam is to Eve) – a Garden which becomes, as Stevie Davies has put it, "an externalisation of the fruitful person of Eve" and perhaps, at least on some level, "an allegory . . . of the psyche itself."[18] Like the headpieces to

Fig. 22 Alexis Smith, granite volume of *Paradise Lost* (detail)

Fig. 23 Alexis Smith, garden and bench (detail)

each book, this design is womblike in its perfect and protective enclosure. And for the moment Groom chooses not to remind us of the scoptophilic gaze of Satan, without which we could not enter, past the rural mound's "hairy sides / With thicket overgrown" to visit this "delicious Paradise" (IV.135–36, 132). She will attend to his destructive agony in later designs.

But here Groom allows us to revel with the lovers in the sheer delight of their innocent, though vulnerable, love. Her Eden, like Milton's – like heaven and unlike Satan's mind – is a world in which there is no tragic gap between desire and fulfillment. To love in this world – the world also of the Song of Songs, which Groom and other members of her circle illustrated – is to possess and be possessed by the beloved without jealousy, mistrust, or the anxiety of potential loss.

With the exception of Bruegel, all the artists we have looked at so far have produced illustrations that have appeared in books. But Alexis Smith brings *Paradise Lost* fully into the postmodern age with her 1992 *Snake Path,* by turning the very idea of textual illustration inside-out. As Milton incorporated the ideal of education into his epic, Smith takes that massive epic and plunks it – in the form of a ten-foot-high granite volume, complete with appropriate call number – in the midst of a university campus, to elicit a walking meditation on the nature of Paradise and its relationship to learning (figures 21–23). There *is* a text in Smith's Milton class. But that text has leaped out from the book onto a path that requires actual walking, and into an Edenic little garden that – on a bench at its center – appropriates an image from Doré's *Paradise Lost* illustrations and a sentimental passage from Gray's "Ode on a Distant Prospect of Eton College": "Where Ignorance is Bliss, / Tis Folly to be wise." But, Smith dares the walker to ask, *is* ignorance bliss? Is it better to stay in this little garden of childlike innocence and avoid the dust and heat of adult life? Or is it better, as Michael suggests in the lines quoted on the front of Smith's *Paradise Lost* volume, to follow the snake's inevitably erroneous route to the library door – and to exercise, like Milton's "true wayfaring Christian," the choice that makes the difference between faith and heresy? Smith provides no definitive answers. The world lies before the reader, with Providence, one hopes, as guide.

NOTES

This chapter is dedicated to Virginia James Tufte, my partner in the study of Milton illustration for almost thirty years.

1 Roland Mushat Frye, *Milton's Imagery and the Visual Arts: Iconographic Tradition in the Epic Poems* (Princeton, 1978), 3–39.

2 Joseph Wittreich, "Illustrators," in *A Milton Encyclopedia*, ed. William B. Hunter, Jr., John T. Shawcross, and John M. Steadman, 9 vols. (Lewisburg, PA, 1978–83), IV:55–78.

3 Humbert Wolfe, *The Observer*, August 8, 1937. From a file set of press clippings collected by the Golden Cockerel Press – owned, and graciously shared, by Professor Roderick Cave of Victoria University, Wellington, New Zealand.

4 Frye, *Milton's Imagery*, 34.

5 In May 1992, when the artist was ninety-one years old, Virginia Tufte, Eunice Howe, and I had the privilege of visiting and talking with her in her Brownsville, Texas home.

6 Frye, *Milton's Imagery*, 34.

7 *Paradise Lost*, 4th edn. (London, 1688).

8 Marcia R. Pointon, *Milton and English Art* (Toronto, 1970), 37–61.

9 *The Poetical Works of John Milton*, 2 vols. (London, 1720).

10 *Paradise Lost*, ed. Thomas Newton, 2 vols. (London, 1749).

11 French artist Jean-Frédéric Schall made a set of color illustrations for *Le Paradis perdu* (Paris, 1792), which follows Hayman's selection of subjects and likewise gives Adam and Eve one extra, narratively non-specific love scene.

12 *The Poetical Works of John Milton, with a Life of the Author*, ed. William Hayley, vols. I and II (London, 1794–97); and *Milton's "Paradise Lost"* (London, 1799). Westall made another set of smaller, less sophisticated designs for an edition published in 1816. Pointon places Westall and Burney in her chapter called "Milton and the Precursors to Romanticism," in *Milton and English Art*, 62–167, which also takes up Fuseli and Blake. On the concepts of the sublime and the beautiful, see Edmund Burke, *A Philosophical Enquiry into the Origin of our Ideas of the Sublime and the Beautiful* (1757), in *The Portable Edmund Burke*, ed. Isaac Kramnick (New York, 1999), 63–81.

13 See W. J. T. Mitchell, *Blake's Composite Art: A Study of the Illuminated Poetry* (Princeton, 1978).

14 The phrase is Diane McColley's. See her "Beneficent Hierarchies: Reading Milton Greenly," in *Spokesperson Milton: Voices in Contemporary Criticism*, ed. Charles W. Durham and Kristin Pruitt McColgan (Selinsgrove, PA, 1994), 231–48.

15 See Ken Hiltner, *Milton and Ecology* (Cambridge, 2003), 26.

16 John Milton, *Paradise Lost and Paradise Regained, with an Introduction by William Rose Benét* (New York, 1936); *Paradise Lost: The Poem in Ten Books* (London, 1937).

17 See Edward S. Casey, *The Fate of Place: A Philosophical History* (Berkeley, 1997), 222–42. The figures of Adam and Eve in Petrina's drawings were modeled on Petrina herself and her husband John Petrina. In 1935, while she worked on the *Paradise Lost* illustrations, he was killed in a car accident, leaving her to raise their small son alone. She never remarried.

18 Stevie Davies, *The Feminine Reclaimed: The Idea of Woman in Spenser, Shakespeare, and Milton* (Lexington, KY, 1986), 210.

PART III

Historical and cultural contexts

CHAPTER 17

Astronomy

Dennis Danielson

On November 11, 1572, Danish astronomer Tycho Brahe looked up into the clear nighttime sky and "noticed that a new and unusual star, surpassing the other stars in brilliancy, was shining almost directly above my head . . . I was so astonished at this sight that I was not ashamed to doubt the trustworthiness of my own eyes."[1] What most jolted Tycho, however, was not the mere appearance of the new star but the realization of what it meant. For Tycho's "discovery was a death knell to the natural philosophy of Aristotle. A change had taken place in that 'solid crystal sphere of the fixed stars,' which had been assumed, during nearly two thousand years, to be subject neither to growth nor to decay."[2] In a word, Tycho now knew – contrary to previous beliefs – that even the highest heavens are in the grip of Time.

That realization came not quite thirty years after the publication of Nicolaus Copernicus' landmark treatise *De revolutionibus* and nearly a century before the appearance of *Paradise Lost*. Milton's lifetime was a period in which many thinkers struggled to re-imagine the universe against the backdrop woven by Copernicus, Tycho, and other pioneering astronomers, and Milton's engagement with that ferment reveals itself in ways that can be poetically and cosmologically breathtaking. His great epic stretches out a macroscopic universal fabric within which the human story unfolds, and also within which earth, like Tycho's supernova, can be seen as a bright new star in the heavens.

The not-yet-triumphant new astronomy of Milton's age had already been introduced in England in the sixteenth century by Thomas Digges (*c.* 1546–95). Two decades before Johannes Kepler or Galileo declared for heliocentrism, Digges published the main principles of Copernicus – and did so in English. His diagram of the extended Copernican cosmos is reprinted in many histories of astronomy (figure 24), but even more remarkable was Digges' achievement as an enthusiastic translator – the first to render Copernicus into any vernacular.

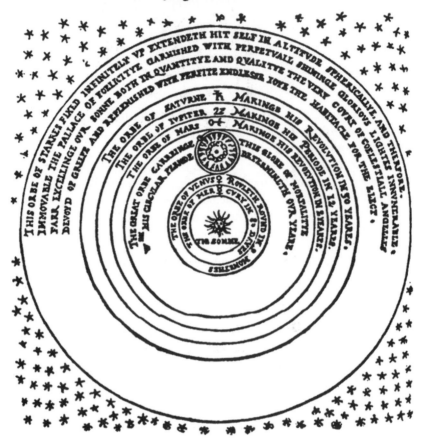

Fig. 24 Thomas Digges' diagram of the extended Copernican cosmos

Digges' *Perfit Description of the Caelestiall Orbes* (1576) praises the "rare wit" of Copernicus, who has showed

that the earth resteth not in the centre of the whole world, but only in the centre of this our mortal world or globe of elements which, environed and enclosed in the moon's orb, and together with the whole globe of mortality, is carried yearly round about the sun, which like a king in the midst of all reigneth and giveth laws of motion to the rest, spherically dispersing his glorious beams of light through all this sacred celestial temple. And the earth itself to be one of the planets, having his peculiar and straying courses turning every twenty-four hours round upon his own centre, whereby the sun and great globe of fixed stars seem to sway about and turn, albeit indeed they remain fixed.

Moreover, Digges presented this Copernican model as no mere saving of the appearances but as a warrantable philosophical (i.e., physically true) system: "Copernicus meant not as some have fondly excused him to deliver the grounds of the earth's mobility only as mathematical principles, feigned and not as philosophical truly averred."[3]

Probably most powerful for the poetic imagination was the Copernican claim that earth is "one of the planets." Classically, the planets were viewed as a class of stars ("wandering stars," from Greek *planetes*). And as Copernicanism unfolded, earth's planetary status – and hence star status – was reinforced not only by heliocentric theory but also by Galileo's *empirical* observations roughly a year after Milton's birth. In his first-ever telescopic examination of the dark side of the moon, Galileo discerned that it is bathed in gentle light reflected from the earth, just as earth reciprocally receives light from the moon. Therefore, contrary to many subsequent science texts and popular histories claiming that Copernicus cosmically demoted the earth, Galileo concluded that earthshine, in combination with earth's literally exalted planetary status, militates against earth's "[exclusion] from the dance of the stars." For earth even "surpasses the moon in brightness, and . . . is not the sump where the universe's filth and ephemera collect."[4]

In this respect Milton – despite the Ptolemaism sometimes attributed to him[5] – is robustly Copernican. In his series of astronomical "what-ifs" in *Paradise Lost*, Raphael clearly implies earth's stellar character:

> What if that light,
> Sent from her [the earth] through the wide transpicuous air,
> To the terrestrial moon be as a star
> Enlight'ning her [the moon] by day, as she by night
> This Earth? Reciprocal . . .
>
> (VIII.140–44)

Even beyond Raphael's hypotheticals, it is apparent in the universe of *Paradise Lost* that earth is a star. At the last stage of his journey to earth, Satan must stop on the sun to ask directions, for earth *qua* planet is not astronomically unique; it is not obvious to a space-traveling observer which of the stars is humankind's habitation, or even if these creatures are confined to a single planet. Satan asks:

In which of all these shining orbs hath man
His fixèd seat, or fixèd seat hath none,
But all these shining orbs his choice to dwell[?]

(III.668–70)

Even if some might doubt Satan's interpretation of his surroundings, Uriel, from his viewpoint on the sun, offers an authoritative response that is thoroughly Copernican, indeed Galilean, in its acknowledgment of earth's star status:

Look downward on that globe whose hither side
With light from hence, though but reflected, shines;
That place is Earth the seat of man, that light
His day, which else as th' other hemisphere
Night would invade, but there the neighboring moon
(So call that opposite fair star) her aid
Timely interposes . . .

(III.722–28)

Galileo was undoubtedly Milton's foremost single astronomical influence; he alone among the poet's contemporaries is mentioned by name in *Paradise Lost*. At some point during his Grand Tour to Italy in 1638 and 1639, Milton met the aging astronomer, then under house arrest. As he wrote in *Areopagitica*, "I found and visited the famous *Galileo* grown old, a prisner to the Inquisition, for thinking in Astronomy otherwise then the Franciscan and Dominican licencers thought" (*CPW* II:538).

Three decades earlier Galileo, already in his mid-forties, had heard reports from the Netherlands of someone constructing what he called a *perspiculum*, or perspective glass, and back-engineered a similar device for his own use. Milton would translate the term quite accurately as "optic glass" or "glazed optic tube" (*Paradise Lost* I.288; III.590). By means of that telescope, as Galileo declared in *Sidereus nuncius* (*Messenger of the Stars*, 1610), "visible objects, although at a great distance from the eye of the observer, [are] seen distinctly as if nearby" (*BOTC* 146).

In this profound little book Galileo set forth four human-consciousness-changing clusters of telescopic discoveries, the first of them touching on the number of the stars. During the two millennia before Galileo, the stars (outside of Hebrew literature) were considered in principle to be countable – in fact, to number roughly 3,000. As Galileo puts it, "To this day the fixed stars which observers have been able to view without artificial powers of sight can be counted. Therefore it is certainly a great thing to add to their number and to expose to our view myriads of other stars never seen before"

(*BOTC* 146). Milton too accepted Galileo's conclusion, at least by the time he wrote *Paradise Lost*, which depicts Satan traveling through space, making "his oblique way / Amongst innumerable stars" (III.564–65).

Galileo's second set of discoveries concerned the moon. Beyond the phenomenon of earthshine, he also observed that the moon has a rough, earth-like surface, and more spots than had been known previously. He subsequently discovered spots on the sun too, a controversial finding because it was taken to imply imperfection in heavenly bodies. "Spot" still occasionally carries the suggestion of blemish (as in a "spot on one's reputation"), an ambiguity Milton happily exploits twice in *Paradise Lost*, both times at Satan's expense. First, Satan's shield

> Hung on his shoulders like the moon, whose orb
> Through optic glass the Tuscan artist views
> At evening from the top of Fesole,
> Or in Valdarno, to descry new lands,
> Rivers or mountains in her spotty globe.
>
> (I.287–91)

And later, when Satan appears on the sun, it is he himself, ironically, who is the blemish:

> a spot like which perhaps
> Astronomer in the sun's lucent orb
> Through his glazed optic tube yet never saw.
>
> (III.588–90)

By means of his lunar discoveries Galileo also offered proof that geometrical dimensions could be applied and calculated in the heavens. Whereas the medieval two-storey universe was divided into two qualitatively different realms, the sublunary and superlunary spheres, Galileo's universe was one in which geometry ("earth measure") applies up there as well as down here. As Copernicus' student Joachim Rheticus wrote some years earlier (echoing the Lord's Prayer), by tracing light and shadows we behold "God's geometry in heaven and on earth."[6] As Galileo's contemporary Johannes Kepler famously declared, "Geometry... shines in the mind of God."[7] It is not surprising, then, that in such an age Milton should imagine Raphael measuring "things in Heav'n by things on Earth," or God himself employing his eternal draftsman's tools – his golden compasses – to shape and "circumscribe / This universe" (*Paradise Lost* VI.893; VII.225–27).

Galileo's third cluster of discoveries pertained to the Milky Way. Observed through the telescope, the milky or cloudy texture of the galaxy could now be resolved into stars: "The stars which absolutely all astronomers until now have called *nebulous* are swarms of small stars astonishingly packed together" (*BOTC* 152). What had been perceived as a semi-opaque plane was thus now recognized as a pattern of points and spaces, or grains and voids. What had seemed a coherent image was now understood to be, as it were, a series of pixels.

The universe accordingly appeared through Galileo's telescope more and more as an array of discrete bits. Little wonder, then, that John Donne should complain that the new science left the world "all in pieces, all coherence gone,"[8] or that those bits, shorn of their beams, deprived of their connective tissue, bereft of their crystalline spheres, should require a new force to hold them all together. And little wonder too that, before a new physical principle (Newton's universal gravitation) was able to reestablish the physical world's coherence, Milton should be thinking about *creatio ex deo* and positing "one first matter" (*Paradise Lost* v.472) that could lend unity to an apparently ever more atomistic and fragmented universe.

Galileo's fourth set of discoveries as recounted in the *Sidereus nuncius* were his observations of the moons of Jupiter. He considered this announcement greater than all the rest, and from a purely Copernican point of view it may well have been. In an unpublished manuscript known as the *Commentariolus*, circulated early in the sixteenth century, Copernicus had presented seven axioms outlining the cosmology he would later expound in *De revolutionibus*, the first of which asserted that "there is no one center of all the celestial circles or spheres."[9] In observing those moons circling about Jupiter, Galileo now had ocular proof of that axiom.

Thus emerged a particular pattern in the history of astronomy. It had been assumed, in keeping with Aristotle's physics, that there was one center in the universe, but Galileo's observations demonstrated that there were at least two. Furthermore, until his time there was thought to be one moon, *the* moon; yet with Galileo's discovery of the Jovian satellites, humans could henceforth speak of *moons*. Other astronomical nouns similarly took on plural forms. Late in the sixteenth century the notorious anti-Aristotelian Giordano Bruno extrapolated (contrary to Copernicus, and not on observational grounds) an infinite universe containing "innumerable suns, and likewise an infinite number of earths circling about those suns."[10] Earth and sun thus acquired plurals. Late in the eighteenth century "galaxy" – a synonym for Milky Way (as its "lactic" etymology suggests) – would likewise begin to acquire a plural form, based on William Herschel's observations of the nebulae. And since the late twentieth century, in the wake of Big Bang cosmology, with its realization that the observable universe is not infinite in space or time, astronomers have also started theorizing about other *universes*, all encompassed within what is now frequently termed the *multiverse*.[11]

Milton took part in such "pluralization" of astronomical categories. Most straightforwardly, Raphael predicts that in future Adam may descry "other suns perhaps / With their attendant moons" (*Paradise Lost* VIII.148–49). But perhaps the most intriguing example of Milton's participation in the pattern is his use of the plural of *world*, which in the seventeenth century could mean either *earth* or *universe* – a cosmos encompassing what biblical language calls collectively "heavens and earth." Milton employs both of these distinct meanings in *Paradise Lost*; and in his hands, both appear in ways that are cosmologically adventuresome – so much so that seventeenth-century astronomical vocabulary is hardly adequate to describe what he depicts.

This is especially true with respect to cosmological questions of *size*. One should start by laying aside the modern suspicion that the pre-Copernican universe was somehow cozy and small. Ptolemy himself claimed that the earth "has the ratio of a point to the heavens." His universe, therefore, was immense – literally *immeasurable*. Ptolemy observed that, no matter how accurately one measured, the horizon (by definition not at the center of the earth) always seemed to bisect the sphere of the fixed stars, which would imply that it *was* at the center. This phenomenon would not occur, he reasoned, "if the earth were of perceptible size in relation to the distance of the heavenly bodies."[12]

Yet Copernicus' universe, with the sun rather than the earth at its center, had to be many orders of magnitude larger than Ptolemy's. For Copernicus realized with astonishment that earth's "orb of annual motion" is also "as a point in respect of the immensity of that immovable heaven."[13] Despite this multiplied immensity, however, Copernicus never said that the universe was "without end." Writers like Digges and Milton, nonetheless, saw that the new cosmology might lead in that direction.

It is here that ordinary astronomical vocabulary evinces signs of strain. What do we mean when we speak of Milton's cosmos? The universe containing the sun, the earth, and all the other stars is – in *Paradise Lost* – large but finite, like the universes of Ptolemy and Copernicus. In fact it is enclosed, accessible only through a hatch that opens at the bottom of a retractable staircase hanging down from the empyreal Heaven. But in this enclosed sense, the cosmos is decidedly not "all that is or ever was or ever will be."[14] For outside of it are God's heaven, and hell, and chaos. And with due caution against the dangers of anachronism, we might not find a better term for that totality than Milton's *multiverse*.

What is not anachronistic about this usage is that Milton presents his multiverse as dynamic, a potential nursery of universes, one that may even be read atheistically, as in Satan's informed if oblique conjecture that "Space may produce new worlds" (1.650) – "worlds" in this case meaning universes. Milton uses the term in the same way and context, though of course theistically, when he describes the primordial materials of chaos, which "must ever fight, / Unless th' Almighty Maker them ordain / His dark materials to create more worlds" (11.914–16).

Moreover, Milton carefully establishes the immense disproportion between the size of his multiverse and the size of our universe. Whereas for Copernicus and Digges the circle of earth's orbit is reduced proportionately to the infinitesimal dimensions of a point in relation to the immensity of the sphere of the fixed stars, Milton applies the same maneuver, but on a hugely larger scale, to the whole sidereal universe. Following Satan's trajectory across chaos, we catch our first glimpse (within the narrative *Paradise Lost*) of our own universe. Indeed, we see it through Satan's eyes – and it appears very small. Even Heaven, despite its genuinely great magnitude, appears (because of its distance) small enough that Satan cannot discern its shape. He beholds

> Far off th' empyreal Heav'n, extended wide
> In circuit, undetermined square or round,
> With opal tow'rs and battlements adorned
> Of living sapphire, once his native seat;
> And fast by hanging in a golden chain
> This pendent world, in bigness as a star
> Of smallest magnitude close by the moon.
>
> (11.1047–53)

"Smallest magnitude" is a technical term – an astronomer would say "sixth magnitude" – for the tiniest star visible to the naked eye. To Satan still out in chaos, our whole cosmos thus appears as a barely discernible speck of light – a mere point within the boundless ocean of Milton's multiverse.

Of course once we are inside that cosmos and returned to earth, the universe that Satan perceived as almost infinitesimally small appears to Adam in Eden as immensely large in contrast to the "punctual" earth. As Adam tells Raphael:

When I behold this goodly frame, this world
Of heav'n and Earth consisting, and compute
Their magnitudes, this Earth a spot, a grain,
An atom, with the firmament compared
And all her numbered stars, that seem to roll
Spaces incomprehensible (for such
Their distance argues and their swift return
Diurnal) merely to officiate light
Round this opacous Earth, this punctual spot,
One day and night; in all their vast survey
Useless besides, reasoning I oft admire,
How nature wise and frugal could commit
Such disproportions, with superfluous hand
So many nobler bodies to create,
Greater so manifold to this one use,
For aught appears, and on their orbs impose
Such restless revolution day by day
Repeated, while the sedentary Earth,
That better might with far less compass move,
Served by more noble than herself, attains
Her end without least motion, and receives,
As tribute such a sumless journey brought
Of incorporeal speed, her warmth and light;
Speed, to describe whose swiftness number fails.

(VIII.15–38)

The reasons Adam gives for being puzzled echo those that Copernicus adduced against Ptolemy, whose view entailed the fixed stars' attaining what Adam calls "incorporeal speed." In this way Milton's geocentrist Adam articulates astronomical difficulties that, among others, would lead to the adoption of heliocentrism and a theory of the moving earth.

A further astronomically exciting feature of Milton's creation combines space flight and the question of extraterrestrial life. Again, Satan serves as prime vehicle for exploring the nature of the physical cosmos, which (as just mentioned) has appeared to him, out in the multiverse, as "[t]his pendent world" (II.1052).

Two features of the new, post-Copernican astronomy bore directly on the question of space flight. Robert Burton brilliantly summed up the new possibilities in his *Anatomy of Melancholy* (1638). Everyone, from Tycho to Bruno, is of "the selfsame opinion about the essence and matter of the heavens: that it is not hard and impenetrable, as Peripatetics [i.e., Aristotelians] hold . . . 'but that it is penetrable and soft as the air itself is.'" By the seventeenth century, the crystalline spheres had melted away, and from the absence of such cosmic glass ceilings Burton drew the inference that is the *sine qua non* of space flight: "If the heavens then be penetrable, as these men deliver, and no lets, it were not amiss in this aerial progress to make wings and fly up."[15]

Once the space-traveling Satan has gained access to our universe through its outer rind – the only thing in Milton's cosmos comparable to a hard crystalline sphere, a "firm opacous globe" (III.418) – he finds that the heavens are indeed penetrable:

> Down right into the world's first region [he] throws
> His flight precipitant, and winds with ease
> Through the pure marble air his oblique way.
>
> (III.562–64)

Satan accordingly bends his course "Through the calm firmament" (574), and the latter term apparently retains no lingering connotation of firmness. Moreover, by saying in the same context that Satan makes his way "[a]mongst innumerable stars" (565) Milton distances himself from the old view that the "fixed stars" were embedded in and borne along by a single great orb. Indeed, it is this lack of any solid means of stellar and/or planetary conveyance that called for some other physical hypothesis concerning their locomotion. The one that Milton chose appears closely analogous to one offered by Kepler, according to which the wandering stars "are turned / By [the sun's] magnetic beams" (582–83).[16]

Satan's space flight, like his exploration of the new world generally, can be read as the devilish embodiment of actual human aspirations articulated widely and respectably in the seventeenth century. As John Wilkins wrote in his *Discovery of a World in the Moon* (1638), "True indeed, I cannot conceive any possible means for . . . sailing to the moon . . . We have not now any Drake or Columbus to undertake this voyage, or any Daedalus to invent a conveyance through the air. However, I doubt not but that time . . . will also manifest to our posterity that which we now desire but cannot know."[17] Wilkins' extrapolations about extraterrestrial "worlds" and their inhabitants typifies much imaginative speculation that flowed from the scientific work of men such as Copernicus and Galileo. For, once the earth was seen as a planet, it was but a short step to thinking of the moon and planets as other earths.

Furthermore, *Paradise Lost* intriguingly adumbrates the possibility that those other worlds, if not inhabited yet, someday may be, even perhaps by Adam and Eve's offspring. The heavenly chorus, celebrating the "new-made world" (i.e., universe), speculates that "every star [is] perhaps a world / Of destined habitation" (VII.617, 621–22). The movement of various extraterrestrials about this created universe certainly enhances the plausibility of space travel by humans, especially if they remain sinless. And the unfallen scenario sketched by Raphael – of humans literally taking wings and ascending angel-like, with choice of earthly or heavenly dwelling places (V.496–500) – indicates that the sort of aerospace exemplified by Satan and the unfallen angels who visit Paradise had real potential to be a growth sector in an unfallen economy.[18]

Finally, what most deeply intrigued Milton about the size and structure of the physical universe was its bearing on divine and human meaning; he reflected creatively, even audaciously, on the significance of the new cosmology. Particularly regarding the size of the cosmos, he struck a quite felicitous balance. From the seventeenth century to the present, often scientists or popularizers of science have taken a grim (and oddly self-congratulatory) pleasure in explaining how insignificant our tiny earth and its inhabitants are within the cosmos as a whole. And of course cultivating humility can be a good thing. But Milton knew that a true assessment of the cosmic significance of earth must flow from a finer analysis than one that shallowly considers magnitudes only. He makes clear, through Raphael, that

> great
> Or bright infers not excellence: the Earth
> Though, in comparison of heav'n, so small,
> Nor glistering, may of solid good contain
> More plenty than the sun.
>
> (VIII.90–94)

Yet in emphasizing the value of earth and what takes place there, Milton does not occlude the lessons in humility afforded by astronomical reflections on earth's small size. Raphael goes on to indicate that there may be much else going on in the universe – and *a fortiori* in the multiverse – than humans know about, and that a degree of modesty, as well as piety, might be a fitting response to this recognition:

> And for the heav'n's wide circuit, let it speak
> The Maker's high magnificence, who built
> So spacious, and his line stretched out so far;
> That man may know he dwells not in his own;
> An edifice too large for him to fill,
> Lodged in a small partition, and the rest
> Ordained for uses to his Lord best known.
>
> (VIII.100–06)

Our edifice, for all its magnificence, reflecting that of the Builder, turns out indeed to be a "small partition."

Thus Milton's engagement with astronomy leads him and his readers outward, even beyond the greatly expanded Copernican cosmos that his age struggled to comprehend. His was a universe, according to *Paradise Lost*, abounding in manifold kinds of potentiality, beauty, excellence, and "solid good" – great things that yet can be loved and enjoyed by the tiny, at once privileged and humble, inhabitants of this particular exquisite wandering star.

NOTES

1 Tycho Brahe, *De nova stella*, trans. John H. Walden, in *A Source Book in Astronomy*, ed. Harlow Shapley and Helen E. Howarth (New York, 1929), 13.

2 Annie Jump Cannon, *The Universe of Stars*, ed. Harlow Shapley and Cecilia H. Payne, 2nd edn. (Cambridge, MA, 1929), 136.

3 Thomas Digges, *A Perfit Description of the Caelestiall Orbes* (London, 1576), sig. M1r–M2v; quoted from *The Book of the Cosmos: Imagining the Universe from Heraclitus to Hawking*, ed. Dennis Danielson (Cambridge, MA, 2000), 133. All subsequent references to this anthology are abbreviated *BOTC*.

4 Galileo Galilei, *Sidereus nuncius* (Venice, 1610); quoted from *BOTC* 149–50. All subsequent references to Galileo's text are from this edition and appear parenthetically within the chapter. On Copernicus' supposed "dethroning" of earth, see Dennis Danielson, "The Great Copernican Cliché," *American Journal of Physics* 69 (2001): 1029–35.

5 See, typically, *The Riverside Milton*, ed. Roy Flannagan (Boston, 1998), 325: Milton "makes the universe of *Paradise Lost* that of Galileo's Ptolemaic forebears, and Milton's cosmology is generally geocentric."

6 See Dennis Danielson, *The First Copernican: Georg Joachim Rheticus and the Rise of the Copernican Revolution* (New York, 2006), ch. 6; and Samuel Y. Edgerton, Jr., *The Heritage of Giotto's Geometry: Art and Science on the Eve of the Scientific Revolution* (Ithaca, NY, 1991), 223–53.

7 *Kepler's Conversation with Galileo's Sidereal Messenger*, trans. Edward Rosen (New York and London, 1965), 43.

8 *An Anatomy of the World: The First Anniversary*, line 213; John Donne, *The Complete English Poems*, ed. A. J. Smith (Harmondsworth, 1971), 276.

9 See Danielson, *The First Copernican*, 60–64.

10 Giordano Bruno, *De l'infinito universo et Mondi*, 1584; reprinted in *Le opere italiane di Giordano Bruno* (Göttingen, 1888). Quoted from *BOTC* 144.

11 See Bernard Carr, ed., *Universe or Multiverse?* (Cambridge, 2007).

12 Claudius Ptolemy, *Almagest*, trans. G. J. Toomer (New York, 1984), 43.

13 I quote Digges' eloquent version of Copernicus, *BOTC* 137. In book 1, chapter 10 of *De revolutionibus*, Copernicus writes that "the fixed stars ... are

immensely distant, for which reason even the motion of the annual revolution, or the appearance thereof, vanishes from sight" (*BOTC* 117).

14 Carl Sagan's famous formulation: *Cosmos* (New York, 1980), 4.

15 Robert Burton, *The Anatomy of Melancholy*, ed. Holbrook Jackson (New York, 1977), Part 2, 50.

16 See Anita Lawson, " 'The Golden Sun in Splendor Likest Heaven': Johannes Kepler's *Epitome* and *Paradise Lost*, Book 3," *Milton Quarterly* 21 (1987): 46–51.

17 John Wilkins, *The Discovery of a World in the Moon: or, A Discourse tending to prove that 'tis probable there may be another habitable World in that Planet* (London, 1638); quoted from *BOTC* 190.

18 For more historical materials on the "plurality of worlds," see *The Extraterrestrial Life Debate, Antiquity to 1915: A Source Book*, ed. Michael J. Crowe (South Bend, IN, 2008).

CHAPTER 18

The book trade

Stephen B. Dobranski

Authors during the seventeenth century had relatively little legal author-ity within the English book trade. The business of producing, selling, and binding printed matter was controlled by the Company of Station-ers, which the crown had chartered in 1557 to prevent the publication of "certain seditious and heretical books . . . moving our subjects and lieges to sedition and disobedience."[1] According to this system of regulation, any text that someone wished to have printed had to be licensed by a government-appointed official, then approved a second time by a member of the Stationers' Company, who, for a fee, officially entered its title and owner's name in the Company's *Register*. The law emphasized ownership, not authorship. Prior to the first copyright act in 1709, a member of the Sta-tioners' Company who obtained a copy of a work did not need to seek the author's permission but could secure legal ownership merely by publishing the book in print or paying the fee and having it officially registered.[2] The one acknowledgment that survives of a writer having rights during this period is a brief stipulation that a person who legally owned a book had to inform the author before having the book reprinted.[3]

It was in response to this system that Milton in November 1644 wrote *Areopagitica*. While not directly calling for authors' increased authority, Milton opposed the intrusive regulations favored by the Stationers and characteristic of Tudor and Stuart press laws. Rather than sanctioning a select group of agents – whether licensers or Stationers – to oversee the book trade, Milton in *Areopagitica* advocates a social process of sharing knowledge that included authors, printers, and readers. He anticipates the central role that the printing press would come to play and allies its unfettered operation "with truth, with learning, and the Commonwealth" (*CPW* II:488). As he recalled his motive ten years later, he was attempting in *Areopagitica* to show "that the judgment of truth and falsehood, what should be printed and what suppressed, ought not to be in the hands of a few men (and these mostly ignorant and of vulgar discernment) . . . at whose will or whim virtually everyone is prevented from publishing aught that surpasses the understanding of the mob" (*CPW* iv:626).

But if Milton in opposing pre-publication licensing ultimately crafted a landmark argument against censorship, he also wrote *Areopagitica* for personal reasons, at least in part in response to critics such as the Presbyterian divine Herbert Palmer. Three months earlier, on August 13, 1644, Palmer had delivered a sermon against toleration before both houses of parliament and cited the "impudent" author of a "wicked booke" about divorce "deserving to be burnt."[4] When later that same month the Stationers' Company submitted a petition to the House of Commons complaining about recent unlicensed and unregistered books, including Milton's divorce tracts, the House of Commons responded by ordering the Committee for Printing to prepare an ordinance and "diligently to inquire out the Authors, Printers, and Publishers, of the Pamphlet against the Immortality of the Soul, and concerning Divorce."[5]

Both the Stationers' petition and the parliament's order also composed part of a broader strategy by which the Company and government were attempting to re-establish control of the book trade. For three years following the assembly of the Long Parliament in 1640, printing in England had experienced a period of diminished regulation. The elimination of the Courts of Star Chamber and High Commission in July 1641 had resulted in "great . . . abuses and frequent disorders in Printing"; without the threat of royal prosecution, printers were virtually free to print whatever they wished, and the quantity of English publications consequently ballooned.[6]

Parliament and the Company responded to the outpouring of printed material by passing the Licensing Order of 1643. Intended to protect the government from misrepresentation while curtailing pirated and seditious pamphlets and books, the new law revived key provisions from the Star Chamber's 1637 Decree Concerning Printing. Parliament assumed the position formerly held by the king; Presbyterian censors replaced royalist, Episcopal licensers; and the master and wardens of the Stationers' Company were once again authorized to apprehend anyone who helped to produce or circulate scandalous or unlicensed works and to search and seize printing presses used to produce such publications. The 1643 law omitted references to corporal punishment, which had been an important part of previous legislation under Charles I, but the new government was still casting a wide net: as with the 1637 decree, parliament's ordinance applied to everyone who participated in the material process of printing, "all Authors, Printers, and other persons whatsoever imployed in compiling, printing, stitching, binding, publishing, and dispersing of the said scandalous, unlicensed, and unwarrantable Papers, Books, and Pamphlets."[7]

Yet, if the 1643 ordinance and much of the period's legislation regarding the book trade seem repressive by our present standards, the extent of the government's actual regulatory practices remains more difficult to measure. During the Tudor and Stuart reigns and under the Long Parliament, the licensing system appears not to have been strictly enforced. The government tried to prosecute anyone who repeatedly published unlawful works, or, as in Milton's case with his divorce tracts, anyone who took egregiously controversial positions or whose works elicited official complaints. But the quantity of manuscripts that the government's licensers would have been expected to examine must have necessitated in practice no more than a cursory review of some tracts; as Milton observes in *Areopagitica*, "there cannot be a more tedious and unpleasing journey-work, a greater losse of time... then to be made the perpetuall reader of unchosen books and pamphlets, oftimes huge volumes" (*CPW* ii:530).

And what was to prevent an enterprising author from first obtaining a license for a work and then slyly inserting a controversial passage without the licenser's knowledge? Or, as Milton did with his unlicensed *Areopagitica*, simply ignoring the law altogether? That in 1644, the year *Areopagitica* was printed, only 20 percent of the published books and pamphlets were registered suggests that in many cases writers did not bother to obtain official approval.[8] The owner of a work who knew that it contained nothing unlawful had little motive to acquire a license, and, conversely, the owner of a work who knew that it would be found subversive had good reason for trying to circumvent the licenser. Presumably, the mere existence of pre-publication licensing discouraged some writers from even attempting to take controversial works to press, but we cannot know how often such self-censorship occurred nor with what frequency licensers redacted or expunged passages they deemed unacceptable from works that they then approved. In this latter regard, the licenser of *Paradise Lost* reportedly raised various "frivolous Exceptions" about the epic's language, and, according to one of Milton's seventeenth-century biographers, almost prevented the poem's publication because of a passage describing how the newly risen sun casts a shadowy "twilight" that "Perplexes monarchs" (1.594–99).[9]

Milton's argument in *Areopagitica* addresses both the effrontery of such interference and the impracticality of the government's policy. Even if an author were not trying to skirt the law, it was inconvenient, Milton notes, for the author to seek approval for every late revision: "what if the author shall be one so copious of fancie, as to have many things well worth the adding, come into his mind after licensing, while the book is yet under the Presse" (*CPW* II:532)? But, even as Milton in *Areopagitica* eloquently argues that books should be "freely permitted . . . both to the triall of vertue, and the exercise of truth" (II:528), he also stipulates that post-publication regulation is sometimes necessary. For books "found mischievous and libellous," he writes, "the executioner will be the timeliest and most effectuall remedy" (II:569). He specifically endorses censoring books about Catholicism, "open superstition," and "that also which is impious or evil absolutely either against faith or maners" because, he reasons, any such book "extirpats all religions and civill supremacies" (II:565). In other words, Milton accepted the suppression of those works which would, in his mind, attempt to undo the principle of toleration on which *Areopagitica* was based.

The qualified nature of Milton's argument against censorship in *Areopagitica* may help to explain how five years after its publication he agreed to work as a government licenser. As Secretary for Foreign Languages under the Commonwealth, Milton licensed one of the government's newsbooks, *Mercurius Politicus*, and was called upon to investigate the papers of various suspicious people, some of them printers and publishers. His apparent change in thinking may have stemmed from the new political circumstances of 1649: when he wrote *Areopagitica*, he could not have imagined that within five years the king would be tried and executed and a Council of State would rule in place of the monarch. We also need to remember that Milton's opposition to pre-publication licensing in 1644 probably grew out of that earlier political climate. Presbyterians striving to consolidate their power within parliament had the most to gain from the Licensing Order of 1643, and Milton may have advocated less regulation for the book trade as an attempt to give voice to opponents of Presbyterianism and thus thwart Presbyterian calls for a settlement with Charles I.[10]

Still, we ought not soft-peddle or downplay Milton's apparent inconsistency. Given that in *Areopagitica* he had roundly criticized pre-publication licensing – he dismissively characterizes all future licensers as "ignorant, imperious, and remisse, or basely pecuniary" (*CPW* II:530) – Milton while Secretary for Foreign Languages was contradicting the spirit if not the letter of his earlier tract. According to the Council of State's Order Books, Milton prepared only seven letters and wrote two translations during his first year in office; for the most part, he oversaw and negotiated with members of the book trade.[11] We also know that Milton licensed more than the newsbook *Mercurius Politicus*: on December 16, 1649 an entry appears in the Stationers' *Register* "under the hand of Master Milton" for the *Histoire entiere et veritable du Proces de Charles Stuart Roy d'Anglitere &c*, and on October 6, 1651 another entry "under the hand of Master Milton" registers a copy of Samuel Pecke's newsbook, *The Perfect Diurnall*.[12]

Probably the most provocative instance of Milton's involvement with members of the book trade while working for the government concerns the publication and suppression of *Catechesis Ecclesiarum quae in Regno Poloniae*, commonly known as *The Racovian Catechism*. On January 27, 1652, the Council of State issued a warrant for the arrest of the printer William Dugard and the seizure of this heretical, Socinian tract.[13] Among the documents examined by the House of Commons' special committee was "a Note under the Hand of Mr. *John Milton*" dated August 10, 1650, and on April 2, 1652 the committee questioned Milton along with Henry Walley, Clerk of the Stationers' Company, and Francis Gouldman, an editor and lexicographer.[14]

According to the Dutch ambassador Liewe van Aitzema, Milton licensed the catechism. Shortly after arriving in England, van Aitzema was told that Milton had approved ("*hadde gelicentieert*") the work's publication, and he goes on to record in his journal that, when questioned, Milton explained, "Yes, and that he had published a tract on that subject, that men should refrain from forbidding books; that in approving of that book he had done no more than what his opinion was."[15] While such an account of Milton's toleration does not entirely accord with his other censorial duties as secretary, certainly he would have approved of the catechism's heretical rejection of the trinity. Milton, though no Socinian, demonstrates his belief in *Paradise Lost* and *De Doctrina Christiana* that the Son was not co-eternal with God, and years later in *Of True Religion* he would not only include Socinians among a list of sects he calls "no Hereticks" (*CPW* VIII:423) but also imply that Anabaptist, Arian, Arminian, and Socinian books should be freely "sold & read as common as our own" (VIII:437).

Most likely, the Council of State often called on Milton to help oversee the book trade as part of his duties as secretary because by 1649 he had so much firsthand experience with printers and booksellers. Milton had already published twelve prose works, and his poetry had appeared in nine collections, including his own 1645 *Poems*. Soon after Milton accepted his appointment with the new government his life-long friend Matthew Simmons became a printer for the Council of State.[16] And that the Council also worked with the printer Thomas Newcomb may similarly reveal Milton's influence: in 1648 Newcomb had married Ruth Raworth, the printer of Milton's *Poems*, and he printed seven of Milton's prose tracts between 1650 and 1660, in addition to printing Walter Raleigh's *The Cabinet-Council* in 1658 when Milton came across the manuscript among his papers and decided to finance its publication.

We can also trace Milton's familiarity with the book trade to his early years growing up in London. Most of the city's bookshops during the sixteenth and seventeenth centuries lined Paul's Cross Churchyard, roughly 600 feet from Milton's boyhood home in Bread Street. In late 1620 when Milton began attending St. Paul's School, he would have walked daily past crowds of printers' and booksellers' shops as he made his way back and forth to the east end of St. Paul's Cathedral. While we cannot pinpoint Milton's earliest working relationship with members of the book trade, he enclosed some printed verses, now lost, in a letter to Alexander Gil from 1628 or 1631, and the publication of Milton's "On Shakespeare" in 1632 in the second folio of Shakespeare's works may indicate that, beginning in his twenties, Milton and his poems were known by some Stationers.

Over the course of his career, Milton would work with more than ten different printing houses and more than twenty booksellers, including Humphrey Robinson and Humphrey Moseley, two of the most prominent and influential literary publishers of the period. The number of Milton's collaborations with Stationers suggests how thoroughly he was engaged with London's publishing community and how widely his works circulated. Even when Milton lived with his parents in the suburbs of Hammersmith and Horton, he maintained connections with members of the book trade; in a letter to Gil dated December 4, 1634, for example, Milton tells his former teacher to "expect me on Monday in London (God willing) among the Booksellers" (*CPW* 1:322). Later in life, Milton also continued to develop lasting friendships with Stationers. In addition to his long friendship with Matthew Simmons and his family, Milton reportedly lived for a period in 1669 or 1670 with the bookseller Edward Millington in Little Britain, another of London's centers for bookshops, and, in a letter to Carlo Dati dated April 21, 1647, Milton refers to "James, the bookseller" and "his master, a most familiar acquaintance of mine" (*CPW* 11:765). Milton also seems to have befriended George Thomason, an influential collector and bookseller. Thomason owned autographed copies of Milton's publications, and Milton wrote Sonnet 14 about the death of Thomason's wife Catherine, a book lover herself who amassed an impressive library.

We ought not assume, however, that Milton's friendships enabled him to control his works' printing. If writers during the seventeenth century had almost no legal rights, they also typically had limited influence over their books' design. In *Mechanick Exercises of the Whole Art of Printing* (1683–84), Joseph Moxon attributes little practical authority to writers during the process of material production.[17] In addition to choosing a book's format and determining the layout, a compositor might follow house styles over a writer's preferences in some places or justify lines of type by creating contractions that unintentionally influenced a work's meaning.

Milton's books in general reflect such a collaborative process. While some of his printed texts retain some of his personal preferences – the 1667 and 1674 editions of *Paradise Lost*, for example, mostly respect Milton's idiosyncratic spelling of "their" as "thir"[18] – Milton, even if he had wished, could not have controlled every aspect of his works' printing: after he went blind in 1652, he would have had to rely on amanuenses to compose his works and on agents to oversee the publication. Thus, a comparison of the surviving manuscript of *Paradise Lost*, book 1, with the same text in the first printed edition of 1667 reveals that members of the printing house made more than 1,000 changes in spelling and roughly 133 changes in punctuation, all apparently attempts to normalize, albeit inconsistently, Milton's manuscript.[19]

I do not mean to suggest, however, that Milton entirely ignored his books' minor details. Milton's nephew Edward Phillips recalls visiting his uncle "for some years" during the composition of *Paradise Lost* and perusing the manuscript "in a Parcel of Ten, Twenty, or Thirty Verses at a Time, which being Written by whatever hand came next; might possibly want Correction as to the Orthography and Pointing."[20] Phillips here suggests that before Milton handed over his manuscript to the printer he understood spelling and punctuation as having a correct form, even if he did not take pains to see these details carried through in his works' published versions. We also know that Milton cared enough about his books' physical appearance to compose a Greek epigraph expressing his disapproval of William Marshall's frontispiece portrait in his 1645 *Poems*. And while members of the printing house would have designed the title pages for all of Milton's books and determined, for example, how or even if the author's name would be used to attract potential buyers, presumably Milton himself provided the quotations that adorn some of his texts.

That some surviving copies of Milton's seventeenth-century publications contain apparently authorial, handwritten corrections also indicates that he cared about but could not entirely control some of his works' minor details. In a copy of *Areopagitica* at the Harry Ransom Humanities Research Center, "wayfaring Christian" has been corrected to "warfaring Christian" with one of Milton's characteristic Rs, and the Ransom Center's copy of *A Mask Presented at Ludlow Castle* has four manuscript changes that look authorial: "my" has been corrected to "by" (line 20), "at" has been corrected to "art" (line 131), "you" has been inserted between "meane" and "that" (line 417), and "reproachfull" has been replaced with "contemptuous" (line 781).[21]

This final, substantive, handwritten revision suggests that Milton did not understand publication as the final step in the creation of a text. He not only published revised and expanded versions of his prose works – *The Doctrine and Discipline of Divorce* (1643, 1644), *The Tenure of Kings and Magistrates* (1649, 1650), *Eikonoklastes* (1649, 1650), *Pro Populo Anglicano Defensio* (1651, 1658), and *The Readie and Easie Way to Establish a Free Commonwealth* (February and April 1660) – but he also continued polishing some of his poems after they were printed. In addition to changing "reproachfull" to "contemptuous" in *A Mask*, Milton revised individual words in "On Shakespeare" between 1632 and 1645; added a headnote to *Lycidas* between 1638 and 1645; fine-tuned two lines in "On the Morning of Christ's Nativity" between 1645 and 1673; and, during the same period, incorporated four additional, slight adjustments in *A Mask*.

Milton also worked with Samuel Simmons to continue improving *Paradise Lost* after its first printing. In a re-issue of the poem's first edition, he added a defense of his verse and the arguments that summarize each book. Then, for the second edition, he restructured the epic from ten to twelve books, added eight lines (VIII.1–3; XII.1–5), revised one line (VIII.4), and appears to have made at least four other substantive revisions (I.504–5, V.636–41, XI.485, XI.551).[22] As with Milton's other texts, *Paradise Lost* reflects a collaborative process of creation. According to a note in the re-issue of the first edition, the printer/publisher Simmons and the book's earliest readers influenced the meaning of Milton's original work. As Simmons explains, "There was no Argument at first intended to the Book, but for the satisfaction of many that have desired it, I have procur'd it, and withal a reason of that which stumbled many others, why the Poem Rimes not."[23]

Perhaps in part because of Simmons' efforts, *Paradise Lost* seems to have sold fairly well: the first edition sold at least 1,300 copies within 17 months, and during this same period Milton may have personally given away an additional 200 complimentary copies. We can infer the book's success from Simmons and Milton's contract in which the Stationer agreed to pay the author £5 up front to publish the poem and an additional £5 at the end of the first three editions.[24] Some scholars have underestimated how quickly *Paradise Lost*'s first edition sold out by assuming that Simmons published Milton's poem in late August 1667, shortly after entering it in the Stationers' *Register*. But even if Simmons began working on the book on April 27, 1667, the day he and Milton signed their contract, and if he worked at the typical rate of a seventeenth-century printer and completed an average of one and a half sheets each week,[25] Simmons would have finished the 43 sheets that compose *Paradise Lost* some time in the middle of November. Apparently all these copies of the first edition had then sold by April 26, 1669, the day on which, in keeping with the terms of their original agreement, Simmons paid Milton £5 for the second edition.[26]

Because Milton received so little money up front for writing *Paradise Lost*, Karl Marx cited the epic's contract to illustrate his notion of "unproductive labour."[27] But Milton and Simmons' agreement is instead notable for treating Milton as the work's owner. Rather than assume the publisher's perpetual right to print Milton's poem, the contract requires that Simmons pay the poet for the epic's subsequent editions. Few English authors were compensated for their works according to such generous terms during the first half of the seventeenth century.[28] Again, there were no laws upholding an author's claims against the rights of a Stationer, and printers and booksellers probably paid authors only when it suited their own interests. With the demise of patronage and the rise of a market system, the economics of printing would have been dictated by the type of book and the number of sales a book's owner could anticipate.

Milton and Simmons' contract for *Paradise Lost* – the earliest surviving formal agreement of its kind in England – thus represents a significant advance in the development of authors' rights during the early modern period. This chapter began by emphasizing how writers had little legal authority within the English book trade, but, with the increased name recognition that came with print publication, they were gradually gaining new power. Looking at Milton's career in the context of seventeenth-century publishing reminds us that even the greatest poets require, as Satan puts it in *Paradise Lost*, "the work / Of secondary hands" (v.853–54). But Milton also represents an important figure within book trade history because his career helps to document the early modern author's emerging status – legally, economically, and symbolically. While more than half of the items published in the 1600s were anonymous, the originality and value of a printed work came to be predicated on the existence of a visible writer. Printers began to include authors' portraits in some books, and some title pages advertised books as the creation of a particular person. In the case of Milton's prose, his first three pamphlets were published anonymously, but the title page of the fourth, *The Reason of Church-Government*, reads, "By Mr. *John Milton*," presumably because the publisher John Rothwell thought Milton's name would appeal to – or at least not dissuade – prospective customers.

With Milton's poetry, his initials first appear in print at the end of *Lycidas* in the 1638 collection *Justa Edouardo King*, and his full name is first printed on the title page of his 1645 collection, *Poems of Mr. John Milton*. Interestingly, at a time when portraits in books most often served as memorials to deceased authors, this collection is one of four texts published during Milton's lifetime that begins with his portrait on the frontispiece; the others are *The History of Britain*, *Artis Logicæ*, and some copies of *Paradise Lost*'s second edition. While all these texts contributed to Milton's contemporary reputation, the 1645 *Poems* emphasized his authorial presence more than any of his other publications. Announcing on the title page, "*Printed by his true Copies*," the book then enhances this sense of authenticity by including various commendatory notices from Milton's friends and acquaintances and by framing seventeen poems with brief, biographical notes, explaining the poet's age when he wrote a specific work or the circumstance of its composition.[29] With the 1645 *Poems* – not for the last time during Milton's career – members of the book trade were helping to create and preserve his works and, in the process, they were helping to construct the Author John Milton.

NOTES

1 *A Transcript of the Registers of the Company of Stationers of London, 1554–1640 A. D.*, ed. Edward Arber, 5 vols. (London, 1875–94), I:xxviii.
2 Stephen B. Dobranski, *Milton, Authorship, and the Book Trade* (Cambridge, 1999), 14–26.
3 *A Transcript of the Registers of the Company of Stationers*, IV:421.
4 Herbert Palmer, *The Glasse of Gods Providence towards His Faithfull Ones* (London, 1644), I1r.
5 *Journal of the House of Commons: Volume 3: 1643–1644* (London, 1802), 606.
6 "An Ordinance for the Regulating of Printing [14 June 1643]," in *Acts and Ordinances of the Interregnum, 1642–1660*, ed. C. H. Firth and R. S. Rait, 3 vols. (London, 1911), 1:184. For statistics about the escalating production of printed texts, see N. H. Keeble's chapter in this volume.
7 "An Ordinance for the Regulating of Printing," 1:185.
8 This statistic is taken from D. F. McKenzie, "The London Book Trade in 1644," in McKenzie, *Making Meaning: "Printers of the Mind" and Other Essays*, ed. Peter D. McDonald and Michael F. Suarez (Amherst, MA, 2002), 131.
9 John Toland, "The Life of John Milton [1698]," in *EL* 180.
10 William Walwyn, *The Compassionate Samaritane* [1644], in *The Writings of William Walwyn*, ed. Jack R. McMichael and Barbara Taft (Athens, GA, 1989), 112–13; and see Dobranski, "Licensing Milton's Heresy," *Milton and Heresy*, ed. Stephen B. Dobranski and John P. Rumrich (Cambridge, 1998), 139–58.

11 See, for example, the *Calendar of State Papers, Domestic Series*, 13 vols., ed. Mary Anne Everett Green (London, 1874–86), 1:474; IV:338.

12 *A Transcript of the Registers of the Worshipful Company of Stationers, from 1640–1708 A.D.*, 3 vols. (1913–15; Gloucester, MA, 1967), 1:333, 380.

13 *Calendar of State Papers, Domestic Series*, IV: 550.

14 *Journal of the House of Commons: Volume 7: 1651–1660* (London, 1802), 113–14.

15 *LR* III:206.

16 See Dobranski, *Milton, Authorship, and the Book Trade*, 105–06.

17 Joseph Moxon, *Mechanick Exercises of the Whole Art of Printing (1683–4)*, ed. Herbert Davies and Harry Carter, 2nd edn. (London, 1962), 192.

18 John T. Shawcross, "Orthography and the Text of *Paradise Lost*," in *Language and Style in Milton*, ed. Ronald David Emma and John T. Shawcross (New York, 1967), 120–53.

19 See Helen Darbishire, ed., *The Manuscript of Milton's "Paradise Lost," Book I* (Oxford, 1931), xxiii–xxxvii; and Mindele Treip, *Milton's Punctuation and Changing English Usage, 1582–1676* (London, 1970), 150–52.

20 *EL* 73.

21 John Milton, *Areopagitica* (London, 1644; shelfmark Pforz 707), B3v; and *A Mask Presented at Ludlow Castle* (London, 1637; shelfmark Pforz 714), B1v, B3r, C4r, E2r.

22 R. G. Moyles, *The Text of "Paradise Lost": A Study in Editorial Procedure* (Toronto, 1985), 21–28. Another approximately thirty-seven, comparatively minor, changes made between the first and second editions may or may not be authorial.

23 John Milton, *Paradise Lost* (London, 1667), $^{\pi}$A2r.

24 The contract is transcribed in *LR* IV:429–31.

25 D. F. McKenzie, "Printers of the Mind: Some Notes on Bibliographical Theories and Printing-House Practices," *Studies in Bibliography* 22 (1969): 1–76.

26 *LR* IV:448.

27 Karl Marx, *Capital: A Critique of Political Economy*, vol. 1, trans. Ben Fowkes (London, 1990), 1044.

28 See Stephen B. Dobranski, *Readers and Authorship in Early Modern England* (Cambridge, 2005), 7.

29 *Poems of Mr. John Milton, both English and Latin, Compos'd at Several Times* (London, 1645), A2r.

CHAPTER 19

The Caroline court

Nicholas McDowell

On February 12, 1625, Milton was admitted to Christ's College, Cambridge, aged sixteen. King James I died some six weeks later. The closest Milton got to writing an epitaph for James are four Latin epigrams *In Proditionem Bombardicam* ("On the Gunpowder Plot") and the 226-line *In Quintum Novembris* ("On the Fifth of November"), Milton's longest Latin poem. The latter was probably written in Cambridge in the autumn of 1626 – the headnote in the 1645 *Poems* informs us that the poet was "*Anno aetatis 17*" – and it has been presumed the epigrams were composed around the same time. Milton's topic in these poems is James' escape from assassination near the beginning of his reign, when the conspiracy of a group of Catholics to blow up king and parliament was foiled on November 5, 1605. The pressure of James' recent death is felt: in the second of the epigrams, addressed at once to Guy Fawkes, the explosives expert in the Catholic group, and the apocalyptic "beast" of Roman Catholicism that Fawkes personifies, the poet declares that James "has indeed without you gone late to his kindred stars, not using the aid of your infernal powder" (lines 5–6). Yet the focus of these Latin poems is relentlessly on the demonic threat of Catholicism: *In Quintum Novembris* features the first appearance of the Miltonic Satan, disguised as a Franciscan friar and counselor to the pope, while one of the literary models for the epigrams is the neo-Latin satirical epitaph on controversial popes, a genre which enjoyed a brief vogue in late sixteenth-century Europe.[1]

How are we to interpret the seventeen-year-old Milton's curious choice of genre and anachronistic choice of topic? He was perhaps trying to imitate the Latin style and theme of his older friend Alexander Gil, whose father taught Milton at St. Paul's School: when scores of Catholic worshipers died in a collapsed secret chapel close to St. Paul's on November 15, 1623, Gil had celebrated the catastrophe as divine revenge for the gunpowder plot in his poem *In ruinam camerae papisticae* (first published, 1632). We could also read Milton's recollection of the Gunpowder Plot in 1626 as indicative of his concern that the Catholic threat to the English state, so vividly embodied for the English by Guy Fawkes, was again urgent in the early years of the reign of Charles I. The anachronistic concern with James as champion of Protestantism thus betrays anxiety about recent signs that Charles may fail to live up to his father's (early) example.[2] In this chapter I will show how we might go about tracing the opposition to Caroline court culture that reaches its furious rhetorical height in the aftermath of regicide in *Eikonoklastes* (1649) back to virtually the very beginning of Milton's career as a writer in the mid 1620s. But I will conclude by suggesting that this interpretation, while attractive in its unity, reads the early poetry in the light of the civil war prose and so always runs the risk of anachronism: the argument (or assumption) that "at every stage [of his life Milton] took up a reformist and oppositional stance which prepared him for the choice he would ultimately make" needs some qualification if it is to be sufficiently sensitive not only to the complexities of religious and political allegiance in Caroline England, but also to the relationship between the young Milton's social experience and poetic development.[3]

What, then, were the circumstances in late 1626 that might have encouraged the teenage Milton to fear that England might succumb to Catholicism under the new king? Immediately after the death of Lancelot Andrewes, Bishop of Winchester, in September 1626, Charles gave William Laud the crucial post of Dean of the Royal Chapel that had been held by Andrewes and promised him the archbishopric of Canterbury. Laud had come to regard zealous anti-Catholic and Calvinist views as inherently extremist and "Puritan," and he had recently represented Puritanism as a threat to ecclesiastical and civil government, the fortunes of which were for Laud inextricably linked: in sermons before parliament and the court in February and July 1626, Laud warned of the danger to the monarchy posed by those who sought further godly reform of the church and "would faine know all the secrets of *Predestination*." He equated the Puritans' curiosity about "God's cause" with a similarly sacrilegious attitude toward the divine authority of the king.[4] Laud and his friends in the Durham House group, a circle of bishops and theologians who were increasingly influential at court in the 1620s and who emphasized ceremonialism and the role of the clergy over preaching and lay biblicism, were in turn stigmatized as "Arminians" – after the Dutch theologian Jacob Arminius, who, against the Calvinist doctrine of double predestination, emphasized the universality of the atonement and the capacity of the human will to reject grace. English Arminianism was represented by Puritans as no better than closet Catholicism, and their fears about pro-Catholic sympathies in the Caroline court, stoked by Charles' marriage to Henrietta Maria of France in 1625, were further fueled by Laud's growing prominence. After he became Archbishop of Canterbury in 1633 Laud would become the key figure in the religious disputes that played a vital role in the outbreak of civil war and the downfall of Charles, who during his "Personal Rule" without parliament from 1628 to 1640 fully backed the Laudian promotion of set prayer, the sacraments, and church decoration.[5] Laud was tried on the charge of treason in 1644 and finally executed, in less than transparent legal circumstances, in January 1645.

Laud received the good news about his promotion in September 1626, from his close ally George Villiers, Duke of Buckingham, to whom Laud acted as chaplain and who maintained with the accession of Charles the status of chief royal favorite to which he had risen in the Jacobean court. Buckingham was the focus of discontent, both religious and political, with the Caroline court in its early years – a discontent that culminated in his murder by a disillusioned soldier in 1628. In May 1626, parliament had sought to have Buckingham impeached on charges of corruption; Charles responded by dissolving parliament and helping to ensure Buckingham was installed as the new chancellor of Milton's Cambridge. A host of libels and satires on Buckingham and his relationship with the Stuart kings circulated anonymously in manuscript in the 1620s. "The Five Senses," probably written in 1623, illustrates how Buckingham was seen to personify a popish influence in the court that manifested itself in undeserved favoritism, fiscal corruption, and moral laxity, in particular disordered sexuality. It was widely believed that the close relationship Buckingham had formed with James I had a sexual element, and the author of "The Five Senses" prays that God will save "My Soveraigne from a Ganimede / Whose whoreish breath hath power to lead / His excellence which way it list" (lines 59–61).[6] Sodomy is linked with judicial corruption as the poet calls on the heavens to

> blesse my King
> From such a bribe as may with drawe
> His thoughts from equitie, and lawe
> From such a smooth, and beardlesse chinn
> As may provoke, or tempt to sinn[.]
> (lines 40–44)

The infiltration of popery is the root cause of these other sins and is placed at the center of the poem, where James is warned away

> From the cand[i]ed poyson'd baites
> Of Jesuites and their deceipts
> Italian Sallets, Romish druggs
> The milke of Babells proud whore duggs[.]
>
> (lines 31–34)

The reader with literary or court connections could recognize in the very form of the poem a reference to Buckingham's centrality in the extravagant, expensive theatrical performances for which the Jacobean court had become known. "The Five Senses" is based on a song from Ben Jonson's masque, *The Gypsies Metamorphosed*, written for Buckingham's entertainment of James in 1621 and featuring Buckingham and his friends dressed as thieving gypsies who are transformed into impeccably loyal (and impeccably well-dressed) courtiers. One anti-Buckingham satire of 1621, "When Charles, hath got the Spanish Gearle," associates the patronage of the lavish Whitehall masques composed by Jonson and staged by Inigo Jones with the indifference of the court to its waste of the nation's wealth:

> When the Banquetting howse is finishd quite
> then Jones Sir Inigo we will call
> & Poetts Ben brave maskes shall write
> & a Parlament shall pay for all[.]
>
> (lines 25–28)

The patronage of court masques continued under Charles and attacks on the theatrical culture of the Caroline court as an embodiment of its moral and spiritual corruption would become a motif of Puritan polemic in the 1630s, most notoriously in William Prynne's *Histrio-mastix* (1633), which condemned female actors as little better than whores at a time when Henrietta Maria was in rehearsal for a new masque performance. Prynne was tried on a charge of treason and was sentenced to have his ears cropped: the episode starkly illustrates the growing politicization of court culture in Caroline England.

"The Five Senses" contains the motifs common to many of the libels on Buckingham but it is also "particularly significant within early Stuart political culture," according to Andrew McRae, "because of its assumption that the identity of the monarch, as well as those of his courtiers, might be fashioned and contested in libels."[7] That this significance was recognized by contemporaries is made clear by an episode that must surely have made an impact on Milton. After his friend Gil publicly toasted the health of Buckingham's murderer and disparaged the king, he was reported to Laud; a subsequent search uncovered a copy of "The Five Senses," along with other manuscript libels, among Gil's papers.[8] In November 1628, the Court of Star Chamber, the official organ of censorship in early modern England, degraded Gil from the ministry, stripped him of his degrees, and sentenced him to lose his ears; in the event, Gil escaped mutilation but remained in prison for two years. It has been argued that the imagery of bodily violence in *Lycidas* (1637) reflects Milton's fear that his thinly veiled attack on the condition of the Church of England in that poem would put him at risk of the sort of public mutilation performed earlier in 1637 on John Bastwick, Henry Burton, and Prynne again (he lost all of his ears this time) for Puritan activism and writing; the Gil episode of nine years earlier, however, was a more personal encounter with the potential consequences of state censorship.[9] Indeed, we might even look for vernacular influences on Milton's Cambridge epigrams in the culture of early Stuart libeling: the universities were the most important centers for the transmission of manuscript libels and the mock epitaph was not only a feature of neo-Latin anti-papal satire but "the most common form employed by libellers" in the 1620s.[10] One 1626 libel, "The Kinge and his wyfe the Parliament," can be compared with Milton's gunpowder epigrams of the same year in its representation of Buckingham as an instrument of Satan, even worse than the sulphuric Guy Fawkes in the popish dangers he poses to the state:

> An art sprunge from a blacker seed,
> then that which he powred in that weed
> Whom we call Guido Faux:
> Who if he fiered had his vessell,
> of Sulphure standeinge on beare tressell,
> in his sepulchrall walkes:
> Could not have soe disperst our state,
> Nor opened Spayne soe wyde a gate,
> as hath his gracelesse grace[.]
>
> (lines 37–45)

The themes of the manuscript libels on Buckingham in the 1620s – courtly corruption, popery, and extravagance – became a staple of parliamentarian propaganda of the 1640s and shape the polemical strategies of *Eikonoklastes*. Milton repeatedly represents the *Eikon Basilike* (1649), supposedly the record of the king's thoughts before his execution, as a piece of typically ornate and artificial Caroline court theatre. Milton mocks the famous frontispiece image of the praying Charles as a

conceited portraiture . . . drawn out to the full measure of a Masking Scene, and sett there to catch fools and silly gazers, and by those Latin words after the end, *Vota dabunt quae Bella negarunt* . . . for though the Picture sett in Front would

Martyr him and Saint him to befool the people, yet the Latin Motto in the end, which they understand not, leaves him, as it were a politic contriver to bring about that interest by faire and plausible words, which the force of Armes deny'd him. But quaint Emblems and devices begg'd from the old Pageantry of some Twelf-nights entertainment at *Whitehall*, will doe but ill to make a Saint or Martyr: and if the People resolve to take him Sainted at the rate of such a Canonizing, I shall suspect thir Calendar more then the *Gregorian*. (*CPW* III:342–43)

Charles' book (which went through an astonishing thirty-five editions within a year of publication) works on the common people – those who have no Latin – in exactly the same way as Catholic (and thus Laudian) cer-emony and decoration: it uses the power of the image to inculcate idolatry in "silly gazers." The representation of Charles as "a Saint or Martyr" is just another clerical trick to deceive the people into an unthinking acceptance of popish tyranny – it is "a civil kinde of Idolatry" (*CPW* III:343). This popish cult of the visual is equated with the theatricality and expense of Jacobean and Caroline court culture – many of Jonson's court masques had been presented on Twelfth Night at Whitehall. This is why the failure of the common reader to see beyond the empty but glittering spectacle of kingship in the *Eikon Basilike* leads Milton to despair of the chances of both religious and political reformation in England.

The association of theatricality and the moral corruption at the heart of Caroline culture and society had been a feature of Milton's earlier anti-episcopal prose. In *An Apology Against a Pamphlet* (1642) Milton biliously recalls how at Cambridge he had witnessed future ministers "so oft upon the Stage writhing and unboning their Clergie limmes . . . prostituting the shame of that ministery which either they had, or were nigh having, to the eyes of Courtiers and Court-Ladies, with their Groomes and *Madamoisel-laes*" (*CPW* I:887). Milton combines his contempt for both the Laudian emphasis on ceremonial religion and the effeminate luxury of the Caro-line court with an expression of puritanical distaste for the immorality of theatrical display. The suggestion of grotesque sexual as well as dramatic performance in the image of the (presumably cross-dressed) student actors "writhing and unboning" recalls the charges of sodomy leveled against Buckingham and the royal court in the 1620s libels. Here Milton sounds like Prynne in his attack on masques in *Histrio-mastix*. But of course Milton himself wrote a masque not long after he left Cambridge and in the imme-diate aftermath of Prynne's sentence: *A Mask Presented at Ludlow Castle* celebrated the installation of the Earl of Bridgewater as President of Wales in September 1634. Those who argue that Milton chose to work within the form of the masque because he sought its "reformation" – to purify it of the spiritual and moral corruptions of Jacobean and Caroline court culture as he later wished to purify the nation – can find some evidence in the connections between *A Mask* and Ben Jonson's court masque, *Pleasure Reconciled to Virtue* (1618): the character of Comus represents unrestrained indulgence in Jonson's masque, although he is more of a Rabelaisian belly-god than Milton's demonic tempter. Milton's Comus and his unruly "rout" have been seen as a representation of the court and a criticism of its "ethos of sensuality and corrupt ritual"; Milton pointedly refuses Jonson's reconciliation of virtue and pleasure.[11] For all the efforts of Charles and Henrietta Maria to project an image of their marriage and court in terms of a Neoplatonic spiritual purity, their court included figures such as Thomas Carew, who had been close to Buckingham and had obtained the sought-after post of sewer-in-ordinary to Charles. Carew's notorious libertine poem "A Rapture," although not published until 1640, was an important influence on the self-consciously erotic and anti-Puritan verse of the "Cavalier" poets of the 1630s and 1640s, while in Carew's 1634 masque *Coelum Britannicum* – in which the same sons of the Earl of Bridgewater who were to perform in Milton's *Mask* a few months later had danced – Momus, the god of ridicule, threatens to reveal the libertine activity behind the platonic veil of the Caroline court by looking into "all the privy lodgings, behind hangings, doors, curtains, through keyholes, chinks, windows, about all venereal lobbies, sconces, or redoubts."[12]

The treatment of virginity and chastity in *A Mask* can thus be opposed to the moral decadence which had been associated with the Jacobean and Caroline courts both in the libels on Buckingham's sexuality and the assaults on the immorality of masque performance in Puritan polemic (although it should be noted, in the light of Prynne's attacks on female participation in masques, that Milton's lead actor was the fifteen-year-old Alice Egerton). While the masque had become closely associated with Jonson and with Jonson's status as James I's poet laureate – Caroline court writers such as Carew represented themselves as the "sons of Ben" – in *A Mask* Milton adopts instead language and themes from Edmund Spenser's *The Faerie Queene* (1590–1609) – Satanic temptation, moral choice, aggressive chastity – associated with a more militantly Protestant poetics. For those who read an evolving radicalism in the early Milton, the Spenserian reformation of a Jonsonian, courtly form in *A Mask* prepares the way for *Lycidas*, which "marks a decisive and unambiguous commitment to the Spenserian tradition" of prophetic, anticlerical pastoral established by *The Shepheardes Calender* (1579). This commitment is retrospectively underlined by the headnote which Milton added to the version of *Lycidas* printed in the 1645 *Poems*, which presents St. Peter's interjection, and thus Milton's poem, as a prophecy of "the ruin of our corrupted clergy then in their height."[13]

This is how we might go about unifying the student Milton composing neo-Latin epigrams in 1626 with the salaried propagandist defending the regicide in vernacular prose in 1649. Yet, tempting as this reading is, it will not quite do. Just before Milton wrote *In Quintum Novembris* and (probably) the gunpowder epigrams, he wrote *In Obitum Praesulis Wintoniensis*, a Latin elegy for Lancelot Andrewes, the bishop whose death opened the way for Laud's rise. Andrewes may have been more circumspect and less public in his criticism of predestination and Puritanism but "Laud and his circle regarded him as an intellectual father figure."[14] In Milton's elegy Andrewes experiences apotheosis, ascension to heavenly glory that was traditionally associated with the canonization of saints: "A starry brightness shone from his radiant face; his white clothing flowed down to his golden ankles, a white fillet girded his divine head" (lines 54–55). The first entry in the *OED* for "apotheosis" is from a reference to the Catholic "Canonization of false Martyrs" in John Foxe's *Acts and Monuments* (1563). Apotheosis was a particular feature of the baroque, Counter-Reformation art favored by Laudians – around 1625 Rubens had painted the (still very much alive) Duke of Buckingham ascending to the heavenly temple of virtue – but it is a favorite topos of the early Milton, found also in the gunpowder epigrams and the 1626 elegy for the Bishop of Ely (and indeed in *Lycidas*). In detailing the baroque effects in Milton's early verse, Graham Parry argues that the poet "who comes nearest to Milton's youthful grand style" in the episcopal elegies is William Drummond of Hawthornden, the leading Scottish poet of the time who is best known for recording his literary conversations with Jonson. It seems that among Drummond's poetic works of the 1620s may have been none other than the libel on Buckingham, "The Five Senses," found in Alexander Gil's papers.[15] Drummond can hardly be described as a Puritan radical: he wrote verses to welcome Charles I on the king's visit to Scotland in 1633 and during the conflicts of the later 1630s and 1640s Drummond was constant in his anti-Presbyterianism and loyalty to the crown.[16] But then the composition and possession of anti-court manuscript libels was no barometer of later radicalism: in 1632 Alexander Gil published a collection of poems dedicated to Charles and including a "profoundly respectful poem addressed to Laud."[17] Milton's gunpowder poems may, then, be (very) oblique criticisms of Charles' perceived weaknesses; but even highly explicit, aggressive libels of the 1620s should not be taken as evidence of anti-monarchical sentiment.

The resemblances between Milton's early verse, including not only the Latin episcopal elegies but vernacular devotional pieces such as "The Passion" and "Upon the Circumcision," and the baroque aesthetic that we now associate with a Laudian devotional style become more intriguing when we take into account the recent discovery that in 1633 Milton's father became a churchwarden of a chapel in Hammersmith consecrated by Laud two years earlier: in the earlier 1630s, in other words, Milton may have worshiped in Laudian style. It has always been assumed that Milton moved from orthodox Calvinism to an Arminian insistence on the role of choice in salvation around 1644, in part in reaction to the hostile Presbyterian and Calvinist reception of his ideas on divorce. But there is little to indicate Milton *ever* subscribed to orthodox Calvinist theology. Indeed *A Mask*, with its external agencies of grace such as the Attendant Spirit and Sabrina, has been recently described as Milton's "most sustained engagement with the theory, as well as the style, of anti-Calvinism."[18] In the 1640s Milton certainly jettisoned any notion that devotional forms could play a role in salvation, but his Arminian soteriology may have been longstanding.

The influential statement that Milton's early poems "oppose the Caroline aestheticization of politics" can actually only be applied with much confidence to *Lycidas*.[19] Milton's *Mask* is, after all, a masque, written for a Caroline courtier, and the circumstances of Milton's commission remind us that his immediate post-Cambridge work was facilitated by courtly connections. Milton collaborated on the production with the musician Henry Lawes: it must have been through Lawes, music master to the Earl of Bridgewater's children, that Milton was invited in the latter half of 1632 to write *Arcades* for the children's grandmother, the Countess of Derby, which then led to the commission to compose the *Mask*. Lawes had since 1631 been a member of the king's music, the inner circle of musicians who played in the monarch's apartments. He was involved during the 1630s in the composition of music for court entertainments and masques, including Carew's *Coelum Britannicum*, and became well known for his setting of "Cavalier" poets. There is no question about Lawes' royalist sympathies during the civil wars. Yet at the beginning of 1646 Milton addressed a sonnet to Lawes, probably sent with a presentation copy of the 1645 *Poems*: the title page of the *Poems* informs the reader that the "Songs were set by Mr Henry Lawes Gentleman of the Kings Chapel, and one of his Majesties Private Musick." It is usually assumed that Milton must have been upset by this Cavalier packaging and that it was imposed by the publisher, Humphrey Moseley, whose editions during the 1640s of court poets such as John Suckling, James Shirley, and Carew tend to invoke nostalgia for a lost golden age of Stuart cultural patronage. This assumption excludes the possibility that Milton actively sought the attention of royalist readers by publishing his poems of the 1620s and 1630s in 1645 – a possibility which is given credence by "To Mr. H. Lawes, on his Airs." Written, significantly, in the style of a Jonsonian epigram like "To William Camden," the sonnet suggests Milton's desire, with the (first) war almost concluded and the bishops overthrown, to reconnect with the cultivated circles in which he had moved before the outbreak of war and his reluctant (or so he assures us) assumption of the role of prose polemicist. Presbyterian intolerance seems to have encouraged Milton during the mid 1640s to look toward a *rapprochement* with royalists who shared his appreciation of wit and poetry.[20]

Milton's anti-episcopal and regicide prose works are perhaps the most rhetorically powerful attacks on the Caroline church and court of the whole civil war period and plainly they must be linked to the apocalyptic anticlericalism of *Lycidas* – although it must be remembered that St. Peter has "mitred locks" (line 112) and that the poem does not show Milton to have abandoned episcopacy. The twenty-five line assault on the Laudian church in *Lycidas* evidently shows Milton to have become to some extent alienated from the Caroline establishment by the end of 1637, and we perhaps need to examine more closely the political and personal events between 1634 and the end of 1637 that might have contributed to this crisis of allegiance. Fresh archival evidence might provide clues, such as the recent discovery that Milton's father was cited in an episcopal visitation of the Horton parish church in August 1637.[21] But claims for Milton's *consistent* opposition to the culture associated with the Caroline court before *Lycidas*, and indeed even during the civil wars, can only be made by simplifying or suppressing crucial historical, literary, and personal contexts.

NOTES

I am grateful to Andrew McRae and William Poole for their comments on a draft of this chapter.

1 Stella Revard, *Milton and the Tangles of Neaera's Hair: The Making of the 1645 "Poems"* (Columbia, MO, 1997), 54–55.

2 *Ibid.*, 56.

3 Barbara K. Lewalski, "How Radical was the Young Milton?", in *Milton and Heresy*, ed. Stephen B. Dobranski and John P. Rumrich (Cambridge, 1998), 49–72 (p. 50).

4 William Laud, *A Sermon Preached before his Maiestie, on Wednesday the Fift of Iuly, at White-hall* (London, 1626), 21.

5 For the Laudian "counter-reformation," see Graham Parry, *The Arts of the Anglican Counter-Reformation: Glory, Laud and Honour* (Woodbridge, 2006).

6 All quotations from libels on Buckingham are from "Early Stuart Libels: an Edition of Poetry from Manuscript Sources," ed. Alastair Bellany and Andrew McRae, *Early Modern Literary Studies*, Text Series 1 (2005), http://purl.oclc.org/emls/texts/libels/.

7 Andrew McRae, *Literature, Satire and the Early Stuart State* (Cambridge, 2004), 82.

8 Public Records Office, State Papers Domestic 16/iii/51; Gordon Campbell, "Alexander Gil," *Oxford Dictionary of National Biography* (Oxford, 2004).

9 John Leonard, "'Trembling Ears': the Historical Moment of 'Lycidas,'" *Journal of Medieval and Renaissance Studies* 21 (1991): 59–81.

10 McRae, *Literature, Satire*, 40–41, 46.

11 Achsah Guibbory, "Milton and English Poetry," in *A Companion to Milton*, ed. Thomas N. Corns (Oxford, 2001), 72–89 (p. 75).

12 *Court Masques*, ed. David Lindley (Oxford, 1995), 169.

13 David Norbrook, *Poetry and Politics in the English Renaissance*, rev. edn. (Oxford, 2002), 256.

14 Nicholas Tyacke, "Archbishop Laud," in *The Early Stuart Church*, ed. Kenneth Fincham (Basingstoke, 1993), 51–79 (p. 62).

15 Graham Parry, "Literary Baroque and Literary Neoclassicism," in *A Companion to Milton*, 54–71 (p. 63); McRae, *Literature, Satire*, 75–76.

16 See John Kerrigan on the qualifications of Drummond's allegiance by his Scottish patriotism in *Archipelagic English: Literature, History and Politics, 1603–1707* (Oxford, 2008), 141–68.

17 Campbell, "Alexander Gil."

18 Thomas N. Corns, "Milton before 'Lycidas,'" in *Milton and the Terms of Liberty*, ed Graham Parry and Joad Raymond (Cambridge, 2002), 23–36 (pp. 27, 34).

19 Norbrook, *Poetry and Politics*, 15.

20 Nicholas McDowell, "Dante and the Distraction of Lyric in Milton's 'To My Friend Mr Henry Lawes,'" *The Review of English Studies* 59 (2008): 232–54.

21 Edward Jones, "'Church-outed by the Prelats': Milton and the 1637 Inspection of the Horton Parish Church," *Journal of English and Germanic Philology* 102 (2003): 42–58.

CHAPTER 20

Catholicism

Joan S. Bennett

A Milton family story tells how the poet's father, John Milton Senior, was cast out of his home by his father for possessing an English Bible.[1] Although the 1559 Act of Uniformity required all subjects' loyalty to the Protestant Church of England, the poet's grandfather adhered to "the old religion"; he was a "recusant" who paid fines rather than attend services at his Anglican parish church. His disinherited son remained a Protestant, but his younger grandson, Christopher, eventually converted to Catholicism. John Milton stayed closely connected throughout his life to his brother.[2] Several of Milton's most deeply treasured friends were artists and scholars whom he met during a stay in Italy, all of whom, being Italian, were Catholic. Although some complained that Counter-Reformation intolerance had "dampt the glory of Italian wits," Milton felt delighted by their brilliance and honored by their kindness to him.[3] He memorialized them in letters, in poems, and eventually in the colloquy between Adam and Raphael in *Paradise Lost.*[4]

Understanding seventeenth-century Catholicism is challenging for readers puzzled to discover that Milton's *Areopagitica,* which deeply influenced the Enlightenment commitment to religious freedom by urging toleration of all other forms of Christianity, excluded English Catholics: "I mean not tolerated Popery, and open superstition, which as it extirpats all religions and civill supremacies, so it self should be extirpat, provided first that all charitable and compassionat means be us'd to win and regain the weak and the misled" (*CPW* II:565). What people were included in Milton's terms "Popery," "open superstition," "the weak," and "the misled"? The answer involves understanding the development of nationalism in early modern Europe.

England's identity as a Protestant nation was initiated by Henry VIII (d. 1547) but did not achieve stability until Elizabeth I (d. 1603) was able to enforce the English church's declaration that "The Bishop of Rome hath no jurisdiction in this Realm of England."[5] Whereas Elizabeth's predecessor,

248

"Bloody" Queen Mary (d. 1558), had violently returned a generally reluctant nation to papal loyalty, the Elizabethan church required a looser kind of religious conformity. Papist clergy were punished severely if apprehended, but lay Catholics were often *de facto* allowed to believe as they wished and even to carry on private worship in the great houses of Catholic nobility as well as the more remote regions of the country. Conformity's most serious issue was reflected in the so-called "bloody question" used to identify suspected Catholics: Would the person being interrogated swear to defend England against the pope – who had ordered Queen Elizabeth's deposition – if papal forces were to invade the country? Such an invasion was attempted by Catholic Spain in 1588, when a naval attack by its Armada was repulsed against formidable military odds in what to the English seemed a providential deliverance. Something of the recusants' dilemma is seen in the incident reported of English Catholics studying in Rome, who burst into cheers when news of the Armada's defeat reached them.[6] Framers of the Elizabethan religious settlement hoped that Englishness would prevail over Catholicism, which would eventually wither away as papist clergy either conformed or emigrated and recusants gradually died out.

For its part, the Roman church was not in a position to recognize what we now think of as national sovereignty, a phenomenon that was then just emerging. As bearer for 1600 years of a Christ-given commission to bring salvation to the world, the papacy felt bound to uphold the faith against waywardness and error; and the Protestantism that the Roman church had battled for the past century was by far the largest and most dangerous error in its history. Therefore, as soon as Catholicism was banned in England, a major international effort, guided by exiled English priests and the Counter-Reformation papacy, undertook a mission to regain the country for Rome by means of a "hidden church of England," where "[holy] fathers disguised themselves as peddlars, to carry on a precious traffic for eternity."[7] English Catholics of means sent their sons to seminaries abroad, where many trained for the priesthood or for the new, missionary Jesuit order. Wealthy English Catholics provided patronage for resident clergy and missionaries of the "hidden church."

Catholic hopes and Protestant fears for restored English subjection to Rome were raised by King James' marriage negotiations for his son, the future Charles I, who finally yielded to domestic pressure not to make an alliance with Catholic Spain but then in 1625 married another Catholic princess, Henrietta Maria of France. In fact, an attempted French or Spanish takeover of English sovereignty on behalf of Rome could not have been met by an uprising of significant numbers of English Catholics to support it. By mid-century, about 31,000 names were on the recusancy rolls, indicating to modern historians that there were somewhere between 60,000 and 360,000 Catholics in a total English population of about five million.[8] But there were no national census data to offer reassurance; and exactly such an uprising was assumed to have been the goal of the shocking Gunpowder Plot of 1604, which attempted to bomb parliament in session, thereby achieving what the Armada had failed to accomplish. To the annual poems celebrating the plot's timely discovery, as a university student Milton contributed *In Quintum Novembris* ("On the Fifth of November"), which shows Satan engineering the papal plot: "Either the ferocious Gaul [France] or the savage Iberian [Spain] will invade them when they are overwhelmed with sudden fear, stunned at the event; so at last the Marian ages will return there."[9] The plot's discovery hardened King James' decision to enforce a 1606 Oath of Allegiance, compelling English Catholics to choose between their nation and their spiritual leader, the pope, who refused to allow them to take the oath, insisting on his right not only to excommunicate their king but also to depose him.

Rome, however, actually advised against terrorist means. On her departure for England, Henrietta Maria was urged by Cardinal Barberini and by her godfather, Pope Urban VIII, to attempt her husband's conversion and the peaceful return of England to papal loyalty. She complied, establishing a prominent Catholic court in London parallel to the court of King Charles, complete with a grand chapel, papal representative, and other foreign dignitaries, making Catholicism notoriously fashionable at court and among the English aristocracy whom, the young Milton exclaimed in *Lycidas* (1637), "the grim wolf with privy paw / Daily devours apace" (lines 128–29).[10] Milton's Commonplace Book reflects the national anxiety caused by the assertively Catholic queen; and his highly unusual *Mask on Comus* may be seen to critique the idolatrous masques of the Stuart court.

Although many in Catholic Europe, especially papal monarchists, believed that civil as well as spiritual authority rested ultimately with the pope, political rulers claimed partial autonomy in some cases. The French solution, called Gallicanism, even allowed a notable Protestant minority to exist, with restrictions, under an absolutist monarchy that overruled the papacy in this matter, declaring France to be a Catholic nation, but on its own terms. Trying to emulate French monarchical absolutism, but without recognizing papal authority, Charles I insisted that he ruled England, as Louis XIII ruled France, by divine right. Once England was on the brink of civil war over this claim, Charles' effort to retain his people's loyalty was handicapped when the English learned that European Catholic powers were offering Charles military aid for his campaign against the Scottish rebellion of 1641. By 1642, England's Presbyterian-controlled parliament was at war with its king and beginning to reshape religious policy in England.[11]

In *Areopagitica* (1644), one of many tracts published during these war years, Milton advocated a religious toleration far more inclusive than that desired even by his own party, the Independents, who opposed a Presbyterian state church; he argued for a very wide toleration of Protestant belief and practice. Yet some voices in these pamphlet wars – albeit extremely few – were willing to go even further than Milton and include toleration of Catholics.[12] Examining the thought and commitments of two of these writers, the "Leveller" William Walwyn and the New England "Seeker" Roger Williams, may illuminate Milton's reasons for excluding Catholicism.

The Levellers sought to persuade first parliament then Cromwell's army generals to adopt a set of legal reforms and common people's rights called an *Agreement of the People*. Although appealing to later generations as early proposals for representative government, the Levellers' demands were, in 1649, practically unworkable, as was their desire to abolish the newly forming Council of State, which was all that stood between England and Charles II's efforts to recapture the country. Working for the Council of State, Milton was committed to making the new government a viable, if imperfect, step toward an English republic. The Council believed that the likely, if unintended, effect of the Levellers' opposition would be to "bring the *Dagon* of Monarchy once more amongst us."[13]

William Walwyn, the Levellers' main theorist, was, like Milton, a middle-class layperson who talked extensively with Puritan speakers without joining a separatist church or reform movement. He sought in the early 1640s to prevent the establishment of a Presbyterian state church under parliament and in 1648–49 to prevent a congregational state church under Independent forces. Walwyn pointed out that the recusancy statute, though "intended against the Papists," was frequently put "in execution against the Separation."[14] But he also held, with the Elizabethan church, that Rome, although benighted, was a genuine part of the House of God. Most English Catholics, he believed, were not likely to join a foreign invasion, and he urged toleration of such of their "opinions as are not destructive to humane society."[15]

Walwyn and other Levellers routinely claimed that toleration worked satisfactorily in other countries such as Calvinist Holland, which minimally (and temporarily) tolerated Catholicism in an effort at national unity with areas remaining under Spain's control; Catholic France with its Gallican allowance for Protestants (revoked by Louis XIV in 1685); and Poland, where the growth of Protestantism among nobility and townspeople had led several Polish kings to support toleration (but where Jesuit missionaries were gradually returning the country to papal control even as the Levellers wrote). Some English Jesuits secretly approached Cromwell, against papal wishes, with an English Gallican plan, called Blacklowism after its instigator.[16] We do not know whether Milton was privy to the unsuccessful Blacklow discussions. However, he would have found neither Gallicanism nor any of the other national arrangements suitable as models for England, which, having been providentially delivered from papal control at the end of the previous century, should never, he felt, risk its return.

Levellers opposed the English effort to quell a Catholic rebellion in Ireland, which had been roughly subject to England since the Norman conquest of Britain in the twelfth century. The rebellion, which Cromwell planned to put down, was being manipulated by royalist forces seeking to use Ireland, along with Scotland, for the exiled Charles II's military efforts. As foreign secretary, Milton wrote "Observations" on behalf of the Commonwealth against "Articles of Peace" offered by the royalist Irish governor. Although he could not have known in advance how brutal Cromwell's forces would be in subduing the rebels, even if he had known, here again, Milton could not have allowed rebel forces to fight for the king.

When the Leveller movement was forcibly ended in 1649, Walwyn returned to private life, recommending to his countrymen the writings of the "honest Papist" Montaigne on "innocent Cannibals," from whom he felt the Independents could learn some needed charity.[17] Meanwhile, Roger Williams, the virtually adopted son of a Narragansett chief, was actively pursuing the welfare of Native Americans along with that of New England colonists.[18] Ordained in the Church of England, Williams' thought moved quickly beyond even the most tolerant reformers'; and he argued, like Walwyn, for toleration of papists. Unlike Walwyn, however, he did not regard the Roman church as part of the House of God; rather he believed with his friend "the Secretarie of the Councell, (Mr. Milton)," that popery bred spiritually "ravenous and greedy *Wolves*."[19] Williams therefore offers perhaps the most illuminating comparison to Milton.

Important to this comparison is Williams' success in building a New England polity where religious toleration was absolute for as long as he was alive. Rhode Island achieved a tumultuous kind of democracy that would have pleased the idealistic Levellers. It remained viable in spite of constant, harsh opposition, and it achieved a religious toleration much more significant than that of the only other English site attempting toleration for Catholics, Maryland, which until 1691 was a feudal-style palatinate of the Catholic Barony of Baltimore.[20]

Williams and Milton agreed that the state must not hinder Christians from continuously searching by "the light which we have gain'd" (*Areopagitica, CPW* II:550); for, said Williams, God would "inclose the *Light* of his holy *Truths,* in dark and obscure, yea and ordinarily in *forbidden Books, persons* and *Meetings,*" and "it is the *Command* of *Christ Jesus* to his *Schollars,* to try all things."[21] Both believed Rome would put an end to such liberty if it could. But Rome was farther away from Providence than from London and not, in Williams' mind, as great a threat to New England consciences as the violent persecution he continually experienced at the hands of the Massachusetts Bay colonists. He allowed, nevertheless, that in England magistrates might guard against Roman influence by requiring Catholics to swear a loyalty oath, yield up their weapons, wear special insignia, live in specified areas, or whatever seemed most likely to ensure public safety and still allow nationally loyal Catholics to pursue their lives in peace.[22] Milton believed also that harsh penalties such as fines and/or corporal punishment should be abjured for non-seditious English Catholics, the "weak" and "misled."[23] Unlike Williams, however, Milton would not permit public or, during the Restoration, even private Catholic worship. And here we are at the heart of our comparison.

Williams' version of Calvinism persuaded him that not only papists but most human beings – Native Americans and Europeans, the people of new England and old – were damned. He reacted to this realization by wanting, out of sheer compassion, to be as kind as possible in this world. Further, because any individual, including a papist, might be called to salvific repentance, Williams wanted to create conditions by which persons would be able to respond to such a call. He also believed that under the influence of natural law most Catholics would respond well to loving behavior directed at them by the state and that civil obedience should be the magistrate's only goal for a citizenry already divided by God into those "naturally *dead in Sin,* or alive in *Christ.*"[24] Moreover, Williams believed that those "alive in Christ" might be divinely required to endure religious persecution; for from his reading of scripture, it seemed to him not unlikely that England and Europe would once again revert to popery before the Beast met its final destruction.[25] Although religious persecutors, "*Soule-killers,*" commit the deepest sin, their victims can be the most powerful bearers of Gospel truth, as were the "*Waldenses,*" Protestants of Lyon who suffered a terrible massacre by Catholic forces in 1655 but whose survivors, in their dispersion, were more effective witnesses to Christ than they would have been if they had won a military victory "on *Horsbacke* with *carnall weapons.*"[26]

Milton did not think it likely that God would require the return of popery to England, and he wanted pragmatic help for the Waldensians. The poet's optimistic readiness to combat oppression came from his belief that the natural law of Creation was not a dead thing. For him, even after the fall, "God and Nature bid the same" (*Paradise Lost* VI.176). Through divine renewal of the natural law of Creation, all people could, with resurrected right reason, answer God's call to repentance and spiritual liberty. God would never revoke the "high decree / Unchangeable, eternal, which ordained / Their freedom" (*Paradise Lost* III.126–28). Therefore, the state must foster the ability of every citizen to exercise that freedom, to try all things and hold fast to that which is good.

Walwyn advised: "If the Papists will have Altars, Priests, Sacrifice and ceremonies . . . let them alone."[27] But Milton believed that for the nation to tolerate idolatry was to foster in its people an inner slavery that eventually empowers political tyranny. Williams accepted that it might "please the jealous God for the sins of his Saints" to allow the return of papal tyranny to England. If so, he held with Milton, there would be "to the tyrant thereby no excuse" (*Paradise Lost* XII.96); and Williams wanted "those *Sons* of *Blood*, the *bloudie Papists*," to know that, among the English, the Catholics' "*bloudy Doctrin of persecution*, was disclaimed by some, whom they call *Sectaries*: That *equall* and *impartiall* favour was pleaded to the *Catholicks*."[28] Even though Milton understood, with Williams, that "suffering for Truth's sake / Is fortitude to highest victory" (*Paradise Lost* XII.569–70), the poet wanted to maintain readiness for divinely offered occasions for effective liberatory action.

Under the restored Stuart monarchy, when it was no longer possible to fight the establishment of a state church, Milton still worked toward a nation that would unite the social order of the state with the spiritual welfare of citizens.[29] In 1673, when a brief break in the Restoration censorship allowed him to publish his last tract, *Of True Religion*, Milton focused on the danger posed to such a vision by Roman Catholicism. Ultimately even more damaging than the papacy's threat to national sovereignty was its enforced idolatry, which Milton saw not as a harmless set of mistaken theological beliefs but as an enforced spiritually enervating practice, leading finally to external enslavement. "At the cost of his own slavery," Milton had argued in *Pro Populo Anglicano Defensio* (1651), Christ "put our political freedom on a firm foundation" (*CPW* IV:376). Yet not even the Son of God could "of inward slaves make outward free" (*Paradise Regained* IV.145).

That papists worshiped idols did not matter to Williams because he believed that when God called his elect individuals, the message of repentance would be suddenly unmistakable to them. But Milton believed that God continually called everyone and that everyone needed, like Jesus, vigorously to exercise freedom of mind and spirit in the wilderness of this world to be able to hear and answer that call. The most effective spiritual exercise, he believed, would come through engaging with scripture, which citizens must interpret with "mutual forbearance and charity one towards the other, though dissenting in some opinions." Thus, for civic and especially for spiritual safety, popery should be uprooted from England. Milton may well have felt that his prose tract's chance of influencing national policy in 1673 was slim. However, he could point out that the most sure way deeply to combat papal influence in England was for "all sorts and degrees" of people to study the Bible "in their Mother Tongue," as Milton's own father had done in the Catholic household in which he was raised. "[I]gnorance in Scripture chiefly upholds Popery," he observed, and the "serious reading thereof will soonest pull Popery down" (*Of True Religion, CPW* VIII:434–35).

Under what he believed to be the faithless, oppressive, Catholic-leaning monarchy of Charles II, anticipating the possible succession of his Catholic brother James, Milton implicitly reminded his readers of the great scriptural poems that he had published in their mother tongue to help England's citizens work with the Bible's "dangerous memory," praying that God would "Irradiate" in each willing reader "the mind through all her powers" with the truth that liberates (*Paradise Lost* III.52–53).[30]

NOTES

1 William Riley Parker, *Milton: A Biography*, 2nd edn., ed. Gordon Campbell, 2 vols. (1968; Oxford, 1996), 686, n. 6.
2 To survey Milton's recorded interactions with his brother, see Barbara K. Lewalski, "Christopher (brother)," in *The Life of John Milton* (Oxford, 2000), 766, *Index*: "Milton, John, family of."
3 *Areopagitica* (1644) in *CPW* II: 538.
4 See Catherine Gimelli Martin's chapter, "Italy," in this volume. See also Anna K. Nardo, "Academic Interludes in *Paradise Lost*," *Milton Studies* 27 (1991): 209–41; and Cedric Brown, "Milton and Civilized Community," in *Milton in Italy: Contexts, Images, Contradictions*, ed. Mario DiCesare (Binghamton, NY, 1991), 329–44.

5 Article 37 of the Articles of Religion, 1571, in *The Book of Common Prayer* (New York, 1990), 876.

6 Kenneth L. Campbell, *The Intellectual Struggle of the English Papists in the Seventeenth Century: The Catholic Dilemma* (Lewiston, NY, 1986), 9. The papal bull "Regnans in excelsis" (1570), which excommunicated Elizabeth, called for her deposition but not, as is commonly believed, for her assassination.

7 *Relation de la Nouvelle France, 1635*, quoted in J. H. Kennedy, *Jesuit and Savage in New France* (New Haven, 1950), 70.

8 John Bossy, *The English Catholic Community 1570–1850* (New York, 1976), 188; Martin J. Havran, *The Catholics in Caroline England* (Stanford, CA, 1962), vii.

9 This translation is taken from *CPEP* 209.

10 Cedric Brown, "Milton and the Idolatrous Consort," *Criticism* 25 (1973): 419–39.

11 See James Loxley's chapter, "The civil wars," in this volume.

12 See Norah Carlin, "Toleration for Catholics in the Puritan Revolution," in *Tolerance and Intolerance in the European Reformation*, ed. O. P. Grell and R. W. Scribner (Cambridge, 1996), 216–30.

13 J. Philolaus, *A Serious Aviso to the Good People of this Nation, Concerning that Sort of Men, Called Levellers* (London, 1649), quoted in Martin Dzelzainis, "History and Ideology: Milton, the Levellers, and the Council of State in 1649," *Huntington Library Quarterly* 68 (2005): 274.

14 *A Demurre to the Bill for Preventing the Growth and Spreading of Heresie* (1646), rpt. in *The Writings of William Walwyn*, ed. J. R. McMichael and B. Taft (Athens, GA, and London, 1989), 243.

15 *The Power of Love* (1643) in *Writings of William Walwyn*, 81.

16 For an account of the Blacklow effort, see Thomas Hughes, *History of the Society of Jesus in North America: Colonial and Federal*, 4 vols. (1917; rpt. Farnborough, UK, 1970) vol. II, Appendix A.

17 *Walwyn's Just Defence* (1649), in *Writings of William Walwyn*, 400.

18 *Testimony of Roger Williams* (1682), rpt. in *The Complete Writings of Roger Williams*, ed. Samuel L. Caldwell, 7 vols. (New York, 1963), VI:407, hereafter *Complete Writings*.

19 *The Correspondence of Roger Williams*, ed. Glenn LaFantasie, 2 vols. (Hanover, NH, and London, 1988), II:393. *The Bloudy Tenent of Persecution* (1644), rpt. in *Complete Writings*, III:142.

20 *Narratives of Early Maryland, 1633–1684*, ed. Clayton Colman Hall (1910; rpt. Washington, DC, 2005).

21 Williams, *The Bloody Tenent Yet More Bloody* (1652), in *Complete Writings*, IV:29.

22 *Ibid.*, IV:313–14.

23 Milton, *Of True Religion* (1673), in *CPW* VIII:431.

24 Williams, *The Bloudy Tenent*, in *Complete Writings*, III:208.

25 *Ibid.*, 326.

26 *Ibid.*, 209; *The Bloody Tenent Yet More Bloody*, in *Complete Writings*, IV:352–53. See Milton's Sonnet 18 "On the Late Massacre in Piedmont" (1655) and the

account of Milton's work with Cromwell on the Waldensians' cause in Robert Fallon, *Milton in Government* (University Park, PA, 1993), 139–51.

27 *Petition of the Papists*, in *Writings of William Walwyn*, 58.

28 Williams, *The Bloody Tenent Yet More Bloody*, in *Complete Writings*, IV:27.

29 See Joan S. Bennett, *Reviving Liberty: Radical Christian Humanism in Milton's Great Poems* (Cambridge, MA, 1989), esp. ch. 1.

30 See Joan S. Bennett, "Asserting Eternal Providence: John Milton Through the Window of Liberation Theology," in *Milton and Heresy*, ed. Stephen B. Dobranski and John P. Rumrich (Cambridge, 1998), 219–43; and Sharon Achinstein, *Milton and the Revolutionary Reader* (Princeton, 1994). Milton's treatment of idolatry in his poetry and prose is very helpfully studied by Barbara K. Lewalski in "Milton and Idolatry," *Studies in English Literature* 43 (2003): 213–32.

CHAPTER 21

The civil wars

James Loxley

Among the majority of those who gathered at Westminster in November 1640 for the beginning of the new parliament a common opinion was evident: Charles I's reign had been dominated for too long by a faction committed to courses of action that were a severe threat to the fundamental laws of the kingdom, the liberties of the subject, and the doctrine and worship of the English church.[1] Throughout the 1630s the Caroline administration had sought outlandish and innovative ways of raising finance, and thus of improving its own prospects of governing strongly and without domestic hindrance. Customarily, revenue would be raised through a parliament, but Charles' ministers resorted instead to a series of strained and unfamiliar extra-parliamentary measures to circumvent the need for one: during the later 1620s, parliaments had not only failed to grant the supply the administration needed but had also served to gather and amplify a series of grievances that Charles had no intention of assuaging. Such royal policies, backed up by aggrandizing and alarming assertions of prerogative powers, appeared to threaten the subject's secure hold on his property as well as permitting the permanent mothballing of the only national forum available to those without power at court. It didn't help that the administration had been seen to compromise the capacity of the law to check such assertions of executive authority, and that in granting monopolies from which it hoped to gain revenue it was fostering discontent in those whose economic prospects and interests it had checked or overridden. When the Long Parliament met, it demonstrated a widely shared determination not only to assert but also to establish an ineffaceable role for parliament in the counsels of the king, and to cut off the legal and administrative means through which Charles had looked to realize his elevated aspirations for monarchical power.

These, though, were not simply secular issues for either the king and his ministers or his newly gathered opponents. Charles' vision of his rule also involved the reformation of a national church that appeared to him and his leading churchmen to be worryingly lax, ill ordered, and prone in parts to unorthodox doctrine and worship. An attempt at comprehensive and thorough reinvigoration was led by the Archbishop of Canterbury, William Laud, with an emphasis on ceremony and hierarchy that was perceived by the "hotter" sort of English Protestant not as reform but as a frightening counter-reformation. Laud and his supporters were understood to be deviating from the dominant Calvinist doctrine of the church, and imposing liturgical practices that smelled suspiciously of unreformed Roman Catholicism.[2] That the king had an openly Catholic wife redoubled such suspicions, as did the fact that he was offering barely lukewarm support for the cause of international Protestantism in the Thirty Years War, an epic European conflict then raging across the continent. By November 1640 these anxieties had convinced many members of the assembling parliament that only fundamental reform of the English church could safeguard, and thus irrevocably complete, the Protestant reformation begun a century before. As part of this process the system of church government that invested power in a hierarchy of bishops had to go, or at the very least be drastically qualified.

So for Charles' opponents this was an opportunity to displace, or to impose constitutional limits on, a leadership in both church and state whose intentions as well as policies they had come to distrust. Distaste for what the episcopate and Charles' government had already done was effective enough, but fear of what they might be plotting was as powerful a driver of reform, and an inducement to pursue more radical measures. Yet there were also others, and not just supporters of Charles' personal rule, who were animated by fears of their own: for them, the constitutional changes that the leading activists among Charles' parliamentary and ecclesiastical opponents thought necessary to curb untrustworthy incumbents were as much of a threat to the kingdom's proper constitutional order. The heated debate over prelacy in which Milton intervened so pungently offers a good example of this: many who were happy to see the deposition of Laud did not wish to pull down episcopacy itself, and rejected not only the claim that it was necessarily contaminated with popery and tyranny but also the vision of a more thoroughly reformed church set out by Milton and his allies. From such as these, as much as from committed theorists and proponents of royal absolutism, the king's party eventually came.[3] One of this party's problems was that it amounted to a coalition of interests with potentially conflicting aims, but its military opponents were, however, no less divided. The opposition to episcopacy that bound staunch Parliamentarians together was not enough to sustain their unity once the bishops were out of the way. For one grouping and their Scots allies, an established Presbyterian church in England was the necessary heart of any viable settlement; for those of a more radical religious persuasion, including Milton, the English Presbyterians were to become almost as contemptible an enemy as the royalists proper in the threat they offered to the liberty of conscience that was the precondition of a free civic life. Profound religious differences were to lead to conflicting attitudes to state and government in general, to monarchy in particular, and to King Charles himself.

By late 1641, the committed pursuit of a still common purpose by the dominant groupings in both Houses of Parliament had done much to clip the wings of bishops and king, and establish parliamentary involvement in, and control over, the royal government. This, though, was not enough for the keenest supporters of parliamentary efforts. To the frustration of many, episcopacy had not yet been abolished. Then alarming news of a rising in Ireland reached Westminster. Charles' dynastic rule over three kingdoms ensured that English politics was affected by the affairs of both Scotland and Ireland in many and unpredictable ways; indeed, it was the failure of his attempts to suppress the resistance to his imposition of ecclesiastical uniformity on Scotland, and his need to finance a further military effort to do so, that had brought him to the dangerous expediency of calling an English parliament in 1640, and had thus given his opponents there the chance they had so eagerly seized. In the light of the threat the Irish rising was deemed to represent to English security, control over military resources became one of the main issues in renewed efforts to implement even more radical reform of church and state. By the spring of 1642, the king and his opponents were deadlocked over the militia, with Charles refusing point blank to assent to a bill allowing parliament to control it. Parliament passed a militia ordinance instead, declaring in doing so its right to act as an executive authority against the king's will and without his approval. Charles then issued commissions of array authorizing the raising of troops for his defense, and local leaders found themselves facing two incompatible demands on their allegiance. The workings of constitutional government had been replaced by a condition in which competing claims to a monopoly of legitimate force inhabited one polity, and both groupings felt that their success and survival alike had come to depend on the forceful overcoming of their opponents. England was now in a state of civil war, even if neither party had yet managed to mobilize the army it needed.

In fact, though, force and the threat of force had long been an important factor in the thinking of many of the actors in these constitutional dramas. Both the king and his opponents used force in ways that deeply alarmed their antagonists, and managed to make it more likely that the other party would resort to similar or equivalent means. The parliamentary leadership resorted to legally dubious proceedings to press home a charge of treason against one of Charles' chief ministers, the Earl of Strafford; the bill authorizing his execution was reluctantly approved by the king, but was taken to be judicial murder even by many who deplored Strafford's policies. A Scottish army that had faced and beaten its own king in the First and Second Bishops Wars (January to June, 1639, August to October, 1640) occupied part of northern England and collaborated with its English allies at Westminster, while the proceedings of government in London were buffeted by both the spontaneous and the managed interventions of city crowds. On the other side, 1641 saw plots and threatened risings by royalist partisans, some from within the army that Charles had assembled to suppress his Scottish opponents, and in January 1642 Charles notoriously violated parliament with a crowd of armed supporters in an attempt to arrest five prominent members of the House of Commons. Both sides maneuvered to secure stores of armaments for themselves, leading to a celebrated and much-debated stand-off at the city of Hull. The sanguinary tendencies of partisans were thus an important factor in political calculations long before the king raised his standard at Nottingham in August 1642. The wars that followed left perhaps 180,000 people dead in England alone, and helped to confirm armed conflict as a customary aspect of domestic politics in England and Scotland for the following century.[4] Yet military struggle was not some unanticipated bolt from the cloudless blue: it happened, and it continued to happen, because there were participants enough in the religious and political disputes of the period willing to engage in a war effort. John Milton, "imbued with the fervor of what he considered to be a just war undertaken in a righteous cause," was one of them.[5]

From the perspective of the literary historian, one of the most significant elements in the rising conflict was the resort to print and to the public by many partisans of the coalescing sides. With the collapse of the system of pre-publication licensing through which Charles' administration had governed the presses, an extended and much denser chorus of voices found itself with a more easily accessible outlet. Crucially, it also found a public interested and large enough to support the publishers who furnished it with its medium. Some literary historians have described this as a crucial moment in the establishment of a "public sphere" in English culture, with varying degrees of fealty to the model set out by Jürgen Habermas, and varying senses too of the extent to which this flowering instantiated a republican promise at this stage only fitfully animating the parliamentarian cause.[6] Milton found one of his voices here, and once this liberty was under threat from the parliamentary leadership he urgently and publicly asserted its benefits. His conjuration of London as "a City of refuge, the mansion house of liberty" in *Areopagitica*, gives rise to a vision of a new "Temple of the Lord" as a free space or forum accommodating many "moderat varieties," "brotherly dissimilitudes," and "neighboring differences" of opinion and expression (*CPW* II:553–54, 555, 565), a tolerated diversity that was helping to restore a nation to its health and vigor.

Yet this pacific vision is not the only way he imagines the exchange made possible by the abolition of pre-publication censorship: elsewhere in the text, he repeatedly invokes not the architecturally ordered spaces of political or religious institutions, nor the proximities of family and locality, but the field of battle. Truth is in conflict with falsehood, and the "true warfaring Christian" must fight with evil in order to become fully virtuous: "that which purifies us is triall, and triall is by what is contrary" (*CPW* II: 515; see also 517, 547, 556, 561, 562, 567). What's more, the force exerted in this conflict is not necessarily metaphorical, or otherwise confined in a separate sphere of letters. If books "contain a potencie of life in them to be as active as that soule was whose progeny they are" (*CPW* II:492), that does not simply invest them with a human dignity deserving of respect; it also ensures that they participate in the kind of danger presented by armies, the threatening physicality of a not always benign life, and that they are liable too to the same kinds of punishment. In opposing pre-publication censorship Milton is keen not to be accused of "introducing licence," and is certainly not advocating a space of reasons untouched by physical force: "I deny not, but that it is of greatest concernment in the Church and Commonwealth, to have a vigilant eye how Bookes demeane themselves, as well as men; and thereafter to confine, imprison, and do sharpest justice on them as malefactors" (*CPW* II:492). And as he states at the tract's end, for "mischievous" and "libellous" books ("libel" here has a much broader application than its modern, purely legal usage, and includes royalist publications such as newsbooks) "the fire and the executioner will be the timeliest and the most effectuall remedy" (*CPW* II:528, 569). So in *Areopagitica* the free space of the city merges with the rather different space of contingency that is the battlefield, just as a Truth that is only strengthened by its encounter with its enemy, and cannot be worsted (*CPW* II:561), must somehow be accommodated to a Truth violently dismembered by "a wicked race of deceivers" and only to be restored by Christ's agency at his second coming (*CPW* II:549). The time and trial of war is therefore the period of the nation's greatest vigor, of its greatest liberty; but it is also the condition of its crisis, its exposure to the threat of its enemies. Liberty is risk, and civility is continuous with hostility.

Other participants in the polemical exchanges of the 1640s found many ways to characterize their engagements, but were often as fond of the language of military force as Milton is here, and capable of demonstrating equivalent ambivalences. And for many of those participants poetry was a weapon or "Engine," as the parliamentarian soldier and writer George Wither put it, with which to fight.[7] Abraham Cowley – eminent poet, secretary to the exiled queen, royalist intelligencer – set out a particularly resonant formulation in the preface to his *Poems* of 1656: "Now though in all *Civill Dissentions*, when they break into open hostilities, the *War* of the *Pen* is allowed to accompany that of the *Sword*, and every one is in a maner obliged with his *Tongue*, as well as *Hand*, to serve and assist the side which he engages in."[8] In context, Cowley's comments seek to excuse his participation in the royalist war effort to a Protectorate audience;[9] nonetheless, his assertion that the conflicts of tongues and hands are continuous with each other, is the articulation of a civil war commonplace.

This is one of the contexts in which Milton's own first published collection needs to be seen. Critics have often been puzzled by features of the 1645 *Poems* that appear to present its author as "a gentleman poet, possibly a member of the landed gentry with close ties to Caroline peerage" and even to the courtly aesthetics of Charles' personal rule: this is someone who writes masques for the aristocracy, collaborates with a composer, Henry Lawes, identified by his courtly role in the King's Music, and even pens respectful elegies for bishops.[10] The fact that the book was published by Humphrey Moseley, whose list came to feature volumes by poets strongly identified with Stuart court culture, has enhanced the sense of strangeness. In 1645 Moseley also published the poems of Edmund Waller, a quondam court poet and moderate member of parliament who had been disgraced for his involvement in a plot to surrender London to the royalist army, so this certainly would appear to be Milton placing himself – or being placed – in patently royalist company.[11] Yet Moseley's brand of apparently nostalgic, recuperative, or memorial royalism was not the only mode of poetical engagement of which royalists were capable, and the compromised Waller actually makes a rather poor exemplar of the wartime royalist writer. A far more illuminating comparison can be made with John Cleveland, also a graduate of Christ's College, Cambridge, acknowledged for his rhetorical mastery, a fellow contributor to the volume of elegies in which *Lycidas* first appeared and possibly the "late court-Poet" whose image of monarchy Milton turns to his own purposes in *The Readie and Easie Way to Establish a Free Commonwealth* (*CPW* VII:361, 426). Cleveland wrote royalist satires in prose and verse excoriating the full range of the king's enemies; his energetic and demanding poetry was first collected and published in 1647 and went through eight editions and re-issues that same year. A new collection of his poems appeared in 1651 and went through fourteen editions and re-issues before the Restoration, making him one of the more popular poets of the Interregnum.[12] Significantly, his royalism was not an untimely attempt to preserve prewar court culture: it adapted and reworked the satirical modes of wartime opponents and radicals, and was of a piece with the innovative inhabitation of the new public spaces demonstrated by other royalists.[13] Unsurprisingly, he was strongly identified as a vigorous prosecutor of the royalist cause, "the grand Malignant of Cambridge."[14]

The peculiarities of Milton's 1645 *Poems* look rather different in this light. It is not that the volume appears to be quasi-royalist, necessarily; instead, the most striking feature is its disengagement of poetic endeavor from the exigencies of the war of the pen, positing poetry as a form of social engagement irreducible to the forceful exchanges of polemic or war. This might even open up the possibility of a rapprochement between enemies through the medium of poetry, a possibility enhanced by his 1646 sonnet praising Henry Lawes.[15] Sonnet 8 does actually imagine an encounter between poetry and armed royalism: the poem is purportedly addressed to a "Captain or colonel, or knight in arms" (line 1) who might have entered London as part of the king's army when Charles seemed able and about to do so in the autumn of 1642. Yet far from being a polemical address, the poem attempts to deflect violence by recalling instances in which poetry or a poet's fame had pacified an enemy, and in so doing refuses the subsumption of verse under the demands of hostility articulated by Wither, Cowley, Cleveland, and other contemporaries. In his *Pro Populo Anglicano Defensio Secunda* Milton could happily boast of how he had met Salmasius "in single combat and plunged into his reviling throat this pen, the weapon of his own choice" (*CPW* IV:556), but this violent attack was committed in prose. As James Turner suggests, though, it would be a mistake to think that prose for Milton is the medium of public engagement, and poetry a social register that evades public demands and concerns.[16] He had a rather different conception of poetry's role in the world, and acknowledging this difference is important to understanding how the demands on different kinds of writing exerted by the civil wars find a distinctive response in Milton's major poetry.

In *The Reason of Church-Government* Milton establishes a clear polarity between his current endeavors "sitting here below in the cool element of prose" and the work of "a Poet soaring in the high region of his fancies with his garland and singing robes about him" (*CPW* 1:808). Polemical pamphleteering is work of the left hand, and therefore lesser than the elevated productions of the right, poetic hand. He hopes he will eventually be able to speak as a national poet in the highest poetic forms, "an interpreter & relater of the best and sagest things among mine own Citizens throughout this Iland in the mother dialect" (*CPW* 1:811–12). Poetry in this proper sense is a Divine gift, and concomitantly grand in capacity and aspiration; indeed, it is "of power beside the office of a pulpit, to inbreed and cherish in a great people the seeds of vertu, and publick civility, to allay the perturbations of the mind, and set the affections in right tune," as well as an organ of worship and a means "to deplore the general relapses of Kingdoms and States from justice and Gods true worship" (*CPW* 1:816–17). But now is not the time for this kind of writing. It is not only that "it were a folly to commit any thing elaborately compos'd to the carelesse and interrupted listening of these tumultuous times," but also that the conditions for the production and circulation of epic poetry are actually lacking: under the "inquisitorius and tyrannical duncery" of episcopacy "no free and splendid wit can flourish" (*CPW* 1:807, 820). The suggestion that poetry is a means by which a free nation can be sustained in its strength and vigor is reinforced in *Of Education*, where poetry accompanies moral, political, and rhetorical education to help produce the good citizens who will not "in a dangerous fit of the commonwealth be such poor, shaken, uncertain reeds, of such a tottering conscience, as many of our great counsellers have lately shewn themselves" (*CPW* 11:398). Yet this pedagogy is still only an ideal, and the public realm bedeviled by uncertain reeds; prose polemic is the mode more suited to combating the forces preventing the nation's restoration to its native strength.

Although Milton can often foresee the triumph of liberty, he is also acutely aware of the dangers that might prevent it. Royalist successes in the early years of the war were checked by decisive battles at Marston Moor, near York, in 1644, and then at Naseby, in Northamptonshire, in 1645. Recognizing that his military cause was lost, the king gave himself up to parliament's Scottish allies in 1646, before being transferred to English custody. But no settlement in church or state was forthcoming, and subsequent negotiations only served to widen divisions affecting the parliamentary coalition. Milton's erstwhile Presbyterian allies had already emerged as inimical to the liberty he championed, as "old *Priest*" gave way to "New *Presbyter*" ("On the New Forcers of Conscience," line 20): book licensing had been maintained, the religious liberty of conscience was threatened, and Milton's reasoned and scholarly arguments for divorce had been the focus of vituperative Presbyterian attacks. During 1647, divisions among parliamentarians, and the growing politicization of the parliamentary New Model Army, provoked new and dangerous instabilities in the uncertain English state. Emboldened by this factionalism, Charles' supporters reignited armed conflict the following year. Although these uprisings were conclusively defeated, parliamentary Presbyterians continued to seek a deal with the king on terms that seemed to radicals to promise nothing more than the renewal of royal tyranny. By late 1648 the possibility of creating the right kind of nation appeared to be receding so starkly that in the "Digression" to his *History of Britain*, probably written around this time, Milton is scathing about the English people's incapacity to embrace the liberty that the wars should have won for them.[17] The military coup of December 1648, and the regicide that followed, were celebrated by Milton as a miraculous opportunity to reinvigorate the cause of freedom. But liberty remained fragile, and polemical labors were still necessary: the English people were all too enamored of their dead king, as the popularity of his book, *Eikon Basilike*, suggested, and Milton took up the role of a breaker of images in *Eikonoklastes*, with its apparent contempt for the poetic, as well as writing in defense of the commonwealth and himself against their foreign enemies. The republic and the succeeding Protectorate found new ways to entwine hope and disappointment until the depressingly secure renewal of the Stuart yoke in 1660 postponed the day of true liberty once again.[18]

The conditions in which Milton might properly assume the mantle of the national poet, then, never became propitious. On occasion, he imagines that his prose celebrations of "at least one heroic achievement of my countrymen" can be compared with the noble work of the epic writer (*CPW* IV:685). Yet neither the moment nor the achievement lasted. Unable in the end to speak from and for a "noble and puissant Nation" (*CPW* II:558), unable to reflect in verse the historical actualization of a promise, Milton conjured an epic instead from the wrong conditions, as the narratorial self-presentation in the proem to book VII of *Paradise Lost* makes clear. There was a strong classical precedent for this kind of difficult epic in Lucan's *De Bello Civili* (or *Pharsalia*), a work that not only chimed with Milton's republican sympathies but was likewise written from a position at odds with the polity it first addressed.[19] By the same token, the identity of Milton's public here is not an easy matter to settle. Instead of the presumed national auditory of the early 1640s was he addressing only the marginalized remnant of the republic's supporters, those few who would be equally perturbed by the way history had turned out? *Samson Agonistes* and *Paradise Regained*, published together in 1671, reflect particularly acutely on the question of right action in fraught circumstances through the choices faced by their central figures, and might reasonably be read as addressing the predicament of Milton's fellow radicals, as a number of recent contextual studies have suggested.[20] It might also be thought that Milton had arrived at his full poetic powers too late, that the moment of true freedom had passed; but perhaps it was still too soon, and he had to speak proleptically for and to a nation that was yet to come?

Whatever his sense of his audience, the epic frame of *Paradise Lost* demanded the reflective placing of recent English history into theological and world-historical narratives that would serve to determine its meaning. The religious, domestic, and civil liberty of which he had been such a strong champion in the 1640s is here elaborated in its full theological and historical significance, and the consequences of its long betrayal are set out both for the emblematic figures of Adam and Eve and for the line of their descendants down to the English of Milton's own day. Here, too, there is an explanation for those whom providence might on the face of it appear to have abandoned, and a re-casting and re-affirmation of the messianic hopes that had animated the zealous reformers of 1641. The events and lessons of the civil war period are folded into an eschatological vision that promises an ultimate triumph for the cause of rational liberty and reformation. In granting himself such synoptic powers Milton offers a pointed riposte to those, such as John Dryden, who presumed to dictate the appropriate forms and modes of poetry from their now authorized and authoritative positions at the heart of the restored monarchical regime.[21] The disengagement here, the turn away from the modes and genres of topicality that had dominated Milton's published writing until 1660, is in fact a renewed engagement with the grandest public concerns on different terrain: the poet proclaims his miraculous ability to soar, to address his public or his nation, even in the face of its historical absence. In doing so, he refuses the uniformity of a Restoration settlement and revives the risky liberty of the early 1640s; now, though, poetry is the means by which this can happen. Though given up to the exigencies of the cause, and buffeted by its defeats and disappointments, the Miltonic poet will not in the end be a helpless or silenced victim.

NOTES

1 Underlying this narrative are both canonical and more recent accounts of the high political aspects of the civil wars: Robert Ashton, *The English Civil War: Conservatism and Revolution 1603–1649*, 2nd edn. (London, 1989); Conrad Russell, *The Fall of the British Monarchies 1637–1642* (Oxford, 1991); Jonathan Scott, *England's Troubles: Seventeenth-Century English Political Instability in European Context* (Cambridge, 2000); Michael Braddick, *God's Fury, England's Fire: A New History of the English Civil Wars* (London, 2008).

2 See Neil Forsyth's chapter in this volume for a more detailed discussion of Laud and his opponents.

3 David Smith, *Constitutional Royalism and the Search for Settlement* (Cambridge, 1994), 62–106.

4 For estimates of casualties in all three kingdoms, see Charles Carlton, *Going to the Wars: The Experience of the British Civil Wars, 1638–1651* (London, 1992), 201–29.

5 Michael Lieb, *Poetics of the Holy: A Reading of "Paradise Lost"* (Chapel Hill, NC, 1981), 265. See also Robert Fallon, *Captain or Colonel: The Soldier in Milton's Life and Art* (Columbia, MO, 1984), 30–71.

6 Jürgen Habermas, *The Structural Transformation of the Public Sphere* (London, 1989); David Norbrook, *Writing the English Republic: Poetry, Rhetoric and Politics, 1627–1660* (Cambridge, 1999), 93–139; Joad Raymond, "The Newspaper, Public Opinion, and the Public Sphere in the Seventeenth Century," in *News, Newspapers, and Society in Early Modern Britain*, ed. Raymond (London, 1999), 109–40.

7 George Wither, *Campo-Musae: or the field-musings of Captain George Wither* (London, 1643), A3r.

8 Abraham Cowley, *Poems* (London, 1656), [A4r].

9 James Loxley, *Royalism and Poetry in the English Civil Wars* (Basingstoke, 1997), 97–98; Nigel Smith, *Literature and Revolution in England 1640–1660* (New Haven, 1994), 216; Martin Dzelzainis, "Literature, War, and Politics, 1642–1668," in *A Companion to Literature from Milton to Blake*, ed. David Womersley (Oxford, 2000), 15–16.

10 Richard Johnson, "The Politics of Publication: Misrepresentation in Milton's 1645 Poems," *Criticism* 36 (1994): 45; Peter Lindenbaum, "John Milton and the Republican Mode of Literary Production," *Yearbook of English Studies* 21 (1991): 121–36; and Stephen B. Dobranski, *Milton, Authorship, and the Book Trade* (Cambridge, 1999), 91–93.

11 Warren Chernaik, "Waller, Edmund (1606–1687)," *Oxford Dictionary of National Biography* (Oxford, 2004), www.oxforddnb.com/view/article/28556, accessed June 23, 2008.

12 See Brian Morris and Eleanor Withington, eds., *The Poems of John Cleveland* (Oxford, 1967), xli–xlix.

13 Smith, *Literature and Revolution*, 306; Jason McElligott, *Royalism, Print and Censorship in Revolutionary England* (Woodbridge, UK, 2007).

14 *The Kingdomes Weekly Intelligencer,* 101 (May 27, 1645), 811.
15 See Nicholas McDowell, *Poetry and Allegiance in the English Civil Wars: Marvell and the Cause of Wit* (Oxford, 2008), 69–90.
16 James Grantham Turner, "The Poetics of Engagement," in *Politics, Poetics and Hermeneutics in Milton's Prose,* ed. David Loewenstein and James Grantham Turner (Cambridge, 1990), 257–75.
17 On the dating of the Digression, see Austin Woolrych, "Dating Milton's *History of Britain,*" *Historical Journal* 36 (1993): 929–43; Nicholas von Maltzahn, "Dating the Digression in Milton's *History of Britain,*" *Historical Journal* 36 (1993): 945–56; and more recently Blair Worden, *Literature and Politics in Cromwellian England* (Cambridge, 2007), 410–26.
18 See David Loewenstein's chapter, "The Interregnum," in this volume.
19 See Anthony Welch's chapter, "Poetic tradition, epic," in this volume.
20 Albert Labriola and David Loewenstein, eds., "*Paradise Regained* in Context," special issue of *Milton Studies* 42 (2003); David Loewenstein, *Representing Revolution in Milton and his Contemporaries* (Cambridge, 2001), 242–95; and Worden, *Literature and Politics,* 358–83.
21 Steven Zwicker, "Milton, Dryden and the Politics of Literary Controversy," in *Culture and Society in the Stuart Restoration,* ed. Gerald Maclean (Cambridge, 1995), 137–58.

CHAPTER 22

Classical literature and learning

Stella P. Revard

Milton's classicism is well known. At St. Paul's School, he would have read Ovid in Form 3, have progressed to Virgil and Cicero in Form 5, and Homer and Hesiod in Form 8.[1] By the time Milton studied these classical authors, there were standard texts and commentaries in place, and clearly Milton would have been influenced by the views expressed in them. Milton's favorite classical poet was Homer, from whom he could reportedly recite almost without book. His daughter Deborah, interviewed not long before her death, stated that after scripture Milton most often called for Homer and Ovid's *Metamorphoses* to be read to him. She remembered and could repeat long passages from both.[2]

Few books survive from Milton's personal library, so we can only speculate which texts Milton would have used for Homer, Virgil, and Ovid.[3] Virgil and Ovid were available in texts printed both on the continent and in England, but Homer was not printed in England until George Bishop's Greek edition of the *Iliad* in 1591.[4] As with most classical texts, the earliest editions of Virgil appeared in Venice, the edition of 1491 with Christopher Landino's commentary being one of the most prominent. Virgil was also printed, however, in Leiden, Frankfurt, Basel, Geneva, Wittenberg, as well as in London in 1593 and 1597. These editions featured the commentary of Marcus Servius, the life of Virgil by Donatus, and usually Vegius' supplement on the *Aeneid*. Renaissance editions of Virgil contained besides the *Eclogues*, *Georgics*, and the *Aeneid* other material attributed to Virgil – the *Culex*, the *Dirae*, epigrams, an elegy on the death of Maecenas, as well as the notorious priapic poems. Standard apparatus included arguments for the major poems as well as marginal notes, often cross-referenced with Homer.

Ovid was printed as early as Virgil both on the continent and in England, with editions from all of the major printing houses. The first annotated edition of Ovid by Raphael Regius appeared in 1492; Aldus Manutius added a life of Ovid to his edition of 1502. Ann Moss has usefully surveyed the editions and commentaries of Ovid printed in France before 1600.[5] As she points out, the individual texts are usually those used by the schools, with *Metamorphoses* and *Tristia* the most popular. The erotic poems less often appear in single copies, for they were not taught in the schools. However, as Moss has observed, Bartholomeus Merola did not censure the erotica in his commentary (1495). The *Amores, Ars Amatoria,* and *Remedia Amoris* also appear in the 1586 *Epistolae* of Ovid printed in London. The young Milton would have read the erotica on his own and by his own confession was an admirer of the erotic Ovid.[6] Like Virgil, Ovid was printed with prefatory arguments and with marginal glosses. Aldus' life of Ovid was included in most editions, sometimes also with Angelo Politiano's epigram on the life and death of Ovid.

Editions of Homer in Greek began to appear at end of the fifteenth century, the *editio princeps* in 1488, edited by Demetrius Chalcondylas and Giovanni Acciaiuoli. Aldus Manutius' two-volume Homer appeared in 1504 and included the pseudo-Herodotean and pseudo-Plutarchan Lives of Homer. In 1610 Niccolò della Valle printed a Latin translation of the *Iliad.* Texts attributed to Homer such as the Homeric Hymns and the *Batrachomyomachia* (the battle of the frogs and the mice) were also regularly included with the *Iliad* and the *Odyssey.* Milton apparently accepted these and the pseudo-Lives as authentic.[7] Editions of Homer appeared in Florence and Rome as well as Venice, and in France were brought forth by the leading French printers, Wechel and Morel.[8] However, two of the most important editions of Homer came forth from Geneva and Basel. Henri Estienne printed a corrected text of Homer with facing Latin translation in Geneva and included Homer with sixteen other Greek poets in the *Poetae Graeci Principes.* In Basel in 1583 an immensely influential edition of Homer appeared with a commentary by Iohannes Spondanus (Jean de Sponde). Although Harris Fletcher asserted that Milton had used Spondanus' edition, there is no authoritative proof of this.[9] Although Milton's classical learning extends far beyond these three poets, they will be the focus of this study.

The favorite poet of Milton's youth clearly was Ovid, whom, as he himself tells us in *An Apology against a Pamphlet,* he enjoyed with the other elegiac poets:

others were the smooth Elegiack Poets, whereof the Schooles are not scarce. Whom both for the pleasing sound of their numerous writing, which in imitation I found most easie; and most agreeable to natures part in me, and for their matter which what it is, there be few who know not, I was so allur'd to read, that no recreation came to me better welcome. (*CPW* I:889)

Milton's preference is clearly reflected in his own Latin elegies, composed before the age of twenty-one, in elegiac couplets, the verse form Ovid had made his own, and printed in the *Elegiarum Liber*, part of the *Poemata*, the second half of Milton's 1645 *Poems*.[10] In these Milton frequently lifts lines from Ovid or closely imitates his Latin idiom. When he intones "fallor" ("am I mistaken?") in Elegies 5 (line 5) and 7 (line 56), we can almost hear Ovid's voice. Also in Elegies 1, 4, 5, 6, and 7, he alludes to situations that recall Ovid's own poetry.[11] Elegy 1 includes a survey of London, comparable to Ovid's surveys of Rome in the *Amores*, and in this elegy and in Elegy 7 Milton, like Ovid, searches out sites where young women congregate. Elegy 4 to his former tutor, Thomas Young, imitates the tone of Ovid's letters of exile in the *Tristia*, particularly the one to his stepdaughter Perilla. Elegy 5 imitates Ovid's exuberant sexual energy in a salute to spring, and Elegy 7 imitates a typical Ovidian encounter with Cupid. Elegy 6 contrasts elegy with more serious forms of poetry, imitating the either–or style of Ovid's *Amores* 3. 1.

In Prolusion 1 Milton calls Ovid the choicest ("elegantissimus") of poets (*CPW* 1:231). Addressing him in Elegy 1 as the "Tarpeian Muse" (line 69), Milton wistfully describes him as potentially Homer's and Virgil's equal, had he not been banished to Tomis (lines 21–24). However, Elegy 6 and the retraction printed in the *Elegiarum Liber* may reflect second thoughts about Ovid, at least the Ovid of the *Amatoria*. In the Retraction Milton wishes to be ranked with those poets of whom Plato would have approved, not with the writers of elegy and light amatory verse. Elegy 6 mentions Ovid directly only once, regretting, as in Elegy 1, that Ovid's poems of exile, lacking the inspiration of Rome's conviviality, were inferior (Elegy 6, lines 19–20). Milton implies, whether seriously or in jest, a separation from those poets whom the Muses of wine inspire – Horace, Anacreon, and, yes, even though he does not name him – Ovid. With his recent composition of the Nativity Ode he declares that he is moving toward the poets of serious religious verse and epic – and among those he names is Homer. Despite this apparent disclaimer, Ovid continues as a presence in later Latin poems, and throughout *Paradise Lost* the Ovid of the *Metamorphoses* is ever at hand in mythic allusions and even lends a pagan enthusiasm to the creation passages of book VII. Moreover, when he hymns the joys of wedded love in book IV Milton lights the bridal torch from Ovid's praise in the *Amores* of Cupid inspiring lovers with mutual joy. In his epic Ovid stands beside Virgil and Homer, poets seemingly closer to his design as an epic poet.

As early as Prolusion 6, Milton praises Homer as "the rising sun or morning star of cultured literature, at whose birth all learning was born also, as his twin" (*CPW* 1:272). Homer's divine mind, Milton comments, made him apt to describe the councils of the gods and deeds done in heaven; yet Homer could also stoop to describe comic events, such the battle of the frogs and mice in the comic epic *Batrachomyomachia*. In the second book of the *Poemata* (1645), the *Sylvarum Liber*, Milton makes clear his epic aspirations, adopting Homer's and Virgil's hexameters as his dominant verse form, and with *In Quintum Novembris* making his first attempt at semi-epic. A highly imitative poem composed at the age of seventeen, *In Quintum Novembris* contains embedded phrases from Homer, Virgil, Ovid's *Metamorphoses*, as well as from a host of other Latin and neo-Latin poets. In tones that suggest Zeus awakening Agamemnon or Virgil's Mercury awakening Aeneas, Milton's Satan calls upon the pope to rise. Milton's Fama, who spreads the report of the Gunpowder Plot, is a cousin of Virgil's Fama. By exchanging a mere two words of Virgil's description Milton turns Virgil's Fama – "malum quo non aliud velociter ullum" (*Aeneid* 4.174) – from an evil into a good, "bonum quo non aliud veracius ullum" (line 195). Such very often is the technique of the young Milton with his Latin sources.

By 1639/40, when he composed *Epitaphium Damonis*, the final poem of the *Sylvarum Liber*, Milton is far more sophisticated. True, the Latin lament for his friend Charles Diodati owes a good deal to Virgil's lament for his friend Gallus as well as Ovid's lament for Tibullus (*Amores* 3.9). As Douglas Bush has pointed out, *Epitaphium Damonis* yields some seventy echoes from Virgil's *Eclogues*, as well as thirty-five from the *Georgics* and forty from the *Aeneid*.[12] Also, to signal that he intends, like Virgil, to turn from pastoral to epic, Milton even adapts his line "vos cedite sylvae" (line 160) from Virgil's famous line – "concedite sylvae" (Eclogue 10.63), expressing thereby his intention to compose an epic on Arthur's wars that would be an English *Aeneid*. Yet despite its extensive borrowing from Virgil, *Epitaphium Damonis* is far more than an imitation of Virgil's eclogues. More than his other Latin poems, it turns to Greek as well as Latin writers for inspiration, deliberately suggesting in its adoption of Thyrsis as his persona Theocritus' first idyll and in its use of the title epitaph Bion's epitaph for Adonis and Moschus' epitaph for Bion. Further, the passages that recall Milton's Italian voyage, or describe the cups that Manso gave him, or look forward to the composition of his British epic, lift his lament for Charles Diodati above the conventional pastoral imitation.

Milton's English poems differ from his Latin poems in their use of classical references and contexts. Although echoes remain and classical precedents are clear, they are often harder to detect in English than in Latin. Milton was not the first poet to place Christ's Nativity in the context of the flight of the pagan deities from their oracles. Mantuan and Tasso had done so before him. However, he is distinctive in contrasting the new sun-god of Christianity with the departing Apollo forsaking his shrine.[13] Moreover, the development of the catalogue of pagan deities in this early poem prepares him for the more sophisticated catalogue of pagan gods in *Paradise Lost*. Unlike the Nativity Ode, *L'Allegro* and *Il Penseroso* do not at first seem classical in either orientation or form. However, Milton manages to infuse both with classical flavor.[14] First, he adopts as his genre the classical hymn to the deity, invoking Mirth as the Grace Euphrosyne in *L'Allegro* and Melancholy as a Muse-like deity in *Il Penseroso*, attaching to both, moreover, classical genealogies. The opening dismissal in *L'Allegro* with its references to Cerberus and the darkness of a Stygian cave or a Cimmerian desert has the aura of a release from an oppressive classical underground. The shepherds and shepherdesses that Allegro sees are both English country-folk and familiar classical types with classical names – Corydon, Thyrsis, Phyllis, and Thestylis. In *Il Penseroso* Philomela inhabits the woods, Cynthia the sky, and Aurora the dawning sky. As Milton had introduced in Elegy I a classical note by alluding to ancient comedy, he makes Penseroso an admirer of "Gorgeous Tragedy," "Presenting *Thebes*, or *Pelops'* line, / Or the tale of *Troy* divine" (lines 97, 98–99). The mythic poet Orpheus has a prominent part in both poems, winning the ear of Pluto in *L'Allegro* and in *Il Penseroso* drawing "Iron tears down Pluto's cheek" (line 107). Milton succeeds in *L'Allegro* and *Il Penseroso* in wedding the classical to the native without overwhelming the native.

In many of his sonnets Milton invites us to interpret personal or political events through specific classical allusions. In the sonnet to Lady Margaret Ley, for example, he heroicizes her father, James Ley, by associating his death (which occurred shortly after Charles I's dissolving of parliament in 1629) with Isocrates' death, which legend attributed to his grief at Athens' loss of liberty after Philip of Macedon's "dishonest victory / At Chaeronéa" (lines 6–7). In his Sonnet 8, "When the Assault was intended to the City," he heroicizes himself and poetry by exhorting the besieger, "Lift not thy spear against the Muses' Bow'r" (line 9), and by invoking the examples of Alexander sparing the house of Pindar at the siege of Thebes and the conquerors sparing Athens' city walls when they heard the singing of Euripides' chorus from *Electra*. A different effect occurs in the second sonnet on *Tetrachordon* when Milton alludes to Latona's transforming into frogs the disrespectful "hinds" who "Rail'd at *Latona's* twin-born progeny" (lines 6–7), thus equating the detractors of his divorce pamphlets with the ignorant peasantry who disrespected Apollo and Diana. In the first case he associates himself as poet with Pindar and Euripides, in the second with the classical gods themselves. Classical allusion does the work for Milton in all these cases by furthering his own and opposing the opposite view.

Milton's *Mask Presented at Ludlow Castle* and *Lycidas* look back on classical models in different ways. The *Mask* takes its plot from a well-known story, told by Homer in the *Odyssey* and retold by Ovid in the *Metamorphoses* – Odysseus' rescue of the men whom Circe turned into swine, a plot used by Ariosto, Tasso, and Spenser in their Renaissance romances and epics.[15] Milton transforms the plot further by turning the female sorceress into Comus the sorcerer, making the Lady resist Comus' charms, and casting her brothers rather than the heroic male Odysseus as her rescuers. The Attendant Spirit, who guides the brothers and supplies the protective herb haemony, takes the place of the god Hermes who aided Odysseus. Further, Milton invents the semi-classical, semi-native nymph Sabrina, who comes, accompanied by classical water deities, to release the Lady.[16] Milton uses a well-known classical plot to serve his own devices to honor the Lady's chastity and heroicize her brothers.

Milton introduces other allusions and asides from classical myth to further classicize his Ludlow *Mask*. To characterize Comus' dangerous and seductive powers Milton alludes to those of his parents, Bacchus and Circe, noting, for example, how Bacchus transformed the Tuscan mariners into dolphins (lines 48–50), a story told both in the *Homeric Hymn to Dionysus* and in *Metamorphoses* (3.650–91). When he describes Circe's singing with "the Sirens three, / Amidst the flow'ry kirtled Naiades" (lines 253–54) near Scylla and the whirlpool Charybdis, he reminds us thereby that it was Circe who transformed Scylla into a monster. Besides being the offspring of Circe and Bacchus, Comus is allied to the classical goddesses of darkness, Cotytto and Hecate (lines 129, 135). The Lady is connected with several classical figures. When she appeals in her song to the "love-lorn Nightingale" (line 234), Milton is recalling Philomela, whose rape by her brother-in-law warns us of the Lady's present danger. Although her Elder Brother compares the Lady to the virgin goddesses Diana and Minerva, the first armed with arrows, the latter protected by the gorgon shield, Comus compares her to the more vulnerable Daphne, "root-bound" to the enchanted chair in his palace (lines 661–62). When Comus tempts her with a drink that he says will stir up joy, his likening it to Nepenthe, the drug used by Helen to induce forgetfulness of pain (lines 674–77), implies its narcotic potential. With these classical allusions Milton makes clear the dangers of the Lady's predicament and the daunting powers of the sorcerer who holds her prisoner.

The epilogue, through use of classical allusion, lends a philosophical dimension to the *Mask*. The Attendant Spirit returns to the semi-classical, semi-Christian garden of the Hesperides where the three daughters of Hesperus, attended by "the Graces and the rosy-bosom'd Hours," dance about the "golden tree" (lines 983, 986). There Venus attends Adonis, who "wax[es] well of his deep wound," and "Celestial Cupid" holds his dear Psyche, who will give birth to the "blissful twins" Youth and Joy (lines 1000, 1004, 1010). Milton chooses here, as he had throughout the *Mask*, to employ classical allusion to underscore one of the work's main themes – that paradisal rewards await those who follow virtue.

Like *A Mask*, *Lycidas* is an amalgam of classical influences. Milton follows Virgil in mourning for a poet-friend (Edward King); but he turns that friend as Lycidas into an archetypal figure for the poet, struck down, like Theocritus' Daphnis, in his prime. From Virgil (*Eclogue* 10.3) Milton draws his query, "Who would not sing for Lycidas?" (line 10); from Theocritus (*Idylls* 1.64) and Moschus (*Epitaph on Bion* 1.8) the refrain addressed to the Muses, "Begin then" (line 15). Nature mourns for Lycidas as for the poet Bion (Moschus 1.1–7), and Milton imitates Theocritus and Virgil (Theocritus 1.66–69; Virgil, *Eclogue* 10.9–12), when he asks where the nymphs were when Lycidas died. Like Virgil (*Eclogue* 1.2), Milton meditates on the muse and has Phoebus Apollo appear (*Eclogue* 6.3–4) to rebuke the shepherd-swain, touching him by the ears. Triton and Hippotades (names drawn from Homer and Virgil) appear to represent the gods of sea and wind, who disclaim responsibility for Lycidas' death, and report that the Nereid Panope with her sisters played upon the level ocean. Milton invokes both Alpheus and Arethusa to represent the pastoral genre and alludes to the myth of Alpheus' safe passage under the sea and union with Arethusa to suggest Lycidas' ultimate salvation. Recalling perhaps the myth of how dolphins saved the poet Arion, he asks the dolphins to waft Lycidas' body to shore. Before passing on to Christian consolation and entrusting Lycidas to "other groves, and other streams along" (line 174), Milton introduces a pastoral consolation and bids the "woeful shepherds weep no more" (line 165). As he employed a conventional opening frame in *Epitaphium Damonis*, he employs a closing frame in *Lycidas*, describing, as Virgil had (*Eclogue* 1.83; 2.67), how "the Sun had stretch'd out all the hills" (line 190). By supplying *Lycidas* with a classical context, Milton endows it with an overarching universality.

In *Paradise Lost*, Virgil and Homer and Ovid are also present, sometimes referred to directly, sometimes indirectly as models or predecessors in the epic genre. At the outset of his poem, Milton announces his theme, "man's first disobedience," just as Homer in the *Iliad* had named "Achilles' wrath" his theme or Virgil "arms and the man" in the *Aeneid*. Like his classical predecessors he calls upon the muse for inspiration, but he also determines to surpass them by soaring "above th' Aonian mount" (1.15). Though he draws the name Urania (VII.1) from the Greek muse of the heavens, he differentiates his muse from the classical muses. Homer is the only classical poet Milton names in *Paradise Lost* – "blind Maeonides" – equating himself with him in blindness and hopefully also in renown (III.34–35). However, in the proem to book IX he once more asserts his determination to surpass both Homer's and Virgil's poems, declaring his argument "Not less but more Heroic than the wrath of stern *Achilles*" or the "rage of *Turnus*" or the ire that caused Neptune and Juno to harass Odysseus or Aeneas (IX.14–19).

Despite this competitive stance Milton relies throughout *Paradise Lost* on Homer and Virgil for epic formulas and other techniques. Famously, he models the catalogue of the fallen angels in book 1 on Homer's catalogue of the ships in the *Iliad* (2.484 ff.). But unlike Homer, Milton is not looking back on heroic leaders and the geographical locations connected with them, but looking forward to those sites the fallen angels will claim as pagan deities and pollute with their idolatry. He does not honor the Olympian gods as princes of heaven, but reminds us that Jupiter (1.512–18) is a usurping ruler, who snatched the power from his father Saturn, just as Satan and his crew attempted to usurp God's rightful rule. Similarly, retelling Homer's poetic version of Zeus' ejection of Hephaestus from Olympus, Milton describes the god's fall as the descent of a falling star – "from Morn to Noon... from Noon to dewy Eve, / A Summer's day" (1.742–44). But he quickly corrects the ancient poets: "Thus they relate, / Erring" (1.746–47). Although, as Milton tells us at the beginning of the epic, Satan, like Hephaestus, was hurled from heaven by an angry god, his fall was fiery (1.44–51). No falling star, he. But, if Milton castigates the errors of the ancients, he also draws details from them. Satan and his crew resemble Hesiod's Titans, similarly ejected from Olympus by Zeus, for like the Titans who fell nine days (*Theogony* 664–735), the rebel angels lay confounded in Hell for nine days (1.50–52). Moreover, Milton likens the fallen angels lying upon the burning lake "in bulk" to the Titans or the giants "that warr'd on *Jove*, / *Briareus*, or *Typhon*, whom the den / By ancient *Tarsus* held" (1.198–200). By endowing Satan's rebels with the likeness of Jove's monstrous enemies Briareus and Typhon, he makes them and their motives also monstrous.

Although Hell with its fires and palpable darkness and burning lake seems in book I a realization of the biblical Hell, Milton finds the classical precedent irresistible. Pandemonium resembles Ovid's palace of the Sun in *Metamorphoses* 2, and in book II the landscape of Hell takes on the features of a Virgilian underworld. The "four infernal rivers" of Virgil's Hades – Styx, Acheron, Cocytus, Phlegethon– "disgorge into the infernal lake" (II.754–55). Classical monsters also inhabit Milton's Hell – "harpy-footed Furies" (II.596) and prodigies "worse / Than Fables yet have feign'd, or fear conceiv'd, / *Gorgons* and *Hydras* and *Chimeras* dire" (II.626–28). While most areas of Milton's Hell alternately burn and freeze, Milton sets aside fields where the fallen angels perform athletic exercise and hills where they engage in philosophical discourse and poetic entertainment, much as the blessed dead would have in a classical Elysium. But the fallen angels also suffer the torments of sinners tortured in a classical Tartarus. They cannot attain the forgetfulness that the classical Lethe would confer. Milton has set Lethe apart from the other rivers of Hell and places Medusa at its ford to terrify the fallen angels. Alluding to Homer's description of the classical sinner Tantalus whom Odysseus saw punished at a pool in Tartarus (*Odyssey* 11.582–92), Milton comments that the waters of Lethe fly "All taste of living wight," as once they "fled / The lip of Tantalus" (II.613–14). Thus the figure of Tantalus becomes something more than a mortal punished for sacrilege.

Classical reference functions in a different way in the Edenic books of *Paradise Lost*, as Milton often uses classical figures to contrast with Adam and Eve or to ironically predict their future. In alluding to "that fair field / Of Enna" (IV.268–69), where Proserpine gathered flowers, Milton looks forward to the scene in book IX when Eve among her flowers was "gathered" by Satan, just as Proserpine, "Herself a fairer flower, by gloomy Dis / Was gather'd" (IV.270–71). Conversely, he both likens Eve to and differentiates her from Narcissus. Although, like Narcissus, Eve was enthralled by her own beautiful image viewed in a lake, she does not pine in self-love like the mythical youth, but after being led to Adam learns "How beauty is excelled by manly grace" (IV.490). Milton also compares Adam and Eve to classical gods, but to different effects before and after the fall. In book IV he has Adam smile on Eve, "as *Jupiter* / On *Juno* smiles, when he impregns the clouds / That shed May flowers" (IV.499–501). The first man and woman here innocently resemble the beneficent nature deities of the classical world. However, in book IX a flowery comparison involving these same gods has sinister implications. When after the fall Eve lures Adam to a flowery bank, Milton echoes the passage in the *Iliad* (14.329–51), where Homer's Hera, deceiving her spouse, entices him to lovemaking on similar flowers (*Paradise Lost* IX.1027–45). By allowing readers to identify specific classical contexts, he complicates our understanding of Adam and Eve and their situation before and after the fall.

As with *Paradise Lost,* Milton employs classical genres to shape biblical material, basing *Paradise Regained* on the Virgilian brief epic and *Samson Agonistes,* as he freely acknowledges in his preface, on Greek drama. However, in these final poems, he restrains his borrowing of lines or devices from classical myth or poetry. His borrowing at the beginning of book IV of *Paradise Regained* of Homer's simile of flies at the milk pails is a rare instance (*Iliad* 16.641). Similarly, when he alludes to Hercules' defeat of Antaeus and Oedipus' quelling the Sphinx with the correct response to her riddle, he not only marks the Son of God's triumph over Satan but also celebrates the Son's superiority over figures from classical myth. Moreover, for the most part the figures from antiquity that he names in *Paradise Regained* are real rather than mythic, whether the conquerors Alexander, Caesar, and Pompey (III.31–42) whom Satan praises or the virtuous Romans such as Cincinnatus, Fabricius, Curius, and Regulus (II.445–49) whom the Son links with virtuous Hebraic leaders. *Samson Agonistes* follows a similar pattern. To celebrate Samson's triumph, Milton alludes to Ovid's phoenix rising from its ashes.[17] However, throughout the drama biblical references replace the classical ones of his earlier poetry. Homer and Virgil and Ovid may have taught Milton his craft as a poet, but in his final poems, while remaining true to their poetic lessons, Milton replaces the context of classical poetry with the context of the Bible.

NOTES

1 See Donald Lemen Clark, *John Milton at St. Paul's School* (New York, 1948), 111–21; Davis P. Harding, *Milton and the Renaissance Ovid* (Urbana, IL, 1948); Harris Francis Fletcher, *The Intellectual Development of John Milton,* 2 vols. (Urbana, IL, 1956–61); Richard DuRocher, *Milton and Ovid* (Ithaca, NY, 1985).

2 "The Life of Milton," in *Paradise Lost,* ed. Thomas Newton (London, 1749), I, lvii–lviii. She could also recite passages from Euripides, another of Milton's favorite classical writers.

3 Milton's copies of Heraclides of Pontus and Lycophron are at the University of Illinois Library, his copy of Euripides in the Bodleian Library, and other

texts at the New York Public Library. For a reconstruction of Milton's library, see Jackson Campbell Boswell, *Milton's Library: A Catalogue of the Remains of John Milton's Library and an Annotated Reconstruction of Milton's Library and Ancillary Readings* (New York, 1975).

4 Philip Ford, "Homer in the French Renaissance," *Renaissance Quarterly* 60 (2006): 4.

5 Ann Moss, *Ovid in Renaissance France. A Survey of the Latin Editions of Ovid and Commentaries Printed in France Before 1600* (London, 1982).

6 See the passage from *An Apology against a Pamphlet*, cited later.

7 See Prolusion 6 in *CPW* 1:272.

8 Ford, "Homer," 2–6.

9 See John B. Dillon and Gordon Teskey, "Milton's Homer," *PMLA* 101 (1986): 857–58. Dillon refutes Fletcher's claim, pointing out that it was based upon the assumption (since proved incorrect) that the marginal notes in the copy of Pindar's *Odes* at Harvard University were by Milton.

10 See my discussion of the influence of Ovid in "Milton's Dialogue with Ovid: The Case for the *Amatoria*," in *John Milton: "Reasoning Words*," ed. Charles W. Durham and Kristin A. Pruitt (New York, 2008), 77–87.

11 Citations of Milton's poetry are from John Milton, *Complete Poems and Major Prose*, ed. Merritt Y. Hughes (New York, 1957).

12 Douglas Bush, ed., "The Latin and Greek Poems," in vol. 1 of *A Variorum Commentary on the Poems of John Milton* (New York, 1970), 285.

13 See Stella Revard, "Apollo and Christ in the Seventeenth-Century Religious Lyric," in *New Perspectives on the Seventeenth-Century English Religious Lyric*, ed. John Roberts (Columbia, MO, 1994), 143–67; also see my discussion of Tasso in *Pindar and the Renaissance Hymn-Ode* (Tempe, AZ, 2001), 223–45.

14 See my discussion of Milton's use of classical hymn in "'L'Allegro' and 'Il Penseroso': Classical Tradition and Renaissance Mythography," *PMLA* 101 (1986): 338–50, re-worked in *Milton and the Tangles of Neaera's Hair: The Making of the 1645 "Poems"* (Columbia, MO, 1997).

15 See Homer, *Odyssey*, 10.233–40, 275–399; Ovid, *Metamorphoses* 14.271–307. The sorceress Alcina in *Orlando Furioso*, her counterpart Armida in *Gerusalemme Liberata*, and Acracia in *The Faerie Queene* (11.xii.69–87) are based on Circe.

16 See my discussion of Sabrina as a classical water nymph in *Milton and the Tangles*, 128–61.

17 Milton's sources for the legend of the phoenix include Ovid, *Metamorphoses* 15.392–407; Lactantius, *De Ave Phoenice*; Claudian, *Phoenix* (27); Tasso, "La Fenice," in "Quinto Giorno," *Il Mondo Creato*, 1278–1591. See *Epitaphium Damonis*, lines 185–89.

CHAPTER 23

Education

Gregory Chaplin

After seven years at Christ's College, Cambridge University, John Milton graduated Master of Arts *cum laude* on July 3, 1632. His farewell to Cambridge survives as Prolusion 7, a Latin oration delivered in the college chapel that would have lasted for more than an hour and satisfied one of his final degree requirements. The assigned topic of the disputation – whether learning brings more blessings to men than ignorance – prompts him to reflect on the education that he has received, an opportunity he seizes to express his frustration and disappointment. His university education has been insufficient for the future he imagines for himself as poet and orator. The "constant interruptions" of academic exercises have "hindered and hampered [him] in the hard and arduous pursuit of learning" (*CPW* 1:289). The curriculum is a relic of the Dark Ages when

> nothing was heard in the schools but the absurd doctrines of drivelling monks, and that profane and hideous monster, Ignorance, assumed the gown and lorded it on our empty platforms and pulpits and in our deserted professional chairs. Then Piety went in mourning, and Religion sickened and flagged, so that only after prolonged suffering, and hardly even to this very day, has she recovered from her grievous wound. (*CPW* 1:293)

Too much time is devoted to the wrong parts of grammar and rhetoric ("despicable quibbles" [*CPW* 1:300]), a distorted view of logic, and metaphysics ("a sinister rock, a Lernian bog of fallacies, devised to cause shipwreck and pestilence" [*CPW* 1:301]). In *Of Education* (1644), Milton goes even further, suggesting that the universities corrupt the young ("instilling their barren hearts with a conscientious slavery" [*CPW* 11:376]) and thus imperil the nation. His plan for reforming education in England simply does away with them.

As his anti-Catholic caricature of the Middle Ages suggests, Milton tends to align the educational reforms of the humanists – the "rebirth of classical learning" central to the idea of the Renaissance – with the reformation of the church and the search for true religion. The former enabled the latter, and it continues to fuel "the reforming of Reformation itself" that he envisions in *Areopagitica* (*CPW* ii:553). Throughout his career, Milton places a rigorous humanist education at the center of his vision of political and religious freedom. In his *Pro Populo Anglicano Defensio Secunda* (1654), he underscores the political significance of educational reform: "For nothing can be more efficacious than education in moulding the minds of men to virtue (whence arises true and internal liberty), in governing the state effectively, and preserving it" (*CPW* iv:625). And in his final impassioned call for republican liberty, *The Readie and Easie Way to Establish a Free Commonwealth* (1660), Milton continues to see the founding of good schools as essential: each English county "should have . . . schools and academies at thir own choice, wherin thir children may be bred up in thir own sight to all learning and noble education not in grammar only, but in all liberal arts and exercises" (*CPW* vii:460). Whether reflecting on his own preparations or the fate of the nation, Milton views education as nothing less than a reformation of the self – the disciplined renewal of a purer state of being, the recovery of the divine image that has been defaced by the fall, and the self-mastery that is the foundation of true liberty.

Milton could be so critical of Cambridge because he had been so well trained at one of the finest grammar schools in England, St. Paul's School, located in the close of St. Paul's Cathedral in London and a short walk from his childhood home on Bread Street. St. Paul's School was at the forefront of humanist education in England: the humanist John Colet, the Dean of the Cathedral and noted Christian reformer, completed the establishment of the school in 1512 with the assistance of Erasmus and made William Lily its first high master. As Renaissance humanists, their principal goal was the preparation of young men for public life through the study of classical languages and literature, which meant the *studia humanitatis* ("the humanities"): grammar, rhetoric, poetry, history, and moral philosophy. From "the outset," Erasmus writes in *De ratione studii* (1511), which provides the theoretical framework for the education at St. Paul's, "boys must be instructed in . . . Greek, of course, and Latin . . . because almost everything worth learning is set forth in these two languages."[1] Since "a true ability to speak correctly is best fostered both by conversing and consorting with those who speak correctly and by the habitual reading of the best stylists," Erasmus makes his recommendations clear: for Greek, he would assign Lucian, Demosthenes, Herodotus, Aristophanes, Homer, and Euripides; for Latin, Terence, Virgil, Horace, Cicero, Caesar, and Sallust.[2] In his

Statutes for the school, Colet concurs, banishing the Latin of the Middle Ages ("all barbary corrupcion . . . which ignorant blynde folis brought into this worlde and . . . poysenyed the olde laten speech") and "charg[ing] the Maisters that they teche . . . suych auctours that hathe with wisdome joyned the pure chaste eloquence."[3]

As Colet's emphasis on both wisdom and eloquence indicates, humanist educators were as interested in the moral formation of their students as they were in their ability to write pure classical Latin and Greek. Quintilian's description of the perfect orator captures their ideal:

> The first essential for such a one is that he should be a good man and consequently we demand of him not merely the possession of exceptional gifts of speech, but of all the excellences of character as well . . . The man who can really play his part as a citizen and is capable of meeting the demands both of public and private business, the man who can guide a state by his counsels, give it a firm basis by his legislation and purge its vices by his decisions as a judge, is assuredly no other than the orator of our quest.[4]

This view that personal morality legitimizes and empowers speech becomes crucial to Milton's conception of himself as poet and orator, and indeed, it may have contributed to his preoccupation with sexual purity in his early works.[5] The autobiographical digressions that mark his polemical prose often serve as ethical proofs that he is a virtuous man whom we should find persuasive. In *An Apology against a Pamphlet* (1642), Milton declares his conviction "that he who would not be frustrated of his hope to write well hereafter in laudable things, ought him selfe to bee a true Poem, that is, a composition, and patterne of the best and honourablest things" (*CPW* 1:890).

We know that Milton completed his studies at St. Paul's School by the end of 1624 because he was admitted to Christ's College on February 12, 1625, two months after he turned sixteen. Donald Clark contends "that Milton entered school in 1615 at the normal age of seven, after having learned to read and write at a petty school or at home with a tutor," but the major biographers suggest that he may have been tutored at home for a longer period and entered as late as 1620.[6] St. Paul's was divided into eight forms (class or grade levels based on student proficiency). The first and second forms focused on Latin grammar and simple Latin texts, including William Lily's *Carmen de Moribus*, a poem on morals and school regulations that illustrated grammatical constructions and expanded vocabulary; Cato's *Disticha Moralia*; and Aesop's *Fables* in Latin. The third and fourth forms continued with Latin grammar. Students in the third also practiced conversational Latin by studying Erasmus' *Colloquies* and Terence's *Comedies* and began poetry with Ovid's *De Tristibus*. Students in the fourth studied more poetry – Ovid's *Epistles* and *Metamorphoses* – and started to read historians such as Caesar and Justinus. Milton would have covered this material one way or another, whether entirely under the care of a private tutor or at St. Paul's with the assistance of an evening tutor.

Employing tutors in either role was quite common, and Milton emphasizes that his "father took care that [he] should be instructed daily both in school and under other masters at home" (*CPW* iv:612). The most significant tutor was Thomas Young, a Scottish Presbyterian, who taught Milton from 1618 to 1620, the period when he would have been studying the curriculum of the third and fourth forms. In *Elegia Quarta*, Milton credits Young with introducing him to Latin poetry ("With him leading me, I first traveled the Aonian retreats and the sacred green precincts of the forked mountain and drank the Pierian waters") and history ("and with Clio's favor sprinkled my happy mouth three times with Castalian wine" [lines 29–32]). This early instruction in elegiac poets such as Ovid seems to have awakened the poet in him: "both for the pleasing sound of their numerous writing, which in imitation I found most easie; and most agreeable to natures part in me, and for their matter . . . I was so allur'd to read, that no recreation came to me better welcome" (*CPW* i:889). Young is almost certainly "the puritan . . . who cutt his hair short" for the portrait painted of Milton at age ten, and his religious politics and knowledge of the early church and church fathers must have had significant influence on him.[7] In *Elegia Quarta*, Milton imagines Young in Hamburg "going through the great volumes of the ancient fathers, or the Holy Bible of the true God" (lines 43–44), and he suggests that Young's decision to leave England for Hamburg in 1620 to serve as chaplain to the Merchant Adventures stems from his inability to find a suitable position due to his Presbyterian sympathies: "you live alone and impoverished in an unknown land, and in your need seek in a foreign home the sustenance which the Penates of your homeland did not provide you" (lines 84–86).

The high master at St. Paul's was Alexander Gil, and Milton completed the last four forms under his direct supervision. In the fifth form, students began Greek grammar and continued their reading of Latin poetry with Virgil and history with Sallust. The sixth form kept up the study of Greek and began reading the *New Testament*, continued with Virgil, and read Cicero's *Epistles* and *De Officiis*. The seventh form completed Greek grammar; read minor Greek poets such as Hesiod, Pindar, and Theocritus; and studied Cicero's *Orations* for Latin prose and Horace for poetry. In the eighth form, students took up Hebrew grammar and the Hebrew Psalter; read Homer, Euripides, and Isocrates; and probably studied the Latin satirists Persius and Juvenal. Gil was educated at Oxford, and his scholarly interests must have shaped his pedagogy. Although he taught Latin, Greek, and Hebrew to his students, and may have introduced them to Aramaic dialects as well, Gil was a proud advocate of English. His *Logonomia Anglica* (1619) is an English grammar and rhetoric written in Latin that includes sections on etymology, syntax, prosody, and the reform of English spelling. The examples he provides are drawn from English poets, and his enthusiasm for vernacular poetry, particularly Spenser, would have encouraged Milton to see the reading and writing of English poetry as a serious and patriotic endeavor. Gil was also a Protestant theologian of a decidedly rationalist cast. In 1635, he published *The Sacred Philosophy of the Scripture*, which included a reprint of his earlier *Treatise Concerning the Trinity in Unity of the Deity* (1601). "Gil carried Christian rationalism to the extreme limits of orthodoxy" in his theology, Douglas Bush concludes, "limits which his quondam pupil Milton was to overstep" in *De Doctrina Christiana*.[8] Milton witnessed his schoolmaster's rationalist habits of mind at work on a vast array of subjects and texts for four years, and he became confident in the power of human reason to examine any issue – including the nature of divine justice – and to challenge any established belief.

The pedagogical structure of St. Paul's encouraged competition. The school building was one long chamber that could be divided into four smaller chambers with curtains, and "[a]t the upper end of the School, facing to the Door, was a decent *Cathedra*, or Chair placed, somewhat advanced, for the high Master to sit in, when he pleased, and to teach and dictate there."[9] The students were seated on benches along the walls. As Erasmus describes, "Each of the boys has his allotted place on steps that rise gradually, with their spaces marked out. Each class contains sixteen, and the head boy in each class has a stool a little higher than the rest."[10] Gil would have sat in that raised chair and assigned seats to students based on their academic performance, awarding the most accomplished student in each form the appropriate stool: "And as every one is more excellent in the gift of learning," all the students would have memorized from Lily's *Carmen de Moribus*, "so he shall sit in the more excellent place."[11] Students who succeeded received praise and rewards in front of the entire school; those who failed to achieve or who were disobedient were disciplined. Even in a period where corporeal punishment was ubiquitous, Gil was known for his "whipping fits."[12] Nonetheless, at St. Paul's School, Milton thrived in an environment – one of few in his culture – that placed merit before birthright, and his commitment to a meritocracy underwrites his later republicanism.

When he founded the school, Colet dedicated it to the boy Jesus: "Above the high master's desk sits a remarkable representation of the boy Jesus in the attitude of a teacher... Above is the Father's face, saying 'Hear ye him.'"[13] The iconoclasm of the Reformation swept away these images, but Milton frequently would have said the prayers that Colet and Erasmus wrote to express that dedication, including: "We pray unto thee, Jesus Christ, who as a boy twelve years old, seated in the temple, taught the teachers themselves, to whom the voice of the Father, sent from heaven, granted authority to teach all men, saying: This is my beloved son in whom I am well pleased: hear him."[14] Scholars have noted the influence of these prayers on the description of Jesus in *Paradise Regained*, who

> went'st
> Alone into the temple; there was found
> Among the gravest Rabbis disputant
> On points and questions fitting Moses' chair,
> Teaching not taught; the childhood shows the man,
> As morning shows the day.[15]
>
> (IV.216–21)

Milton certainly found the idea of Jesus as an exemplary student advanced to the role of teacher more conducive to his imagination than contemplating the horrors of the Passion and Crucifixion. In both *Paradise Lost* and *Paradise Regained*, the heroism of the Son stems first and foremost from his intellectual and moral clarity. Likewise, there may be some truth in Alexander Pope's complaint that Milton made God the Father sound too much like a "school-divine" in *Paradise Lost*, or at least a humanist schoolmaster testing the intellectual faculties of his creatures – most notably, the Son in book III and Adam in book VIII – and holding out advancement as the reward for obedience and discipline.[16]

By the time he left St. Paul's, Milton had the technical training necessary to be a great poet. (Shakespeare and Ben Jonson had no more than a sound grammar-school education.) Milton would have devoted considerable time to analyzing literary models – identifying the grammatical, rhetorical, prosodic, and logical principles of the texts he was studying – and translating, memorizing, paraphrasing, and imitating these models. He would have engaged in the standard technique of double translation (Latin to English to Latin) as well as translating Greek or Hebrew texts into English and then from English into Latin. So while Milton spoke Latin in school, he would have worked with English as well. He would have been asked to turn poetry into prose, prose into poetry, and poetry written in one meter into another. He would have been required to memorize a vast amount of material, including his Latin and Greek grammars and rhetoric textbook. The powers of mind that this strenuous education cultivated help explain Milton's technical brilliance as a poet as well as his ability to compose his late masterpieces while blind. Imitation was at the center of humanist education: students were taught to write with the eloquence of Cicero or Virgil through the careful study and emulation of their works. As a result, in ways that often seem paradoxical to modern readers, Renaissance writers can be indebted to earlier authors and profoundly original at the same time. Milton's declaration that *Paradise Lost* "pursues / Things unattempted yet in prose or rhyme" in a line translated from Ariosto's *Orlando Furioso* exemplifies this competitive imitation: it simultaneously acknowledges his debt to his predecessor and his desire to surpass him (1.15–16).

Milton formed two important friendships while at St. Paul's. The first was with Alexander Gil, Jr., the son of the headmaster, who started teaching the first two forms at St. Paul's in 1621. Young Gil was an accomplished Latin poet with a militantly Protestant outlook. For instance, he wrote poems celebrating not only the successes of Protestant military heroes but also the collapse of a covert Catholic chapel in Blackfriars in 1623.[17] He was an informal literary mentor for Milton, who credits him as "the keenest judge of Poetry" (*CPW* 1:314) and would have seen him as an example of the repressive nature of the Jacobean regime: young Gil was imprisoned and nearly had his ears cut off for toasting the health of John Felton, who assassinated the Duke of Buckingham, the unpopular favorite of Charles I, in 1628.[18]

The second friend was Charles Diodati, whom, Christopher Hill argues, "Milton clearly adored . . . more than he ever adored any human being except possibly his second wife."[19] Their surviving correspondence, including the Latin and Italian poems that Milton addressed to Diodati, and *Epitaphium Damonis*, which laments Diodati's untimely death in 1638, provide crucial evidence about Milton's intellectual, emotional, and poetic evolution during these years. Diodati's father was a successful physician whose family fled religious persecution in their native Lucca; his uncle was a famous theologian and Professor of Hebrew in Geneva. Although slightly younger than Milton, Diodati completed his education at St. Paul's two years earlier and went on to take his Bachelor's and Master's degrees at Trinity College, Oxford by 1628. As schoolboys, they lived a short walking distance from one another in London, and they probably shared a private tutor in Italian (and perhaps French and Spanish as well).[20] In any case, the surviving evidence demonstrates that they shared an abiding interest in Italian language, literature, and culture, and in the *Epitaphium*, Milton stresses Diodati's Tuscan roots.[21]

The value of these friendships became increasingly clear to Milton during his early years at Cambridge, where he felt alienated from the curriculum, his fellow students, and his first tutor, William Chappell. Milton alludes to a conflict with Chappell in *Elegia Prima*, addressed to Diodati: "Nor do I now have any interest in returning to the reedy Cam... How badly that place suits Phoebus's followers. It is not pleasing to keep bearing the threats of a harsh master and other things intolerable to my talent" (lines 11, 14–16). Although the details are unclear, this rift between tutor and student was so severe that Milton was reassigned to another tutor, Nathaniel Tovey, probably through the intercession of Diodati's father.[22] In this context, where he found "almost no intellectual companions," Milton began to idealize intimate conversations with friends and mentors, as his 1628 letters to Gil and Young attest, and he eventually places them at the center of his educational philosophy (*CPW* 1:314). In Prolusion 7, Milton depicts a Platonic universe in which "a mind trained and ennobled by Learning and study" can "contemplate the Ideas of things human or divine" and ascend to "the heaven whence it had come," and he suggests that the proper friendships can facilitate this process: "what can we imagine more delightful and happy than those conversations of learned and wise men, such as those which the divine Plato is said often to have held in the shade of that famous plane-tree?" (*CPW* 1:291, 295). Such conversations reoccur throughout Milton's poetry: in *A Mask*, between the Attendant Spirit and "a certain shepherd lad" (line 619); in *Epitaphium Damonis*, between Milton and Diodati; and in *Paradise Lost*, between Adam and Raphael.[23]

For all of his complaints, Milton acquired considerable expertise in rhetoric, logic, philosophy, and theology at Christ's College. He became familiar with the Puritan theological works of former Fellows William Perkins and William Ames, which were important touchstones for his *De Doctrina Christiana*, and he received extensive training in Ramist logic, the basis of his own *Artis Logicae*. Christ's College was a strong center for Cabbalistic studies and biblical languages, so by the time Milton left he was an accomplished Biblical scholar.[24] He would also have been acquainted with Joseph Mede, the most distinguished Fellow at Christ's, whose apocalyptic work *Clavis Apocalyptica* (1627) fueled millennial speculation.[25] In addition to the studies directed by their tutors, students were required to develop their rhetorical prowess by taking part in numerous orations and disputations, and Milton's surviving Prolusions demonstrate him perfecting the skills that he would go on to use as a polemicist. They reveal how successfully he mastered techniques that he found dubious: arguing for arbitrary positions, which cultivates a talent for "mak[ing] the worse appear / The better reason" (*Paradise Lost* II.113–14), and utilizing the Scholastic reasoning he abhorred, as in Prolusion 4: "In the Destruction of any Substance there can be no Resolution into First Matter." At the same time, the Prolusions display his desire to champion a worthy cause and willingness to attack the status quo, and as James Holly Hanford observes, "they contain . . . elements of his later conception of himself as a being set apart from others and bound to cultivate himself for special uses."[26]

In *Of Education* (1644), Milton offers his plan for reforming the standard sequence of schooling that he had undergone – as many as eight years of grammar school and seven years at university – in light of his own studies and experience as a private tutor, which he began after his return from Italy in 1639. The overt occasion for the tract was a request from Samuel Hartlib, a follower of educational reformer John Amos Comenius. The principal goal of Comenian reform was a more utilitarian education, so that students were prepared "to do and execute the duties of a vocation and trade of living."[27] In effect, it sought to replace the traditional literary education ("that inveterate custome, or rather disease of Schooles, whereby all the time of youth is spent in Grammaticall, Rhetoricall, and Logicall toyes") with vocational training; the reading of original texts of all sorts, except the Bible, would be replaced by compilations.[28] At first glance, there seem to be points of connection between Milton and the Comenians: Milton feels that the current approach to teaching Latin and Greek takes too long, students are forced to compose poetry and prose too soon ("the plucking of untimely fruit" [*CPW* II:373]), and study should begin with mathematics and geometry as well as texts on agriculture, natural philosophy, astronomy, and geography. But Milton is no Comenian; he seeks to perfect the humanist model of education, not replace it with vocational studies. The existing system has failed to produce leaders who can navigate the political and military challenges of the English civil war and secure the existence of a free commonwealth. What Milton proposes, Martin Dzelzainis convincingly argues, is "a New Model education."[29]

"The end then of learning," Milton declares, "is to repair the ruins of our first parents by regaining to know God aright, and out of that knowledge to love him, to imitate him, to be like him, as we may the neerest by possessing our souls of true vertue, which being united to the heavenly grace of faith makes up the highest perfection" (*CPW* II:366–67). The process that he outlines is "a complete and generous Education that which fits a man to perform justly, skillfully and magnanimously all the offices both private and publike of peace and war" (*CPW* II:377–79). These two statements declare his debt to the northern humanism that gave birth to St. Paul's School, which "baptised the classical idea of the *vir humanus* [the virtuous man] by subsuming it under the biblical ideal of Man as the image of God."[30] The pursuit of classical civic virtues initiates the process through which one seeks to counteract the effects of the fall. Thus Milton does not depart from the goals of a humanist education; he reformulates, intensifies, and expands the curriculum so as to "lead and draw [students] in willing obedience, enflam'd with the study of learning, and the admiration of vertue; stirr'd up with the high hopes to be brave men, and worthy patriots, dear to God, and famous to all ages" (*CPW* II:384–85). Rather than simply reading about heroic endeavors, the students will have the physical and intellectual training to perform them. After twelve years of study, students will have mastered Greek, Latin, Italian, and Hebrew and moved through a dizzying array of subjects that culminate in the study of politics, theology, rhetoric, and poetry. Milton concludes by acknowledging that his educational model "is not a bow for every man to shoot in [*sic*] that counts himselfe a teacher; but will require sinews almost equall to those which Homer gave Ulysses" (*CPW* II:415). For both teacher and student, then, this education is a heroic undertaking. And it is his own education that has prepared Milton – as student, teacher, and ultimately as poet – to pursue epic ambitions.

NOTES

1 Erasmus, *On the Method of Study*, trans. Brian McGregor, in *Collected Works of Erasmus*, ed. Craig R. Thompson, 86 vols. (Toronto, 1974–), XXIV:667.

2 *Ibid.*, XXIV:669.

3 Quoted in Donald Lemen Clark, *John Milton at St. Paul's School* (New York, 1948), 101.

4 Quintilian, *The Institutio Oratoria of Quintilian*, trans. H. E. Butler, 4 vols. (Cambridge, MA, 1963), I:9–11.

5 See E. M. W. Tillyard, *Milton* (London, 1949), 374–83; Ernest Sirluck, "Milton's Idle Right Hand," *Journal of English and Germanic Philology* 60.4 (1961): 749–85; and William Kerrigan, *The Sacred Complex* (Cambridge, MA, 1983), 22–72.

6 Clark, *John Milton*, 32. See Barbara K. Lewalski, *The Life of John Milton* (Oxford, 2000), 5–6; and James Holly Hanford, *John Milton, Englishman* (London, 1950), 23.

7 *EL* 2.

8 Douglas Bush, *English Literature in the Earlier Seventeenth Century* (Oxford, 1945), 321.

9 Quoted in Clark, *John Milton*, 39.

10 Erasmus, "To Justus Jonas 1521," trans. R. A. B. Mynors, in *Collected Works of Erasmus*, VIII:236.

11 Quoted in Clark, *John Milton*, 52.

12 Quoted in Lewalski, *Life*, 30.

13 Erasmus, "To Justus Jonas 1521," VIII:236.

14 Quoted in Clark, *John Milton*, 45.

15 See Clark, *John Milton*, 46; and S. H. Steadman, "Milton and a School Prayer," *Times Literary Supplement* (August 1927): 548.

16 Alexander Pope, "The First Epistle of the Second Book of Horace Imitated," in *Alexander Pope: A Critical Edition of the Major Works*, ed. Pat Rogers (Oxford, 1993), 102.

17 See Leo Miller, "On Some Verses by Alexander Gil which John Milton Read," *Milton Quarterly* 24 (1990): 22–25.

18 Christopher Hill, *Milton and the English Revolution* (New York, 1977), 28.

19 *Ibid.*, 31.

20 Harris Francis Fletcher, *The Intellectual Development of John Milton*, 2 vols. (Urbana, IL, 1956–61), 1:420–21.

21 See chapter 26 in this volume, Catherine Gimelli Martin's "Italy," for a fuller account of Milton's friendship with the Diodati family and his interest in Italian culture.

22 See Leo Miller, "Milton's Clash with Chappell: A Suggested Reconstruction," *Milton Quarterly* 14 (1980): 77–87; and Gordon Campbell, "Milton's Second Tutor," *Milton Quarterly* 21 (1987): 81–90.

23 For a discussion of Plato's influence on Milton's thought, see Pitt Harding's chapter in this volume.

24 Fletcher, *Intellectual Development*, 11:289–99.

25 See John Peter Rumrich, "Mead and Milton," *Milton Quarterly* 20 (1986): 136–41.

26 James Holly Hanford, "The Youth of Milton," in *John Milton, Poet and Humanist: Essays by James Holly Hanford* (Cleveland, OH, 1966), 1–74 (p. 19).

27 Quoted in *CPW* 11:190.

28 Quoted in *CPW* 11:189.

29 Martin Dzelzainis, "Milton's Classical Republicanism," in *Milton and Republicanism*, ed. David Armitage, Armand Himy, and Quentin Skinner (Cambridge, 1995), 3–24 (p. 11).

30 Brendan Bradshaw, "Transalpine Humanism," in *The Cambridge History of Political Thought 1450–1700*, ed. J. H. Burns (Cambridge, 1991), 95–131 (p. 103).

CHAPTER 24

The English Church

Neil Forsyth

Everything about the English church in the seventeenth century was contested, even whether there should be such an institution – or such a building. Quakers and Ranters met in private houses or barns, even taverns. Others formed "gathered churches" apart from the official institution, or went out onto hillsides and moors to listen to itinerant preachers. The Church of England, or Anglican church as it came to be called, barely survived the years of war and commonwealth: its forms of governance were transformed, and the interiors of many parish churches were ripped out, windows and decorations smashed and the walls whitewashed. During the 1640s and 1650s, the high point of Puritan power, ordinances made it a criminal offence to use the Book of Common Prayer or openly to celebrate the birth, death, and resurrection of Jesus Christ. A third of the parish clergy lost their livings. The Archbishop of Canterbury, like his king soon afterwards, was tried, convicted, and beheaded. Other bishops were imprisoned or exiled. Episcopacy itself was abolished and the lands and possessions of the bishoprics and cathedrals sold off. How are we to account for these unthinkable events?

The catastrophic cleavage in western Christendom that was the sixteenth-century Protestant Reformation was still dividing Europe a hundred or more years later, and still exciting strong feeling. For many Protestants the Bishop of Rome was the Antichrist: worship of God had been supplanted by idolatry.[1] In England execution of priests and overtly practicing Catholics was more common than in any other country in Europe.[2] Many of the more extreme events of the period can be explained if we remember this savage background and the paranoia it fostered. Roman Catholicism was, for the mature Milton, not so much a religion as a political system, and a constant threat. He argued in *A Treatise of Civil Power*, part of his last-ditch effort to prevent the Restoration of the monarchy, that popery cannot "be acknowledged a religion; but a Roman principalitie rather, endevouring to keep up her old universal dominion under a new name and meer shaddow of a catholic religion . . . supported mainly by a civil, and, except in Rome, by a forein power" (*CPW* VII:254).

How soon did Milton adopt these views? As a boy, he attended All Hallows Church near his home in London, where Richard Stock, a respected and eloquent Puritan, was minister. The word "puritan," let us be clear, refers not to an organized sect but to those who wanted to continue the Protestant mission of *purifying* the church from Roman Catholic ceremony and trappings. It was also a term of abuse for those opposed both to high-church ceremonial and to entertainments (it is so used in *Twelfth Night* of Malvolio, for example).[3] Those of Puritan tendency preferred to call themselves "the godly." Milton may well have taken on Stock's antipapist views but he would later repudiate the minister's conservative views on marriage, his sabbatarianism (insistence on dour Sundays), and his defense of tithes (payment of a tenth of one's income to maintain the church and pay the minister's salary).

There is little evidence, however, that this background had any special bearing on Milton's early religious practice. Milton's earliest English poems are psalm paraphrases, obviously written under his musical father's influence, and one of them will be familiar to anyone with even the slightest Christian upbringing. It converts the words of Psalm 136, "O give thanks unto the Lord, for he is good, for his mercy endureth forever," into

> Let us with a gladsome mind
> Praise the Lord, for he is kind,
> For his mercies aye endure,
> Ever faithful, ever sure.
>
> (lines 1–4)[4]

In the Calvinist churches, psalm singing had become a popular part of the service of worship.[5] Although some extremists followed Zwingli and were hostile to any music in church, hymn singing was widespread and did not mark the singer as a member of any particular Protestant branch or tendency. Another of Milton's early compositions, the paired poems *L'Allegro* and *Il Penseroso*, contains little to differentiate Milton from other practicing members of the Church of England. The favorite places of Il Penseroso, the Melancholy man, are dimly lit churches, perhaps like the great cathedral of St. Paul's near Milton's home, or the magnificent "chapels" of some Cambridge colleges like King's, where there are

> storied windows richly dight,
> Casting a dim religious light.
> There let the pealing organ blow,
> To the full-voiced choir below,

In service high, and anthems clear,
As may with sweetness, through mine ear,
Dissolve me into ecstasies,
And bring all Heav'n before mine eyes.
                                        (lines 159–66)

There had been a good deal of controversy about whether the beautiful stained glass of England's churches – in so far as it had survived the iconoclasm of the Reformation – was an aid to worship, as George Herbert tried to show in "The Windows," or an insidious kind of idolatry. But Milton did not, as yet, seem interested or partisan. If he were, it is unlikely he could have written poems on the deaths of the Bishop of Ely and of Lancelot Andrewes, Bishop of Winchester, whose views on the office of bishop he later attacked (*CPW* 1:768–74). And the themes of his poem on the Gunpowder Plot (1626) were common to most Protestants: Satan was behind the pope's efforts to blow up the parliament and the king. Antipopery of this kind could be used to play down the significance of internal divisions within the English church in the face of the common adversary.[6]

Although most Puritans, or "the hotter sort of Protestants," were still working within the fold of the official church, within a few years the broad Calvinist consensus that had held the church together under Elizabeth and James I – especially since the terror of the Gunpowder Plot of 1605 – came apart.[7] Almost as soon as he came to the throne in 1625 Charles tried to impose a revolution from on high.[8] His henchman William Laud, who held a series of bishoprics culminating with his appointment as Archbishop of Canterbury, head of the English church, in 1633, feared Puritanism and insisted on high-church rituals, including a full set of elaborate vestments. Disputing doctrine in sermons was discouraged and "correct" preaching was enforced by ecclesiastical courts beyond the reach or protection of the Common Law. Puritan pamphleteers were liable for brutal punishments: William Prynne, for example, author of *Histrio-mastix* (1632), an attack on Laudian ritual and stained-glass windows, as well as the Caroline fashion for public entertainments, was tried by the Star Chamber in 1633 and sentenced to imprisonment, a £5,000 fine, and the removal of part of his ears. Very soon, and probably in response, on October 18, James I's controversial *Book of Sports* was reissued as *The King's Majesty's declaration to his subjects concerning lawful sports to be used*. It listed those sports that were permissible, indeed encouraged, as soon as church was out: these included "dancing, either men or women, archery for men, leaping, vaulting, or any other such harmless recreation," along with "May-games, Whitsun-ales and

Morris-dances, and the setting up of May-poles."⁹ The declaration rebuked Puritans and "precise people," and was issued to counteract growing calls like Prynne's for strict abstinence on the Sabbath. Charles ordered that any minister who refused to read it out loud would be deprived of position.

Those two books exemplify the increasingly bitter opposition between the two tendencies in the church. Although Puritans often quarreled fiercely among themselves, they were brought together by the urgent need to oppose what they saw as Laud's revival of popery and idolatry. If the English nation did not now complete the Reformation as God wanted, the people would see the Bible replaced by the Mass, Magna Carta by the laws of Castile, and the gentry would find themselves in the chain-gangs of Peru and the galleys of the Mediterranean.¹⁰

Laud also tried to impose a new theology, one with which Milton would later find himself in some sympathy. The name given to this system is Arminianism, since it derives its anti-Calvinist arguments from the Dutch theologian Jacobus Arminius. The dominant religious paradigm in the English church since the time of Elizabeth had been orthodox Calvinist predestination: God had decided in advance that only a few among the faithful are saved and are thus in fact the elected saints who run the church through their evident sanctity. This view, though widely held on the official level, created enormous anxiety: no one really knew whether he or she belonged to the chosen elite. In the Arminian system, on the other hand, Christ died for everyone, not only the elect, and mankind was free to choose, or reject, the offered grace. Sacraments were the main vehicle for the saving grace: infant baptism began the process, to be followed by regular participation in communion open to all who confessed their sins.

The focus of these elaborate rituals, using the liturgy in the Book of Common Prayer, was the communion table, which thus became an altar again. As Laud put it, with a swipe at the Puritan love of preaching, the altar is "the greatest place of God's residence upon earth. I say the greatest, yea greater than the pulpit; for there 'tis *Hoc est corpus meum*, This is my body; but in the other it is at most but *Hoc est verbum meum*, This is my word."¹¹ From Elizabethan times, the communion table had usually been set lengthwise, and the congregation could gather around it. Laud thought this disrespectful:

Should [the Holy Table] be permitted to stand as before it did, churchwardens would keep their accounts on it, parishioners would despatch the parish business at it, schoolmaster will teach their boys to write upon it, the boys will lay their hats, satchels and books upon it, many will sit and lean irreverently against it in sermon time, the dogs would piss upon it and defile it.¹²

In Laud's churches, the altar was railed off at the east end of the chancel in a separate and sacred space that only the minister could enter. A crucifix could now be placed on it. And one had to kneel to the priest to receive the bread and wine.

These practices were anathema to Puritans and brought a swift reaction from them. John Pym and the other leading Calvinists in parliament argued that it was they who were the loyalists and that the new Arminian religion was both heterodox and the means of re-introducing Roman Catholicism into England – creeping popery. An Arminian, said Francis Rous in a parliamentary debate of January 26, 1629, "is the spawn of a papist."[13] Soon the system of church governance known as Presbyterianism, strongly Calvinist and powerful in Scotland since Elizabeth's time, became the chief means of opposition, both within parliament and outside it, to the Laudian Church of England. Bishops should be abolished and replaced by the locally elected church officials known as presbyters.

Milton was a student at Cambridge when many of these Puritan ideas were being promulgated by such teachers as John Preston, master of Emmanuel College. Milton's own college, Christ's, itself had a Puritan tradition, and he may have been sent there because Richard Stock had also been at Christ's. Yet Milton does not seem, while at Cambridge, to have taken sides in these increasingly acrimonious disputes, even when in 1626 the Duke of Buckingham was foisted on the university as its chancellor and all predestination teaching was forbidden. When Milton graduated with his BA in 1629 and his MA in 1632, he was automatically required to sign the subscription book and thus acknowledge three Articles of Religion: the king is the head of the church, the Book of Common Prayer is the lawful liturgical text, and the Thirty-Nine Articles which had defined the Church of England since the Elizabethan compromise contained nothing contrary to the word of God. A few years later, Milton could not have agreed to any of those propositions. Unless he signed with his fingers crossed, it does not look as if he was yet committed to the Puritan cause.

Milton wrote later that he had been "Church-outed by the Prelats" (CPW 1:823) – by which he meant, not that he was thrown out of the church, but that his distaste for the Laudian priests forced him to give up any idea of a career in the ministry. He does not say exactly when this is supposed to have happened, and in retrospect it may have seemed more like a decisive moment than the longer process it probably was. The process may have already started at Cambridge. Milton made witty attacks on the university in his Prolusions, and clearly thought that the church was so badly governed because of what the gentry who supported the status quo had learned there. The "monkish and miserable sophistry" of that education incapacitated them for "all true and generous philosophy," as he wrote later (1642) in *The Reason of Church-Government* (*CPW* 1:854). As Milton well knew, a majority of the young men graduating from Cambridge went into the ministry and collected a salary for doing not very much. They often lived elsewhere and left the parish in the care of uneducated or incompetent substitutes.

The first clear sign of Milton's entry into the controversy of the time is *Lycidas*. St. Peter, swinging his keys at the heavenly gates, "shakes his mitred locks" and tells the arriving Edward King (like Milton, one of those Cambridge graduates, and actively preparing for the ministry) how different he is from those who "for their bellies' sake / Creep and intrude, and climb into the fold" (lines 114–15). These animals are, we soon learn, the clergy who do not fulfill their proper function as pastors, i.e., to feed their sheep, as Simon Peter is told at John 21:15–16, but instead offer an unpleasant-sounding alternative to this pastoral verse: "And when they list, their lean and flashy songs / Grate on their scrannel pipes of wretched straw" (lines 123–24). It is central to the pastoral convention of the poem that bad preaching should be equated to bad singing, and that those lines stand out vividly in the midst of the mostly mellifluous verse. They continue with a direct and memorable image – "The hungry sheep look up, and are not fed" – and then denounce "the grim wolf" who "Daily devours apace" what the sheep ought to be eating (lines 125, 127–28).

Who is that "grim wolf"? On one level he is obviously the pope, exerting pervasive influence over the corrupt Church of England.[14] Particularly perhaps, the wolf represents the Jesuits, since their founder, Ignatius Loyola, had two grey wolves on his coat of arms. Jesuits still carried on illegal proselytizing in England, and thus contributed to Protestant paranoia. Within the poem the wolf is also kin to those creatures whose bellies were just mentioned in language that echoes the parable in John 10:1–28 about corrupt preachers as wolves; Matthew 7:15 about "false prophets, which come to you in sheep's clothing, but inwardly they are ravening wolves"; and Matthew 10:16 about "sheep in the midst of wolves." At the time, such language was widely used for Laud's usurpation of the church: "these are the men that should have fed Christ's flock, but they are the wolves that have devoured them."[15]

Differences over how the church was to be governed, exacerbated now by Laud's reforms, were one of the causes of the civil wars that spanned the middle years of the seventeenth century. The instigating cause of these wars was the attempt of Charles and Laud, with Catholic support from

Ireland, to impose the English episcopal structure on the Scottish Presbyterian system. Following his humiliating defeat, Charles had to summon what came to be called the Long Parliament. Quickly this newly assembled body acted to compensate the Puritan victims of Archbishop Laud's persecution, and began impeachment proceedings against Laud for "subversion of the laws... and of religion."[16] He was sent to the Tower and eventually executed in 1645.

Milton immediately joined in the struggle to get rid of the bishops not only from the ecclesiastical hierarchy but from the House of Lords. He wrote five antiprelatical tracts over the next two years in favor of the "Root and Branch" petition, signed by 15,000 Londoners and handed in to parliament on December 11, 1640. According to the petition there has been a "great increase of idle, lewd and dissolute, ignorant and erroneous men in the ministry, which swarm like locusts of Egypt over the whole kingdom." The text goes on to denounce in Laud's church the "growth of popery and increase of papists, priests, and Jesuits in sundry places, but especially about London since the Reformation; the frequent venting of crucifixes and popish pictures both engraven and printed, and the placing of such in Bibles." The list of Romish practices includes, as well as the bishops' elaborate clothing, "the standing up at Gloria Patri and at the reading of the Gospel, praying towards the East, the bowing at the name of Jesus, the bowing to the altar, the sign of the cross in baptism, the kneeling at the Communion."[17] There is a good deal more in the same vein. The tone was set.

Milton was not yet as radical either in politics or theology as he soon became: like most Englishmen he still recognized the king and thought of his power as shared with the Lords and the Commons.[18] But parliament, he argued, should be the sole agent of church reform. If not, the king would impose his own high-church ceremonial and doctrine, through his control of the appointment of bishops. Milton's pamphlets helped to generate an extraordinary explosion of tract and counter-tract, a war of words on everything from the imminence of the apocalypse, the renewed power of Satan, to how the people could take power from their rulers.

In May 1641, at the height of the controversy, appeared the first of Milton's five pamphlets (actually more of a short book), *Of Reformation Touching Church-Discipline in England*. With this fiercely eloquent treatise, Milton announced himself as one of the great writers of English prose. He implores the "*Tri-personall* GODHEAD! looke upon this thy poore and almost spent, and expiring *Church*, leave her not thus a prey to these importunate *Wolves*" (*CPW* 1:614 – a passage which shows he was still an orthodox Trinitarian[19]). The echo of *Lycidas* is unmistakable, and the same biblical references stand behind it. As for the bishops, those "Vassals of Perdition" (*CPW* 1:617), they should be executed, and will in any case spend eternity being tortured in Hell.

In a further tract, known for short as *Animadversions*, Milton places himself, not for the last time, in the line of prophets "transported with the zeale of truth to a well heated fervencie" (*CPW* 1:663) – he is thinking, he later says, of Daniel against Nebuchadnezzar and Elijah against Baal (*CPW* 1:700). He attacks this hireling clergy and urges them to "Wipe your fat corpulencies out of our light" (*CPW* 1:732). He also imagines God coming down among us again: "When thou hast settl'd peace in the Church, and righteous judgement in the Kingdome, then shall all thy Saints address their voyces of joy, and triumph to thee, standing on the shoare of that red Sea into which our enemies had almost driven us" (*CPW* 1:706). Clearly the language allows for little compromise. Nevertheless, in a reversal of the previous policy announced in "The Grand Remonstrance" of December 1, 1641, which often uses Milton's language, parliament allowed the bishops to return to the House of Lords on December 29. Milton was incensed and sat down again to write, to denounce this backsliding.

The resulting tract, *The Reason of Church-Government*, takes a different approach from the vitriolic satire of the earlier texts. Milton here makes a broad argument against episcopacy based on an ideal church order including the equality of clergy and laity that he takes to be anticipated in the gospel. The degree of his advancing radicalism may be judged by the way he defends the sects called by their enemies "Puritans, and Brownists." He claims that "the Primitive Christians in their times were accounted such as are now call'd Familists and Adamites" (*CPW* 1:788), both of which sects believed in the possibility of recovering prelapsarian innocence. The Adamites, at least according to their enemies, went naked whenever they could (rare enough and courageous in the English climate, but a sign of their regained purity and simplicity), and were baptised as adults, a practice condemned as heretical. Milton clearly feels no need to distinguish his own views from those of these extreme sects (and we know from his theological treatise that he opposed infant baptism). His target is the priesthood. To oppose the claim of the bishops that episcopacy had developed over time in order to counter schism during the early years of the church, he argues that the priesthood itself is the chief promoter of schism, labeling opposing sects as Puritans or Adamites and denouncing heretics instead of encouraging controversy as a way to truth. Unlike the civil magistrate, the church has power over only the inner man, and so must plead and cajole and reprove, perhaps even excommunicate if necessary, but always "reason." Like Calvin, Milton speaks of "a company of Saints." Any Christian, not just a speciously sanctified priesthood, should be able to teach and expound scripture "though never so laick, if his capacity, his faith, and prudent demeanour commend him" (*CPW* 1:841, 844).

In the five years since he wrote *Lycidas*, where he attacks the greed of the clergy but still allows for a national church hierarchy, Milton had progressed rapidly toward the radical positions he would now be identified with. In the first of his antiprelatical tracts, he wrote not exactly as a Presbyterian but as if he expected the Presbyterians to be on his side in the struggle for reform. But in the space of a few months he had moved beyond the idea of an established and centrally controlled church.

In January 1643 the Long Parliament did abolish episcopacy and convened the Westminster Assembly of Divines to advise on church settlement. It was stacked with Presbyterians, and in the *Solemn League and Covenant*, it attempted to establish a unified Reformed Church throughout the realm, yet still allowing for the king's authority "in the preservation and defence of the true Religion and liberties of the Kingdoms."[20] There were many to disagree. Independents were becoming stronger, especially in the army, and argued for broad-based toleration of all Protestant sects, and some even for all Christians, including Roman Catholics. Independents such as John Goodwin generally wanted separate and autonomous churches "gathered" under elected ministers and democratically run. William Walwyn, one of the Leveller leaders, warned parliament against what he saw as "a very inquisition" trying to stifle debate about religion and dispose men to believe "whatsoever the Synod and learned Church-men shall hold forth." These differences gave rise to some of the sharpest and most unforgiving polemics of the period.[21]

Milton's growing disillusion with the Presbyterian-dominated parliament had much to feed on. The attacks on his divorce tracts of 1643–45 came initially from those same "puritanical" Presbyterians, such as William Prynne and Robert Baillie, on whose support he had initially counted. The attacks pushed Milton's own views closer to what was emerging as the tolerationist Independent line soon endorsed by Cromwell. Although some of these were separatists, others such as the five "Dissenting Brethren" who signed, in 1643, what was to become the manifesto of all Congregationalism, *An Apologeticall Narration*, wanted a unified church. Roger Williams (whom Milton probably met and befriended at this time) took a different line. An eloquent tolerationist, he wanted no national church. Although there is no evidence of Milton's having joined them, or indeed any church, his sympathy for Independency is plausible, if for no other reason than his commitment, so clear in *Areopagitica* (1644), to liberty of conscience (*CPW* II:554, 560). Milton there further confirmed his scorn for the Presbyterians, who had forgotten their own persecution and now wanted to inflict it on others (*CPW* II:568–69), although he never could agree, with Williams, to tolerate "Popery, and open superstition" (*CPW* II:565). Then in a 1646 sonnet, "On the New Forcers of Conscience," Milton wittily attacked the Presbyterians, proposing that "New *Presbyter* is but old *Priest* writ large" (line 20), and again, during the trial of the king in December 1648, he saved his real fury in *The Tenure of Kings and Magistrates* for the "dancing Divines" of the Westminster Assembly and Sion College (*CPW* III:195). They had been foremost in stirring up the revolt against Charles: they "devested him, disannointed him, nay curs'd him all over in thir Pulpits and thir Pamphlets" (*CPW* III:191). But now they had turned their coats, and were worthy only of contempt.

In the years of the Interregnum, the weakness of parliament and the lack of any other central authority allowed radical religious activity to proliferate even more rapidly – Baptists, Ranters, Quakers, Muggletonians, Fifth Monarchists, Levellers, even the proto-communist Diggers, were holding meetings in private houses or disrupting public services. On February 10, 1652, a "Committee for the Propagation of the Gospel" was appointed, including Cromwell, to attempt to impose some limited order on the state of religion. Immediately, however, a group of Independents, flushed with their new sense of power, themselves proposed an Established Church with a paid clergy and restrictions on liberty of worship and publication. Though now almost totally blind, Milton vigorously opposed this position, arguing once again "that men should refrain from forbidding books."[22] He also sent a sonnet to Cromwell in May. In the Trinity Manuscript the sonnet carries a title that makes a protest against this new threat to freedom of worship: "On the Proposals of Certain Ministers of the Committee for Propagation of the Gospel." What especially annoyed Milton was the proposition that no one should be permitted to speak on any religious question unless two divines at least had certified his orthodoxy. Milton urges Cromwell to defend religious liberty and to make no provision for a stipendiary clergy. The enemies of these positions are identified with the hireling wolves in sheep's clothing of Matthew 7:15 and those denounced in Philippians 3:19 "whose God is their belly." These are among the same biblical texts Milton had in mind when he had written, fifteen years earlier, the passage about the clergy's bellies in *Lycidas*.

Following the Restoration, Milton's circumstances were much straitened but his religious views and practice changed little. He worked on the great poem, on his theological treatise, and continued not belonging to any church. In the first years of the new dispensation parliament and the crown increased the repression of sects – no group of more than five persons could meet for a service of worship that did not conform to the Church of England liturgy. The Act of Uniformity obliged even Presbyterian incumbents, whom Milton had long seen as latter-day Pharisees and in part responsible for the Restoration, to resign their ministries. And later nonconformists found themselves banished from towns to obscure villages. Only after Milton's death did the Toleration Act of 1689 finally permit worship in non-episcopal congregations, and the tradition of Puritanism could pass into "Dissent."

Milton dissented in radical ways throughout his adult life. Yet it seems he rarely joined with others in worship. There was a large Quaker community in Chalfont St. Giles, where Milton lived briefly in 1665 to escape the London plague while he was finishing *Paradise Lost,* and many features of the Quaker meeting would have been to his liking – its informality and lack of authoritarian structure and ritual, the absence of a clergyman, the quiet waiting on the spirit to move the people, the freedom to speak out. Yet for the last thirty years or more of his life, and even among the sympathetic Quakers of Chalfont St. Giles, there is no record of Milton's membership of a church or meeting-house. There was none to suit.

The established church was the main reason. The last book of *Paradise Lost* (1674) imagines the struggle between godly sheep and anti-Christian wolves in language that had not changed very much since *Lycidas.* If anything, it had become more vehement. "Wolves shall succeed for teachers, grievous wolves, / Who all the sacred mysteries of Heav'n / To their own vile advantages shall turn / Of lucre and ambition, and the truth / With superstitions and traditions taint" (XII.508–12). This is exactly the reproach Milton always had against Catholicism, that it was mere superstition and respect for tradition, "outward rites and specious forms" (XII.534) – but this was also what the Laudian church had been, and what the Restoration church had again become. The whole passage is instinct with Milton's sadness at what had happened to the "good old cause."

NOTES

1 Achsah Guibbory, *Ceremony and Community from Herbert to Milton: Literature, Religion, and Cultural Conflict in Seventeenth-Century England* (Cambridge, 1998), 147.
2 Diarmaid MacCullough, *Reformation: Europe's House Divided 1490–1700* (London, 2003), 392.

3 Henry Parker's *Discourse Concerning Puritans* of 1641 bewails the scurrilous uses of the word "to cast dirt in the face of all goodness," in Lawrence Sasek, *Images of English Puritanism: A Collection of Contemporary Sources* (Baton Rouge, LA, 1989), 167. Christopher Hill, "The Definition of a Puritan" (1964), in *Society and Puritanism in Pre-Revolutionary England* (London, 1969), 15–30, brought together various senses of the word, and John Spurr extended and qualified the list in *English Puritanism, 1603–1689* (Basingstoke, 1998), 3–8, 17–27.

4 The tune one knows is Monkland, by John Antes, and dates from around 1790.

5 Robert Weeda, *Le Psaultier de Calvin* (Turnhout, Belgium, 2002), 99; MacCullough, *Reformation*, 308.

6 Peter Lake, "Anti-popery: The Structure of a Prejudice" (1989), in *The English Civil War*, ed. Richard Cust and Ann Hughes (London, 1997), 187.

7 John Morrill, "The Religious Context of the English Civil War" (1984), in Cust and Hughes, *English Civil War*, 165.

8 Nicholas Tyacke, *Anti-Calvinists: The Rise of English Arminiamism, c. 1590–1640* (Oxford, 1987). For opposition to Tyacke's argument see, e.g., Christopher Haigh in *The English Historical Review*, 103.407 (1988): 425–27, for whom, as for John Morrill, Protestantism itself was an elitist religion of the literate imposed from above on an unwilling people broadly content with medieval Catholicism; and Kevin Sharpe, *The Personal Rule of Charles I* (London and New Haven, 1992), 286–87, who puts emphasis on the wider appeal of Puritanism.

9 *The Constitutional Documents of the Puritan Revolution 1625–1660*, ed. Samuel Rawson Gardiner, 3rd edn. (Oxford, 1906), 99–102. Available online at www.constitution.org/eng/conpur_.htm. The 1634 text has recently been published with introduction, notes, and brief commentaries, by Stephen Orgel's "History of the Book" class at Stanford University: see *The Book of Sports*, ed. Andrew Bricker *et al.* (Stanford, 2008), quotations on pp. 4 and 10.

10 Robert Baillie, *The Canterburians Self-Conviction* (1641), cited in John Morrill, "The Impact of Puritanism," in *The Impact of the English Civil War*, ed. John Morrill (London, 1991), 53.

11 *The Works of William Laud*, ed. W. Scott and J. Bliss, 7 vols. (Oxford, 1847–60), VI:57 (quoted in Tyacke, *Anti-Calvinists*, 202).

12 *Works of William Land*, VI:59 (quoted in Graham Parry, *The Seventeenth Century* [London, 1989], 185).

13 Quoted in Nicholas Tyacke, "Puritanism, Arminianism and Counter-Revolution," in *The Origins of the English Civil War*, ed. Conrad Russell (London, 1973), 135.

14 Soon in *Of Reformation* Milton says the pope "suttl'y acted the Lamb" but then "threw off his Sheepes clothing, and started up a Wolfe" (*CPW* I:595).

15 John Rushworth, *Historical Collections of Private Papers of State*, 8 vols. (London, 1721–22), IV:122, quoted in Morrill, "Religious Context," 167. All quotations from the Bible in this chapter are from the King James version.

16 Quoted in Barbara K. Lewalski, *The Life of John Milton* (Oxford, 2000), 126.

17 This along with many other such texts is available on line from the Hanover Historical Texts Project at http://history.hanover.edu/project.html.

18 On differences between Milton's early and late political thinking, see also Nicholas McDowell's chapter in this volume.

19 In *De Doctrina Christiana*, begun years later, Milton opposes the Trinity (and many other orthodoxies). The argument occupies the very long book 1, ch. 5 (*CPW* vi:208–75). See William Poole's chapter in this volume.

20 This is the third provision. The text is accessible on line in several places; try www.constitution.org/eng/conpur058.htm.

21 David Lowenstein, "Toleration and the Spectre of Heresy," in *Milton and Toleration*, ed. Sharon Achinstein and Elizabeth Sauer (Oxford, 2007), 58. Lowenstein ably summarizes Walwyn's views (57–63) and then compares them (63–71) with views held by Goodwin, Milton, and Thomas Edwards, author of the vitriolic *Gangraena* (1646).

22 *LR* 3:206.

CHAPTER 25

The Interregnum

David Loewenstein

The Interregnum in England (1649–60), following the execution of King Charles I, was a period of acute political crisis, volatility, and experimentation, as well as a period of growing sectarianism and religious tension. The tumultuous political and religious changes during these years tested Milton's talents as a controversial prose writer in new ways. The experimental political years of the Interregnum offered the English people unprecedented opportunities for liberty and yet, in Milton's view, ended disastrously with the collapse of the commonwealth and the return of the English monarchy and church in 1660. How would Milton respond to this period of great volatility when the mighty Protestant English nation – hailed by Milton in the 1640s as a "Nation chos'n before any other" (CPW II:552) – showed such great promise and yet seemed to squander the remarkable opportunity it had to fashion itself into a robust republican commonwealth? 1649 especially was a year of climactic revolutionary upheaval and tensions. It was preceded by the purging of parliament (on December 6, 1648) and followed by the trial and execution of Charles I, the abolition of kingship and the House of Lords, and establishment of the English republic. These traumatic political events were supported by many religious radicals and vigorously defended in Milton's controversial prose works. Yet 1649 was a year fraught with tensions: the experimental republic that emerged from it was far from secure. Consequently, when the most popular royalist text of the period, *Eikon Basilike*, first appeared a week after the execution of Charles I in January 1649, the enormous popularity this tear-jerking book, which presented the king as a Christ-like martyr and claimed to record his meditations and devotional exercises during his final captivity, only underscored the vulnerability of the infant republic. 1649 was also a year of acute internal tensions as Leveller agitation in the army and press posed a serious threat to the fledgling republic established by a *coup d'état* and lacking popular support.[1] Milton the controversialist positioned himself both boldly and carefully during this remarkable year as he used his pen to justify the revolutionary political events and the new regime, while not attacking its most vocal and popular radical critics, notably the Levellers.

Published two weeks after the regicide, Milton's *Tenure of Kings and Magistrates* (February 1649) presented a vigorous defense of revolution and tyrannicide, as well as an assault on the counter-revolutionary politics of the Presbyterians, the orthodox Puritans who had favored a negotiated settlement with the king and opposed the regicide. Here Milton insisted, much like the Levellers, that "the power of Kings and Magistrates is nothing else, but what is only derivative, transferr'd and committed to them in trust from the People . . . in whom the power yet remains fundamentally, and cannot be tak'n from them, without a violation of thir natural birthright" (*CPW* III: 202), a claim Milton would assert to a wider European audience two years later in his *Pro Populo Anglicano Defensio* (February 1651);[2] and with marvelous bluntness he defended natural rights and liberties since no one "can be so stupid to deny that all men naturally were borne free" (*CPW* III:198). Nonetheless, Milton does not attempt to reconcile the contradiction between the claim made by the Commons that the people are "the original of all just power"[3] and the fact that power was being wielded at this critical moment by the Rump Parliament and army, by no means representative bodies.[4] Rather, Milton's most pungent prose derives from his animus against the shifting Presbyterians who had "juggl'd and palter'd with the world" (*CPW* III:191), as Milton echoes the equivocal language of Shakespeare's *Macbeth* (5.8.19–22): they had first waged zealous war against Charles during the 1640s, their fiery preachers urging parliament to fight the Lord's battles and invoking the curse upon Meroz in the Song of Deborah (Judges 5:23) against those who did not; then they had reversed course, supporting negotiations with the king, since he had agreed to accept Presbyterian religion in Scotland and establish it in England, and incited sedition against the Rump.[5] The Presbyterians had claimed that their "discipline" was more demanding than the episcopal government they rejected: so why, Milton scornfully asks, were they ready to absolve a king who had levied war against parliament and his people and who was tainted by blood guilt and yet remained "unrepentant" (*CPW* III:235)? Milton's strategy as a polemicist in *The Tenure* (reinforced in the second edition of 1650) involves citing eminent Protestant authorities – including the zealous sixteenth-century John Knox, the original Presbyterian defender of regicide – to assault the present-day prevaricating divines who have assumed their "new garbe of Allegiance" (*CPW* III:193).

Thus in one memorable passage, Milton presents the doubling divines as "nimble motionists," London militiamen who easily shift ground with "cunning and dexterity" for their own political advantage-taking; they invoke providence, as godly preachers and soldiers so frequently did during the civil war years, though in this case to justify equivocal means and covetous ends:

> For Divines, if ye observe them, have thir posture, and thir motions no less expertly, and with no less variety then they that practice feats in the Artillery-ground. Sometimes they seem furiously to march on, and presently march counter; by and by they stand, and then retreat; or if need be can face about, or wheele in a whole body, with that cunning and dexterity as is almost unperceavable. (*CPW* III:255)

Milton's military trope vividly conveys the doubleness of Presbyterian political behavior during the turbulent years of the civil wars as he characterizes these guileful, serpentine clergymen who "winde themselves by shifting ground into places of more advantage" (*CPW* III:255). Where did the author of *Paradise Lost* learn about equivocal political behavior and language, exemplified by Satan and his "calumnious art" (v.770)? Certainly his engagement with "prevaricating [Presbyterian] Divines" (*CPW* III:232) in *The Tenure* and other prose tracts contributed something to his imaginative rendering of slippery political behavior and rhetoric in his greatest poem.

The Tenure is also a notable contribution to early modern political theory. Milton attacks not only Stuart divine right theory supporting the notion that "Kings are accountable to none but God" but also any claims to a sphere of royal prerogative outside the law. When it comes to the issue of sovereignty and the right of revolution, surely one of Milton's most radical conclusions is

> that since the King or Magistrate holds his autoritie of the people, both originaly and naturally for their good in the first place, and not his own, then may the *people as oft as they shall judge it for the best, either choose him or reject him, retaine him or depose him though no Tyrant, meerly by the liberty and right of free born Men, to be govern'd as seems to them best.* (*CPW* III:206; emphasis added)

In other words, it is the people's sovereign right to change *any* government – and not just a tyrannical one – at their will and when they choose to do so. This touches on an issue debated by early modern Protestant resistance theorists: who may lawfully resist an idolatrous or tyrannical leader? Even such notable sixteenth-century resistance theorists as John Ponet, John Knox, and Christopher Goodman (Milton cites the latter two in the second edition of *The Tenure*) argue that the most fitting leaders of any resistance movement should be inferior magistrates, rather than the ordinary body of citizens or the whole body of the people (although Ponet and Goodman also discuss when it is lawful for the people to resist – i.e., when "magistrates and other officers cease to do their duty").[6] But Milton is not just arguing here about lawful resistance by another ordained magistrate to a notorious tyrant; he is arguing for the right – the people's right and *choice* as freeborn citizens – to depose a ruler whether or not he or she is a tyrant. So much for revolutionary caution: Milton is making here a powerful populist revolutionary argument, a very radical one indeed. Interestingly, at a moment when the English republic is about to be born, Milton never invokes Leveller writers to support this argument (nor did he attack them when parliament requested him to do so in March 1649), but they surely would have been impressed by this bold, populist justification for political revolution.

Nevertheless, in *The Tenure* Milton never confronts, as the Levellers would do, the political ambiguities of identifying the authority and power of the Rump, despite its truly revolutionary origins – the Purge, the regicide, the abolition of monarchy and the House of Lords – with the just and the supreme power of the people and the "natural and essential power of a free Nation" (*CPW* III:237). Why? No doubt there is an element of political realism to Milton's position in 1649: for the moment and in such exhilarating but traumatic times, the Rump probably seemed like the best hope for the struggling English nation and the experimental infant republic. Other radical writers, including the Levellers, expressed skepticism over the new regime's ability to re-forge the nation, and especially to close the gap between its ideal profession of popular sovereignty and a more sinister reality of political and religious power. In political and religious terms, Milton was more radical than the cautious new government he chose to support (for example, he never regretted the unpopular regicide, as most Rump MPs did, and he fervently opposed a national church supported by tithes).[7] However much Milton justified political revolution in the controversial writings he published in 1649, he did not probe there the ambiguities of this experimental regime claiming to represent the sovereign power of the people. Those tensions would continue to trouble the English nation and its republican regime, resulting in further political instabilities during the Interregnum.

Milton's attack on counter-revolutionary politics in *The Tenure* no doubt helped to secure his government appointment in March 1649 as Secretary for Foreign Tongues to the Council of State and as propagandist for the republic. During March Milton was asked to exercise his polemical talents to combat the external threat to the republic believed to emanate from

Ireland, where a major rebellion had broken out in 1641 and intensified anti-Catholic hysteria in England. Milton's first official piece of writing on behalf of the new regime, *Observations upon the Articles of Peace with the Irish Rebels* (May 1649), was written in response to a treaty of January 1649 between the king's Lord Lieutenant, James Butler, the Earl of Ormond, and the Confederate Catholics of Ireland, an "Articles of Peace" which posed a military threat to the new regime and which Milton, with caustic irony, refers to "as one of [the late king's] last Masterpieces" made with the "inhumane Rebels and Papists of *Ireland*" (*CPW* III:301). Milton's polemical response to the Irish crisis was partly fueled by his perception of the late king's treacherous politics and verbal equivocation. Even when Charles was finally in custody, and parliament's supporters expected "his remorse at last ... of all the innocent bloud shed ... for his meer wilfulness," he engaged (like the unrepentant Satan of *Paradise Lost*) in "contriving and fomenting new plots," including plans to encourage Irish rebels (*CPW* III:332). Milton's portrait of the Irish rebels as demonic blurs the boundary between the imagined and political, conveying the exigencies of polemical propaganda, which attempted to link the royalists and the Irish resistance with popery, anti-Christian tyranny, and monstrous rebellion. Milton's *Observations,* which plays upon English anti-Catholic fears, consequently helped to prepare for Oliver Cromwell's punitive and vengeful military expedition in the second half of 1649 to re-conquer Ireland and combat the forces of Antichrist. Milton's republican tract about Ireland thus remains one of his most disturbing texts for twenty-first-century readers. It is not easy, after all, to reconcile his militant Protestant response to the Irish rebellion (which he could never see as a war of national liberation) to our sense of Milton as a towering author of courageous, often fierce intellectual independence, a fervent defender of religious freedom and civil liberty.

During 1649, Milton was also given by the government the unenviable task of answering *Eikon Basilike: The Portraiture of His Sacred Majesty in His Solitudes and Sufferings,* an experience that shattered his belief that his countrymen and women consisted of discerning, rather than credulous, readers who would quickly see through the artfulness of a royalist frontispiece or a sentimental piece of propaganda. The king's book (co-fashioned by the divine John Gauden) went through no fewer than thirty-five editions in 1649; its appeal confirmed widespread conservative sentiment when it came to the institution of kingship and the narrowly based support for the infant republic. *Eikon Basilike* presented the martyred King Charles as a patient Davidic and Christic figure, suffering yet constant in the midst of turbulent, revolutionary times; it was one of those "shrewd books, with dangerous Frontispices" (*CPW* II:524) displaying the pious king kneeling at his prayers in a basilica, gazing at the heavenly crown of glory, while holding the crown of thorns, setting aside his own crown, and treading under foot the things of this world. Such was the enticing power of royalist representation, and Milton responded as a zealous iconoclast in an era when iconoclasm, in an effort to dismantle Laudian church innovations, had been sanctioned by the Puritan Commons.[8] In *Eikonoklastes* (October 1649), Milton attempted to break to pieces, through his own verbal polemic, the king's seductive words and image, thereby demystifying the potent language and iconicity of monarchy.

Moreover, Milton was acutely aware of the dramatic appeal of the king's visual and emblematic representation with his "great shew of piety" (*CPW* III:536). Consequently, Milton in *Eikonoklastes* contemptuously evokes the court masque, that lavish theatrical form which had been instrumental in projecting the power of the Stuart monarchy. Milton characterizes *Eikon Basilike* as a deceptive piece of "Stage-work": its "conceited portraiture before [the king's] Book" is drawn out "to the full measure of a Masking Scene," and yet "quaint Emblems and devices begg'd from the old Pageantry of some Twelf-nights entertainment at *Whitehall*, will doe but ill to make a Saint or Martyr" (*CPW* III:530, 342–43). Milton attempts in *Eikonoklastes* to expose the disjunction between seductive image and dangerous reality, between Charles' "fair spok'n words" and "his own farr differing deeds" (*CPW* III:346–47). In that sense, the guileful Stuart king, with his "cunning words" (*CPW* III:600), anticipates Milton's portrait of the theatrical and rhetorically slick Satan of *Paradise Lost*: under his "saintly show" (*Paradise Lost* IV.122), Milton's Charles is willful, revengeful, unrepentant, guilty of prevaricating, full of rage and malice, imperious and violent.

Nonetheless, despite the seductive power of the king's image, Milton badly wants to believe (like Adam at the end of *Paradise Lost*; see book XII.64–71) that servility is *not* the natural inclination of humankind, and certainly not the English people. Instead, the source of servility – including the worse kinds of mental servility and degradation – is to be found in both courts and clerics, though the people themselves bear a crucial element of responsibility and needed to "bethink themselves," to break free from the mind-forged manacles of monarchy and clerical authority: "Which low dejection and debasement of mind in the people, I must confess I cannot willingly ascribe to the natural disposition of an English-man" (*CPW* III:344). Tested by the unprecedented revolutionary events of 1648–49, and offered a genuine alternative to monarchical power and a servile court, many of Milton's compatriots (at his most scornful the radical Puritan calls them an

"Image-doting rabble") had nevertheless allowed themselves to succumb to the "glozing words," "illusions," and Circean powers of the king's "Sorcery" (*CPW* III:582, 601) – "inchanted," as Milton caustically observes, "with the *Circaean* cup of servitude" – and were, again, "running thir own heads into the Yoke of [regal] Bondage" (*CPW* III:488). Yet in Milton's eyes it was also "thir own *voluntary*... baseness" (emphasis added) that was to blame; the "credulous and hapless herd" (*CPW* III:601) who had fallen for the king's enchanting book and its counter-revolutionary narrative of recent history were not simply passive victims: they had *chosen* servility. Consequently, there is a tension in Milton at this great crisis of the revolution in 1649: servility is not the natural inclination of the English people, yet the people, inconstant in their judgments, are in danger of too easily being seduced into it again, even after all the bloodshed of the civil war years. The crisis of the English revolution and the impact of the king's hugely successful book profoundly affected Milton's sense that the virtuous – even if they were a minority – had the right to resist ecclesiastical and monarchical servility and the right to remain free and the right to keep power.

The Interregnum years not only saw Milton translating letters of state and other documents on behalf of the governments he served; they also brought new challenges to Milton as he engaged in polemical warfare by defending the English nation and its experimental regimes on a wider European stage. In his *Pro Populo Anglicano Defensio* (*A Defence of the English People*), authorized by the Council of State, Milton took on one of the most famous European classical scholars, Salmasius or Claude de Saumaise, author of *Defensio Regia pro Carlo I* (1649). Presenting himself as a chivalric warrior defending England and his *Defence* as a heroic undertaking, Milton savagely attacked Salmasius in his roles as scholar, orator, historian, and panegyricist for the late King Charles.[9] Polemical writing was itself warfare: "our little *English David*," Milton's nephew and early biographer observed, was showing his wider European audience that he "had the courage to undertake [the] great *French Goliath*."[10] The English Protestant polemicist aimed to confound and crush his opponent, destroying both his professional credentials and his personal character: Milton forms his "battle line of Luthers, Zwinglis, Calvins, Bucers, Martyrs and Paraeuses"; and he writes prophetically of divine wrath and vengeance as he associates both Salmasius and Charles I with the beasts of Revelation 13 (*CPW* IV:396, 459, 499, 534). The "heroic Samson" rising up against the Philistines serves as a crucial model of biblical tyrannicide and would later receive fuller realization in Milton's drama, *Samson Agonistes*, where the Old Testament warrior of God destroys "at one stroke not one but a host of his country's tyrants," along with the idolatrous Temple of Dagon, "having first made prayer to God for his aid" (*CPW* IV:402). Milton's inspiration as godly republican writer consequently came from both the scriptures and classical authors. In the *Defensio* he invokes such authorities as Euripides, Sophocles, the Greek lyric poet Alcaeus (via Horace), Theognis, Seneca, and Pliny the Younger to attack tyrannical rulers and justify tyrannicide (*CPW* IV:440–42, 446–49, 455); he also invokes Tacitus and Cicero, the latter the selfless defender and orator of the ancient republic after whom Milton, savior of the endangered English republic, partly models himself (see *CPW* IV:536). Milton's *Defensio* was immensely successful: publicly burned in France, it nonetheless won praise from the Low Countries to Greece; Milton felt especially vindicated in this mighty battle of words after the Protestant Queen Christina of Sweden expressed admiration for his performance in Latin polemic (*CPW* IV:604–06, 655–56). From a rhetorical standpoint, however, Milton's most versatile and dazzling defense of the English people and himself was yet to come.

Having routed the famous Salmasius, Milton continued to wage polemical warfare on an international front with his vigorous response to the anonymously published *Regii Sanguinis Clamor ad Coelum Adversus Parricidas Anglicanos* (August 1652) or *The Cry of the Royal Blood to the Sky against the English Parricides*, a reply to Milton's *Defensio* by the English royalist clergyman, Peter du Moulin. By the time he was attacked in the *Clamor*, Milton was completely blind, a personal crisis he would struggle with in some of his greatest prose and poetry. The *Clamor* viciously maligned Milton, the republican detractor of the martyred king and great Salmasius, as a vile adversary, a depraved wretch, an obscure rabbler, and a monstrous Polyphemus.[11] Milton, however, mistook the true author of the *Clamor*, attacking instead its editor-publisher, Alexander More, and again addressing his text to the European community at large. In his *Pro Populo Anglicano Defensio Secunda* (*Second Defense of the English People*, May 1654), Milton produced one of his most complex controversial works, a skillful mixture of invective, autobiographical self-justification, panegyric, and hard-nosed political advice. Milton's tract celebrated the heroic achievements of virtuous revolutionary leaders and godly parliamentarians, including the ardent republican John Bradshaw – President of the High Court of Justice which had so daringly tried Charles I – and Cromwell himself, leader of the Protectorate, the new experimental regime that assumed power at the end of 1653. The *Defensio Secunda* became an occasion for revolutionary mythmaking: there Milton presents himself as a fearless chivalric warrior who, with his mighty pen, has borne arms in the struggle for liberty and who compares himself to the epic poet creating a national literary monument "that will not soon pass away" to extol the glorious deeds of his countrymen (*CPW* IV:685). The *Defensio Secunda* reveals Milton's impulse, during the Interregnum, to write an epic based upon the major actors and events of the English revolution: Milton presents Cromwell as a classical-style military hero, as *pater patriae* ("the father of his country," the honorific title given to Romans, like Cicero, who performed outstanding service to the state) and as a Puritan saint known for his "devotion to the Puritan religion and his upright life." His military and political exploits have outstripped not only those of English kings, but "even the legends [*fabulas*] of our heroes" (*CPW* IV:667, 672). At the same time, Milton, identifying his own personal crises and trials with those of Cromwell and the godly nation, defends himself against royalist detractors who interpreted his blindness as a sign of God's judgment against a writer who justified the regicide. Milton presents his blindness as a mark of sacredness and an occasion for internal illumination, enabling him to show strength "made perfect in weakness," a Pauline phrase (2 Cor. 12:9) that became the writer's personal motto.[12] Like Cromwell, he remains "tireless" in his work – his work for the Council of State continued unabated during this period – and willing to risk great danger in polemical combat (*CPW* IV:591).

Milton also counters attacks on the new quasi-regal Protectorate, with its single-person executive, from disenchanted Independents and inflamed radical sectarians, as well as from religious Presbyterians who were fueling factions. But despite working for the new regime, Milton does not hesitate to issue warnings and advice to his fellow countrymen and to Cromwell himself: although hard won through the traumatic events of the revolution, political liberty remains vulnerable. Milton urges Cromwell and his countrymen to separate church and state, reduce and reform laws, see to the education and morals of the young, allow free inquiry and a more open press, protect liberty of conscience, refrain from factions, and resist succumbing to "royalist excess and folly," as well as other vices which would enable corrupt, incompetent men to assume power and influence in the government (*CPW* IV:681). The *Defensio Secunda* consequently balances skillful panegyric with a realistic assessment of the volatile political situation under the experimental Protectorate. Thousands of radical Puritans – many more than the fiery ones who protested that King Oliver was usurping the role of King Jesus – looked to Cromwell's regime with hope.[13] Milton was one of them, although he employed his formidable literary talents both to defend the regime's authority (as did such writers

as Andrew Marvell, George Wither, and Marchamont Nedham) and to
voice a note of political realism and uneasiness about the Protectorate's
precarious stability.

After the verbal mud-slinging of his final defense (his *Pro Se Defensio*
of 1655, a tract likewise devoted to attacking Alexander More), Milton did
not engage in further public polemic until the final two unstable years of
the Interregnum. Oliver Cromwell's death in September 1658 was followed
by a period of great political flux: Richard Cromwell's Protectorate, which
antagonized the army and more radical Independents and sectaries, was
short-lived; the Rump returned to power in May 1659, but was no more
popular than before and proved ineffective; George Monck (commander
of the army in Scotland) marched into London in February 1660 and
reassembled the Long Parliament which met and dissolved itself in March
1660; with mounting popular enthusiasm for the return of the king, the
newly elected parliament summoned Charles II from exile in May 1660.[14]
Despite the backsliding trends of these late Interregnum years, Milton's
radical political and religious voice remained "unchanged / To hoarse or
mute" (*Paradise Lost* VII.24–25); in some ways it became even more radical.

Milton published companion pieces in 1659 highlighting his radical
spiritual convictions: *A Treatise of Civil Power in Ecclesiastical Causes*,
addressed to the conservative Puritan parliament of Richard Cromwell, and
*Considerations Touching the Likeliest Means to Remove Hirelings out of the
Church*, published in August when intensified fears and escalation of radical
pamphleteering (especially from militant Quakers) had led to a pro-royalist
uprising.[15] In *Civil Power* Milton gives voice to his radical Protestantism by
vigorously challenging ecclesiastical and political authorities when it comes
to spiritual matters and inward religion: no church authority should employ
outward force to constrain inward conscience or faith. Milton's emphasis
in *Civil Power* on the guidance of the "inward perswasive motions" of the
Spirit (*CPW* VII:261), rather than on the laws and commandments of men,
reminds us of his close relation to other religious radicals – notably the
Quakers – who were following the impulses of the Spirit within; and it
anticipates the radical spiritualism of Milton's great poems, expressed in
the "strong motion" by which Jesus is led into the wilderness in *Paradise
Regained* (1.290), or the "rousing motions" (line 1382) Samson feels just
before he destroys the idolatrous Philistine temple in *Samson Agonistes*.
Milton did not join a separate congregation during the Interregnum, yet
he remained staunchly opposed to a national church: both *Civil Power*
and *Likeliest Means* are notable for neglecting the role of the church in
Protestant experience. Milton resembles contemporary religious radicals,

including Quakers, in his biting attack on the hireling clergy as wolves and "greedy dogs" (*CPW* vii:296, echoing Isa. 56:110), and in his rejection of compulsory tithes (tax-payments of one-tenth of income by the laity to the church) in order to maintain an established ministry and national church. Tithes became one of the most contentious issues of the English revolution;[16] religious radicals, including Milton (*CPW* vii:281–90), argued that they had lost their divine sanction when the ceremonial Law was superseded by the Gospel and the Levitical priesthood by an apostolic ministry. Milton preferred an inwardly inspired ministry, but to remove hirelings and find ministers prepared to preach the Gospel *gratis* (as St. Paul did), he tersely remarks in *Likeliest Means*, would not be easy, since "few such are to be found" (*CPW* vii:280). In this sense, Milton's late Interregnum tracts anticipate the end of *Paradise Lost* where the poet grimly depicts "grievous wolves" succeeding teachers and making the Gospel a cloak of carnal interest at a time when "works of faith / Rarely be found" (xii.508, 536–37).

The greatest crisis Milton confronted at the end of this volatile decade was the collapse of the Commonwealth and the inevitable restoration of the Stuart monarchy, along with a new age of political servility and idolatrous rites. As the rising flood of enthusiasm for the monarchy increased, Milton produced one of his most daring prose works with its valiantly optimistic – yet ironic – title: *The Readie and Easie Way to Establish a Free Commonwealth,* first hastily published in late February 1660 (when the Rump was still sitting), and then revised, enlarged, and published in a second edition in April (when the Rump no longer existed), just weeks before Charles II was recalled to England and entered London. As the Commonwealth was rapidly collapsing – undone by its own internal strife – Milton dared to cry out prophetically against its dangerous backsliding, as he urged his impulsive countrymen to "consider whether they are rushing" (*CPW* vii:463). Nonetheless, in April 1660 Milton could expect little and yet he wanted his compatriots to be without excuse: with so many eager to embrace the thralldom of kingship, his countrymen would soon begin "so long a Lent of Servitude" (*CPW* vii:408). Writing once again with the radical voice of *Eikonoklastes*, Milton ridicules the spectacle of semi-divine kingship and absolute power promoted by the Stuarts, "wheras a king must be ador'd like a Demigod, with a dissolute and haughtie court about him, of vast expence and luxurie, masks and revels" (*CPW* vii:425). With mocking scorn for "the new royaliz'd Presbyterians," he presciently warns that the return of monarchy would fuel a backlash of royalist revenge in the form of "imprisonment, fines, banishment, or molestation," and aimed not only at radical nonconformists and republicans but at the Presbyterians themselves. In response to the volatile and grim political situation, Milton proposes a commonwealth whose main foundation would be not a single person (that is, an authoritarian monarch or even a quasi-regal Protector), but a perpetual senate of meritorious men inspired by such ancient classical and Jewish models as the Areopagus and the Sanhedrin.

Milton was acutely conscious in *The Readie and Easie Way* that he was writing "the last words of [his nation's] expiring libertie" before the Stuart Restoration and the loss of the republican *"good Old Cause"* to which he had devoted many years of his career as a controversial writer. Milton was bidding farewell to a revolutionary era, even as, at the end of his pamphlet, he evokes the elegiac words of the prophetic Jeremiah to convey a sense of the national tragedy: *"O earth, earth, earth!* to tell the very soil it self, what her perverse inhabitants are deaf to" (see Jer. 22:29; *CPW* VII:462–63). Milton the controversialist had not only given moving expression to republican ideals – the vision that England might "be another *Rome* in the west" (*CPW* VII:423) – but also to a generation of radical Puritans who had sought to act according to the divine light: "after all this light among us," his countrymen were "now chusing... a captain back for *Egypt*" (*CPW* VII:462–63). Milton's pamphlet concludes with a terrifying sense of great forces rushing out of control. Milton would soon publish, in the Restoration, his great epic about the fall in which a rash act would have tragic consequences for all of human history; just weeks before the Restoration, as his compatriots faced "a precipice of destruction," Milton, with reckless disregard for his own safety,[17] chose to cry out against "the deluge of epidemic madness" (*CPW* VII:463) and the tragic loss of freedom signified by the impetuous rush toward monarchy.

NOTES

1　For a discussion of the Levellers, see Joan Bennett's chapter in this volume.
2　See *CPW* IV:388, 484, 485, 500.
3　J. P. Kenyon, ed., *The Stuart Constitution*, 2nd edn. (Cambridge, 1986), 292.
4　Colonel Thomas Pride, having forcibly purged parliament of MPs in December 1648, left a remnant or "rump" who supported the army and voted that the king be brought to trial.
5　Milton alludes to the theme of the famous bloodthirsty apocalyptic sermon by Stephen Marshall, *Meroz Cursed* (1641): *CPW* III:234–35, 242, IV:334–35. See Robert Ashton, *Counter-Revolution: The Second Civil War and its Origins, 1646–48* (New Haven, 1994), ch. 8.

6 Quentin Skinner, *Foundations of Modern Political Thought*, 2 vols. (Cambridge, 1978), II:234–35.

7 The fullest account of the Rump Parliament and its cautious conservatism remains Blair Worden, *The Rump Parliament, 1648–1653* (Cambridge, 1974).

8 On ordinances passed in 1641, 1643, and 1644 to purify churches of popish and superstitious objects, see *Acts and Ordinances of the Interregnum, 1642–1660*, ed. C. H. Firth and S. R. Rait, 3 vols. (London, 1911), I:265, 425; John Morrill, *The Nature of the English Revolution* (Harlow, 1993), 73, 154.

9 The symbolic frontispiece to the *Defensio* displays a shield with a cross and a harp, conveying intersecting meanings associated with Milton: the chivalric-warrior defender of his nation (like St. George) was using his literary, prophetic talents (the harp evokes both the figures of Orpheus and the prophet David) to defend the English republic against enemies at home and abroad.

10 *EL* 70.

11 For selections from the *Clamor,* see *CPW* IV:1041–81.

12 King James version.

13 See Austin Woolrych, *Commonwealth to Protectorate* (Oxford, 1982), 390.

14 Valuable accounts of the politics of these volatile years include Austin Woolrych's introduction to *CPW* VII:1–176; Godfrey Davies, *The Restoration of Charles II, 1658–1660* (1955; Oxford, 1969); and Ronald Hutton, *The Restoration* (Oxford, 1985).

15 This was the uprising led by Sir George Booth to overthrow the Commonwealth regime in the summer of 1659.

16 See, e.g., Morrill, *Nature of the English Revolution*, 170–71.

17 On June 16 Milton was ordered to be arrested and his *Eikonoklastes* and *Defensio Prima* were ordered to be burned.

CHAPTER 26

Italy

Catherine Gimelli Martin

Despite his well-known tour of Venice, Florence, Rome, Naples, and spots along the way (May 1638–July 1639), Milton and Counter-Reformation Italy have never seemed a very logical match.[1] Not long afterward (1644), he used the Italian Inquisition as a negative example of what England should never become: the persecutor of original thinkers like Galileo (*Areopagitica, CPW* II:538). The strongly anti-Catholic tenor of this treatise and other Miltonic prose leads Barbara Lewalski to remark that "Arriving in Calvinist Geneva, after being for so long attracted and repelled by Catholic Italy, must have afforded Milton some psychic relief," especially in freely speaking about religion and politics.[2] Lewalski's biography accords with the standard "puritanical" or staunch Protestant interpretation of Milton and his Italian sojourn, yet he actually recorded only regret, not relief, upon leaving the peninsula, and left behind no positive opinion of Geneva. *Areopagitica* certainly condemns Galileo's "Franciscan and Dominican licencers," but this opinion was shared by Milton's Florentine friends, "lerned men" who considered him "happy to be born in such a place of *Philosophic* freedom, as they suppos'd England was, while themselves did nothing but bemoan the servil condition into which lerning amongst them was brought" (*CPW* II:537–38). Sadly, Milton soon learned that his own land was not "happy" or fortunate enough to permit the freedom of the press he advocated.

Milton's sole recorded criticism of his Italian tour was that some Catholics found him too "free" in defending his religion, and some Jesuits plotted against him in Rome (*WJM* VIII:125). But these were English, not Italian Jesuits, who in any case failed to prevent his subsequent return to Rome. Some scholars even speculate that he exaggerated these plots to conceal his extremely cordial relations in Italy from his Puritan audience at home, but he never actually concealed his high estimation of Italy. We know that he amicably dined with both English and native Italian Jesuits at the English college in Rome, enjoyed the witty, learned, and occasionally bawdy by-play of the Florentine academies, and became friends with some of Italy's most serious poets, scholars, and reformers.[3] In mid-life he praised their "liberal sentiments" in his *Defensio Secunda* (1654, *CPW* IV:555, n.33), and in the preface to his final work, *Samson Agonistes* (1671), re-affirmed his early esteem for both ancient and modern Italian poetic models. His early treatise *Of Education* also shows that he taught his pupils to admire "that sublime art which in *Aristotles poetics*, in *Horace*, and the *Italian* commentaries of *Castelvetro*, *Tasso*, *Mazzoni*, and others, teaches what the laws are of a true *Epic* poem, what of a *Dramatic*, what of a *Lyric*" (*CPW* II:404–05).

Milton's close friendship with the Anglo-Italian Diodati family probably led him to study Italian sometime before 1625 and to begin reading Dante and other Italian poets both before and after his Cambridge years (*CPW* I:366, n.2). To his closest boyhood and college friend Charles Diodati, he addressed some of his finest Italian poems, and in another expressed love for his relative or friend Aemilia, although she may be a poetic fiction. Not so with the subject of three other Italian poems, Leonora Baroni, one of the most beautiful and famous Roman singers of the era. Milton may have heard her sing at the Barberini palace in the fall of 1638, since a surviving letter effusively thanks Cardinal Francesco Barberini, nephew of Pope Urban VIII, for his musical entertainment. It also praises the cardinal's "great virtues, and regard for what is right," his patronage of "all the liberal arts," and the "submissive loftiness of mind" that makes him a shining example to "most other princes" (*WJM* XII:45). These were apparently not empty compliments; he published them just before he died (*WJM* XII:3). Yet music, beauty, and grace were not all that Milton appreciated on the Italian peninsula; he says he equally admired the elegant tongue and wit of Florence and its academies, where he met "Jacopo Gaddi . . . Carlo Dati, Frescobaldi, Coltellini, Buonmattei, Clementillo, Francini, and many others." Later in Naples he became friends with Giovanni Battista Manso, benefactor of the great Italian poet Torquato Tasso and his own host before "melancholy tidings . . . of civil war" canceled his trip to Sicily and Greece and led him back to revisit Roman and Florentine friends who "longed no less to see me, than if I had returned to my own country" (*WJM* VIII:123–27).

Such friendships were virtually unique for young Englishmen of the day, who were usually warned against visiting Italy at all.[4] Roger Ascham's *The Schoolmaster* explains why:

Virtue once made that country mistress over all the world. Vice now maketh that country slave to them that before were glad to serve it . . . and doth breed up every where common contempt of God's word, private contention in many families, open factions in every city, and . . . [a willingness] to bear the yoke of serving strangers abroad. Italy now is not that Italy that it was wont to be and therefore now not so fit a place as some do count it for young men to fetch either wisdom or honesty from thence.[5]

Most English visitors (Thomas Coryat, James Howell, John Evelyn, John Raymond, and Richard Lassel) similarly record "incomprehension and criticism of a kind of life they found fantastic, Catholic, pagan, superstitious, wicked" – if at times admirable.[6] Milton not only voiced no such objections but actually recommended Italy's example in promoting both private academies and public performances in theaters and church porches (*CPW* I:809–10, 819–20).[7] He continued this early advocacy both in his *Defensio Secunda* (*WJM* VIII:123) and his final pre-Restoration tracts (1659–60), which encourage public funding for similar institutions. His *Defensio Secunda* is especially remarkable for declaring eternal friendship with Galileo's son Vincenzo and many other Italians who sent greetings in Carlo Dati's letter six years earlier, some of whose "names do not survive even in standard reference books" (*CPW* IV:617, n.285). Equally remarkable, he inverts the standard anti-Italian rhetoric common among all Protestants in claiming that France or Holland would make better refuges for the critic who accused him of "fleeing" to Italy after being "expelled" from Cambridge: "Italy . . . [is] not, as you imagine . . . the place of refuge to the profligate, but [as] . . . I knew . . . before . . . it is the retreat of civility and of all polite learning" (*WJM* VIII:115).

Milton initially prepared for his visit (and for his major poems) through private, postgraduate studies in music, mathematics, and, most likely, astronomy – at the time, closely related branches of study (*WJM* VIII:121). The results clearly impressed Dati and another Florentine, Antonio Francini. Both praise Milton's deep knowledge of astronomy and his great "passion for glory," which Dati predicts he will achieve partly through "eloquence," and partly through his capacity to hear "the harmonious strains of the heavenly spheres," that is, to interpret "the true meaning of those marvels of nature by which the greatness of God is portrayed." He also praises Milton's grasp of history and his Baconian ambition to probe "the hidden mysteries of bygone days," restore "what the lapse of the ages has laid low," and recover "the intricacies of learning" (*WJM* I:167). Francini agrees that desire for "beauteous Fame" brought Milton from his "native skies, in quest of Sciences and Arts" and "of Italy the most worthy heroes." This quest will be rewarded as he reaches "the deepest secrets which Nature hides" and the furthest "boundaries of moral . . . wisdom" (*WJM* I:161–63).

Some of this praise is formal extravagance, yet standards for admission to the Florentine academies were quite high, and Francini correctly predicts that Milton's masterpiece would combine a learned treatment of cosmology with a profound moral vision. He probably possessed a copy of Milton's Latin Prolusion 7, in which the young poet first proclaims his pursuit of the same "scale" of natural/scientific and human knowledge.[8] Hence Milton was eager to meet Galileo, an ambition facilitated by his Diodati connections. Eli Diodati was Galileo's close friend and ally as well as a second cousin to Charles Diodati's father, Theodore, who grew up with him in Geneva. Eli met Galileo in Italy around 1620 and they continued to correspond for twenty years. He also served as Galileo's foreign agent and translator, most famously, of his *Dialogue on the Two Major World Systems* (1632). He completed the standard Latin Elzevir edition in 1635 and provided unflagging moral support after Galileo's imprisonment. Galileo called him his most beloved and true friend in a letter to Hugo Grotius, the famed expert on international law Milton also met while on tour.

The Diodatis also seem to have influenced the Latin poem Milton likely recited at the Svogliati academy in Florence, *Naturam non pati senium,* "That Nature does not suffer from old age."[9] Originally composed to support George Hakewill's side in the Cambridge graduation debates of 1628, the poem declares that nature's laws are constant and scientifically knowable because nature is *not* decaying, as John Donne among others believed. Siding instead with Bacon and Galileo, the poem supports a steady-state universe where scientific progress is limited only by human ignorance and sloth (Milton's "Custom from without, and blind affections within" [*CPW* III:190]). Hakewill's defense of these views required a huge body of evidence, some of which he obtained from the distinguished physician, Theodore Diodati. By "drawing off of a pint or more of blood on three successive days," Theodore had not only saved "a man nearly eighty years old," but proved in the process that "moderns" were not inferior to "ancients": neither doctors nor their patients had "decayed" since Galen's day.[10] Milton's poem opens with Bacon's most frequently reiterated point: man's mind is *not* the measure of all things, as all four of Bacon's famous "Idols" or deterrents to progress falsely claim, so there can be no real comparison between human and cosmic lifespans. Nature's "face" is as eternal as "adamant" (lines 4–9) – not, like Diodati's patient, "covered with furrowing wrinkles" – or limping "with uncertain steps" (lines 8–14).

Another physician-friend of Milton's who belonged to the Florentine academy of "the Indifferent" (meaning "the uncommitted" or unbiased, not the uncaring) also defended scientific progress, supported Galileo's works and intellectual stance, but remained a staunch Roman Catholic. That stance stressed dispassionate, skeptical inquiry in scientific and even some moral matters, so that much like the Milton of *Areopagitica,* Agostino Coltellini believed that good and evil are so inevitably intertwined that "those who wished to make ill use of a thing had only themselves to blame."[11] Yet also like Milton under Cromwell, he eventually became an unwilling censor. Such situations seem to explain why Milton's "damning" association of censorship with the Catholic church did not apply to individual Catholics.[12] He actually gave pride of place to Dante for proving that "the combining of ecclesiastical and political government . . . is equally destructive to both religion and the State," and he linked the burning of Dante's *De Monarchia* to Rome's acquisition of censorial powers (*CPW* 1:476, 438). Perhaps most extraordinarily of all, he begged his Italian friends to pardon him when "he may be speaking of your religion in our peculiar [English] way," and to grant him the same tolerance they gave to "proto-Protestants" like Dante and Petrarch (*WJM* xii:51). These circumstances suggest that Milton was "probably, beneath his literary/polemic mask, more complex, more tolerant than we take him to be."[13] His support for contemporary Italian reformers such as Paolo Sarpi, "the great Venetian Antagonist of the *Pope*" (*CPW* 1:581) and "the great unmasker of the *Trentine* Councel" (*CPW* ii:501), is less surprising, especially since Sarpi showed how the church wrongly became involved in the regulation of marriage and divorce (*CPW* 1:406–07). His friend Dati implicitly agreed that legally preserving the "brazen yoke [of] forms and minds unequal" was unjust (*WJM* xii:301), but Milton's main Italian authority in his divorce arguments was the ancient Roman law code of Theodosius, whose generous provisions made him the civil equivalent of Moses for Milton. Later, he applied another precedent enacted by "*Theodosius . . .* that a Prince is bound to the Laws" (*WJM* v:13) to justify resistance to European tyrants.[14]

In the end, however, Milton's admiration for a nation that gave rise to both the Renaissance and the Reformist doctrines of the Waldensians was not just political and spiritual but literary, although these domains were never separate. By then, however, Italy's great age of humanist glory had faded, although the Florentine Benedetto Buonmattei tried to counter its decline through linguistic studies which (among many other things) showed that her northern intruders had not corrupted but fortified Tuscany's language.[15] Milton's 1638 letter to Buonmattei reveals a similar interest in combining the best of the "barbarian" north with the Greek and Italian past through cultivating vigorous vernacular language, itself a standard humanist goal. Ben Jonson cites Seneca's warning that "Where-soever, manners, and fashion are corrupted, Language is. It imitates the publicke riot. The excesse of Feasts, and apparel, are the notes of a sick State; and the wantonnesse of language, of a sick mind."[16] Yet both Seneca and Jonson are more stoic than Milton, whose admiration of Tuscany's tongue extends to its beautiful countryside, music, and poetry. He frankly tells Buonmattei that these things have made him "so great a lover of your nation that . . . I think, there is no other more so," as shown by his search for the best Florentine writers of drama, dialogues, and history (*WJM* XII:35). Politically, both Milton and Buonmattei believe that a flourishing state first demands leaders who know "how to form wisely the manners of men and to rule them at home and at war with excellent institutes," and second, educators who "establish in maxims and rules the method and habit of speaking and writing received from a good age of the nation." Great politicians make citizens "just and holy," but great educators make them "splendid and beautiful, – which is the next thing to be wished." By banishing illogical, inaccurate language, they reform humanity from within, a far more important concern than the mere changes in "manner and habit of dressing" (*WJM* XII:31–33) that worried Plato, Jonson, and the Puritans alike. Both "Attic Athens . . . with her pellucid Ilissus" and "old Rome with her bank of the Tiber" once modeled these ideals, but Milton now finds them in the Arno and its surrounding hills (*WJM* XII:35).

Charles Diodati unfortunately died while his friend toured his home-land, but the similarly named Carlo Dati seemed partly to compensate for his loss. Greatly relieved by the belated arrival of a letter from Dati, Milton re-affirms how very painful their separation has been, how

> it planted stings in my heart which now rankle there deeper, as often as I think with myself of my reluctant parting, my separation as by a wrench, from so many companions at once, such good friends as they were, and living pleasantly with each other in one city, far off indeed, but to me most dear. I call to witness that tomb of Damon [Diodati], ever to be sacred and solemn to me, whose adornment with every tribute of grief was my weary task . . . I call that sacred grave to witness that I have had no greater delight all this while than in recalling to my mind the most pleasant memory of all of you, and of yourself especially. (*WJM* XII:49)

Dati reciprocated by expressing "joy immeasurable" that "so fresh and affectionate a memory is maintained in the gentle soul of John Milton," and in for what high "esteem you held my country, which counts it among its greatest treasures to have in that great England . . . one who magnifies our glories, loves our citizens, celebrates our writers, and who writes and speaks in so correct and polished a fashion in our beautiful idiom." He also

admires one "so singularly gifted to revive the dead languages and make
foreign ones your own" (*WJM* XII:297). His final surviving letter records
his great pleasure at receiving two copies of Milton's first volume of verse,
"than which there could not have reached me a more welcome gift; for,
however little, it contains infinite value, from being a gem from the treasury
of John Milton" (*WJM* XII:313).

   The "Epitaph for Damon," the English title of Milton's elegy for Diodati,
still voices regret for his voyage: "Alas, what inconstant error dragged me to
unknown shores . . . !" (line 113). "Ah, surely it would have been permitted
to touch his hand at the end . . . and to have said, 'Farewell'" (lines 121, 123).
Yet it also celebrates those "shepherds of Tuscany, young men devoted to
the Muses," especially since

you also were a Tuscan, Damon, whence you take your ancestry from the ancient
city of Lucca. O, how grand I felt, stretched out by the murmurs of the cold Arno
and the poplar grove . . . I even dared to compete . . . [with] Dati and Francini . . .
and they were both of them famous for voice and learning, and both of Lydian
blood. (lines 126–30, 133, 137–38)

The Latin lament also records Milton's ambition to write an epic linking
Troy and England through Inogene of Italy, the wife of the Trojan Brutus
(lines 162–63), and it expresses Milton's gratitude to the great patron Manso
for treating him so generously (lines 182–83). In another Latin poem,
Mansus, Milton again exults that Manso has not spurned "a distant Muse,
who, barely nourished of late under the frigid Bear, imprudently dares
to fly through the cities of Italy" (lines 27–29). He writes that he and
Manso share the same gift of hearing that he earlier praised in Buonmattei:
"We also believe that we have heard swans singing in our river in the
dark shadows of night, where silver Thames pours forth her blue-grey
hair broadly from pure urns in Ocean's stream" (lines 30–33). "Tityrus" or
Chaucer once visited both shores, thus symbolically linking the Thames,
Tiber, and Arno and soothing Milton's lifelong anxiety about England's
"cold" inhospitality to Apollonian genius. So, too, do his claims that his
people have worshiped Phoebus since the time of the Druids (lines 34–41),
and that through Manso, he is linked to Tasso (Spenser's chief inspiration)
(lines 49–53, 78–80).

   Yet Milton's great poem may already have been fated to depart from
the romance epic genre of Spenser or Tasso and to revive the clas-
sical/cosmological mode of Dante, which Buonmattei and Dati both
defended. Irene Samuel shows that both Dante's final vow to write a
great epic in the *Vita Nuova* and Boccaccio's *Vita di Dante* gave Milton

a powerful role model: a studious youth, early imitator of Latin poets, a great believer in the "high office of poetry," and stalwart pursuer of his epic despite every adversity – political, marital, careerist. Although preferring books and music to politics, Dante similarly participated in the great religious and political crises of his age despite hardship and ultimate exile, "but nevertheless produced his great work." Significantly, Milton's interest in Dante among other "choice poets" continued even in his later years; his last notes on him appear in the hand of the amanuensis who transcribed *Paradise Lost,* book I. Hence "There is good reason to believe that the poet who... wished to write what would be 'doctrinal to a nation'... found Dante a better teacher than Calvin and far more helpful to the composition of *Paradise Lost.*"[17] Antony Cinquemani shows that even Milton's negative associations with Italy are Dantean: most can be traced to the *Purgatorio*'s "long jeremiad on what Milton might call the 'wearied virtue' of the Valdarno" (*Purgatorio*, canto 14, lines 29–66), where the lovely Florentine countryside is transformed into its opposite, the site where the destruction of paradise and the corruption of republican principles begins. Galileo is dissociated from this corruption since his optic tube reveals the "orb" of satanic envy (*Paradise Lost* I.287), so that like Dante's Virgil, he guides and protects readers on their perilous way. Appropriately, Galileo, the great astronomer, humanist, poet, and promoter of human freedom, was among the first to compose a defense of Dante (1588) and the very first to calculate the depths of his hell.[18]

Building on Galileo, Buonmattei defended the Dantean view that the sublime soul should scorn "the narrow confines of the epic," go "beyond every known path, and with the incisiveness of his very profound genius penetrate... the most remote secrets of God's high mind."[19] Milton repeats this idea in the first invocation of the muse in *Paradise Lost*, while in the second, taught by the same "Heav'nly Muse" Dante invoked as Urania, he dares to "venture down / The dark descent, and up to reascend, / Though hard and rare." Here he addresses the sun as a "sov'reign vital lamp" (*Paradise Lost* III.19–22), an analogy much noted and debated by Dante's critics, while the golden censors of book XI seem to recall Dati's defense of Dante's depiction of "lamps burning oil as fuel... hung, as the noblest of ornaments, facing the altars of God, perhaps in the manner in which the beautiful lamp of the sun shines... to the glory of the Creator."[20] After naming Urania in his third invocation, Milton's fourth and final oration recalls Buonmattei's rejection of Giraldi Cinthio's somewhat "shallow" list of epic topics: "*furious loves, unaccountable wraths, bloody battles, cruel spectacles, and vain, improbable fictions and chimeras.*"[21] Great poets like

Dante eschew such nonsense and write for a "fit . . . though few" readership (*Paradise Lost* VII.31) – Dante's "*Voi alti poche*" ("Ye other few").[22] Broader continuities between the two epics include cosmic journeys; symbolic use of stars, comets, and constellations; dialogic or dramatic structure (absent from most English or Italian heroic poetry); and a heroine or mortal goddess, "the quintessence of Paradise," whose "smile can easily dazzle and overwhelm."[23] Milton's unfallen Eve may not guide him through Paradise like Dante's Beatrice, but she similarly transfers attention from God's transcendence to his immanence. After her fall and repentance, like the Son she shows that the "*vision* of God gives rise to love (and then successively ardor, brightness, and motion)"; and this vision is shared by the nine angelic orders discarded by Calvin but retained in Dante's *Paradiso* and the central books of *Paradise Lost*, where they celebrate God in feast, song, and dance.[24] Milton also owned the first copy of Dante's *Convivio* in England, and first cited his political works or mentioned Boccaccio's *Vita de Dante* at a time when Dante enjoyed "little favor, even in Italy . . . and outside Italy, he was scarcely named."[25] As Samuel notes, Milton's "nephew and pupil Edward Phillips was one of the few other [English] writers to make any mention of Dante."[26]

Near the end of his political career Milton concludes his reiterated admiration for the "serene and self-controlled magnanimity of the Italians" with a prophetic claim "to be bringing home again everywhere in the world, after a vast space of time, Liberty herself, so long expelled and exiled." Yet while referring to liberty as a "product from my own country," he does not claim to have invented it; that honor belongs to *Liberi Patris*, "Father Liber," the early Italian god of the soil usually identified with Dionysus (*WJM* VIII:14– 15; *CPW* IV:555, n.32). Like Milton's motto that one's country is wherever it is well with one – and the entirety of his Italian journey, correspondence, and poems – these sentiments firmly contradict the traditional image of a parochial and intolerant Milton. By freely admitting his ongoing debts to Italy, including major debts to more numerous Italian poets than can be cited here, we can read him more like the poet of the *Commedia*, as someone who can "combine scripture's assurance about historicity with fiction's freedom to raise an eyebrow, conceal a guffaw, and introduce a spirit of sublime play (angelic and otherwise) into an ultimately serious journey of redemption."[27]

NOTES

1 See John Arthos, *Milton and the Italian Cities* (New York, 1968), 55.
2 Barbara K. Lewalski, *The Life of John Milton* (Oxford, 2000), 108.

3 Edward Chaney, *The Grand Tour and the Great Rebellion* (Geneva, 1985), 249.

4 See Joseph Hall (Milton's prelatical opponent), *Quo Vadis? A Just Censure of Travell, As It Is Commonly Undertaken by the Gentlemen of Our Nation* (London, 1617).

5 Roger Ascham, *The Schoolmaster* (London, 1571), ed. L.V. Ryan (Ithaca, NY, 1967), 60–61.

6 Arthos, *Milton and the Italian Cities,* 109.

7 John W. Stoye, *English Travellers Abroad, 1604–1667* (rpt. 1952; New York, 1968), 223; and Arthos, *Milton and the Italian Cities,* 52.

8 Estelle Haan, *From "Academia" to "Amicitia"* (Philadelphia, 1998), 19–20, 48–51.

9 Donald Clayton Dorian, *The English Diodatis* (New Brunswick, NJ, 1950), 171–73; and Haan, *From "Academia" to "Amicitia,"* 25–28.

10 Dorian, *The English Diodatis,* 58, 61.

11 Arthos, *Milton and the Italian Cities,* 25.

12 A. M. Cinquemani, *Glad to Go for a Feast* (New York, 1998), 46.

13 *Ibid.,* 2, 49, 118.

14 Martin Dzelzainus, "'In These Western Parts of the Empire': Milton and Roman Law," in *Milton and the Terms of Liberty,* ed. Graham Parry and Joad Raymond (Cambridge, 2002), 47–68 (pp. 62–63, 67–68).

15 Cinqumani, *Glad to Go for a Feast,* 15–16.

16 *Ben Jonson,* ed. Percy Simpson and Evelyn Simpson, 11 vols. (Oxford, 1925–52), VIII:954–58.

17 Irene Samuel, *Dante and Milton* (Ithaca, NY, 1966), 43–45.

18 Cinquemani, *Glad to Go for a Feast,* 149–55, 157–58, 153–54.

19 *Ibid.,* 17, 146.

20 Dati, quoted *ibid.,* 144.

21 Samuel, *Dante and Milton,* 51.

22 *Ibid.,* 52.

23 Peter S. Hawkins, "All Smiles: Poetry and Theology in Dante," *PMLA* 121 (2006): 371–87 (p. 380).

24 *Ibid.,* 372–73, 381; Robert H. West, *Milton and the Angels* (Athens, GA, 1955), 13.

25 Samuel, *Dante and Milton,* 33–34.

26 *Ibid.,* 34.

27 Hawkins, "All Smiles," 382. Milton's debts to major and many minor Italian poets are extensively covered by Frank T. Prince, who pays less attention to Dante: *The Italian Element in Milton's Verse* (Oxford, 1954).

CHAPTER 27

Law

Lynne Greenberg

In his copy of Harrington's translation of Ariosto's *Orlando Furioso*, Milton scrawled: "Tu mihi Jure tyo Justiniane vale" ("Farewell, Justinian, with your law book") (*WJM* xviii:330). This tag line, inserted perhaps in jest, perhaps in seriousness, suggests his formal and definitive renunciation of the study, practice, and even interest in law in favor of literary pursuits. His relationship to England's legal institutions, however, would be of lasting concern. He would participate personally and professionally, individually and as part of collective bodies, in legal agons, legislative changes, and quasi-legal matters throughout his lifetime. His statement also belies his formidable working knowledge of legal history, comparative law, and seventeenth-century British law, and its competing administrations, procedures, terminologies, and foundational principles. While his knowledge may not have equaled that of practicing jurists or legal theorists, it did inform his writing in complex and sophisticated ways. Further, he developed detailed categorizations of its different jurisdictions (natural, divine, and human), offered trenchant critiques of the abuses made of the law, and defined specific limits to his uses and purposes.

Milton's fluidity with legal discourse, history, and practices grew not from formal training. In many ways, he is a product of seventeenth-century society in which the majority of men of his class and education had a working knowledge of the intricacies of common, legislative, equitable, and manorial law. Married under three separate systems of marriage formation, a legatee and heir, an owner and renter of real property, affiliated with the profession of scrivening, and a debtee, Milton was equipped with a working knowledge of domestic, property, and contract law. Nevertheless, Milton's knowledge was more specialized than is typical of his peers, gleaned not just from his marital experiences and commercial endeavors, but also from his rigorous self-study, prose writing, lawsuits in the Court of Chancery, negotiations with printers, experiences both as licensee and licensor, and employment as Secretary for Foreign Tongues.

While presumably intended for a career in the ministry, upon refusing to take ordination upon his graduation from Cambridge, Milton may well have received the suggestion to consider an alternative career in law. Although Milton does not seem to have taken this option seriously, he does disclose in 1637 in Letter 7 to Charles Diodati, that he was planning "migrating into some Inn of the Lawyers," although not for the purposes of instruction but rather for housing and "companions" (*WJM* vii:29). In this period, it was a fairly routine practice for young men beginning their professional careers to live for brief periods at one of the Inns of Court without actually engaging in the study of law. While Milton never actually moved to one of the Inns, his dalliance with this idea indicates his interest in being part of a coterie of legally minded peers. His seeking out of such relationships would culminate later the following year when he visited Hugo Grotius in Paris in May or June 1638.[1]

Milton signaled his definitive rejection of law as a career option in his Latin poem *Ad Patrem*, the date of which has been surmised as falling somewhere in the 1630s.[2] I personally date the composition to 1638, as the poem seems to allude to the end of his retirement at Horton and initial preparation to travel abroad. The poem equably offers both abundant praise to his father for providing him with his education and a veiled critique of his father's perceived intrusions into his vocation choices. Milton, by turns, credits his father for not insisting on his pursuing a legal career and cautions his father to adhere to this neutral stance: "nor do you hurry me off to law and the nation's badly kept statutes, nor do you condemn my ears to that ridiculous clamor" (lines 71–72). His younger brother Christopher instead fulfilled this paternal ambition, engaging in a distinguished legal career. Admitted to the Inner Temple in 1671, Christopher was later made Serjeant-at-Law and Baron of the Exchequer in 1686 and ultimately appointed a Justice of Common Pleas in 1687.

While Milton would reject a career in law, we are nonetheless given significant indicia of Milton's enduring interest in the law as early as 1639. His Commonplace Book includes two separate compilations, "Laws" and "Of Laws, Dispensations from Them, and Indulgences," that form a part of his Political Index written in the period 1639 to 1645. These entries were noted by Ruth Mohl as significant both for their range and iteration of tenets that would occupy Milton's thinking on legal matters throughout his lifetime.[3] The citation of sources attests to the breadth of Milton's exposure to legal history, comparative law, and contemporary British practice, as he moves in patchwork fashion from Roman to Anglo-Saxon, from canon to common, from Italian to Spanish, and from medieval to early modern law.

These entries also facilitate defining what Milton means when referring to the "law," although his discriminations would become more finely honed over time. Milton records Justinian's distinctions between the three major branches of law delineated in book I of the *Institutes*: natural, international, and civil law (*WJM* xvIII:166). This framework is foundational to Milton's later thinking; he relies on Justinian explicitly on sixteen separate occasions in his other prose works and, arguably, by proxy throughout his writings.

Milton strives to distinguish between and, importantly, to hierarchize the different areas of the law that ground his antiprelatical, divorce, and political tracts. His pattern is to define and in a later tract to re-define distinctions between branches of the law in legalistic arguments that justify the jettisoning of certain laws in favor of higher, thereby privileged, ones. His antiprelatical tracts argue for the complete abrogation of Mosaic law (further divided between the "politicall" and "morall") by the law of the Gospel (*CPW* I:764). By 1643, in *Doctrine and Discipline of Divorce*, in order to justify grounds for divorce, he has altered his argument, calling instead for the continuing viability of moral law (*CPW* II:283–84, 292, 301–04). In *De Doctrina Christiana*, he further refined his thinking, emphasizing that "[o]n the introduction of the gospel, or new covenant through faith in Christ, the whole of the preceding covenant, in other words the entire Mosaic law, was abolished" (*WJM* xvi, I:125).[4] *Tetrachordon* also clarifies Milton's definition of natural law. He discriminates between a primary law of nature that existed only before the fall which "made us all equall . . . coheirs by common right and dominion over all creatures" and a secondary law of nature to which mankind has been subjected since the fall (*CPW* II:661).

In *Tenure of Kings and Magistrates*, he would further refine his comparison of natural and civil law to set out the extent and limits of kingship and to justify the people's enduring right to keep, and when necessary, depose their rulers. As Milton describes, natural law acts as an unwritten code of justice superior to man-made, or civil, law. He makes two salient points, seemingly at odds with each other. First, the people are not bound by civil laws but by the law of nature only, when the king has broken this covenant with his people (*CPW* III:254). Second, the king is subject to both civil and natural law in concert with "right reason" (*CPW* III:197). In other words, *lex* is not *rex*. "[T]o say Kings are accountable to none but God, is the overturning of all Law and government. For if they may refuse to give account, then all cov'nants made with them at Coronation; all Oathes are in vain, and meer mockeries, all Lawes which they sweare to keep, made to no purpose" (*CPW* III:204–05).

In *Tenure of Kings and Magistrates* and *Pro Populo Anglicano Defensio*, he argues that the king's trial for treason was legal, as Charles was accused of having breached his promise to the people, explicitly acknowledged in the coronation oath by which the king promises both to obey and uphold the civil law. Should he breach this "trust" with the people, thereby breaking his oath by behaving tyrannically, then the people have the right to depose him (*CPW* III:211). Milton concludes that King Charles is "a rebell to Law" (*CPW* III:230), and, in more vitriolic rhetoric, writes in *Eikonoklastes* that King Charles I "disables and uncreates the Parlament it self, with all our laws and Native liberties that ask not his leave" (*CPW* III:347). As late as 1660, on the brink of the Restoration, Milton would argue all the more fervently in *The Readie and Easie Way* that civil law could not bind parliament either, but the law of nature only, which reigns "supreme" and is "the beginning and the end of all Government" (*CPW* VII:411, 413). *De Doctrina Christiana* makes a further critical point that "Christian liberty," while loosing the individual from both the rule of law and civil law, does not lead to license but to stricter internal codes, "divine law written in the hearts of believers" (*WJM* XVI, 1:149). Christian liberty thereby mandates following the spirit, rather than the letter, of the law (*WJM* XVI, 1:145), suggesting that the man who follows natural law and right reason need obey no other law but that of his own conscience. Milton explores this question in several of his poetic works as well, including Sonnet 12, in which he cautions "License they mean when they cry liberty" (line 11), and most centrally in *Samson Agonistes*.

The distinctions between various branches of the law would be of relevance not just to Milton's prose writings but also to him practically. England's civil system was housed in at least sixteen separate jurisdictions during the early modern period. Milton's personal, professional, and intellectual involvement with the law was in several of these legal jurisdictions and their substantive laws, most importantly, in common law, equity, statutory law, and ecclesiastical law. Milton took part routinely in domestic quasi-legal matters, witnessing and acting as the signatory to several legal documents, including the marriage settlement of his sister Anne to Edward Phillips (November 27, 1623) and the wills of William Blackborough (April 11, 1645) and his father-in-law Richard Powell (December 30, 1746). His father John Milton Senior was appointed Assistant of the Scriveners' Company in 1616 and had a long career as a scrivener, which included money-lending, perfunctory contract law, and notary work, until his retirement in 1636. Milton also participated in his father's work, charged with the control, administration, and collection of several interest-bearing bonds, indentures, and mortgages. In 1627, he signed an indenture for the purchase of property in St. Martin in the Fields and owned and rented properties in St. Martin in the Fields, Aldersgate, and London. He lent money and took interest-bearing bonds for their re-payment from several individuals, including Sir John Cope (February 1, 1638), Robert Warcupp (February 16, 1650), George Foxcroft (May 13, 1651), Thomas Maundy (January 14, 1657/8), and Richard Hayley (July 27, 1674).[5]

Milton's most intimate engagement with the practical side of legal proceedings was undoubtedly in equity. His entanglements in Chancery, both as plaintiff and defendant, revolved around unpaid bonds, thereby giving him an intricate knowledge of actions of covenant, or contract, and debt. In brief, Milton found himself the defendant in two lawsuits over lands in Forest Hill and Wheatley that he had taken over from Richard Powell, his father-in-law, for failure to pay back a debt to John Milton Senior, upon which he had received as security a staple bond for £500 made payable to Milton (June 11, 1627). On February 11, 1647, Sir Robert Pye, having taken possession of Forest Hill after Richard Powell's death, alleged that he had the rightful possession of this property; Pye would eventually drop the suit and the court issued a formal decree dismissing the suit on June 16, 1649. Mrs. Elizabeth Ashworth brought suit in February 1654, alleging that by taking over Wheatley, Milton had deprived her of the right to collect on Richard Powell's debt to her. The Court of Chancery settled the action, ordering Anne and Richard Powell to repay the debt and Milton to withdraw from and return Wheatley to the Powells. Milton, as plaintiff, brought suit against Lady Elizabeth Cope on June 16, 1654 to recover the unpaid portion of a loan made to her husband in 1638. This suit was never settled despite years of litigating. The last record is dated June 11, 1659, in which the Court of Chancery prepares to make depositions available to both sides in the suit.[6]

Milton would also have had an intimate working knowledge of licensing matters, not only from his eloquent defense of pre-publication freedom of the press in *Areopagitica*, but also from his own confrontations with censorship and, ironically, his work as a licensor.[7] Early modern printing and licensing acts, warrants, and orders were complex, at times purely subjective, and always political, in their application, and changed in substance dramatically during Milton's lifetime. On August 24, 1644, the Company of Stationers sent a petition against unlicensed and unregistered books to parliament that listed *Doctrine and Discipline of Divorce* amongst the texts (both the first and second editions of the tract had been published anonymously and without licensing or registration). The House of

Commons referred the matter to the Committee for Printing, which seemed to let the matter drop. The matter was revived, this time in the House of Lords, and on December 28, 1645, Milton was called to appear before judges appointed by the House of Lords. No extant records exist, however, to indicate what occurred at Milton's examination or how the Committee thereafter acted.[8] In November 1670, Milton also faced censorship of his work; this time the controversy revolved around passages in *The History of Britain*, referred to as the "Digression," that Milton agreed to suppress for printing.[9] Upon the Restoration, Milton felt the full effect of censorship, as *Eikonoklastes* and *Pro Populo Anglicano Defensio* were both burned at the Session-house of the Old Bailey by the hangman on September 10, 1660.[10]

Conversely, Milton's initial work as Secretary of Foreign Tongues was in the arena of licensing. Particularly in the period March 1650/51 through January 1651/52, Milton acted as a government censor, a role that, as Stephen Dobranski has argued, cannot simply be excused as pro forma, but instead suggests that he "participated in the government's regulation of the book trade to a greater extent than critics commonly recognize."[11]

Milton's most threatening exposure to the criminal arm of the law was his arrest and imprisonment in November 1660 for his publications in support of the execution of Charles I. The House of Commons examined his case, ultimately finding that he was not excluded from the Indemnity Bill (which officially pardoned the people of England from responsibility for King Charles I's execution). Milton was quickly released on December 15, and thereafter received an official pardon.[12]

It is not surprising, given Milton's negotiations with legal matters, that he would harbor hostility to the machinations of the legal system; his prose writings, nevertheless, are distinctive for their extensive treatment and critique of the law. Milton vociferously recorded his general dislike of the legal profession and lawyers in several of his prose tracts. He regularly denigrated legal education, writing early on in Prolusion 7: "Jurisprudence in particular suffers much from our confused methods of teaching" (*CPW* 1:301). He also disparaged the morality and character of those who practiced law, referring, for example, to lawyers as "tricksters" (*CPW* IV:319). His Commonplace Book is spattered with reminders of the duplicitous and selfish motivations of lawyers whose "opinions turn with the times for private ends" (*WJM* XVIII:166). In *Of Reformation* he cautions that "the sufferance and subjection of the people" is vulnerable to the "modern politician"; further, "the puny Law may be brought under the wardship, and controul of lust, and will ... To make men governable in this manner their precepts mainly tend to break a nationall spirit, and courage by count'nancing upon riot, luxury, and ignorance" (*CPW* I:571–72).

Nevertheless, Milton at times praises specific individuals engaged in the practice of law. Sonnet 10 offers an encomium of Earl James Ley, Lord High Treasurer under James I, for his integrity at carrying out governmental functions "unstained with gold or fee" (line 3). Sonnet 17 lauds Sir Henry Vane the Younger, a member of the Council of State, for championing the separation of "spiritual power and civil" (line 10). Former Chief Justice of the King's Bench and legal theorist Sir Edward Coke, whose advocacy of the supremacy of English common law over parliamentary, royal, and ecclesiastical law led in 1616 to his ousting as a jurist and in 1620 to his imprisonment, receives Milton's highest accolades in Sonnet 21. Addressed to Coke's grandson Cyriack Skinner, the poem both commends Coke and simultaneously contains a larger critique of the administration of justice: "Cyriack, whose grandsire on the Royal Bench / Of British Themis, with no mean applause / Pronounced and in his volumes taught our laws, / Which others at their bar so often wrench" (lines 1–4). Milton reserves his highest praise for John Bradshaw in an extended panegyric in *Defensio Secunda* and in other works heralds Sir Thomas Smith as a "skilled jurist and a statesman" (*CPW* IV:476), Hugo Grotius as "one of the best learned" (*CPW* II:238), and John Selden as "learned" (*CPW* II:350).

Milton's critique of the law is particularly heated in his descriptions of legalese, the Latin French that was the official language of the courts. This "jargon," he writes,

one might well take for some Red Indian dialect, or even no human speech at all. Often, when I have heard our lawyers shouting at each other in this lingo, it has occurred to me to wonder whether men who had neither a human tongue nor human speech could have any human feelings either. I do indeed fear that sacred Justice will pay no attention to us and that she will never understand our complaints and wrongs, as she cannot speak our language. (*CPW* I:301)

Milton reserved his most trenchant critique of legal power for the ecclesiastical courts. Ecclesiastical jurisdiction, separate from the jurisdiction of the common law, regulated the laws of marriage and inheritance and had extensive disciplinary power over a wide range of religious, moral, and sexual offenses. His objection to this illegitimate commingling of ecclesiastical and legal power grounds much of *Of Reformation*. Of the ecclesiastical courts, he writes: "What a Masse of Money is drawne from the Veines into the Ulcers of the Kingdome this way; their Extortions, their open Corruptions, the multitude of hungry and ravenous Harpies that swarme about their Offices declare sufficiently" (*CPW* 1:590–91). In *Animadversions*, he compares the Ecclesiastical Court of High Commission to "Gehenna at *Lambeth*" (*CPW* 11:674), signifying the tortuous tyranny of the ecclesiastical courts. He characterizes ecclesiastical laws as "*Rotchet Apothegmes*" and the pecuniary punishments as "sordid Fees" (*CPW* 1:587, 591). As to corporeal punishments, he writes: "They pray us . . . that it would please the *Parliament* that they may yet have the whipping, fleecing, and fleaing of us in their diabolical Courts to tear the flesh from our bones" (*CPW* 1:612). Specifically, he viewed the ecclesiastical courts as impinging upon both parliamentary and common law: the prelates "trample under foot all the most sacred, and life blood Lawes, Statutes, and Acts of *Parliament* that are the holy Cov'nant of Union, and Marriage betweene the King and his Realme, by proscribing, and confiscating from us all the right we have to our owne bodies, goods and liberties" (*CPW* 1:592–93). He calls for a complete separation of church and state, so that "the Common, and Civill *Lawes* shall be both set free, the former from the controule, the other from the meere vassalage and *Copy-hold* of the *Clergie*" (*CPW* 1:601).

The historicizing of Milton's work with seventeenth-century legal discourse is an approach that has not received adequate attention in Milton studies to date, unlike the larger field of early modern studies that has persistently taken advantage of legal contextualizations.[13] Nevertheless, a handful of articles approach the question of Milton's political thought from a legal perspective, including his position on slavery, divorce, usury, the limits of governmental authority, tyrannicide, republicanism, censorship, and licensing. Milton's relationship to the law has enduring significance not only for literary scholars but also for legal theorists and practicing lawyers. Milton's work has received extended discussion in law review articles,[14] and his prose writings, particularly *Areopagitica*, are regularly cited in legal briefs, case law, and Supreme Court decisions. Some tangible indicia of his influence on legal matters during his lifetime exist. Notably, "an eminent member of the House of Lords" consulted him in March 1670 about the divorce proceedings for Lord Roos, suggesting that in the area of marital relations, Milton was considered a legal expert.[15] Further, Samuel von Pufendorf cited *Doctrine and Discipline of Divorce* as authoritative in *De Jure Naturali* (1672). And, Milton's publishing contract for *Paradise Lost*, argues Peter Lindenbaum, is a significant moment in an emerging conception of the writer as the exclusive owner of intangible, or intellectual, property.[16]

The reach of Milton's influence on legal matters remains a significant gap in current research and merits further investigation. One of the greatest holes in our scholarship is just how influential a role Milton played in legislative reform and foreign relations in his official capacity as Secretary of Foreign Tongues. So, too, we are not fully versed in Milton's thoroughgoing knowledge of legal matters. At the time of his widow Elizabeth Milton's death, eleven folios of law books that presumably belonged to him were listed in the inventory of her goods, suggesting his ongoing interest in legal thought.[17] And, while Milton frequently cites legal treatises in his work, there has been no comprehensive interpolation of these works with his prose and poetry. For example, Milton relied extensively, amongst numerous other legal tracts, on the works of Sir John Fortescue of Selden, Sir Thomas Smith, Sir Edward Coke, Sir Francis Bacon, Henry de Bracton, and William Lombard; their influence on his thinking merits further study. The extent of Milton's knowledge of Roman law and Flavius Anicus Justinian's work has been the subject of one of the few articles on this subject.[18] Milton studies is also long overdue for a definitive treatment of Milton's indebtedness to natural rights theories, particularly those of Hugo Grotius.

There too remains the question of the "Index Legalis" (1659), a brief smattering of Latin citations from contemporary legal treatises, most of which refer to procedural matters, found in the Columbia Manuscript. In the Columbia edition of *The Works of John Milton*, this Index was printed as an "Addition" to the Commonplace Book; the Yale edition of the *Complete Prose Works of John Milton*, however, relegated it to an Appendix, because, as Maurice Kelly argued, "its right to inclusion in the Milton canon has yet to be clearly established" (*CPW* 1:954). While the Columbia Manuscript contains three works definitively attributable to Milton, it also contains a number of other works by other authors, calling into doubt the authorship of the "Index Legalis." Should the Index be definitively attributed to Milton, it would add to our understanding of Milton's interest in and knowledge of legal matters.

Finally, both Milton's poetry and prose are infused with the specialized language and argumentative and rhetorical style and methods of legal discourse. Further analysis of his deployment of legal discourse, both its form and substance, would permit myriad contextualizations of his work that would broaden our sense of Milton as scholar, pamphleteer, political theorist, and poet.

Exploring Milton's knowledge of and relationship to the law is still an adventure in largely uncharted waters. While I have offered an abbreviated guided tour of the current state of Milton studies and the law, this chapter in many ways demonstrates just how incomplete our scholarship is to date and intends to act as a call to future critics. More definitive mappings of Milton's relationship to both seventeenth-century British law and comparative legal systems, historical and contemporary to Milton, are necessary in order to appreciate Milton's legal vision and his influence on British legal thought.

NOTES

1 *LR* 1:368.
2 For the poem's possible years of composition, see the appendix in this volume.
3 Ruth Mohl, *John Milton and His Commonplace Book* (New York, 1969), 224.
4 For further discussion of the influence of Mosaic law on Milton's work, see Jason P. Rosenblatt, *Torah and Law in "Paradise Lost"* (Princeton, 1994).
5 See *LR* for these documents.
6 For a detailed account of Milton's lawsuits, see J. Milton French, *Milton in Chancery: New Chapters in the Lives of the Poet and His Father* (New York, 1939).
7 For a fuller discussion of Milton's relationship to the book trade, see Stephen Dobranski's chapter in this volume.
8 William Riley Parker, *Milton: A Biography*, 2nd edn., ed. Gordon Campbell, 2 vols. (1968; Oxford, 1996), 264.
9 David Masson, *The Life of John Milton*, 7 vols. (London, 1877–96), VI:806–12.
10 Parker, *Milton*, 574.
11 Stephen B. Dobranski, "Licensing Milton's Heresy," in *Milton and Heresy*, ed. Stephen B. Dobranski and John P. Rumrich (Cambridge, 1998), 144.
12 Parker, *Milton*, 567–76.
13 Some notable exceptions include Mary C. Fenton, *Milton's Places of Hope: Spiritual and Political Connections of Hope With Land* (New York, 2006); Lynne A. Greenberg, "*Paradise Lost* and the Enclosure of the Feme Covert," in *Milton and the Grounds of Contention*, ed. Mark R. Kelley, Michael Lieb, and John T. Shawcross (Pittsburgh, PA, 2003), 150–73; Greenberg, "Dalila's 'feminine assaults': The Gendering and Engendering of Crime in *Samson Agonistes*," in *Altering Eyes: New Perspectives on Milton's "Samson Agonistes,"* ed. Joseph A. Wittreich and Mark R. Kelley (Newark, NJ, 2002), 192–219; and Gary D. Hamilton, "*Paradise Regained* and the Private Houses," in *Of Poetry and Politics: New Essays on Milton and His World*, ed. P. G. Stanwood (Binghamton, NY, 1995), 239–48.
14 See, for example, Stanley Fish, "Unger and Milton," *Duke Law Journal* (1988): 975.
15 *LR* V:11–14.
16 Peter Lindenbaum, "Milton's Contract," in *The Construction of Authorship: Textual Appropriation in Law and Literature*, ed. Martha Woodmansee and Peter Jaszi (Durham, NC, and London, 1994), 175–90.
17 *LR* V:124.
18 Martin Dzelzainis, "'In These Western Parts of the Empire': Milton and Roman Law," in *Milton and the Terms of Liberty*, ed. Graham Parry and Joad Raymond (Cambridge, 2002), 57–68.

CHAPTER 28

Literary contemporaries

Albert C. Labriola

There are numerous ways to situate Milton historically, one of which is to compare his writings with his contemporaries'. To limit the scope of such analysis, I will choose Shakespeare, Spenser, and Donne. For the first two authors, Milton himself supplies evidence of admiration. In *Areopagitica* (1644), he contends that "our sage and serious Poet *Spencer*" is "a better teacher then *Scotus* or *Aquinas*" (*CPW* II:516). And in "On Shakespeare," a commendatory sixteen-line epigram published in the front matter of the Second Folio of the plays (1632), Milton lauds Shakespeare as an author who transcends anyone's ability to eulogize him. Finally, while a student at St. Paul's School in London, Milton may have heard John Donne's sermons at the cathedral nearby.

By examining Milton and his literary contemporaries historically, one does not reject other critical methodologies but complements them. Reviving a historical approach, no longer popular in the postmodern era of cultural and critical studies, redresses an imbalance resulting from the prevalent use of more recent critical methodologies. Postmodern methodologies downplay literary and aesthetic elements: genre, theme, imagery, characterization, paradox, irony, allusion, allegory, and symbolism. They also downplay the intellectual milieu in which literary historians tend to situate works, a milieu including the history of ideas, which recurs through various eras and in diverse cultural circumstances. In the postmodern era, moreover, literature as such is no longer privileged, but perceived as another text in the broadest sense: visual or verbal, intellectual or popular. For instance, one of the newer critical methodologies, new historicism or cultural materialism, broadens the historical milieu in which to juxtapose and interrelate literary and non-literary texts. Politics, law, medicine, economics, religion, travelogues, journals, and material means of production (printing, illustration, licensing, censorship, and dissemination of texts) have added significantly to the historical framework, often popular, in which literature is interpreted. Although the insights that emerge from this approach cannot be denied or minimized, the present chapter emphasizes literary history and the history of ideas as the framework for comparative and intertextual analysis of Milton and his contemporaries, a process that will revive lines of inquiry that may be pursued or adapted by the postmodern generation of critics.

The interrelation of Shakespeare and Milton has long intrigued scholars, for Milton was seven years old when Shakespeare died.[1] In addition to Milton's epigram lauding Shakespeare in the Second Folio of the plays, Milton refers to Shakespeare's dramas admiringly in *L'Allegro*, particularly the comedies: "sweetest Shakespeare, Fancy's child / Warble[s] his native wood-notes wild" (lines 133–34). And in *Eikonoklastes* (1649), Milton refers to the Duke of Gloucester who becomes Richard III, a duplicitous character in Shakespeare's play and, from Milton's perspective, a prototype of King Charles I, whose pious pretenses depicted in the *Eikon Basilike* concealed his treacherous heart.

Despite these acknowledgments that Milton knew Shakespeare's plays, the influence of the playwright on the younger author is uncertain. The typical method of adducing influence has been to compile and increase the number of verbal resemblances between the two authors. Alwin Thaler, for instance, compiled hundreds of parallels between Shakespeare's plays and Milton's poems. These resemblances often center upon a word or a phrase: for example, "pillars of the state" in *2 Henry VI* (1.i.72) and "pillar of state" in *Paradise Lost* (11.302); "sad despair" in *3 Henry VI* (11.iii.9) and "flat despair" in *Paradise Lost* (11.143).[2]

Sometimes, resemblances include characters, themes, and settings in Shakespeare's plays and in Milton's poems. Evil ambition is aroused in *Macbeth* when Duncan names Malcolm as the Prince of Cumberland and heir apparent; and Satan becomes envious and rebellious when the Son is proclaimed vicegerent and king of the angels, a proclamation that the archfiend interprets as an affront to his own dignity. Juxtaposing the characters of Macbeth and Satan and citing the overarching theme of inordinate ambition as the cause of downfall do provide some comparative insight. Thaler also likens the witches in *Macbeth* to Comus and his followers in *A Mask*, both groups engaged in casting spells and practicing necromancy. And the so-called green world in Shakespeare's comedies and romances anticipates some elements of Milton's Garden of Eden, sites in which the fancy of characters exceeds rational self-control, including Eve's encounter with the Tree of Knowledge as Satan tempts her. Despite their proliferating numbers, the likenesses and parallels to which I refer – verbal echoes, characters, themes, or setting – are tenuous, tendentious, or commonplace, surely not clear-cut and cogent enough to assert that the playwright significantly influenced the epic poet and polemicist.

Rather than merely enumerating intertextual parallels between Shakespeare and Milton, beyond which there is little or no elaboration nor any historical context, the more productive way of comparing Shakespeare and Milton is to analyze their writings from the broader perspective of literary history, including the history of ideas. For instance, governance, an all-pervasive idea from classical antiquity to, through, and beyond the early modern era, is embedded in Shakespeare's histories and tragedies and in Milton's prose and poetry. Both authors focus on the idea of monarchical governance, through which authority, not only political but often religious, was wielded. Benevolent monarchs who promoted the commonweal and tyrants whose oppression was inimical to liberty appear in Shakespeare's plays and Milton's works.

Another related feature in the writings of the two authors is regal spectacle: how and why it projects authority and whether and when it is idolatry. In Shakespeare's *Richard II* (III.iii) the king atop Flint Castle is likened to the rising sun dispelling the clouds that would dim its glory or impede its progress through the firmament. This figurative language invites comparison with the solar imagery describing Satan in *Paradise Lost*, who after the War in Heaven is arrested in his ambition to rival the godhead: "as when the sun new ris'n / Looks through the horizontal misty air / Shorn of his beams" (1.594–96). Prior to Satan's downfall, the narrator describes his imperious presence "in his sun-bright chariot" as an "Idol of majesty divine" (VI.100–01). Like Richard II, Satan believes that external trappings and accouterments of royalty convey, if not confer, sovereignty. Unlike Henry V, whose rejection of "idol ceremony" (IV.i.238) is an enlightening moment, Satan is self-indulgently preoccupied with the semblance of his kingship, sometimes deluded by his own pretenses.[3]

Indeed, Henry V's soliloquies and Satan's provide access to their interior selves, whether at moments of self-awareness or self-delusion, not to mention the processes by which each one of them crafts a public persona and calculates his relationships with others. Accordingly, a public persona and a private self distinguish Richard II, Henry V, and Satan. Henry V and Satan, despite their private doubts of success, incite their followers by adopting a public persona of self-confidence, in contrast to Richard II, whose descent from his sunlike eminence atop Flint Castle – "Down, down I come; like glistering Phaëthon" (III.iii.178) – reflects a breakdown because of psychological duress. Richard's downfall is described by imagery not unlike Lucifer's fall from splendor, an event recounted in Isaiah 14:12:

"How art thou fallen from heaven, O Lucifer, son of the morning!" *Paradise Lost* incorporates the same biblical imagery: Satan did "fall like lightning down from heav'n" (x.184).

In addition, both Henry V and Satan use similar methods to energize their cohorts, whether on the battlefield at Agincourt or during the War in Heaven. Both leaders chide their followers, but the effect is positive. Henry galvanizes his warriors by reminding them of their heroic forebears, whom they should emulate; and Satan incites his cohorts by recalling their former grandeur, which they must struggle to regain. To differentiate the two leaders, one might contend that Henry's public persona manifests bravura, whereas Satan's projects bravado.

Other resemblances between Henry V and Satan entail conscientious dilemmas that they face, so-called cases of conscience for which casuistry was an early modern means of deliberation and resolution. In the historical context of seventeenth-century England, no idea received greater attention than the conscientious dilemma or case of conscience. On the eve of the Battle of Agincourt, Henry V resolves the dilemma of Williams, Bates, and Court, three commoners in his army whose determination to stand and fight is being tested by their belief that after their deaths, the king, if captured, will be ransomed. They, then, will have died in vain. Disguised under the cloak of Sir Thomas Erpingham, Henry engages their dilemma by urging them to be shriven, so that if they were to die on the battlefield, their souls would be prepared for judgment. He rejects their claim to withdraw from the conflict, a decision not theirs to make. Instead, the decision to wage war issues from the conscience of the king, who "himself hath a heavy reckoning to make" (iv.i.135) on Judgment Day. Paradoxically, the metal of the crown, or "idol ceremony" (iv.i.238), elicits homonymic wordplay with "mettle," the substance of character enabling one to withstand, if not prevail over, adversity. To Henry, moreover, the weight of the crown signifies the burdens, anxieties, and conscientious dilemmas that befall a king.

Contrasting with Henry is Satan, who will suffer the deity's judgment, an event foreseen in the protevangelium of Genesis (3:14–15) and incorporated allusively in Milton's epic. In cursing the serpent, the Son announces that Eve's progeny, notably the Son, "shall bruise [its] head" (x.181). When Abdiel strikes his sword against Satan's helmet in hand-to-hand combat (vi.191), his action anticipates the ultimate capital bruise that will be inflicted upon the archfiend, from whose head Sin was born. But the aforementioned consequences that will befall Satan eventuate from his conscientious dilemmas or, more aptly, from his sinful resolution of them.

These conscientious dilemmas unfold during his two major soliloquies: the first in book IV, the second in book IX. In the first, he struggles with the possibility of repentance but rejects that course of action. In the second, he is tormented by the idea of imbruting himself after having been among the loftiest of angels, the light-bearer Lucifer. Grudgingly, Satan resolves this dilemma by pursuing the debased means of inhabiting a serpent to pursue revenge against the deity.

Spenser, the *magister bonus* whom Milton cites in *Areopagitica*, also affected the younger author in several ways. Echoing Milton's praise of Spenser, Dryden in the Preface to *Fables Ancient and Modern* contends:

> *Milton* was the Poetical Son of *Spencer*, and Mr. *Waller* of *Fairfax*; for we have our Lineal Descents and Clans, as well as other Families: *Spencer* more than once insinuates, that the Soul of *Chaucer* was transfus'd into his Body; and that he was begotten by him Two hundred years after his Decease; *Milton* has acknowledg'd to Me, that *Spencer* was his Original.[4]

Probably the dual nature of Satan in *Paradise Lost* – his overconfident public persona and his guileful inward self – derives from several characters in *The Faerie Queene*. Satan's stand-off against Death in book II of *Paradise Lost* and his hand-to-hand combat against Abdiel and Michael in book VI reflect many like encounters in Spenser's epic, including Redcrosse Knight's battle with Sansfoy and later with Sansjoy, and Guyon's various struggles. These forceful conflicts, however, are secondary to the guileful engagements of evil-fair-seeming. In *Paradise Lost*, Satan is more successful when guileful than while forceful. His various transformations, like Archimago's, project a kaleidoscopic range of personae that seduce others. Also anticipating Satan's use of force and guile is Radigund in book 5 of *The Faerie Queene,* who triumphs over adversaries by one means or another. And her androgynous nature glances at the interrelationship of Satan and Sin, whereby the latter, a female, emerged from Satan's head as if the fission of the one character from the other dramatizes a split in what had been a hermaphroditic being, not unlike Eve's emergence from Adam.

Juxtaposing the epics of Spenser and Milton, one discerns that the former author inclines more toward romance and to the explicit use of allegory. The latter emphasizes psychological verisimilitude and inwardness, a conspicuous progression toward subjectivity that entrances a reader by soliloquies of self-analysis, interpersonal relationships, dramaturgical dialogue, and profoundly rich elements of characterization such as prolonged deliberation, assessment of motivation in oneself and in others, cases of conscience, and processes of decision-making. Despite the dramatic origins from which it eventuated as an epic, *Paradise Lost* sometimes anticipates novelistic techniques of characterization, at least to the degree that it, though not *The Faerie Queene*, may be called a psychological epic.

In effect, Milton mediates between Shakespeare and Spenser by portraying the inner depth and psychological verisimilitude of characters in a manner not unlike the dramatist and by superseding the allegoresis of his English epic forebear. One way of highlighting Milton's progression in developing characters is to compare the relationship of Amoret and Scudamor from book 3 of *The Faerie Queene* (especially the 1590 edition) and that of Adam and Eve. Clearly the former couple manifest a complementary relationship, tested by separation but rewarded by reunion. While the events that impinge on their relationship appear to be contrived and lack the depth of lifelike being, Spenser's characters nevertheless become the analogues of other couples in Shakespeare and Milton, couples whose separation and reunion create the very framework in which to chart their unfolding relationship. When, for example, Macbeth and Lady Macbeth, having been separated by his involvement in military conflict, are reunited at Inverness Castle, their psychosexual interaction inflames Macbeth to implement his criminal ambitions as a traitor to the king, after he had seemingly resolved his conscientious dilemmas by remaining loyal to Duncan. Interaction with Lady Macbeth, accompanied by sexually charged language and fleshly intimacy, emboldens Macbeth to perform the misdeed that he had shunned. Preceded by Macbeth's long soliloquy, his reunion, dialogue, and interaction with his wife constitute pivotal points in his decision-making.

Similarly, in *Paradise Lost* the parting in the garden in book ix and the eventual reunion of Adam and Eve manifest psychological verisimilitude in which the wife affects the husband's decision-making, what some commentators call uxoriousness. In rapid succession Adam errs twice: by failing to command Eve to remain with him (a command, without physical restraint, that she was free to obey or not) and by partaking of the forbidden fruit that Eve offers him. The first error in judgment enables Eve to work alone, a condition in which she is more susceptible to Satan's duplicity and treachery; the second is a knowing lapse by Adam after having been overcome by Eve's female charm.

Along the continuum that I have outlined, when Amoret and Scudamor are examined, their depth as characters is questionable though their significance in the allegoresis of Spenser's epic is clear. Reinforcing this appraisal is the prevalent use of onomastics to identify and interpret Spenser's allegorical characters. With Milton, the relationship of Adam and Eve is an enactment – verbally, emotionally, and psychologically – that resonates with the personal experience of readers. Although Spenser's and Milton's works may be termed romantic epics, *The Faerie Queene* is the purer and more traditional example of that genre; whereas *Paradise Lost* may be perceived as an ironic or satiric adaptation, or critique, of loving relationships in Spenser's epic.

Not to be overlooked is the *locus amoenus* or *hortus conclusus* that distinguishes Spenser's and Milton's epics. Among other examples, the Bower of Bliss in book 2 of *The Faerie Queene* and the Garden of Adonis in book 3 may be juxtaposed with Milton's Garden of Eden and the "blissful bower" in which Adam and Eve consummate their marriage (IV.690). Beyond the loco-descriptive similarities of such gardens, the greater significance centers upon their resemblances to the *hortus mentis*, or garden of the mind. Placed along a continuum of literary gardens – classical, medieval, and early modern – these settings, particularly in *Paradise Lost*, afford interpretive keys to understanding the characters' subjectivity. Less a setting and more a state of mind, the Garden of Eden in *Paradise Lost* enables Adam and Eve to celebrate the bounty of Nature, laud the beneficence of the Lord, and promote fecundity. The same site, however, occasions a lustful postlapsarian encounter, where a myriad of vices predominate and supplant the virtues that had prevailed earlier in the minds of Adam and Eve. Indeed, the vices and virtues embodied in Adam and Eve may be construed within the framework of Christian morality and ethics in *The Faerie Queene*. In several ways, the courtesy book that *The Faerie Queene* presumes to be does anticipate *Paradise Lost*, not to mention Milton's disquisition on vices, virtues, morality, and ethics in *De Doctrina Christiana*.

Whether by reference to *The Faerie Queene* or *Paradise Lost*, conscientious dilemmas also provide a framework in which to examine the same phenomena in John Donne's religious poems. The dilemmas in the Holy Sonnets are almost always eschatological, for they recount struggles by a speaker or speakers who deliberate on sinfulness and repentance but whose ultimate orientation inclines toward salvation and damnation. Compressed into the briefest poems, these dilemmas are resolved in the sestet of the Italian sonnet structure that Donne imitates or in the epigrammatic closing couplet of the Shakespearean sonnet structure that he sometimes adopts. Across the fourteen lines of the sonnets are proliferating ironies, striking paradoxes, vivid imagery, and conceits, whether protracted or concise. Dilemmas likewise engage the speakers in Donne's longer religious poems, such as "Good Friday, 1613. Riding Westward" and "Hymne to God my God in my sickness." In the former, the speaker who acknowledges profound sinfulness ponders how and why he might be saved. In a remarkable *tour de force*, he presents his sinful self for the Lord to punish until justice is appeased and mercy proffered. In the latter, the speaker who anticipates imminent death seeks assurance of salvation by having himself wrapped in a purple shroud that variously signifies the blood, mercy, and saving grace of Christ.

In fact, Milton and Donne have not yet been comparatively studied across their careers as casuistical authors. Even in their juvenilia, both authors practiced a form of debate or equivocation that evolved into casuistry in their mature writings. Milton's Prolusions and Donne's *Paradoxes and Problems* are precisely the youthful ventures into certain topics that recur in their later works. Donne's *Paradox* I, "A Defence of Womens Inconstancy," informs at least two of his poems, "Womans Constancy" and "The Indifferent." And Milton's Prolusions likewise anticipate his later writings. Prolusion 1, "Whether Day or Night is the More Excellent," contains commentary on chaos, darkness, and personifications that inhabit those realms, an effective framework in which to investigate book II of *Paradise Lost*. Furthermore, Prolusion 2, "On the Music of the Spheres," supplies a context for understanding "On the Morning of Christ's Nativity," "At a Solemn Music," and the ethereal music that the Lady of *A Mask* hears and to which she harmonizes her song.

In addition to the separate analysis of Milton and Donne, who re-use but adapt certain ideas over time, a more direct comparative analysis of the authors' use of the same ideas is illuminating. The process of regeneration, for example, is an ongoing topic of Donne's religious poems. The stages of regeneration including, among others, contrition, the infusion of grace, and atonement involve the collaborative endeavor of the sinner and the Lord. Through imagery, Donne blends the penitent's contrite tears and the merciful blood of Christ into a sacramental drink, the spiritual counterpart of an imbibed elixir or balm. In *Paradise Lost*, Milton dramatizes the regenerative process in the interaction of Adam and Eve after the fall, a counterpoint to their cooperative endeavor in sinfulness at the fall. In this case, the process of regeneration also involves the Son firsthand as a character in the epic, who serves as judge and comforter, administering punishment and mercy, respectively. And if one subscribes to the regenerationist interpretation of Samson – that he manifests contrition, acquires an influx of grace, and enters into atonement[5] – then Milton's dramatic poem reflects the positive outcome of being reinstated as God's "faithful champion" (*Samson Agonistes*, line 1751) and as his scourge and minister of vengeance against the unfaithful Philistines.

When the theology of Donne and Milton are comparatively studied in their prose works, not merely in their poems, then the overlap of coverage by the two authors is remarkable. Donne's *Essays in Divinity*, *Devotions Upon Emergent Occasions*, and *Sermons*, on the one hand, and Milton's *De Doctrina Christiana*, on the other, engage many of the same topics. Their Trinitarian theology, for instance, is vitally important to the seventeenth-century conception of an ontological hierarchy of the Divine Persons, a view advocated by Donne and Milton. This view was regularly espoused by the ante-Nicene Fathers. Only after the Council of Nicea (325 CE) was so-called orthodox Trinitarian theology formulated, whereby the Divine Persons were deemed co-equal, co-essential, co-substantial, co-eternal. Aligned more with the ante-Nicene rather than post-Nicene Fathers, Donne and Milton engage the topics of anthropomorphic and anthropopathic renditions of the Divine Persons.[6] In line with these views, both authors comment on divine deliberation: the processes of thought and decision-making that humankind imputes to the godhead. Accordingly, the very conscientious dilemmas that beset humankind typify deliberation in, and among, the Divine Persons, notably at the creation of humankind but especially at the prospect of redemption. Redeeming fallen humankind involves the necessity to exact justice but the desire to afford mercy. Resolved by the Son's voluntary humiliation, which is depicted in the works of Donne and Milton, the dilemma ultimately highlights the godhead's self-sacrificing love.

Both Donne and Milton likewise employ economic metaphors to recount the inestimable value of the Son's bloodshed. For Donne in "Good Friday, 1613. Riding Westward," one moist drop of blood is sufficient to transform dust to dirt, malleable earth from which the regeneration (or re-genesis) of humankind may occur. For Donne, both the Father and the Son are artificers, and humankind becomes their artifact. And the Son's imperative in Milton's epic – "Account me man" (*Paradise Lost* III.238) – is an economic metaphor whereby the Second Person's merits are imputed not only to relieve humankind's so-called indebtedness after the fall but also to generate fiscal solvency, if not inestimable value. Comparative study of Donne and Milton on many fronts suggests that both authors portray a thinking, speaking, and passible deity.

In line with this view, both authors derive their understanding of an anthropomorphic and anthropopathic deity from their analysis of scripture. Donne and Milton cite countless proof-texts from scripture, so that studies might be conducted of their citations of the same biblical passages and their inferences therefrom. Whether in Donne's prose works, especially the sermons, or in Milton's *De Doctrina Christiana*, the methods of rational theology or apologetics of the two authors come to the fore. To select one instance, both Donne and Milton cite biblical passages acknowledging that the pre-existent Christ, or the Son, was manifested as an angel in the Old Dispensation, the so-called angel of the Lord who interacted with the Israelites. If the Son is the *theangelos* or the deity represented as angelomorphic, then Donne and Milton may be espousing an ontological hierarchy of Divine Persons whereby the *theangelos* eventually descends to become the *theanthropos*.

This process of the Son's gradual humiliation or descension accords with Neoplatonism. If, that is, Neoplatonic ascent is a rarefied and sublimated progression, then voluntary descent is a loving process of benign degradation enacted by the Son, who assumes the forms and nature of lesser beings, angelic and human. The demonic counterpart in *Paradise Lost* is Satan's constrained degradation, not only in book x when he is transmogrified on his throne in Hell but also in book ix when pride compels him to imbrute himself in order to pursue revenge against the godhead.

Whether the emphasis is on literary elements such as characterization, imagery, irony, and the like, or on the history of ideas, commentary on Milton and his literary contemporaries generates lines of inquiry applicable to the postmodern era. Subjectivity, selfhood, and conscientious dilemmas, for instance, may be approached from present-day models of analysis, or revaluated by comparison with Milton's contemporaries. But both approaches, the traditional and postmodern, may develop a symbiotic relationship, whereby the differences among early modern authors come into view along the trajectory of history, so that our own era more fully understands whether and when the past is prologue, or whether and when originality or continuity is the thrust of the postmodern achievement.

NOTES

1 Milton's relationship with Shakespeare is discussed more fully in Ann Baynes Coiro's chapter in this volume.
2 See Alwin Thaler, "The Shaksperian Element in Milton," *PMLA* 40 (1925): 645–91.
3 Shakespeare's plays are cited from *The Complete Works of Shakespeare*, ed. David Bevington, 6th edn. (New York, 2006).
4 Preface, *Fables Ancient and Modern*, in *The Works of John Dryden, Volume* VII: *Poems, 1697–1700*, ed. Vinton A. Dearing (Berkeley, 2000), 25.

5 See, for example, F. Michael Krouse, *Milton's Samson and the Christian Tradition* (Princeton, 1949); and Anthony Low, *The Blaze of Noon: A Reading of "Samson Agonistes"* (New York and London, 1974).
6 Milton's ideas about God, His decrees, and the Son are discussed in detail in William Poole's chapter in this volume.

CHAPTER 29

Logic

Phillip J. Donnelly

The effects of Milton's formative education in the liberal arts of grammar, logic, and rhetoric appear in various ways throughout his poetry and prose. The precise character of Milton's relation to the art of logic, however, remains a matter of ongoing debate.[1] The reasons for this are multiple, including, as we shall see, the conflicting historical accounts of the pedagogical tradition in which Milton situated his own logic text, the logic of Peter Ramus (1515–72). Even after that pedagogical context has been somewhat clarified, however, questions persist regarding how Milton viewed logic: specifically regarding his view of the extent to which logical inferences could reliably lead to truth but also regarding the role of such reasoning in poetry. Such questions cannot be avoided; much of what readers encounter in Milton's major poetry and prose will be shaped directly by what we assume to be his attitude toward logic. When *Paradise Lost* begins by referring to its main subject as an "argument" (1.24) and by asking "what cause / Moved" Adam and Eve to fall, does Milton expect his readers to apply the definitions of "argument" and "cause" (1.28) that he formulated in his introductory logic text, *Artis Logicae*? The short answer is that Milton's epic and his logic text are indeed related, but not primarily in the direct ways that we might expect. This chapter first considers the Ramist pedagogical tradition in which Milton locates his *Artis Logicae Plenior Institutio* (1672), commonly translated as *A Fuller Course in the Art of Logic*. In light of that tradition, I show how Milton's logic text responds to some of the characteristic traits of Ramism. I then consider specific points in *De Doctrina Christiana* that engage Milton's Ramism. Finally, I explain how an appreciation for Milton's view of logic can improve our understanding of his major poetry.

Peter Ramus has been alternately hailed as a revolutionary pedagogue whose approach to texts became a crucial context for modern scientific thinking or denounced as a "bold and clever ignoramus" whose logic text was a "farrago of *a priori* nonsense."[2] To understand these contrasting reactions, one needs to appreciate that Ramism developed as part of the Renaissance humanist response to the perceived excesses of scholastic logic and its culture of disputation. The scholastic tradition had developed the study of logic based on a collection of Aristotle's works, commonly referred to as the *Organon* ("tool").[3] The first four of these (six) works concerns the establishment of a rigorous method of demonstration. The first work presents a detailed discussion of how terms function (*Categories*), followed by a study of semantics and categorical propositions (*On Interpretation*), and the relations between propositions in a syllogism (*Prior Analytics*), all of which culminates in an attempt to establish what constitutes a demonstrative "science," in Aristotle's sense (*Posterior Analytics*): that is, knowledge based on inferences from universal first principles. The final two works in the *Organon*, the *Topics* and *Sophistical Refutations*, however, are quite different from the others. The *Topics* does not focus on scientific demonstration but on how to conduct arguments based on "reputable opinions," rather than first principles.[4] The final text of the *Organon*, *Sophistical Refutations*, focuses on fallacies that may be involved in such arguments based on reputable opinions. The crucial point to appreciate here is that Renaissance humanists effectively adopted a "rhetorical logic" derived from Cicero's appropriation of Aristotle's *Topics* (hence, "topical logic"): that is, a logic aimed at persuasion based on plausibility. Conversely, humanists rejected the scholastic emphasis on the first four parts of the *Organon* as either superfluous to understanding truth or an impediment to Christian virtue. This humanist emphasis on such rhetorical logic was based on the adaptations of Aristotle's *Topics* specifically by Cicero (106–43 BCE) and Boethius (480–524), and later mediated through humanist writers such as Lorenzo Valla (1407–57) and Rudolph Agricola (1443–85).[5] Ramist logic was directly indebted to Agricola's *De inventio dialectica*.[6] This context is crucial in order to understand the character of the disagreement between Ramism and its critics, both then and now. Ramism, in its most sweeping formulations, extended such rhetorical, or "topical," logic to all subject areas; as a result, Ramist practice could deny the very possibility of a demonstrative science.

The crux of the disagreement between the scholastics and Ramus has been described by Howard Hotson in this way: "in replacing the rigorous demonstrative logic of Aristotle with the topical logic derived from Agricola [Ramus] abandoned a tool capable of dealing with scientific problems for a humanist dialectic of little use beyond merely literary pursuits."[7] The choice of the word "merely" suggests where Hotson is inclined to locate truth; whereas a skeptic like Lorenzo Valla might insist that, given the nature of human knowing and the arts of discourse, "dealing with scientific problems" is always necessarily a kind of "literary pursuit."[8] Although not constituting a formal logic, the genius of Ramism was to "provide a method of reading which identifies and groups thoughts and illustrations so that the argument or arguments" of a given text may be "accessible to the reader"; in short, Ramist logic helped students to grasp the "discursive organization" of texts.[9]

In order to appreciate the appeal of this kind of topical logic, one might consider how Ramist logic could enable a student today to analyze an advertisement, an admittedly debased form of deliberative argument. For Ramus, every advertisement would be viewed as, in effect, a rhetorical syllogism which aims to move people toward a given action, based on generally held assumptions. The "topics" identify the different kinds of "arguments" that could constitute the "middle term" in a suasive discourse: that is, the term that connects the inductive premise to a given conclusion. Thus, for example, an advertisement for a specific beverage might refer to the ingredients (material cause) or to a healthy lifestyle (biological final cause of drinking). In the first case, the "argument," or middle term, would be the material cause, in the latter case, the final cause. In either case, the goal of the ad is to persuade (sell), and the viability of its "argument" would depend on generally held opinions regarding either food or health. Analyzing or composing texts in this manner would not result in absolute knowledge, but such skills were useful for training civil servants and other participants in the new information culture of early modern Europe. This broad appeal of Ramism should not, however, be taken to imply that humanist logic was limited to "non-rigorous" discourse.[10] Such rhetorical analysis could also be applied, for example, to an empirical lab report. The contrast, however, between the respective aims of demonstrative Aristotelian science and humanist topical logic is, in effect, part of "the story of the unresolved tension" between scholastic logic and humanist rhetoric.[11] Interpretations of Ramus and his legacy will therefore often depend on whether a given historian assumes that logic or rhetoric is the supreme discursive art.

Because a Ramist logic text is a topical, or rhetorical, logic aimed to help Renaissance students analyze texts, students of modern logic who take up Milton's *Artis Logicae* may be puzzled by much that seems unfamiliar. Instead of exploring the nuances of the syllogism, or the modes of inference, *Artis Logicae* begins, in Ramist fashion, by first defining the art of logic and then dividing it into pairs of subdividing topics. The ensuing chapters of the text, in Part 1, then consider the various kinds of "arguments" that may be used to support or deny any given claim. The first part of logic was called *inventio*, or the "discovery," of arguments. The second part of logic concerned *dispositio*, or the "arrangement," of the arguments. Thus, chapters 3 through 8 consider aspects of the four causes (efficient, material, formal, and final), but they do so specifically with a view to helping students understand how these causes can be used to "argue" something. As Milton explains, by "arguing" he means: "with a view to showing, explaining or proving something." Thus according to the well-known quotation, "'Fear argues degenerate souls,' *Aeneid* 4" (*CPW* VIII:220). As his example suggests, Milton assumes that "argument" may include but is not limited to strict logical inference, or even to the verbal sense of "debate." An argument may not strictly "prove," but it may "show" or "explain" – that is, it may describe the constitution of a given thing or its causes without conclusively demonstrating the truth of that description. Indeed, conclusive demonstration in a given case may not be available. Instead, Milton maintains the broadest possible meaning of "argument," as a relation between or among words and/or things, whether real or feigned; moreover, he uses "arguments," in this sense, as a synonym for "reasons" (*CPW* VIII:220).

Comparing the text of the *Artis Logicae* with those works from which Milton drew can suggest how he altered the Ramist tradition while participating in it. In the Ramist textbook tradition, the axioms of a given art were generally adopted from earlier texts, while the writer's explanation and clarification of those axioms typically provided the occasion for unique reflection. There are at least four known texts upon which *Artis Logicae* draws. The two main sources are *Dialecticae Libri Duo* (1572), by Peter Ramus, and *Commentarii in P. Rami Dialecticam* (1601), by George Downame.[12] The first text provided the framework of main axioms, while Downame's commentary was the major source for the explanations that Milton wove into the Ramus text. Beyond these two major sources, Milton also explicitly engages Bartholomew Keckermann's *Systema Logicae Tribus Libris Adornatum* (1613) (*CPW* VIII:330, 374). Evidence regarding Milton's selection of examples from Downame also suggests that Milton may have known *The Logician's School-Master* (1629), by Alexander Richardson.[13] The main innovation that Milton claims for his own work is the textual format, in that he has "woven" the commentary directly into the main text, noting that he does revise the commentaries where he disagrees (*CPW* VIII:209–10).

Given this relationship between the axioms and the commentaries in the textbook tradition, we might be surprised to find that Milton alters the first and most basic axiom in defining the art of logic: "Logic is the art of reasoning well [*ars bene ratiocinandi*]" (*CPW* VIII:217). The Ramus source text reads: "the art of discoursing well" [*ars bene disserendi*].[14] Walter Ong argues that Milton's use of *ratiocinandi* rather than *disserendi* "situates him farther out than Ramus had been along the trajectory moving logic from an art of communication [as part of rhetoric] to an art of presumably solipsistic [proto-Cartesian] thought."[15] Ong assumes that by the term *ratio* Milton means something reductive, something less than *disserere*; but Milton actually rejects *disserendi* because, like the term "dialectic," it is too limited: it refers only to "the art of questioning and answering, that is, of debating" (*CPW* VIII:218). Milton simply insists that logic includes *more* than debating, so that to limit logic to *disserere* "is too narrow" (*CPW* VIII:218).[16] This distinction is pivotal for Milton because, in his view, not even the art of persuasion, or rhetoric, is reducible to "debating," and, as we shall see, rhetoric is the practical context in which Milton situates the study of logic, in the 1640s and the 1670s.[17]

Although Milton published *Artis Logicae* only in 1672, evidence supports the consensus that the text was first composed between 1641 and 1647.[18] In *Of Education* (1644) Milton situates the study of logic within a broad account of the means and end of learning. The goal of learning, he says, is "to repair the ruins of our first parents" – that is, to restore the divine image in humans. The two specific means by which that restoration occurs is through the saving knowledge of God, "and out of that knowledge to love him, to imitate him, to be like him, as we may the neerest by possessing our souls of true vertue, which being united to the heavenly grace of faith makes up the highest perfection" (*CPW* II:366–67). This statement is, in some respects, typical of a Ramist Protestant, and yet, in other ways, it clearly opposes the trajectory of later Ramism. At one level, the means that he designates for repairing the effects of the fall are conveniently twofold: knowledge (doctrine, or faith) and virtue (charity, or works). The emphasis upon the way that sanctification (works) arises from justification (faith) is a Protestant commonplace; however, the insistence that faith and works are properly united in governing the structure of theology is a characteristic of Ramist theology.[19] The key point to notice here is that, for Milton, formal education is ancillary to the process of sanctification, the cultivation of virtue subsequent to and dependent upon saving faith, or knowledge of God.[20] This emphasis upon moral formation, however, contrasts sharply with the broader cultural trajectory of Ramism, in which Ong locates the origins of modern rationalist encyclopedic and technological culture.[21] Whatever the accuracy of Ong's claims regarding the broader cultural effects of Ramist method, his suggestion that Milton follows the modern aspiration for a totalizing "methodical knowledge" of a "closed field" is not warranted.[22]

As Milton describes the curricular details of this education whose aim is the moral formation of students, he departs from Ramist norms by giving logic a limited rather than comprehensive role. After students have completed rudimentary studies, they are to turn to "the morall works" of philosophers (*CPW* II:396). Only after the study of moral philosophy should students then turn "lastly" to "those organic arts which inable men to discourse and write perspicuously, elegantly, and according to the fitted stile of lofty, mean, or lowly":

Logic therefore so much as is usefull, is to be referr'd to this due place withall her well couch't heads and Topics, untill it be time to open her contracted palm into a gracefull and ornate Rhetorick... To which Poetry would be made subsequent [in time], or indeed rather precedent [in dignity], as being less suttle and fine, but more simple, sensuous and passionate. (*CPW* II:401–03)

In connecting rhetoric to poetry, Milton specifies that he is not referring to mere versification, but to the "art," or knowledge of causes, which includes an understanding of the poetic genres and, above all, knowledge of "decorum," "which is the grand master peece to observe" (*CPW* II:404, 405). The most crucial point in the above passage, however, is that Milton clearly locates the fulfillment of logic in rhetorical practice. In a similar departure from Ramist norms, *Artis Logicae* insists that orators and poets may have "their own account of method" (*CPW* VIII:395); this directly qualifies the initial characterization of logic as "first" among the arts (*CPW* VIII:216). Moreover, for Milton, true rhetoric depends on moral conduct. In his *Apology against a Pamphlet* (1642), Milton maintains that those who are "most eloquent" are those who "express nature best, who in their lives least wander from [nature's] safe leading, which may be call'd regenerate reason" (*CPW* I:874). Such "regenerate reason," or restored "right reason," is, according to Milton, the faculty which enables the arts of logic and rhetoric.[23] Thus, when we encounter the term "reason" in Milton's writing, he may not necessarily mean "logic" but may be indicating the moral faculty of "right reason." We may therefore be justly skeptical of Ong's claim that the frequent "references to 'reasoning'," in Milton's major poems "are all to logic."[24]

If Milton maintains that logic finds its fulfillment in the practice of rhetoric, why does he, in the second part of *Artis Logicae*, follow the Ramist custom of strictly dividing between the art of logic (*inventio* and *dispositio*) and the art of rhetoric (*elocutio* and *pronuntiatio*)?[25] The answer is that

Milton is describing here the division between "arts," that is, between the theoretical presentation of two subjects as they are taught in the classroom; he is not referring to discursive practice. In practice, for Milton, logic and rhetoric, like faith and works, are united.[26] Against such a view, John Connor argues for a sharp contrast between a public "rhetorical" Milton of the 1640s and an inward "logical" Milton of the 1670s.[27] There are textual reasons to doubt Connor's appeal to publication chronology, most notably *Of Education*'s unrevised re-publication in 1673;[28] but the deeper issue here is the assumption that Milton's rejection of "debating" in *Artis Logicae* entails a rejection of all rhetoric, as though disputation were the only mode of interpersonal communication. Just as "logic" is more than "debating" (or "dialectic") for Milton (*CPW* VIII:217–18), so also "rhetoric" is more than debating because it includes poetry, which has the capacity to be morally doxological. In other words, rhetoric, rooted in the faculty of right reason, extends to include not only debating but all manner of poetry and its capacity for participation in divine glory, or beauty.

   Artis Logicae departs from its Ramist source texts in two further ways that should be noted. First, Milton explicitly rejects the Ramist practice of naming the second part of logic *iudicium* ("judgment"), choosing instead to follow the ancient practice of naming it *dispositio* ("arrangement"). By rejecting the Ramist tendency to pit invention and judgment against each other, in a manner anticipating the modern contrast between knowledge of facts and judgment of values, Milton insists instead that judgment is an effect of both invention and arrangement. Hence, for Milton, "reason also is choice" (*Paradise Lost* III.108; cf. *CPW* II:527), not because reasoning is merely arbitrary, but because it involves judgments regarding the good and therefore presumes volition. A second major way in which Milton departs from his source texts is in rejecting the typically sweeping claims made for Ramist "method." Against the customary Ramist claim that there is only one correct "method," which involves moving from universals to singulars, Milton notes that the Ramist approach is only one possible "method of teaching" among others (*CPW* VIII:391–92).

   The theology of *De Doctrina Christiana* indicates the influence of Milton's Ramism in the overall arrangement of the text, in its treatment of the doctrine of creation, and in its arguments against the doctrine of the Trinity.[29] The arrangement of material in *De Doctrina* could easily be mapped onto the kind of bifurcating table of topics that was so typical of Ramist texts. This structure is due in part to the Ramist character of the theological works by William Ames and Johannes Wolleb upon which *De Doctrina* is apparently based.[30] This arrangement is not merely formal; as we have noted, Milton indicates appreciation for the theological meaning of the unity between doctrine and ethics that governs the structure of Ramist theology (*CPW* VI:129). The account of creation in *De Doctrina* also seems to bear a direct connection to the treatment of "material cause" in *Artis Logicae*. *De Doctrina* rejects the traditional doctrine of creation *ex nihilo* (out of nothing), insisting that the universe must have a material (not corporeal) cause.[31] Because Milton is equally committed, however, to avoiding the pantheism and the ontological dualism that normally accompanies the rejection of creation *ex nihilo*, he attempts to argue that matter is "from God" (*ex deo*) without being God (*CPW* VI:307–08). This argument draws upon the distinction in *Artis Logicae* between "proper" and "common" essence (*CPW* VIII:234). In effect, by interpreting the Father as God's "proper essence" and creation's first matter as God's "common essence," Milton attempts to explain how creation can participate in God's goodness without being God.[32]

The third notable way in which *De Doctrina* bears the influence of Milton's Ramism is in the way that the theological treatise handles the doctrine of the Trinity. In the chapter "On Form" *Artis Logicae* states: "Therefore, things which differ in number also differ in essence, and never do things differ in number without also differing in essence. *Here let the Theologians take notice*" (*CPW* VIII:233, original emphasis). *Artis Logicae* takes "form" ("proper essence"), rather than "matter," as the principle of individuation; *De Doctrina* seems to draw on this particular equation of numerical identity with form in order to argue against the doctrine of the Trinity, by equating also hypostasis, substance, and person with essence (*CPW* VI:139–42, 205–39).[33] In the Preface to *Artis Logicae*, Milton criticizes those who "stuff in random rules which come from theologians rather than from logic" (*CPW* VIII:211). Milton never implies, however, that logic has no bearing on theology; he insists that logical principles should not be specially shaped to accommodate a doctrinal position that would otherwise be deemed illogical.

How does an appreciation for Milton's view of logic help us to understand his poetry? Rather than view *Paradise Lost* as a presumptuous subjection of providence to a kind of demonstrative analysis that would prove divine justice beyond doubt, we can now better understand the kind of question posed for readers by the use of the term "argument." The request by the narrative voice to be raised and supported, "That to the highth of this great argument / I may assert eternal providence, / And justify the ways of God to men" (1.24–26) may now appear in a new light. A Ramist analysis of the poem might recast these lines as a question: "Assuming the reality of providence, what 'argues,' or shows, divine justice?" For readers today, this might seem like an odd argument to attempt, until we realize that Milton understood himself to be surrounded by Calvinists who failed on precisely this point: that is, they ostensibly believed in providence, but their theology of predestination, in Milton's estimation, failed to show God's justice (*CPW* VI:192–93). The "argument" of *Paradise Lost*, therefore, in a Ramist sense, is in the entire poem's disclosure of how providence shows rather than obscures divine justice.

Paradise Lost presents two episodes that highlight the contrast between "reason" as an ethico-cognitive faculty and the use of that faculty to follow a given train of argument. In book V.99–121, Adam appeals to the categories of faculty psychology, including "Reason" and "Fancy," to explain Eve's troubling dream of temptation the previous night. Some attempt has been made to show how this passage actually draws upon Ramist epistemological vocabulary.[34] But such an attempt arguably misses the more basic twofold point of the passage regarding the operations of reason. On the one hand, Adam's inability to deduce a correct conclusion regarding the efficient cause of Eve's dream is a function of blameless finitude; the influence of Satan whispering in Eve's ear is a contingent event that Adam could never infer from his general knowledge. The action of the poem thus foregrounds the impossibility of inferring certain kinds of knowledge regarding a contingent event based on general or categorical knowledge. On the other hand, Adam's factual error does not impinge on his moral clarity, as he concludes that, despite whatever doubts he may have about the source of the dream, he knows that evil which is "unapproved" by the will leaves "No spot or blame" (V.118–19).

Another key passage that refers directly to "reason" is the statement by Eve, amid the climactic temptation scene, when she explains to Satan, "But of this Tree we may not taste or touch; / God so commanded, and left that command / Sole daughter of his voice; the rest, we live / Law to ourselves, our reason is our law" (IX.651–54). Eve's point is that reason guides all their action, except for the prohibition regarding the Tree of the knowledge of good and evil. The prohibition was revealed and could be neither known intuitively nor inferred; nevertheless, the divine prohibition is among the things that Eve knows. As with Adam's situation in book V, Eve began this scene by attempting to discover the cause of a contingent event, the new ability of the snake to speak. Eve, however, has the additional challenge of being required to judge the testimony of a witness, what Milton calls an "inartificial" argument (*CPW* VIII:318–22). Moreover, she is being subjected to active deception and temptation by a character who deploys sophistical reasoning.[35] The poem does not imply that Eve would have been okay if only she had studied *Artis Logicae* and learned that the reliability of testimony depends on ascertaining the "authority of the one giving testimony" (*CPW* VIII:322). Rather, the dramatic action suggests that inferences aimed at knowledge, whether based on categorical propositions, empirical observation, or testimony, may be innocent in themselves, but they cannot result in human happiness if the quest for knowledge violates a known divine command.

By appreciating Milton's claim that logic involves the discovery of "arguments," in the broadest sense, and that its practice is fulfilled in a rhetoric that includes but is not reducible to debating, we can also understand *Paradise Regained* and *Samson Agonistes* in new ways. The puzzling rhetorical stance of the Son in *Paradise Regained* becomes more intelligible once we appreciate that Milton presents the Son as the incarnation of the divine *Ratio* and *Oratio* (*Logos*). The Son's refusal to debate directly with or attempt to persuade Satan is an indication of Milton's insistence that logic and rhetoric cannot be reduced to mere debate; instead, the Son, guided by right reason, expresses and embodies faith in the Father's love.[36] By contrast, *Samson Agonistes* largely consists of debate. A Ramist analysis would consider not only the direct arguments deployed but also the implicit claims presented by the dramatic action. In particular, what is "argued" by Samson's final act of destroying the temple of Dagon? Does the supernatural strength required for Samson to perform his act "argue" for the genuine character of his repentance? Whether answered positively or negatively, such questions engage in the kind of rhetorical reasoning that Milton would have expected from fit readers.

NOTES

The author is grateful to Emma Wilson for her comments on a draft of this chapter.

1 See, for example, John T. Connor, "Milton's *Art of Logic* and the Force of Conviction," *Milton Studies* 45 (2006): 187–209.

2 See, respectively, Perry Miller, *The New England Mind* (New York, 1939), 116, and Norman E. Nelson, *Peter Ramus and the Confusion of Logic, Rhetoric, and Poetry* (Ann Arbor, MI, 1947), 2, 4. These two contrasting assessments of Ramus appear united in Walter J. Ong, *Ramus, Method, and the Decay of Dialogue* (Cambridge, MA, 1958), 1–49, 92–112.

3 The reception of the individual texts that make up the *Organon* varied widely among late medieval philosophers. See E. J. Ashworth, "Traditional Logic," in *The Cambridge History of Renaissance Philosophy*, ed. Quentin Skinner and

Eckhard Kessler (Cambridge, 1988), 143–53. My account of the relation between the components of Aristotle's *Organon* is indebted to Paul V. Spade, *Thoughts, Words and Things: An Introduction to Late Medieval Logic and Semantic Theory*, version 1.1, 2002, 10–15. April 18, 2008. www.pvspade.com/Logic/index. html.

4 Aristotle, *Topics*, trans. W. A. Pickard-Cambridge, in *The Complete Works of Aristotle*, ed. Jonathan Barnes (Princeton, 1984), 100a20–102a1. The difference between Aristotle's and Cicero's respective understandings of the topics arises from the fact that Aristotle views topics as part of "dialectical deduction" whereby first principles may be discovered (100a20–101b5), whereas Cicero rejects the Socratic detachment of dialectic from persuasion. See Cicero, *On the Ideal Orator [De Oratore]*, trans. James M. May and Jakob Wisse (Oxford, 2001), book 3, 58–62.

5 Peter Mack, *Renaissance Argument: Valla and Agricola in the Traditions of Rhetoric and Dialectic* (Leiden, 1993), 74–95, 117–88, 334–55.

6 *Ibid.*, 344–49.

7 Howard Hotson, *Commonplace Learning: Ramism and its German Ramifications, 1543–1630* (Oxford, 2007), 17.

8 Regarding Lorenzo Valla, see Mack, *Renaissance Argument*, 74–95; and Brian P. Copenhaver and Charles B. Schmitt, *Renaissance Philosophy* (Oxford, 1992), 223–30.

9 Lisa Jardine, "Humanist Logic," in *The Cambridge History of Renaissance Philosophy*, ed. Quentin Skinner and Eckhard Kessler (Cambridge, 1988), 189.

10 *Ibid.*, 187.

11 Ong, *Ramus, Method*, 49.

12 Ong, *CPW* VIII:184–86.

13 Brian Weiss, "Milton's Use of Ramist Method in his Scholarly Writings," PhD Diss. (City University of New York, 1974), 157–58.

14 Ong, *CPW* VIII:217, n.

15 Ong, Introduction, *CPW* VIII:155.

16 Phillip J. Donnelly, *Milton's Scriptural Reasoning: Narrative and Protestant Toleration* (Cambridge, 2009), 41.

17 *Of Education* was published in 1644 and re-published in 1673, while *Artis Logicae* was apparently composed in the 1640s and published in 1672. See the appendix in this volume for more information on the dates of composition.

18 Ong, Introduction, *CPW* VIII:145.

19 Donald K. McKim, "The Functions of Ramism in William Perkins' Theology," *The Sixteenth Century Journal* 16 (1985): 508–09.

20 Donnelly, *Milton's Scriptural Reasoning*, 29–30.

21 Ong, Introduction, *CPW* VIII:178–79. Cf. Hotson, *Commonplace Learning*, 6–9, 169–277.

22 Ong, Introduction, *CPW* VIII:179.

23 Donnelly, *Milton's Scriptural Reasoning*, 46.

24 Ong, Introduction, *CPW* VIII:200.

25 *CPW* VIII:333; see Ong, *CPW* VIII:156–59.

26 Kees Meerhoff, "'Beauty and the Beast': Nature, Logic and Literature in Ramus," in *The Influence of Petrus Ramus*, ed. Mordechai Feingold, Joseph S. Freedman, and Wolfgang Rother (Basel, 2001), 202, makes a claim regarding the logical and rhetorical practice of Ramus that is comparable to my point here about Milton.

27 Connor, "Milton's *Art of Logic*," 188–89.

28 Donnelly, *Milton's Scriptural Reasoning*, 28.

29 For a fuller discussion of Milton's theology, see the chapter by William Poole in this collection.

30 Maurice Kelley, Introduction, *CPW* VI:18–22; cf. Maurice Kelley, "Milton's Debt to Wolleb's *Compendium Theologiae Christianae*," *PMLA* 50 (1935): 156–65.

31 Phillip J. Donnelly, "'Matter' versus 'Body': the Character of Milton's Monism," *Milton Quarterly* 33 (1999): 79–85.

32 Donnelly, *Milton's Scriptural Reasoning*, 52–55.

33 Thomas S. K. Scott-Craig, "The Craftsmanship and Theological Significance of *Milton's Art of Logic*," *Huntington Library Quarterly* 17 (1953): 1–6; see also Gordon Campbell, "The Son of God in *De Doctrina Christiana* and *Paradise Lost*," *Modern Language Review* 75 (1980): 507–14.

34 William O. Scott, "Ramism and Milton's Concept of Poetic Fancy," *Philological Quarterly* 42 (1963): 183–86.

35 Regarding Satan's use of logical fallacies in this passage, see Richard Arnold, *Logic of the Fall: Right Reason and [Im]pure Reason in Milton's "Paradise Lost"* (New York, 2006), 59–71.

36 Donnelly, *Milton's Scriptural Reasoning*, 189–91.

CHAPTER 30

London

Ian W. Archer

John Milton was a Londoner. Born on December 9, 1608 at the sign of the
Spread Eagle in the wealthy inner city parish of All Hallows Bread Street,
he was the son of John Milton senior, a moderately prosperous Scrivener,
and Sara Jeffrey, herself the daughter of a merchant tailor, Paul Jeffrey.
John Milton of Oxfordshire yeoman stock had become a freeman of the
Scriveners' Company in 1600, and was to rise through the *cursus honorum*
to become an assistant in the 1620s. Although the precise dates are unclear,
the young John spent part of his schooling under Alexander Gil at St.
Paul's School, run by the Mercers' Company, and just around the corner
from the family home. He was at Cambridge between 1625 and 1632, but
seems to have spent the vacations in London; "the city which the Thames
washes with retreating waves holds me," he writes in Elegy 1 to Charles
Diodati (line 9). Milton enjoyed the pleasures of the theater and watching
the pretty girls in the fields outside the city. On leaving Cambridge with
his MA degree in 1632, he joined his father at Hammersmith, where the
family seems to have moved the previous year, just seven miles east of the
city. Between 1635 and 1638 they resided at Horton, a little further afield,
but still within easy striking distance of the capital. Milton was absent on
his continental travels for about fifteen months from May 1638, but on his
return took up residence in the city once more, at first in a house in the
churchyard of St. Bride Fleet Street belonging to one Russell, a tailor, and
then from November 1640 in "a pretty garden house" at the end of an entry
in Aldersgate Street. From October 1645 he leased a larger house in the Barbican just off the same street.[1] Here he stayed until August 1647, when he
moved to a smaller house in High Holborn backing on to Lincoln's Inn
Fields. The "private and quiet life" he is said to have lived there came to an
end when he took up the post of Secretary for Foreign Tongues in 1649.[2] He
now moved closer to the center of government, dwelling successively at one
"Thomson's next door to the Bull Head Tavern at Charing Cross opening
into the Spring Garden" (March–November 1649), then to official lodgings

in Scotland Yard (November 1649–December 1651), and finally "a pretty garden house in Petty France [now York Street] in Westminster, next door to the Lord Scudamore's, and opening into Saint James' Park" (December 1651–May 1660).[3] As Charles II's Restoration loomed, and Milton's life came under threat he went into hiding, but significantly he did not abandon the capital, seeking refuge in an unidentified friend's house in Bartholomew Close, West Smithfield. Once the Act of Oblivion had removed the shadow of the death penalty, he was able to move in September 1660 to a house in Holborn near Red Lion Fields (now Red Lion Square); not long before his pardon having passed the seal, he removed to Jewin Street, off Aldersgate Street, where he had lived for much of the 1640s. In February 1663, after his third marriage, he moved to a house in the Artillery Walk leading to Bunhill Fields, a few streets north of Jewin Street, and this was to be his London home for the rest of his life. He left the city during the plague of 1665 to take the cottage at Chalfont St. Giles secured by his friend the Quaker Thomas Ellwood, but he returned to the London property in February/March 1666, and died there in 1674. Apart from his time at Cambridge and on the continental tour, he had hardly ever been more than a few miles from London.

Milton's mobility within the capital, dictated by changing household size, financial circumstances, and employment, was not unusual among Londoners. His differing residences exposed him to a variety of metropolitan experiences. Bread Street, where he had been brought up, was according to John Stow "wholy inhabited by rich marchants, and diuers faire innes bee there."[4] All Hallows was one of London's characteristically small inner city parishes: with just seventy-two households in 1638, and a dense complement of parish and precinct officers, it was subject to the "strict and punctual government" that so many middling Londoners found satisfying in their drive for order.[5] In the parish church under the watchful eye of the godly rector, Richard Stock, noted for his "discreet carriage" in catechizing youth, Milton would have been bombarded with powerful denunciations of the popish menace, but he would have also become aware of the underlying currents of social criticism in the godly conscience, for Stock was also well known for his "freedom of speech" in reproving sin, "even to the faces of the greatest, in public and private, when occasion required it."[6] London, for all that the government sought to limit the freedom of expression, was also already a vibrant emporium of intellectual exchange. The young Milton's school was located at the east end of St. Paul's churchyard with the bookstalls just a few yards away, and the theater whose "chatty stage" he enjoyed as a young man opened up a world of competing and often indeterminate viewpoints.[7]

The London of Milton's lifetime was a rapidly expanding city. Its population when he was born was about 200,000; by 1650 it was 400,000, and by the time of his death about 500,000. Most of this population increase took place beyond the city's core, in the suburban areas. Whereas at Milton's birth over 50 percent of the metropolitan population had lived in the area under the lord mayor's jurisdiction, by 1680 perhaps less than a quarter did so. When Milton took up residence in the capital after 1639 it was to these growing suburban parishes that he gravitated. The suburbs were a byword for iniquity, and Milton's critics seized the opportunity to blacken his name by association: it was claimed that "having grown to an Impostume in the brest of the University, he was at length vomited out thence into a Suburbe sinke about London . . . He that would find him after dinner, must search the Playhouses or the Bordells for there I have traced him."[8] But we need to be wary of generalizing about the characteristics of the suburbs. St. Botolph Aldersgate, for example, was one of the more salubrious residential districts. Its main thoroughfare was described in 1657 by James Howell as resembling "an Italian street, more than any other in London, by reason of the spaciousness and uniformity of the buildings; and the straightness thereof with the convenient distance of the houses."[9] The parish had a marked gentry and aristocratic presence: no fewer than 17 of the 63 persons with the status of knight or above resident in the city, according to the tithe assessment of 1638, lived in this parish, a reminder that we should not predate the westward drift of the social elite. Among its residents in the 1630s were Lord Petre, the Earls of Thanet (whose house was faced with Ionic pilasters in 1641) and Winchelsea, and the Countesses of Kent and Westmorland. But in moving to High Holborn in 1645 Milton was reflecting that shift in the center of gravity for the social elite, as more fashionable housing developments, including that of Lincoln's Inn Fields onto which Milton's house opened, took off in the later 1630s. Several of the parliamentary peers, including the Earl of Warwick, had their town houses in this neighborhood. By the time that Milton died the area between the Strand and Holborn had witnessed extensive re-development. There were still many green spaces in spite of this infilling, and it is notable that Milton seems to have sought out properties with points of access to these sites of retreat. Among the new recreational facilities for the fashionable town society were the Spring Gardens, carved out of part of St. James' Park, where there were orchards, lawns, a bowling green, and bathing facilities.

Milton's Charing Cross property was nearby, and the Petty France garden house was likewise close to the open space of St. James' Park enclosed by Henry VIII. Perhaps it was London's pollution that prompted Milton to compare Satan's arrival in Paradise to a townsman

> ... long in populous city pent,
> Where houses thick and sewers annoy the air,
> Forth issuing on a summer's morn.
> (*Paradise Lost* IX.445–47)

In moving back to the northern suburbs as the regime changed, Milton was moving to an area that was becoming déclassé. St. Giles Cripplegate was one of the London's poorest parishes: 26 percent of the male inhabitants in the later seventeenth century were involved with the textile and clothing trades, another 6 percent in shoemaking. It was always one of the areas hardest hit by plague: in 1665 mortality levels were over seven times the norm, while inner city parishes were much less severely hit with levels at three times the norm. But even St. Giles had its pockets of affluence: 6 percent of the males dying in the later seventeenth century were described as gentlemen. Milton might have been attracted by the fresh air of Bunhill Fields close by his house, but during the plague of 1665 the aldermen had it walled in and turned into a cemetery to cope with the pressure on space in the traditional burial grounds.

So London offered a bewildering variety of social experiences. As Donald Lupton remarked in 1616, "London is grown so great I am almost afraid to meddle with her; she is certainly a great world; there are so many little worlds with her,"[10] and historians have in recent years tended to follow him in studying the smaller units of identification, at the level of neighborhood and craft, which assisted newcomers in assimilating to the demands of metropolitan life. But the processes of social and topographical polarization were somewhat muted; the rich needed servicing, so the poor tended to cluster not far away even from the more exclusive areas, while, as we have seen, parishes we might otherwise class as poor retained a share of desirable residences, even in the mid seventeenth century. And for all that London was a sprawling patchwork, it was, as Pepys' diary reminds us, still traversable. Where we can track individuals and their patterns of sociability across the metropolis, they tend to be geographically and socially diverse.

Milton of course is no exception. Recent scholarship has gone a long way to debunk the self-fashioned myth of the lonely scholar called to his people's service "to imbreed and cherish in a great people the seeds of vertu, and publick civility" (*CPW* 1:816), and, if we cannot go as far as Christopher Hill in seeing Milton rubbing along with every species of urban radical in London's rich tavern culture, we have gained a much more rounded picture of him as a convivial and companionable being.[11] The poet's early biographers stress his sociability. Aubrey claimed he was "of a very cheerful humour . . . extreme pleasant in his conversation . . . but satirical."[12] According to his nephew Edward Phillips, at the time he was writing the antiprelatical tracts in 1641, Milton "would drop into the society of some young sparks of his acquaintance, the chief whereof were Mr. Alphry and Mr. Miller, two gentlemen of Gray's Inn, the beaus of those times."[13] It was perhaps at this time that he forged his friendships with the future parliamentarian army officers, Robert Overton and Charles Fleetwood, both Gray's Inn men. Another close associate also from Gray's Inn was the lawyer John Bradshaw ("a friend whom threats cannot move from the path of justice"), who achieved prominence in city politics as undersheriff after a controversial election in 1643, and, as a leading war party radical, presided at Charles' trial, becoming president of the Rump's council of state (*CPW* iv:639). Phillips tells us that in the 1650s Milton was regularly visited by his "particular friends," among whom he numbers Marchamont Nedham ("a great crony," according to Aubrey), Andrew Marvell, Edward Lawrence, and Cyriack Skinner.[14] Milton has also been located in the networks of intellectual exchange connecting London with continental scholars, and here his associations with Samuel Hartlib's circle of thinkers and writers seem to have been crucial. He also enjoyed the company of "that exemplary woman," Katherine Jones, Lady Ranelagh, daughter of Richard Boyle, Earl of Cork;[15] her house in fashionable Pall Mall was a meeting place for London intellectuals, including many associated with the Hartlib circle, and she entrusted the tuition of her son and nephew to Milton.

Our dependence on the selective accounts of the early biographers and chance allusions in Milton's own writings may, however, be distorting, skewing the reconstruction of Milton's social network toward high society and international connections, and underplaying its civic dimension. Milton did have city connections, but those we know about were overwhelmingly through the print trade. Stephen Dobranski's study of Milton's relationship to the processes of textual production has revealed his dependence on his printers and booksellers.[16] The contract for the printing of *Paradise Lost* with Samuel Simmons reinforced a longstanding relationship with that family of printers, who were based in Aldersgate, a short walk from Milton's home in Artillery Walk. His book collecting brought him into the circle of George Thomason, the Presbyterian bookseller and common councillor, whose involvement in the importation of Italian books probably explains the "most familiar acquaintance" he enjoyed with Milton (*CPW* II:765). But for someone who had grown up in a busy scrivener's shop, Milton's civic connections are strikingly elusive. Just how much we are missing is not clear. It is noticeable that a substantial amount of the correspondence that Milton translated for the republic in his role as Latin secretary dealt with commercial matters. Of course, he may have had little to do with the process of composition, but he was required to attend on the committees where the merchants lobbied. It is hard to believe that he could have fulfilled the Council of State's requirement that he look for evidence concerning the exportation of prohibited goods without talking to some merchants, but proving that Milton talked to merchants is in fact no easy task. There are tantalizing glimpses of possible connections, such as the highly plausible – but still speculative – brokering of his second marriage in 1656 by the banker and alderman Sir Thomas Vyner, who had acted as treasurer for the relief of the Waldensians.

Milton maintained an ambivalence about London. While in Italy he presented himself as "alumnus ille Londini Milton," and in one of the poems he wrote there, he celebrated the place where "the silver Thames pours forth her blue-gray hair broadly from pure urns in Ocean's stream."[17] The title page to the Latin verse published in his collection of poems in 1645 described Milton as "Londiniensis," and David Norbrook has suggested that he is attempting to counter royalist claims that London has collapsed into unlettered chaos.[18] On the other hand, there are distancing features of his writing and his career. In *Ad Patrem* in the early 1630s he thanked his father for sparing him a career in the law and pursuing the "golden hope of making money" (line 70), allowing him instead to depart from the "city's noise" to pursue his intellectual interests (line 74). He showed little interest in the city's history: in the Commonplace Book there is a single reference drawn from Holinshed to Henry III's charter giving the citizens freedom from toll.[19] He never took up the freedom of the city to which he was entitled by patrimony, and there is no evidence of his holding local office. And apart form some passages in *Areopagitica* to which we shall come in a moment, there is relatively little in his writings where he might be said to adopt a distinctive civic voice. Although the Presbyterians in the city became major targets of his writings, he did not, as the Levellers did, enter into the debates over the forms of the city constitution, which were germane to the outcome of the political conflict. Nor do we get much sense of a bottom-up perspective of the revolution: the bread and butter concerns of the ordinary Londoner in the street were rather beneath him.

And yet it was Milton who produced the most famous depiction of the freedom of the citizens in *Areopagitica* (1644):

Behold now this vast City; a City of refuge, the mansion house of liberty, encompast and surrounded with his protection; the shop of warre hath not there more anvils and hammers waking, to fashion out the plates and instruments of armed Justice in defence of beleaguer'd Truth, then there be pens and heads there, sitting by their studious lamps, musing, searching, revolving new notions and idea's wherewith to present, as with their homage and their fealty the approaching Reformation: others as fast reading, trying all things, assenting to the force of reason and convincement. (*CPW* II:553–54)

London is a divinely favored city (the reference to the city of refuge recalled Numbers 35); it is also a new Athens where the citizens enjoyed the right to speak out freely on any issue. It is of a piece with the conviction elsewhere expressed in the early prose pamphlets of the capacities of the citizens for independent political judgment. The antiprelatical tracts had celebrated London's petitioning. The root and branch petition of December 1640 in which 15,000 citizens subscribed to the call for the abolition of episcopacy was celebrated by Milton as "the honour of our cheif Citty"; his episcopal antagonists (the "great Clarks" like John Hall who dismissed the "Libelling Separatist" tradesmen), were sent up for their view that "these men, because they have a Trade (as *Christ himselfe*, and Saint *Paul* had) [they] cannot therefore attaine to some good measure of knowledge and to a reason of their actions" (*CPW* I:676–77). In *An Apology against a Pamphlet* Milton praised the "wisdome" of a parliament which could admit petitions from "the meanest artizans and labourers, at other times also women" (*CPW* I:926).

The imagery of *Areopagitica*, where the limits to human knowledge that pre-publication licensing entailed were compared to the monopolistic practices of the great trading companies, shows Milton drawing on the rhetorics by which elements of the London oligarchy were criticized. As Blair Hoxby has argued, by constructing reading and writing as forms of labor, Milton was able to present attacks on them as restraints on man's God-given duty to labor.[20] "Truth and understanding," he argued, "are not such wares to be monopoliz'd and traded in by tickets and statutes, and standards. We must not think to make a staple commodity of all the knowledge in the Land, to mark and licence it like our broad cloath, and our wooll packs" (*CPW* II:535–36). The general appeal to the anti-monopoly feeling which ran high among Londoners is also strengthened by a specific application, for he also claimed that the demand for tighter regulation of printing would serve the interests of the oligarchs, "some old *patentees* and *monopolizers* in the trade of book-selling," who ran the Stationers' Company. They sought to "exercise a superiority over their neighbours, men who doe not therefore labour in an honest profession to which learning is indetted, that they should be made other mens vassalls" (*CPW* II:570). Milton was making a direct intervention in the bitter conflicts raging within the Stationers' Company over the booksellers' tightening grip on the structures of governance.

But there may have been a disjunction between Milton's high style and his audience. In his Sonnet II, "A book was writ of late," he complains about the reception of his *Tetrachordon*, a book

> . . . woven close, both matter, form and style;
> The subject new: it walked the town a while,
> Numb'ring good intellects; now seldom pored on.
> Cries the stall-reader, "Bless us! What a word on
> A title page is this!" and some in file
> Stand spelling false, while one might walk to Mile-
> End Green.
>
> (lines 2–8)

The image of bookstall browsers stubbornly rejecting Milton's high-minded efforts to instruct them resonates powerfully. Norbrook notes that the tract *Of Education* (in spite of its dedication to Hartlib) was not received with unreserved enthusiasm by Hartlib's friends, probably because it did not treat its subject in the down-to-earth utilitarian manner which was their custom. And, he reminds us, "*Areopagitica* would have been still less accessible to the artisans who were enthusiastically entering political debate. It speaks for, rather than to, them; the community it speaks of is that of intellectuals deeply versed in literary culture."[21] In any case, as Larry Manley has pointed out, there is a powerful non-local element to Milton's argument in *Areopagitica*. It is the free circulation of ideas throughout the kingdom, what Manley calls London's centrifugal, anti-sedentary role in the revolutionary process, that Milton celebrates.[22] He rejected the Presbyterians' localized and insular understanding of church order in favor of the new covenant of grace. London might be the "city of refuge," but "he who thinks we are to pitch our tent here, and have attain'd the utmost prospect of reformation . . . that man by this very opinion declares, that he is yet farre short of Truth" (*CPW* II:549).

The populist rhetoric of 1644 had given way to a much darker mood by 1649. *Eikonoklastes* famously attacks "an inconstant, irrational, and

Image-doting rabble"; the English have been subject to a "perpetual infusion of servility," a legacy of subjugation by the Romans, but lately reinforced by the scandalous behaviour of their clergy (*CPW* iii:601, 344). The people were now "worse & more disordinate, to receave or to digest any libertie at all" (*CPW* v:449). In the tracts justifying the regicide Milton finds himself addressing a virtuous minority, the "staid and well-principl'd men" who are to be set against the "mad multitude," the "miserable, credulous, deluded thing that creature is, which is call'd the Vulgar" (*CPW* iii:339, 345, 426). In a passage in the *Defensio Secunda* probably written soon after the dissolution of the Rump Milton expresses his disdain for popular elections, where bribed and drunken voters produce a parliament of "inn-keepers and hucksters of the state from city taverns or from country districts ploughboys and veritable herdsmen" (*CPW* iv:682).

Milton's disillusionment owes a great deal to the populace's surrender to the Presbyterian clergy, exemplified by "shallow Edwards," an allusion to Thomas Edwards, arch-heresiographer and author of *Gangraena*;[23] but there were particular reasons why the Londoners, in Milton's eyes, would be unreliable custodians of liberty. It is true that his position fluctuates according to the polemical needs of the moment. In answering Salmasius' attacks on the republic, he sees virtue as lying in the "middle class, which produces the greatest number of men of good sense and knowledge of affairs" (*CPW* iv:471). But it was a weakness of the Rump's Council of State, he told Hermann Mylius, the ambassador from Oldenburg in 1651, that it was dominated by "mechanics, soldiers, home grown, strong and bold enough, in public political powers mostly inexperienced."[24] And in the *Digression* in his *History of Britain* he attributed the corruption of the Long Parliament to the prominence of tradesmen among its councils: "Some who had bin calld from shops & warehouses without other merit to sit in supreme councel[s] & committies, as thir breeding was, fell to hucster the common-wealth" (*CPW* v:445).

Tradesmen were conventionally narrow-minded and preoccupied with profit. As Hugh Peter put it, too many Londoners "never looked beyond the smoke of their own Chimnies, that measure States and kingdoms with their interests, by their private shopwards."[25] Milton gave this narrow-mindedness another twist, for in his eyes their concern with profit meant that they were predisposed to foster habits of luxury, which as he knew from his readings of Sallust and Machiavelli would sap republican virtue. By the time he wrote *The Readie and Easie Way* in 1660 he saw the tradesman's preoccupation with profit (he was perhaps thinking of the apprentices' *Remonstrance* of December 1659 which called attention to the stagnation of trade) as fatal to the cause of liberty. Londoners were prepared to

> prostitute religion and libertie to the vain and groundless apprehension, that nothing but kingship can restore trade... [I]f trade be grown so craving and importunate through the profuse living of tradesmen, that nothing can support it, but the luxurious expences of a nation upon trifles or superfluities, so as if the people generally should betake themselves to frugalitie, it might prove a dangerous matter, least tradesmen should mutinie for want of trading, and that therefor we must forgoe & set to sale religion, libertie, honor, safetie, all concernments Divine or human to keep up trading. (*CPW* vii:461–62)

But more important than the stagnation of trade in London's swing to the right in 1658–60 was the fear of radical sectarianism, and it was this that gave Milton's Presbyterian opponents their leverage over their congregations.

The priority that tradesmen gave to profits over piety blinded Londoners to true religious freedom. For all that it celebrates the virtue of inquiring citizen minds, even *Areopagitica* recognizes that not all Londoners properly embraced the freedom offered to them. It attacks the tradesman "in the shop trading all day without his religion" who seeks to compartmentalize his spiritual life, treating it as a "dividuall movable" and failing to appreciate that economic, civic, and spiritual roles were inseparable (*CPW* ii:544–45). "A wealthy man addicted to his pleasure and to his profits, finds Religion to be a traffick so entangl'd, and of so many piddling accounts, that of all mysteries he cannot skill to keep a stock going upon that trade." So he surrenders the "whole ware-house of his religion" to "som factor, to whose care and credit he may commit the whole managing of his religious affairs... som Divine of note and estimation" (*CPW* ii:544). Milton was thinking of the complacent godly among London's tradesmen, who had formed close relations with their parochial ministers, but whose enemies saw them as hypocrites. These men were so blinded to truth that they were easy dupes for the Presbyterian clergy. It was the failure of his fellow Londoners to embrace religious liberty, and the power of the Presbyterian clergy over so many of them, that explains Milton's progressive disillusionment with his fellow Londoners. That the people should have been content on choosing a "captain back for *Egypt*" was a response to the bitterness of the religious divisions opened up by the "earnest and zealous thirst after knowledge and understanding" celebrated in *Areopagitica* (*CPW* vii:463, ii:554). Unfortunately for Milton his fellow Londoners chose incorrectly.

NOTES

1 *EL* 62.
2 *EL* 68.
3 *EL* 69–71.
4 John Stow, *A Survey of London*, ed. C. L. Kingsford, 2 vols. (London, 1908), 1:346.
5 Ian W. Archer, *The Pursuit of Stability: Social Relations in Elizabethan London* (Cambridge, 1991), 226.
6 *Oxford Dictionary of National Biography*, s.n. Richard Stock.
7 Elegy 1, line 28.
8 John Hall, *A Modest Confutation* (London, 1642), A3r–v.
9 James Howell, *Londinopolis* (1657), 342.
10 Donald Lupton, *London and the Countrey Carbonadoed* (London, 1632), B2v.
11 See Christopher Hill, *Milton and the English Revolution* (London, 1977).
12 *EL* 5, 6.
13 *EL* 62.
14 *EL* 74.
15 *Oxford Dictionary of National Biography*, s.n. Katherine Jones, Lady Ranelagh.
16 Stephen B. Dobranski, *Milton, Authorship, and the Book Trade* (Cambridge, 1999).
17 *Ad Salsillum*, line 9; *Mansus*, lines 32–33.
18 David Norbrook, *Writing the English Republic: Poetry, Rhetoric, and Politics, 1627–1660* (Cambridge, 1999), 158–67.
19 *CPW* 1:447.
20 Blair Hoxby, *Mammon's Music: Literature and Economics in the Age of Milton* (London and New Haven, 2002), 38–47.
21 Norbrook, *Writing the English Republic*, 122–25.
22 Lawrence Manley, *Literature and Culture in Early Modern London* (Cambridge, 1995), ch. 10.
23 "On the New Forcers of Conscience," line 12.
24 Leo Miller, *John Milton and the Oldenburg Safeguard* (New York, 1985), 134–35.
25 Cited by Valerie Pearl, "London's Counter-Revolution," in *The Interregnum: The Quest for a Settlement, 1646–1660*, ed. G. E. Aylmer (London, 1972), 34.

CHAPTER 31

Manuscript transmission

Randall Ingram

Any essay on the transmission of Milton's works in manuscript must confront a daunting, if often tacit, consensus, expressed with characteristic clarity by Peter Beal: "Milton is not a poet whose works one would normally associate with MS circulation."[1] Unlike, say, Philip Sidney or John Donne or Katherine Philips, early modern poets who are understood as transmitting their poetry through manuscript rather than print, Milton is associated with his printed volumes. Indeed, he is often considered a pivotal figure in the birth of print authorship, as when Leah Marcus argues that his first printed collection *Poems* of 1645 "helped to invent literary subjectivity as we have traditionally been taught to understand it."[2] Milton's dissociation from one of his culture's primary means of disseminating literary texts has contributed to his image as an isolated titan whose words are broadcast mechanically rather than shuffled about in what some early modern stationers dismissed as "loose imperfect Manuscripts."[3] Yet both recent scholarship and documentary evidence offer a more complicated image of Milton's involvement in contemporary practices of manuscript transmission, an involvement especially clear in examples from his early poetry.

This involvement may have been unavoidable. Produced long before typewriters and word processing, all early modern literary documents can be said to have begun as handwriting, either autograph manuscripts, when writers put their words to paper, or scribal manuscripts, when writers dictated their words to amanuenses. Milton famously did both. The most important manuscript of Milton's literary career and, according to Beal, "the most important poetical autograph of the [seventeenth] century,"[4] the Trinity Manuscript, a collection of Milton's writings given to Trinity College, Cambridge, soon after Milton's death, contains both autograph and scribal texts. Some of the writing in Milton's own hand shows Milton revising his best-known early works. In addition to its drafts and notes in Milton's hand, the Trinity Manuscript also contains a number of his poems in other hands, some of them apparently finished and carefully transcribed. Several poems, such as the sonnet that would later be Sonnet 13 "To Mr. H. Lawes, on His Airs," exist in multiple states within a few pages of the manuscript: an autograph draft with revisions, an autograph fair copy, and a copy prepared by a scribe. Miltonists continue to debate the complicated evidence presented by the Trinity Manuscript, but it clearly shows Milton's reliance on pen and paper to refine his early poetry and on scribes to prepare his poems for other readers.

That second step, the use of a scribe to help polish a handwritten text, brings Milton's poetry into the realm of manuscript transmission. Unlike the autograph drafts and notes, the scribal copies of Milton's poems in the Trinity Manuscript resemble other documents circulating among readers of poetry in Milton's England. Manuscript transmission remained an important means of literary production and consumption throughout the seventeenth century, when, as Beal and others demonstrate in a number of studies, "the age of the scribe was far from over."[5] These scholars have sought to complicate pat narratives that position print as the triumphal endpoint of all writing, the inevitable goal of every writer's labor, and the invention that brought a quick stop to the circulation of handwritten texts. Michael D. Bristol and Arthur F. Marotti list some of the needs satisfied by manuscript transmission in the "multimedia world" of early modern England: "manuscript transmission belonged to a culture that valued personal intimacy, sociality, and participation, if not also intellectual and social exclusivity – all features that generally distinguished it from print transmission."[6] Bristol and Marotti, like other analysts of early modern manuscript culture, do not equate handwritten texts with privacy and secrecy. If some earlier scholarship had categorized manuscript transmission as a primarily defensive gesture, a way to hide texts from an ill-wresting world or from punitive authorities, scholars now tend to examine the broader uses of handwriting as an occasionally preferable alternative to print. For example, H. R. Woudhuysen critiques the notion that early modern writers might choose to circulate their texts in manuscript to avoid "the stigma of print," the shame of offering one's writing as a commodity available to anyone able to buy it.[7] Woudhuysen argues instead that writers chose manuscription for its strengths more than for worries about print's shortcomings. Seen as Woudhuysen and others suggest, manuscript circulation becomes not simply a retreat from the risks of printing, but an alternative medium with benefits of its own, benefits not eclipsed but highlighted by the expansion of print.

Because printing could be, in Peter Stallybrass' provocative phrase, "a revolutionary incitement to writing by hand," early modern agents apparently appreciated the interplay among media.[8] Unlike modern scholars, these agents seem to have imagined manuscript and print as complements more than substitutes. Savvy entrepreneurs could recognize the advantages of profiting as broadly as possible from the literary marketplace: some stationers sold manuscripts alongside the printed books in their stalls, while some scriveners sold printed books along with their services as scribes.[9] Moreover, because the movement from manuscript to print was not unidirectional, booksellers might both buy manuscripts to produce printed books and lend printed books for transcription.[10] These instances may have been exceptional; many, likely most, stationers and scriveners stuck to their media, mid seventeenth-century stationers selling mostly printed books and scriveners selling a wide variety of scribal services. Yet the ease with which early modern purveyors crossed a boundary that has seemed firm to some historians raises questions about the divisions themselves. Although early modern writers tend to be associated with particular media, such as print, manuscript, or performance, why would enterprising writers accept a level of confinement that stationers and scriveners rejected? More specifically for Milton, would an iconoclast who resisted locating value in material objects limit the range of his expression to a single medium – and to the medium most likely to offer the stability of icons? What better test case for the ways seventeenth-century artists worked across media than the son of a scrivener and a composer?

Beal's *Index* implicitly addresses such questions. Immediately after noting that Milton is not usually linked to manuscript transmission, the *Index* acknowledges some "rare instances" of that transmission:

His Hobson poems, which had some degree of MS circulation, bear witness to his participation in at least one thoroughly characteristic student activity; and isolated MS copies of *On Time* and *An Epitaph on the Marchioness of Winchester* reflect a similar impingement on student common-place book culture. In the special case of *A Mask Presented at Ludlow Castle* (*Comus*) transcripts were evidently made besides [the extant manuscripts].[11]

The two poems on the death of the coachman Thomas Hobson and *A Mask* help illustrate the involvement of Milton's poetry in contemporary manuscript transmission, as well as the challenges that this involvement poses for modern scholarship. In particular, the contrasts between these early works in surviving manuscripts and in the 1645 *Poems* map some of the divergent models of authorship and readership available to Milton and his contemporaries.

Milton's were among the numerous poems occasioned by Hobson's death on January 1, 1631, when the university was closed because of the plague. There is no indication that Milton was particularly close to Hobson, a popular figure remembered for offering customers the horse nearest the door or none at all, hence the phrase "Hobson's choice." Like other poems on Hobson, Milton's were almost certainly written in 1631, but the date of their publication is a more complex matter. Modern readers tend to link "publishing" with "printing," and by that standard the Hobson poems as a pair were printed in 1645, when Milton's *Poems* presented on facing pages two poems on Hobson, entitled "On the University Carrier who sickn'd in the time of his vacancy, being forbid to go to *London*, by reason of the Plague" and "Another on the same."[12] Five years earlier, however, the second poem had been printed in *A Banquet of Jests* (1640), apparently without Milton's participation in the volume's production and with no attribution, implying its availability in manuscript.[13] And in fact, variants of "Another on the same" can be found in at least four extant manuscript verse miscellanies as an independent poem rather than as "Another."[14] These manuscripts, some of which date from the 1630s, before any printed versions of Milton's Hobson poems appeared, suggest that at least one of the poems was introduced into manuscript circulation, a process that Harold Love has called "scribal publication." Love characterizes "publication" not as an effect of a particular medium but "as a movement from a private realm of creativity to a public realm of consumption."[15] Love recognizes that the transition between "private . . . creativity" and "public . . . consumption" is not always clear:

> The problem is to determine whether any given text – in our case a text transmitted through handwritten copies – has made this transition. We will need to recognize both a "strong" sense in which the text must be shown to have become publicly available and a more inclusive "weak" sense in which it is enough to show that the text has ceased to be a private possession. A further condition is that scribal publication should be something more than the chrysalis stage of an intended print publication. This would exclude manuscripts circulated for comment and correction prior to printing or in order to attract a sheaf of commendatory verses.[16]

Read according to Love's influential taxonomy, the poems of the Trinity Manuscript do not qualify as scribal publication, although its scribal fair copies mark an important stage between drafts and public texts. But the poem later entitled "Another on the same" offers a clear instance of Milton's making one of his poems public as a handwritten text.

Rather than only chancing to undergo scribal publication, Milton's poem seems to have been designed for manuscript circulation. Its repetition of the formula "Here lieth" (line 1) refers not only to "On the University Carrier" but also to other epitaphs, a genre profoundly appealing to the compilers of manuscript miscellanies. A miscellany held at St. John's College, Cambridge, includes Milton's poem as one of numerous epitaphs, some later canonical, such as a version of Jonson's "Epitaph on Elizabeth, L. H.," and some less familiar now, such as the popular "Epitaph on a Fart."[17] The pith of epitaphs made them suitable for transcription; they were portable discourse pretending to be situated in a specific place, the "here" of the *hic jacet* convention. It should therefore come as no surprise that Milton's other epitaph, "An Epitaph on the Marchioness of Winchester," also found its way into at least one manuscript collection.[18] That the epitaph is a paradoxical form, both monumental and mobile, made it all the more attractive to compilers who valued paradoxes, which are likewise prevalent in the St. John's miscellany. In fact, immediately before the verses on Hobson is a poem entitled "A paradox that love is not a fire." Of Milton's Hobson poems, "Another on the same" especially relishes the paradoxes of Thomas Hobson's death, starting with the central paradox that Hobson's stopping caused his death rather than vice versa: "Here lieth one who did most truly prove, / That he could never die while he could move" (lines 1–2). Some central lines of the poem are packed with paradoxes:

> Rest that gives all men life, gave him his death,
> And too much breathing put him out of breath;
> Nor were it contradiction to affirm
> Too long vacation hastened on his term.
>
> (lines 11–14)

Taking death and misfortune as occasion for wit was a frequent practice of manuscript poets such as Donne, whose poems appear repeatedly in the St. John's miscellany and many others. Based on the extant English poetry in miscellanies, it would seem that a seventeenth-century poet who wished to succeed in manuscript could hardly choose more shrewdly than to write a paradoxical epitaph. The example of the poem entitled in print "Another on the same" suggests that by the early 1630s Milton was already sensitive to the material conditions of publication and that his writing reflected that sensitivity. Instead of an isolated figure with no concern for how his texts might be received or reproduced, this poem shows a more calculating poet, willing to shape his writing to suit a medium and its particular aesthetics.

A poet designing texts for compilers of manuscripts might also anticipate that those compilers could alter the texts as they transcribed them. If – and it is by no means certain – Milton's manuscript of 1631 was identical to the poem printed in 1645 as "Another on the same," that manuscript underwent significant changes on its way to the St. John's miscellany. Comparing the miscellany to the 1645 *Poems* shows that, among other changes collated by John Shawcross, the manuscript rearranges the lines of the printed poem to the following order: lines 1–12, 27–28, 13–14, 21–24, 29–34.[19] This arrangement omits lines 15–20 of the printed poem, a section in which Hobson speaks. In the verse miscellany the poem is less concerned with what Hobson might have to say than with what might be wittily said of him. The manuscript accordingly opts to emphasize the poem's paradoxes. It inserts within the dense series of paradoxes quoted above a couplet from later in the printed poem ("But had his doings lasted as they were, / He had been an immortal carrier") so that lines 27–28 of the printed poem interrupt lines 11–14. Consequently, in the manuscript the poem's paradoxes are not so tightly concentrated but are a sustained element, offered as public discourse, without Hobson's individuating voice. The St. John's miscellany attributes the poem to "Jo: Milton," but the significant differences between the text in manuscript and the text in print make the authority of the earlier text uncertain: is it a rearrangement of Milton's poem as it would later be printed, a prior draft of the printed poem, or a version of the poem crafted specifically for the proclivities of manuscript circulation? As is often the case in manuscript transmission, the handwriting on the pages of the St. John's miscellany do not lead clearly to a specific lineage or a specific agent.

The issue of doubtful authorship arises again in another poem on Hobson. In *A Banquet of Jests* of 1640 Milton's acknowledged poem is followed by a poem entitled "Hobson's Epitaph," which Shawcross has traced to over twenty manuscript sources, including the St. John's miscellany.[20] Shawcross notes the proximity of "Hobson's Epitaph" to one or both of Milton's Hobson poems in multiple manuscript and printed sources, and, although no source attributes the poem to Milton, Shawcross observes that this silence does not preclude the "interesting possibility" that Milton wrote "Hobson's Epitaph."[21] Shawcross presents "Hobson's Epitaph" "with qualification" in his edition of Milton's complete poetry.[22] Granting the poem even a qualified spot in Milton's canon remains controversial (Beal skeptically refers to the poem as "only one of a number of humorous poems by Milton's contemporaries"[23]), yet Shawcross' edition has the advantage of representing the fuzzy contours of Milton's oeuvre, enmeshed as it was in a network of textual exchange – a network, that is, typical of manuscript transmission.

These issues of tangled authority become even more intricate in the case of *A Mask Presented at Ludlow Castle*, which Roy Flannagan has called "the most complicated to edit of all of Milton's texts."[24] The difficulty arises in part from the origin of *A Mask* on Michaelmas, September 29, 1634, when it was performed to commemorate John Egerton, Earl of Bridgewater's assuming the position of Lord President of Wales and the Marches. Comparable to the instability of other early modern theatrical texts – an instability rooted in the collaborative, fluid nature of performance – *A Mask* survives in multiple forms: a draft mostly in Milton's hand found in the Trinity Manuscript; a carefully prepared scribal manuscript usually thought to have been a presentation copy to the Bridgewater family; two manuscripts of five songs from the masque, one in the hand of Henry Lawes, who set Milton's texts to music; a text printed anonymously in 1637; and Milton's first acknowledgment of the masque in print in his 1645 *Poems*. According to a prefatory letter by Lawes in the 1637 printing and reproduced in Milton's 1645 volume, there were likely other manuscripts of *A Mask* that have not survived because Lawes claims that *A Mask* was "so lovely, and so much desired, that the often Copying of it hath tir'd my Pen to give my severall friends satisfaction."[25] *Poems* adds another prefatory letter, this one from Sir Henry Wotton to Milton, recording Wotton's appreciation for a copy of *A Mask*, which Milton had sent him in 1638, further testimony to the ongoing circulation of *A Mask*.[26]

These texts vary across time, medium, and local context, leaving modern editors to sort out their relative authority. The differences between the Bridgewater Manuscript and the 1645 *Poems* have seemed especially significant. For example, as Cedric Brown notes, the Lady's opening soliloquy is much longer in the 1645 *Poems*, where it is an "explicitly religious" meditation that specifies both her fears and her chastity as the best defense against those fears.[27] As in the case of the Hobson poems, explanations for the differences among the texts of *A Mask* vary. Although he admits that the relation between the manuscript and the masque printed in 1645 "is bound to remain conjectural," Brown hypothesizes that for the purposes of the Bridgewater Manuscript "a censor" may have purged Milton's text of passages that could have embarrassed the Bridgewater family.[28] Conversely, Shawcross notes that the text of the masque continues to change in the Trinity Manuscript even after the performance of *A Mask* in 1634, indicating that Milton continued to refine it.[29] The apparently "missing" portions of the Bridgewater Manuscript thus might not have been suppressed but still unwritten in 1634. If, as Shawcross implies, the Bridgewater Manuscript represents a crucial moment in the textual history of *A Mask* – one phase of the masque rather than a censoring of an already complete work – it is nonetheless a scribal publication and a record of performance, "something more than the chrysalis stage of an intended print publication."

Like the version of Milton's Hobson poem in the St. John's miscellany, the Bridgewater Manuscript requires Miltonists to consider who wrote (or erased) what and when. Both manuscripts could reflect Milton's primary agency, his work on an early arrangement of the Hobson poem in the St. John's miscellany and on an early, briefer masque in the Bridgewater Manuscript. The two manuscripts could thus offer instances of the "gradualistic" creativity that Love locates in manuscript transmission: "the scribal author-publisher is able both to polish texts indefinitely and to personalize them to suit the tastes of particular recipients."[30] Conversely, both manuscripts could point to the intervention of other agents, a rearranger of Milton's Hobson poem or a censor of his masque. The possibility of these intervening agents is consistent with seventeenth-century literary manuscripts generally, which Beal describes as "open; still fluid and living . . . [with] clients encouraged to participate, to be themselves engaged in the process of collecting, even writing, as well as reading."[31] As representative manuscripts, these handwritten texts of Milton's poems expose the gap between manuscript transmission and some fundamental assumptions of modern scholarship, between "gradualistic," "open" texts and the editorial standard of the author's final intentions.

The 1645 *Poems* is sometimes understood as a rejection of this uncertainty, a founding affirmation of a proprietary subject, set against the textual and authorial instability of manuscript transmission. Yet, as Ann Coiro has observed, the poems of that volume regularly draw attention to their prior status as works in manuscript, the "manuscript life" that preceded and enabled the volume.[32] A number of the Latin poems, for example, were written and circulated during Milton's travels in Italy, revealing a world of social connections forged through manuscription. These poems, along with contemporary letters, provide some of the essential details of Milton's biography in the late 1630s. Because the manuscripts have long since disappeared, J. Milton French reproduced selections from the 1645 *Poems* in *The Life Records of John Milton*.[33] The examples of the St. John's miscellany and the Bridgewater Manuscript reveal the dangers of assuming that the 1645 volume and handwritten texts differ only in medium. With no manuscripts, however, French faced a Hobson's choice. The printing

of texts that had circulated in manuscript may have allowed Milton to
assert his sole authorship of those texts as completed poems and, as Coiro
contends, may have allowed him to demystify manuscript transmission as
the privilege of a few.[34] But printing also inevitably recalls the poems' first
material settings, when now-dead friends such as Charles Diodati handled
now-lost manuscripts such as a handwritten copy of the Nativity ode. From
the perspective of manuscript transmission, Milton's first printed collection of poetry not only registers his ownership of his writing; it conveys
too another central theme of his career, an acute sense of what has been
lost.

NOTES

1 Peter Beal, *Index of English Literary Manuscripts, 1625–1700*, vol. II, part 1
   (London, 1987), 86.
2 Leah S. Marcus, *Unediting the Renaissance: Shakespeare, Marlowe, Milton*
   (London, 1996), 221.
3 This example, particularly relevant for Milton's *Poems*, comes from Humphrey
   Moseley's "An advertisement to the Reader" in Edmund Waller's *Poems*
   (London, 1645), A1r.
4 Beal, *Index*, 70.
5 Peter Beal, *In Praise of Scribes: Manuscripts and their Makers in Seventeenth-
   Century England* (Oxford, 1998), 2.
6 Michael D. Bristol and Arthur F. Marotti, Introduction, in *Print, Manuscript
   and Performance: The Changing Relations of Media in Early Modern England*,
   ed. Arthur F. Marotti and Michael D. Bristol (Columbus, OH, 2000), 13.
7 H. R. Woudhuysen, *Sir Philip Sidney and the Circulation of Manuscripts, 1558–
   1640* (Oxford, 1996). For Woudhuysen's critique of J. W. Saunders' phrase
   "stigma of print," see 13–14. For Saunders' discussion of that phenomenon, see
   his book *The Profession of English Letters* (London, 1964).
8 Peter Stallybrass, "Blank Pages, or Why Printing is a Revolutionary Incitement
   to Writing by Hand," A. S. W. Rosenbach Lecture, University of Pennsylvania
   Library, Philadelphia, February 2006.
9 Woudhuysen, *Sidney and the Circulation of Manuscripts*, 45–49 and 60–61.
10 *Ibid.*, 49–50.
11 Beal, *Index*, 86.
12 John Milton, *The Poems of Mr. John Milton, Both English and Latin* (London,
   1645), 28–29.
13 [Archie Armstrong?], *A Banquet of Jests* (London, 1640), 129–31.
14 Beal, *Index*, 91.
15 Harold Love, *Scribal Publication in Seventeenth-Century England* (Oxford,
   1993), 36.
16 *Ibid.*
17 St. John's College, Cambridge, MS S.32, ff. 7r and 8v.

18 The manuscript collection, held at the British Library (Sloane MS 1446), includes a version of "An Epitaph on the Marchioness of Winchester" on ff. 37v–38v.

19 John T. Shawcross, "A Note on Milton's Hobson Poems," *The Review of English Studies* 18 (1967): 433–37, cited 434. See also Shawcross' textual notes in the revised edition of his *The Complete English Poetry of John Milton* (New York, 1971), 627–28.

20 See Shawcross, "A Note," 435–37, and *Complete Poetry*, 628.

21 Shawcross, "A Note," 437.

22 Shawcross, *Complete Poetry*, 628.

23 Beal, *Index*, 88.

24 Roy Flannagan, ed., *The Riverside Milton* (Boston, 1998), 114.

25 Milton, *Poems*, 69.

26 *Ibid.*, 71–73. Wotton offers even more evidence for the circulation of *A Mask* when his letter states that he first came across *A Mask* at the end of Thomas Randolph's *Poems* (1638), "in the very close of the late R.'s Poems" (72).

27 Cedric C. Brown, *John Milton's Aristocratic Entertainments* (Cambridge, 1985), 173.

28 *Ibid.*, 171–78.

29 On pp. 115–16 of *The Riverside Milton*, Flannagan cites a letter of August 23, 1992 in which Shawcross summarizes his view of the texts of *A Mask*.

30 Love, *Scribal Publication*, 53.

31 Beal, *In Praise of Scribes*, 25. For more on these practices, see Juliet Lucy's chapter in this volume.

32 Ann Baynes Coiro, "Milton and Class Identity: The Publication of *Areopagitica* and the 1645 *Poems*," *Journal of Medieval and Renaissance Studies* 22 (1992): 261–89 (p. 286).

33 See, for example, French's citation of *Mansus* from the 1645 *Poems* as the poem Milton gave Manso in December of 1638 (*LR* 1:394–97).

34 Coiro, "Milton and Class Identity," 286–88.

CHAPTER 32

Marriage and divorce

Shigeo Suzuki

When Charles Diodati died in 1638, Milton lost his most intimate confidant, a man whose close companionship, he confessed in *Epitaphium Damonis* (lines 37–39, 43, 45–47), had driven away the cares and loneliness in his own daily life. The sudden death of Diodati, "a youth without stain" (line 212), might have inspired the young Milton to devote himself to celibacy, but three years later in 1641, he was willing to announce that "marriage must not be call'd a defilement" (*CPW* 1:893), adding that he would prefer "a virgin of mean fortunes honestly bred, before the wealthiest widow" (*CPW* 1:929). Milton's stated wish became a reality around June 1642, when he left for Oxfordshire, probably to do some work in the Bodleian Library and to visit relatives. Likely at the request of his father, a notary and money-lender, he would also recover an outstanding debt due from Richard Powell.

About a month later, Milton, thirty-three years old, returned home to London with a seventeen-year-old bride, Mary Powell. Only a few weeks later, the marriage was for the time being at an end. She went back to her parents' home and stayed there for about three years, until the summer of 1645. There has been much surmising about the motives for Mary Powell's sudden departure, based upon a memoir which Edward Phillips, Milton's pupil and co-resident in London, wrote fifty-two years later.[1] The young bride might have felt homesick for the lack of jovial family activities, abhorred her husband's austere rigorous personality, or was opposed to his sympathies regarding the impending civil war. We might also speculate whether she was too inexperienced as a housewife to marry, for the average age at marriage for women during this era was twenty-three and a half.[2] Powell's father should at least have pondered Robert Filmer's contention that a daughter should "be not marri[ed] until [she] be skilfull in huswifrie."[3]

It may well have been under the influence of this initial experience that Milton almost immediately argued for a deeper understanding of marriage and divorce. He claimed in *The Doctrine and Discipline of Divorce* in 1643 that marriage was instituted by God to provide a congenial helpmate rather than to establish a family lineage and to avoid sexual misconduct. He also argued that if through careless but perhaps inevitable lapses in judgment a marriage were far from satisfying this primary purpose, divorce should be permitted. Much opposition to this view led him to write three further pamphlets in a more assertive vein over the following two years: *The Judgment of Martin Bucer* (a partial summary of the lengthy theological writing of the Protestant theologian a century earlier), *Tetrachordon* (a detailed collation of biblical references to marriage and divorce in the manner of biblical expositions), and *Colasterion* (an abusive reply to an anonymous opponent who concisely summarized and examined the issues of Milton's first divorce pamphlet). Far from being greeted with acclamation, these pamphlets quickly brought Milton renown as a ringleader of what would be called the "Divorcers" or "Miltonists," a group who would supposedly loosen the bonds of marriage in the service of inordinate lust.[4]

Despite the initial breakdown, Milton's marriage to Mary Powell ultimately lasted seven years and produced three daughters, ending with Mary's death in childbirth in 1652, by which time Milton was totally blind. Four years later, he took a second wife, Katherine Woodcock, who a year later also died in childbirth. It was probably after this brief second marriage that Milton wrote Sonnet 23, "Methought I saw my late espousèd saint," in which the blind poet relates a dream of his wife appearing with her face veiled, although he doesn't specify which of his wives this was or whether it was an oneiric amalgamation of both. Deviating from English Renaissance love poems such as Spenser's *Epithalamion* in which wedded love is idealized within the public sphere, Milton's work presents a private vision of married life. He depicts an endearing wife with the refined domestic virtues of "Love, sweetness, goodness" (line 11) who immediately vanishes when she tries to embrace her husband. The speaker fashions himself as a considerate husband, deeply afflicted by his wife's death and displaying a sincere affection for her. The wedded love depicted here bears no signs of the Lady's vigorous dedication to virginity in *A Mask*, a private masque probably written as a cleansing ritual for a family beleaguered by the sexual misconduct of a relative.

The death of his second wife must have added personal grief to political disillusionment for Milton in a period marked by tensions and rifts in the republican government. His life as a pamphleteer advocating individual civil liberty substantially came to an end with the restoration of the monarchy under Charles II. The aged writer was arrested, detained, but shortly

after released with the aid of his relatives and loyal friends. The change of
the regime reduced his assets so seriously that he faced the prospect of a very
frugal life with his three teenage daughters, who Christopher Milton, the
poet's brother, later reported to be "undutiful and unkind" to their father.[5]
Despite his old age, blindness, and strained domestic circumstances, both
financially and personally, Milton was introduced to a twenty-five-year-old
widow named Elizabeth Minshull, the second cousin of one of his friends.
Not pursuing an imaginary marital life with his deceased wife, as did the
Puritan theologian Richard Baxter or the royalist poet, Henry King, Milton, now fifty-five years old, took Elizabeth as a third wife in 1663. Despite
a considerable age difference between the couple, something ridiculed as a
cause of marital failure in Renaissance literature, Milton's life after his marriage to Elizabeth was, according to Cyriack Skinner, Milton's biographer
and beloved student, quieter, more settled, and more orderly.[6]

Milton spent his last twelve years with Elizabeth as he worked on the
final stage of *Paradise Lost*. Indeed, the completion of his *magnum opus*
could be partially attributed to Elizabeth's management of the household.
This may have influenced Milton's writing of a domestic relationship
using the figures of Adam and Eve in which repeated emphasis is given
to an apparently ideal interaction between marriage partners (v.129–36,
viii.48–58, x.1096–100). He later expressed his considerable affection and
tenderness for Elizabeth by bequeathing her almost all his estate. If Milton
had harbored some traumatic effects of the initial breakdown of his first
marriage and mourned the brevity of the second, his life with Elizabeth
may well have had a restorative effect.

To furnish a better understanding of Milton's ideas about marriage and
divorce respectively, I would like to examine in detail his texts and his immediate circumstances, both public and private, with reference to historical
resources concerning these matters from his time. I should note, though,
that any unified picture that may emerge here derives from reconstructions
based on numerous facts culled from fragmented historical sources and
refracted through ideological changes.

We can glean an idea of the church's position on matrimony at the time
of Milton's first marriage as it was summarized in the *Constitutions and
Canons* (1604), which codified earlier regulations and ecclesiastical customs, among which three canons were mainly concerned with matrimony.
Couples intending to marry should not have had "any impediment of pre-
contract, consanguinity, affinity," and they needed "the express consent of
their parents" if they were under the age of twenty-one.[7] There was no
such impediment between Milton and Mary Powell, who were not closely

related and neither of whom had been previously married. Milton presumably obtained consent from her parents while she was living with them. The laws also specified that ministers must marry a couple in a church in the area where one of them was living after they proclaimed banns (public announcements of the couple's intention to marry) thrice before the wedding ceremony. This directive was a measure against the custom of clandestine marriages entered into privately with the mutual consent of both parties, where even a simple verbal promise to marry in the future, succeeded by voluntary sexual intercourse, often made the couple married. The Powells came to stay with Milton for several days to celebrate his marriage to Mary, which means there was no secret in regard to the bride's family. The canons required that a registration book with the dates and years of weddings be kept at each church, but there are no surviving church records of Milton's marriage to Mary to prove that this marriage was sanctified at a church by a priest.[8]

Two years before this marriage, the Root and Branch Petition by the Puritans to the House of Commons in 1640 inveighed against priests who were arbitrarily prohibiting "marriages without their license" and granting "marriages without banns."[9] The petition led to the establishment of the Directory for Public Worship (1645), whereby a couple could be man and wife after exchanging the brief, specified phrases of consent in the present tense. Neither taking communion nor exchanging rings was necessary, but the wedding had to be conducted by a lawful minister. These new religious edicts were not enough to satisfy Puritan resentment of the marital procedure, which, under the influence of canon law, still gave priests the authority to determine when a marriage could occur. A major legal reform was carried out under the Cromwellian government in An Act Touching Marriages (1653) three years before Milton's second marriage. It disqualified the clergy from conducting wedding ceremonies and provided the justices of the peace, secular officials such as Mary Powell's father, with exclusive powers in presiding over a wedding, although parliament ultimately voted against giving control over divorce to the justices in the Act.[10] Milton, probably motivated strongly to justify his previous arguments concerning marriage, eulogized this legislation as a recovery of "the civil liberty of marriage from thir [the clergy's] incroachment" (*CPW* vii:300). A parish register in his local church in London shows that he actually put his second marriage into practice "according to the Act."[11] This new legislation was invalidated seven years later under the Restoration, although parliament under Charles II declared that marriages entered into according to the laws of 1645 and 1653 remained valid. Consequently, Milton's third marriage took place at a church in London in 1663, perhaps under an Anglican clergyman.[12]

Despite the apparent instability in marriage law, most Protestants and Catholics in the sixteenth and seventeenth centuries agreed upon three purposes of marriage: the begetting of children, prevention of sexual misconduct, and mutual assistance. Protestants rejected the Catholic idea that marriage is a sacrament, a sacred bond which Christ instituted to confer grace upon wedded couples, and held that marriage was a social institution for all persons which God had ordained as a necessary remedy for sexual sins.[13] Calvin valued marriage not only as a covenant established by voluntary consent between two people, but also as "the holiest bond" in which God participated as the third party.[14] The effect of holy, contractual marriage was to add to the mundane union of husband and wife a spiritual dimension of love and sacrifice for the heavenly kingdom.

The English Puritans gave significant support to this idea, emphasizing that marriage could not be properly maintained without "hearty affection" and sexual activity.[15] As for corporeal union, Protestant writers generally considered sexual intercourse as a means to fulfill the purpose of marriage in propagating the human race and thereby to enlarge the number of church members, although it was also assessed by some theologians, Luther for example, as inherently sinful because it was the fruit of original sin. The Puritans went further by identifying marital sex with the honorable and loyal interaction of spouses. William Whately came to speak of sex as "the best means to continue and nourish their mutuall naturall love."[16] In this context, sex was an expression of the emotional content of a marital relationship where affection reigned from the beginning and developed over time. Sexual pleasure within marriage was respected not simply as a means of driving away lust, but also as a means of cultivating mutuality and harmony between the husband and wife.

Milton, sharing these ideas, delineated the meaning of "one flesh" (Gen. 2:24) as more of a harmonious union of compatible souls than of two bodies. He suggested in his divorce tracts that the concord of sentiments and desires between spouses was not just a happy byproduct of marital relations, but also an essential requirement in matrimony. Marriage, Milton claimed, must answer the need of satisfying the soul's "pure and more inbred desire of joyning to it self in conjugall fellowship" (*CPW* II:251). He even suggests that sexual activity without a union of minds threatens to become a disgusting "quintessence of an excrement" (*CPW* II:248) and that sexual inability or inadequacy cannot cause serious frustration as long as "the minde and person pleases aptly" (*CPW* II:246).

Milton evaluates the relationship of a male with a female consort in marriage along the lines of the spiritual joys obtainable through the model of male friendship: "one society of grave freindship, and another amiable and attractive society of conjugal love" (*CPW* II:740). The idea of male friendship goes back to the classical period, where two autonomous souls equal in status were seen to unite to become one soul in two bodies.[17] Humanists in the sixteenth-century, such as Thomas Elyot, revived this idea with all its trappings, and proclaimed its centrality to men's lives.[18] The sixteenth- and seventeenth-century advocates of friendship, most prominently Montaigne, promoted masculine friendship as the antithesis of the heterosexual marriage partnership.[19] They praised a sincere male relationship and remarked the difficulty of its attainment, while claiming an inadequacy in the nature of women and the unlikelihood that a heterosexual relationship could satisfy both the emotional and the moral needs of men. But Juan Luis Vives, a wandering Spanish humanist, and Heinrich Bullinger, an influential Swiss theologian, included the classical idea of friendship in their definition of marriage.[20] Edmund Tilney, an Elizabethan courtier, also embraced this view in his book on conduct in marriage, and later the Anglican and the Puritan divines perpetuated the notion of companionship as a core element of a proper marriage.[21] In fact, several English treatises on marriage in the seventeenth century discuss the affectionate life of spouses as a form of fellowship. Milton participated in the same tradition in installing the vocabulary of fellowship across genders in the language of matrimony.

Milton seems to have rendered the companionate marital relationship as an entirely equal partnership at a time when the traditional subordination of female to male authority and the characterization of women as lighter, less serious than men had long been figured and justified in religious and political thought. Certainly, Milton's claim for a degree of equality within wedlock is reflected in the remarks and behavior of the female characters in his poetry, such as Eve in *Paradise Lost* and Dalila in *Samson Agonistes*, both of whom are able to defy blind subordination and to control the shape and direction of their relationships with their spouses. Nevertheless, this laudable egalitarianism is in conflict with the persistent assumption of a gender hierarchy that pervades his works: "the will and consent of both parties, or of the husband alone" (*CPW* II:344) or "He for God only, she for God in him" (*Paradise Lost* IV.299). Milton's partial negotiation of this apparent inconsistency involves the notion of an actively premeditated obedience. The wife obeys by her own rational choice rather than from a sense that she is a creature innately subordinate to her husband. Her behavior and words are not to exhibit a critical judgment that does not match that of her husband, who is rationally and expediently obeying God. Consequently, Milton's writings proclaimed marriage as a union of congenial and in a sense equal partners, but simultaneously approved of male dominance and female effacement as complementary obligations in a marriage.

Milton thus aligned himself with a contemporary position on companionate marriage, which held that a marital relationship did not share the equality of status and intellect or the moral intensity believed to characterize early modern male friendships. Yet, at the same time, following what he saw in the Bible and the secular laws, he believed marriage required "a fit conversing soul" (*CPW* II:251). Milton's apparently conflicting positions here imply that all marriage must fall short of genuine compatibility unless the spouses are able to liberate themselves from conventional notions of gender hierarchy and sexual difference, entrenched assumptions almost impossible to overthrow in Milton's time. This must have suggested to his contemporaries, then, that marriage would be a radically unstable institution if divorce were allowed on the grounds of incompatibility.

In fact, no proper ecclesiastical and secular laws in late medieval and Renaissance Europe permitted divorce or separation on grounds of incompatibility of disposition. The Directory of 1645, which was intended to replace the Common Prayer Book, followed the same line as the Book in ruling out the possibility of divorce. Anglican priests such as Edmund Bunny adamantly opposed divorce on any grounds, including adultery and desertion, in the early seventeenth century. The Anglican church maintained the Catholic belief in the indissolubility of marriage and dictated that a married couple should direct themselves toward being "loving and faithful" to each other "until God shall separate us [them] by death."[22]

Around the late thirteenth century, the Catholic church had solidified its position against "severance of marriage bond" (*divortium a vinculo matrimonii*) on the basis that marriage was a sacrament.[23] Although the church made divorce virtually impossible, it permitted a victimized spouse the right to "separation from bed and board" (*divortium a mensa et thoro*). Moreover, the church had the authority to issue annulments, which declared that a marriage did not exist because it had, for a variety of possible reasons, been contracted improperly. Still, annulments were particularly difficult to obtain, as in the case of Henry VIII, if the spouses had consummated their marriage and had children.[24]

Continental reformers challenged this anti-divorce doctrine by claiming that impediments to divorce were, as Luther argued, "follies" the Catholics "thought up."[25] They also insisted that separation (*divortium a mensa et thoro*) was the same as divorce (*divortium a vinculo matrimonii*) since it deprives the husband and wife of interaction in this life, the formal reason for marriage. The Protestant tenets, which presented continence as the most prominent of the three main purposes of marriage, resulted in adultery being considered the most serious violation of the marital bond, and this was especially true in the case of a wife because it cast doubt upon legitimate lineage, another important purpose of marriage as it was viewed at that time. Reformers concentrated on Matthew 19:9 to demonstrate that Christ had permitted divorce only in cases of adultery. Most Protestant theologians also agreed that desertion (1 Cor. 7:15), which might lead to a sexual relationship with another partner, justified revoking a marriage. Some reformers argued for divorce on other grounds: impotence, contagious diseases, cruel violence, insanity, witchcraft, and differing religions. Yet, judging from the meager number of divorce cases, this legal departure from the Catholic canons did not have a serious impact on marital customs in Protestant countries.[26]

There was a movement in the burgeoning Anglican church to bring about a change in the canon law to permit divorce on the basis of adultery and to provide the innocent spouse a right to remarry. This proposal, *Reformatio Legum Ecclesiasticarum*, was submitted to but rejected by parliament in 1552. After 1552, no significant official action was taken to permit complete divorce with a right to remarry until parliament passed the act to allow Charles Gerard, the Earl of Macclesfield, to dissolve his marriage to his adulterous wife in 1698. This bill, though only applicable to the suppliant, set a legal precedent for divorce obtained by an innocent husband against an adulterous wife through a private legal suit to parliament, a procedure which was affordable only for the affluent.[27]

In the first half of the seventeenth century many Puritan clergy wrote that divorce should be permitted in the event of adultery or desertion. But they also warned that the separation of a man and wife due to emotional difficulties should be avoided on the grounds that working through the difficulties was a task assigned by God as a trial.[28] Anglicans must have shared the same views, since their honored *Reformatio* prescribed that no permission to separate should be given to a couple even when their emotional discords "boil up to the point that the married couple do not wish to live together in the same house."[29] The couple was to remember, as Rachel Speght remarked, that marriage was an estate formed for the "mutual participation of each other's burden" and that the spouses must observe their divinely ordained roles and duties.[30] The preachers recommended endurance and charity for the innocent party and repentance for the guilty party, even after permission was given to live apart from a common bed and table.

The emphasis on overcoming emotional difficulties in marriage goes a long way toward explaining Milton's overwhelming conviction in his divorce tracts that a lack of emotional compatibility and of mutual respect and love was not simply an undesirable situation but manifest grounds for divorce. Milton came to speak of marital affliction in the case of an incompatible mate as a form of suffering at "the very foundations of his inmost nature," a different kind of hardship from the "thousand outward and intermitting crosses" which the couple must bear (*CPW* II:259). What for the established churchmen stood as pious advice was in Milton's eyes a perverted exhortation to hypocrisy, a "dissimulation against his soul in the perpetuall and ceaseles duties of a husband" (*CPW* II:259). Moreover, Milton engrafted the notions of conjugal compatibility onto "a meet and happy conversation" (*CPW* II:246), a humane interchange comprising a broad range of elements, from spiritual care and kindness to sexual contact. Conversation, "the chiefest and the noblest end of marriage," works as a remedy "to comfort and refresh . . . against the evill of solitary life" (*CPW* II:246, 235). The absence of compatibility restrains conversation and thereby limits the possibility of mutual negotiation of problems, promoting rather a retreat into solitude and rendering marriage a merely formal commitment that serves only to move each party away from God. So a clash of natural temperaments which militated against natural concord, the sine qua non of a proper marriage, justifies divorce.

Milton's argument for divorce did not meet with approval, partly because, as was mentioned earlier, his conclusion was regarded as allowing the indiscriminate gratification of human capriciousness, and partly because the principal interpretive method he applied to biblical texts – assessed by one of his opponents as an "intolerable abuse of Scripture" – might have exceeded what was deemed reasonable argumentation at that time.[31] We should add that Milton tried to bring the positions of theological and legal authorities into line with his notion of "just and reasonable desires" (*CPW* II:342) by interpolating, remixing, and making partial omissions from the authors' written texts.[32] He used sleight of hand even when he "epitomiz'd" (*CPW* II:478) Bucer's work *On Christ's Kingdom* (*De Regno Christi*). The reformist theologian allowed for divorce with mutual consent, but not simply because of emotional incompatibility, consistently regarding marriage as an indissoluble bond and divorce as a last resort to save distressed wives in seriously and irreparably dysfunctional personal relationships.[33] No major Puritan writer apart from Milton ever stated adamantly that spiritual incompatibility with a wife as judged by her husband was sufficient reason for divorce.[34]

Milton's proposal for divorce was not legalized in England until more than three centuries later, when parliament passed the Divorce Reform Act (1969), making irreconcilable differences a grounds for divorce.[35] The Act was passed under social pressure to eliminate the sense of guilt and public humiliation afflicting estranged couples. A married couple could now legally obtain a "divorce at pleasure" (as one of Milton's opponents put it[36]), if they found emotional ties crumbling. However, an alarming divorce rate of one in three marriages and the apparently unfavorable effects of divorce on spouses and their children led to the introduction of the Family Law Act in 1996, which aimed at making people better understand "the consequences of divorce and the effects of divorce on children" through the mediation of family counselors and solicitors.[37] Certainly, granting permission for divorce and remarriage on a non-fault basis served to reduce physical and psychological havoc between spouses, and to provide unprecedented opportunities for creating better relationships. Nevertheless, while the Act of 1969 could be viewed as endorsing Milton's argument, the need to introduce the Act of 1996 suggests that his ideal divorce would not alone necessarily ensure "the good of husband, wife, or childern" (*CPW* II:353).

NOTES

1 *EL* 64–65.

2 Peter Laslett, *The World We Have Lost: Further Explored*, 4th edn. (London, 2005), 82–83; and E. A. Wrigley, *et al.*, *English Population History from Family Reconstitution 1580–1837* (Cambridge, 1997), 134.

3 Robert Filmer, "In Praise of the Vertuous Wife" (manuscript, n.d.), in J. M. Ezell, *The Patriarch's Wife: Literary Evidence and the History of the Family* (Chapel Hill, NC, 1987), 169–90 (p. 176).

4 William Riley Parker, *Milton's Contemporary Reputation* (1940; New York, 1971), 73–79.

5 *LR* v:3.

6 *EL* 33.

7 *Constitutions and Canons (1604)*, ed. H. A. Wilson (Oxford, 1923), CII.

8 William Riley Parker, *Milton: A Biography*, 2nd edn., ed. Gordon Campbell, 2 vols. (1968; Oxford, 1996), 230.

9 Samuel R. Gardiner, ed., *The Constitutional Documents of the Puritan Revolution: 1625–1660*, 3rd edn. (Oxford, 1906), 141 (article 20).

10 *Journal of the House of Commons: Volume 7: 1651–1660* (1802): 307–08. www.british-history.ac.uk/report.aspx?compid=24241.

11 *LR* IV:126.

12 Parker, *Milton*, 583, 1095.

13 John T. Noonan, Jr., *Contraception: A History of Its Treatment by the Catholic Theologians and Canonists* (Cambridge, MA, 1966), 314–15.

14 John Witte, Jr., *From Sacrament to Contract: Marriage, Religion, and Law in the Western Tradition* (Louisville, KY, 1997), 110.

15 Henry Smith, "A Preparative to Marriage" (1591), in *The Sermons of Master Henry Smith* (London, 1637), 40; William Perkins, *Christian Oeconomie* (London, 1609), 110–11; William Gouge, *Of Domesticall Duties* (London, 1622), 215; and John Preston, *The Breast-Plate of Faith and Love* (London, 1637), 76.

16 William Whately, *A Bride-Bush or A Direction for Married Persons* (London, 1617), 43–45, cited in James G. Turner, *One Flesh: Paradisal Marriage and Sexual Relations in the Age of Milton* (Oxford, 1987), 74.

17 Aristotle, *Nicomachean Ethics*, trans. Horace Rackham (Cambridge, MA, 1926), 9.4.5; and Cicero, *De Amicitia*, trans. William Armstead Falconer (Cambridge, MA, 1953), 7.32.

18 Sir Thomas Elyot, *The Book Named the Governor* (1531), ed. S. E. Lehmberg (London, 1962), 2.134.

19 Michel de Montaigne, "Of Friendship," in *The Complete Essays of Montaigne* (1588), trans. Donald M. Frame (Stanford, CA, 1958), 138.

20 Juan Luis Vives, *The Education of a Christian Woman: A Sixteenth-Century Manual* (1524), trans. Charles Fantazzi (Chicago, 2000), 175; and Heinrich Bullinger, *The Golde[n] Boke of Christen Matrimonye*. trans. Theodore Basille [i.e., Thomas Becon] (London, 1543), sigs. A5, B4–5.

21 Edmund Tilney, *The Flower of Friendship: A Renaissance Dialogue Contesting Marriage* (1568), ed. Valerie Wayne (Ithaca, NY, 1992), 104–05; Robert Cleaver, *A Godly Forme of Houshold Gouernment* (London, 1598), 172–73; Gouge, *Of Domesticall Duties*, 216, 361; and Anthony Ascham, *Of Marriage* (1647), ed. J. M. Perlette, *English Literary Renaissance* 3 (1973): 284–305 (p. 288).

22 *The Directory for Public Worship* (1645), n.p. www.british-history.ac.uk/report. aspx?compid=56006.

23 James A. Brundage, *Law, Sex, and Christian Society in Medieval Europe* (Chicago, 1987), 370–71, 453–55.

24 R. H. Helmholz, *The Spirit of the Classical Canon Law* (Athens, GA, 1996), 240–41.

25 Kate Aughterson, ed., *Renaissance Woman: A Sourcebook: The Construction of Femininities in England 1520–1680* (London, 1995), 101, 103.

26 Merry E. Wiesner-Hanks, *Christianity and Sexuality in the Early Modern World* (London, 2000), 78–79.

27 Joan Perkin, *Women and Marriage in Nineteenth-Century England* (London, 1989), 22–23; and Roderick Phillips, *Putting Asunder: A History of Divorce in Western Society* (Cambridge, 1988), 414–17.

28 Cleaver, *A Godly Forme*, 199; Gouge, *Of Domesticall Duties*, 363–64.

29 Gerald Lewis Bray, ed., *Tudor Church Reform: The Henrician Canons of 1535 and the "Reformatio Legum Ecclesiasticarum"* (Rochester, NY, 2005), 244–45.

30 Rachel Speght, *A Mouzell for Melastomus* (1617), in *The Women's Sharp Revenge: Five Women's Pamphlets from the Renaissance*, ed. Simon Shepherd (New York, 1985), 70.

31 *An Answer to a Book [by J. Milton] Intituled "The Doctrine and Discipline of Divorce"* (London, 1644), 28.

32 Shigeo Suzuki, "Milton's Legitimatized Divorce and its (Un)creative Interaction," in *Milton, Rights, and Liberties,* ed. Christophe Tournu and Neil Forsyth (Bern, Switzerland, 2006), 155–67 (p. 166); and *An Answer*, 37.

33 V. Norskov Olsen, *The New Testament Logia on Divorce: A Study of Their Interpretation from Erasmus to Milton* (Tübingen, 1971), 78–79, 84–85; H. J. Selderhuis, *Marriage and Divorce in the Thought of Martin Bucer*, trans. John Vriend and Lyle D. Bierma (Kirksville, MO, 1999), 264–72.

34 Edmund Leites, *The Puritan Conscience and Modern Sexuality* (New Haven, 1986), 176, n. 83; and Phillips, *Putting Asunder*, 91.

35 Stephen Cretney, *Family Law in the Twentieth Century: A History* (Oxford, 2003), 391.

36 Parker, *Milton's Contemporary Reputation*, 73.

37 Great Britain, Lord Chancellor's Department, *Looking to the Future: Mediation and the Grounds for Divorce* (London, 1995), 56.

CHAPTER 33

Music

Diane McColley

John Milton's life, like his poems, was full of music – at his father's house in London, in the streets with their criers, in churches and college chapels, in theatrical performances – during a time when the music of such composers as Thomas Tallis, William Byrd, Thomas Tomkins, Orlando Gibbons, Thomas Weelkes, Thomas Morley, and John Amner provided musical riches for church and court and for sociable singing, playing, and dancing. During their outpouring of glorious and still treasured settings of sacred texts, Puritan reformers opposed choral services on the grounds that music obscures the words of the liturgy. Dedicated to the revolutionary and parliamentary side of the civil wars, but opposed to censorship and deeply attached to music, Milton collaborated with a court composer, praised the church music that Puritans attempted to destroy, and in his epics represented choral and instrumental music in Heaven, Hell, and Paradise.

What Milton in "At a Solemn Music" calls the "Sphere-borne harmonious sisters, Voice and Verse" (line 2) were linked together in church music, court entertainments, and much singing at private gatherings of psalms, catches, madrigals, and airs, many with texts by courtly "Cavalier" poets. In *Ad Patrem* the young poet defends his vocation to his composer father: "what good is an empty modulation of the voice, lacking words and sense and expressive meter?" (*CPEP* 222). In Milton's poems, words are linked to music both descriptively and by their own intrinsic song.

Milton's musical experience began at home. His father, John Milton Senior, a Scrivener and a composer of music who had been schooled as a chorister at Christ Church College, Oxford, held music meetings at his London house on Bread Street, near St. Paul's Cathedral.[1] In 1599, Milton's father was invited to the music meetings at the home of Nicholas Yonge, a chorister at St. Paul's, where he may have met Thomas Morley – madrigalist, musician of the Chapel Royal, and organist at

St. Paul's – to whom Elizabeth I had granted the right to print music, and who invited the elder Milton to contribute to *The Triumphs of Oriana* (1601), a collection of madrigals in honor of the queen.[2] Milton also set three of Thomas Ravenscroft's much-sung texts in *The Whole Book of Psalmes* (1621), and he composed four settings for William Leighton's *Teares, or Lamentations of a Sorrowfull Soule* (1614), to which such notable composers as William Byrd, Alphonso Ferrabosco, Martin Peerson, John Dowland, and Orlando Gibbons also contributed. Thomas Myriell, who transcribed 192 compositions by the best English composers of his time into one collection, the *Tristitia Remedium*, included ten by John Milton Senior.[3]

The gatherings in which Milton's father participated were musical commonwealths, drawing people together into a harmonious community. Music for these occasions was sometimes printed in "table books" so that four singers, or three singers and a lutenist, could sit facing each other at one rectangular table with the book lying open. Milton's "Thou God of Might" in Leighton's *Teares*, for example, was printed in this way (see figure 25). In Richard Alison's *The Psalmes of David in Meter* (1599), the cantus part is printed across the table from the citterne player's, and next to them the altus and tenor also face each other while the bassus sits at the end between them.

Part-singing creates an audible empathy. The friendly intimacy of such gatherings provides a place where "pure concent" ("At a Solemn Music," line 6), the perfect pitches, without vibrato, required by Renaissance and early baroque music, could be pleasantly practiced. Part-singers, whether of psalms or madrigals, have to listen carefully to achieve such harmony, as must members of a body politic and readers of Milton's harmonious verse.

Barbara Lewalski suggests that *Il Penseroso* describes what Milton may have heard passing St. Paul's Cathedral on his daily walk to school, with the organ played perhaps by John Tompkins or Adrian Batten.[4] Written in 1631, when choral singing and organ accompaniment in church were matters of controversy, partly because reformers thought such music obscured the text, Milton's poem includes a defense of both, including anthems and settings of the liturgy, modified by the word "clear":

> There let the pealing organ blow,
> To the full-voiced choir below,
> In service high, and anthems clear,
> As may with sweetness, through mine ear,
> Dissolve me into ecstasies,
> And bring all Heav'n before mine eyes.
>
> (lines 161–66)

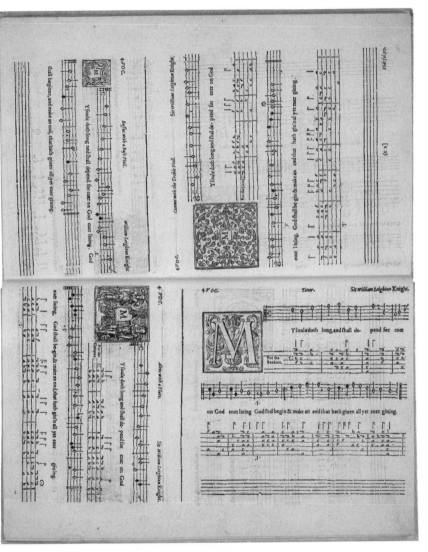

Fig. 25 John Milton Senior's "Thou God of Might" from William Leighton's *The Teares or Lamentacions of a Sorrowfull Soule* (1614)

In "At a Solemn Music" Milton similarly endorses musical settings by invoking the "Blest pair of sirens, pledges of Heav'n's joy, / Sphere-borne harmonious sisters, Voice and Verse" (lines 1–2). He asks them to raise our imaginations to the heavenly song of "pure concent" (line 6) – perfect intonation, but suggesting also the "concent" of voice and verse, or words and music:

> Wed your divine sounds, and mixed power employ
> Dead things with inbreathed sense able to pierce,
> And to our high-raised fantasy present
> That undisturbèd song of pure concent,
> Ay sung before the sapphire-colored throne
> To him that sits thereon.
>
> (lines 3–8)

Milton in this poem goes on to describe seraphic trumpeters and the thousand cherubic choirs with golden harps. His call for a human response endorses such music both as itself and as a metaphor of the regeneration of the harmony broken by man's fall:

> That we on earth with undiscording voice
> May rightly answer that melodious noise;
> As once we did, till disproportioned sin
> Jarred against nature's chime, and with harsh din
> Broke the fair music that all creatures made
> To their great Lord, whose love their motion swayed
> In perfect diapason, whilst they stood
> In first obedience, and their state of good.
> O may we soon again renew that song,
> And keep in tune with Heav'n, till God ere long
> To his celestial consort us unite,
> To live with him, and sing in endless morn of light.
>
> (lines 17–28)

If sin is absence of harmonic proportions, earthly words set to music help prepare humankind to rejoin the celestial consort, not as angels but as ourselves, retuned.[5]

In "On the Morning of Christ's Nativity" (1629) the angels sing with "heav'n's deep organ" in "ninefold harmony" (lines 130–31); in 1640 the parliament which Milton largely supported forbade both organs and polyphony in conformity with the emphasis on intelligibility and sobriety in the reformed Book of Common Prayer. In spite of verbally appropriate settings of the English liturgy like William Byrd's and Thomas Tomkins' and intelligible anthems that musically unfolded the meaning of the text, such as Tallis' "If Ye Love Me, Keep My Commandements," church music was outlawed, organs smashed, and choirs disbanded. Oliver Cromwell, then member of parliament for Cambridge, to whom Milton would later write a sonnet beginnng "Cromwell, our chief of men," cautioned the dean and chapter at Ely as "your loving friend," "Lest the soldiers should in any tumultuous or disorderly way attempt the reformation of your cathedral church I require you to forbear altogether your choir service, so annoying and offensive, and this as you will answer it if any disorder should arise thereupon."[6] In churches, at least, the twin-born harmonious sisters' wedded "divine sounds" were divorced.

Although Milton would side with parliament against Charles I, he wrote two courtly masques for the family of Sir John Egerton, Earl of Bridgewater, set by Henry Lawes, music tutor to the Egerton children who performed in them and a court composer known for his skill at setting words both enhancingly and intelligibly.[7] A Gentleman of the Chapel Royal, Lawes was born in Wiltshire in 1596 and educated at Salisbury Cathedral – a fount of sacred music based on the Sarum Rite – where Lawes' father became "a bass lay vicar" in 1605 and was promoted to priest vicar in 1631 "perhaps because of his son Henry's presence at court, or through the influence of the Herbert family at Wilton."[8]

According to Ian Spink, "From what we know of Lawes's relationship with the [Egerton] family and his reputation compared with Milton's (who was still at the beginning of his career) it seems pretty certain that it would have been Lawes who approached Milton with the 'libretto' rather than the other way around," having perhaps known of him through Milton's father. Lawes would have appealed to Milton in part because his music is "through-composed" rather than strophic, Spink points out, so that each verse or stanza gets its own word-coloring.[9]

In 1632 Milton and Lawes first collaborated on *Arcades*, a pastoral masque probably performed at Harefield by the children of Sir John Egerton in honor of their grandmother, Alice, Dowager Countess of Derby. The entertainment included songs of praise for the countess, inviting the nymphs and shepherds to leave Arcadia for the better soil of her estate. The masque, which is only part of the entertainment, has one long speech, in rhymed couplets, by "the Genius of the Wood," whose task is to nurse and protect the young trees and plants and "visit every sprout / With puissant words, and murmurs made to bless" (lines 59–60). But at night,

> ... then listen I
> To the celestial sirens' harmony,
> That sit upon the nine enfolded spheres,
> And sing to those that hold the vital shears
>
>   ...
>
> And keep unsteady Nature to her law,
> And the low world in measured motion draw
> After the heavenly tune, which none can hear
> Of human mold with gross unpurgèd ear.
>
> (lines 62–73)

The Genius nevertheless asserts that "such music" is "for her [the countess] most fit" (lines 74, 76). Music in *Arcades* is thus the audible expression not only of the structure of the universe but of the consonant nature of virtue.

Two years later, the Egerton family invited Milton again to collaborate with Lawes, producing *A Mask Presented at Ludlow Castle*, in which the Attendant Spirit finds the lost Lady by her singing. The song "Sweet Echo," by which she helps her brothers to find her, addresses the "sweetest Nymph that liv'st unseen" (line 230) and asks Echo to "Tell me but where" (line 240) her brothers are:

> Sweet queen of parley, daughter of the sphere,
> So may'st thou be translated to the skies,
> And give resounding grace to all heav'n's harmonies.
>
> (241–43)[10]

William Shullenberger remarks that "The harmonic reciprocities that Milton achieves in his seemingly effortless interweaving of multitudinous classical and biblical sources make the text a figural counterpart to the perfected ecological dynamism of the garden it evokes, and to the fructifying abundance of life and joy now incarnated in the living body of the Lady."[11] "Harmonic reciprocities" suggests that Milton's use of literary sources, as well as his language and his conceptions of nature and virtue, is rooted in his sense of "concent" or harmonious concord.

The place-based title of this work when it was printed, "A Mask ... Presented at Ludlow Castle, 1634," may have political resonances. Although "in 1644 the Lords and Commons decreed that 'all Organs, and the Frames or Cases where they stand in all Churches or Chappels ... shall be taken away, and utterly defaced,'" Ludlow "remained in Royalist hands until June 1646 and it was not until April 1650 that the Town Council ordered that 'the organ pipes remaininge useless in the church' were to be sold off by weight," fetching £5 3s 8d.[12]

In 1638, Milton traveled to Italy, where he discovered the *stile nuovo* with its freedom of expressiveness in the musical setting of words; heard the singing of the famous soprano soloist Leonora Baroni, to whom he wrote three Latin epigrams; and discovered the works of Claudio Monteverdi, Luca Marenzio, Antonio Cifra, Orazio Vecchi, and other composers, copies of whose works he sent back to England.[13]

In 1645/46 Milton published his early *Poems, both English and Latin,* including among other pertinent works the epigrams to Leonora, "At a Solemn Music," and a sonnet, "To Mr. H. Lawes, on his Airs," as the composer whose songs "first taught our English music how to span / Words with just note and accent" (lines 2–3).[14] In this volume, as throughout Milton's poetry, the love of music, the politics of music, and music itself are deeply embedded in both the gist and the sounds of words, as in the sonnet's suspension of "span / Words" and the staccato of "just note and accent."

Reducing censorship to the absurd in *Areopagitica* (1644), Milton wrote,

If we think to regulat Printing, thereby to rectifie manners, we must regulat all recreations and pastimes, all that is delightfull to man. No musick must be heard, no song be set or sung, but what is grave and *Dorick*...It will ask more then the work of twenty licencers to examin all the lutes, the violins, and the ghittarrs in every house...And who shall silence all the airs and madrigalls, that whisper softnes in chambers? (*CPW* II:523–24)

Although such ransacking of secular music did not occur during the civil wars and controversies of the 1640s, church music, for which the cathedrals and college chapels of England were and are justly famed, was both forbidden and materially destroyed.

In 1642, Peter le Huray reports, Puritan revolutionaries confronted Charles I "with an ultimatum – the Propositions for Peace – in which he was required to agree to 'taking away of all archbishops, bishops, and their chancellors and prebendaries, and all vicars choral and choristers'"; choral services gradually came to an end.[15] Composers expressed their grief in anthems and psalm-settings unsingable in church, among them perhaps Henry Lawes' setting of Thomas Carew's adaptation of Psalm 137, "Sitting by the Streams of Babylon," from the Bridgewater collection now at the Huntington Library. Reading Carew's poem, anyone who plays an instrument or sings in a choir would feel the wrench of

Holy *Salem*, if thy love
    Fall from my forgetful heart,
May the skill by which I move
    Strings of music tun'd by art,
From my wither'd hand depart.[16]

By forbidding polyphony as well as Latin services, the Reformation made the entire liturgy intelligible to the commons. For the singer, or the attentive listener, however, polyphonic settings of familiar texts can be made more responsive to words than monophonic ones by using more kinds of "word coloring" and expressiveness. Secular madrigals (unaccompanied part-singing) like sacred motets require singers to listen to each other and achieve "just concent." This phrase may also be applied to the body politic, to the relationships of human beings to God, each other, and other beings, and to the relations of words to music in Milton's poems.

But, despite or perhaps in response to contemporary restrictions on church singing and song, music occurs in every venue of *Paradise Lost*. Even in Hell, Satan's mustering of the fallen angels not only starts with "Trumpets loud and Clarions" but proceeds by tempering their passions and assuaging their fear and pain in the "mood" or mode prescribed:

> . . . anon they move
> In perfect phalanx to the Dorian mood[17]
> Of flutes and soft recorders; such as raised
> To highth of noblest temper heroes old
> Arming to battle, and instead of rage
> Deliberate valor breathed, firm and unmoved
> With dread of death to flight or foul retreat,
> Nor wanting power to mitigate and swage
> With solemn touches, troubled thoughts, and chase
> Anguish and doubt and fear and sorrow and pain
> From mortal or immortal minds. Thus they
> Breathing united force with fixèd thought
> Moved on in silence to soft pipes that charmed
> Their painful steps o'er the burnt soil.
>
> (1.549–62)

The rhythms of this description tend to halt and lurch. Similarly, when "Hell's dread Emperor" (11.510) goes off to try to "waste [God's] whole creation, or possess / All as our own, and drive as we were driven" (11.365–66), some of the fallen angels retire to sing

> With notes angelical to many a harp
> Their own heroic deeds and hapless fall
> By doom of battle; and complain that fate
> Free virtue should enthrall to force or chance.
> Their song was partial, but the harmony
> (What could it less when spirits immortal sing?)
> Suspended Hell, and took with ravishment
> The thronging audience.
>
> (II.548–55)

This devilish music is "partial" in at least three ways: it adheres to the devil's party, its text is only partly true, and it is part music. Music of self-praise for aggressive warfare that complains of fate and ravishes the listeners is dangerous propaganda. "Partial" and "ravishment" chime aptly with Satan's plot to find Adam and Eve and "seduce them to our party" (II.368). Ravishing polyphony was suspect among advocates of church reform. But the devils' party-music also "suspended Hell"; perhaps it could have been used to seduce them away from evil as well.

In Heaven, having heard the prophecy of the fall and the Son's offer to become incarnate and redeem the world by paying the price of Man's foretold lapse, the angels, with "Harps ever tuned" and beginning with "preamble sweet / Of charming symphony," introduce "Their sacred song, and waken raptures high; / No voice . . . but well could join / Melodious part, such concord is in Heav'n" (III.366–71). This passage links harmonious part-singing with good government as well as heroic action. The angels' song is a great *Te Deum*:

> Thee Father first they sung omnipotent,
> Immutable, immortal, infinite,
> Eternal King; thee Author of all being,
> Fountain of light, thyself invisible.
>
> (III.372–75)

In Milton's Heaven, God does not keep his Sabbath "in silence holy":

> the harp
> Had work and rested not, the solemn pipe,
> And dulcimer, all organs of sweet stop,
> All sounds on fret by string or golden wire
> Tempered soft tunings, intermixed with voice
> Choral or unison: of incense clouds
> Fuming from golden censers hid the mount.
>
> (VII.594–600)

"Choral or unison" could have raised the hackles of the radical iconoclasts who had left English churches with bare ruined choirs – some with the faces of saints sliced off the finials. But when God's angels rejoice that His human images will "multiply a race of worshippers," and "the empyrean rung / With halleluiahs," the narrator, who is the Archangel Raphael, concludes pointedly "thus was Sabbath kept" (VII.630, 633–34).

In Eden, Adam assures Eve that "Millions of spiritual creatures walk the Earth / Unseen, both when we wake, and when we sleep" and comments

> how often from the steep
> Of echoing hill or thicket have we heard
> Celestial voices to the midnight air,
> Sole, or responsive each to other's note
> Singing their great Creator: oft in bands
> While they keep watch, or nightly rounding walk
> With Heav'nly touch of instrumental sounds
> In full harmonic number joind, their songs
> Divide the night, and lift our thoughts to Heaven.
>
> (IV.680–88)

With solos, antiphons, full choir, and instrumental accompaniment, the angels fill the Edenic air at night as richly with music as the day gives odorous perfumes and beauteous flowers, and both come together when

> With flowers, garlands, and sweet-smelling herbs
> Espousèd Eve decked first her nuptial bed,
> And heav'nly choirs the hymenaean sung.
>
> (IV.709–11)

The Edenic night is filled with music as is Heaven's "twilight" while the angels rest in "Celestial tabernacles . . . / . . . save those who in their course / Melodious hymns about the sov'reign throne / Alternate all night long" (V.654–57).

In *Paradise Regained,* what Adam and Raphael place among the daily and nightly pleasures of Eden and Heaven, Satan includes among the temptations by which the Redeemer is tried. In Greece, Satan insinuates, he could not only learn poetry and philosophy but would "hear and learn the secret power / Of harmony in tones and numbers hit / By voice or hand, and various-measured verse" (IV.254–56). Jesus replies:

> . . . [I]f I would delight my private hours
> With music or with poem, where so soon
> As in our native language can I find
> That solace? All our law and story strewed

With hymns, our psalms with artful terms inscribed,
Our Hebrew songs and harps in Babylon
That pleased so well our victors' ear, declare
That rather Greece from us these arts derived

. . .

Such are from God inspired, not such from thee;
Unless where moral virtue is expressed
By light of nature not in all quite lost.

(IV.331–53)

And finally, having reversed the fall by standing with perfect balance against all temptations, the Son incarnate is given a celestial banquet,

. . . and as he fed, angelic choirs
Sung Heav'nly anthems of his victory
Over temptation, and the tempter proud.

(IV.593–95)

NOTES

1 Ernest Brennecke, Jr., imaginatively reconstructs this education in *John Milton the Elder and His Music* (New York, 1973), ch. 1.

2 *Ibid.*, 54–58.

3 British Library, Add. MSS. 299372–28377 (Brenneke, *John Milton*, 82, n.5).

4 Barbara K. Lewalski, *The Life of John Milton* (Oxford, 2000), 7. See also Cedric C. Brown, *John Milton: A Literary Life* (Basingstoke and London, 1995).

5 On the roles of the sirens in this poem and both of Milton's masques, see Stella P. Revard, *Milton and the Tangles of Neaera's Hair: The Making of the 1645 "Poems"* (Columbia, MO, 1997), 143–46.

6 Peter Le Huray, *Music and the Reformation in England, 1549–1660* (Cambridge, 1985), 53–54.

7 Cedric C. Brown gives a full account of the masques in *John Milton's Aristocratic Entertainments* (Cambridge, 1985).

8 Ian Spink, *Henry Lawes: Cavalier Songwriter* (Oxford, 2000), 1. Spink includes notations for some of Lawes' settings.

9 *Ibid.*, 56.

10 The musical setting of this song may be found *ibid.*, 58–59, and other sources listed under "Further reading" in the present volume.

11 William Shullenberger, "Milton's *Primavera*," in *Renaissance Ecology: Imagining Eden in Milton's England*, ed. Ken Hiltner (Pittsburgh, PA, 2008), 63–89.

12 Richard Francis and Peter Klein, *The Organ and Organists of Ludlow Parish Church* (Ludlow, 1982), 11. Church music manuscripts were also saved and deposited in the Shrewsbury County Record Office.

13 On Milton and Italian music, see M. N. K. Mander, "The Music of *L'Allegro* and *Il Penseroso*," in *Milton in Italy: Contexts, Images, Contradictions*, ed. Mario

A. DiCesare (New York, 1991), 281–91; as well as Margaret Byard, "'Adventrous Song': Milton and the Music of Rome," in *Milton in Italy*, 305–28.

14 Humphrey Moseley, who published Milton's early poems, also published Henry and William Lawes' *Choice Psalmes Put into Musick* (London, 1648).

15 Le Huray, *Music and the Reformation*, 53.

16 Performed on *Sitting by Streams: Psalmes, Ayres and Dialogues by Henry Lawes*, The Consort of Musicke, dir. Anthony Rooley (CDA66135, London). The psalm is included in Scott Nixon, "Henry Lawes's Hand in the Bridgewater Collection: New Light on Composer and Patron," *Huntington Library Quarterly* 62.3–4 (2001): 232–72. It is difficult to imagine anyone singing Carew's version of the painful conclusion of the Psalm, which seeks vengeance for the sufferings of Zion: "Happy shall he be, that taketh and dasheth thy little ones against the stones"; and which he intensifies:

> Men shall bless the hand that tears
> > From the Mothers' soft embraces
> Sucking Infants, and besmears
> > With their brains the rugged faces
> > Of the rocks and stony places.

See *The Poems and Masque of Thomas Carew*, ed. Joseph Woodfall Ebsworth (London, 1893), 207.

17 "Dorian: (1.) The first church mode. (2.) A Greek mode that may be represented by a scale descending through the white keys from é to e" (Theodore Karp, *Dictionary of Music* [Evanston, IL, 1983], 128). The Dorian mode represents valor in Plato's *Republic*.

CHAPTER 34

The natural world

Karen L. Edwards

As a beetle's beautiful, light-refracting carapace is made of translucent keratin laid over pigment, so the rich natural world represented in *Paradise Lost* is made of layer upon layer of texts. The refraction of meaning that results from such layering demands attentive reading – ideally, reading so attentive that it becomes conscious of its own interpretive activity. In representing a wholly textual natural world, Milton re-animates the ancient commonplace that Creation is "God's Other Book." A reader's encounter with the natural world depicted in the poem is thus an engagement with the process of how we arrive at meaning when we read. In *The Faerie Queene*, Spenser shows the Red Cross Knight and Una wandering into a "shadie grove" of meaningful trees: "The Mirrhe sweete bleeding in the bitter wound, / The warlike Beech, the Ash for nothing ill, / The fruitfull Olive, and the Platane round, / The carver Holme, the Maple seeldom inward sound."[1] In *Paradise Lost*, trees are not circumscribed or bound by epithets; they and other elements of the natural world *mean* in a very different way. How they do so is the subject of this chapter. I will approach it by considering what seems at first glance to belong to the built environment rather than the natural world: the wall of Paradise. Questions about the meaning of bounds and the bounds of meaning are central to Satan's transgressive leap into the Garden of Eden in book IV of *Paradise Lost*. It is thus crucial to ask in what sense the garden is enclosed, a question that leads to others: the size of the enclosure and what it encloses, the relationship between the garden and that which lies outside the garden's bounds, where in the world the garden is located, and whether or how far the portrayal of the garden is touched by the New World explorations and the origins of modern science that are a feature of Milton's own historical moment.

A pun on "bound," appropriately, marks Satan's entry into the Garden of Eden:

Due entrance he disdained, and in contempt,
At one slight bound high over leaped all bound
Of hill or highest wall, and sheer within
Lights on his feet...

(*Paradise Lost* IV.180–83)

His entry into the garden is also an entry into the complex symbolism of the *hortus conclusus*. For centuries the enclosed garden had persisted in a kind of symbolic stasis. Through dozens of biblical, classical, medieval, and early Renaissance representations, one can trace similar preoccupations: safeguarded fertility, spiritual refreshment, the secret pleasures of love (chaste or erotic), the emblematic language of flowers and herbs. These preoccupations are not abandoned when the early modern period evokes the enclosed garden, but they are affected by the insertion of the garden into new cultural and political discourses. In the sixteenth and seventeenth centuries, great princely gardens were established throughout Europe, designed and laid out on ideological lines.[2] The plants and animals carried back to Europe from Asia, Africa, and the Americas, arriving on foreign soil as specimens, commercial products, and exotic rarities, were meant to testify to the wealth and power of their new possessors. Symbolic language is not immune from external pressures; indeed, one could argue that symbols are constituted by such pressures. As the enclosed garden was identified increasingly with exclusive property and seen as a repository for living exotica, its symbolic field began to shift.[3] This shift has a profound impact on Milton's representation of the Garden of Eden in *Paradise Lost*. The enclosed garden, which had for earlier ages symbolized a protected and nurturing space, began in the early modern period also to symbolize exclusion from – or at best a contested right to – such a space.

The site of Milton's negotiation between the garden's old and new symbolic roles is the wall that Satan confronts in book IV. There has been greater critical interest in the figurative than in the material bound that Satan contemptuously overleaps, for in the poetic tradition of the enclosed garden, the wall often "implies the life-giving separation between nature [that is, fallen human nature] and Grace."[4] In the prelapsarian world of *Paradise Lost*, however, the material bound deserves our attention, for there is as yet no separation between "nature and Grace." Joan Thirsk has commented that in sixteenth-century protests against the enclosing of common grazing land, "anger was directed mainly at the hedges and fences – outward and visible signs of enclosure."[5] This is understandable, for in the demarcation of property, a wall, especially of brick or stone, is the supreme sign of actual and figurative place and, in the case of the enclosure movement, of actual and figurative displacement. The higher and longer the wall (which itself becomes, by literal extension, a costly object), the greater the area of land it encloses, and the higher the status of its owner may therefore be assumed to be. Allowing those outside the wall to draw such an inference is one of the many benefits to be derived from erecting a high wall around one's estate. There are others, such as attempting to intimidate or impress beholders, or to induce in them subservience, voyeuristic envy, or the desire to be identified with what proclaims itself to be exclusive. Walls, of course, confer the power to exclude upon which exclusivity depends: chief among the rights of owning a high wall is the ability to decide who does and who does not have access to the area it encloses. All of these are political benefits, in the largest though not the most generous sense of "political." It is not surprising that the fencing off of land – whether to end common grazing rights, to enlarge a princely estate, or to claim a stake in a new world – often entails violence.

Satan's overleaping in book IV results from his assumption that the wall is intended both to mark off God's property and to keep out intruders.

> So on he fares, and to the border comes,
> Of Eden, where delicious Paradise,
> Now nearer, crowns with her enclosure green,
> As with a rural mound the champaign head
> Of a steep wilderness, whose hairy sides
> With thicket overgrown, grotesque and wild,
> Access denied; and overhead up grew
> Insuperable highth of loftiest shade,
> Cedar, and pine, and fir, and branching palm,
> A sylvan scene, and as the ranks ascend
> Shade above shade, a woody theater
> Of stateliest view. Yet higher than their tops
> The verdurous wall of Paradise up sprung:
> Which to our general sire gave prospect large
> Into his nether empire neighboring round.
> And higher than that wall a circling row
> Of goodliest trees loaden with fairest fruit,
> Blossoms and fruits at once of golden hue
> Appeared, with gay enameled colors mixed.
>   (*Paradise Lost* IV.131–49)

As in an Impressionist painting, the depiction of the wall seems clear enough from a distance. Studied closely, however, the details begin to take on an independent life, and one loses the sense of how they are related to the whole. What *is* a "verdurous" wall? It is certainly not made of brick or stone, but is it then a "hedge,"[6] "a cliff masked by foliage,"[7] or, simply, verdure growing so thickly that it appears to be a wall?[8] Whatever it is, the wall recedes further and further from precise definition (in both senses) as Satan's gaze ascends and reads it *as* a wall. Our gaze ascends with his, beginning with the masses of entangling thickets covering a steep hill, moving on to the ranks of lofty cedars, firs, pines, and palms standing above them, then to the "verdurous wall of Paradise," and ending at the tops of an encircling row of fruit-bearing trees. The proper response to this description surely ought to be some degree of uncertainty. What in fact distinguishes the "verdurous" wall from the thick verdure around it? The passage does not provide an answer. The noun "wall" asserts a distinction that the adjective "verdurous" has already complicated. The effect is to suggest, simultaneously, that the wall bounds and does not bound. Inevitably, Satan's adversarial hermeneutic leads him to assume, with no hint of a second thought, that the wall is a material manifestation of the Great Forbidder's will and that it encloses the Great Forbidder's property. Satan's is the perspective of the outlaw: a wall (or anything that he can construe as a wall) declares to him that he is beyond the pale. The Satanic reading process is in thrall to that assumption; every detail Satan encounters is made to confirm it. There is no revision, no room for ambiguity in his reading, no speculative consideration of other interpretive possibilities.

Yet there is much in the description of the wall that undermines Satan's fixed assumptions, as if his reading generates its own counter-readings. A succession of alternative perspectives on the wall emerges in the passage, each flashing briefly into view and quickly being replaced by another. With its abundance of horizontally branching trees, the wall can be read as a ladder providing a means to ascend, which may imply an invitation to enter rather than a command to keep out. The wall can also be read as "a woody theater," both stately to view and allowing a stately view. By thus providing Adam with "prospect large / Into his nether empire neighboring round" (144–45), the wall acts as a frame or an infrastructure whose main function is to raise and support so as to illumine. As James Turner has remarked, in the seventeenth century "the prospect from a high place was well-established as an image of political foresight and inquiry."[9] Even the "ranks" of trees ascending "shade above shade" constitute an implicit rebuke of Satan's (literally) vaulting ambition: unlike the former archangel, these great, noble trees are content to stand in the shade of those above them.[10] Perhaps the richest and most suggestive possibility of all, however, is implicit in line 143: "The verdurous wall of Paradise up sprung." The wall itself here takes on the attributes of a living creature, of a green and vigorous plant, shooting (rather than bounding) from the earth. Animate, growing, and vital, *this* wall is as far removed as possible from Satan's fixed reading of it as a rigid barrier.

In its springing up, the wall of Paradise most closely resembles its heavenly counterpart, the wall of Heaven. When after flying through Chaos Satan sees Heaven afar off, it extends "wide / In circuit, undetermined square or round, / With opal tow'rs and battlements adorned / Of living sapphire" (II.1047–50). Milton alludes here to the description of John's vision of the heavenly Jerusalem in Revelation 21: the city "had a wall great and high" (verse 12), built on twelve foundations, all of them "garnished with all manner of precious stones" (verse 19).[11] "Undetermined" may be a Satanic adjective, in that Satan cannot determine whether Heaven is square or round. But it may also be a narrational one, which implies that the circuit, or wall, of Heaven does not determine whether Heaven is square or round. Similarly, "living" may mean "unhewn," as Alastair Fowler suggests, but it may also mean what in fact it usually means, that is, "animate" or "alive."[12] The behavior of the wall of Heaven during Satan's rebellion fully supports these more radical meanings of "undetermined" and "living." The Son, recounts Raphael, pursued Satan and his fellows

> to the bounds
> And crystal wall of Heav'n, which op'ning wide,
> Rolled inward, and a spacious gap disclosed
> Into the wasteful deep . . .
> (VI.859–62)

This is a wall of lively, animate crystal, a wall that encloses *and* discloses. It does not mold heaven into square or round. It neither rigidly bounds nor rigidly excludes but moves responsively to the exigencies of the place it surrounds.

If, as I am suggesting, the wall that Satan confronts is like the wall of Heaven, then we need to consider the possibility that the wall of Paradise gives dynamic form to what it embraces. Ostensibly the wall separates the Garden of Eden from the rest of Eden, a separation or distinction implied by Genesis 2:8: "And the Lord God planted a garden eastward in Eden." Biblical commentators did not fail to observe that the Hebrew phrase was ambiguous, however, and that "eastward in Eden" could be (and sometimes was) translated as "from the beginnings of the earth."[13] Perhaps in response to this biblical ambiguity, *Paradise Lost* does not maintain a systematic distinction between Eden and the garden within it. The garden itself is represented as at once intimate and vast in scale – so intimate that Eve has "bred up" all her flowers "[f]rom the first op'ning bud" and given them names (XI.276–77), so vast that in his survey of it, Satan roams "[t]hrough wood, through waste, o'er hill, o'er dale" (IV.538). Common sense might suggest that Adam and Eve know intimately only the small portion of the garden that two human beings can tend, but representation, not common sense, is at issue here. If the garden itself is represented, even if not consistently, as covering a huge and indeterminate area, how is it possible to distinguish between it and the rest of Eden?

The border between Eden and the rest of the world is equally difficult to distinguish. We remember that Satan arrives at "the border . . . / Of Eden" as he prepares to trespass on what he regards as God's property:

> So on he fares, and to the border comes,
> Of Eden, where delicious Paradise,
> Now nearer, crowns with her enclosure green,
> As with a rural mound the champaign head
> Of a steep wilderness . . .
>
> (IV.131–35)

This "border" is generally assumed to mark the division between Eden and the rest of the world, with Paradise being "a walled garden situated on the level summit (*champaign head*) of a hill (steep wilderness) on the eastern border of Eden."[14] The hill itself is not merely steep; it is overgrown with thicket, "grotesque and wild" (IV.136). Its labyrinthine and monstrous entanglement is re-affirmed as Satan considers "th'ascent of that steep savage hill" and finds no way through,

> so thick entwined,
> As one continued brake, the undergrowth
> Of shrubs and tangling bushes had perplexed
> All path of man or beast that passed that way.
>
> (IV.174–77)

According to the standard critical view, this hill, lying within Eden, is overgrown, unlike the carefully tended garden that also lies within Eden. Yet in an influential essay on Milton's Paradise, Barbara Lewalski defines the steep, tangled wilderness as "the mountain *outside* Eden."[15] That is, she merges Eden and the garden, and distinguishes only between Eden/garden and the rest of the world: "[t]he Garden, like the entire earth, is a place of profuse growth and tremendous fecundity, and it too tends to wild, though not to the same degree."[16] Her point is that the garden would revert to the overgrown state of the rest of the world if Adam and Eve did not tend it. They are "gardeners also of their own paradise within, that is, responsible for perfecting their own natures."[17] The necessity for daily lopping, pruning, propping, and binding (*Paradise Lost* IX.210) symbolizes the unending necessity for Adam and Eve to tend the garden of their minds.

Lewalski's is a persuasive reading; there can be little doubt that every "place" in *Paradise Lost* reflects the mind of its inhabitant. Satan is never *not* entangled in a thicket or its equivalent, so that even in Paradise, he is "involved in rising mist" (IX.75) or hidden in the serpent's "mazy folds" (IX.161). As if in reiteration of this fact, all of Satan's modes of entanglement combine as he readies himself for tempting Eve:

> through each thicket dank or dry,
> Like a black mist low creeping, he held on
> His midnight search, where soonest he might find
> The serpent: him fast sleeping soon he found
> In labyrinth of many a round self-rolled,
> His head the midst, well stored with subtle wiles.
> (IX.179–84)

The contrast with Eve's experience of the garden is subtle but explicit. Satan creeps through thickets; Eve is surrounded by a "spring of roses intermixed / With myrtle" (IX.218–19). He is like "a black mist"; she is "[v]eiled in a cloud of fragrance" (IX.425). He seeks the head of the serpent amidst its complicated, self-rolled rounds; she stands and "upstays" the heads of her flowers "bushing round / About her" (IX.430, 426–27). Eve's garden is not Satan's garden – and it can never *become* Satan's garden. After the fall, Adam and Eve seek cover not in thicket but in "thickest wood" (IX.1100), perhaps an allusion to that very differently signifying wood of *The Faerie Queene*. Adam and Eve's disobedience does not cause the garden to revert to the overgrown and tangled condition of Satan's world, in other words, for that world is satanic; it reflects and embodies Satan's mind. After the fall, Adam and Eve inhabit our world, and it, unlike Satan's world, is a mixture of tended and wild, tangled and cleared. Before the fall, wherever Adam and Eve dwell is Paradise; it is, from the beginning, "a paradise within" that manifests itself in the place of their dwelling. Just as Satan is always in Hell, so an unfallen Adam and Eve are always in Paradise, which means that the garden, and Eden, and the rest of the world are all Paradise before the fall. Insisting on strict or rigid boundaries between the garden and Eden, or between Eden and the world, or even between the garden and the world is futile – as is trying to limit Paradise to a point on a map.

In the sixteenth and seventeenth centuries, where Paradise was located became the subject of intense speculation. "It is difficult for the secular mind of modern times," notes Arnold Williams, "to conceive how seriously the Renaissance took the search for the true location of Paradise."[18] Although there was rough consensus "that Eden, of which Paradise was a part, was somewhere between Palestine and Persia,"[19] another strand of thinking held that Paradise encompassed the entire world.[20] Milton's representation of Paradise allows it be understood both as a place (at least formerly) to be pinpointed on a map *and* as an expanse so unbounded that it coincides with the globe itself. Sitting on the Tree of Life, Satan sees

> A Heav'n on Earth, for blissful Paradise
> Of God the Garden was, by him in the east
> Of Eden planted; Eden stretched her line
> From Auran Eastward to the royal tow'rs
> Of great Seleucia, built by Grecian kings,
> Or where the sons of Eden long before
> Dwelt in Telassar: in this pleasant soil
> His far more pleasant Garden God ordained.
>
> (IV.208–15)

Eden extends, so the passage indicates, from Auran to Seleucia or to Telassar, and the garden lies in the eastern part of this area. Even leaving aside the presence of the alternative (Seleucia or Telassar), these place names lack genuine referential precision. Auran (or Hauran or Haran) is the name both of Abraham's brother (Gen. 11:26) and of his ancestral home (Gen. 11:31); Seleucia is sometimes confused with Babylon, a place whose symbolic importance for Judaism and Christianity overwhelms its historical and geographical specificity; and Eden and Telessar (Isa. 37:11) seem at once synonymous and distinct.[21] In other words, the names in the passage above are significant, but what they signify, other than "the East," is difficult to say. They seem simply to mean that Milton's Paradise lies to the east of the East, a "location" that belongs to myth rather than geography. Thus Auran, Seleucia, and Telassar imply that Eden's intangible line extends eastward into the invisible distance until it merges, finally, with the circumference of the globe.

There is further support for this reading of Paradise in Satan's view of the wall, when he sees "delicious Paradise" crowned "with her enclosure green, / As with a rural mound the champaign head / Of a steep wilderness" (*Paradise Lost* IV.132–35). "Mound" does not mean, as we might first assume, an earthy elevation, which is a later sense of the word. It means here a hedge or a fence around a field.[22] As we have seen, this mound is much larger and more complex than anything we normally think of as a hedge or a fence, a fact that suggests the influence in the passage of another "mound," the substantive derived from Latin *mundus*, meaning a representation of the globe.[23] Mounds of *this* sort, made of gold or other precious metals, were designed to "crown" regal crowns. "Mound" thus acts as a conduit between two views of Paradise: a discrete, walled garden crowning an unenclosed, or champaign, plateau; and a garden as vast and complete as the globe, a world surmounting the world, even perhaps a world superimposed upon the world, "enclosed" only by its circumference. From the latter perspective, Satan's attempt to break into and enter Paradise is absurd.[24]

It is not surprising, then, to find that the plants and animals of Paradise belong to every part of the globe. It is instructive to compare the practice of Andrew Marvell, Milton's friend and contemporary, in his poem "Upon Appleton House." Marvell often uses colloquial, familiar, or regional names for the creatures on Fairfax's estate, thus emphasizing its particular and unique character. Among its fowls, he mentions the rail and the hewel, the throstle and the stock-dove; among its flora are the sensitive plant (*herba mimosa*) and the strawberry, the hazel, and the ash.[25] In *Paradise Lost*, in contrast, the representation of creatures is governed by the word *all*: "All trees of noblest kind for sight, smell, taste" (IV.217); "Flow'rs of all hue" (IV.256); "all kind / Of living creatures" (IV.286–87). The animals that frisk before Adam and Eve are "[a]ll beasts of th'earth, since wild, and of all chase / In wood or wilderness, forest or den" (IV.341–42). Those specifically named are drawn from the widest range of historical, literary, and geographical sources:

> Sporting the lion ramped, and in his paw
> Dandled the kid; bears, tigers, ounces, pards,
> Gamboled before them, th'unwieldy elephant
> To make them mirth used all his might . . .
>   (IV.343–46)

The lion and the elephant are found in the biblical East, in classical literature's depictions of the Colosseum and of Africa, and in ancient and modern symbols of royalty and ferocity in warfare; the kid figures prominently in Aesop's fables, in the Bible, and in everyday early modern English life; the bear is an inhabitant of the New World and the Old, and is mentioned in biblical and classical literature; the Asiatic tiger, the European ounce, and the myth-encrusted pard are signifiers of the felines found in all centuries and all climates; and the serpent has been represented in human culture as far back as any kind of record, visual, oral, or written, has been kept. The presence of these beasts in Paradise may signify that the garden's prelapsarian climate is suitable to all creatures of the earth, but it may also signify that the garden and the earth are one. By creating menageries, botanical gardens, curiosity cabinets, and paper museums, wealthy Renaissance collectors were seeking to bring the whole world into the strict compass of an enclosed space. By creating a paradise that reaches out to and embraces *all* creatures, Milton imparadises the whole earth.

And after the fall? Let us look again at the fate of Paradise, as foretold by Michael:

> then shall this mount
> Of Paradise by might of waves be moved
> Out of his place, pushed by the hornèd flood,
> With all his verdure spoiled, and trees adrift
> Down the great river to the op'ning gulf,
> And there take root an island salt and bare,
> The haunt of seals and orcs, and sea-mews' clang.
> To teach thee that God attributes to place
> No sanctity, if none be thither brought
> By men who there frequent, or therein dwell.
>
> (XI.829–38)

By definition, an island is bounded by water. This bare postlapsarian rock would thus seem to be as far removed as possible from the boundless, fertile prelapsarian garden. But we need to look closely at Michael's prediction. The island, he states, will "take root," a phrase implying and promising growth. Even this rock, that is, seems to partake of the vitality of heaven's living sapphire wall and the up-springing wall of Paradise. Moreover, Michael's prophecy contains a crucial "if": "God attributes to place / No sanctity, if none be thither brought." If sanctity (from Latin *sanctus*, "holy") *is* brought, however, any place in the fallen world – a bare rock, an estate in Yorkshire, the suburbs of London – may be holy. The Bible repeatedly proclaims that "the Lord our God *is* holy" (Ps. 99:9). Those who dwell in holiness dwell with God, and it is the presence of God within that creates Paradise on earth. Satan's unsanctified bound over the wall does not allow him to enter Paradise. He would have been equally unable to enter Paradise had he walked in at the gate.

It is a condition of creatureliness to inhabit place, a condition figured in Genesis' evocation of beasts of the earth, birds of the air, and fish of the sea. In *Paradise Lost*, a corollary of this principle underpins the representation of the natural world: as God created Adam and Eve in his image, Adam and Eve create their earthly habitation in *their* image. Because God made them free – "I formed them free, and free they must remain, / Till they enthrall themselves" (III.124–25) – the prelapsarian natural world is also free, unbounded, and dynamic. Yet liberty, Milton insists repeatedly in his works, is not license. The wall of Paradise functions for the natural world as God's command (not to eat of the fruit of the forbidden tree) functions for Adam and Eve: the command, like the wall of Paradise, serves not to restrict but to define freedom.

NOTES

1 Edmund Spenser, *The Faerie Queene*, ed. A. C. Hamilton *et al.* (Harlow, UK, 2001), 1.1.9.
2 See, for instance, David R. Coffin, *The Villa D'Este at Tivoli* (Princeton, 1960).
3 To some extent, the development of botanical gardens exerts a counter-pressure on the establishment of gardens intended to demonstrate political and social power. See John Prest, *The Garden of Eden: The Botanic Garden and the Re-Creation of Paradise* (New Haven, 1981).
4 Stanley Stewart, *The Enclosed Garden: The Tradition and the Image in Seventeenth-Century Poetry* (Madison, WI, 1966), 59.
5 Joan Thirsk, ed., *The Agrarian History of England and Wales. Vol. IV: 1500–1640* (Cambridge, 1967), 200.
6 Charlotte Otten, "'My Native Element': Milton's Paradise and English Gardens," *Milton Studies* 5 (1973): 255.
7 G. Stanley Koehler, "Milton and the Art of Landscape," *Milton Studies* 8 (1975): 7.
8 The *Oxford English Dictionary* cites *Paradise Lost*, IV.43, as the first occurrence of the word "verdurous" in English and defines it as "consisting of or composed of verdure" (*Oxford English Dictionary* [hereafter *OED*], 2nd edn., 1989), s.v. verdurous, a., def. 2.
9 James Grantham Turner, *The Politics of Landscape: Rural Scenery and Society in English Poetry 1630–1660* (Cambridge, MA, 1979), 5.
10 See *OED*, s.v. shade, sb., def. 1.1.c, a sense of the word relatively new in the mid seventeenth century.
11 King James version.
12 Alastair Fowler, ed., *Paradise Lost*, by John Milton, 2nd edn. (London, 1998), II.1049–50, n.
13 Philip Almond, *Adam and Eve in Seventeenth-Century Thought* (Cambridge, 1999), 65.
14 *CPEP* 388 (IV.132–45, n.).
15 Barbara K. Lewalski, "Innocence and Experience in Milton's Eden," in *New Essays on "Paradise Lost,"* ed. Thomas Kranidas (Berkeley, 1971), 90.
16 *Ibid.*

17 *Ibid.*, 93.
18 Arnold Williams, *The Common Expositor: An Account of the Commentaries on Genesis 1527–1633* (Chapel Hill, NC, 1948), 95–96.
19 *Ibid.*, 99.
20 Alessandro Scafi, *Mapping Paradise: A History of Heaven on Earth* (London, 2006), 264–66.
21 See Fowler, *Paradise Lost* iv.209–16, n.
22 See *OED*, s.v. mound, sb.³, def. 1 and 3.
23 See *OED*, s.v. mound, sb.¹, def. 1.
24 For an alternative reading of Eden – and this passage – see Amy Boesky's chapter in this volume.
25 Andrew Marvell, *The Poems of Andrew Marvell*, ed. Nigel Smith (London, 2003), stanzas 45, 50, 67–68 (226, 227, 232).

CHAPTER 35

The New World

Amy Boesky

To what extent did *Paradise Lost* participate in the imperial imaginary of
seventeenth-century Britain? Over the past fifteen years, since the publication of David Quint's *Epic and Empire*, discussions of *Paradise Lost* and the
New World have become an increasingly important part of Milton's critical canon.[1] While Samuel Johnson may have maintained that *Paradise Lost*
does not involve "the conduct of a colony, or the foundation of an empire,"
readers today are less willing to accept the possibility that Milton's references to Columbus (IX.1116), Montezuma (XI.407), and Atabalipa (XI.409)
are unrelated to British imperial ventures in the seventeenth century.[2] An
important moment in the critical understanding of Milton's relation to the
New World came in 1996, when J. Martin Evans published *Milton's Imperial Epic*. In this study, Evans argues that *Paradise Lost* participates in the
ideology of its culture and must be read alongside the "recurring themes"
of colonialism – "the nature of the colony, the status of the colonized,
the character of the colonizers" – as well as alongside a "common body of
linguistic practices, descriptive tropes, narrative patterns, and conceptual
categories." For Evans, Milton's "great Argument" is integrally connected
to "the rhetorical and argumentative strategies deployed by the promoters
and agents of European imperialism."[3] Evans' study is one of a number in
recent years that takes Milton and colonialist discourse as subject. Increasingly, the epic's interests in space, boundaries, and world-making are being
seen as part of a larger contemporary "discourse of Western colonialism."[4]

How do these contexts matter to our reading of *Paradise Lost*? Is the
poem critical of imperial discourses, affiliating the enterprises of empire
with the epic's great antihero, Satan, and in this way (subtly or unsubtly)
denouncing contemporary colonialist agendas? Or is it rather the case
that "Milton's use of the terminology of colonies, plantations, and long-
distance trade betrays a certain complicity in the designs of empire"?[5]
Yet another possibility – are the allusions to empire in *Paradise Lost* finally
morally neutral – is the poem conversant with colonialist discourse without

either accepting or condemning it? In reading Milton's relationship to the New World, critics today often proceed by using what Balachandra Rajan calls "cautious contextualization," trying to take these questions into account without overstating them.[6] Without forgoing that necessary caution, my aim here is to point to some of the differences that Milton's New World contexts make to our reading of *Paradise Lost*, and to some possible directions for further inquiry.

First, we need to consider what Milton knew about British colonial ventures during the period in which he was planning and writing his epic. Thanks to extensive scholarship by critics such as Evans, Robert Fallon, Balachandra Rajan, and Paul Stevens, we know much more than we once did about this subject. Milton was living and writing during a period of intense interest in colonial venture. As Evans notes, "the crucial first phase of English empire building in the New World coincided more or less exactly with Milton's lifetime."[7] The years during which Milton lived saw both a consolidation and an intensification of British overseas ventures, and many of the travel narratives produced in or after these expeditions focused new energies on the subject of the control, management, and subjugation of indigenous peoples. After a series of overseas experiments under Elizabeth, many of them failures, the Stuart period witnessed a new seriousness in imperial design. According to Kenneth R. Andrews, "it was the reign of James that saw the effective beginnings of the British empire: the establishment of colonies in North America, the development of direct trade with the East, and even the first annexation of territory in a recognized Spanish sphere of influence – the West Indies."[8] In the seventeenth century, the English organized colonial enterprises by forming most of the great joint-stock and trading companies: the East India Company (1600), the Virginia Companies (1607), the Dorchester Company (1624), the Newfoundland Company (1610), the Massachusetts Bay Colony (1629), and the Royal African Company (1660).[9] From Stuart endorsements of joint-stock companies and colonial settlements to Oliver Cromwell's nationalist Western Design (a policy in which Cromwell supported the seizure of Spanish holdings in the West Indies), the 1650s saw encounters outside of Britain becoming organized on a larger and more serious scale. "Planting" (a term suggesting the organic nature of installing colonies), expansion, and colonial management were recurrent topics in seventeenth-century British discourse, from Bacon's essay "Of Plantations" to Margaret Cavendish's laudatory descriptions of subdued multicolored peoples in exotic lands. Dozens of texts published in the 1650s and 1660s took up the imperial theme, including travel narratives such as George

Warren's "Impartial Description of Surinam," romances such as Cavendish's *The Blazing World*, and utopias such as Henry Neville's *Isle of Pines*.

Would Milton have known about these ventures merely because they were taking place? Evans maintains that Milton was exposed to the colonization of the Americas through at least three different avenues: personal acquaintances, intensive reading, and political work done under Cromwell in the 1650s. In the first instance, Milton was acquainted with several men who "had promoted, or emigrated to, the colonies" – Ralph Hamor, Samuel Hartlib, Sir Henry Vane, and Roger Williams among them.[10] In the second instance, extensive reading would have deepened Milton's awareness of British ventures overseas. "Milton could hardly avoid being aware of events taking place on the other side of the Atlantic" given the extensive number of tracts and treatises on England's plantation in Virginia alone in the middle decades of the seventeenth century.[11] Finally, Milton's official work with Cromwell in the 1650s may have implicated him personally and professionally in British expansion overseas.

Objections to these claims have come from several directions. Some critics believe that Evans overemphasizes the Americas in assessing Milton's "discourse of colonialism." Balachandra Rajan and Paul Stevens, for instance, see Milton's imperial scope extending eastward, to India and beyond, rather than merely to the American or Atlantic locus. Stevens believes that the "new world" of the Americas which appears so vexingly in book IX of *Paradise Lost* is allied with ignominy more than with glorious gain, and that colonization for Milton meant more than "the colonization of America"; to argue otherwise is to lose entirely "Milton's eastward gaze."[12] Stevens and Rajan in particular note the importance of allusions in *Paradise Lost* to India – Rajan analyzes six in brilliant detail – suggesting that India and the East were as important to Milton's evocation of imperial adventure and expansion as the Americas.[13] Other critics note the importance of Milton's imperial discourse within the British isles, rather than outside of them. Sharon Achinstein, wondering whether Milton was in fact "concerned about the rights of . . . conquered peoples," points out that he was "unequivocally in favor of conquest in Ireland."[14] Willy Maley observes that Ireland for Milton was, along with being "a key component of the British state [and] a bridge between Scotland and England, [a] focal point of empire, and a crucible of colonial otherness."[15]

There also has been disagreement about the significance of Milton's work with Cromwell in terms of imperial expansion. Historians such as Christopher Hill and David Armitage have proposed that Cromwell (and

Milton along with him) was working toward a unified imperial vision of British global expansion in the 1650s, but Robert Fallon disagrees, arguing that Milton's work under Cromwell must not be read anachronistically. Fallon notes that the word "empire" was used differently in the mid seventeenth century than it is today. He contends that Cromwell's vision was neither global nor unified, and reminds readers to be cautious in drawing conclusions. While there is some suggestion that Milton disapproved of the expansion of empire, such as an English translation published by Milton's nephew John Phillips (*The Tears of the Indians*), "it is too great a leap to conclude that the poet deplored all empires as well."[16] Milton's prose is "disappointingly empty of any reference to English colonies in the New World," and though the poetry is more promising for gleaning hints of Milton's dispositions, Fallon contends "the political imagery of *Paradise Lost* is an unreliable reflection of the poet's judgment on the events of his time."[17]

There are, then, significant disagreements among critics both as to the extent and the implications of Milton's "colonialism," despite the fact that most critics admit Milton could hardly have been impervious to contemporary discourses of empire. Further disagreements arise over how to read the allusions in *Paradise Lost* to India and the Americas. Are these references merely part of what has been referred to as an "encyclopedic" epic's interest in encyclopedic places?[18] If the allusions are more than mere decoration, can they be read as part of a coherent ideology, or are they inconsistent? And what ideology do they promote? Do they work to support the causes of colonialism or to critique them? Quint, who sees empire-building as the central work of epic as a genre, argues that *Paradise Lost* offers a stringent critique of imperial practices through the figure of Satan, whose hunger for power ends in humiliation and bitter defeat. Other Miltonists who number themselves among the "anti-imperialists" include Janel Mueller, who sees the epic proceeding from "an imperial to a post-imperial construction of the course of human history," and Diane McColley, who believes that Milton is "an ecological poet, doing battle with the intemperate implementation of the Baconian conception of empire over nature as he does with tyrannical monarchy."[19] For these critics, Milton participates in colonial discourse primarily to denounce it. Here, as in other discussions of Milton in context, it is worth recalling that *Paradise Lost* is a poem that encompasses contradictory positions. Like Milton's God or his Eve for critics in earlier periods, Milton's "new world" today seems both to invite and to baffle fixed conclusions. Places (earthly or celestial) are rarely fixed or fully knowable in *Paradise Lost*, and it is worth remembering that the moments in which America or India appear – fascinating and disturbing as they may be – are moments of analogy, in which a non-synchronous event is set forth by way of "future" example, comparing something that has happened at a point thousands of years beyond the history that the Bard narrates in a place distant from the epic's main events as well as from the poet's own habitus. The poem's "new worlds," in other words, belong to the epic's imaginary, and, while they invite our speculation, they simultaneously confound it.

My interest here lies in extending in one specific way the thoughtful and provocative recent criticism on Milton and colonialism by considering a set of concerns adjacent to – but I think importantly involved with – representations of the new world in Milton's epic. Imperial analogy in Milton's poem often centers on the body – a body vulnerable, open, naked, or longed for; a body degraded, shamed, covered or discovered. The most famous colonialist moment in the epic, talked about by almost every critic who confronts the subject, is very much a "bodily" moment. It occurs just after the fall, when Adam and Eve realize they are naked – "destitute and bare / Of all their vertue" (IX.1062–63), and Adam "counsels" that they find:

> Some tree whose broad smooth leaves together sewed,
> And girded on our loins, may cover round
> Those middle parts, that this newcomer, Shame,
> There sit not, and reproach us as unclean.
>
> (IX.1095–98)

The body is itself a "new world" here, newly recognized ("those middle parts") and at once denounced as abject. The narrator's description of the body's covering and its comparison to the couple's "first naked glory" is what incites the famous reference to how "Columbus found th'American" (IX.1115–16). Like other significant moments in the epic – Satan meeting Sin, Satan first seeing Eve – this moment in book IX is a point in which an imperial journey ends (and/or begins again) in the confrontation of a body, open, naked, abject. Bodies in *Paradise Lost* are lost as they are found, covered as they are discovered. References to bodies continuously deepen and disturb the epic's colonial subtexts, suggesting to my mind deep affiliations in the poem between subjecthood and empire.

Bodies matter in discussions of new worlds in ways that might usefully extend the critical conversation about Milton and colonialism. As Annette Kolodny and Patricia Parker have argued, a close connection emerged in the early modern period between sexual and territorial conquest.[20]

Corporeal and colonialist discourses often borrowed from and re-shaped each other. Medical tracts drew frequently from travel narratives to describe the "mapping" of the body, and the early medical explorers such as Johann Fallopius laid claim to their discoveries by naming body parts for themselves. As Jonathan Sawday writes, "Like the Columbian explorers, these early discoverers dotted their names, like place-names on a map, over the terrain which they encountered. In their voyages, they expressed the intersection of the body and the world at every point, claiming for the body an affinity with the complex design of the universe."[21] If the body could be described as a land mass – "O my America, my new found land!," Donne's lover exclaims in Elegy 15, describing his exploration of his lover's naked body[22] – the land mass could in turn be described as a body ("Guiana," Sir Walter Ralegh wrote in his letter describing the country to Elizabeth, in terms that she might especially appreciate, "is a country that hath yet her maidenhead, never sacked, turned, nor wrought"[23]). Samuel Purchas and Thomas Morton each compared Virginia to a "modest virgin... now valid with wild Coverts and shadie Woods, expecting rather ravishment than Mariage from her Native Savages."[24] The intersection of bodily and colonialist discourses in *Paradise Lost* emphasizes the powerful need in the epic for dominion, mastery, and control over a new body/new world whose charms unsettle that need even as it is exhorted. The permeability of the body – its access to touch, light, music, taste, and fragrance – makes it susceptible to penetration, weakness, and ruin. As Denise Albanese notes, "the body under siege in *Paradise Lost* is always feminized – even when it is Adam's body," as when Adam expresses his anxiety to Raphael that in "sub-ducting" his rib in order to create Eve, God may have taken "perhaps / More than enough" (VIII.536–37).[25] The epitome of the "terrifying absence of corporeal boundaries" in the epic, Albanese observes, is Sin, whose "openness to rape, incest, and base appetite marks her as troublingly permeable."[26] But this openness becomes one of the more suggestive tropes in the poem, and one of the richest nodes of intersection for Milton between corporeal and colonial fantasy.

It is the garden, of course – at once open and closed, a "woody theater" (IV.141), a "sylvan scene" (IV.140), a "view" (IV.142), a site of congruencies where nature is at once in first bloom and full harvest – that most richly evokes the ideality and terror of easy entrance. As Albanese phrases it, "when paradise is designated, as Milton's Eden is, to be God's 'new world' (2.403), its placement within the thematics of colonialist novelty marks it as an alternative topography."[27] The garden is at once a new world and a body. For all its "Native perfumes" (IV.158) dispensed by "odoriferous wings" of gentle gales (IV.157), Eden's border is impenetrable, "grotesque and wild" (IV.136), a terrain that evokes the image of *hortus conclusus* in its deliberate evocation of female genitalia:

> So on he fares, and to the border comes,
> Of Eden, where delicious Paradise,
> Now nearer, crowns with her enclosure green,
> As with a rural mound the champaign head
> Of a steep wilderness, whose hairy sides
> With thicket overgrown, grottesque and wild,
> Access denied.
>
>   (IV.131–37)

Satan, of course, "At one slight bound over leaped all bound" (IV.181) and "sheer within / Lights on his feet" (IV.182–83). Like Eve in book IX, when Satan's words "Into her heart too easy entrance won" (IX.734), the garden is tragically permeable. Paradoxically, only after the fall will God defend Eden with "Cherubic watch," "Lest Paradise a receptacle prove / To Spirits foul" (XI.120–24). Eden must be both open and closed, not only for Milton's drama of "free will" to play itself out, but for the paradoxical fantasies of colonial power to be reenacted in the poem. Like Eve's body – so closely associated with the luxurious fecundity of the garden, as well as with its vulnerability – Eden is both the site of temptation and punishment, of opportunity and of curtailment.[28]

What connections can be drawn between this representation of access and violation and its colonial contexts? In 1667, the year that *Paradise Lost* was published, an Englishman named George Warren visited Guiana (made famous by Ralegh's voyages) and published his impressions in a tract called *An Impartial Description of Surinam upon the Continent of Guiana*. Unlike Ralegh, who believed Guiana to be the legendary site of El Dorado and hoped to discover the Garden of Eden there, Warren found Surinam a fallen place, "swarming with so many severall kinds of Vermin," including "Snakes, Crocodiles, Scorpions, Bats, Ants, Musketoes, Toads, and Frogs." The Indians whom Warren met struck him as a "People Cowardly and Treacherous," the women "naturally lascivious, and some so truly handsome, as to Features and Proportions" that the colonists needed "more than Joseph's continency" to avoid embracing them.[29] Warren's tract describes (and newly sexualizes) a landscape teeming with possibility. Decades earlier, Ralegh's Guiana had been figured as lush with access and offerings. Goods offer themselves up, like the fruit that jumps into guests' hands in Ben Jonson's "To Penshurst":

On both sides of the river, we passed the most beautiful country that ever mine eyes beheld... I never saw a more beautiful country, nor more likely prospects, hills so raised here and there over valleys, the river winding into divers branches, the plains adjoining without bush or stubble, all fair green grass, the ground of hard sand easy to march on, either for horse or foot, the deer crossing in every path... and every stone that we stooped to take up, promised either gold or silver by his complexion.[30]

Like Ralegh and Warren, Milton in *Paradise Lost* interweaves the fecundities of new worlds and new bodies. New worlds in the epic are often signaled by new bodies, and vice versa. In book IX Adam and Eve, having covered themselves in their shame with the leaves of the fig tree, are compared by the narrator, as Rajan summarizes it, "to the Taino people whom Columbus encountered on the periphery of the New World":[31]

> Such of late
> Columbus found th'American so girt
> With feathered cincture, naked else and wild
> Among the trees on isles and woody shores.
> (*Paradise Lost* IX.1115–18)

This passage layers different versions of covering, discovering, and re-covering, wrenching the reader's gaze away from one primal scene (the naked, postcoital bodies of our first parents, guilty and abject) and displacing it with another, which Rajan notes conjoins a double confusion:

The "of late" refers to an event that took place a hundred and seventy-five years before *Paradise Lost* was published; Milton's powers of intimidation are such that annotators pass over this majestic minimization in silence. The distant event is also misperceived. Columbus did not find the American girt at all but clad "in native honor," as Adam and Eve were before taking refuge in the banyan tree. The alteration is crucial and it too has passed unnoticed.

This elision, Rajan observes, separates the Amerindians from innocence and instead places them "at the beginnings of fallenness."[32]

The passage Rajan points to here – and the one that has become the best-known and most problematic moment of imperial discourse in the epic – is made all the more complex by layering analogies within analogies. Adam and Eve wake, "and each the other viewing, / Soon found their eyes how opened, and their minds / How darkened" (IX.1052–54). This passage supposes, with its own intricacies and complexities, that the couple rises together like Samson, "the Danite strong," "Shorn of his strength" (IX.1059, 1062). But only after almost forty lines of bitter reproach from Adam does the couple take action: "both together went / Into the thickest wood; there soon they chose / The fig tree" (IX.1099–101). From line 1066 to 1098, Adam berates Eve, laments his own inability to behold the face of God or angel again, and imagines a solitary recovery in which he might disavow her and live alone:

> O might I here
> In solitude live savage, in some glade
> Obscured, where highest woods impenetrable
> To star or sunlight, spread their umbrage broad
> And brown as evening.
>
> (IX.1084–88)

Sensing his body as newly shameful, Adam envisions a kind of devolution, a fantasy of becoming "savage" (IX.1085). Earlier he had convinced God to make him a companion fit for him, and not the beasts; now he longs for double solitude, alienated from Eve as well as from God. In his fantasy of living savage, he imagines the woods covering him with their shadows, spreading "broad / And brown as evening" (IX.1087–88). Both the use of the word "brown" to modify evening and the word "savage" suggest that Adam in his initial fallen state conflates himself with the poem's representation of a "fallen" Amerindian. While the concluding part of this invective suggests both he and Eve need to hide "the parts of each from other, that seem most / To shame obnoxious, and unseemliest seen" (IX.1093–94), the fact that the words come from Adam underscores the extent to which it is Eve's body whose "middle parts" (IX.1097) are now seen both as shameful and "unclean" (IX.1098).

The conflation of colonialist and misogynist discourse in this passage is useful in retracing a larger problematic in the poem's treatment of Eve, who is constantly bound up in the rhetoric of expansion and desire that expresses itself most richly, and most problematically, in the epic's depictions of "inside" and "outside." Space and place in the epic are continually described in terms that intuit "place as a property of the body," as John Gillies suggests: Milton is thus unlike Donne, who "deplacializes and etiolates his lovers in the process of expanding them to cosmic proportions or collapsing the cosmos into them, while Milton is profoundly corporeal."[33] Eve's body is like the garden in which it finds its closest "placial" identification, a "new world" to Adam, who is at once its creator and its colonist. Having watched himself be opened in order to extract the "streaming rib" that gives Eve material form, he is consequently disarmed by her, feeling before her strangely incomplete. Raphael chastises him for overvaluing "an outside" (VIII.568), and Adam, in the most important moment of disagreement in their exchange, insists that Raphael has misunderstood him. Adam compares Eve to a world:

> Under his forming hands a creature grew,
> Manlike, but different sex, so lovely fair,
> That what seemed fair in all the world, seemed now
> Mean, or in her summed up, in her contained.
>
> (VIII.470–73)

Eve is, in other words, the epic's most important new world, and Adam's clear mandate – though he defies it – is to establish dominion over her. The consequence of his refusal is the fall. His mandate is to manage well, so that Eve will acknowledge him "her head" "and to realities yield all her shows" (VIII.574–75). Raphael sharply warns Adam to reign in his passions, noting that the same "sense of touch whereby mankind / Is propagated" (VIII.579–80) is enjoyed by cattle and "each beast" (VIII.582). That Raphael can imagine Eve in these terms is astonishing. "For . . . what transports thee so, / An outside?" he asks Adam, denouncing Adam's love and through it, its object (VIII.567–68). It is no wonder that Adam's reply is "half abashed" (VIII.595). For God's ambassador to describe Adam's new world in these terms – a mere "outside" – is to reproduce the baffling paradox at the center of the poem. Through Raphael's eyes, as through Satan's, we see new worlds as outsiders, we are reminded that our task is to subdue, and that every "inside" is only another layer we believe we have the right to call our own.

NOTES

1 David Quint, *Epic and Empire: Politics and Generic Form from Virgil to Milton* (Princeton, 1993). J. Martin Evans reviews the critical literature on this theme in chapter 13 of this volume.
2 See John Leonard, "Hatching Empires," *Milton Quarterly* 31.4 (1997): 145–47 (p. 145).
3 J. Martin Evans, *Milton's Imperial Epic: "Paradise Lost" and the Discourse of Colonialism* (Ithaca, NY, 1996), 3.
4 Paul Stevens, review of Anne-Julia Zwierlein, *Majestic Milton: British Imperial Expansion and Transformation of "Paradise Lost," 1667–1837*, *Modern Language Review* 98 (2003): 961–63 (p. 961).
5 Zwierlein, *Majestic Milton*, quoted in Stevens, review of *Majestic Milton*, 962.
6 Balachandra Rajan, "Milton Encompassed," *Milton Quarterly* 32.3 (1998): 86–89 (p. 86).
7 Evans, *Milton's Imperial Epic*, 11.

8 Quoted in Amy Boesky, *Founding Fictions: Utopias in Early Modern England* (Athens, GA, 1996), 12.

9 A joint-stock company, begun during this period, was a company held collectively by its shareholders.

10 Evans, *Milton's Imperial Epic*, 11.

11 *Ibid.*, 12.

12 Paul Stevens, "Milton and the New World: Custom, Relativism, and the Discipline of Shame," in *Milton and the Imperial Vision*, ed. Balachandra Rajan and Elizabeth Sauer (Pittsburgh, PA, 1999), 90–111 (p. 91).

13 Balachandra Rajan, *Under Western Eyes: India From Milton to Macaulay* (Durham, NC, 1999), 50–66.

14 Sharon Achinstein, "Imperial Dialectic: Milton and Conquered Peoples," in Rajan and Sauer, *Milton and the Imperial Vision*, 67–89 (p. 70).

15 Willy Maley, "Milton and 'the Complication of Interests' in Early Modern Ireland," in Rajan and Sauer, *Milton and the Imperial Vision*, 155–68 (p. 168).

16 Robert Fallon, "Cromwell, Milton, and the Western Design," in Rajan and Sauer, *Milton and the Imperial Vision*, 133–54 (p. 148).

17 *Ibid.*, 150.

18 Rajan, *Under Western Eyes*, 50.

19 Janel Mueller, "Dominion as Domesticity: Milton's Imperial God and the Experience of History," and Diane Kelsey McColley, "Ecology and Empire," in Rajan and Sauer, *Milton and the Imperial Vision*, 25–47 (p. 26) and 112–29 (p. 113).

20 Quoted in Evans, *Milton's Imperial Epic*, 65.

21 Jonathan Sawday, *The Body Emblazoned: Dissection and the Human Body in Renaissance Culture* (New York, 1995), 23–24.

22 Elegy 15, "Going To Bed," in *The Complete Poetry of John Donne*, ed. John Shawcross (New York, 1967), 57–58, line 27.

23 Quoted in Boesky, *Founding Fictions*, 163.

24 Quoted in Evans, *Milton's Imperial Epic*, 66.

25 Denise Albanese, *New Science, New World* (Durham, NC, and London, 1996), 134.

26 *Ibid.*, 133–34.

27 *Ibid.*, 121.

28 For an alternative reading of Eden's permeability, see Karen Edwards' chapter in this volume.

29 Quoted in Boesky, *Founding Fictions*, 165.

30 Quoted *ibid.*, 163.

31 Rajan, review of Evans, *Milton's Imperial Epic*, *Modern Philology* 96.2 (1998): 248.

32 *Ibid.*

33 John Gillies, "Space and Place in *Paradise Lost*," *ELH* 74.1 (2007): 27–57 (pp. 32, 38–39).

CHAPTER 36

Pamphlet wars

N. H. Keeble

The Milton who, heir of Moses, Homer, and Virgil (*CPW* 1:812), invoked a time of oral culture and manuscript circulation, aspired to timelessness: "with his garland and singing robes about him," he sought "an immortality of fame" by leaving "something so written to aftertimes, as they should not willingly let it die" (*CPW* 1:327, 808, 810). This same Milton was, however, also the most topically immediate of authors, addressing himself not to posterity but to his contemporaries. By utilizing press technology to take up current issues of public concern through the prompt publication of pamphlets and controversial tracts, this most traditional of authors was yet among the most innovative of early modern writers, becoming the first master of print culture in English literary history.

The publishing opportunity of which Milton took such creative advantage had never before been available. His early literary career coincided with, and was shaped by, an unprecedented increase in press activity associated with the gathering momentum of the English revolution. The political and religious tensions of the early decades of the century were articulated through what, assuming ironically the voice of a would-be controller of the press, Andrew Marvell later described as "the seditious meetings of Letters": "*O Printing*! How hast thou disturb'd the Peace of Mankind! that Lead, when moulded into Bullets, is not so mortal as when founded into Letters!" Both Milton and Marvell likened the output of the press to the dragon's teeth sown by Cadmus that "sprang up armed men."[1] It was a time, in the words of Edward Hyde, Earl of Clarendon, of "paper-skirmishes," of pamphlet wars.[2]

In 1648 the Puritan minister Richard Baxter exclaimed in dismay at the result: "Every ignorant, empty braine... hath the liberty of the Presse, whereby... the number of bookes is grown so great that they begin with many to grow contemptible." By 1653, he had come to fear that the "Luxuriant Fertility, or Licentiousness of the Press of late" is "a design of the Enemy to bury and overwhelm in a croud... Judicious, Pious, Excellent

Writings."[3] The revolutionary and radical ideas published in the tracts of Levellers, Anabaptists, Ranters, and, later, Quakers, disclosed to Baxter's orderly Puritanism a prospect of anarchy, of, in the oft-quoted words of Acts 17:6, "a world turned upside down."[4] While Baxter's dismay at the consequences of its "Luxuriant Fertility" might be challenged, there is no disputing the press' extraordinary increase in productivity in the 1640s: an annual output of 625 titles in 1639 jumped to 850 in 1640, to over 2000 in 1641, and over 3,666 in 1642.[5] A unique record of this output is preserved in the remarkable collection of broadsides, tracts, pamphlets, and books assembled by Milton's friend the bookseller George Thomason, who, between 1640 and 1661, amassed 22,000 publications. Never before had so many people turned to writing, never before had so many seen their thoughts into print, and never before had what they printed generated such extensive interest and public debate.[6]

A condition of this sudden upsurge in press productivity was the collapse of pre-publication censorship following the sitting of the Long Parliament in November 1640 and the subsequent abolition of the Court of Star Chamber in August 1641. The Long Parliament, however, quickly found that it had no more liking for a free press than had earlier regimes and by an ordinance of June 14, 1643 licensing of texts before publication was re-instituted. This was the immediate occasion of Milton's *Areopagitica: A Speech of Mr. John Milton for the Liberty of Unlicensed Printing, to the Parliament of England* (1644), which construed the disputatious ferment that so distressed Baxter not as the work of Satan but as vital to continuing Christian commitment: "Truth is compar'd in Scripture [Psalm 85:11] to a streaming fountain; if her waters flow not in a perpetuall progression, they sick'n into a muddy pool of conformity and tradition" (*CPW* II:543). What animates *Areopagitica* is not the revelation of truth but the excitement of its pursuit: "[t]o be still searching what we know not, by what we know, still closing up truth to truth as we find it . . . is the golden rule in *Theology*" (*CPW* II:551). Rather than retreat, "fugitive and cloister'd," the true Christian presses on in the Pauline "race, where that immortall garland is to be run for, not without dust and heat" (*CPW* II:515), for "our faith and knowledge thrives by exercise, as well as our limbs and complexion" (*CPW* II:543). What Baxter shunned, Milton welcomed:

Where there is much desire to learn, there of necessity will be much arguing, much writing, many opinions; for opinion in good men is but knowledge in the making. Under these fantastic terrors of sect and schism, we wrong the earnest and zealous thirst after knowledge and understanding which God hath stirr'd up in this City. What some lament of, we rather should rejoyce at. (*CPW* II:554)

"[S]ects and schisms," he wrote elsewhere, "are but as the throws and pangs that go before the birth of reformation" (*CPW* I:795). The fecundity of a free press, the availability of cheap print, pamphleteering – these Milton took to be the marks of a "Kingdome of free spirits" (*CPW* I:669). "Give me the liberty to know, to utter, and to argue freely according to conscience, above all liberties" (*CPW* II:560).[7]

Milton's confidence in the potential of free debate – "Let [Truth] and Falshood grapple; who ever knew Truth put to the wors, in a free and open encounter" (*CPW* II:561) – was founded on an equally idealistic opinion of his readers, or, at least, of their responsibility. To substitute for heresy and disobedience custom and tradition as the obstacles to religious and political well-being was to identify searching personal interrogation of received opinion as a primary Christian duty, leading to Milton's paradoxical, but understandable, assertion that a person "may be a heretick in the truth . . . if he beleeve things only because his Pastor sayes so . . . though his belief be true, yet the very truth he holds, becomes his heresie" (*CPW* II:543). Milton's pamphlets hence participate in a revolution not simply in press productivity but in reading practices and expectations. In the words of 1 Thessalonians 5:21, which Milton quotes (*CPW* II:511–12), his readers are to "Prove all things, hold fast that which is good," to assess, weigh, and analyze evidence before adopting or accepting contentions or arguments. The true Christian exercises an independent intelligence in critical and self-aware reading.[8]

Milton's apparently democratic confidence in his readers sits awkwardly, however, with his many disparaging and dismissive comments elsewhere on the incapacity of the "ruder sort" with their "thousand idle descants and surmises" to recognize the force of his arguments, and his apprehension that it might have been better to withhold his more radical ideas from "vernacular readers" by writing in Latin (*CPW* II:224, 233; IV:610). The "numerous and vulgar train" of "Error and Custome . . . make it their chiefe designe to envie and cry-down the industry of free reasoning" (*CPW* II:224) while the "blockish vulgar" (*CPW* III:339) accept whatever they hear or read. Milton dismisses as a "credulous and hapless herd," "an inconstant, irrational, and Image-doting rabble" (*CPW* III:601), those impressed by *Eikon Basilike*, even though these are the very readers he would win from their royalist allegiance. Despite his commitment to pamphleteering, popular opinion did not in fact count for much with Milton. "If a majority in Parliament prefer enslavement and putting the commonwealth up for sale, is it not right for a minority to prevent it if they can?" was his response to the accurate observation that in Pride's Purge "The officers did it with their troops": "We should then thank the officers for standing by the state, and for driving off the raging mob of London hirelings and hucksters" (*CPW* IV:457–58).[9] Milton's characterization of the readers of *The Reason of Church-Government* (1641) as "intelligent and equal [impartial]," "elegant & learned," "the gentler sort" (*CPW* I:806, 807, 808) is no doubt a compliment, but it is not a hollow compliment. His pamphlets place their confidence in "the wise and right understanding handfull of men," "the choisest and the learnedest" (*CPW* II:232, 233), rather than in the multitude, just as later *Paradise Lost* would address a "fit audience . . . though few" rather than the riotous (royalist) train of Bacchus and his revellers (VII.30–38).

There is a similar tension between the high valuation of pamphleteering in *Areopagitica* and Milton's slighting comments in other tracts on the business of controversial prose. He has no opinion of the "wretched projectors . . . that bescraull their Pamflets every day with new formes of government for our Church" (*CPW* I:753) and professes "small willingnesse" to take on such controversial work himself (*CPW* I:821). "[T]he genial power of nature" draws him rather to "versing" than "prosing." If he "hunted after praise by the ostentation of wit and learning," he would not work in "the cool element of prose" "wherin knowing my self inferior to my self . . . I have the use, as I may account it, but of my left hand." Were he "wise only to mine own ends" he would not engage in controversies which demand hasty composition since "the not deferring is of great moment to the good speeding" of the work. He would choose instead "such a subject as the publishing whereof might be delayd at pleasure, and time enough to pencill it over with all the curious touches of art, even to the perfection of a faultlesse picture" (*CPW* I:807–08).

These disclaimers, however, may not be quite all they seem, for Milton's pronouncements about poetry and prose can be contradictory and are often at odds with his practice.[10] He can exalt poetry as capable of "Religious . . . glorious and magnificent use" (*CPW* II:405), but in *Eikonoklastes* he associates it with fatuity, fabrication, and hypocrisy to discredit Charles I: "Poets indeed use to vapor much" (*CPW* III:502). "Cool" is hardly the characterization one would choose for his own prose style which can display just those "knotty Africanisms, the pamper'd metafors; the intricat, and involv'd sentences" that he deplored in the Church Fathers (*CPW* I:568). Though he avers that "it were a folly to commit any thing elaborately compos'd to the carelesse and interrupted listening of these tumultuous times" (*CPW* I:807) that, in fact, is what he does, expending upon this supposedly inferior medium great rhetorical ingenuity. Indeed, a key part of his business is to demonstrate by his practice that critics of the political and religious establishment are not "grosse-headed, thick witted, illiterat, shallow," in need of tuition "to speak good English" and to "order a set of words judiciously" (*CPW* 1:873). On the contrary, "fond utterances" and specious "metaphoricall compellations" are characteristic of his opponents' incapacity "to write, or speak in a pure stile" (*CPW* 1:877, 934). He himself is "not unstudied in those authors which are most commended" and knows "the rules of best rhetoricians," which he can impudently demonstrate in an extended passage illustrating what his opponent, were he as skilled as Milton, might have said to promote his case (*CPW* 1:889, 899, 922–28; cf. 949). He rehearses the range of his reading as a recommendation to his readers (*CPW* 1:888–93) and in the tracts reaches not only for the generically predictable historical and theological sources, but for classical, medieval, and Renaissance dramatists and poets. His titles – *Areopagitica, Tetrachordon, Colasterion* – appeal to the learned, and (as he recognized) could affront the "vulgar": "Bless us! What a word on / A title page is this!" (Sonnet 11, lines 5–6). This is a writer at "the elite end of the pamphleteer's spectrum."[11]

In short, the business of Milton's autobiographical passages of methodological comment is affective, not confessional. His apparently personal interventions serve to establish his own exceptional vocation and credentials in contrast to his contemptible adversaries, mere drudges and hired laborers (*CPW* 1:822), and to flatter his implicitly – indeed, explicitly – learned and gentle readers. The extended, and seemingly irrelevant, autobiographical passage in *The Reason of Church-Government* in which Milton discourses on classical and Renaissance literary theory, and expatiates on the didactic mission and civilizing force of high culture, is not in fact the digression from his main business that it might appear (*CPW* 1:806–23). By entering into a "covnant with any knowing reader" that he will in due course produce a great work consistent with these principles (*CPW* 1:820–21), he situates his tract in a cultural context such readers would recognize and impresses on them how serious the case must be that compels him to turn aside from this work. Rather than disparaging pamphleteering, his distinction between "learned pains" and "unlearned drudgery" (*CPW* 1:822), between the exalted and enduring didactic mission of poetry and the ephemeral carping of controversy, in fact elevates the latter.

To the same end, Milton constructs a pamphleteering persona of conscientious integrity with the highest of literary motives: "the enforcement of conscience only" compels him to his prose writings, to exercise the "honest liberty of free speech" against tyranny and hypocrisy (*CPW* 1:806, 804). While he might himself prefer to continue his preparations for his great work, yet "were it the meanest under-service, if God by his Secretary conscience injoyn it, it were sad for me if I should draw back, for me especially, now when all men offer their aid" to fight tyranny in church and state (*CPW* I:822). Hence, by his own account, in the summer of 1639 he returned early from his Italian journey because of "the sad tidings of civil war from England . . . For I thought it base that I should travel abroad at my ease . . . while my fellow-citizens at home were fighting for liberty." He resolved to commit himself to the struggle and with *Of Reformation* (1641) began his series of five tracts opposing episcopacy (by its opponents derogatively called "prelacy") as a form of church government (*CPW* IV:618–22).

Given that their occasion was the defense of five Presbyterian divines who, as "Smectymnuus" (a pseudonym constructed from their initials) contested the claims of episcopacy, these tracts are, with the exception of *The Reason of Church-Government*, curiously uninterested in ecclesiology. They have a very great deal to say about bishops, and none of it good, but almost nothing to say about what church polity should replace them. Hence, while Milton may be supposed in 1641–42 to have had Presbyterian sympathies, evidence of firm Presbyterian commitment is wanting. It is not ecclesiology but the prospect of the corrupt and tyrannical exercise of power which animates his writing, as it will do throughout his life. The target is the bishops, or prelates; the alternative, "*Presbytery*, if it must be so call'd" (*CPW* I:610), receives little attention. It is less rival ecclesiastical systems that are opposed than the despotism of coercive authoritarianism and the heroism of the individual conscience. This takes us to the heart of Milton's prose enterprise and to the core value championed by all his tracts, to, indeed, their high seriousness whatever their immediate occasion. It would be for "crowding free consciences and Christian liberties into canons and precepts of men" that in 1644 Milton would condemn the "Prelaticall tradition" in *Areopagitica* (*CPW* II:554), and that theme drives these earlier tracts. By preferring the externalities of uniformity in profession and worship to the sincerity of inner commitment, episcopacy creates not a communion of believers but "a grosse conforming stupidity," the "iron yoke of outward conformity," "the ghost of a linnen decency," "the gripe of custom" (*CPW* II:563–64). Milton presents himself as a test case: convinced that "tyranny had invaded the Church," he refused to "subscribe slave" to secure his ordination and so found himself "Church outed by the Prelats" (*CPW* I:822–23).[12]

In retrospect, Milton came to see these antiprelatical tracts as the first components of a literary enterprise that worked out in prose a coherent libertarian system covering in sequence the "three varieties of liberty without which civilized life is scarcely possible, namely ecclesiastical liberty, domestic or personal liberty, and civil liberty" (*CPW* IV:624). Biographers and commentators have been unpersuaded by this intellectualistic account and have supposed that it was Milton's recent experience of abandonment by his first wife that prompted him to move on to "domestic" liberty in his next series of tracts. The target of *The Doctrine and Discipline of Divorce* (1643) was the law's restriction of divorce to a single physical cause – adultery – which implies that marriage is "a work of the flesh" (*CPW* II:236). Milton's counter-argument, that divorce should be available for incompatibility as well as for infidelity, construes mutual companionship, not sexual intimacy, as the essence of marriage: "*mariage is not a meer carnall coition, but a human Society*" (*CPW* II:275). This leads him to a characteristic formulation: "Love in marriage cannot live nor subsist, unlesse it be mutual; and where love cannot be, there can be left of wedlock nothing, but the empty husk of an outside matrimony; as undelightfull and unpleasing to God, as any other kind of hypocrisie" (*CPW* II:256). While the latent patriarchal prejudice of this and the ensuing three divorce tracts jeopardizes their talk of mutuality,[13] they do undertake a wonderful exercise in Miltonic "free reasoning" in countering the obvious objection based on the absolute dominical prohibition of divorce "saving for the cause of fornication" (Matthew 5:32, 19:9) by elevating as the interpretive key for all biblical texts the "supreme dictate of charitie," the "command above all commands" (*CPW* II:250, 355, alluding to Matthew 22:36–8; Romans 13:10; 1 Timothy 1:5) which is frustrated, not fulfilled, by the "polluting sadnes and perpetuall distemper" of a loveless marriage (*CPW* II:258).[14]

As Stanley Fish remarks, to "show that when Christ *says* a man can put away his wife only for reason of fornication, he *means* that a man can put away his wife for any reason" requires an exercise in hermeneutics "so strenuous that even the word 'manipulation' is too mild to describe it."[15] That after 1600 years Milton should be the "first [who] found out, or at least with a fearlesse and communicative candor first publisht" a "discount'nanc't truth" by rescuing "the words of Christ with other Scriptures of great concernment from burdensom & remorsles obscurity" (*CPW* II:224, 226, 340) seemed equally preposterous to contemporaries, and dangerous besides. Traduced and berated in print as a heretic and libertine proponent of divorce at pleasure, condemned in the Westminster Assembly of Divines and investigated by the Long Parliament, Milton found that the Presbyterians were quite as determined to outlaw dissent from their views as the episcopalians: "Bishops and Presbyters are the same to us both name and thing" (*CPW* II:539).

The third of Milton's "varieties of liberty" – the "civil" – is articulated in just the terms of *Areopagitica* in his 1649 defenses of regicide and in his 1659–60 tracts attempting to prevent the restoration of monarchical government:

> he who holds in religion that beleef or those opinions which to his conscience and utmost understanding appeer with most evidence or probabilitie in the scripture, though to others he seem erroneous, can no more be justly censur'd for a heretic then his censurers . . . To protestants therfore whose common rule and touchstone is the scripture, nothing can with more conscience, more equitie, nothing more protestantly can be permitted then a free and lawful debate at all times by writing, conference or disputation of what opinion soever, disputable by scripture. (*CPW* vii:248–49)

For Milton, it is the business of republican government to facilitate believers' exercise of this intellectual independence: parliamentary supremacy is but a means to the end of religious toleration. To secure this fundamental and unlimited "Christian and euangelic liberty" (*CPW* vii:270) Milton was prepared severely to limit civil liberty: while the former encompasses all (biblically derived) opinions, in the public sphere only a very restricted range of political views is admitted. In his various constitutional models of 1659–60 his self-perpetuating supreme council is elected by, and consists of, those who hold appropriate (that is, Miltonic) political and religious convictions.[16]

The elitism and exclusivity that are consequent marks of Miltonic republicanism were biblically founded. Milton shared with many radical Puritans a fondness for the Old Testament notion of the "godly remnant," reserved by the Lord to fulfill his purposes despite the ungodly and hostile majority.[17] Just so, in *The Tenure of Kings and Magistrates* (1649) he had applauded the exercise of unrepresentative power in bringing Charles I to trial and execution: "If God and a good cause give them Victory" then these "Worthies" are justified in pressing ahead regardless of "the throng and noises of Vulgar and irrational men" (*CPW* iii:192). By empowering Milton to dismiss the views of the "rable" who objected to rule by a small and unrepresentative junto (*CPW* vii:365–66), this conviction that "God hath yet his remnant" (*CPW* vii:363) fatally undermined the polemical force and political persuasiveness of the 1659–60 tracts: it was precisely the right of the "revolutionary elite" to exercise power that royalists and Presbyterians did not accept and was the point to be argued.[18]

The 1659–60 republican tracts, then, hardly succeed as political manifestos. However, as Thomas N. Corns has remarked, republicanism for Milton was, as Presbyterianism had been, more an attitude of mind than a political system.[19] It embodied and articulated a set of values about human nature and potential. As the restoration of monarchy became ever more probable, Milton assumed the role of a prophet bearing witness against a backsliding nation.[20] This witness is structured in *The Readie and Easie Way to Establish a Free Commonwealth* (1660) by a binary rhetoric that opposes, on the one hand, "the noblest, the manliest, the equallest, the justest government, the most agreeable to all due libertie and proportiond equalitie, both humane, civil and Christian" (*CPW* VII:359), conducted by men who "are not elevated above thir brethren, live soberly in thir families, walk the streets as other men, may be spoken to freely, familiarly, friendly, without adoration" (*CPW* VII:360), against, on the other, the government of a king who "must be ador'd like a Demigod, with a dissolute and haughtie court about him, of vast expence and luxurie . . . to set a pompous face upon the superficial actings of State, to pageant himself up and down in progress among the perpetual bowings and cringings of an abject people, on either side deifying and adoring him" (*CPW* VII:360–61). This opposition between republican freedom and monarchical servitude is re-worked and reinforced insistently in *The Readie and Easie Way*, less in political terms than through metaphor, metonymy, and association. Within the register of the former lie: manliness, strength, resilience, nobility, freedom, glory, friendship, confidence, service, magnanimity, integrity, order, naturalness, plainness; and within the latter: womanliness, weakness, softness, debasement, enslavement, ignominy, sycophancy, fear, tyranny, indulgence, hypocrisy, chaos, monstrosity, affectation. Distinguishing good from evil in just these terms, *Paradise Lost* would be the continuation of the pamphlet wars by other means as the right-handed epic bard took up the work of the left-handed pamphleteer.

NOTES

1 *CPW* II:492; and *The Prose Works of Andrew Marvell*, ed. Annabel Patterson *et al.*, 2 vols. (New Haven, 2003), 1:46.
2 Edward Hyde, Earl of Clarendon, *The History of the Rebellion and Civil Wars*, ed. W. Dunn Macray, 6 vols. (1888; Oxford, 1992), II:13, 206.
3 Richard Baxter, *Aphorismes of Justification* (1649), prefatory epistle, A1–A1v; and *The Right Method for a Settled Peace of Conscience* (1653), prefatory epistle, A11. The "Enemy" is, of course, Satan.
4 The phrase provides the title of Christopher Hill's *The World Turned Upside Down: Radical Ideas during the English Revolution* (London, 1972).
5 For statistical data, see John Barnard, D. F. McKenzie, and Maureen Bell, *The Cambridge History of the Book in Britain: Vol. IV: 1557–1695* (Cambridge, 2002), chs. 1, 2, and 26 (esp. 557–67), and appendix 1, from which these figures are taken.

6 See Joad Raymond, *Pamphlets and Pamphleteering in Early Modern Britain* (Cambridge, 2003), esp. 161–201; and Sharon Achinstein, "Texts in Conflict: the Press and the Civil War," in *The Cambridge Companion to Writing of the English Revolution*, ed. N. H. Keeble (Cambridge, 2001), 50–68. Stephen Dobranski discusses seventeenth-century printing practices and censorship in chapter 18 of this volume.

7 For a reading that problematizes this idealism, see e.g. Stanley Fish, "Driving from the Letter: Truth and Indeterminacy in Milton's *Areopagitica*," in *Remembering Milton*, ed. Mary Nyquist and Margaret W. Ferguson (London, 1987), 74–96.

8 Joad Raymond, "The Literature of Controversy," in *A Companion to Milton*, ed. Thomas N. Corns (Oxford, 2001), 202, 205.

9 On Pride's Purge, see David Loewenstein's chapter in this volume.

10 See James Grantham Turner, "The Poetics of Engagement," in *Politics, Poetics and Hermeneutics in Milton's Prose*, ed. David Loewenstein and James Grantham Turner (Cambridge, 1990), 257–75.

11 Raymond, "Literature of Controversy," 201, 202.

12 See Neil Forsyth's chapter in this volume for further discussion of Milton's opposition to the established episcopal church.

13 As noted by e.g. Annabel Patterson, "Milton, Marriage and Divorce," in Corns, *Companion to Milton*, 285–89. See also Shigeo Suzuki's chapter, "Marriage and divorce," in this volume.

14 King James version.

15 Stanley Fish, "Wanting a Supplement," in Loewenstein and Turner, *Politics, Poetics and Hermeneutics*, 54, 55.

16 For the 1659–60 tracts see Laura Lunger Knoppers, "Late Political Prose," in Corns, *Companion to Milton*, 309–25; N. H. Keeble, "'Nothing nobler then a free Commonwealth': Milton's Later Vernacular Republican Tracts," in *The Oxford Handbook to Milton*, ed. Nicholas McDowell and Nigel Smith (Oxford, forthcoming).

17 See e.g. Isaiah 10:20–6; Jeremiah 23:3; Micah 5:7–8; and Zephaniah 3:13.

18 The phrase is from Thomas N. Corns, *Uncloistered Virtue: English Political Literature, 1640–1660* (Oxford, 1992), 197, which quotes this passage.

19 Thomas N. Corns, "Milton and the Characteristics of a Free Commonwealth," in *Milton and Republicanism*, ed. David Armitage, Armand Hiny, and Quentin Skinner (Cambridge, 1995), 25–42 (p. 41).

20 For this view, see James Holstun, *A Rational Millennium: Puritan Utopias of Seventeenth-Century England and America* (Oxford, 1987), 246–65; Laura Lunger Knoppers, "Milton's *Readie and Easie Way* and the English Jeremiad," in Loewenstein and Turner, *Politics, Poetics and Hermeneutics*, 213–25.

CHAPTER 37

Philosophy

Pitt Harding

Given the age-old quarrel between philosophy and poetry, it might be tempting to take as Milton's final judgment on philosophy the rejection of the Athenian academy by his Jesus in *Paradise Regained*: whoever seeks wisdom there, we are told, finds "An empty cloud" (IV.321). The rebuke seems consistent with Adam's view in *Paradise Lost* that lofty speculation is mere "fume, / Or emptiness, or fond impertinence" (VIII.194–95). Uninspired by revelation, it seems, philosophical inquiry leads to a vaporous nothing. With characteristic ambivalence, though, the musically sensitive Milton first allows the Satan of *Paradise Regained* to tempt Jesus by investing "the olive grove of Academe" with pleasing aural sensations: "the Attic bird / Trills her thick-warbled notes the summer long," and the "bees' industrious murmur oft invites / To studious musing" (IV.244–46, 248–49). Albeit from the Tempter's lips, this association of philosophy with a peaceful place of retirement, where spontaneous natural music encourages musing, directs us back to the "shady spaces of philosophy" that Milton visited in his youth, according to his own testimony in *An Apology against a Pamphlet* (*CPW* I:891), and to the Second Brother in *A Mask* who exults: "How charming is divine philosophy! / Not harsh and crabbèd as dull fools suppose, / But musical as is Apollo's lute" (lines 476–78). Earlier still, in his seventh Prolusion, Milton invokes "divinus *Plato*" for the image of Socrates and Phaedrus discussing friendship "in the shade of that famous plane-tree" ("*sub illa platano*") – wordplay that gives philosophical discourse another attractive local habitation (*CPW* I:295; *WJM* XII:264). We know that Milton felt that students in his day were introduced too soon to the "intellective abstractions" of scholasticism, that Spenser was a better teacher than Duns Scotus, and that poetry should take precedence (in esteem, if not in sequence) over classical rhetoric, as being "more simple, sensuous and passionate" (*CPW* II:374, 516, 403). From these instances we might infer an impatience with bodiless abstraction and a desire to sensualize the activities of the mind.

The philosophical trend most attractive to English poets in the decades before Milton's birth, Renaissance Neoplatonism, ran in the opposite direction. It led from the illusory world of the senses to ecstatic union with an incorporeal Ideal. A tradition extending from the *Enneads* of Plotinus had elaborated the mystical elements of Platonism (chiefly visible in *Timaeus*) and augmented them with hermeticism to produce a body of doctrines bordering on the occult. The Platonism received in early modern England by way of Marsilio Ficino and the Florentine Academy is epitomized by the transformation of Diotima's lesson to Socrates (*Symposium*) into Peter Bembo's elaborate meditation on love in the fourth book of Hoby's translated *Book of the Courtier* (1561), where the *scala amoris* elevates the lover from sensual desire to contemplation of ideal Beauty.[1] The poetry of Sidney and Spenser, to name but two sixteenth-century figures influenced by this version of Platonism, frequently sustains a tension between the competing claims of earthly and heavenly bliss. In any case, beginning with the doctrine of Christ as the incarnate *logos*, Christianity was so deeply infused with Greek philosophy – Nietzsche called it "Platonism for 'the people'" – that theology students such as Milton could scarcely escape its influence.[2] Platonized Christianity shapes the opening stanzas of the Nativity Ode, which place emphasis on *kenosis*, the voluntary emptying-out of divinity, by which the heavenly Son surrenders his "glorious form" to enter the body's "darksome house of mortal clay" (lines 8, 14). A Platonist dualism is voiced, too, by the speaker in *Il Penseroso* when he invokes "thrice-great Hermes" (Hermes Trismegistus, putative author of ancient esoteric texts) and in the next breath longs to "unsphere / The spirit of Plato" to disclose "what vast regions hold / The immortal mind that hath forsook / Her mansion in this fleshly nook" (lines 88–92). Plato, like Hermes, here serves mainly as a convenient custodian of a realm of pure spirit. A similar dichotomy between the spiritual and the earthly appears when the *Phaedo* supplies the opening image of *A Mask*: the Attendant Spirit (called a "daemon" in the manuscripts) arrives from a palace of eternal composure where "bright aërial spirits live ensphered / In regions mild of calm and serene air, / Above the smoke and stir of this dim spot, / Which men call earth" (lines 3–6). However vividly expressed in sensory imagery, the early poetry's sharp distinction between matter and spirit falls within the conventions of the day.

Beyond this youthful Platonizing, though, Milton apparently devoted serious study to the rational arguments in the Socratic dialogues, before and during the years of civil war, for he cites Plato with increased specificity as a respected authority in his antiprelatical writings and in the divorce tracts.[3] Describing the formation of his views on chastity in *An Apology*, for example, he credits the "divine volumes of *Plato*," chiefly the *Symposium*, for his awareness that "the first and chiefest office of love, begins and ends in the soule" (*CPW* 1:891–92). From this source too (perhaps by way of the *scala amoris*) would eventually come Raphael's lesson to Adam in *Paradise Lost* that "love refines / The thoughts" and "is the scale / By which to Heav'nly love thou may'st ascend" (VIII.589–90, 591–92). On the question of what constitutes the good life, Milton adopts Plato's hierarchy of values and uses it to attack the Laudian church. If pleasure gratifies the lowest level of the soul, as Plato held, then Milton could argue that idolatry perverts religion in the same way that hedonism perverts ethics: "they pamper what they should restrain," in Irene Samuel's memorable formulation.[4] Where Milton might be expected to dissent most sharply from Plato, the banning of poets from the ideal republic, Samuel observes that in fact Milton accepts Plato's contention that poetry exerts a powerful ethical influence, is too often misused, and should serve a didactic purpose – or, as Milton puts it in *An Apology*, "a true Poem" must be "a composition, and patterne of the best and honourablest things" (*CPW* 1:890). In *The Reason of Church-Government* he endorses the Platonic view that persuasion serves the cause of moral improvement better than force, and advises "them in autority" to encourage recreation and moral instruction rather than merely prohibiting incitements to vice (*CPW* 1:816–20). Poetry's power of persuasion turns poets into teachers if they direct it toward its proper ends, which Milton enumerates in *Reason* while substituting Christian worship for the pagan subjects in book 7 of Plato's *Laws*. In *Areopagitica* he endorses Plato's reliance on what he calls the "laws of vertuous education, religious and civill nurture" as the basis of all just legal codes (*CPW* II:526). Thus he shares Plato's respect for poetry's power to persuade and instruct, but he transfers the censoring function from civil and religious authorities to poets themselves.[5] Although Milton never explicitly embraced the Platonic theory of forms, which he playfully mocked in an academic exercise (*De Idea Platonica*), he does use the terms "idea" and "form" and "essential form" throughout his prose in a plausibly Platonic sense, to signify a perfected or inner reality distinct from imperfect outward appearances.[6] The creation of the earth out of formless elements by a single divinity (as in *Timaeus*), the ethical value of various musical modes (*Republic*), and the music of the spheres (a conception derived from Plato by way of Pythagoras) all inform his thinking; they share the theme that the disposition of elements into harmonious order has both aesthetic and ethical dimensions. In the soul, according to Plato, disharmony arises when reason fails to subordinate the passions. Milton's Raphael says of the soul that "reason is her being" (*Paradise Lost* v.487), and Michael refers to "virtue, which is reason" (xii.98), while informing Adam that the inner tyranny of unbridled passion and appetite will result in political tyranny: "true liberty / Is lost" when "upstart passions catch the government / From reason, and to servitude reduce / Man till then free" (xii.83–84, 88–90). As in the Platonic republic, the condition of the state mirrors the condition of the soul. Milton urges his compatriots in *Defensio Secunda* to "learn to obey right reason, to master yourselves" (*CPW* iv:684). The alternative is the anarchy of "barbarous dissonance" (*A Mask*, line 550; *Paradise Lost* vii.32) – a disruptive possibility that seems to have haunted Milton all his life. He continued to hold Plato in high regard, repeatedly giving him the epithet "divine" in a more than merely conventional nod to his preeminence. While denying that Greek philosophers attained wisdom, the Jesus of *Paradise Regained* still terms Socrates "The first and wisest of them all" (iv.293).

The chief alternative to Platonism in Milton's day was the Aristotelian tradition. Mediated by centuries of commentary and modified by scholastic philosophy, the works of Aristotle remained so entrenched in the curriculum that Milton could call him "our chief instructer in the Universities" (*CPW* vii:448). He cites Aristotle even more frequently than he does Plato, sometimes pairing them in support of the same view. Hence, Aristotelian concepts can be found across the range of his writing; a few examples must suffice. First, Aristotle's attempt to delineate the structural principles of various literary modes bears fruit in Milton's approach to composition. John Steadman observes that an orientation toward Aristotelian rationalism makes *Paradise Lost* "more logical, more tightly conceived and articulated, than any of the epics or tragedies lauded in the *Poetics*." From the Aristotelian principles underlying early modern poetic theory came the demand that narrative writing should pass muster intellectually – that characters should speak and act in a manner appropriate both to their station and to their moral character, and that the action should unfold plausibly, with a causal relationship between character and plot: "[t]he tight logical structure of Milton's epic and the prominence he assigns to the analysis of the causes and effects of the central action reflect this rationalistic approach."[7] The defining features of the tragic plot described in the *Poetics* – *hamartia* (error of judgment), *anagnorisis* (recognition), *peripeteia* (reversal of fortune) – have been traced by Barbara Lewalski within the action of Milton's epic.[8] Milton's Preface to *Samson Agonistes* cites the famous discussion of tragedy in the *Poetics* and extends its definition of the tragic effect to encompass both homeopathic and musical meanings: to "purge" pity and terror, Milton says, is to "temper and reduce them to just measure" (*CPEP* 707) – aggravating the passions so as to restore mental balance and harmony.[9]

Aristotelian influence is most visible in Milton's treatment of ethics. His praise of Cromwell in *Defensio Secunda* for "magnanimity" and for being "victor over himself" (*CPW* IV:672, 668) invokes the virtues of the magnanimous man described in the *Nicomachean Ethics*, who restrains himself through *sophrosyne* or wise self-government.[10] The exposition of ethics in book 2 of *De Doctrina Christiana* draws from Aristotle the method of defining virtue as the mean between contrasting pairs: magnanimity strikes a balance between pride and pusillanimity; liberality avoids the extremes of niggardliness and prodigality (*CPW* VI:735–37, 779). Perhaps the most important concept derived from Aristotle's elaboration of Plato is "that act of reason which in *Ethics* is call'd *Proairesis*," as Milton writes in his tractate *Of Education* (*CPW* II:396). *Proairesis*, or rational choice preceded by deliberation, can be exercised only by free beings. The liberty to choose underlies *Areopagitica*'s argument against pre-publication licensing; moreover, it supports Milton's theodicy by negating determinism: "many there be that complain of divin Providence for suffering *Adam* to transgresse, foolish tongues! when God gave him reason, he gave him freedom to choose, for reason is but choosing; he had bin else a meer artificiall *Adam*" (*CPW* II:527). The sufficiency of Adam's power to choose is so key to the theodicy of *Paradise Lost* that Milton has God affirm the Aristotelian principle by stating it parenthetically: "(reason also is choice)" (III.108).

In the realms of physics and metaphysics, Milton can again be found negotiating with Aristotle to enlarge the scope of free will. On the one hand, in *De Doctrina Christiana* he explicitly dissents from Aristotle's conception of God as pure actuality (*actus purus*), for to deny God potentiality would be to circumscribe his freedom to act in ways other than those he has chosen (*CPW* VI:145–46). On the other hand, as John Rumrich demonstrates, the divine creative process discussed in the treatise and dramatized in *Paradise Lost* shows basic points of agreement with Aristotle. Milton's argument against creation *ex nihilo* parallels certain passages in the *Metaphysics*, and his Chaos resembles Aristotle's "first matter." Notably, in both treatise and epic, Milton adopts an Aristotelian shift in emphasis: in place of a cosmos defined by a dichotomy between appearance and reality, as in Plato, we find a dynamic interaction between potency and act. As "the mode of reality's progress from chaos to perfection," says Rumrich, change is fundamental to Milton's cosmos: "creatures *must* change in order to become what God wants."[11]

It is on this question of substance (*ousia*) that Milton obliquely addressed the most pressing philosophical issues of his day. Although he never took part publicly in philosophical debate, new developments in seventeenth-century philosophy appear to have altered his thinking during the 1640s and 1650s, resulting in a new conception of the relation between spirit and body. As Stephen Fallon has shown, Platonists such as Henry More and Ralph Cudworth, centered at Milton's college at Cambridge, were alarmed by a resurgence of Epicurean atomism, which was thought to undermine the foundation of morality, and even more by the new mechanistic philosophy of Thomas Hobbes (1588–1679).[12] Hobbes posited that nothing exists but matter in motion. Even mental events should be understood as purely material phenomena: "*Conceptions* and *apparitions* are nothing *really*, but *motion* in some internal substance of the *head*."[13] All else was mere superstition. Hobbes denied being an atheist, but his denial of incorporeal spirit was widely viewed as tending in that direction: "*No Spirit, no God*," wrote More.[14] In what amounts to a secularized version of Calvinist determinism, Hobbes argued that we act only out of necessity, for to believe otherwise would set limits on God's omnipotence. Englishmen troubled by this denial of human freedom initially welcomed the writings of René Descartes (1596–1650), whose radical dualism preserved human reason and will within an incorporeal domain (*res cogitans*) distinct from the material world (*res extensa*). Yet Descartes too posited a mechanistic universe and so, it was thought, left ample room for Hobbesian determinism. The Cambridge Platonists offered systematic refutations of these new mechanistic philosophies by arguing for various versions of Incorporealism: Cudworth's "plastic nature" and More's "spirit of nature" were proposed as forces acting upon material bodies to give them form and movement.[15]

In all his published work Milton never mentions Hobbes or Descartes by name; he was not, strictly speaking, a philosopher, and though deeply engaged with philosophical issues he never set forth a systematic philosophy. Yet he knew men who were involved in the debate over substance and free will, and it is during the 1650s when this debate raged that he formulated, explicitly in *De Doctrina Christiana* and implicitly in *Paradise Lost*, a metaphysics of animist materialism. This view of substance breaks with centuries of Christian orthodoxy, rather startlingly, by dispensing with the dichotomy between spirit and matter.[16] The human being, he writes, "is not double or separable: not, as is commonly thought, produced from and composed of two different and distinct elements, soul and body. On the contrary, the whole man is the soul, and the soul the man: a body, in other words, or individual substance, animated, sensitive, and rational" (*CPW* VI:318). Finding no scriptural warrant for the idea that spirit exists separately from the body, Milton embraces mortalism, the belief that the soul dies with the body to await their simultaneous resurrection (*CPW* VI:319, 404). This radical monism, which unites spirit and body as manifestations of one substance, accepts Hobbes' assumption that everything is material, but it invests matter with a potential for transformation defined by its moral standing in relationship to God. Thus Raphael in *Paradise Lost* describes to Adam a continuum along which, within limits, all created things may rise or fall to conditions of greater or lesser spiritual refinement. All things were formed by God from "one first matter," says Raphael, and living creatures are simply "more refined, more spiritous, and pure, / As nearer to him placed or nearer tending... / ... Till body up to spirit work" (v.472, 475–76, 478). To illustrate the vital potency by which living matter may become more "spiritous," Raphael adduces a flowering plant: from its root springs a stalk, thence leaves "More airy," and "last the bright consummate flow'r / Spirits odorous breathes" (v.479–82). The botanical image is more than metaphorical: not only do earthbound roots aspire to produce more spiritous flowers, but by partaking of the flower's fruit, the human body initiates a digestive process that yields "vital spirits" enabling thought and movement. Ontologically, body and spirit differ only in degree: even the most "spiritous" substance retains material form. Hence Milton's angels, unlike the immaterial beings of tradition, are able to eat, blush, and enjoy an angelic version of sex. Conversely, all matter holds the potential to become more attenuated. Raphael instructs Adam that metabolic processes might eventually dissolve any distinction between the human and the angelic: "from these corporal nutriments perhaps / Your bodies may at last turn all to spirit, / Improved by tract of time" (v.496–98).[17]

This remarkable teleology blends metaphysics and ethics, for Milton's sapient creatures determine their own position along the material continuum by giving or withholding loving obedience to its creative source. Unlike Raphael, the rebellious angels become grossly corporeal by moving farther from God: their hearts literally harden, and their forms congeal into an oppressive materiality. They end in Hell, a "universe of death" (II.622), because they have chosen to inhabit a mechanistic Hobbesian universe. Satan then resorts to a diabolical Cartesian dualism: "Though changed in outward luster," he claims to retain his "fixed mind," and asserts that "The mind is its own place" (I.97, 254). Insofar as his desperate embrace of duality begets a world of woe, Satan could be said to pioneer the fallen state of being wherein Milton's isolated narrator will entertain nightly visitations from his muse while compassed round with dangers, and Adam's consolation for relinquishing outward Eden must be "a paradise within" (XII.587). But Satan's own position is undermined by the deterioration of his body, until, in the course of the poem, he descends through progressively grosser and more corporeal forms. Given the fate of the fallen angels, Fallon perhaps understates the case when he observes that "[m]oral choices in *Paradise Lost* have implications for choices about where one wishes to be placed along the continuum of the one first matter."[18]

That Milton's animist monism was formulated in response to contemporary debates may have eluded previous commentary because it is not glaringly inconsistent with his earlier views. As early as *A Mask* he had expressed the idea that moral status determines ontological status: the Elder Brother says that for chaste souls, heavenly vision enlightens the body, "And turns it by degrees to the soul's essence, / Till all be made immortal" (lines 462–63). Conversely, by indulging base appetites "The soul grows clotted by contagion, / Embodies and imbrutes" (lines 467–68). Furthermore, Milton would have found versions of monism in the course of his vast reading. Among the Church Fathers, Origen dismissed "imaginary" Platonic ideas and "an incorporeal world that exists solely in the mind's fancy or the unsubstantial region of thought," holding instead that

material substance possesses such a nature that it can undergo every kind of transformation. When therefore it is drawn down to lower beings it is formed into the grosser and more solid condition of body . . . But when it ministers to more perfect and blessed beings, it shines in the splendour of "celestial bodies" and adorns either the "angels of God" or the "sons of the resurrection" with the garments of a "spiritual body."[19]

While this materialistic monism might have given the Cambridge Platonists pause, Origen was the Father they esteemed most highly, and he had earlier been accepted as well by the Florentine Neoplatonists.[20] Whatever sources might have influenced Milton's thinking, though, he took a position that sought to resolve the contemporary debate: it accepted Hobbesian materialism while investing matter with spiritual potency, and explained the mind–body gulf identified by Descartes as a function of morality. Grounded in a Platonized Christianity that elevates being over becoming – and bound by a creation myth that traces human origins to a single, fully formed male adult – Milton nonetheless tried to account for organic growth and development, to the extent of allowing bodily functions to participate in his salvific scheme. Philosophical merit aside, it brilliantly unifies an epic cosmos in which the cataclysmic event is an act of eating.

In a mechanistic universe, Nietzsche chillingly remarks, "the living being is only a species of the dead – and a very rare species."[21] For Milton, though, life is not an anomaly in a world of dead matter; it is matter's usual condition. He strips the soul of its special status, and even its immortality, so as to celebrate this vitality. In Fallon's words, "It is as if he is saying that the deadness of the material world is too great a price to pay for the immortality of a separable soul."[22] Perhaps it testifies to Milton's generosity of spirit that, in his later years when disability lodged him in the truly "darksome clay" of a sightless body, plagued by painful gout, he could not only exalt celestial light but also find in material forms an abundant spiritual potential.

NOTES

1 *The Book of the Courtier, from the Italian of Count Baldassare Castiglione: done into English by Sir Thomas Hoby, anno 1561* (New York, 1967).
2 Friedrich Nietzsche, *Beyond Good and Evil*, trans. R. J. Hollingdale (Harmondsworth, 1973), 14.
3 Irene Samuel, *Plato and Milton* (Ithaca, NY, 1947), 3–25. No English translation of Plato appeared until 1675, but Ficino's editions in Greek and Latin, with commentary, were available from the early sixteenth century onwards.
4 *Ibid.*, 73.
5 *Ibid.*, 45–67.
6 *Ibid.*, 131–47.
7 John M. Steadman, *Milton's Epic Characters* (Oxford, 1968), x, ix.
8 Barbara K. Lewalski, *"Paradise Lost" and the Rhetoric of Literary Forms* (Princeton, 1985), 225–53.
9 John K. Hale, "Milton's Preface to *Samson Agonistes*," *Explicator* 52.2 (1994): 73–75.
10 James S. Baumlin, "The Aristotelian Ethic of Milton's *Paradise Regained*," *Renascence* 47.1 (1994): 41–57 (p. 41).
11 John Rumrich, *Matter of Glory: A New Preface to "Paradise Lost"* (Pittsburgh, PA, 1987), 54–5, 70.
12 Stephen M. Fallon, *Milton Among the Philosophers: Poetry and Materialism in Seventeenth-Century England* (Ithaca, NY, 1991), 20, 30–41.
13 Thomas Hobbes, *De Homine* 7.1, quoted *ibid.*, 34.
14 Henry More, *An Antidote Against Atheism* (London, 1653), quoted in C. A. Patrides, ed., *The Cambridge Platonists* (Cambridge, MA, 1970), 32.
15 Fallon, *Milton Among the Philosophers*, 37, 21–30, 53–54.
16 *Ibid.*, 8–10, 98.
17 *Ibid.*, 103–06.

18 *Ibid.*, 203–09, 202.
19 Origen, *On First Principles [De Principiis]*, trans. G. W. Butterworth (New York, 1966), 90, 81–2; see also Harry F. Robins, *If This Be Heresy: A Study of Milton and Origen* (Urbana, IL, 1963).
20 Patrides, ed., *Platonists*, 5.
21 R. J. Hollingdale, ed. and trans., *A Nietzsche Reader* (Harmondsworth, 1977), 201.
22 Fallon, *Milton Among the Philosophers*, 107.

CHAPTER 38

Reading practices

Elizabeth Sauer

This chapter reviews the confluence of writing and transgressive reading practices in two complementary but traditionally unpaired works by John Milton: his Commonplace Book and *Areopagitica*. Conscious of his civic, intellectual, and moral responsibilities in an emerging nation and heavily invested in the politico-religious conflicts and intellectual debates of the day, Milton documented his "judicious conversing" (*CPW* ii:373) with ancient and contemporary continental readers, historians, travel writers, mathematicians and scientists, jurists, musicians, tragedians, philosophers, poets, geographers, orientalists, patriarchs, and theologians through which he paradoxically established his Englishness. Early modern "distinctions between writers – poets, historians, dramatists – were far less rigid than our own" and nationhood was likewise more porous, developing alongside various allegiances, consciousnesses, and practices.[1] The habits of reading and authorship documented here are exercises in education, liberty, and citizenship. Milton aligns his intellectual pursuits not only with the cultivation of civility but also the "reforming of Reformation" through active engagement with books "promiscuously read" and digested.[2] Redirecting the focus of "internationalists" such as Thomas More and Erasmus, Milton applies humanist principles and translates his involvement in a republic of letters to the writing of a Protestant national identity.[3]

As he rehearses the earlier achievements of his left hand up to *Areopagitica*, Milton in the *Defensio Secunda* (1654) celebrates the advances he made to the "cause of true and substantial liberty" and specifically England's "ecclesiastical liberty, domestic or personal, and civil liberty" (*CPW* iv:624). That the *Defensio* also commends Oliver Cromwell's cultivation of the true religion and preservation of liberty (*CPW* iv:666–75) reinforces the correspondence between the writer's and the politician's national contributions. In the Commonplace Book and *Areopagitica*, such accomplishments are represented by a program of reading, writing, and education modeled for an active citizenry, a liberty-loving Reformation nation.[4]

Originally a holograph and then the product of scribal hands, the manuscript of Milton's Commonplace Book records his sources and annotations on his reading from his college years until 1665.[5] More than half of the entries, however, date from the early middle period – 1640 up to the publication of *Areopagitica* in 1644 – thus underscoring its relationship to Milton's treatise on the impediments to and liberty of reading. Both works offer evidence of extensive, yet also discontinuous, reading and of the correspondences between reading and the "labour of book-writing" (*CPW* II:532). The interrelationship of these practices testifies to what Stephen Dobranski has characterized as the "ill-defined" boundary between reading and writing during the seventeenth century.[6] The authorities Milton quotes, annotates, and applies also bridged that divide, thus making writing a habit of reading.[7]

Stephen Orgel describes marginalia as "the legible incorporation of the work of reading into the text of the book," a definition that could as readily be applied to commonplacing, which displays a confluence of reading and writing.[8] "Reading and writing were . . . inseparable activities," Robert Darnton asserts; "they belonged to a continuous effort to make sense of things, for the world was full of signs: you could read your way through it; and by keeping an account of your readings, you made a book of your own, one stamped with your personality."[9] Judged as "perhaps the most reliable account of his reading that we have," Milton's Commonplace Book has been interpreted accordingly.[10] William Riley Parker summarizes the observations made by James Holly Hanford's 1921 biographical study of Milton's private studies that first discussed the Commonplace Book. Parker supports Hanford's claim that the work offers considerable information about Milton's reading in 1642–45 undertaken for the purpose of self-education rather than for practical or controversial purposes: "The object was self-cultivation, the general enrichment and maturing of the mind through liberal study . . . He was preparing himself intellectually . . . for service the future might bring."[11] In the Preface to her edition of Milton's Commonplace Book, Ruth Mohl likewise distances the Book from Milton's controversialist roles, affirming instead that the work exhibits its author's "essential oneness of purpose and the continuity of thought that make his prose, poetry, and drama so unmistakably his" (*CPW* I:358). She applies the same interpretation in her monograph on the Commonplace Book published a year after Parker's biography, and concludes that the entries from some 90 authors and 110 books were employed for intellectual not polemical purposes.[12] Mohl's reading upholds the standard definition of the commonplace book as "a private compilation."[13]

Miltonists occasionally reference the Commonplace Book as a gloss and mine it for evidence of Milton's sources, but since Mohl's 1969 study, it has rarely been cited in scholarship on Milton, book history, readerships, and book culture. Acknowledging this oversight, Kevin Sharpe determines that the work "awaits full study as a document of reading" that yields information on "how [Milton] extracted passages, and how they fashioned his own writings and thought."[14] In his argument about Sir William Drake, Sharpe demonstrated the function of active reading in the process of self-fashioning and in the act of preparation for Drake's vigorous participation in the volatile and politically charged climate of seventeenth-century England. While still approaching commonplacing as an exercise in self-formation, as early Milton scholars had done, Sharpe ascertains that Milton, who like Drake understood that "ways of reading were implicated with the exercise of power," read himself into a political role. "To Milton reading *was* politics,"[15] and that is also the thrust of Barbara Lewalski's brief though astute remarks on the Commonplace Book in her biography of Milton.[16] Drawing on the critical tradition from Milton's Commonplace Book, the next part of this chapter investigates transgressive reading practices in terms of the negotiation of humanist and nationalist thinking.

Through the art of commonplacing, humanists sought to compartmentalize knowledge in terms of *communes loci* or "common places." Synonymous since Aristotle's time, "arguments" and "places" were "'building blocks of common knowledge and *thus* basic elements of social cohesion,'" but subject to individual assembly, often resulting in associations particular to the early modern era and unfamiliar to ours.[17] *Of Education* teaches that Milton's study of pedagogical methods and philosophies was derived in part from Erasmus, the Dutch humanist, whose *Adagia, Colloquia, De duplici copia*, and the adaptations thereof formed part of the curriculum. The importance of reading the best classical writers, of which Milton boasts, and the moral spiritual benefits derived thereby, reveal an indebtedness to *De copia verborum*, which offered a method for disciplined reading, classification, digestion, and assembly of literary subjects.[18] According to the humanist Erasmus, "right reading" was "an ethical practice, an inculcation and practice of virtue and prudence"; it was moreover, a means of cultivating and modeling citizenship "in a Christian commonweal."[19] For Milton, however, that commonwealth would be defined by a specifically Protestant ethic and linguistic nationalism. Unlike his predecessor, Milton also championed the study of the vernacular – "I beare to my native language . . . ere

I assay the verdit of outlandish readers" (*CPW* II:233) – and thereby helped delineate the contours and language of England's Reformation nation.

An examination of the social nature of reading practices also needs to address material culture – the bookshops, libraries, and the marketplace of print in which the works are or are not available and affordable. As *Areopagitica* demonstrates, the material context is shaped by the socio-political conditions that encouraged or frustrated the production of books and the book trade. Milton's reading history includes visits to publishing houses and London booksellers, with whom he was also acquainted.[20] His "continu[ous] reading" (*CPW* I:327) was fed and directed not only through a humanistic education, for which reading is the primary medium, but also through visits to libraries, through the amassing of his own library, and through correspondence with teachers and scholars, acquaintances, and editors.[21] An early letter addressed to Thomas Young thanks the teacher for a copy of the Hebrew Bible (*CPW* I:312). 1637 correspondence with Charles Diodati refers to the Greek and Italian histories Milton read, and mentions his request for a copy of Giustiniani Bernardo's *De Origine Urbis Venetiarum Rebusque ad Ipsa Gestis Historia* (Venice, 1492). Correspondence with Lukas Holste in 1639 acknowledges indebtedness to the Vatican librarian for access Milton was granted to "the invaluable collection of Books, and also the numerous Greek Authors in manuscript" annotated by Holste (*CPW* I:333). *An Apology* (1642) justifies Milton's deliberately selective reading of the volumes on the reign of Constantine: "surely to sit out the whole extent of their tattle in a dozen volumes, would be a losse of time irrecoverable . . . I have not therefore I confesse read more of the Councels save here and there, I should be sorry to have bin such a prodigall of my time." Extensive reading being a means of establishing one's authority, as Erasmus earlier testified, Milton professes to his opponent thereafter: "but that which is better, I can assure this Confuter; I have read into them all" (*CPW* I:944–45).

That Milton conceptualizes reading as a communal experience is apparent in his definition of the practice as "a well continu'd and judicious conversing among pure Authors digested" (*CPW* II:373). The digestion metaphor is originally Senecan but popular in Milton's time. Resisting medieval scholasticism and passive reception, digestion is evidenced in the Commonplace Book in Milton's annotations and in the assembly of entries featuring classical and humanist works alongside biblical entries and selected contemporary writings. As such, the Commonplace Book is more than a "topic folio" dismissed in *Areopagitica* as one of the props used by "parochiall" clergy, the modifier connoting geographic and intellectual narrowness (*CPW* II:546). Milton's Book is also distinguished by its arrangement as a social and educational manual, as well of course by the application of most of the entries in other writings – a further stage in the acts of consumption and digestion.[22]

The processing and synthesis of readings through the use of topics and headings was recommended by Erasmus and by Francis Bacon, who likely adopted an Aristotelian model in developing his own moral, domestic/private (or economic), and political indexes. In the medieval period Aristotle's political and moral philosophy had informed Giles of Rome's mirror for princes, *De Regimine Principum*, the first book of which treats the moral or religious; the second, the domestic; the third, the political.[23] The *ethica-oeconomica-politica* scheme was adapted by the humanist intellectual tradition, which emphasized the serviceable nature of reading and connected educational theory and rulership. Milton applies the scheme in the Commonplace Book, suggesting that readers and reading are the foundations for a nation conceptualized in terms of the tripartite structure. The Commonplace Book thereby assumes a public dimension, while also complementing Milton's writing program designed to advance national liberty within three contexts – ecclesiastical, personal, and civil.

Milton cites and annotates a larger number of secular than religious writings, although he likely compiled a theological index for the latter. The undiscovered index is cited six times in the Commonplace Book, including in the Ethical Index where "Of Church Property" is referenced alongside "Avarice" (*CPW* 1:365), and in the Political Index where a heading on church–state relations has a marginal reference to "Of Not Forcing Religion" (*CPW* 1:477). The cross-referencing of headings – "Marriage" and "Divorce" (*CPW* 1:393), and "Of the Education of Children" and "Of the Knowledge of Literature" (*CPW* 1:405), for example – and the illustrations of composite readings suggest the simultaneous use of multiple works as well as their fragmentation and investment with new significances through their arrangement.[24] The fluidity of Milton's epistemology is conspicuous in such sections as "Marriage," which concludes with entries from the imaginative literature of Geoffrey Chaucer, the *Historia* of Italian Paolo [Pietro] Sarpi, and John Selden's *Uxor Hebraica*, cross-referenced with a heading from the theological index (*CPW* 1:402). The patterns of assembly in the Commonplace Book thus depend both on the creation of reading units and on segmental and discontinuous rather than linear or sequential reading habits.

The sacred and civil or political, the radical and orthodox are juxtaposed under the same headings throughout the Book, thereby showcasing the "ideas and ideals of a well-informed, judicious liberal."[25] Detailing his early liberal engagement with books, Milton defends extensive, transgressive reading as an exercise in virtue: "So that even those books which to many others have bin the fuell of wantonnesse and loose living, I cannot thinke how unlesse by divine indulgence prov'd to me so many incitements as you have heard, to the love and stedfast observation of that vertue which abhorres the society of Bordello's" (*CPW* 1:891). The practice has historical precedents which Milton amasses: contained in the Ethical Index, "Of the Knowledge of Literature," which represents among the earliest of the headings in the Commonplace Book, includes quotations from such early Greek historians as Eusebius and Evagrius on questions of reading of profane writers (*CPW* 1:376). Socrates Scholasticus' example of the Apostle Paul's use of Greek literature, Eusebius' example of Dionysius of Alexandria, and Theodoret's quotation from Julian the Apostate justify immersion in pagan literary traditions. That Eusebius makes his way into each index of the Commonplace Book reveals the interconnectedness of the issues outlined and categorized in the work, while also highlighting the discontinuous nature of reading practices and the partitioning of Milton's sources and knowledge generally.[26]

In formulating a theory of transgressive reading as expression and validation of liberty, Milton turns to an examination of secular and political evidence. The opening entries under "Gentleness" in the Political Index are units, producing conjoined, even interwoven, sites of reading. Sir Henry Savile's *Rerum Anglicarum Scriptores post Bedam Praecipui* (1596) includes five histories of which William of Malmesbury's *De Gestis Regum Anglorum* is the first, and which in turn is juxtaposed with John Stow's *Annales, or Generall Chronicle of England* (1580; 1615 folio edn.) on the dangers of clemency. A compound entry featuring Tacitus' anti-censorship pronouncement and Francis Bacon's 1641 observation, "forbidden writing is thought to be a certain spark of truth that flyeth up in the faces of them that seek to chok and tread it out, wheras a book authorized is thought to be but the language of the time," exhibits the dangers of failed clemency (*CPW* 1:450).[27] Histories by de Thou (Jacobus Augustus Thuanus) and Sarpi, an opponent of papal secular authority, are cited for evidence of the advantages of reading books by one's rivals: "What benefit can be derived for the glory of God from the books of our opponents" (*CPW* 1:451). Together, the entries under "Gentleness" propose an exploration of the topic from various angles, the juxtaposition of contraries providing the means for approaching truth, which supports "more shapes then one" (*CPW* 11:563).

In the Commonplace Book Milton extracts from Bacon's oeuvre one key quotation that he then uses in support of *Areopagitica*'s main theme on transgressive reading: "*authoriz'd books*" represent "*but the language of the times*" (*CPW* 11:534).[28] The commonplaces in *Areopagitica* generally encourage engagement with unauthorized, unlicensed books as an ethical act and civil/political right, and as a practice integral to the educational program onto which the reading habits are mapped in the Commonplace Book. *Areopagitica* thus continues the work of the Commonplace Book by featuring books as the material, epistemological, and philosophical media for liberty and citizenship.

In *Of Education* Milton reconciles the classical and Christian traditions, adding transgressive reading to the education theory of John Amos Comenius and Juan Luis Vives, both of whom condemned heathen writers. Deriving his authority from "many studious and contemplative yeers altogether spent in the search of religious and civil knowledge," Milton judges that the reformation of learning is the key to the health of the nation and the "repa[ration of] the ruins of our first parents" (*CPW* 11:366–67).[29] Accordingly, the educational model he furnishes is designed to fashion "stedfast pillars of the State" (*CPW* 11:398). Published in the same year as his treatise on education, *Areopagitica* designates reading and writing as exercises in education and civic participation. "[T]hose unwritt'n, or at least unconstraining laws of vertuous education, religious and civill nurture" serve as "the bonds and ligaments of the Commonwealth, the pillars and the sustainers of every writt'n Statute" (*CPW* 11:526). Sublimating his authorial identity in *Areopagitica*, Milton appeals instead in the exordium to a public cause to "promote" the "Countries liberty" through the exercise of "civill liberty" and civil duty (*CPW* 11:487). This assurance diverts attention from personal motives for presenting the argument, like that of responding to attacks on his divorce tracts: "this is not therefore the disburdning of a particular fancie, but the common grievance of all those who had prepar'd their minds and studies above the vulgar pitch to advance truth in others" (*CPW* 11:539). In fashioning a social identity, Milton characterizes the favorable reception of his appeal to the Areopagus as validation of civil rights: "when complaints are freely heard, deeply consider'd, and speedily reform'd, then is the utmost bound of civill liberty attain'd, that wise men looke for" (*CPW* 11:487). Representing "lerned men at home" who were echoing "lerned men of other parts" (*CPW* 11:539), the public orator imagines his relationship to his readers in social terms and identifies his audience as the elite members of the Court of the Areopagus, newly invested with authority.[30]

A series of composite reading acts produces dialogues between classical and Christian traditions. Evidence from scripture reveals that "*Moses,*

Daniel & Paul...were skilfull in all the learning of the Ægyptians, Caldeans, and Greeks, which could not probably be without reading their Books of all sorts, in *Paul* especially, who thought it no defilement to insert into holy Scripture the sentences of three Greek Poets" (*CPW* II:507–08). Milton cites Socrates Scholasticus to ground the anti-censorship thesis in the history of the primitive church: "So great an injury they [the Apollinaires] then held it to be depriv'd of *Hellenick* learning; and thought it a persecution more undermining, and secretly decaying the Church, then the open cruelty of *Decius* or *Dioclesian*" – second-century Roman emperors and persecutors of Christians (*CPW* II:509).[31] Transgressive and promiscuous reading is then judged as fundamentally Christian. "And perhaps it was the same politick drift that the Divell whipt St. *Jerom* in a lenten dream, for reading *Cicero*" (*CPW* II:509–10).[32] Milton turns to Eusebius' account of *Dionysius Alexandrinus*, Bishop of Alexandria, who "had wont to avail himself much against hereticks by being conversant in their Books." The exercise is sanctioned, as he testifies: "Read any books what ever come to thy hands, for thou art sufficient both to judge aright, and to examine each matter. To this revelation he assented the sooner, as he confesses, because it was answerable to that of the Apostle to the Thessalonians, Prove all things, hold fast that which is good" (*CPW* II:511–12). Supplementing and validating the reading act through recourse to scripture, Milton determines that the evangelist "might have added another remarkable saying of the same Author; To the pure all things are pure, not only meats and drinks, but all kinde of knowledge whether of good or evill; the knowledge cannot defile, nor consequently the books, if the will and conscience be not defil'd." The metaphor of digestion is extended to distinguish the practices of contemporaries judged as "judicious" – a modifier used throughout *Areopagitica* to relate authorship and reading, and describe Milton's ideal reader: "Bad meats will scarce breed good nourishment in the healthiest concoction; but herein the difference is of bad books, that they to a discreet and judicious Reader serve in many respects to discover, to confute, to forewarn, and to illustrate" (*CPW* II:512–13). The history of transgressive reading culminates in the example of Milton's contemporary compatriot, John Selden, "the chief of learned men reputed in this Land," whose *De Jure Naturali* is cited in defense of the anti-censorship argument and of the exercise of conscience and reason (*CPW* II:513). Milton's use of Selden thus links the parliamentarian-jurist-historian's epistemology and theories of active interpretation to those advanced throughout *Areopagitica* generally.

After first showcasing the classicist, the humanist, and internationalist, the treatise channels humanist learning into an appeal by a Protestant

English apologist and nationalist. When Milton hopes for the "reforming of Reformation it self" (*CPW* II:553) through "books promiscuously read" – the subject of the oration's confirmation (*CPW* II:517) – he concentrates on national policies on the assumption that a true Nation or "well instituted State" (*CPW* II:521–22) would never resort to licensing: the "best and wisest Commonwealths" have forborne to apply censorship; those who have, have sought "to obstruct and hinder the first approach of Reformation" (*CPW* II:507). The value attributed to books, reading, and education establishes the bounds of liberty and sutures for an elect nation – God having revealed himself "first to his English-men" (*CPW* II:553). The defining practices of "the mansion house of liberty" are thus enacted by the mutual participation of writers and readers: "pens and heads there, sitting by their studious lamps, musing, searching, revolving new notions and idea's wherewith to present, as with their homage and their fealty the approaching Reformation: others as fast reading, trying all things, assenting to the force of reason and convincement" (*CPW* II:553–54).

The first readers of *Areopagitica* consisted of "an admittedly limited audience of humanists."[33] Undistinguished as a material object, the work generated little attention, and wasn't reprinted until it appeared in collected editions of Milton's prose at the very end of the seventeenth century. The Commonplace Book lacked readers other than the compiler himself until the late nineteenth century. It may, therefore, seem unusual to ascribe to the Commonplace Book, a purportedly personal work, and to *Areopagitica*, a work appealing to an elite Areopagus and specifically designed for private reading, a civic, national function. Yet both works engage in "judicious conversing" with the cultural, political, material, and national and international contexts in which they were produced. While a point of contention for Reformers, Milton staunchly defended promiscuous reading, maintaining that together the secular and sacred writings can best serve the cause of liberty, education, religion, and thus of the nation. Citizenship becomes an exercise of ecclesiastical, domestic or private, and civil (or political) liberty by virtuous readers engaged in "disputing, reasoning, reading, inventing, discoursing . . . [about] things not before discourst or writt'n of" (*CPW* II:557).

NOTES

1 Kevin Sharpe, *Reading Revolutions: The Politics of Reading in Early Modern England* (New Haven, 2000), 293.

2 *CPW* II:553, 517. Active reading spread through the Reformation; see Stephen
   B. Dobranski, *Readers and Authorship in Early Modern England* (Cambridge,
   2005), 31.
3 Cathy Shrank, *Writing the Nation in Reformation England 1530–1580* (Oxford,
   2004), 13.
4 Citizen (*civis* Latin) was "originally nearer in meaning to our modern sense
   of a 'national'" (Raymond Williams, *Keywords: A Vocabulary of Culture and
   Society*, rev. edn. [1976; New York, 1985], 56.)
5 Alfred J. Horwood, who discovered the manuscript in 1874, produced an 1876
   edition thereof and a revised, corrected version in 1877 (*A Common-Place Book
   of John Milton*, rev. edn. [1877; New York, 1965]).
6 Dobranski, *Readers and Authorship*, 55.
7 Steven N. Zwicker, "Habits of Reading and Early Modern Literary Culture," in
   Cambridge History of Early Modern English Literature, ed. David Loewenstein
   and Janel Mueller (Cambridge, 2002), 176.
8 Stephen Orgel, "Margins of Truth," in *The Renaissance Text: Theory, Editing,
   Textuality*, ed. Andrew Murphy (Manchester, 2000), 107.
9 On the disjunctions between reading and writing, see Keith Thomas' "The
   Meaning of Literacy in Early Modern England," in *The Written Word: Literacy
   in Transition*, ed. Gerd Baumann (Oxford, 1986), 97–131; and Robert Darnton,
   "Extraordinary Commonplaces," review of Kevin Sharpe's *Reading Revolutions*
   and *Geoffrey Madan's Notebooks*, ed. J. A. Gere and John Sparrow (Oxford,
   1981), in *The New York Review of Books* 47 (December 21, 2000): 82.
10 Annabel Patterson, "Couples, Canons, and the Uncouth: Spenser-and-Milton
   in Educational Theory," *Critical Inquiry* 16 (1990): 779.
11 William Riley Parker, *Milton: A Biography*, 2nd edn., ed. Gordon Campbell,
   2 vols. (1968; Oxford, 1996), 249; see also James H. Hanford, "The Chronology
   of Milton's Private Studies," *PMLA* 36 (1921): 286, 287, 305.
12 Ruth Mohl, *John Milton and His Commonplace Book* (New York, 1969); and
   Ruth Mohl, Preface, *Milton's Commonplace Book* (1953), in *CPW* I:344–59.
13 Peter Beal, "Notions in Garrison: The Seventeenth-Century Commonplace
   Book," in *New Ways of Looking at Old Texts*, ed. W. Speed Hill (Binghamton,
   NY, 1993), 133.
14 Sharpe, *Reading Revolutions*, 292–93.
15 *Ibid.*, 291, 292.
16 Barbara K. Lewalski, *The Life of John Milton* (Oxford, 2000), 126–27, 160–61,
   252.
17 Mohl, *Milton and His Commonplace Book*, 17; and Sharpe, *Reading Revolutions*, 278, quoting M. T. Crane, *Framing Authority* (Princeton, 1993), 18. For
   the classical definitions, see Ann Moss, *Printed Commonplace-Books and the
   Structuring of Renaissance Thought* (Oxford, 1996), 2–6. Moss, however, does
   not cite Milton.
18 Erasmus, *De Copia*, in *Collected Works of Erasmus: Literature and Educational
   Writings 2: De Copia/De Ratione Studii*, ed. Craig R. Thompson (Toronto,

1978), 635; and Mohl, *Milton and His Commonplace Book*, 16–17. See also Milton's *An Apology* (*CPW* 1:889, 914).

19 Sharpe, *Reading Revolutions*, 40; Moss, *Printed Commonplace-Books*, 164; Anthony Grafton and Lisa Jardine, *From Humanism to the Humanities: Education and the Liberal Arts in Fifteenth- and Sixteenth-Century Europe* (London, 1986), 146–49. Milton also took exception to Erasmus' criticism of Luther (*CPW* 1:901).

20 On Milton's relationships with printers and booksellers, see Stephen Dobranski's chapter in this volume.

21 On reading and education as "expressive and constitutive of community," see Thomas Festa, "Repairing the Ruins: Milton as Reader and Educator," *Milton Studies* 43 (2004): 35.

22 Cf. the Confuter's abuse in his argument of "a shred" from "his common place-book" (*CPW* 1:893). Mohl indexes Milton's unused entries (*Milton and His Commonplace Book*, 255).

23 Beal, "Notions in Garrison," 145; and Mohl, Preface, *CPW* 1:349–50, n. 21.

24 Sharpe, *Reading Revolutions*, 184; and Lisa Jardine and Anthony Grafton, "'Studied for Action': How Gabriel Harvey Read His Livy," *Past and Present* 129 (1990): 30–78. For examples of composite reading, see Hanford, "The Chronology of Milton's Private Studies," 297.

25 Mohl, Preface, *CPW* 1:357.

26 On discontinuous reading see Peter Stallybrass, "Books and Scrolls: Navigating the Bible," in *Books and Readers in Early Modern England*, ed. Jennifer Andersen and Elizabeth Sauer (Philadelphia, 2002), 42–79.

27 Francis Bacon, *An Advertisement Touching the Controversies of the Church of England*, in vol. 1 of *The Letters and Life of Francis Bacon*, ed. James Spedding (London, 1862), 74–95 (p. 78).

28 A paraphrase from Bacon's *A Wise and Moderate Discourse, Concerning Church-Affaires* (1641), 11 (originally *An Advertisement Touching the Controversies of the Church of England* [1589]); see also *CPW* 1:23.

29 See Guari Viswanathan, "Milton and Education," in *Milton and the Imperial Vision*, ed. Balachandra Rajan and Elizabeth Sauer (Pittsburgh, PA, 1999), 273–93.

30 Ernest Sirluck notes the limited authority enjoyed by the ancient court, authority which Isocrates sought to restore (*CPW* 11:486, n.1).

31 Socrates Scholasticus, *Ecclesiastical History* (London, 1853), 191–92 (book 111, ch. 16).

32 Sarpi's *Historia del Concilio Tridentino* was translated by Nathaniel Brent into English as *The Historie of the Councel of Trent* (London, 1620), 472.

33 David Norbrook, "*Areopagitica*, Censorship, and the Early Modern Public Sphere," in *The Administration of Aesthetics: Censorship, Political Criticism, and the Public Sphere*, ed. Richard Burt (Minneapolis, 1994), 15; see also 10, 30, n. 39; and Leo Miller, "A German Critique of Milton's *Areopagitica* in 1647," *Notes and Queries* 234 (1989): 29–30.

CHAPTER 39

The Restoration

Joad Raymond

The Restoration began with Charles II processing through the tapestry-
and troop-lined streets of London on May 29, 1660, past crowds of citizens
and wine flowing through fountains and conduits, to popular acclamation,
the burning of animal rumps and the acrid smell of bonfires bearing
republican effigies. Except, of course, that it began several weeks earlier
with the last in a series of military coups, this one led by General George
Monck. Support of parliamentary government and hostility to religious
toleration combined with royalist principles (among a minority) to create
a coalition that overwhelmingly favored a return of the king, under the
apprehension that this would bring about a parliamentary settlement and
forgiveness for anti-royalist activity over the preceding two decades. A "free
and general pardon" had been promised in Charles Stuart's Declaration of
Breda on April 4, along with liberty of conscience.[1] Once the ticker tape
had been cleared up, the recriminations began: the list of those exempted
from a general indemnity swelled, those who were perceived as threats
to the new regime were imprisoned, parliament clamped down on godly
Protestants opposed to episcopacy and the service of the established church,
and regicides, living and already dead, were executed at Tyburn.[2]

Some time in May Milton went into hiding. At the beginning of March
he had published *The Readie and Easie Way to Establish a Free Commonwealth*, and in early April he published a second, revised version of this
pamphlet resolutely opposed to a return of monarchy.[3] Milton adopted the
voice of a Jeremiah, speaking out dutifully to mark his opposition in the
arena of public print – just as Cavalier pamphleteers were calling for the
blood of republicans and regicides in increasingly inflammatory rhetoric –
more than in hope of preventing the event.[4] On June 16 parliament issued
a warrant for his arrest, and ordered *Pro Populo Anglicano Defensio* (1650)
and *Eikonoklastes* (1649) to be burned. His books were removed from the
Bodleian. He may have felt that worse lay ahead. Milton cut a notorious
figure in the pamphlet noise of the spring of 1660, a champion of regicide

singled out as deserving punishment. On August 29, however, the Act of Free and General Pardon, Indemnity and Oblivion was passed, identifying named exemptions from the promised pardon for treasonable offenses committed in the preceding decades. Milton's name was not included among those exempt, and so he appeared to have escaped punishment for his regicide tracts and other duties undertaken for the commonwealth and protectorate. Shortly thereafter he came out of hiding. In the autumn, however, he was arrested and briefly imprisoned in the Tower, where he spent his fifty-second birthday before being released on December 15, perhaps in return for "good promises."[5] His books were burned and condemned in print.

Blind, his name reviled, his religion threatened, his politics disappointed, Milton spent the remainder of his life living in internal exile. His latest surviving letter, from 1666, regrets that his patriotism had almost "expatriated" him, and offers melancholy reflections on what "home" means.[6] The invocation to book VII of *Paradise Lost* perhaps speaks of his feelings at this time:

> fall'n on evil days,
> On evil days though fall'n, and evil tongues;
> In darkness, and with dangers compassed round,
> And solitude.
>
> (VII.25–28)

At this time he may have ceased work on his systematic theology now known as *De Doctrina Christiana*, a work he described as *"melius aut pretiosius nihil habeo"* or "my best and richest possession," perceiving that the religious climate was inclement for publication.[7] Though he continued to write, he published nothing until 1667.

There is one qualified exception. George Sykes' *The Life and Death of Sir Henry Vane* (1662), published anonymously and surreptitiously, is one of a series of trial and execution pamphlets from the first half of the decade that constitute a martyrology for commonwealthsmen and republicans. Sykes' unconventional life of Vane eschews a more traditional narrative of Puritan struggles and providential suffering, and offers instead an intellectual portrait "treating mostly of the principles and course of his hidden Life amongst the sons of God."[8] In this context Sykes prints in full Milton's previously unpublished sonnet to Vane, attributing it only to "a learned Gentleman" who sent it to Vane on July 3, 1652. Sykes interprets the sonnet's exemplary observations on Vane's character in a language that shows how 1650s commonwealth politics translated into 1660s nonconformism and political opposition. His interests, imagery, and conceptual vocabulary are suggestively close to Milton's: he praises Vane's "angelical intuitiveness"; allegorically interprets Vane's writing on the two trees of Eden; and turns to Roman history and ancient English rights in discussing the proper separation of church from state.[9] Whence Sykes received his copy of the poem he does not say, but the proximity of the language, his interests in angels, and Milton's familiarity with the pamphlets reporting on the punishment of the regicides – they reverberate in the tragedy of *Samson Agonistes* (1671)[10] – intimate that Sykes and Milton may have been acquainted. Sykes turns the poem from 1650s republican panegyric to 1660s nonconformist lament. Like many of Milton's publications, this passed without comment, though at least one copy has impassioned and sympathetic annotations by a near-contemporary reader (see figures 26 and 27).

The years of Milton's silence were defined by a series of acts passed by the Cavalier Parliament, now known as the Clarendon Code (after Edward Hyde, first Earl of Clarendon, Charles II's Lord Chancellor). These pressed closely upon Milton's circumstances and shaped his experience and understanding of the character of these years. The first piece of legislation comprehended within the Clarendon Code was the Corporation Act of December 1661: this required all office-holders to acknowledge royal supremacy and forswear political resistance, abjure the Solemn League and Covenant, and take communion in the established church. Dissenters were thereby prevented from holding public office. The second was the Act of Uniformity in May 1662, which required all ministers and schoolmasters to take the same oath renouncing political resistance and conforming to the church. All clergy who objected to episcopacy were deprived of their livings. These acts created and defined nonconformity, a confessional and political identity for those disenfranchised on the grounds of religious dissent.[11] This took effect on St. Bartholomew's Day, and the irony of this black anniversary for Protestants was not lost on the 1,800 ministers expelled on August 24, 1662. In 1660 Presbyterians, Quakers, and separatists had been divided by their various antipathies to toleration and military rule, which had assisted the return of the king; now they were united by the oppression of a Cavalier and Anglican regime. The Conventicle Act of 1664 extended the repression of nonconformists to laymen. Endeavoring to prevent worship outside churches, it imposed fines, on a sliding scale and with increments for subsequent offenses, for all religious meetings of more than four persons beyond the members of a household. The fines were increased in a second Conventicle Act in 1670. The Five Mile Act of 1665 required all nonconformist ministers to swear an oath renouncing the pursuit of

(92)

disabled to perform one title of the Law in the single activity of our corruptible (though renewed) mind, we come to do fulfil the whole Law in the continuing and incorruptible principle of new-creature life, that against us there is no Law, that hath any thing to say, *Gal.* 5. 23. *Do ye then walk in the Law through faith? God forbid: yea*, we come by this means another to establish and fulfil the Law, *Rom.* 3. 31. *Mat.* 5. 17. They that believe in God, must be careful to maintain such good works, to wit, the works of faith, *Tit.* 3. 8. This is the *laying our light so shine before men, that they may see our good works, and glorifie our father which is in heaven*, *Mat.* 5. 16. We knew hereby that God's spirit which is set up in man by the new creation, is better at working righteousness, than mans spirit that was set up in him by the first-creation.

Any works we do, as born of God in the new-creation, are better on all accounts, than what we can do, as made of God in the first, whatever work is good in the honest Heathen or legal Christian, shall be owned and out-done by the spiritual believer, in his more excellent principles and way. The highest Principles of Life in man, unclude, purifie, and out-do all that righteousness that is performable in the lower.

In such Principles was this Sufferer a worker of righteousness, such a worshipper of God as the Father feeds and approves of; such a true Son of peace, & such a peacemaker at hand him described; but reckoned a man of contention, for that very reason. He was content with *Paul* to be a fool for Christ, despised for Christ, the poor and needy man, with *David*. As a true Embassador of Christ, and minister of the everlasting Gospel, he warned and besought the sons of men, to consider their own true interest in becoming not onely almost but altogether such as he was, except his bonds. His Life was not like other mens, (*Wisd.* 2. 15.) therefore have I writ his Life after another fashion than mens Lives use to be written, creating motly of the principles and course of his hidden Life amongst the sons of God, that the sons of men may the better know and consider what manner of man it was they have betrayed, persecuted and slain. For this read on from verse 15, to 23, of *Wisd.* 2. (which I quote not as Scripture, but as a notable character of mens rational conviction and acknowledgements, together with their false reasonings, and most perverse deductions therefrom, in the present case) *ye are esteemed of him as counterfeit; He maketh his boast that God is his Father. Let us see if his words be true. If to be the*

(93)

Son of God, he will help him and deliver him from his enemies. Let us examine him with despitefull and torture, that we may know his meekness and prove his patience. Let us condemn him with a shamefull death, for he shall be respected, by his own saying. Such things they did imagine, and were deceived, for their own wickedness hath blinded them. As for the mysteries of God, they knew them not, nor discerned the reward of blameless souls.

Thus, not owning my net-self an Apology for having been so large in the exposition of his divine Life, Principles, and Doctrine, (save onely this, that I have spoken these things, rather as an instruction to the living than an Apology for the dead) I return to the more publick and overt acts of his humane pilgrimage, and conversation amongst men, having mentioned the private passages thereof in the beginning.

Would you know his Title in reference to his countrey? He was a *Common-wealth-Man.* That's a dangerous Name to the Peace and Interest of Tyranny.

I have lately met with two new State Paradoxes in Print, which speak mine to all that own that Title.

1. *That the Common-Wealth-men's are safe, while Common-Wealth-Men are alive.*

2. *That the Lawes are not safe, while they are alive that every day call forth and stifle the Law.*

These Affections carry with them such an appearance of contradiction, to say no more, that I cannot for much in *Oedipus* as to unriddle them.

The Character of this deceased Statesman, (with whose Principles those two sayings carry little harmony) I shall exhibite to you in a paper of Verses, composed by a learned Gentleman, and sent him, *July* 3. 1651.

VANE, young in years, but in sage counsell old,
Then whom a better Senatour n'er held
The helme of Rome, when Gowns not Armes repell'd
The fierce Epirot and the African bold:

Som-

Figs. 26–27 Opening from George Sykes' *The Life and Death of Sir Henry Vane* (1662), showing Milton's sonnet to Vane, with annotations by a near-contemporary reader

Fig. 27

alteration in church and state. Ministers who did not comply were prevented from teaching in a school or coming within five miles of a corporation or borough. Those who looked back on Charles' 1660 Declaration of Breda, which Milton had viewed with skepticism, felt its promises of religious toleration and "Liberty to Tender Consciences" were broken.[12]

The Printing Act of 1662 possessed the same complexion as the Clarendon Code and facilitated its successful operation. It re-introduced pre-publication licensing, extensive powers of search for the Stationers' Company, stringent fines, and strict controls on the periodical press. The same year, Roger L'Estrange, who had mounted a propaganda campaign against Milton in 1660, was appointed Surveyor of the Press. Pre-publication licensing was only one of an armory of weapons that suppressed opinions, republican and nonconformist, that L'Estrange found opprobrious.[13] The long reach that Secretary of State Sir Joseph Williamson exerted in 1675–76 to thwart Daniel Skinner's efforts to publish Milton's manuscript *De Doctrina Christiana* suggests the efficacy of the Restoration state in suppressing dissidence when motivated. When the laws reached their limit, then personal intervention could be relied upon, from the smashing of presses to the use of gangs to threaten and assault nonconformists and political enemies.[14]

When Clarendon was impeached and fled into exile in 1667, the enforcement of these laws was temporarily relaxed; it remained less rigorous until 1670. The royal Declaration of Indulgence of 1672 provided some relief for nonconformists, as well as Roman Catholics, while provoking hostility among dissenters and Anglicans. The debate around this royal promise of religious toleration prompted Milton's *Of True Religion* (1673), the two parts of Marvell's *The Rehearsal Transpros'd* (1672–73), Samuel Butler's *The Transproser Rehearsed* (1673), and Samuel Parker's *A Reproof to the Rehearsal Transprosed* (1673). From these we can glean some insight into the continuing significance of Milton's reputation in the early 1670s. Milton, Marvell tells us, lived in "retired silence" (though he had published several books over the preceding years).[15] Any relaxation in the circumstances of nonconformists was reversed in 1673 when Charles withdrew the Declaration and parliament introduced the Test Act, which once again enforced office holders to take the Oaths of Allegiance and Supremacy, to take the sacrament, and to deny the doctrine of transubstantiation. The timing of Milton's publications after 1660 – and his eloquent silences – should be interpreted within the constraints affecting publication, as well the atmosphere of state hostility to nonconformists, social disenfranchisement, threatened violence, and the spectacular displays of royal authority in entries, progresses, and public executions.

The Restoration state was based not on religious comprehension, indulgence, or toleration of zealous Protestantism and nonconformity but on compulsion, and the last thirteen years of Milton's life were spent living under the same coercive parliament. What opposition there was – within parliament and the Corporation of London – centered on nonconformity. The major arguments of the Restoration period, and the most sensitive political topics, concerned the nature of the church settlement, the extent of civil authority, and liberty of conscience.

Milton broke his silence in 1667. He may have delayed publication of *Paradise Lost* for a few years, waiting for a more clement time. Thus it may be no coincidence that it was published a few weeks after Clarendon's fall (though it had already been contracted, licensed, and entered in the Stationers' Register). As his first publication since *The Readie and Easie Way*, the epic poem was the work not of a known poet but of a notorious republican and defender of regicide. His friends feared that his poem would provoke recriminations or sanctions – hinted at in Marvell's commendatory poem of 1674 – and were relieved when they learned that it was a Genesis epic (ironically, one German reader judged that they had been right at first, and that it was precisely a lament for the fallen republic).[16] According to Milton's early biographer John Toland, the licenser Thomas Tomkins searched *Paradise Lost* for offense, and "we had like to be eternally depriv'd of this Treasure by the Ignorance or Malice of the Licenser; who, among other frivolous Exceptions, would needs suppress the whole Poem for imaginary Treason in the following lines":

> as when the sun new ris'n
> Looks through the horizontal misty air
> Shorn of his beams, or from behind the moon
> In dim eclipse disastrous twilight sheds
> On half the nations, and with fear of change
> Perplexes monarchs.
>
> (1.594–99)[17]

Either Milton, or his printer Samuel Simmons, found it necessary to approach a licenser, suggesting that one or both felt their enterprise was ideologically vulnerable. Nevertheless the poem appeared with these lines intact, perhaps because of the political thaw.

The nature and extent of its political engagement are disputed: most modern historicist critics divide into those who interpret its spiritual interests as a retreat from worldly concerns and an implicit rejection of political engagement; those who find in it an attack on satanic Cromwellian ambition; and those who see it as encoding consistently republican or anti-monarchical values and rejecting Restoration culture. There are certainly grounds, more than Tomkins found, for seeing it as critical of the political and devotional arrangements of the 1660s.[18] Milton's narrator has fallen on "evil days," and the consistent championing of liberty and the poem's hostility to displays of grandeur and authority, to titles, and to authority founded on status, even if they do not articulate a theory of political resistance, nonetheless speak against the foundations of Restoration monarchy.

As Jonathan Scott has written, "It was, in practical terms, the struggle which had retreated from Milton, not vice versa."[19] But Milton's godly republicanism had been incorporated, within the context of Restoration culture, into the broad spectrum of nonconformism, sounding rather different but by no means apolitical. Milton's turn to the spirit – sometimes identified as a turn away from worldly politics – identifies the individual conscience as the source of true belief and redemption. Michael promises Adam "A paradise within thee, happier far" (*Paradise Lost* XII.587) than the Edenic paradise, and this paradise within is secured not through unfree obedience to the law but by actively choosing and willing good (III.103–11). The most resonant theological passages of the poem, and the crux of its visionary argument, stress the role of the conscience in realizing the good. The spirit, the narrator tells us in his invocation, prefers "Before all temples th' upright heart and pure" (I.18), which is to say that the spirit of prophecy attends to the individual conscience rather than places or institutions of worship. This reiterates an argument from numerous Independent tracts from the 1640s, some of them Milton's: the compulsion of belief, even in matters that happen to be true, cannot result in true belief, because belief relies on the choice of the individual, and institutions that suppress the process of choosing can only result in the forcing of conscience, the "professing" of beliefs, and thus to spiritual darkness. Whether this "inward" light (III.52) is specifically associated with Quaker theology, and thus peaceful non-resistance, matters not: the toleration of nonconformity on the grounds of liberty of conscience was the most intractable political issue of the 1660s. Parliamentary legislation sought to impose outward religious conformity against the opposition of individual consciences, and, moreover, associated such conformity, performed through oaths and taking of Anglican sacraments, with professing allegiance to the crown. In its account of conscience, far from turning away from the world, *Paradise Lost* addresses the issues that brought about the Restoration and defined the political world of the 1660s, and does so in a way that sides its author with London nonconformists who were opposed to the Cavalier government.[20] It is no surprise that its author should have felt this way, but it is necessary to emphasize the worldly significance of the spiritual arguments of the poem, and how they fitted into the language of the political opposition.

There was another Milton during these years, as far the reading public were concerned: the humanist scholar and teacher. His other publications included *Accedence Commenc't Grammar* (1669), *The History of Britain* (1670), *Artis Logicæ Plenior Institutio* (1672), *Epistolarum Familiarium Liber Unus* (1674), and the translation *A Declaration, or Letters Patents of the Election of this present King of Poland* (1674). The complexion of these works is very different from that of the intensively engaged series of pamphlets from 1659 to 1660. They do not have a strong ideological orientation and whatever comments Milton wished to pass on the times were discreetly made. He was clearing out his files, putting into print works that, the last excepted, had probably been complete or near-complete for some years. In 1673 he also issued an expanded version of his 1645 *Poems*, to which he appended the tract *Of Education*. He probably wanted to publish them as educative materials, ones that reflected his humanist credentials.

This is not the case with the 1671 volume, *Paradise Regain'd. A Poem. In IV Books. To which is added Samson Agonistes*, which speaks hard words against Restoration culture. The second work in the volume, the "addition" and yet the most charged, was probably the first to be written. Though little is known for certain about the dates of Milton's post-1660 works, it seems likely that *Samson* was commenced after the completion of *Paradise Lost* around 1664: it resonates with pamphlets about the sufferings of the regicides in the early 1660s. It contemplates the appropriate nature of political resistance to the Philistines in terms that would have been familiar to a nonconformist audience required to submit to the Anglican church and swear obedience to the king. The brief epic was probably written after this, between about 1667 and 1670,[21] though placed first in the volume and given more prominence on the title page. *Paradise Regained* locates the triumph of the Son in his private role, prior to the Sermon on the Mount and long before the Passion, through successfully consistent passive resistance to temptation. It demonstrates the importance of spiritual reflection, but this cultivation of the spirit is presented as a preparation for action. The Son's struggle associates salvation with an inner light, resembling the doctrine of Milton's quietist Quaker friends; however, martyrdom and conquest lie in his future.[22]

Samson Agonistes also concerns waiting, but its waiting is human. Critics are divided on whether Samson is regenerate – which is to say, receives spiritual illumination so that his final actions are indeed justified of God – or is a flawed hero who acts dreadful violence on his own impulse in the absence of God's.[23] This dichotomy points to a potential limitation within current literary studies: scholarship is disengaged from the experiences of early modern radical theology, and privileges a conception of critical sensibility that discourages the admiration of a text that endorses genocide. From either perspective, however, the tragedy reflects on Restoration culture, on the "Great pomp" with which "th' idolatrous rout amidst their wine" celebrate a false deity and dishonor the true God (lines 436, 443); and on the reversal of fortunes that the chosen ones of God face, when he tests them by leaving them "to the hostile sword / Of heathen and profane" and to the condemnation of "unjust tribunals" and the "condemnation of the ingrateful multitude" (lines 692–96).

Aesthetically, *Paradise Regained* is challenging: after the baroque indulgences of *Paradise Lost* it offers a biblical epic stripped down to plain language. The plot is superficially simple while bearing a complex symbolic structure (the nature of the temptations and the boundaries between them are obscure). Its audience were more likely to be consumers of Joseph Caryll's voluminous *Exposition* on the Book of Job, a venture that began in the 1640s and was not concluded until the 1660s, than readers of Restoration heroic or satirical verse. The aesthetics of *Samson Agonistes* are articulated in its Preface, which takes a swipe at the "infamy" tragedy is brought into "at this day" through the "error of intermixing comic stuff with tragic sadness and gravity." Milton eschews modern innovations, introduced "without discretion, corruptly to gratify the people," preferring "the ancient manner." His is a drama "never intended" for the stage, which takes place in a rarefied mental space, the conscience of the fit reader (*CPEP* 707–08). Three years earlier, when asked to introduce a note on the verse of *Paradise Lost*, because, as Simmons put it, many readers "stumbled" upon it, Milton penned a similarly contentious condemnation of the "barbarous age" that masked poor meter behind the "jingling sound" of rhyme, and proclaimed his form to be "an example set, the first in English, of ancient liberty recovered to heroic poem from the troublesome and modern bondage of rhyming" (*CPEP* 291). Milton defied the literary fashions of his day and emphasized that this was not a matter of taste but the expression of true liberty. Both prefatory notes stress the ideology of literary form, associating Restoration literature with slavish politics, and profess to seek purity through a restoration of ancient tradition, much as some republican argument in the 1650s presented monarchy as a modern innovation that ruined ancient liberties.[24]

Paradise Lost and *Samson Agonistes* contemplate the means by which liberty succumbs to slavery. According to Michael, when "right reason" is obscured:

> . . . upstart passions catch the government
> From reason, and to servitude reduce
> Man till then free. Therefore since he permits
> Within himself unworthy powers to reign
> Over free reason, God in judgement just
> Subjects him from without to violent lords;
> Who oft as undeservedly enthrall
> His outward freedom.
>   (*Paradise Lost* XII.84, 88–95)

Liberty is first lost inwardly, and then outwardly. Samson reflects:

> But what more oft in nations grown corrupt,
> And by their vices brought to servitude,
> Than to love bondage more than liberty,
> Bondage with ease than strenuous liberty.
>   (*Samson Agonistes* 268–71)

The principles of literary excellence are consistent with the political analysis of the descent into internal bondage then servitude. Milton wrote a cognate account of this, in *The Readie and Easie Way*, amidst the turmoil that led to the Restoration:

Monarchs . . . aim is to make the people, wealthy indeed perhaps and wel-fleec't for thir own shearing, and for the supply of regal prodigalitie; but otherwise softest, basest, vitiousest, servilest, easiest to be kept under; and not only in fleece, but in minde also sheepishest . . . if . . . after all this light among us, the same reason shall pass for current to put our necks again under kingship, as was made use of by the *Jews* to return back to *Egypt* and to the worship of thir idol queen . . . our condition is not sound but rotten, both in religion and all civil prudence; and will bring us soon, the way we are marching, to those calamities which attend alwaies and unavoidably on luxurie, that is to say all national judgments under forein or domestic slaverie[.] (*CPW* VII:384, 386–87)

This polemic was written, swiftly and purposefully, during the slower composition of *Paradise Lost*; the texts overlap in time and content. Throughout the decade Milton was still angry about 1660. The Restoration poems hark back to this decisive step toward monarchy, and the forms they take express Milton's resistance to the outcome.

That Samson's waiting is the drama's focus reminds readers that serving God may consist not solely in action. In the meantime the godly have to live with what freedom they have, bear His yoke, nourish their inner vision, and wait for the hour of deliverance. *Samson* ruminates on the fates of the godly, particularly those regicides and republicans who had been executed, and it is a dark drama, brimful of danger, repression, intolerance, and violence. But it is also a love poem. It is the lament of a man cast down in the eyes of a distant loved one. Samson is wounded by his pride and circumstances, but he is most hurt by the fact he can no longer see or feel the being he loves. Without God he cannot give up the world, and yet he must give up any sense of agency in the world to find his God again. It is a love poem about being deserted and waiting for the return of the loved one. And, like all great love poems, its end is not a simple reunion, but an act of terrible, destructive violence.

The pairing of the two works in the 1671 volume juxtaposes perspectives on preparation and action, and on the nature of resistance. If asked under what circumstances the Oath of Allegiance can be broken, the volume answers: when God instructs. This moment is not subject to political analysis, but lies in individual revelation and inspiration. As we cannot see into another's soul in order to assess whether this experience is true or false, perhaps it is appropriate that there is no consensus over Samson's state of grace. Only through our own inspiration can we accurately assess another's. The sequence of the volume privileges the brief epic as the greater work, but also means that the volume ends on the discordant note of cataclysmic violence. It suggests that the action that follows the preparation of the self will be a human action, not an angelic one. What that action is – the publication of *De Doctrina*, perhaps, or even of the 1671 volume itself – we do not know, and it is probably wrong to ask: neither of the protagonists knows what their path will be until they take it.

Milton published his last new work shortly before the 1673 *Poems* and the revised version of *Paradise Lost* (1674). Responding to Charles II's withdrawal of his Declaration of Indulgence, *Of True Religion* (1673) is an attack on Roman Catholicism and a plea for the toleration of Protestants. The grounds of the argument are consistent with *Areopagitica* (1644), but the rhetoric is adapted to the less visionary and more pragmatic political languages of the 1670s. His selective intolerance is coherent: the nature of the attack on Catholicism is determined by the defense of non-orthodox (or heretical) Protestant doctrine. Conscience must be founded upon scripture, insists Milton. No belief that is founded upon a reasonable interpretation of scripture, as opposed to "implicit faith," can be heretical, though it may be erroneous; and therefore it must be allowed. Catholicism disavows the sole authority of scripture and allows "implicit faith"; and, in abjuring the ground of true faith, "Popery is the only or the greatest Heresie," and therefore toleration cannot logically be extended to it (*CPW* VIII:421). Milton reiterates, in plainer language, the arguments of *Areopagitica* with respect to the liberty of printing:

> We suffer the Idolatrous books of Papists . . . to be sold & read as common as our own. Why not much rather of Anabaptists, Arians, Arminians, & Socinians? There is no Learned man but will confess he hath much profited by reading Controversies, his Senses awakt, his Judgement sharpn'd, and the truth which he holds more firmly establish't . . . all controversies being permitted, falshood will appear more false, and truth the more true . . . (*CPW* VIII:437–38)

Milton had no hopes that the printing of popish books would be stopped, but wished to justify the toleration of Protestant "errors," many of which could be found in the unpublished theological treatise that sat, neatly organized, among his other papers. It was in part because of his own radical enthusiasm, and in part because of his contempt for monarchy, that Milton found himself adopting a quite contrary argument to Marvell in *The Rehearsal Transpros'd*, where his friend argued, pseudonymously and not without ironical twists, in favor of the king's policy of tolerating moderate Protestants and Catholics. Although his language and arguments are adapted to the times – Milton was profoundly sensitive to polemical context, though sometimes contemptuous of its limitations – Milton had returned to his habit of challenging royal policy and judgment.

In *Of True Religion*, Catholicism means a great deal more than the institution or a theological position: "popery" is a metaphor for spiritual corruption and slavery. The secular ideology in this argument cannot be unpicked from the religious fervor: "The last means to avoid Popery, is to amend our lives: it is a general complaint that this Nation of late years, is grown more numerously and excessively vitious then heretofore; Pride, Luxury, Drunkenness, Whoredom, Cursing, Swearing, bold and open Atheism every where abounding" (*CPW* VIII:438). The passage echoes *Paradise Lost* and *Samson Agonistes* in particular: inner bondage will lead to the external chains of popery, which is incompatible with both liberty and truth. Throughout his Restoration writings, while unable, or reluctant, to confront contemporary British politics in a direct and explicit manner, Milton comments insightfully and acerbically on the cultural foundations of that politics.

After issuing the revised *Paradise Lost*, Milton died. *The London Gazette*, the sole newspaper of the day (press control was once again moderately effective) did not comment on the fact. Milton's revolution would be a long one.

NOTES

1 Samuel Rawson Gardiner, *Constitutional Documents of the Puritan Revolution, 1625–1660* (Oxford, 1906), 465–67.
2 Gary S. De Krey, *London and the Restoration, 1659–1683* (Cambridge, 2005); and Ronald Hutton, *The Restoration: A Political and Religious History of England and Wales, 1658–1667* (Oxford, 1985).
3 Gordon Campbell, *A Milton Chronology* (Basingstoke, 1997), 187–90.
4 Laura Lunger Knoppers, "Milton's *The Readie and Easie Way* and the English Jeremiad," in *Politics, Poetics, and Hermeneutics in Milton's Prose*, ed. David Loewenstein and James Grantham Turner (Cambridge, 1990), 213–25; Joad Raymond, "The Cracking of the Republican Spokes," *Prose Studies* 19 (1996): 255–74.
5 *EL* 4–5; Campbell, *Milton Chronology*, 193–94.
6 *WJM* XII:114–15; *CPW* VIII:3–4.
7 *CPW* VI:121; *WJM* XIV:8–9; Gordon Campbell, Thomas N. Corns, John K. Hale, and Fiona J. Tweedie, *Milton and the Manuscript of "De Doctrina Christiana"* (Oxford, 2007), 33, 64, 66.
8 [George Sykes], *The Life and Death of Sir Henry Vane* ([London], 1662), 92.
9 *Ibid.*, 78, 92–95, 103, 98–101.
10 Blair Worden, "Milton, *Samson Agonistes*, and the Restoration," in *Culture and Society in the Stuart Restoration: Literature, Drama, History*, ed. Gerald MacLean (Cambridge, 1985), 111–36.
11 A. G. Matthews, *Calamy Revised* (1934; Oxford, 1988); Neil H. Keeble, *The Literary Culture of Nonconformity in Later Seventeenth-Century England* (Leicester, 1987); De Krey, *London and the Restoration*, 72, 87–90.
12 *King Charles II. His Declaration... Dated from His Court at Breda* (London, 1660).
13 Harold M. Weber, *Paper Bullets: Print and Kingship under Charles II* (Lexington, KY, 1996); Joad Raymond, *Pamphlets and Pamphleteering in Early Modern Britain* (Cambridge, 2003), ch. 8.
14 Campbell *et al.*, *Milton and the Manuscript*, 5–38; Mark Goldie, "The Hilton Gang and the Purge of London in the 1680s," in *Politics and the Political Imagination in Later Stuart Britain*, ed. H. Nenner (Rochester, NY, and Woodbridge, UK, 1999), 43–73.
15 Annabel Patterson, ed., *The Prose Works of Andrew Marvell, Vol. 1: 1672–1673* (New Haven and London, 1993), 417–18.
16 David Norbrook, *Writing the English Republic: Poetry, Rhetoric and Politics, 1627–1660* (Cambridge, 1999), chs. 5, 9.

17 *EL* 180; Nicholas von Maltzahn, "The First Reception of *Paradise Lost* (1667)," *The Review of English Studies* 47 (1996): 479–99.

18 See James Loxley's and Neil Forsyth's chapters in this volume.

19 Jonathan Scott, *England's Troubles: Seventeenth-Century English Political Instability in European Context* (Cambridge, 2000), 347.

20 De Krey, *London and the Restoration*, 100–14.

21 See the appendix in this volume.

22 John T. Shawcross, ed., *John Milton: The Critical Heritage*, 2 vols. (1970; London, 1995), 1:223–24; Sharon Achinstein, *Literature and Dissent in Milton's England* (Cambridge, 2003), ch. 5; David Loewenstein, *Representing Revolution in Milton and his Contemporaries: Religion, Politics, and Polemics in Radical Puritanism* (Cambridge, 2001), ch. 8.

23 Contrary views are stated in Mary Ann Radzinovicz, *Toward "Samson Agonistes": The Growth of Milton's Mind* (Princeton, 1978); and Joseph Wittreich, *Interpreting "Samson Agonistes"* (Princeton, 1986); these arguments have been defended and adapted by many critics.

24 Norbrook, *Writing the English Republic*, chs. 5, 9.

CHAPTER 40

Theology

William Poole

There were two opposing textual traditions on which Milton and his contemporaries could draw in order to describe or compare theological beliefs. The first was the genre of systematic theology, always compiled by defenders. The second was the genre of heresiography, always compiled by attackers. The structure of systematics in Milton's age was dictated by sixteenth-century developments in logic, notably the reforms of Petrus Ramus; the structure of heresiography relied on the revival of patristic taxonomies, revamped to include the ever-proliferating sects of the radical reformation. Systematics tended to the scholarly dissection of belief with an emphasis on the probative force of logic and philology; heresiography preferred colorful lists of heretics and blasphemers, often anecdotal in character. Hence, too, systematics were usually first composed in Latin, whereas heresiographies adopted the vernacular.[1]

Until recently, it has been customary to discuss Milton in the context of heresiography, because it places Milton among vivid company. Commentators have therefore followed heresiographers contemporary to Milton, who corralled believers into named sects (Arminians, Baptists, Seekers, Quakers, Ranters, Diggers), and slotted in newcomers real or imagined. Hence we hear of "Divorsers" from 1645, as a result of Milton's own unfortunate publications on that subject between 1643 and that year.[2] Heresiographers also employed the metaphor of travel, each successive heresy representing the next stop on the primrose path. Milton disdained such an approach, protesting "I follow no... heresy or sect" (*CPW* VI:123), and he assembled in Latin his own systematic theology. In this work, the *De Doctrina Christiana*, he defended his beliefs in scholarly form, eschewing sectarian nomenclature, a policy he usually adopted in his English prose too. Worked on in its current form until around 1660, it was then abandoned and remained unpublished in his lifetime. Structurally, Milton's *De Doctrina* manuscript replicated both the order and much of the content of prior systematics. Hence a given base text, itself the product of similar prior processes, was gradually metamorphosed through a series of local transformations into a succeeding body of doctrine.[3] This is a superior way of understanding not only Milton's formal theology as adumbrated in the *De Doctrina*, but also its evolution over his lifetime. As it is beyond the scope of this short chapter to discuss all Milton's oeuvre, I shall concentrate on the *De Doctrina* with some comparisons drawn from the major poems.[4] But my opening consideration of generic shape should warn us not to discuss Milton's theology independently of the two considerations of chronology and genre: the old Milton differed from the young; and comparisons between intellectual speculation occurring within epic, dramatic, lyric, pastoral, polemic, didactic, and systematic genres may reveal considerable tensions.

Systematics on the Ramist model by Milton's time was usually divided into two complementary investigations. The first concerned the knowledge of God, or faith; the second the worship of God, or works. This is how Milton divides up his manuscript too. (The worship of God will not concern us here; in Miltonic terminology it comprises not "doctrine" [theology] but "discipline" [worship].) The following discussion, then, will roughly track the order of standard investigations into faith, starting with God, and descending down through his decrees, the Son, Creation, angels, man, the fall, and finally scripture.

God, Milton unsurprisingly claims, is in himself unknowable. The uncaused divine nature is indefinable, because to define is to adduce causes (*CPW* VI:133, 137). And although he rejected an anthropomorphic God, Milton did endorse some level of anthropomorphism in our imaginings of the deity:

It is safest for us to form an image of God in our minds which corresponds to his representation and description of himself in the sacred writings. Admittedly, God is always described or outlined not as he really is but in such a way as will make him conceivable to us. Nevertheless, we ought to form just such a mental image of him as he, in bringing himself within the limits of our understanding, wishes us to form. Indeed, he has brought himself down to our level expressly to prevent our being carried beyond the reach of human comprehension, and outside the written authority of scripture, into vague subtleties of explanation. (*CPW* VI:133–34)

Milton therefore insists on one level on our lack of access to God-in-himself. But on another level he also insists that the God of the Bible, the God who is angry, who forgives, who even repents and fears – the examples are all Milton's – must be *imagined* as really such, because he must have some purpose in arranging for scripture to be written so. The difference is that God's emotions are shorn of all the negativity they have in human heads.

Milton the theologian was nervous about straying "outside the written authority of scripture" in such imaginings. But Milton the epic poet breaks that ban. The God of both his epics may therefore be seen as extrapolated from Milton's view of biblical accommodation, but an extrapolation that transgresses the very exegetical decorum out of which it arose: "they understand best what God is like who adjust their understanding to the word of God, for he has adjusted his word to our understanding, and has shown what kind of an idea of him he wishes us to have" (*CPW* vi:136). Hence it is crucial for Milton that God repeatedly describes himself as one throughout scripture (*CPW* vi:146–49): both logic and scripture then dictate that the orthodox doctrine of the Trinity is both illogical and unscriptural.

God's decrees were a controversial topic for Milton's contemporaries. Orthodox Calvinists insisted that God had decreed a number of people to salvation and a (larger) number of people to damnation before he created the world. Milton was deeply unhappy about this. His solution was to decide that God offered the chance of salvation to all, but that they were free to refuse it. In theological terminology, Milton equated predestination and election, but insisted that such election is general and resistible as opposed to the Calvinist notion that it is particular and irresistible. As Milton put it: "Peter is not predestined or elected as Peter, or John as John, but each only insofar as he believes and persists in his belief" (*CPW* vi:176). We can identify this as an Arminian position, which Milton may have derived from William Chappell and Joseph Mede during his time at Christ's College, Cambridge.[5] Following Milton's peroration on the necessity of free will in *Areopagitica* (1644), he never wavered from this conviction. But Milton also thought that the wicked too exercised free will in rejecting God's offer of grace, and that predestination and election are terms never applied to damnation. This was a seemingly unique move in contemporary systematic theology, but it is consistent with Milton's overriding sense that all men must be able to exercise free will.[6] The parascriptural God of *Paradise Lost* is passionate on the point:

> Such I created all th' ethereal Powers
> And spirits, both them who stood and them who faild;
> Freely they stood who stood, and fell who fell.
> Not free, what proof could they have givn sincere
> Of true allegiance, constant faith or love,
> Where only what they needs must do, appeared,
> Not what they would?
>
> (iii.100–06)

Milton's most obvious heresy is his Arianism, or his belief that the Son is "a God who is not self-existent, who did not beget but was begotten, is not a first cause but an effect, and is therefore not a supreme God" (*CPW* VI:263–64). For Milton the Trinity was a late and unscriptural notion, and so sensible was he of the importance of this discussion that he equipped it with its own preface, and the resultant chapter on the Son is easily the longest in the *De Doctrina*. Milton's Arianism was consistently registered by the earliest readers of *Paradise Lost*, although necessarily its presence in the public poem is "implicit, not effaced."[7] It is explicit in Milton's systematic theology, and is once again proved by both logical and scriptural means. Milton's exact argumentation need not be rehearsed here, but we should note on the logical side Milton's insistence that "since a numerical difference is the result of a difference in essence, if two things are two numerically, they must also be two essentially" (*CPW* VI:216). Therefore the Father and the Son cannot be one. Although Milton does assert earlier in the chapter "let us disregard reason when discussing sacred matters" (*CPW* VI:213), we may in turn disregard this assertion: Milton once again shows that logic typically dictates theological reasoning, and not the other way around. We shall not work through Milton's scriptural arguments, but we can note that Milton deals with the problem of the seemingly Trinitarian 1 John 5:7–8 ("the Johannine Comma") by dismissing it, correctly, as a textual accretion (*CPW* VI:221–22). This textual decision had been rendered notorious by its endorsement in the first two editions of Erasmus' Greek New Testament. The Comma was also doubted in Milton's day most notably by Socinian critics and by the Arminian theologian Hugo Grotius, and was one of the texts later demolished by Isaac Newton in his celebrated letter "Two Notable Corruptions of Scripture."[8]

Milton's anti-Trinitarianism might lead us to suspect that Milton was correspondingly lukewarm about the atonement, the doctrine that Christ's sacrifice atones for the sins of mankind. The traditional argument, stemming from the medieval theologian Anselm's celebrated *Cur Deus Homo?*, was that a just God required "satisfaction" for the fall into sin of all mankind through Adam, but that this sin was so great that no single man could make amends for it. Hence, argued Anselm, infinite God needed to become finite man so that God-as-man could punish a man for a sin that only a God could recoup. Now an anti-Trinitarian is in difficulty here, because the whole Anselmic theory of atonement/satisfaction relies on the notion that God can really become a man. Take that away, and the theory falls too. This was the heresy most associated with Socinians in Milton's day, for in denying the divinity of Christ, Socinians also rejected the idea of his atonement, and also correspondingly the idea that original sin existed at all.[9]

Milton is a staunch anti-Socinian in this respect. Christ redeems us not as a mere moral teacher but by virtue of his death, "redeem[ing] all believers at the price of his own blood." Christ "must have existed before his incarnation, whatever subtleties may have been invented to provide an escape from this conclusion, by those [i.e., Socinians] who argue that Christ was a mere man" (*CPW* vi:415, 419). Milton was not sure how Jesus could be both a kind of God and a specific man, but he was sure that this was so:

There is, then, in Christ a mutual hypostatic union of two natures or, in other words, of two essences, of two substances and consequently of two persons. And there is nothing to stop the properties of each from remaining individually distinct. It is quite certain that this is so. We do not know how it is so, and it is best for us to be ignorant of things which God wishes to remain secret. (*CPW* vi:424)

Christ's death, moreover, "fully satisfied divine justice by fulfilling the law and paying the just price on behalf of all men" – not just for the elect (*CPW* vi:444–49). This position Milton implicitly locates as lying between the two extremes of the Socinians and the Trinitarians:

Those who maintain that Christ sought death not in our place and for the sake of redemption, but only for our good and in order to set an example, try in vain to evade the evidence of these texts. Moreover I confess that I cannot see how those who hold that the Son is of the same essence as the Father manage to explain either his incarnation or his satisfaction. (*CPW* vi:444)

In *Paradise Lost*, God too speaks in rigidly Anselmic terms: "Die he or Justice must; unless for him / Some other able, and as willing, pay / The rigid satisfaction, death for death" (iii.210–12).

Why was Milton so unbendingly supportive of the atonement when he had dismantled so much of its traditional Trinitarian scaffolding? There is a political possibility. It has recently been demonstrated that in the aftermath of the regicide, some pro-regicidal theologians felt obliged to re-affirm a model of justice that required strict retribution.[10] Their supposed opponents had protested that "rigid satisfaction" was not required in all cases, and that England could have forgiven Charles I. Certain pro-regicidal theologians associated such political leniency with the theological analogue that God could have forgiven his Son. This shrewd polemic maneuver allowed Independent theologians such as John Owen to elide their Presbyterian enemies, who did not want Charles executed, with the feared and hated Socinians, for the most notorious Socinian tenet was indeed that it made no sense to claim that an omnipotent God was somehow forced to exact vengeance on man, let alone on himself. Milton, the foremost literary apologist for the regicide, here affirms the theological corollary: "Die he or Justice must."[11]

Creation takes place in Milton as in most orthodox accounts *through* the Son. Orthodox accounts would also add that the Holy Spirit assisted too, and that this event marked the beginning of time, because there was no time when God was not with his Son and his Spirit.[12] But because Milton insisted that "father" and "son" are relational terms, and can have no other status in human languages, God's use of them in scripture can only mean that there was a time when there was a father who had no son (a belief flowing from Milton's understanding of accommodation as quoted above: "for he has adjusted his word to our understanding" [*CPW* VI:136], hence fathers must beget, as opposed to sons who are begotten). Thus the Son, though the second of all created things, is not eternal, and when God created through the Son he must first have created the Son, and so he was creating the universe in time (and seemingly without the assistance of a mysterious third Spirit).

The most interesting aspect of Milton's creation, however, is his insistence that God did not create out of nothing. As ever, Milton's objections are both logical and scriptural. Logic dictates that nothing cannot act as a cause. As God was the only being in positive existence at the time of the creation, the requisite matter must have come out of God himself, creating through his recently begotten Son. Philological scrutiny of the biblical text produced the same answer. It had long been recognized that the second word of Genesis (*bara*), past tense of the Hebrew verb "to create," meant in every other occurrence of its use "to create out of something" (such as to make a pot out of clay).[13] This particular site had traditionally been granted immunity from the lexical objection on the philosophical presumption that if God had created out of pre-existent matter then God and matter may have existed together from eternity as two opposed principles, the intolerable specter of dualism. In the preface to his own textbook on logic, the *Artis Logicae Plenior Institutio* (1672), Milton derided the kind of evasive theological trick whereby a philosophically palatable conclusion was fixed in advance, and then logic was bent to enforce it (*CPW* VIII:211); the orthodox position here was exactly that. Milton revoked this immunity, commenting that it is better to think that body can emanate out of spirit than out of nothing. So Milton endorses the orthodox notion that God created a Chaos out of which all substances excepting empyreal or angelic entities were made, but he finds the origin of Chaos in God himself, not in nothing. This is not as outlandish as is often claimed. As Gordon Campbell has recently reminded us, the idea that all comes *from* (*ex*, the preposition

Milton uses) as opposed to *out of* (*de*) God is a familiar Platonic doctrine, witnessed from Justin Martyr right up to the Cambridge Platonists.[14] It is also an Aristotelian commonplace that the universe depends on God, but this dependence is not posterior in time: "as we see the *light*, though it *flows* from the *Sun*, yet the *Sun* is never without *light*."[15] The difference is that while Platonists speak of necessary and eternal emanations, and Aristotelians of an eternal world coeval with its creator, Milton shifts the emphasis onto volition in time: God willed the creation of his Son at a specific moment.[16] This position is also to be distinguished sharply from the pantheism intermittently visible among some Interregnum radicals, in which the creation was indeed identified as materially God. Milton is talking of the filiation of origin, rather than of pure consubstantiality.

In the orthodox tradition, creation resulted in two distinct classes of beings. Created things, says William Ames, are either "immediately" or "mediately perfect." Immediate perfection belongs to those things "having their principles, both materiall and formall, at the first ingenerated in them, and that in a compleat existence." Creatures of "mediate perfection" have a "double existence; first a rude and incomplete, then afterwards a compleat, distinct, and beautified existence." In the highest Heaven, where God lives, all the angels belong to the first category and are subject to no essential change. As beings-perfect-at-once, angels also possess perfection of reason, strength, and speed. Creatures of mediate perfection, on the other hand, suffer change and corruption, and all such things emanate from the Chaos or "that masse which in the beginning was created, without forme, void, and involved in darknesse, which is called Earth, Waters, the Deepe."[17]

The angels, however, for Milton, were not created with but before the rest of the universe. Traditional commentators placed the creation of the angels on the first day, so that "In the beginning, God created the heavens and the earth" was spiritual shorthand for "the highest heavens/the angels, and [then] the material universe." But, as in *Paradise Lost*, the material universe as we know it was created *as a result* of the angelic fall, and hence Milton's angels are slightly older beings than their orthodox counterparts, created before the opening verses of Genesis and undiscussed by them. Their perfection, however, is not of the maximal kind that Milton ascribes to popish teaching: "The good angels do not see into all God's thoughts, as the Papists pretend. They know by revelation only those things which God sees fit to show them, and they know other things by virtue of their very high intelligence, but there are many things of which they are ignorant" (*CPW* vi:347–48). They enjoy cogitating on man's salvation (*CPW* vi:344). But most peculiarly of all, they are material beings. This is obviously a consequence of Milton's views on creation as "from" God, but the angels of *Paradise Lost* are not material in any abstract way: notoriously, they eat, defecate, and even have sex (V.401–43, 461–503; VIII:615–29).[18] Indeed, on this last idea, Milton may also be having a literary joke. Raphael explains that in sex angels can melt entirely into each other. Is he recalling Lucretius' line on the absurdity of human sex, "nor can they penetrate right through and get body entirely into body – for that is what they sometimes seem to wish and strive for"?[19] Milton's angels are therefore far more like humans than any other early modern angels, but equipped with an elasticity of body and mind toward which even unfallen man could only strive.

Milton's Adam and Eve in both *De Doctrina* and *Paradise Lost* are theologically unexceptionable, and I shall not dwell on them. They are created adults, not children. Adam is extremely clever, as one might expect, but unlike some commentators, Milton does not fill Adam's head with all human knowledge.[20] Adam debates with Raphael about astronomy, rather than simply accessing inbuilt knowledge, and Raphael tells him not to think too hard about it. Eve is more troubling: she is created mute, looking down, and unable to make the right decision without divine intervention. Adam, by contrast, is created upright, vocal, physically and philosophically nimble. In so distinguishing the creations of Adam and Eve, Milton treads a dangerous path, as his Eve is more obviously fitted to fall. As for their fall, it is a bleak affair in both epic and treatise, and Milton endorses the gloomy Augustinian/Calvinist maximal judgment of the fall and its consequences.[21] Man is entirely blighted by original sin. This is the corollary to Milton's views on the atonement and is in contrast to the views of many radicals of the age.[22]

Milton opens his discussion of scripture by affirming its inspired status and its complete clarity on matters pertaining to salvation to those who are not already on the high road to damnation. This is a conventional note. Milton then stresses that a good reader of the Bible must possess biblical languages, rhetorical and grammatical sensitivity, knowledge of sources and context, and of parallel texts (*CPW* VI:582–83). Again, this is conventional. Where Milton starts meandering from the high road is in his views on textual integrity, and on the "double scripture." Milton accepts that the Bible contains many textual errors, adducing the huge number of extant manuscripts of the Bible, especially of the New Testament (*CPW* VI:587–89). This is a Socinian view, especially when we remember that for both parties the sole unequivocal proof-text for the Trinity turns out to be one of these very errors. But Milton's real surprise is in his distinction between the external scripture, or the Bible, and the internal scripture, or the Spirit (*CPW* VI:587). The latter is the rule of the former, Milton insists, and can therefore correct it: "on the evidence of scripture itself, all things are eventually to be referred to the Spirit and the unwritten word" (*CPW* VI:590). This is an explosive idea, for in the middle of a treatise consisting mainly of biblical quotation, Milton suggests that biblical text, if found repugnant to the inner conscience, may be safely ignored.

If Milton in this case is echoing the Socinian view of textual fallibility, the question remains whether his theology in general confirms such a sectarian allegiance. Milton's theology has often been called Socinian, from his own time to ours. Modern commentary is ambivalent.[23] Milton's materialism finds Socinian counterparts, and his anti-Trinitarianism perforce overlaps with Socinian arguments. One of the only theologians Milton controverts by name in the *De Doctrina*, Josué de la Place (Placæus), was renowned as an *anti*-Socinian authority.[24] There are many suggestive "parallel passages" between Socinian and Miltonic texts too: the much-discussed exaltation of the Son in *Paradise Lost*, for instance (v.600–15), receives the perfect anti-Trinitarian gloss from the discussion of the dependent texts in *The Racovian Catechisme*, of which Milton licensed the Latin translation.[25] Nevertheless we can now see that Milton was firmly anti-Socinian in the crucial and interconnected areas of the fall, original sin, and the satisfaction, three doctrines affirmed by Milton and denied by Socinians: the Miltonic Son is still bound to most of the jobs from which the Socinian Son has been freed. This, I have also suggested, has a political index.

Moving from doctrine to criticism, Milton's theory of interpretation strikes me as authentically Socinian.[26] His views on textual corruption and his strong philological emphasis are Socinian traits. So is his rejection of institutional or patristic authority (*CPW* VI:591).[27] But most important is Milton's attitude to logic.[28] I have noted frequently how Milton regards logic as theologically decisive, because for Milton logic *is* reason (as he explicitly states [*CPW* VI:159]); and reason, I suspect, is for Milton the manifestation of the "internal scripture." The Socinian tic is to declare a false doctrine to be simultaneously irrational (because implying contradiction) and unscriptural: "for that is repugnant not onely to sound Reason but also to the holy Scriptures."[29] This is of course Milton's controlling methodology in the *De Doctrina* too, and it can be rephrased as the attempted harmonizing of the "internal" and "external scriptures." And when Milton stated that equality implied difference, he was quoting from *The Racovian Catechisme*: "For if Christ be equall to God, who is God by Nature, he cannot possibly be the same God."[30] As both Milton and the Socinians knew, they were in turn both merely repeating a logical

commonplace, which Milton includes in his own *Artis Logicae* and sets off
for emphasis with his famous italic snarl, *evigilent hic theologi*: "*Here let the
Theologians take notice*" (*CPW* VIII:233). When around the turn of the century Milton's acquaintance Abraham Hill declared in one of his commonplace books that Milton was a Socinian, it is crucial that he documented
his claim by quoting the lines from *Paradise Lost* of the Exaltation of the
Son – and then by quoting from Milton's *Art of Logic*.[31]

NOTES

1 The best recent discussion of systematic theology as it pertained to Milton
   is Gordon Campbell, "The Theology of the Manuscript," in Gordon Campbell, Thomas N. Corns, John K. Hale and Fiona J. Tweedie, *Milton and the
   Manuscript of "De Doctrina Christiana"* (Oxford, 2007), 89–120, to which this
   chapter is indebted; see also Maurice Kelley's superb introduction and commentary to *CPW* VI. For the heresiographical tradition see William Poole,
   Milton and the Idea of the Fall (Cambridge, 2005), 58–60, 83–86.
2 Ephraim Pagitt, *Heresiography* (London, 1645), 142. Milton's views on marriage and divorce are discussed in Shigeo Suzuki's chapter in this volume. On
   polygamy, see Leo Miller, *John Milton Among the Polygamophiles* (New York,
   1974).
3 Campbell, "Theology of the Manuscript," 92–98. As his nephew Edward
   Phillips first noted, Milton's treatise is based primarily on the base texts of
   William Ames and Johannes Wolleb (*EL* 61), i.e., William Ames, *Marrow of
   Sacred Divinity* (London, 1642) and Johannes Wolleb, *Abridgment of Christian
   Divinitie* (London, 1650), my broad standards of "orthodox" teaching.
4 See also Maurice Kelley, *This Great Argument: A Study of Milton's "De Doctrina
   Christiana" as a Gloss upon "Paradise Lost"* (Princeton, 1941).
5 For Milton's Arminianism, see Dennis Danielson, *Milton's Good God: A Study
   in Literary Theodicy* (Cambridge, 1982); and Jeffrey Jue, *Heaven Upon Earth:
   Joseph Mede (1586–1638) and the Legacy of Millenarianism* (Dordrecht, 2006),
   28–30.
6 Campbell, "Theology of the Manuscript," 117. It is sometimes claimed that a
   third class of "specially" elected exists in the theology of *Paradise Lost*: "Some
   I have chosen of peculiar grace / Elect above the rest; so is my will" (*Paradise
   Lost* III.183–84). But this couplet is merely God's summation of the previous
   ten lines on the "normally" elected.
7 John P. Rumrich, "Milton's Arianism: Why it Matters," in *Milton and Heresy*,
   ed. Stephen B. Dobranski and John P. Rumrich (Cambridge, 1998), 75–92
   (p. 89); B. Eugene McCarthy, "Milton, Defoe, and Heresy," *Milton Newsletter*
   3 (1969): 71–73. The authoritative account of Milton's Arianism is Michael
   Bauman, *Milton's Arianism* (Frankfurt, 1987).

8 *The Racovian Catechisme* ("Amsterledam" [London], 1652), 23; Johann Crell, *Two Books... touching One God the Father* ("Kosmoburg" [London], 1665), 186; Hugo Grotius, *Opera Theologica*, 3 vols. (London, 1679), II:1143.

9 H. John McLachlan, *Socinianism in Seventeenth-Century England* (Oxford, 1951).

10 Sarah Mortimer, "The Challenge of Socinianism in Mid Seventeenth-Century England" (Oxford DPhil thesis, 2007), 182–96.

11 L. W. Grensted, *A Short History of the Doctrine of the Atonement* (Manchester and London, 1920), 290–98; compare Campbell, "Theology of the Manuscript," 112–13. This emphasis on retribution should also be distinguished from the milder form of juridical atonement espoused by Hugo Grotius in the period, the so-called "Governmental" or "Rectoral" theory.

12 Time and space, in Ames' typical formulation, are only "concreated, or annexed, knit to the things created: because they have not an absolute, but only a relative entitie or being" (*Marrow*, 33).

13 Arnold Williams, *The Common Expositor* (Chapel Hill, NC, 1948), 45; G. N. Conklin, *Biblical Criticism and Heresy in Milton* (New York, 1949), 68.

14 Campbell, "Theology of the Manuscript," 108. For "ex Deo," see *De Doctrina* 1.7, "fuisse omnia ex Deo" (*WJM* xv:20).

15 Edward Stillingfleet, *Origines Sacrae* (London, 1662), K3v.

16 *Ibid.*, 437. Hugh MacCallum, *Milton and the Sons of God: The Divine Image in Milton's Epic Poetry* (Toronto, 1986), 51. MacCallum's general discussion of Milton as lying between the Platonists and the Socinians is excellent (50–56).

17 Ames, *Marrow*, 34–5; cf. Wolleb, *Abridgment*, 39–40.

18 Robert H. West, *Milton and the Angels* (Athens, GA, 1965).

19 Lucretius, *On the Nature of Things [De rerum natura]*, trans. W. H. D. Rouse and rev. Martin F. Smith (Cambridge, MA, 1992), 4.1111–12.

20 Peter Harrison, *The Fall of Man and the Foundations of Modern Science* (Cambridge, 2007).

21 N. P. Williams, *The Ideas of the Fall and of Original Sin* (London, 1927).

22 Poole, *Milton and the Idea of the Fall*, 58–82.

23 Michael Lieb, "Milton and the Socinian Heresy," in *Milton and the Grounds of Contention*, ed. M. R. Kelley, Michael Lieb, and John T. Shawcross (Pittsburgh, PA, 2003), 234–83. The best contemporary analysis is George Ashwell, *De Socino et Socinianismo Dissertatio* (Oxford, 1683).

24 J. P. Pittion, "Milton, La Place, and Socinianism," *The Review of English Studies* 23 (1972): 138–46. La Place should otherwise have been a congenial theologian for Milton (Campbell, "Theology of the Manuscript," 91).

25 *Racovian Catechisme*, 33–34. On the licensing, see most recently Martin Dzelzainis, "Milton and Antitrinitarianism," in *Milton and Toleration*, ed. Sharon Achinstein and Elizabeth Sauer (Oxford, 2007), 171–85, esp. 180–84.

26 Klaus Scholder, *The Birth of Modern Critical Theology: Origins and Problems of Biblical Criticism in the Seventeenth Century* (London, 1990), ch. 2.

27 Cf. Christopher Arnold's comment on Milton: "Of the old English theologians and their commentaries on the Books of Holy Scripture... he seemed to me

altogether to entertain a too harsh, if not an unjust, opinion" (see David
Masson, *The Life of John Milton*, 7 vols. [London, 1859–94], IV:351).

28 Gordon Campbell, "Milton's Theological and Literary Treatments of the Creation," *Journal of Theological Studies* 30 (1979): 128–37. See further Phillip
Donnelly's chapter in this volume.

29 *Racovian Catechisme*, 28.

30 *Ibid.*, 59.

31 William Poole, "The Early Reception of *Paradise Lost*," *Literature Compass* 1
(2004) 17C III:1–13, 8, quoting from MS Sloane 2894, fol. 70v, www.literature-
compass.com.

Appendix: chronology of Milton's major works

Juliet Lucy

This Chronology does not attempt definitively to identify the dates of composition of Milton's works, or to identify all the participants in the debates about the dating of Milton's works. Instead, it paints a broad picture of Milton's patterns of composition over his lifetime and indicates some of the different dates of composition proposed by representative scholars. When read in conjunction with chapter two, the Chronology helps to illustrate the range of Milton's authorial practices.

The following abbreviations are used in the Chronology to refer to scholarly works in which dates of composition are proposed. The number following the abbreviation refers to the page number in the relevant scholarly work where the dating of Milton's work is discussed. For example, "Lewalski 26" means page 26 in Barbara Lewalski's biography, *The Life of John Milton*.

Abbreviation	Scholarly work
Bush	Douglas Bush, "The Date of Milton's *Ad Patrem*," *Modern Philology* 61 (1964): 204–08.
Campbell	Gordon Campbell, *A Milton Chronology* (London, 1997).
CCHT	Gordon Campbell, Thomas N. Corns, John K. Hale, and Fiona J. Tweedie, *Milton and the Manuscript of "De Doctrina Christiana"* (Oxford, 2007).
Coiro	Ann Baynes Coiro, "Fable and Old Song: *Samson Agonistes* and the Idea of a Poetic Career," *Milton Studies* 36 (1998): 123–52.
Dahlo	Rolf Dahlo, "The Date of Milton's 'Artis Logicae' and the Development of the Idea of Definition in Milton's Works," *The Huntington Library Quarterly* 43 (1979): 25–36.
Flannagan	Roy Flannagan, *The Riverside Milton* (Boston, 1998).
Hanford	James Holly Hanford, "The Chronology of Milton's Private Studies," *PMLA* 36 (1921): 251–314.
Hunter	William B. Hunter, Jr., *Milton's "Comus": A Family Piece* (Troy, 1983).
Lewalski	Barbara K. Lewalski, *The Life of John Milton* (Oxford, 2000; rev. edn., 2003).

(cont.)

Abbreviation	Scholarly work
Low	Anthony Low, "Milton's 'Samson' and the Stage, with Implications for Dating the Play," *The Huntington Library Quarterly* 40 (1977): 313–24.
Parker	William Riley Parker, *Milton: A Biography*, 2nd edn., ed. Gordon Campbell, 2 vols., (1968; Oxford, 1996).
Patrick	J. Max Patrick, "The Date of Milton's 'Of Prelatical Episcopacy,'" *The Huntington Library Quarterly* 13 (1950): 303–11.
Raffel	Burton Raffel, "'On the Death of a Fair Infant': Date and Subject," *Milton Quarterly* 34.3 (2000): 93–97.
Revard	Stella P. Revard, *Milton and the Tangles of Neaera's Hair: The Making of the 1645 "Poems"* (Columbia, MO, 1997).
Shawcross *Self*	John T. Shawcross, *John Milton: The Self and the World* (Lexington, KY, 1993).
Shawcross *With Mortal Voice*	John T. Shawcross, *With Mortal Voice: The Creation of "Paradise Lost"* (Lexington, KY, 1982).
Wolfe and Alfred	Don M. Wolfe and William Alfred, "Preface and Notes to *Of Reformation*," *CPW* 1:514–617.
Worden	Blair Worden, "Milton, *Samson Agonistes* and the Restoration," *Culture and Society in the Stuart Restoration*, ed. Gerald MacLean (Cambridge, 1995): 111–36.

CHRONOLOGY OF COMPOSITION OF MILTON'S MAJOR WORKS

Date of composition	Date of publication	Work/Life event	Scholar
Dec. 9, 1608		**Milton born**	
1623 or 1624	1645	Psalms 114 and 136 (translations)	Flannagan 48 – 1623 or 1624; Lewalski 13 – 1623/4 – Milton claims to have written them at age 15
Before Dec. 1624	1645, 1673	Philosophus ad regem, the Apologus De Rustico et Hero and two poems, Carmina Elegiaca and Ignavus satrapam	Campbell 24 – in Milton's schooldays, before Dec. 1624; Revard 10–13 – composed at school
Feb. 12, 1625		**Milton admitted to Christ's College, Cambridge**	
1626	1645, 1673	Elegy 1	Lewalski 21 – 1626; Campbell 27 and Parker 31 – April 1626; Revard 13 – Spring 1626; CPEP xxxi – early April 1626?
1626	1645, 1673	In Quintum Novembris	Lewalski 24 – 1626; Campbell 30 – completed by Nov. 1626; CPEP xxxi – Nov. 1626
1626	1645, 1673	Elegies 2 & 3	Lewalski 23 – Elegy 2 soon after Sept. 26, 1626, Elegy 3 completed by early Dec. 1626; Campbell 29 – Elegy 2 & 3 after late Sept. 1626; CPEP xxxi – autumn 1626
1627	1645, 1673	Elegy 4	CPEP xxxi – between March 11 and April 28, 1627; Lewalski 25 – March 1627
1627	1645, 1673	Elegy 7	CPEP xxxi and 194 – May 1627?; Lewalski 26 – probably spring 1627
1628? or 1625–26?	1673	"On the Death of a Fair Infant Dying of a Cough"	Lewalski 27 – 1628; Campbell 34 – probably after Jan. 22, 1628; Raffel 96 – 1625–26
1628	1674	Prolusion 6	Lewalski 29 – 1628
1628	Performed July 4, 1628; published 1673	"At a Vacation Exercise"	Campbell 35 – oration read July 4, 1628

(cont.)

Date of composition	Date of publication	Work/Life event	Scholar
Dec. 9, 1628		**Milton's 20th Birthday**	
1629	1645, 1673	Elegy 5 & 6	Lewalski 35–36 – 1629; Campbell 37 and Revard 17 – Elegy 5 spring 1629; CPEP xxxi and xxxii – Elegy 5 spring 1629, Elegy 6 late Dec. 1629
1629 or 1630	1645, 1673	Sonnet 1 ("O Nightingale")	Lewalski 39 – 1630; Campbell 37 – probably May 1629 or May 1630; CPEP xxxii – spring 1629 or 1630
1629	1645, 1673	"On the Morning of Christ's Nativity"	Lewalski 38, Campbell 39, and CPEP xxxii – completed by Dec. 25, 1629
1630	1645, 1673	"The Passion"	Lewalski 38 – probably Lenten season of 1630; CPEP 30 – probably 1630, perhaps at Easter
1630	1632, 1640, 1645, 1664, 1673	"On Shakespeare"	Campbell 39, CPEP xxxii and Lewalski 41 – 1630
1631	1645, 1658, 1673	"On the University Carrier" and "Another on the Same"	Lewalski 41–42 – 1631; CPEP xxxii – soon after Jan. 1, 1631
1631–32	1645, 1673	"An Epitaph on the Marchioness of Winchester"	Lewalski 42 – 1631; Campbell 42 and CPEP xxxii – Easter term 1631; Revard 61 – after 1632
June 1631? June 1628?	1645, 1673	De Idea Platonica	Campbell 43 – June 1631?; CPEP xxxi, 218 – June 1628 or 1631
Summer 1631? 1629–35?	1645, 1673	L'Allegro and Il Penseroso	Campbell 43–44 – any time in 1630s, probably summer 1631; Lewalski 42, 559n – between 1629 and 1634, most likely summer 1631; Revard 91 – usually assigned to the years 1632–35; CPEP xxxii – summer 1631?; Parker 98, 769n61 – possibly 1629–33, probably 1631

Date	Work	Publication	Authorities
July 3, 1632	*Milton's graduation from Cambridge, and move to Hammersmith shortly afterwards*		
Dec. 1632 or Dec. 1631	Sonnet 7 ("How soon hath Time")	1645, 1673	Lewalski 60 – upon or after Dec. 9, 1632; Campbell 48 – possibly around Dec. 9, 1632, could be Dec. 9, 1631; *CPEP* xxxii – Dec. 1631
1632–33 or 1633–37	"On Time"	1645, 1673	Revard 91 – 1632–33; *CPEP* xxxii and 58 – 1632–33; Shawcross *With Mortal Voice* 175 – 1633–37
1632–33 or 1633–37	"Upon the Circumcision"	1645, 1673	Lewalski 62 – about Jan. 1, 1633; Revard 91 – 1632–33; *CPEP* xxxii – 1633; Shawcross *With Mortal Voice* 175 – 1633–37
1632–33 or 1633–37	"At a Solemn Music"	1645, 1673	Revard 91 – 1632–33; *CPEP* xxxii – 1632?; Shawcross *With Mortal Voice* 175 – 1633–37
1632? 1629–30? 1632–34?	*Arcades*	Performed Aug.–Oct. 1632? Published 1645, 1673	Parker 80 – possibly as early as 1629, probably 1630; Lewalski 58 – probably performed Aug.–Oct. 1632; Campbell 47 – probably performed Aug. 1632, but perhaps July 1632 – July 1634; *CPEP* xxxii – late summer 1632; Hunter 20 – probably performed May 3, 1634, and completed during summer of 1634
1631–38?	*Ad Patrem*	1645, 1673	Parker 788–89 – 1634?; Lewalski 71, 568n – 1637–38; Shawcross *Self* 68 – spring 1638; *CPEP* xxxii and 220 – probably first half of decade of 1630s, perhaps 1631; Bush 207–08 – spring 1631 – summer 1632
1634	*A Mask Presented at Ludlow Castle*	Performed 1634; published 1637, 1645, 1673	Lewalski 63 – received commission in 1634; *CPEP* xxxii – Sept. 1634
Nov.–Dec. 1634	Psalm 114	1645, 1673	*CPEP* xxxii – Nov. 1634; Lewalski 64 – week before Dec. 4, 1634

(cont.)

Date of composition	Date of publication	Work/Life event	Scholar
Commenced between 1634 and 1637, completed 1644–46		Commonplace Book	Parker 801 – 1634–35 until Milton became blind; Lewalski 65, 160 – commenced 1635–36, largely complete 1646; Shawcross *Self* 76–78 – commenced around Sept. 1637; Hanford 286 – began about 1636, making occasional additions after 1644
May 1636? Nov. 1637	1638	*Milton's move to Horton* *Lycidas*	Lewalski 70 and *CPEP* xxxii – Nov. 1637
Apr./May 1638 *Dec. 9, 1638* 1638–39	1645, 1673	*Milton's tour of the Continent begun* *Milton's 30th Birthday* *Mansus*	*CPEP* xxxiii – Dec. 1638 or Jan.–Feb. 1639
Jul/Aug. 1639 1639–40	1645, 1673	*Milton's return to London* *Epitaphium Damonis*	*CPEP* xxxiii – autumn 1639; Lewalski 109 – late 1639 or early 1640; Revard 226 – 1639–40
Early 1641	May 1641	*Of Reformation*	Lewalski 129 (publication date); Wolfe and Alfred – partly written after April 24, 1641, most probably written Jan. and Feb. 1641
June 1641	July 1641	*Animadversions*	Lewalski 131 – drafting around June 1641, probably published July 1641
Before June–July 1641	June–July 1641	*Of Prelatical Episcopacy*	Lewalski 130 – published June or July 1641; Patrick 304 – written early 1641, published June or July 1641
Nov.–Dec. 1641	Jan.–Feb. 1642, 1654	*The Reason of Church-Government*	Lewalski 135 – Nov.–Dec. 1641; Parker 212 and 223 – Dec. 1641
1642?	After first week April 1642; 1654	*Apology against a Pamphlet*	Lewalski 136 and Parker 223 (for the publication dates)

July 1642?	***Marriage to Mary Powell***		
1643?	Doctrine and Discipline of Divorce, 1st edn.	Aug. 1, 1643	Lewalski 164 and Campbell 78 (for the publication date); Parker 239 – Milton working on draft in July 1643
1643–44	Doctrine and Discipline of Divorce, 2nd edn.	Feb. 2, 1644	Lewalski 169
Apr. 1643–June 1644	Of Education	June 5, 1644	Lewalski 172–73 – commenced after Apr.–Sept. 1643
Mid 1640s	Accedence Commenc't Grammar	June 28, 1669	Lewalski 207, 490 – begun and mostly written in mid 1640s
Apr.–July 1644	Judgment of Martin Bucer	Aug. 6, 1644	Lewalski 175–76 (for the publication date)
Before Nov. 1644	Areopagitica	Nov. 23, 1644	Lewalski 180 (for the publication date)
1644–45?	Tetrachordon and Colasterion	On or before Mar. 4, 1645	Lewalski 182
1645	Poems of Mr. John Milton	1645	Lewalski 199–200 – volume prepared before Sept.–Oct. 1645
1645?–1647?	Sonnet 11 ("A book was writ of late")	1673	Shawcross Self 167 – 1645?; CPEP xxxiii – 1647?; Lewalski 203–04 – probably early months of 1646
1645–49?1625–32?	Artis Logicae	1672	Lewalski 208 – probably mostly drafted when he was teaching Latin (1645–49?); Parker 325 – perhaps 1648; Dahlo 26, 34 – 1625–32 1647
Early 1647	Ad Joannem Rousium	1673	Revard 237 – early 1647; Lewalski 209 – Jan. 1647
Late 1647? – 1649?	The History of Britain	1670, 1677	Lewalski 212, 216 – probably begun late 1647; Parker 295, 1:613 – commenced around 1645–46, reflecting reading undertaken 1639–41, four books finished by mid-March 1649
Months after Nov. 1647	A Brief History of Moscovia	1682	Lewalski 212, 216 – commenced after Nov. 1647, perhaps finished late 1647; Parker 325 – probably 1648

(cont.)

Date of composition	Date of publication	Work/Life event	Scholar
April 1648	1673	Psalms 80–88 (translations)	Shawcross *Self* 164, Campbell 95, and *CPEP* xxxiii – April 1648
July–Aug. 1648	1694	Sonnet 15 ("On the Lord General Fairfax at the siege of Colchester")	Campbell 95 – July 1648; *CPEP* xxxiii – between July 8 and Aug. 17, 1648
Dec. 9, 1648		**Milton's 40th Birthday**	
Jan. 15–29, 1649? early Feb. 1649	Feb. 13, 1649	*Tenure of Kings and Magistrates*, 1st edn.	Lewalski 216, 224 – largely written during king's trial, completed early Feb. 1649; Campbell 97 – largely written between Jan. 15 and 29, 1649
1649?	Before Sept. 30, 1649	*Tenure of Kings and Magistrates*, 2nd edn.	Lewalski 246, Campbell 102 (for the publication date)
1649?	Oct. 6, 1649 or early Nov. 1649	*Eikonoklastes*	Campbell 102 – published Oct. 6, 1649; Lewalski 248 – published Oct. or early Nov. 1649
Mar. 13, 1649		**Milton appointed Secretary for Foreign Tongues**	
?1649 ?1650	May 16, 1649 After June 19, 1650	*Observations on the Articles of Peace* *Eikonoklastes*, 2nd edn.	Lewalski 240 (for the publication date) Campbell 108 – after June 19, 1650; Parker 384 – after late 1650 or early 1651
1650	Feb. 24, 1651	*Pro Populo Anglicano Defensio*	Campbell 104, 111, 113 – commissioned Jan. 8, 1650, registered Dec. 31, 1650; Lewalski 251 – working on it throughout 1650
1652 1652–54	May 30, 1654	**Milton became completely blind** *Defensio Secunda*	Campbell 153 and Lewalski 288–301 – after August 1652, still drafting early 1654, published May 30, 1654
May 1652	1694	Sonnet 16 ("Cromwell, our chief of men")	Parker 412, Campbell 137 and *CPEP* xxxiii – May 1652

Sonnet 17 ("Vane, young in years")	1662, 1694	July 3, 1652	Campbell 139 – July 3, 1652; *CPEP* xxxiii – June–July 1652
Psalms 1–8 translated	1673	Aug. 8–14, 1653	Campbell 149 and *CPEP* xxxiii – 8–14 August 1653
Sonnet 18 ("On the Late Massacre in Piedmont")	1673	May–June 1655	Campbell 160 and *CPEP* xxxiii – shortly after June 20, 1655; Lewalski 331 – May–June 1655
Latin thesaurus	Unpublished	Aug, 1655?, 1645–59?, 1665?	Campbell 161 – probably begun around Aug. 1655; Lewalski 207 and 332 – may have worked on during years of teaching around 1645–59, and around 1665?; Parker 468 – by 1656 had assumed considerable proportions, but far from complete
Pro Se Defensio	Aug. 8, 1655	1655	Campbell 161 – published Aug. 8, 1655; Lewalski 322 – substantially finished mid-May 1655, published Aug. 8, 1655
De Doctrina Christiana	1825	1645–46?, 1656–65?	Parker 293, 481, 1055–57 – probably begun 1645–46, continued 1656, completed 1658–60; Lewalski 125, 319, 357, 398, 415–16 – commenced drafting 1640–46, worked on 1654–60, brought close to completion 1660–65; CCHT 65, 157–58 – working on it mid to late 1640s, late 1650s, finished around 1660
Sonnet 19 ("When I consider")	1673	1655? 1651–52?	Shawcross *Self* 168–69 – Oct. 1655?; Campbell – likely July–Oct. 1655 but possibly written as early as 1651; *CPEP* xxxiii – July–Oct. 1655; Lewalski 290–91 – probably late 1652; Parker 1042n140 – 1655?, perhaps late 1651 to early 1652

(cont.)

Date of composition	Date of publication	Work/Life event	Scholar
1655–56?	1673	Sonnet 20 ("Lawrence of virtuous father")	Campbell 162 – early winter 1655?; *CPEP* xxxiii – Oct.–Nov. 1655?; Lewalski 333 – winter 1655–56; Parker 1043–44n – usually assigned to 1655–56, possibly winter 1654–55
Nov. 12, 1656		**Marriage to Katherine Woodcock**	
1652–63	1673	Sonnet 23 ("Methought I saw")	Campbell 178 – probably in 1658 but possibly between May 1652 and the end of 1656; *CPEP* xxxiii – 1652 or 1658; Lewalski 351 – weeks following Feb. 3, 1658; Parker 475, 1045n – possibly between Feb. 1658 and Feb. 1663, probably between 1652 and 1656
1658?	Oct. 1658	*Pro Populo Anglicano Defensio*, revised edn.	Campbell 181 – 1658
1640–42, mid to late 1650s, and developed to 1665?	1667	*Paradise Lost*, 1st edn.	Shawcross *Self* 173 – conceived and partly written 1640–42, developed to 1645, around 1653 and later 1655 to 1658, then 1661 to 1665; *CPEP* xxxiii – 1640s?, 1658–63?; Parker 296 – begun about 1642; Lewalski 332, 449, 645n45 – perhaps begun 1658, making final revisions after February or early March 1666
Dec. 9, 1658		**Milton's 50th Birthday**	
1658–59	Feb. 17, 1659	*A Treatise of Civil Power*	Campbell 182 (for the publication date); Lewalski 361 – composed Dec. 1658 – Jan. 1659
1659	Aug. 1659	*Considerations Touching the Likeliest Means to Remove Hirelings out of the Church*	Campbell 185 – published Aug. 1659; Lewalski 365 – probably begun in June 1659, published Aug. 1659
Oct. 20, 1659	1698	*Letter to a Friend Concerning the Ruptures of the Commonwealth*	Campbell 186, Lewalski 369 (for the publication date)
Nov. 1659?	1938	*Proposals of Certain Expedients for the Preventing of a Civil War*	Campbell 186 – composed Nov. 1659; Lewalski 370, 661n – begun Nov.–Dec. 1659; Parker 1070n – Nov. 1659?; 1st publication date 1938

Feb. 18–21, 1660	*The Readie and Easie Way*, 1st edn.	Last week Feb. 1660	Campbell 188 (for the publication date); Lewalski 373 – draft finished around Feb. 1660
1st week Mar. 1660	*The Present Means . . . of a Free Commonwealth*	1698	Lewalski 377, 663n84 – perhaps drafted early March 1660
May 1660 **Feb. 24, 1663**	**Restoration of the Monarchy** **Marriage to Elizabeth Minshull**		
Later 1640s?, after 1665	*Paradise Regained*	1671	Shawcross *Self* 166 – later 1640s, reworked after 1665; *CPEP* xxxiv – Aug. 1665–1670?; Lewalski 449–51, 492 – worked on after February or early March 1666, draft finished some time in 1666 after 25 June; Parker 616 – uncertain, but probably some of it dictated between 1665 and July 1670, and the rest perhaps earlier
Later 1640s, then 1667–70?	*Samson Agonistes*	1671	Shawcross *Self* 166– composed later 1640s, then returned to 1667–70; *CPEP* xxxiv – 1660s?; Lewalski 492 and 691n11 – probably 1667–70; Parker 313, 902–17 – commenced around 1647; Worden 111–36 – early 1660s; Low 323 – commenced after 1645, no substantial work until after 1658; Coiro 124 – after *Paradise Lost*
Dec. 9, 1668	**Milton's 60th Birthday**		
Mar. 8–May 6, 1673	*Of True Religion*	Before May 6, 1673	Lewalski 501 – probably commenced after Mar. 8, 1673; Parker 622 – spring 1673
After May 1673	*Poems, &c. Upon Several Occasions*	1673	Lewalski 504 – commenced preparing volume soon after *Of True Religion*
1673–74	*Paradise Lost*, 2nd edn.	6 July 1674	Lewalski 507–08 – revisions for 2nd edn. 1673 or early 1674
Nov. 9 or 10, 1674	**Milton's death**		

Further reading

1. BIOGRAPHY

Lewalski, Barbara K. *The Life of John Milton*. Oxford, 2000.
Fletcher, Harris F. *The Intellectual Development of John Milton*. 2 vols. Urbana, IL, 1956–61.
Masson, David. *The Life of John Milton*. 7 vols. London, 1859–94.
Parker, William Riley. *Milton: A Biography*. 2nd edn. Ed. Gordon Campbell. 2 vols. 1968; Oxford, 1996.

2. COMPOSITION PROCESS

Campbell, Gordon. *A Milton Chronology*. London, 1997.
Coiro, Ann Baynes. "Anonymous Milton, or, *A Maske* Masked." *ELH* 71 (2004): 609–29.
Dobranski, Stephen B. *Milton, Authorship, and the Book Trade*. Cambridge, 1999.
Hale, John K. *Milton as Multilingual: Selected Essays, 1982–2004*. Dunedin, New Zealand, 2005.
Marcus, Leah S. *Unediting the Renaissance: Shakespeare, Marlowe, Milton*. London, 1996.
Shawcross, John T. *John Milton: The Self and the World*. Lexington, KY, 1993.

3. EARLY LIVES

Brown, Cedric C. *John Milton: A Literary Life*. London, 1995.
Campbell, Gordon. "The Life Records." In *A Companion to Milton*. Ed. Thomas N. Corns. Oxford, 2001. 483–98.
Darbishire, Helen, ed. *The Early Lives of Milton*. London, 1932.
Hunter, Michael. *John Aubrey and the Realm of Learning*. New York, 1975.
Rajan, Tilottama. "Uncertain Futures: History and Genealogy in William Godwin's *The Lives of Edward and John Phillips, Nephews and Pupils of Milton*." *Milton Quarterly* 32 (1998): 75–86.
Shawcross, John T. *The Arms of the Family*. Lexington, KY, 2004.

4. LETTERS, VERSE LETTERS, AND GIFT-TEXTS

Davies, Natalie Zemon. *The Gift in Sixteenth-Century France.* Oxford, 2000.

Daybell, James. "Recent Studies in Seventeenth-Century Letters." *ELR* 36 (2006): 135–70.

"Recent Studies in Sixteenth-Century Letters." *ELR* 35 (2005): 331–62.

Dobranski, Stephen B. *Readers and Authorship in Early Modern England.* Cambridge, 2005.

Jardine, Lisa. *Erasmus, Man of Letters: The Construction of Charisma in Print.* Princeton, 1993.

Jardine, Lisa, and Anthony Grafton. "'Studied for Action': How Gabriel Harvey Read His Livy." *Past and Present* 129 (1990): 30–78.

5. MILTON ON HIMSELF

Diekhoff, John. *Milton on Himself.* New York, 1939.

Edmundson, Mark. *Towards Reading Freud: Self-Creation in Milton, Wordsworth, Emerson, and Sigmund Freud.* Princeton, 1990.

Fallon, Stephen M. *Milton's Peculiar Grace: Self-Representation and Authority.* Ithaca, NY, 2007.

Ferry, Anne Davidson. *Milton's Epic Voice: The Narrator in "Paradise Lost."* Chicago, 1963; rpt. 1983.

6. POETIC TRADITION, DRAMATIC

Brown, Cedric C. *John Milton's Aristocratic Entertainments.* Cambridge, 1985.

Dubrow, Heather. "The Masquing of Genre in *Comus.*" *Milton Studies* 44 (2005): 62–83.

McGuire, Maryann Cale. *Milton's Puritan Masque.* Athens, GA, 1983.

Norbrook, David. "The Reformation of the Masque." In *The Court Masque.* Ed. David Lindley. Manchester, 1984. 94–110.

7. POETIC TRADITION, EPIC

Burrow, Colin. *Epic Romance: Homer to Milton.* Oxford, 1993.

Greene, Thomas M. *The Descent from Heaven: A Study in Epic Continuity.* New Haven, 1963.

Quint, David. *Epic and Empire: Politics and Generic Form from Virgil to Milton.* Princeton, 1993.

Revard, Stella Purce. *The War in Heaven: "Paradise Lost" and the Tradition of Satan's Rebellion.* Ithaca, NY, 1980.

8. POETIC TRADITION, PASTORAL

Alpers, Paul. *What is Pastoral?* Chicago, 1996.

Knott, John R. *Milton's Pastoral Vision: An Approach to "Paradise Lost."* Chicago, 1971.

Lewalski, Barbara K. "Milton's *Comus* and the Politics of Masquing." In *The Politics of the Stuart Court Masque.* Ed. David Bevington and Peter Holbrook. Cambridge, 1998. 296–320.

"Paradise Lost" and the Rhetoric of Literary Forms. Princeton, 1985.

Patterson, Annabel. *Pastoral and Ideology: Virgil to Valéry.* Berkeley, 1987.

Poggioli, Renato. *The Oaten Flute: Essays on Pastoral Poetry and the Pastoral Ideal.* Cambridge, MA, 1975.

Revard, Stella P. *Milton and the Tangles of Neaera's Hair: The Making of the 1645 "Poems."* Columbia, MO, 1997.

9. PROSE STYLE

Kerrigan, William. *The Prophetic Milton.* Charlottesville, VA, 1974.

Kranidas, Thomas. *Milton and the Rhetoric of Zeal.* Pittsburgh, PA, 2005.

Loewenstein, David, and James Grantham Turner, eds. *Politics, Poetics, and Hermeneutics in Milton's Prose.* Cambridge, 1990.

10. VERSE AND RHYME

Burnett, Archie. *Milton's Style: The Shorter Poems, "Paradise Regained" & "Samson Agonistes."* London, 1981.

Emma, Ronald David. *Milton's Grammar.* The Hague, 1964.

Emma, Ronald David, and John T. Shawcross, eds. *Language and Style in Milton.* New York, 1967.

Hale, John K. *Milton's Languages: The Impact of Multilingualism on Style.* Cambridge, 1997.

Houston, John Porter. *The Rhetoric of Poetry in the Renaissance and Seventeenth Century.* Baton Rouge, LA, 1983.

Ricks, Christopher. *Milton's Grand Style.* Oxford, 1963.

11. CRITICAL RESPONSES, EARLY

Griffin, Dustin. *Regaining Paradise: Milton and the Eighteenth Century.* Cambridge, 1968.

Keeble, N. H. *The Literary Culture of Nonconformity in Late Seventeenth-Century England.* Athens, GA, 1987.

Parker, William Riley. *Milton's Contemporary Reputation.* Columbus, OH, 1940.

Stevenson, Kay Gilliland. "Reading Milton, 1674–1800." In *A Companion to Milton.* Ed. Thomas N. Corns. Oxford, 2003. 447–62.

Von Maltzahn, Nicholas. "Milton's Readers." In *The Cambridge Companion to Milton.* 2nd edn. Ed. Dennis Danielson. Cambridge, 1999. 236–52.

12. CRITICAL RESPONSES, 1825–1970

Abrams, M. H. "Five Types of *Lycidas*." In *Milton's "Lycidas": The Tradition and the Poem.* Ed. C. A. Patrides. Rev. edn. 1961; Columbia, MO, 1983. 216–35.

Alpers, Paul. "*Lycidas* and Modern Criticism." *ELH* 49 (1982): 468–96.

Dyson, A. E. "The Interpretation of *Comus.*" *Essays and Studies* new ser. 8 (1955): 89–114.

Peter, John. "Reflections on the Milton Controversy." *Scrutiny* 19 (1952): 2–15.

Wilkes, G. A. "The Interpretation of *Samson Agonistes.*" *Huntington Library Quarterly* 26 (1963): 363–79.

Wittreich, Joseph. *Interpreting "Samson Agonistes."* Princeton, 1986.

13. CRITICAL RESPONSES, RECENT

Creamer, Kevin J. T., and Roy Flannagan. *The Milton-L Home Page.* 1991. http://johnmilton.org.

Danielson, Dennis. *The Cambridge Companion to Milton.* 2nd edn. Cambridge, 1999.

Dobranski, Stephen B., and John P. Rumrich, eds. *Milton and Heresy.* Cambridge, 1998.

Evans, J. Martin, ed. *John Milton: Twentieth Century Perspectives.* 5 vols. New York, 2003.

Hill, Christopher. *Milton and the English Revolution.* London, 1977.

Huckabay, Calvin. *John Milton: An Annotated Bibliography, 1968–1988.* Ed. P. J. Klemp. Pittsburgh, PA, 1996.

Hughes, Merritt Y., gen. ed. *A Variorum Commentary on the Poems of John Milton.* Vols. I, II, and IV in 5 vols. New York, 1970–75.

Martin, Catherine Gimelli, ed. *Milton and Gender.* Cambridge, 2004.

Shawcross, John T. *Rethinking Milton Studies: Time Present and Time Past.* Newark, NJ, 2005.

14. LATER PUBLISHING HISTORY

Oras, Ants. *Milton's Editors and Commentators from Patrick Hume to Henry John Todd (1695–1801). A Study in Critical Views and Methods.* London, 1931; New York, 1964.

Parker, William Riley. *Milton: A Biography.* 2nd edn. Ed. Gordon Campbell. 2 vols. Oxford, 1996.

Sensabaugh, George. *Milton in Early America.* Princeton, 1964.

Shawcross, John T. *Milton: A Bibliography for the Years 1624–1700 (Revised) and for the Years 1701–1799.* 4 vols. Tempe, AZ, forthcoming. Available online at *Iter: Gateway to the Middle Ages and Renaissance.* Toronto, 2007. www.IterGateway.org.

Wickenheiser, Robert J. *The Robert J. Wickenheiser Collection of John Milton at the University of South Carolina. A Descriptive Account with Illustrations.* Columbia, SC, 2008.

15. TRANSLATIONS

Einboden, Jeffrey. "A Qur'ānic Milton: From Paradise to al-Firdaws." *Milton Quarterly* 43 (October 2009), forthcoming.

Hale, John K. "John Milton, the English Revolution (1640–60) and the Dynamics of the French Revolution (1789)." *Prose Studies* 4.3 (2001): 18–38.

"The Significance of the Early Translations of *Paradise Lost.*" In *Milton as Multilingual: Selected Essays by John K. Hale.* Ed. Lisa Marr and Chris Ackerley. Dunedin, New Zealand, 2005. 157–80.

Mouchard, Claude. "Chateaubriand, Milton, l'épopée et la prose." *Revue de littérature comparée* 70 (1996): 497–505.

16. VISUAL ARTS

Behrendt, Stephen C. *The Moment of Explosion: Blake and the Illustration of Milton.* Lincoln, NE, 1983.

Dunbar, Pamela. *William Blake's Illustrations to the Poetry of Milton.* Oxford, 1980.

Labriola, Albert C., and Edward Sichi, Jr., eds. *Milton's Legacy in the Arts.* University Park, PA, 1988.

McColley, Diane Kelsey. *A Gust for Paradise: Milton's Eden and the Visual Arts.* Urbana, IL, and Chicago, 1993.

Wittreich, Joseph Anthony, Jr. *Angel of Apocalypse: Blake's Idea of Milton.* Madison, WI, 1975.

17. ASTRONOMY

Martin, Catherine Gimelli. "'What If the Sun Be Centre to the World?': Milton's Epistemology, Cosmology, and Paradise of Fools Reconsidered." *Modern Philology* 99 (2001): 231–65.

Nicolson, Marjorie. *Science and Imagination.* Ithaca, NY, 1956. (Chapter 4, "Milton and the Telescope," first published in *ELH* 2 [1935]: 1–32.)

Sarkar, Malabika. "'The Visible Diurnal Sphere': Astronomical Images of Space and Time in *Paradise Lost.*" *Milton Quarterly* 18 (1984): 1–5.

Singh Marjara, Harinder. *Contemplation of Created Things: Science in "Paradise Lost."* Toronto, 1992.

Tanner, John. "'And Every Star Perhaps a World of Destined Habitation': Milton and Moonmen." *Extrapolation* 30 (1989): 267–79.

18. THE BOOK TRADE

Clegg, Cyndia Susan. *Press Censorship in Caroline England.* Cambridge, 2008.

Dobranski, Stephen B. *Milton, Authorship, and the Book Trade*. Cambridge, 1999.

McKenzie, D. F. "The London Book Trade in 1644." In D. F. McKenzie, *Making Meaning: "Printers of the Mind" and Other Essays*. Ed. Peter D. McDonald and Michael F. Suarez. Amherst, MA, 2002. 126–43.

McKitterick, David. *Print, Manuscript and the Search for Order, 1450–1830*. Cambridge, 2003.

Milton, Anthony. "Licensing, Censorship, and Religious Orthodoxy in Early Stuart England." *The Historical Journal* 41 (1998): 625–51.

Moyles, R. G. *The Text of "Paradise Lost": A Study in Editorial Procedure*. Toronto, 1985.

19. THE CAROLINE COURT

Brown, Cedric C. *John Milton's Aristocratic Entertainments*. Cambridge, 1985.

Corns, Thomas N. "Milton before 'Lycidas.'" In *Milton and the Terms of Liberty*. Ed. Graham Parry and Joad Raymond. Cambridge, 2002. 23–36.

Lewalski, Barbara K. "How Radical Was the Young Milton?" In *Milton and Heresy*. Ed. Stephen B. Dobranski and John P. Rumrich. Cambridge, 1998. 49–72.

McDowell, Nicholas. "Dante and the Distraction of Lyric in Milton's 'To My Friend Mr Henry Lawes.'" *The Review of English Studies* 59 (2008): 232–54.

Parry, Graham. "Literary Baroque and Literary Neoclassicism." In *A Companion to Milton*. Ed. Thomas N. Corns. Oxford, 2001. 54–71.

20. CATHOLICISM

Achinstein, Sharon, and Elizabeth Sauer, eds. *Milton and Toleration*. New York, 2007.

Barker, Arthur E. *Milton and the Puritan Dilemma, 1641–1660*. Toronto, 1942.

Jordan, W. K. *The Development of Religious Toleration in England*. 4 vols. Cambridge, MA, 1932–40.

Zagorin, Perez. *How the Idea of Religious Toleration Came to the West*. Princeton, 2003.

21. THE CIVIL WARS

Achinstein, Sharon. *Milton and the Revolutionary Reader*. Princeton, 1994.

Corns, Thomas N. *Uncloistered Virtue: English Political Literature 1640–1660*. Cambridge, 1992.

Hill, Christopher. *Milton and the English Revolution*. London, 1977.

McDowell, Nicholas. *Poetry and Allegiance in the English Civil Wars: Marvell and the Cause of Wit*. Oxford, 2008.

Wilding, Michael. *Dragons' Teeth: Literature in the English Revolution*. Oxford, 1987.

22. CLASSICAL LITERATURE AND LEARNING

Blessington, Francis C. *"Paradise Lost" and the Classical Epic*. London, 1979.

Burrow, Colin. *Epic Romance: Homer to Milton*. Oxford, 1993.

Haan, Estelle. *John Milton's Latin Poetry: Some Neo-Latin and Vernacular Contexts*. Belfast, 1987.

Hale, John K. *Milton's Languages: The Impact of Multilingualism on Style*. Cambridge, 1997.

Martindale, Charles. *John Milton and the Transformation of the Ancient Epic*. London, 1986.

23. EDUCATION

Chaplin, Gregory. "'One Flesh, One Heart, One Soul': Renaissance Friendship and Miltonic Marriage." *Modern Philology* 99.2 (2001): 266–92.

Clark, Donald Lemen. *John Milton at St. Paul's School*. New York, 1948.

Fletcher, Harris Francis. *The Intellectual Development of John Milton*. 2 vols. Urbana, IL, 1956–61.

Hanford, James Holly. "The Youth of Milton." In *John Milton, Poet and Humanist: Essays by James Holly Hanford*. Cleveland, OH, 1966. 1–74.

Rumrich, John P. "The Erotic Milton." *Texas Studies in Literature and Language* 41.2 (1999): 128–41.

24. THE ENGLISH CHURCH

Cust, Richard, and Ann Hughes, eds. *The English Civil War*. London, 1997.

Hill, Christopher. *Society and Puritanism in Pre-revolutionary England*. London, 1969.

MacCullough, Diarmaid. *Reformation: Europe's House Divided 1490–1700*. London, 2003.

Spurr, John. *English Puritanism, 1603–1689*. Basingstoke, 1998.

Tyacke, Nicholas. *Anti-Calvinists: The Rise of English Arminianism, c. 1590–1640*. Oxford, 1987.

25. THE INTERREGNUM

Corns, Thomas N. *Uncloistered Virtue: English Political Literature, 1640–1660*. Oxford, 1992.

Loewenstein, David. *Representing Revolution in Milton and His Contemporaries: Religion, Politics, and Polemics in Radical Puritanism*. Cambridge, 2001.

Loewenstein, David, and James Grantham Turner, eds. *Politics, Poetics, and Hermeneutics in Milton's Prose*. Cambridge, 1990.

Worden, Blair. *Literature and Politics in Cromwellian England: John Milton, Andrew Marvell, Marchmont Nedham*. Oxford, 2007.

26. ITALY

Boocker, David. "'According to Our Custom': Milton's Papal Attacks and Their Italian Sources." *Explorations in Renaissance Culture* 22 (1994): 19–39.

Di Biase, Carmine G., ed. *Travel and Translation in the Early Modern Period.* Amsterdam, 2006.

Di Cesare, Mario, ed. *Milton in Italy: Contexts, Images, Contradictions.* Binghamton, NY, 1991.

Hunt, Clay. *"Lycidas" and the Italian Critics.* New Haven, 1979.

Prince, Frank T. *The Italian Element in Milton's Verse.* Oxford, 1954.

27. LAW

Dzelzainis, Martin. "'In These Western Parts of the Empire': Milton and Roman Law." In *Milton and the Terms of Liberty.* Ed. Graham Parry and Joad Raymond. Cambridge, 2002. 57–68.

French, J. Milton. *Milton in Chancery: New Chapters in the Lives of the Poet and His Father.* New York, 1939.

Kahn, Victoria. *Wayward Contracts: The Crisis of Political Obligation in England, 1640–1674.* Princeton, 2004.

28. LITERARY CONTEMPORARIES

Borris, Kenneth. *Allegory and Epic in English Renaissance Literature.* Cambridge, 2000.

Hardin, Richard F. *Civil Idolatry: Desacralizing and Monarchy in Spenser, Shakespeare, and Milton.* London, 1992.

Sherwood, Terry G. *Self in Early Modern Literature.* Pittsburgh, PA, 2007.

Slights, Camille Wells. *The Casuistical Tradition in Shakespeare, Donne, Herbert, and Milton.* Princeton, 1981.

29. LOGIC

Donnelly, Phillip J. *Milton's Scriptural Reasoning: Narrative and Protestant Toleration.* Cambridge, 2009.

Feingold, Mordechai, Joseph S. Freedman, and Wolfgang Rother, eds. *Ramus.* Basel, 2001.

Skalnik, James Veazie. *Ramus and Reform: Church and University at the End of the Renaissance in France.* Kirksville, MO, 2002.

Wilson, Emma, and Steven Reid, eds. *Ramus and the Liberal Arts: Ramism in Britain and the Wider World.* London, forthcoming.

30. LONDON

Dobranski, Stephen B. *Milton, Authorship, and the Book Trade.* Cambridge, 1999.

Hughes, Ann. *Gangraena and the Struggle for the English Revolution.* Oxford, 2004.
  "Religious Diversity in Revolutionary London: Politics, Religion, and Commu-
  nities." In *The English Revolution, c. 1590–1720: Politics, Religion and Commu-
  nities.* Ed. Nicholas Tyacke. Manchester, 2007. 111–28.
Lindley, Keith. *Popular Politics and Religion in Civil War London.* Aldershot,
  England, 1997.
Pearl, Valerie. "London's Counter-Revolution." In *The Interregnum: The Quest for
  Settlement, 1646–1660.* Ed. G. E. Aylmer. Hamden, CN, 1972. 29–56.

31. MANUSCRIPT TRANSMISSION

Beal, Peter. *In Praise of Scribes: Manuscripts and Their Makers in Seventeenth-
  Century England.* Oxford, 1998.
Bridgewater Manuscript and Trinity Manuscript. In Harris Francis Fletcher, ed.
  *Complete Poetical Works [of John Milton], Reproduced in Photographic Facsim-
  ile.* Vol. 1. Urbana, IL, 1944.
Love, Harold. *Scribal Publication in Seventeenth-Century England.* Oxford, 1993.
McKitterick, David. *Print, Manuscript and the Search for Order, 1450–1830.*
  Cambridge, 2003.

32. MARRIAGE AND DIVORCE

Crawford, Katherine. *European Sexualities, 1400–1800.* Cambridge, 2007.
Halkett, John. *Milton and the Idea of Matrimony: A Study of the Divorce Tracts and
  "Paradise Lost."* New Haven, 1970.
Harris, Frances. *Transformations of Love: The Friendship of John Evelyn and Mar-
  garet Godolphin.* Oxford, 2003.
Ingram, Martin. *Church Courts, Sex, and Marriage in England, 1570–1640.*
  Cambridge, 1987.
Stone, Lawrence. *The Family, Sex and Marriage in England, 1500–1800.* 2nd edn.
  London, 1990.

33. MUSIC

Heninger, S. K., Jr. *Touches of Sweet Harmony: Pythagorean Cosmology and Renais-
  sance Poetics.* San Marino, CA, 1974.
Le Huray, Peter. *The Treasury of English Church Music, 1545–1650.* Cambridge,
  1982.
Willetts, Pamala J. *The Henry Lawes Manuscript.* London, 1969.
Winn, James Anderson. *Unsuspected Eloquence: A History of the Relations between
  Poetry and Music.* New Haven and London, 1981.
Wulstan, David. *Tudor Music.* Iowa City, 1986.

34. THE NATURAL WORLD

Delumeau, Jean. *History of Paradise: The Garden of Eden in Myth and Tradition.* Trans. Matthew O'Connell. Urbana, IL, 1995.

Edwards, Karen L. *Milton and the Natural World: Science and Poetry in "Paradise Lost."* Cambridge, 1999.

Leonard, John. *Naming in Paradise: Milton and the Language of Adam and Eve.* Oxford, 1990.

Rumrich, John Peter. *Matter of Glory: A New Preface to "Paradise Lost."* Pittsburgh, PA, 1987.

Thomas, Keith. *Man and the Natural World: A History of the Modern Sensibility.* New York, 1985.

35. THE NEW WORLD

Albanese, Denise. *New Science, New World.* Durham, NC, and London, 1996.

Evans, J. Martin. *Milton's Imperial Epic: "Paradise Lost" and the Discourse of Colonialism.* Ithaca, NY, 1996.

Hulme, Peter. *Colonial Encounters: Europe and the Native Caribbean 1492–1797.* London, 1986.

Quint, David. *Epic and Empire: Politics and Generic Form from Virgil to Milton.* Princeton, 1993.

Rajan, Balachandra, and Elizabeth Sauer, eds. *Milton and the Imperial Vision.* Pittsburgh, PA, 1999.

36. PAMPHLET WARS

Achinstein, Sharon. *Milton and the Revolutionary Reader.* Princeton, 1994.

Corns, Thomas N., ed. *A Companion to Milton.* Oxford, 2001.

Loewenstein, David, and James Grantham Turner, eds. *Politics, Poetics, and Hermeneutics in Milton's Prose.* Cambridge, 1990.

Norbrook, David. *Writing the English Republic: Poetry, Rhetoric and Politics, 1627–1660.* Cambridge, 1999.

Raymond, Joad. *Pamphlets and Pamphleteering in Early Modern Britain.* Cambridge, 2003.

37. PHILOSOPHY

Cassirer, Ernst. *The Platonic Renaissance in England.* Trans. James P. Pettegrove. Austin, TX, 1953.

Fletcher, Harris Francis. *The Intellectual Development of John Milton.* 2 vols. Urbana, IL, 1956–61.

Hogan, Patrick G. "Aristotle." *Milton Encyclopedia.* Ed. William B. Hunter, Jr., John T. Shawcross, and John M. Steadman. 9 vols. Lewisburg, PA, 1978–83. 1: 77–83.

Kerrigan, William "Milton's Place in Intellectual History." *The Cambridge Companion to Milton*. Ed. Dennis Danielson. 2nd edn. Cambridge, 1999. 253–67.

Mintz, Samuel I. "The Motion of Thought: Intellectual and Philosophical Backgrounds." In *The Age of Milton: Backgrounds to Seventeenth-Century Literature*. Ed. C. A. Patrides and Raymond B. Waddington. Manchester, 1980. 138–69.

38. READING PRACTICES

Andersen, Jennifer, and Elizabeth Sauer, eds. *Books and Readers in Early Modern England*. Philadelphia, 2002.

Dobranksi, Stephen B. *Milton, Authorship, and the Book Trade*. Cambridge, 1999.

Mohl, Ruth. *John Milton and His Commonplace Book*. New York, 1969.

Norbrook, David. "*Areopagitica*, Censorship, and the Early Modern Public Sphere." In *The Administration of Aesthetics: Censorship, Political Criticism, and the Public Sphere*. Ed. Richard Burt. Minneapolis, 1994. 3–33.

Sharpe, Kevin. *Reading Revolutions: The Politics of Reading in Early Modern England*. New Haven, 2000.

39. THE RESTORATION

Campbell, Gordon, Thomas N. Corns, John K. Hale, and Fiona J. Tweedie. *Milton and the Manuscript of "De Doctrina Christiana."* Oxford, 2007.

De Krey, Gary S. *London and the Restoration, 1659–1683*. Cambridge, 2005.

Knoppers, Laura. *Historicizing Milton: Spectacle, Power, and Poetry in Restoration England*. Athens, GA, 1994.

MacLean, Gerald, ed. *Culture and Society in the Stuart Restoration: Literature, Drama, History*. Cambridge, 1985.

40. THEOLOGY

Campbell, Gordon. "Milton's Theological and Literary Treatments of the Creation." *Journal of Theological Studies* 30 (1979): 128–37.

Campbell, Gordon, Thomas N. Corns, John K. Hale, and Fiona J. Tweedie. *Milton and the Manuscript of "De Doctrina Christiana."* Oxford, 2007.

Danielson, Dennis. *Milton's Good God: A Study in Literary Theodicy*. Cambridge, 1982.

Kelley, Maurice. *This Great Argument: A Study of Milton's "De Doctrina Christiana" as a Gloss upon "Paradise Lost."* Princeton, 1941.

MacCallum, Hugh. *Milton and the Sons of God: The Divine Image in Milton's Epic Poetry*. Toronto, 1986.

Poole, William. *Milton and the Idea of the Fall*. Cambridge, 2005.

Index

Abrams, M. H. 501
Accedence Commenc't Grammar 10, 161, 468, 493
Acciaiuoli, Giovanni 271
Achinstein, Sharon 420, 503, 507
Ad Joannem Rousium ("To John Rouse") 41, 42,
    121, 493
Ad Leonoram Romae Canentem ("To Leonora
    singing in Rome") 319, 400
Ad Patrem ("To my Father") 5, 41–42, 329, 366,
    394, 491
Ad Salzillum ("To Salzilli") 41, 366
Adamites 299
Adams, Robert Martin 120, 130
Addison, Joseph 125, 159, 162, 163, 166, 167, 168,
    173
Aeschylus 66, 134
Aesop 283
Agar, Thomas 7
Agricola, Rudolph 350
Aitzema, Liewe van 36, 230
Albanese, Denise 423, 507
Alcaeus 312
Aldrich, Henry 157, 185
Aldus Manutius 270, 271
Alfray [Alphry], Thomas 365
Alfred, William 487
Alison, Richard 405
Alpers, Paul 499, 501
amanuenses 21, 23, 36; *see also* Milton,
    composition process
Americas, Americans *see* New World
Ames, William 288, 355, 481, 484, 485
Amner, John 394
Anabaptists 230, 430
Anacreon 272
Anderson, Jennifer 508
Andreini, Giambattista 64
Andrewes, Lancelot 238, 244, 294
Andrews, Kenneth R. 419
Anglesey, Arthur Annesley, Earl of 160
Animadversions 47, 159, 299, 335, 489

"Another on the Same" (second Hobson poem)
    374–77, 378, 379, 490
Anselm 478, 479
Antes, John 303
anti-Catholicism 239–40, 241, 244, 248, 252, 255,
    259, 281, 292–93, 294, 295, 297, 298, 303,
    309, 318, 362, 471–72; *see also* Catholics,
    Catholicism
antimasque 62
anti-Miltonists 131, 132–35
antiprelatical controversy 7, 8, 95–99, 122, 227,
    259–60, 265, 292, 296–300, 306, 330,
    367, 434, 435, 440; *see also the titles of
    Milton's individual tracts*
antitheatricality 240, 241–42
anti-Trinitarianism 145, 477–80, 483; *see also*
    theology *and* Arianism
Apologeticall Narration, An 300
Apologus de Rustico et Hero ("The Fable of the
    Peasant and the Lord") 489
Apology against a Pamphlet, An xxiv, 46, 47–50,
    51, 121, 242, 271, 283, 284, 354, 367, 433,
    439, 441, 452, 492
Aquinas, Thomas 338
Arcades 60–61, 82, 84, 174, 245, 398–99, 491
Areopagitica 9–10, 48, 50, 228–29, 232, 262–63,
    322, 332, 335, 338, 342, 366, 367–68, 370,
    400, 432, 433, 435, 441, 449, 493
    author's authority 17, 119, 120, 226
    collaboration 110, 226
    later editions 156, 161
    in translation 169, 170, 171, 172, 173, 174, 175,
        176
    reading practices 430–31, 449, 450, 452,
        454–57, 477
    religious freedom 216, 248, 251, 253, 282, 301,
        318, 434, 471–72
Arian, Arianism 126, 127–28, 145, 166, 177, 230,
    477–78
Ariosto, Ludovico, *Orlando Furioso* 69, 71, 75,
    275, 287, 328

Aristophanes 282
Aristotle, Aristotelian 66, 69, 71, 213, 218, 319,
    350, 351, 359, 442–43, 451, 453, 481
Arminian, Arminianism 103, 145, 230, 238–39,
    245, 295, 296, 475, 477
Arminius, Jacob 238, 295
Armitage, David 150, 420
Armstrong, John 149
Arne, Thomas 165
Arnold, Christopher 485
Arnold, Matthew 132
Artis Logicae (*Art of Logic*) 10, 235, 288, 349,
    351–53, 354–55, 356, 358, 359, 468, 480,
    484, 493; *see also* logic *and* Ramism
Ascham, Roger, *The Schoolmaster* 106, 319–20
Ashworth, Elizabeth 332
astronomy 213–25, 320–21
Atabalipa 418
"At a Solemn Music" 18, 174, 345, 394, 395, 397,
    400, 491
"At a Vacation Exercise" 60, 71, 489
Atterbury, Francis 127, 157
Attridge, Derek 111
Aubrey, John 16, 26, 27, 28, 107, 124, 134, 365
Augustine 47, 145, 482
authors, authorship 226, 228–29, 231–32, 234–35
Aylmer, Brabazon 44

Bacon, Francis 321, 336, 419, 421, 453, 454
Bagehot, Walter 134, 135
Baillie, Robert 300
Bale, John 64
Banquet of Jests 375, 377
Baptists 301, 475
Barberini, Francesco, Cardinal 250, 319
Barker, Arthur E. 57, 144, 146, 503
Baron, Richard 164
Baroni, Leonora 319, 400
Bastwick, John 241
Batten, Adrian 395
Bauman, Michael 145
Baxter, Richard 384, 429–30
Beal, Peter 27, 372, 374, 377, 379, 506
Beer, Anna 4
Behrendt, Stephen C. 502
Bellerophon 54–56
Bennett, Joan S. 149
Bentley, Richard 120, 164–65
Berry, Herbert 58
Bigot, Emeric 38
biographers, early xxi, 4, 15, 17, 26–34, 160, 161,
    163, 365; *see also individual biographers'
    names*
Bion 273, 276
Birch, Thomas 162, 164

Bishop, George 270
Bishops' Wars 7, 246, 261
Blackborough, William 331
Blacklowism 252, 256
Blake, William 133, 145, 189–95, 209
blank verse 105–06, 111–14, 155; *see also Paradise
    Lost*, versification
Blessington, Francis C. 504
Blount, Charles 156
Boccaccio, Giovanni 324, 326
body 241, 422–27
Boethius 350
Boétie, Etienne de la 39
Boiardo, Matteo Maria 69, 71
Boocker, David 505
Book of Common Prayer 292, 295, 296, 388, 397
Book of Sports 294–95
book trade 226–36, 261–62, 332, 333, 362, 365,
    367–68, 373–74, 429–31, 452, 472
Booth, George 317
Borris, Kenneth 505
Boswell, Jackson Campbell 280
Bouchard, Donald 143
Bouche, Paul 157
Boyle, Richard 365
Bracton, Henry de 336
Bradshaw, John 11, 312, 334, 365
Brass, Henry de 38
Bridgewater Manuscript 21, 165, 378–79, 506
Brief History of Moscovia, A 10, 161, 493
Bristol, Michael D. 373
Brown, Cedric C. 28, 378, 498, 499, 503
Brown, Lancelot ("Capability") 185
Brownists 299
Bruegel, Jan, the Elder 181, 182, 208
Bruno, Giordano 218, 221
Buchanan, George 64
Buckingham, George Villiers, Duke of 239–40,
    241, 242, 243, 244, 287, 296
Bullinger, Heinrich 387
Bunny, Edmund 388
Bunyan, John 53
Buonmattei, Benedetto 37, 319, 322–23, 324, 325
Burbage, Richard 59
Burghers, Michael (Burgesse) 157
Burnett, Archie 144, 500
Burney, Edward 186, 189, 191, 192, 209
Burrow, Colin 499, 504
Burton, Henry 241
Burton, Robert 221–22
Bush, Douglas 130, 132, 134, 135, 137–38, 273, 285,
    487
Butler, James 309
Butler, Samuel 73, 465
Byrd, William 394, 395, 397

Cabinet-Council, The 159, 230
Cable, Lana 95–96
Caesar, Gaius Julius 282, 284
Calvinism (John Calvin) 145, 238, 245, 251, 253,
  259, 293, 294, 295, 296, 300, 311, 318, 325,
  326, 357, 386, 444, 477, 482
Cambridge Platonists 444, 446, 481
Cambridge University 4, 5, 59, 60, 86, 134, 239,
  241, 242, 282, 288–89, 293, 296, 319, 320,
  321, 329, 361, 362, 376; *see also* Christ's
  College
Camden, William 246
Camões, Luís Vaz de 71, 73, 110
Campbell, Gordon 28, 145, 146, 147, 480, 487,
  498, 508
Campion, Thomas, *Observations* 106
Carew, Thomas 62, 243, 245, 400–01, 405
Carey, John 144, 151, 152, 166
Carmina Elegiaca ("Elegiac Verses") 489
Caryll, Joseph 469
Cassirer, Ernst 507
Castelvetro, Lodovico 66, 319
Castiglione, Baldassare, *The Book of the Courtier*
  440
Catholics, Catholicism 97, 156, 157, 229, 237–38,
  242, 248–57, 259, 296, 300, 302, 303,
  318–20, 322, 386, 388–89, 465, 481;
  see also anti-Catholicism
Cato 283
Cavalier poets 243, 245, 394
Cavendish, Margaret 419, 420
censorship 159, 160, 241, 262–63, 322, 379, 454;
  see also licensing
Chalcondylas, Demetrius 271
Chapelain, Jean, *La Pucelle* 69, 74
Chaplin Gregory 504
Chappell, William 288, 477
Character of the Long Parliament, The ("The
  Digression") 156, 161, 164, 333, 369
Charles I 9, 10, 164, 227, 238, 244, 274, 294, 295
  civil wars and 3, 229, 258–61, 297, 306, 309,
    398, 400
  court of 62, 82, 238, 239–40, 241–42, 243, 244,
    249, 250, 263, 287
  Milton's criticism of 101, 123, 156, 160, 161,
    309–11, 339, 432
  trial and execution of 10, 11, 65, 94, 122, 124,
    152, 159, 250–51, 265, 266, 292, 301, 305,
    312, 331, 333, 365, 436, 479
Charles II 3, 11, 12, 32, 161, 251, 252, 255, 314, 315,
  362, 383, 385, 460, 462, 465, 471
Charlett, Arthur 160
Chateaubriand, François-René 176–78
Chaucer, Geoffrey 324, 453
Chéron, Louis 185, 186

Christina, Queen of Sweden 312
Christopher, Georgia 145
Christ's College 4, 5, 237, 263, 281, 283, 296, 444,
  477; *see also* Cambridge University
Church of England 87, 241, 248, 251, 252,
  258–60, 292–304, 310, 315, 384–86, 388,
  389–90
Cicero 95, 270, 282, 284, 287, 312, 313, 350, 359,
  456
Cifra, Antonio 400
Cinquemani, Antony 325
Cinthio, Giraldi 325
civil wars, English 7, 9, 10, 70, 123, 127, 238, 239,
  246, 251, 258–69, 289, 297–98, 307, 311,
  400
Clarendon Code 462–66
Clarendon, Edward Hyde 160, 429, 462, 465,
  466
Clark, Donald Lemen 283, 504
classicism 270–80, 281; *see also the names of
  individual writers*
Claudian 71, 73
Clegg, Cyndia Susan 502
Clementillo 319
Cleveland, John 263–64
Codner, David ("Selvaggi") 167
Coiro, Ann Baynes 379, 380, 487, 498
Coke, Edward 43, 334, 336
Colasterion 129, 383, 387, 433, 493
Coleridge, Samuel Taylor 46
Colet, John 282–83, 286
Colman, George 165
Coltellini, Agostino 319, 322
Columbus, Christopher 222, 418, 422, 425
Comenius, John Amos 289, 455
Commonplace Book, Milton's 7–8, 11, 63, 166,
  250, 329, 333, 336, 366, 449–55, 457, 492
Connor, John 355
Considerations Touching the Likeliest Means 156,
  162, 314, 496
Constable, John 187
Constantine 452
Conventicle Act 462
Cope, Elizabeth 332
Cope, John 332
Copernicus, Nicolaus 213–16, 218, 219, 220, 221,
  222, 224
Copyright Act of 1709 156, 226
Coras, Jacques de, *Josué* 69
Corns, Thomas N. 26, 27, 114, 144, 146, 436,
  438, 487, 503, 504, 507, 508
Corporation Act 462
Coryat, Thomas 320
Cowley, Abraham 6, 14, 107, 263, 264
  Davideis 53, 70, 72, 126

Cowper, William 163
Crashaw, Richard 80, 120
Crawford, Katherine 506
Creamer, Kevin J. T. 501
critical responses 120–29, 130–42, 143–53; *see also individual critical approaches*
Cromwell, Oliver 3, 162, 164, 252, 300, 301, 312, 385, 419
    military leader 10, 152, 251, 252
    Milton and 12, 13, 109, 122, 123, 124, 159, 257, 301, 313–14, 398, 420–21, 443, 449, 467
Cromwell, Richard 12, 314
Cruden, Alexander 163
Cudworth, Ralph 444
Cust, Richard 504

Dahlo, Rolf 487
Dalton, John 165
Daniel, Samuel, *A Defence of Rhyme* 106
Danielson, Dennis 144, 501, 508
Dante Alighieri 48, 134, 319, 322, 324–26, 327
Darbishire, Helen 26–27, 28, 166, 498
Darnton, Robert 450
Dati, Carlo 37, 38, 40, 231, 319, 320, 322, 323–24, 325
daughters, Milton's 27, 164, 270, 279, 384
Davenant, William, *Gondibert* 70, 106, 107, 115, 126
Davies, Natalie Zemon 499
Daybell, James 499
De Doctrina Christiana (*Christian Doctrine*) 23, 139–40, 146–47, 166, 230, 285, 288, 304, 330, 331, 344, 346, 347, 349, 355–56, 443, 444, 461, 465, 471, 475–86, 495; *see also* theology
De Idea Platonica ("Of the Platonic Idea") 12, 441, 490
De Krey, Gary S. 508
De Quincey, Thomas 132, 139
Decius 456
Declaration of Indulgence 465, 471
Declaration, or Letters Patents, A 161, 468
Defensio Regio pro Carolo I 11
Defoe, Daniel 128
Delumeau, Jean 507
Demaray, Hannah D. 149
Demosthenes 282
Denton, William 156
Descartes, René 444, 446
Di Biase, Carmine G. 505
Di Cesare, Mario 505
Diekhoff, John S. 4, 121, 499
Diggers 301, 475
Digges, Thomas 213–15, 219, 220
Dillon, John B. 280

Diodati, Charles 4, 37, 38, 39–40, 59, 88, 273, 287–88, 319, 323, 324, 329, 361, 380, 382, 452
Diodati, Eli (second cousin to Charles' father) 321
Diodati, John (uncle of Charles) 287
Diodati, Theodore (father of Charles) 287, 288, 321
Dionysius 56
Dionysius of Alexandria, Pope 454, 456
divorce controversy 9, 16, 122, 156, 227, 228, 245, 300, 322, 330, 335, 383, 386, 388–93, 435, 440, 453, 475; *see also the titles of Milton's individual tracts*
Dobranski, Stephen B. 17, 145, 152, 333, 365, 450, 498, 499, 501, 503, 505, 508
Doctrine and Discipline of Divorce, The 9, 18, 47, 50–53, 64, 122, 129, 134, 233, 330, 332, 335, 383, 386, 387, 390, 431, 432, 435, 493
    in translation 170, 174, 176
Donatus, Aelius 270
Donne, John 35, 80, 119, 218, 321, 338, 344–47, 372, 376, 423, 426
Donnelly, Phillip J. 505
Doré, Gustave 170, 173, 174, 178, 208
Downame, George 352
Downland, John 395
Drake, Francis 222
Drake, William 451
drama 58–65, 67, 279, 310, 319, 342–43, 476; *see also* theaters
Drayton, Michael 80
Driscoll, James P. 143
Drummond, William 244, 247
Dryden, John 58, 68, 76, 106, 109, 110, 127, 145, 157, 167, 267, 342
    Annus Mirabilis 107, 110
    State of Innocence, The 66, 107–09, 113, 114, 155
Du Bartas, Guillaume de Saluste, *La Semaine* 71, 74
Dubrow, Heather 499
Dugard, William 169, 230
Dunbar, Pamela 502
Dunster, Charles 163–64
Duran, Angelica 144
DuRocher, Richard J. 149
Dyson, A. E. 501
Dzelzainis, Martin 289, 505

eclogues 80; *see also* Virgil, *Eclogues*
ecology 149–50, 195, 421
Edmundson, Mark 499
Edwards, Karen L. 149, 507
Edwards, Thomas 369

Egerton, Alice, Dowager Countess of Derby 60, 84, 245, 398–99
Egerton, John, Earl of Bridgewater 6, 85, 242, 378, 398
Egerton, John, Lord Brackley 21, 122
Egerton family 20, 21, 62, 165, 243, 245, 378, 398, 399
Eiboden, Jeffrey 175
Eikon Basilike 11, 156, 160, 164, 266, 305, 309–11, 339, 368–69
  frontispiece 11, 241–42, 309, 310, 431, 432
  in translation 169
Eikonoklastes 13, 65, 123, 159, 238, 266, 310–11, 315, 317, 331, 333, 339, 431, 432, 460, 494
  critique of frontispiece 11, 241–42
  in translation 169
  Pamela's prayer 160, 161
  subsequent editions 18, 160, 161, 162, 164, 233, 494
Einboden, Jeffrey 502
elegies, Milton's 272
  Elegia prima (Elegy 1) 37, 39, 59, 274, 288, 361, 490
  Elegia secunda (Elegy 2) 490
  Elegia tertia (Elegy 3) 244, 245, 489
  Elegia quarta (Elegy 4) 37, 41, 284, 489
  Elegia quinta (Elegy 5) 490
  Elegia sexta (Elegy 6) 37, 39, 490
  Elegia septima (Elegy 7) 489
Eliot, T. S. 123, 125, 133, 144
Elizabeth I 3, 248–49, 256, 294, 295, 296, 395, 419, 423
Ellison, Ralph 134
Ellwood, Thomas 13, 362
Elyot, Thomas 387
Elys, Edmund 159
Emerson, Ralph Waldo 131, 132, 139
Emma, Ronald David 500
Empson, William 133
epic 68–77, 109–14, 273, 277–79, 313, 319, 324–26, 342–44, 447, 466, 476; *see also Paradise Lost*
  brief 71, 75, 279, 421; *see also Paradise Regained*
  mock 73
  neoclassical 69–70, 71–72, 76
Epistolarum Familiarum (*Familiar Letters*) 36–40, 44, 60, 468; *see also* letters
Epitaphium Damonis ("Epitaph for Damon") 6, 37, 38, 40, 71, 82, 88, 273, 276, 287, 288, 324, 382, 492
"Epitaph on the Marchioness of Winchester, An" 374, 376, 490
Erasmus 282, 284, 286, 449, 451, 453, 478
Estienne, Henri 271
Euripides 63, 66, 275, 279, 282, 285, 311

Eusebius 454, 456
Evagrius Scholasticus 454
Evans, J. Martin 149, 150, 418, 419, 420, 501, 507
Evelyn, John 320

Fairfax, Thomas 13, 124, 414
Faithorne, William 157
Fallon, Robert T. 150, 419, 421
Fallon, Stephen M. 444, 446, 447, 499
Fallopius, Johann 423
Familists 299
Fawkes, Guy 237, 238, 241
Feingold, Mordechai 505
Felton, John 287
Felton, Nicholas, Bishop of Ely 244, 245, 294
feminist, feminism 147–48, 200–08; *see also Paradise Lost*, Adam and Eve
Fenton, Elijah 163
Ferrabosco, Alphonso 395
Ferry, Anne Davidson 499
Ficino, Marsilio 440, 447
Fifth Monarchists 301
Filmer, Robert 100, 382
Fiore, Peter 145
Fish, Stanley 73, 97–98, 135, 139, 143, 144, 147, 151–52, 435
Five Mile Act 462–65
"Five Senses, The" 239–40, 244
Flannagan, Roy C. 28, 153, 224, 378, 487, 501
Fleetwood, Charles 365
Fletcher, Giles, *Christ's Victory and Triumph* 71, 75
Fletcher, Harris Francis 5, 166, 271, 280, 498, 504, 506, 507
Fletcher, John, *Faithful Shepherdess, The* 62, 80, 82
Fletcher, Phineas, *Apollyonists* 71, 73
Forsyth, Neil 145
Fortescue, John 336
Foxcroft, George 332
Foxe, John 244
Fowler, Alastair 166, 172, 410
Fragonard, Jean-Honoré 186
Francini, Antonio 319, 320–21, 324
Freedman, Joseph S. 505
French, J. Milton 30, 31, 32, 379, 505
Frénicle, Nicolas, *Jésus Crucifié* 75
Frescobaldi, Pietro 319
Freud, Sigmund 123, 143
friendship 387, 388
Froula, Christine 147, 148
Frye, Northrop 132, 134, 138
Frye, Roland M. 180
Fuseli, Henry 209

Gaddi, Jacopo 319
Galilei, Vincenzo 320
Galileo Galilei 213, 215–18, 222, 318, 321, 322, 325
Gallagher, Philip J. 148
Gallicanism 250, 252
Garber, Marjorie B. 149
Gascoigne, George 106
Gauden, John 160, 309
Geneva Bible 182–85
Georgeson, P. 160
georgic 89, 90, 180, 189; *see also* Virgil, *Georgics*
Gerard, Charles, Earl of Macclesfield 389
Giamatti, Bartlett 149
Gibbons, Orlando 394, 395
Gil, Alexander (high master at St. Paul's School) 284, 285, 361
Gil, Alexander, Jr. 17, 37, 231, 237, 240–41, 244, 287, 288
Gilbert, Sandra H. 143, 147, 148
Giles of Rome 453
Gillies, John 426
Giraud, Jane 195–96, 197–200
Giustiniani, Bernardo 452
Goodman, Christopher 307–08
Goodman, Ellen 149
Goodwin, John 300
Gouldman, Francis 230
Grafton, Anthony 499
Gray, Thomas 208
Greene, Thomas M. 499
Griffin, Dustin 500
Groom, Mary Elizabeth 180, 200, 203–08
Grotius, Hugo 6, 64, 158, 321, 329, 334–35, 336, 478, 485
Guarini, Giovanni Battista 80
Gucht, Michael vander 162
Guiana 423, 425
Gunpowder Plot 16, 72, 237–38, 250, 273, 294

Haan, Estelle 504
Habermas, Jürgen 261
Haigh, Christopher 303
Hakewill, George 321
Hale, John K. 146, 169, 487, 498, 500, 502, 504, 508
Halkett, John 506
Hall, John 367
Hall, Joseph 8
Hamilton, K. G. 97
Hammersmith 361
Hamor, Ralph 420
Handel, Georg Friedrich 162
Hanford, James Holly 289, 450, 504
Hardin, Richard F. 505
Hare, Henry 156

Harrington, John 328
Harris, Frances 506
Hartlib, Samuel 289, 365, 368, 420
Haug, Ralph A. 95, 97
Hayley, Richard 332
Hayley, William 163
Hayman, Francis 163, 186, 187, 189, 209
Heath, Richard 38
Heimbach, Peter 38
Heninger, S. K., Jr. 506
Henrietta Maria, Queen 62, 82, 84, 93, 239, 240, 243, 249, 250, 259, 263
Henry VIII 364, 388
Heraclides of Pontus 279
Herbert, George 120, 294
heresy *see* theology *and individual heterodox beliefs*
Herman, Peter C. 143, 148, 152
Hermes Trismegistus 440
Herodotus 282
heroic couplets 107, 108, 109, 126, 127
Herschel, William 218
Hesiod 270, 284
Hickes, George 160
Hill, Aaron 125
Hill, Christopher 143, 146, 287, 365, 420, 437, 501, 503, 504
Hiltner, Ken 149
History of Britain, The 10, 16, 235, 266, 332, 333, 369, 468, 493
  later editions 156, 157, 159, 161, 162
Hobbes, Thomas 108, 109, 115, 444, 445, 446
Hobson, Thomas 374–77, 379
"Hobson's Epitaph" 377–78
Hoby, Thomas 440
Hog, William 158, 167, 169
Hogan, Patrick G. 507
Hojeda, Diego de, *La Christiada* 75
Holinshed, Raphael 7, 8, 366
Holste, Lucas 37, 452
Homer 53, 65, 68–77, 105, 110, 136, 157, 158, 270, 271, 272–73, 275, 276, 279, 282, 285, 429
  Iliad 53, 54, 68, 110, 270, 271, 277, 279
  Odyssey 55, 68, 74, 110, 271, 275, 277, 278, 290
Honigman, E. A. J. 166
Hopkins, John 167
Horace 55, 79, 272, 282, 284, 312, 319
Horton 7, 329, 361
Horwood, Alfred J. 166, 458
Hoston, Howard 350
Houston, John Porter 500
Howard, Henry, Earl of Surrey 106
Howard, Robert 106
Howell, James 320, 363
Hoxby, Blair 143, 367

Huckabay, Calvin 501
Hughes, Ann 504, 505, 506
Hughes, Merritt Y. 166, 501
Hulme, Peter 507
Hume, Patrick 158–59
Hunt, Clay 505
Hunt, John D. 149
Hunt, Thomas 156
Hunter, Michael 498
Hunter, William B., Jr. 146, 487
Huntley, John F. 98
Huray, Peter le 400
Hutchinson, Lucy, *Order and Disorder* 75
Hyman, Lawrence 148

Ignavus satrapam ("Kings should not oversleep")
    489
Il Penseroso 59–60, 83–84, 162, 165, 274, 293–94,
    395, 440, 490
  in translation 171, 173, 174
  illustrations 157, 159, 162, 163, 165, 170, 173, 174,
    178, 180–82, 183, 184, 186, 187, 188, 190,
    191, 192, 193, 194, 196, 197, 198, 199, 201,
    202, 203, 204, 214, 396
imperialism 150
In Effigiei Ejus Sculptorem ("On the Engraver of
    His Portrait") 157, 232
In Obitum Praesulis Eliensis ("On the Death of
    the Bishop of Ely") 244, 245, 294
In Obitum Praesulis Wintoniensis ("On the
    Death of the Bishop of Winchester") *see*
    elegies, Milton's, *Elegia tertia*
In Proditionem Bombardicam ("On the
    Gunpowder Plot") 237–38, 241, 244
In Quintum Novembris ("On the fifth of
    November") 72, 237–38, 241, 244, 250,
    273, 294, 489
Indemnity and Oblivion Act 461
Independents 251, 300, 301, 313
"Index Legalis" 336
India 420, 421, 422
Ingram, Martin 506
Ingram, Randall 21
Interregnum 159, 301, 305–17, 481
Ireland, Irish 11, 33, 152, 163, 164, 252, 260, 298,
    309, 420
Isocrates 285, 459
Italicus, Silius 70
Italy *see* Milton, Italian journey

James I 237–38, 239–40, 243, 249, 250, 294, 334,
    419
James II 157, 160, 255
James, Henry 138
Jardine, Lisa 499

Jeffrey, Paul 361
Job, Book of 71, 75
Johnson, Samuel 107, 125, 127, 128, 136, 158, 418
Jones, Inigo 240
Jones, Katherine *see* Ranelagh, Katherine Jones
Jones, Richard 36, 38, 39
Jonson, Ben 62, 81, 107, 127, 240, 243, 244, 246,
    286, 323, 376, 424
Jordan, W. K. 503
Joseph, Miriam, Sister 145
Judgment of Martin Bucer, The 174, 383, 390, 493
Julian the Apostate 454
Justa Edouardo King Naufrago 20, 85, 235
Justin Martyr 481
Justinian 328, 330, 336
Justinus 284
Juvenal 285

Kahn, Victoria 505
Keckermann, Bartholomew 352
Keeble, N. H. 500
Kelley, Maurice 140, 146, 336, 484, 508
Kepler, Johannes 213, 217, 222
Kermode, Frank 144
Kerrigan, John 247
Kerrigan, William 4, 143, 145, 500, 507
"King and his wife the Parliament, The" 241
King, Edward 20, 58, 85, 86, 87, 276, 297
King, Henry 384
Knoppers, Laura Lunger 508
Knott, John R. 149, 499
Knox, John 306, 307
Kolodny, Annette 422
Kranidas, Thomas 500

Labadie, Jean de 38
Labriola, Albert C. 151, 502
Lactantius 63
L'Allegro 59–60, 82, 83–84, 162, 165, 274, 293,
    339, 490
  in translation 170, 171, 173, 174
Lamb, Charles 18
Landino, Christopher 270
Landor, Walter Savage 134, 137
Landy, Marcia 147, 148
Lassel, Richard 320
Latin thesaurus 495
Laud, William (Laudian) 238–39, 240, 242, 244,
    245, 246, 259, 292, 294, 295–96, 297–98,
    310, 441
Lauder, William 158
law 328–37, 384–86, 388, 389, 391, 397–98, 399;
    see also natural law
Lawes, Henry 6, 20–21, 61, 62, 165, 245–46, 263,
    264, 378, 398–99, 400, 405

Lawrence, Edward 43–44, 365
Le Huray, Peter 506
Leavis, F. R. 130, 138, 144
Leighton, William 395, 396
Lens, Bernard 157, 184, 185
Leonard, John 501
L'Estrange, Roger 465
Letter to a Friend Concerning the Ruptures of the Commonwealth 161, 496
letters, Milton's
  familiar 17, 35–40, 248, 329, 379, 452
  gift-texts 35, 37, 38, 40–44
  "Letter to a Friend" 44
  state 13, 35, 43, 44, 156, 159, 162, 311
  verse 35, 37, 38, 39, 40–42; *see also Epistolarum Familiarum*
Levellers 251–52, 300, 301, 305–06, 308, 366, 430
Lewalski, Barbara K. 4, 28, 75, 146, 148, 318, 395, 411–12, 442, 451, 487, 498, 500, 503
Lewis, C. S. 73, 131, 132, 135, 136, 137, 139, 145
Ley, James, Earl of Marlborough 41, 274, 334
Ley, Margaret 40, 274
licensing 17, 156, 216, 226–30, 261, 266, 332–33, 443, 465, 466; *see also* censorship
Lieb, Michael 146, 151
Lily, William 282, 283, 285
Lindenbaum, Peter 335
Lindley, Keith 506
literary contemporaries, Milton's 338–48; *see also individual writers' names*
locus amoenus 79, 80, 86, 89, 90, 344
Loewenstein, David 146, 151, 500, 504, 507
logic 349–60, 475, 477, 478, 480, 483–84
Lombard, William 336
London 361–71
Long Parliament 10, 227, 228, 258, 259, 260, 298, 300, 314, 369, 430, 435
Louis XIII 40
Louis XIV 252
Love, Harold 375–76, 379, 506
Low, Anthony 487
Loyola, Ignatius 297
Lucan, *De Bello Civili* 70, 73, 106, 266
Lucian 282
Lucretius 482
Lucy, Juliet 149
Lünig, Christian 159
Lupton, Donald 364
Luther, Martin 102, 104, 311, 386, 388
Lycidas 6, 18–20, 63, 107, 233, 235, 244, 245, 263, 275, 492
  critique of clergy 87, 241, 243–44, 246, 250, 297, 298, 300, 301, 302
  in translation 167, 171, 174, 176
  pastoral and 82, 85–88, 91, 105, 276–77

Lycophron 279
Lytellton, George 124

Macaulay, Catherine (Graham) 156
Macaulay, Thomas Babington 131, 132, 135, 139
MacCallum, Hugh 508
McChrystal, Deirdre 148
McColley, Diane Kelsey 22, 143, 148, 149, 209, 421, 502
MacCullough, Diarmaid 504
McDowell, Nicholas 503
MacGuire, Maryann Cale 499
Machiavelli, Niccolò 369
MacKeller, Walter 166
McKenzie, D. F. 235, 503
McKitterick, David 503, 506
MacLean, Gerald 508
McRae, Andrew 240
Maley, Willy 420
Malory, Thomas 136
Manifesto of the Lord Protector, A 162
Manley, Larry 368
Manners, John, Lord Roos 335
Manso, Giovanni Battista 6, 37, 42, 273, 319, 324, 381
Mansus ("Manso") 6, 41, 71, 74, 324, 381, 492
Mantuan 81, 85, 274
manuscript transmission 372–81, 404, 429, 482; *see also the titles of individual manuscripts*
Marcus, Leah S. 22, 372, 498
Marcus Servius 270
Marenzio, Luca 400
Marino, Giambattista, *L'Adone* 71, 74
Marlowe, Christopher 63, 79, 80, 106
marriage 366, 382–93, 453; *see also the names of Milton's three wives*
Marrotti, Arthur F. 373
Marshall, John 128
Marshall, Stephen 316
Marshall, William 121, 162, 232
Martin, Catherine Gimelli 148, 501, 502
Martin, John 195–97
Martindale, Charles 504
Marvell, Andrew 12, 134, 156, 314, 365, 414, 429, 465, 472
  "On *Paradise Lost*" 105, 108, 466
Marx, Karl 234
Mary I 249
Mask Presented at Ludlow Castle, A (also called *Comus*) 82, 84–85, 131, 149, 245, 275–76, 288, 339, 345, 399, 439, 440, 442
  as courtly drama 58, 60, 61–62, 122, 242–43, 245, 250, 383; *see also* masque
  composition and publication 6, 20–21, 120, 232–33, 374, 378–79, 381, 491

in translation 170, 173, 174, 176, 446
later editions 164, 165, 166, 167
masque 60–62, 240, 242–43, 310, 398–99
Masson, David 28, 30, 31, 123, 139, 498
materialism, animist *see* monism
Maundy, Thomas 332
Mazzoni, Jacopo 319
Mede, Joseph 288, 477
Medina, John Baptist 157, 185, 189
Mercurius Politicus 229
Merola, Bartholomeus 271
Miller, John 365
Miller, Leo 32
Millington, Edward 231
Milton, Anthony 503
Milton, Christopher (brother) 9, 23, 28, 30, 31, 248, 255, 329, 384
Milton, Deborah (daughter) 27, 164, 270, 279
Milton, John
  authorial authority 119, 120, 234–35
  blindness 23, 31, 36, 54, 56, 180, 232, 287, 301, 312, 313, 325, 383, 384, 447, 461
  chronology of works 489–97
  composition process 15–24; *see also Paradise Lost*, composition
  education 5, 281–91
  Italian journey xxii, 5, 6–7, 16, 37–38, 63, 64, 71, 121, 149, 216, 248, 273, 289, 318–27, 361, 366, 379, 400, 434
  on himself 4, 6, 8, 15, 21, 46–57, 63, 102, 121, 123, 283, 312, 313, 433–34
  Secretary for Foreign Tongues (Latin Secretary) 11–12, 16, 35, 229–30, 251, 252, 308–14, 328, 333, 336, 361, 366
  spelling 232
Milton, John, senior (father) 5, 22, 29, 59, 245, 246, 248, 255, 284, 293, 329, 331, 332, 361, 366, 382, 394–95, 396
Milton, John, III (son) 12, 31, 33
Milton, Richard (grandfather) 248
Milton, Sarah (née Jeffrey, mother) 361
Miltonicks 156
Minshull, Elizabeth (Milton's third wife) 12, 27, 336, 384
Minturno 66
Mintz, Samuel I. 508
Mohl, Ruth 329, 450–51, 508
Monck, George 12, 314, 460
monism 126, 127, 145, 444–47, 480–82
Montagu, Walter, *The Shepherd's Paradise* 82
Montaigne, Michel de 39, 64, 252
Monteverdi, Claudio 395, 400
Montezuma 418
More, Alexander 39, 312, 314
More, Henry 444

More, Thomas 449
Morel, Frederic 271
Morley, Thomas 394
Morrill, John 303
mortalism 145, 445
Morton, Thomas 423
Moschus 273, 276
Moseley, Humphrey 10, 120–21, 231, 245, 263, 380, 405
Moss, Ann 270
Mouchard, Claude 502
Moulin, Peter du 312
Moxon, Joseph 231
Moyles, R. G. 503
Moyne, Pierre Le, *Saint Louis* 71–72
Mueller, Janel 421
Muggletonians 301
Murry, John Middleton 131, 132–33, 134, 135
music 22, 64, 85, 162, 165, 245, 263, 293, 319, 320, 323, 345, 378, 394–405, 439, 443
Mylius, Hermann 32, 33, 35–36, 369
Myriell, Thomas 395

nationalism 248–51, 254, 262–63, 265, 449, 451–52, 457
natural law 100–01, 253, 254, 306, 321, 330–31, 336
natural world 149, 195–200, 204, 205, 206, 207, 406–17, 421, 423–24, 425, 445
Naturam non pati senium ("That Nature does not suffer from old age") 321
Nedham, Marchamont 4, 11, 314, 365
Neoplatonism 347, 440–42, 446
Neville, Henry 420
New World 149, 150, 162, 180, 252–53, 406, 407, 414, 418–28
Newcomb, Thomas 230
Newton, Isaac 218, 478
Newton, Thomas 53, 159, 163
Nicolson, Marjorie 502
Nietzsche, Friedrich 440, 447
Norbrook, David 366, 368, 499, 507, 508

Observations on the Articles of Peace 252, 309, 494
Of Education 9, 161, 162, 163, 173, 174, 265, 281, 289–90, 319, 353–54, 355, 359, 368, 432, 439, 443, 451, 452, 455, 468, 493
Of Prelatical Episcopacy 492
Of Reformation 8, 95, 298–99, 303, 333–34, 432, 434, 492
Of True Religion 161, 176, 230, 254, 255, 465, 471–72, 497
Oldenburg, Henry 35, 36, 38–39
"On Shakespeare" 5, 58, 59, 66, 155, 231, 233, 338, 490
"On the Death of a Fair Infant" 489

"On the Morning of Christ's Nativity" (the Nativity Ode) 5, 16, 82–83, 105, 174, 233, 272, 274, 345, 380, 397, 440, 490
"On the New Forcers of Conscience" 266, 301
"On the University Carrier" 155, 374–77, 378, 490
"On Time" 374, 491
Ong, Walter 353–54
orality 22–23, 429
Oras, Ants 501
Orgel, Stephen 450
Origen 446
Orpheus 53, 56, 86, 87, 274, 317
orthodoxy, Christian 145, 298, 480, 481; *see also* theology
Otten, C. F. 149
Overton, Robert 365
Ovid 39, 270–72, 273, 277, 284
    Metamorphoses 56, 79, 273, 275, 278, 279
Owen, John 479

Palmer, Herbert 122, 227
pamphlet wars 429–38; *see also the names of individual controversies*
Paradise Lost 4, 119–20, 123, 205, 206, 207, 213, 339, 356–58, 418–28, 442
    Adam and Eve 65, 133–34, 183, 186, 187, 188, 191, 193, 194, 197, 201, 203, 204, 343–44, 345, 412, 416, 482
        Adam's knowledge 220–21, 248, 288, 357–58, 422, 423, 425–27, 439
        Eve's status 73, 147–48, 190, 192, 196, 202, 357–58, 384, 387, 423, 425, 426–27
    angels 46, 53, 56, 277–78, 289, 345, 481–82; *see also Paradise Lost*, Raphael
    audience and reception 125–28, 130, 132, 135–39, 145, 147, 180, 267, 469, 478
    classical influences 272, 274, 277–79
    composition and publication 13, 16, 21, 22, 23, 27, 228, 232, 233–34, 325, 384, 468, 489
    contract for 233–34, 335, 365
    cosmology 215–24
    creation in 443, 444, 481, 482
    dramatic influences 64–65
    Eden and Paradise 149, 180–209, 278–79, 406–17, 423–24
    epic qualities 68, 71, 73–75, 76, 150
    free will in 97, 109–11, 254, 443
    God 132–33, 134, 286, 477, 479
    in translation 155, 170–74
    invocations and narrator xxi, xxii, 15, 38, 47, 53, 54–56, 70, 266, 287, 325–26, 349, 356–57, 432, 442, 461, 467
    later editions 120, 155, 156–59, 162–63, 165, 166, 167

music in 401–03
    pastoral in 82, 89–91, 180
    political context 3, 63, 254, 255, 267, 302, 315, 437, 466–68, 470, 472
    Raphael 184, 193, 194, 197, 215, 223–24, 248, 288, 441, 442, 445
    Satan 27, 56, 157, 217, 234, 309, 421
        as hero 46, 53, 65, 130, 134, 140, 145
        deception 192, 307, 310, 358
        epistemology 215–16, 220, 221, 222, 325, 408, 409–11, 412, 413–14, 445–46
        in Eden 192, 364, 406–07, 415
        literary precursors 62, 65, 70, 71–73, 74, 237, 340–42
    second edition 18, 105, 155, 233, 235, 236, 471, 473, 497
    Sin 55–56, 96, 132–33, 423
    Son 230, 286, 345, 483, 484
    Urania 22, 54, 55
    "Verse, The" 105, 113, 126, 127, 469–70
    versification 105–06, 107–08, 111–14, 126–27, 155, 469; *see also poetic style and* blank verse
Paradise Regained 3, 13, 16, 57, 65, 68, 75–76, 122, 130, 144, 255, 267, 279, 286, 314, 358, 403–04, 439, 442, 468, 469, 497
    God 477
    in translation 170, 171, 172, 173, 174, 175, 176
    later editions 155, 157, 158, 163–64
    pastoral in 91
Pareus, David 311
Parker, Henry 303
Parker, Patricia 422
Parker, Samuel 465
Parker, William Riley 28, 30, 31, 32, 131, 450, 498, 500, 501
Parry, Graham 244, 503
"Passion, The" 5, 75, 245, 490
pastoral 74, 78–93, 149, 273, 276, 297, 398–99, 476; *see also Paradise Lost*, pastoral in, *and Paradise Regained*, pastoral in
Patrick, J. Max 487
Patterson, Annabel 500
Pattison, Mark 132, 133
Pearce, Zachary 165
Pearl, Valerie 506
Pechter, Edward 148
Pecke, Samuel 230
Peerson, Martin 395
Pepys, Samuel 364
Perkins, William 288
Perrinchief, Richard 122
Persius 285
Peter, Hugh 369
Peter, John 501

Petrarch, Francesco 48, 69, 85, 322
Petrina, Carlotta 182, 200–03, 209
Philaras, Leonard 23, 36
Philips, Katherine 372
Phillips, Anne (Milton's sister) 7, 29, 331
Phillips, Edward (Milton's brother-in-law) 29, 331
Phillips, Edward (Milton's nephew) 7, 8, 13, 16, 22, 23, 26, 27, 29–31, 32, 33, 159–60, 161, 232, 326, 365, 382, 484
Phillips, John (Milton's nephew) 7, 21, 23, 27, 161
Philosophus ad regem ("A Philosopher to a King") 157, 489
philosophy 439–48
Pigné, Nicholas 162
Pindar 55, 274, 275, 280, 284
Place, Josué de la (Placæus) 483
Plato 272, 288, 323, 405, 439, 440–42, 443, 447
Platonism 440, 446, 481
Pliny the Younger 312
Plotinus 440
Plutarch 55
Poems (1645) 41, 42, 374, 400, 468
    authorial presence 120–21, 128, 232, 235, 237, 263, 372, 378
    Latin section 272, 273, 366
    publication process 10, 230, 245–46, 264, 493
    revisions in 20, 244, 375, 377, 379–80
Poems, &c. (1673) 13, 21, 43, 60, 355, 468, 471, 497
    later editions 157–58, 160, 162, 163
poetic style, Milton's 144; *see also* blank verse *and Paradise Lost*, versification
Poggioli, Renato 500
Pointon, Marcia 185, 209
Politiano, Angelo 271
Ponet, John 307–08
Poole, Matthew 156
Poole, William 508
Pope, Alexander 158, 164, 286
portraits, Milton's 157, 159, 163, 232, 234, 235, 284
postmodernism, postmodernist 119, 143, 152, 338–39, 347
"Postscript" to *An Answer to . . . An Humble Remonstrance* 8
Poussin, Nicolas 149
Powell, Anne 332
Powell, Mary (Milton's first wife) 8–9, 10, 12, 29, 30, 31, 32, 33, 50, 57, 382, 383, 384–85
Powell, Richard 8, 29, 331, 332, 382, 385
prelacy, prelates *see* anti-prelatical controversy
Presbyterians, Presbyterianism
    and church reform 8, 95, 251, 296, 298

Milton's association with 96, 97–98, 284, 300, 434
Milton's criticism of 12, 100, 103, 229, 260, 300, 301, 302, 306–07, 313, 315–16, 366, 368, 369, 370, 435
political conservatism 9, 10, 227, 246, 265–66, 300, 436, 462, 479
Present Means . . . of a Free Commonwealth, The 161, 497
Preston, John 296
Pride, Thomas 10, 316, 431
Prince, Frank T. 327, 505
printing *see* book trade
Printing Act 465
Pro Populo Anglicano Defensio (First Defence) 12, 100, 122, 156, 159, 160, 161, 233, 254, 306, 311–12, 317, 331, 333, 432, 460, 494, 496
    in translation 170, 174, 175, 176
Pro Populo Anglicano Defensio Secunda (Second Defence) 12, 36, 120, 159, 264, 282, 312, 319, 320, 334, 369, 442, 443, 449, 494
    autobiographical digression xxi, 6, 7, 47, 312, 431, 435
    in translation 174, 175
Pro Se Defensio 12, 39, 314, 495
Prolusions 5, 44, 60, 272, 273, 281, 288, 289, 296, 321, 333, 345, 439, 489
Proposals of Certain Expedients 496
prose style, Milton's 94–104, 144, 146; *see also the titles of individual works*
Prynne, William 9, 240, 241, 242, 243, 294, 295, 300
psalm translations, Milton's 17, 37, 127, 293, 491, 494, 495
Ptolemy 215, 219, 221
publishing history, later 155–68; *see also the titles of individual works*
Pufendorf, Samuel von 335
Pulci, Luigi 71
Purchas, Samuel 423
Puritans, Puritanism 240, 243, 306, 314, 461
    and marriage 385, 386, 389, 391
    and Milton 284, 299, 313, 316, 323
    church reform 238–39, 244, 251, 292, 294, 295, 296, 298, 303, 310, 400
    defined 293, 318; *see also* anti-Catholicism
Puttenham, George 81
Pye, Robert 332
Pym, George 296
Pythagoras 441

Quakers 292, 301, 302, 314, 315, 430, 462, 467, 468, 475
Quint, David 150, 151, 418, 421, 499, 507
Quintilian 283

Racovian Catechism, The 230, 483
Raffel, Burton 487
Rajan, Balachandra 131, 132, 135, 137, 139, 140, 143, 145, 150, 152, 419, 420, 425, 507
Rajan, Tilottama 498
Ralegh, Walter 80, 159, 423, 425
Raleigh, Walter 130, 132, 133, 134, 230
Ramism, Ramist (Peter Ramus) 288, 349, 475, 476
Randolph, Thomas 6, 14, 62, 381
Ranelagh, Katherine Jones, Viscountess 36, 39, 365
Ranters 292, 301, 430, 475
Rapaport, Herman 143
Rapin, René 79
Ravenscroft, Thomas 395
Raworth, Ruth 230
Raymond, Joad 507
Raymond, John 320
readers, reading practices 70, 102, 119, 120, 122, 142, 226, 255, 406, 449–59, 462, 466, 482
  of Milton 97–98, 126, 138–39, 267, 358, 368–69, 431–32, 433, 473, 478
  women readers 141, 147–48
Readie and Easie Way, The 12, 102, 161, 162, 233, 264, 282, 315–16, 331, 369–70, 436, 437, 460, 466, 470, 497
  in translation 169, 174, 175
reason 354, 355, 357–58, 443, 470, 483; *see also* logic
Reason of Church-Government, The 61, 64, 94, 95–99, 101, 103, 174, 234, 297, 299–300, 364, 432, 434, 441, 492
  autobiographical digression 6, 8, 16, 47, 48, 63, 71, 75, 119, 120, 121, 146, 265, 433–34
Regii Sanguinis Clamor 312
Regius, Raphael 270
Reid, Steven 505
republic, republicanism 43, 102, 103, 111, 261, 266–67, 286, 305, 308–09, 312, 316, 436–37, 451, 462, 466, 467, 470
Restoration 3, 38, 53, 55, 63, 109, 123, 125, 253, 254, 267, 301–02, 315–16, 331, 333, 362, 385, 460–74
Revard, Stella P. 487, 499, 500
Rheticus, Joachim 217
Rhodius, Apollonius 71
Richardson, Alexander 352
Richardson, Jonathan 22
Ricks, Christopher 144, 500
Roberts, William 126
Robinson, Humphrey 231
Rogers, John 127
romance 69, 70, 74
Romantics, Romanticism 130, 133, 186, 189, 200

Rother, Wolfgang 505
Rothwell, John 234
Rous, Francis 296
Routh, Bernard 164
Rovai, Francesco 40
Rubens, Peter Paul 244
Rump Parliament 10, 12, 306, 308, 312, 314, 315, 317, 369
  defined 316
Rumrich, John 145, 146, 147, 152, 443, 501, 504, 507
Rymer, Thomas 76, 126

Sagan, Carl 225
St. Jerome 456
St. John, J. A. 166
St. Paul 47, 102, 367, 454, 456
St. Paul's Church 231, 293, 362, 394–95
St. Paul's School 37, 59, 231, 237, 270, 282–88, 290, 338, 361, 362
Saint-Amant, Antoine Girard de, *Moyse sauvé* 74
Sallust 282, 284, 369
Salmasius [Claude Saumaise] xxi, 11, 16, 38, 39, 156, 160, 163, 311, 312, 369
Salzilli, Giovanni 37, 41
Samson Agonistes 3, 13, 16, 57, 58, 65, 130, 134, 267, 279, 331, 358, 387, 462, 468–69, 470–71, 472, 497
  and 9/11 attacks 151
  in translation 170, 171, 172, 173, 174, 175, 176, 178
  later editions 155, 157, 158, 162, 163
  Preface 66, 319, 442, 469–70
  Samson 46, 311–12, 314, 345
  verse 105, 144
  violence in 151–52
Samuel, Irene 66, 324, 326, 441
Sarkar, Malabika 502
Sarpi, Paolo (Pietro) 7, 322, 453, 454
Sauer, Elizabeth 143, 150, 152, 503, 507, 508
Saunders, J. W. 380
Saurat, Denis 131, 139
Savile, Henry 454
Sawday, Jonathan 423
Scaliger, Julius Caesar 81
Scarron 73
Schall, Jean-Frédéric 209
scholasticism, scholastic 289, 350, 351, 439
Scotland, Scottish 7, 33, 244, 252, 260, 261, 265, 296, 298, 306, 420
Scott, Jonathan 467
Scotus, John Duns 338, 439
Scriveners' Company 331, 361
Scudamore, John (Viscount Sligo) 6, 32, 33
Seekers 251, 475

Selden, John 334, 453, 456
Seneca 312, 323, 452
Sensabaugh, George 501
Shakespeare, William 5, 46, 58, 63, 65, 66, 135, 155, 171, 231, 286, 338, 339–41, 343, 344
  Antony and Cleopatra 66
  As You Like It 80, 81
  2 Henry VI 339
  3 Henry VI 339
  Macbeth 306, 339, 343
  Measure for Measure 62
  Midsummer Night's Dream 62
  prosody 111, 112
  Richard II 340–41
  Richard III 339
  Tempest, The 62, 134
  Twelfth Night 293
  Winter's Tale, The 80, 81
Sharpe, Kevin 303, 451, 508
Shawcross, John T. 17, 18, 23, 143, 146, 172, 173, 377–79, 487, 498, 500, 501
Shelley, Percy Bysshe 133, 145
Shepherd, Fleetwood 163
Sherwood, Terry G. 505
Shirley, James 245
Shubarnov, Alexander 177
Shullenberger, William 148, 399
Sichi, Edward, Jr. 502
Sidney, Philip 71, 80, 81, 92, 372, 440
  Arcadia 80, 81, 160
Simmons, Matthew 13, 230, 231
Simmons, Samuel 13, 105, 126, 233, 365, 466, 469
Singh Marjara, Harinder 502
Sirluck, Ernest 459
Skalnik, James Veazie 505
Skinner, Cyriack 13, 26, 27, 28, 32, 39, 43, 334, 365, 384
Skinner, Daniel 465
Slights, Camille Wells 505
Smart, John S. 166
Smectymnuus 434
Smith, Alexis 180, 200, 205, 206, 207, 208
Smith, Logan Pearsall 130
Smith, Thomas 334, 336
Socinian, Socinianism 161, 230, 478–80, 482–84
Socrates 439, 440, 442
Socrates of Constantinople (Socrates Scholasticus) 454, 456
Sonnets, Milton's 5, 10, 13, 37, 42–44, 105, 166, 173, 174, 176
  Sonnet, 1 "O Nightingale" 490
  Sonnet, 2 "Donna leggiadra il cui bel nome onora" 319
  Sonnet, 7 "How soon hath Time" 5, 6, 44, 491

Sonnet, 8 "Captain or colonel" 23, 264, 274–75
Sonnet, 10 "Daughter to that good Earl" 40, 274, 334
Sonnet, 11 "A book was writ of late" 129, 368, 433, 493
Sonnet, 12 "I did but prompt the age" 129, 275, 331
Sonnet, 13 "To Mr. H. Lawes, on his Airs" 245–46, 264, 373, 400
Sonnet, 14 "When Faith and Love" 41, 231
Sonnet, 15 "On the Lord General Fairfax" 124, 157, 160, 494
Sonnet, 16 "Cromwell, our chief of men" 124, 157, 160, 301, 398, 494
Sonnet, 17 "Vane, young in years" 157, 160, 334, 461–62, 473, 495
Sonnet, 18 "On the Late Massacre in Piedmont" 107, 256, 495
Sonnet, 19 "When I consider" 107, 175, 495
Sonnet, 20 "Lawrence of virtuous father" 43–44, 496
Sonnet, 21 "Cyriack, whose grandsire" 27, 43, 334
Sonnet, 22 "Cyriack, this three years' day" 27, 43, 157, 160
Sonnet, 23 "Methought I saw" 5, 16, 383, 496
Sophocles 63, 66, 312
Spanheim, Ezekiel 38
Spanish Armada 249, 250
Speed, John 8
Speght, Rachel 389
Spencer, T. J. B. 76
Spenser, Edmund 79, 85, 285, 324, 338, 342, 344, 439, 440
  "Epithalamion" 80, 383
  Faerie Queene, The 69, 70, 71, 74, 81, 243, 275, 342–44, 406, 412
  Shepheardes Calendar, The 80, 81, 243
Spink, Ian 398
Sponde, Jean de (Iohannes Spondanus) 271
Sprott, S. E. 166
Spurr, John 504
Stallybrass, Peter 374
Starkey, John 13
Stationers' Company 226, 227, 229, 230, 332, 368, 465, 466
Statius 71
Stavely, Keith W. 144
Steadman, John 442
Stein, Arnold 137, 138
Stevens, Paul 150, 419, 420
Stevenson, Kay Gilliland 500
Stock, Richard 293, 296, 362
Stoll, E. D. 145

Stone, Lawrence 506
Stow, John 8, 362, 454
Strafford, Thomas Wentworth, Earl of 261
Strier, Richard 102, 104
Suckling, John 80, 245
Summers, Claude 143
Summers, Joseph H. 138, 145
Sumner, Charles R. 166
Swift, Jonathan 120, 121, 164
Sykes, George 461–62, 473
Symmons, Charles 166

Tacitus 312, 454
Tallis, Thomas 394, 398
Tanner, John 502
Tasso, Torquato 6, 42, 80, 110, 274, 319, 324
    Gerusalemme Liberata 69, 71, 72, 73, 275
    Le sette giornato 106
Tassoni, Alessandro 73
Tenure of Kings and Magistrates, The 11, 13, 16, 18, 94, 100–02, 103, 124, 156, 159, 161, 233, 301, 306–08, 330–31, 436, 494
Terence 64, 282, 284
Test Act 465
Tetrachordon 52, 330, 368, 383, 433, 493
Thaler, Alwin 339
theaters 58, 63, 320, 361, 362, 363; *see also* drama
Theis, Jeffrey 149
Theocritus 78, 85, 273, 276, 284
Theodoret 454
Theodosius 322
Theognis 312
theology 145, 146–47, 166, 167, 288, 295, 304, 346–47, 355–56, 440, 443, 444–45, 446, 461, 467, 475–86; *see also individual theological categories*
Theophrastus 57
Thirsk, Joan 407
Thirty Years War 259
Thirty-Nine Articles 256, 296
Thomas, Keith 507
Thomason, Catherine 41, 231
Thomason, George 41, 231, 365, 430
Thomson, James 106, 161
Thou, Jacques Auguste de 454
Tickell, Thomas 163
Tillyard, E. M. W. 131, 134, 136, 145
Tilney, Edmund 387
Todd, Henry John 165
Toland, John 27, 160, 161, 466
Tomkins, Thomas 105, 394, 397, 466, 467
Tompkins, John 395
Tonson, Jacob 157, 158
Tovey, Nicholas 288

Townshend, Aurelian 62, 82
translations
    Arabic and Farsi 175–76
    Baltic languages 171
    Bulgarian 172
    Chinese 175
    Czech 171–72
    Dutch 170
    French 176
    German 155, 169–70
    Greek 164, 174
    Hebrew 173
    Hungarian 172
    Iberian languages 173
    Indian and Urdu 175
    Italian 159, 173–74
    Japanese 174–75
    Korean 175
    Latin 155, 157–58, 167, 169
    Polish 171
    Romanian 172
    Russian 172–73
    Scandinavian languages 170–71
    Serbo-Croatian 172
    Slovenian 172
    Turkish 174
Treatise of Civil Power, A 156, 162, 292–93, 314, 436, 496
Trinity College Manuscript 4, 15, 16, 18–20, 21, 23, 27, 28, 41, 44, 63–64, 65, 164, 166, 372–73, 375, 378, 506
Trissino 106
Tufte, Virginia James 208
Turner, Francis 122
Turner, James Grantham 146, 148, 264, 409, 500, 504, 507
Tweedie, Fiona J. 146, 487, 508
Tyacke, Nicholas 303, 504
Tycho Brahe 213, 221
Tyrrell, James 159

Uniformity Act 462
"Upon the Circumcision" 245, 491
Urban VIII, Pope 250, 319

Valla, Lorenzo 350
Valle, Niccolò della 271
Valmarana, Odorico, *Daemonomachiae* 73
Valvasone, Erasmo di, *Angeledida* 69
Vane, Henry 13, 160, 334, 420, 461–62, 473
Vaudois *see* Waldensians
Vecchi, Orazio 400
Vegius, Maphaeus 270
Vertue, George 163
Vida, Marco Girolamo 71, 75

Virgil 53, 65, 68, 71, 85, 105, 134, 157, 158, 270, 271, 272, 273, 279, 282, 284, 287, 429
  Aeneid 53, 68–69, 71, 72, 74, 75, 79, 91, 106, 110, 270, 277, 278, 352
  Eclogues 78–79, 81, 82, 88, 270, 276
  Georgics 79–80, 88, 270
Vives, Juan Luis 387, 455
Voltaire 164
Von Maltzahn, Nicholas 500
Vondel, Joost van den 64, 74
Vyner, Thomas 366

Waldensians 253–54, 257, 366
Waldock, A. J. A. 133, 135, 136, 145
Walker, Robert 156
Walker, William Sidney 166
Wall, Moses (called John) 164
Waller, Edmund 263, 342, 380
Walley, Henry 230
Walpole, Robert 162
Walwyn, William 251, 252, 254, 300
Warcupp, Robert 332
Ward, John 164
Warren, George 419, 425
Warton, Thomas 165
Washington, Joseph 160, 161
Watteau, Jean-Antoine 186
Webber, Isabel 30–31
Webber, Joan 143, 148
Webber, John 30
Webber, Thomasine 30
Wechel, Chrestien 271
Weelkes, Thomas 394
Westall, Richard 186–89, 190, 209
Westminster Assembly 300
Whately, William 386
"When Charles, hath got the Spanish Gearle" 240
"When the Assault was intended to the City" *see* Sonnets, Milton's, Sonnet 8
White, Robert 157

Wickenheiser, Robert J. 501
Wilding, Michael 503
Wiles, John 160
Wilkes, G. A. 501
Wilkins, John 218
Willets, Pamala J. 506
William of Malmesbury 454
Williams, Arnold 413
Williams, Charles 132
Williams, Roger 251, 252–54, 300–01, 420
Williamson, Joseph 465
Wilson, A. N. 28
Wilson, Emma 505
Winn, James Anderson 506
Winstanley, William 124
Wither, George 263, 264, 314
Wittreich, Joseph A. 143, 148, 151, 152, 180, 501, 502
Wolfe, Don M. 8, 146, 487
Wolleb, Johannes 355, 484
Wollstonecraft, Mary 167
Wood, Anthony à 26, 27, 32, 124
Woodcock, Katherine (Milton's second wife) 12, 287, 383
Woolf, Virginia 35, 147
Worden, Blair 4, 11, 487, 504
Wordsworth, William, *The Prelude* 106
Wotton, Henry 6, 21, 120–21, 165, 378, 381
Woudhuysen, H. R. 373
Wright, William Aldis 166
Wroth, Mary, *Urania* 81
Wulstan, David 506

Yalden, Thomas 125
Yonge, Nicholas 394
Young, Thomas 8, 37, 41, 272, 284, 288, 452

Zagorin, Perez 503
Zwierlein, Anne-Julia 150
Zwingli, Ulrich 311